DOING QUALITATIVE RESEARCH

DAVID SILVERMAN 5E

SAGE

Los Angeles | London | New Delhi
Singapore | Washington DC | Melbourne

Los Angeles | London | New Delhi
Singapore | Washington DC | Melbourne

SAGE Publications Ltd
1 Oliver's Yard
55 City Road
London EC1Y 1SP

SAGE Publications Inc.
2455 Teller Road
Thousand Oaks, California 91320

SAGE Publications India Pvt Ltd
B 1/I 1 Mohan Cooperative Industrial Area
Mathura Road
New Delhi 110 044

SAGE Publications Asia-Pacific Pte Ltd
3 Church Street
#10-04 Samsung Hub
Singapore 049483

Editor: Mila Steele
Assistant editor: Alysha Owen
Assistant editor, digital: Chloe Statham
Production editor: Victoria Nicholas
Copyeditor: Neville Hankins
Proofreader: Andy Baxter
Marketing manager: Ben Sherwood
Cover design: Shaun Mercier
Typeset by: C&M Digitals (P) Ltd, Chennai, India
Printed in the UK

Library of Congress Control Number: 2017939357

British Library Cataloguing in Publication data

A catalogue record for this book is available from the British Library

ISBN 978-1-4739-6698-7
ISBN 978-1-4739-6699-4 (pbk)
ISBN 978-1-5264-4161-4 (pbk & interactive ebk) (IEB)

DOING QUALITATIVE RESEARCH

Why lecturers recommend David Silverman's *Doing Qualitative Research*, fifth edition:

'Whether you are a scared neophyte research student or a more experienced qualitative researcher this is an excellent and invaluable and most importantly accessible text that will open the lid of a treasure box of resources. You need this book.'
Thérèse A.G. Lewis
Senior Lecturer in Research Methodology, Northumbria University

'In principle, it is impossible to write a method book that will be valid forever. In practice, David Silverman did just that. Adjustments in new editions only fine-tune the text that contains everything that a qualitative researcher needs to know.'
Barbara Czarniawska
Senior Professor of Management Studies, University of Gothenburg

'This is an excellent textbook that gives students very practical advice on how to conduct qualitative analysis in a thoughtful way. Silverman's vast experience within qualitative methods gives the text a clarity and overview that one can only admire.'
Nanna Mik-Meyer
Department of Organization, Copenhagen Business School

'An essential guide for anyone new to or brushing up on qualitative methodology. This clear, student-centred guide offers first person insights and true-to-life stories that prepare readers for all of the surprises that await researchers in the field. From the ins and outs of designing a study to writing up and publishing analysis (and much more), this book is an accessible, soup-to-nuts account of a complex set of methods we call qualitative research.'
Katie Headrick Taylor
College of Education, University of Washington

For Laurence Silver, a lovely man and a great friend

If this stone won't budge at present and is wedged in, move some of the other stones round it first ... All we want to do is to straighten you up on the track if your coach is crooked on the rails. Driving it afterwards we shall leave to you.

(Wittgenstein, 1980: 39e)

Contents

About the Author

David Silverman trained as a sociologist at the London School of Economics and the University of California, Los Angeles. He taught for 32 years at Goldsmiths, University of London. He is interested in conversation and discourse analysis and he has researched medical consultations and HIV-test counselling.

He is the author of *Interpreting Qualitative Data* (fifth edition, 2014) and *A Very Short, Fairly Interesting and Reasonably Cheap Book about Qualitative Research* (second edition, 2013). He is also the editor of *Qualitative Research* (fourth edition, 2016) and the SAGE series 'Introducing Qualitative Methods'. In recent years, he has offered short, hands-on workshops in qualitative research for universities in Europe, Asia, Africa and Australia.

Now retired from full-time work, he aims to watch 100 days of cricket a year. He also enjoys voluntary work in an old people's home where he sings with residents with dementia and strokes.

Preface to the Fifth Edition

Some people suspect that new editions of textbooks are more to do with publishers' priorities of maintaining market share than with readers' needs. In this preface, I will try to avoid 'the usual blather' and to demonstrate the original features that this edition makes available to you, the reader. So I will begin with a statement about what is different about this fifth edition.

Mixed methods research is becoming more widespread, particularly in disciplines like health, education and business and management. While I remain critical of most attempts to 'triangulate' data and cautious about the way in which qualitative data is seen as subsidiary to quantitative findings, it is important to show fruitful ways in which different kinds of data may be combined. As a result, I have expanded my discussion of the role of qualitative research in discovering social phenomena and then using quantitative data to show 'inputs' and 'outputs' from these phenomena. In my chapter on research design (in Chapter 6, Section 8) and on choosing a methodology (in Chapter 9, Section 6), I have, therefore, extended my discussion of mixed methods both in terms of working with different kinds of qualitative data and combining qualitative findings with quantitative data.

A distinctive feature of previous editions of this book is my use of multiple student examples, often combined with my advice and answers to questions they have asked me. In this edition, many new student examples are used with a particular emphasis on the practicalities of doing research – particularly within organizations – which should appeal to disciplines that are more practice based, like education and business and management. Requesting permission to use their work has led to many interesting discussions where students have asked new questions and I have made new suggestions. So has developed a fascinating dialogue over time as students raise new concerns and I see how their research has developed.

This edition also attempts to increase its friendliness to student use in five ways:

- A more logical chapter order which places ethical issues near the beginning of the book and moves chapters on getting support to an earlier position.
- Reflective questions at the end of each chapter in the form of a checklist to help student revision.
- Model answers provided to many student exercises.
- A refined text design to showcase the practical, hands-on advice and tips in a consistent format so that colour, bold, bullet points, headings and other signposting tools are used in a consistent, elegant format that allows the reader to follow easily along a set of learning points.
- To bring the pedagogy of this edition to new levels of innovation, accessibility and practicality, I offer an interactive Field Guide free with any paperback purchase of the book.

The Field Guide provides students with a fully immersive learning experience and creates numerous opportunities for more personalization and interactive learning. Features include:

- Video tips and tutorials from myself.
- Links to videos featuring other researchers.
- Links to relevant websites and SAGE journal articles for further reading.
- Checklists.
- Interactive 'test yourself' questions or self-assessment questions with answer keys.
- Links to samples of available secondary data.
- Practical exercises with model answers new to this edition.
- Pop-up glossary terms.

In addition to other interactive functionality, students using the Field Guide will be able to click directly on icons and links in the book (what you 'see' through the binoculars) that connect to resources on the Online Resources website (https://study.sagepub.com/dqr5). This type of connectivity will allow you to link directly to exercises and further reading instead of having to flip to another page or type in a complicated hyperlink. It will also enable more linking to websites, relevant organization links and other third-party content, some of which could be sourced through SAGE cases and video products.

Throughout this new edition I have tried to pay attention to new literature and new sources of data. One of the features of the book most highlighted by users and reviewers is the student examples (marked as 'What I did'), which 'put flesh on the bones' of otherwise very theoretical issues. However, it is important not to let these examples dominate the book, so readers will find that many have been shortened and, I hope, made more pithy. A more extended example is my discussion with a marketing student in Chapter 9. This nicely illustrates what I see as the appeal of naturalistic data.

As in previous editions, the content of this book derives from my experience of supervising many MA dissertations and around 30 successful PhDs. Supervision and course teaching have convinced me that the only way to learn the craft skills of qualitative research is to apply classroom knowledge about different methodologies to actual data (found here in the case studies and exercises provided in each chapter).

Over 30 years of teaching methodology courses and supervising research projects at both undergraduate and graduate levels have reinforced the wisdom of the old maxim that true learning is based upon doing. In practice, this means that I approach taught courses as workshops in which students are given skills to analyse data and so to learn the craft of our trade. Like many contemporary teachers, I believe that assessments of students' progress are properly done through data exercises rather than the conventional essay in which students are invited to offer wooden accounts of what other people have written.

When I teach new research students, I find that many assume that qualitative research begins with hypotheses and operational definitions in the same way as quantitative research. Among other things, this may mean that a good qualitative research study may simply begin with the question, 'What is going on here?' It will avoid early hypotheses and definitions and instead will seek to understand how participants define the situation. Unlike quantitative studies, it will pride itself in finding unexpected, new cases and be ready to change direction during the course of the research. None of this means that qualitative studies should be any less rigorous or critical than conventional research. But it does mean that they will take different paths and be judged by different yardsticks.

It follows that I have little time for the conventional trajectory of the PhD in which students spend their first year 'reviewing the literature', gather data in the second year and then panic in the third year about how they can analyse their data. Instead, my students begin their data analysis in year 1 – sometimes in week 1. In that way, they may well have 'cracked' the basic problem in their research in that first year and so can spend their remaining years pursuing the worthy but relatively non-problematic tasks of ploughing through their data following an already established method.

During the past 15 years, I have taught workshops for research students in a range of disciplines from sociology to management and community medicine in the UK, France, Belgium, Finland, Norway, Sweden, Switzerland, Denmark, Poland, Switzerland, Sri Lanka, Malaysia, Australia and Tanzania. I have been struck by the energy and originality that a new generation of students is bringing to our field. This book draws upon the lessons I have learned from that experience, including thinking through whether qualitative research is properly fitted to your research problem (see Chapter 2) and understanding the ways in which doing qualitative research is always a theoretically driven undertaking (Chapter 7).

Qualitative research is a contested terrain in which very different models and methods compete for attention. My own biases have been made explicit in my book *A Very Short, Fairly Interesting, Reasonably Cheap Book about Qualitative Research* (second edition, 2013). By contrast, in this book, while I do not claim neutrality, I have tried to be reasonably even-handed and, thereby, to reach out to a wide range of readers.

My focus here on completing a research project complements the discussion of the uses and limitations of different qualitative research methods in *Interpreting Qualitative Data* (fifth edition, 2014). Both are supplemented by the readings in my edited collection *Qualitative Research* (fourth edition, 2016) and by the authoritative texts on different disciplines and a range of research methods published in my Sage series 'Introducing Qualitative Methods'.

Chapter 16 of this book on computer-assisted qualitative data analysis was written (and updated) by Clive Seale. I am most grateful for his skilful exposition of the subject. I also want to thank Amir Marvasti for his generous permission to allow me to use some of the material that he prepared for a North American version of this book. Jay Gubrium kindly commented on Chapter 7, Anne Ryen made available some of her unpublished data, and Anne Murcott allowed me to quote from her unpublished paper on writing a student dissertation. I also want to thank Moira Kelly, Sally Hunt, Simon Allistone, Seta Waller, Kay Fensom and Vicki Taylor for allowing me to quote from their research diaries. The Economic and Social Research Council (ESRC) kindly gave me permission to reproduce its guidance on research ethics in Chapter 4.

Many students in four continents have allowed me to quote from their workshop papers and others have written short pieces about their work which are included here. I thank them all and hope I have followed their wishes in terms of providing or concealing their identity. I am most grateful to Stewart Clegg, Jay Gubrium, Katarina Jacobsson, Paul Luff, Amir Marvasti, Jonathan Potter and Gary Wickham for helping me find such material from their own students.

My Sage editor, Mila Steele, has been very helpful. Her suggestions have invariably been stimulating and useful. I also wish to thank Alysha Owen for her great help with the digital material which is such an important part of this new edition. Victoria Nicholas always organizes the production of my books with considerable efficiency. Finally, thanks are due once again to Sara Cordell for keeping my back in working order.

CONTENTS

PART I
INTRODUCTION

Part I provides a context for thinking about doing qualitative research. A brief introduction to the themes of this book and how best to use it is provided in Chapter 1. Chapter 2 compares qualitative and quantitative research and raises questions about how to decide whether qualitative methods are appropriate for your research topic. Chapter 3 offers examples of early and late stages of research students' work and shows what you can learn from their experiences and ideas.

ONE
How to Use This Book

In this short chapter, I outline the structure of this book and provide some suggestions about how to make optimum use of it.

Part I is aimed at the beginning research student. Part II assumes that you have overcome your initial doubts and now need to deal with the nitty-gritty issues that arise when you start to design a research study. Ethical issues are rightly coming much more to the fore in all research and are discussed at length in Chapter 4. Chapter 5 seeks to reassure you about the degree of originality required in a student research dissertation. Chapter 6 uses multiple student examples to discuss how to design a credible piece of research.

Many students are puzzled and even over-awed by 'theory'. Chapter 7 provides a guide to what 'theory' means in practice and how to use theoretical models to guide your research. Having thought through ethical issues and grappled with different **theories**, you are in a much better position to design a credible and doable research project. Chapter 8 addresses the basic question of formulating a good research question. Chapter 9 explains what is meant by 'methodology' and helps you think about how to select appropriate methods. The final chapter in Part II considers how to write a research proposal.

Doing a piece of student research can be a very lonely activity. Part III looks at how to maximize the support you can get. Your faculty supervisor is your obvious first port of call and Chapter 11 discusses what is involved in the supervisor–student relationship and how to make the most use of it. However, other means of help are available to the student researcher. So Chapter 12 looks at how to get feedback on your research from your fellow students and by giving talks at conferences.

Part IV focuses upon the period when you have begun to gather and analyse data. Students doing qualitative research are perennially troubled that they do not have enough data. In Chapter 13, I discuss how many cases you need and show you why these are often fewer than you think. Using many student examples, Chapter 14 shows you what is involved in collecting the various kinds of qualitative data. The next chapter outlines what is to be gained by working early with datasets and shows you how to develop your early analysis.

Computer-assisted qualitative data analysis software (**CAQDAS**) can be very useful and Chapter 16 discusses its various forms and how they may be used appropriately. Chapter 17 examines quality issues in research and shows you how to make your work credible. The next chapter shows you how to apply what you have learned in Part IV to evaluate journal articles using qualitative research. The final chapter of Part IV, Chapter 19, provides a discussion of effective qualitative research and, thereby, offers an overview of the main themes of this book.

Pertti Alasuutari describes writing a thesis as rather like learning to ride a bicycle through gradually adjusting your balance:

> Writing is first and foremost analyzing, revising and polishing the text. The idea that one can produce ready-made text right away is just about as senseless as the cyclist who has never had to restore his or her balance. (1995: 178)

Following Alasuutari, Part V is concerned with the 'writing-up' stage of research. Before you can begin to write anything, you always need to think about the audience for whom you are writing. Chapter 20 offers you a guide to the various audiences for research and how to address them differently. The remaining five chapters of Part V help you think through the different parts of your thesis: how to begin your research report; how to write an effective literature review and methodology chapters; how to structure your data chapters; and how to produce a lively concluding chapter.

The two chapters in Part VI consider the aftermath of a finished piece of research. Depending on the level of your work, this may involve an oral or a viva. This is often shrouded in mystery, like some weird Masonic ritual! Chapter 26 attempts to demystify the PhD examination. Whether or not you face an oral examination in the aftermath of submitting your dissertation, your supervisor and examiners should encourage PhD students to think about publishing their research. Indeed, more and more PhDs are now awarded to a collection of published journal articles. Chapter 27 helps you think about how to select parts of your works for different publications and how to make use of reviewers' suggestions about rewrites.

From Part II onwards, the order of this book very roughly follows the likely chronological sequence of doing a piece of research. However, I recognize that textbooks are not usually read in the same way as novels. For instance, although you may want to resist the temptation to skip to the final chapter of a whodunnit, no such prohibitions are sensible when using a textbook. So, for example, you may want to consult Chapter 11 on making good use of your supervisor quite early on. Or, if you want a quick summary of the story this book offers, you may turn at once to Chapter 19. Each chapter is more or less self-contained and so there should be no problems in zigzagging through the book in this way, using the Glossary provided where appropriate.

Zigzagging also makes sense because qualitative research rarely follows a smooth trajectory from hypothesis to findings. As we shall see, this is less a drawback than a chance to refocus your work as new ideas and opportunities arise in the field. Consequently, most readers will want to move backwards and forwards through the book as the occasion arises. Alternatively, you may find it useful to skim-read the book in advance and then work through certain chapters in greater detail to correspond with different stages of your research. Words written in bold (e.g. **methods**) are defined in the Glossary located at the end of this book.

The examples and exercises in this book are designed to allow the novice to emerge with practical skills rather than simply the ability to write good examination answers. The exercises mostly rely upon the stage of your research coinciding with the chapters where they are found. So when you are zigzagging through the book or skimming it, it will usually make sense to return to the exercises at a relevant stage of your work, using your supervisor for feedback and advice.

One of the special features of this new edition is the Field Guide that accompanies it. Please take advantage of the additional readings, links and exercises available there.

Ultimately, of course, no book can or should provide for how it will be read. Complete anarchy is nonetheless rarely very useful to anybody. In this spirit, the structure I have provided tries to give you an initial orientation. From then on, it is up to you. As the philosopher Ludwig Wittgenstein wrote:

> All we want to do is to straighten you up on the track if your coach is crooked on the rails. Driving it afterwards we shall leave to you. (1980: 39e)

TWO

What You Can (and Can't) Do with Qualitative Research

Learning Outcomes

By the end of this chapter you will be able to:

• Recognize that there is no simple distinction between 'qualitative' and 'quantitative' research.
• Understand the uses and limitations of both forms of research.
• Work out whether qualitative methods are appropriate to your research topic.

1 INTRODUCTION

This chapter offers practical help in answering three very concrete questions that you should consider before you think of beginning a qualitative research study. These are:

• Why do students start to use qualitative **methods**?
• Is qualitative research appropriate to the topic in which you are interested?
• If so, how should it influence the way you define your research problem?

In a way, this book as a whole is dedicated to answering these kinds of questions. However, some initial answers will help to give you a good sense of the issues involved. As in the rest of the book, I will set out my argument through examples of actual student research.

2 WHY DO RESEARCHERS USE QUALITATIVE METHODS?

We would like to think that research design depends upon cool, rational assessment of alternatives. After all, we are taught that methods cannot be always 'right' or 'wrong', only more or less appropriate.

Often, however, chance factors related to your biography can sometimes count for more than logically defined choices. Negative experiences of courses in statistics may predispose you towards choosing qualitative methods. Or you might have acquired a preference for using research to understand others and find quantitative research's pursuit of **variables** too mechanistic.

The implied depiction of qualitative research as 'subjective' is, as we will see, a caricature. Qualitative research consists of many different endeavours, many of which are concerned with the 'objective' (i.e. scientific) study of realities which in some sense are 'objective' (e.g. how **culture** works; the logic of conversations).

Nonetheless, the simplistic subjective/objective polarity may inform a preference for qualitative methods. We see this in Michelle Day-Miller's story about realizing that the subjects had all but disappeared in the survey research she conducted prior to her PhD.

WHAT I DID: MICHELLE
Capturing 'Experience'

Like many students, I began my graduate training being socialized within a positivist paradigm. I was learning my statistics and how to conduct surveys and develop quasi-experimental designs. But one day I experienced a transforming moment in graduate school. Donna, one of the participants in a survey-based study I conducted, was reading a manuscript I had written reporting the findings of this study when she exclaimed, 'Where is the depth? Where is the feeling? Where am I in all of these words?'

(Continued)

(Continued)

She was absolutely right! Donna, along with the other participants, provided a unique voice during the collection of the data, yet that voice was ultimately muted by the deadening 'thud' of an aggregate statistic. In my research report she was nowhere to be found.

This experience occurred only a few months before I took my first qualitative research methods course. In that course I found my home. While my education to that point was focused on teaching me to collect information and understand social behaviour, I wasn't getting at the understanding human experience part of my aspiration. I realized that to truly capture experience I needed to embrace the subjective and, along with it, the humanity of social science. [Michelle Day-Miller, USA]

Michelle's emphasis on 'voice' and 'subjectivity' shows how an interest in subjectivity and the authenticity of human experience is a strong feature of some qualitative research. As I show shortly, this kind of naturalist **model** is one of the dominant **paradigms** within qualitative research.

Like Michelle, Roslyn began by participating in a quantitative study. In such studies, the interaction between researcher and subjects is seen as a technical matter where the researcher attempts to follow a protocol in order to limit bias. By contrast, Roslyn began to see how what was happening in the **field** could become a topic in its own right.

WHAT I DID: ROSLYN
What Happens When You Collect Data

I chose my research topic in a way that I think most qualitative researchers really choose their topics, whether they admit it or not: by stumbling across something that fascinated me while I was already in the field. In my case, I had gone to the field as a research assistant to an anthropologist doing a quantitative demography project. Here we were, collecting data on fertility, dowry, land use, and household economics, but it was our very presence that provoked the most interesting conversations of the day. I wanted to know more about the spaces we occupied in the minds of our respondents. I had so many new questions: What was happening? How is women's position in labour articulated? When and where can women work outside of the home? Why might this be changing? How might it be changing? And what happens in households after women work outside of the home? Thus, my research topic emerged from a curiosity that developed while in the field. [Roslyn Fraser, Sociology, University of Missouri-Columbia]

Roslyn's experience in the field showed her that survey interviews could not simply be defined by a good research protocol. Qualitative research topics often emerge by coming to see that apparently 'obvious' features of the social world depend upon intricate social organization. In this way, Roslyn was drawn towards a model of **constructionism** quite different from Michelle's **naturalism**. A good test of whether you will make an insightful constructionist researcher is whether you can make out the extraordinary features of ordinary life (see Silverman, 2013: Chapter 1).

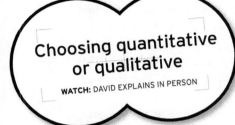

Choosing quantitative or qualitative

WATCH: DAVID EXPLAINS IN PERSON

David's Top Tip 1

Quantitative methods are usually the most appropriate if you want to find out social facts or the causes of some phenomenon. If you are more interested in how social phenomena arise in the interactions of their participants, then qualitative methods should be your choice.

In my own case, the places I studied and the people who supervised me had a key influence on how I did my graduate research. My undergraduate work was at the London School of Economics (LSE) where my only experience of research methods was an excellent introductory course in survey methods taught by Claus Moser. Although not particularly numerate, I was enticed by Moser's use of risqué examples drawn from topics like dating behaviour, guaranteed to fascinate a young man of 18!

After completing an MA in the USA, I returned to LSE to do my PhD. I then discovered that one of my undergraduate teachers (Robert McKenzie, a political sociologist) expected that I would be supervised by him on a topic close to McKenzie's own interests (e.g. voting behaviour). However, by this time, my interests had shifted away from political sociology and towards social class and status. Influenced by my survey course and by sociologists of the 1960s (like C. Wright Mills and David Lockwood), I planned to conduct an interview study of white-collar workers at four different kinds of workplace, focusing on their lifestyles and aspirations. Not wishing to upset my undergraduate tutor (McKenzie), I chose him as supervisor together with an industrial relations specialist, Ben Roberts.

Without any real research training I began my research interviews and, after two years, published a short note on my initial findings in the *British Journal of Sociology* (Silverman, 1968a). As I shall argue in Chapter 15, this shows the value of beginning data analysis at an early stage rather than allowing the data to accumulate.

Early data analysis has a further advantage: it allows you to reconsider the direction in which your research is heading. In my case, such reconsideration had quite a drastic result:

- I started to worry about the **reliability** of data gathered from semi-structured interviews. How far did my respondents' answers to my prepared questions actually reflect their own experiences? Moreover, didn't my own assumptions come into play when I interpreted their answers to some open-ended questions?
- I now had a junior post at Goldsmiths College, where I unexpectedly found myself teaching a course on the sociology of organizations. As a result, I published a paper on organization theory in *Sociology* (Silverman, 1968b). Was this a better topic for my PhD?

My joint supervisor, Ben Roberts, settled the matter. Having read my published paper, he suggested that it might make sense to develop it in the form of a library-based, theoretical PhD. Seeing how quickly such a dissertation could be written, given my reading for the course I was teaching, I switched topics. This example shows what you can gain by discussing the direction of your research with your supervisor.

Two years later, I was awarded my PhD at about the same time as my dissertation was published as a book (Silverman, 1970). So, as a result of chance factors and my own research experience, my research topic was totally redefined.

EXPLORE:
MIXED METHODS EXAMPLES

Through biographical events, I moved out of quantitative research towards a purely theoretical PhD. By 1970, I had a vague curiosity about qualitative research but no real understanding of it. So, while the final chapter of my book twitters on about the importance of understanding people's 'meanings', the only method it refers to is a purely quantitative method of 'measuring' meaning deriving from the positivist psychologist Charles Osgood.

While the context today is very different, I have no doubt that biographical factors continue to play an important part in how students plan their research.

WHAT I DID: JOHAN, PENNY, ANH AND CHARLES
Moving on from Quantitative Research

Here are further examples of students who began by doing quantitative research which inspired them to do a qualitative study:

- When small firms collaborate, does this affect how innovative they become? Beginning from statistical data, the research now focuses on case-studies of new start-ups by small businesses. [Johan Lidström, Umeå School of Business and Economics]
- What are the healthcare needs and experiences of women leaving prison? Beginning with a quantitative medical record review and moving on to qualitative interviews with women prior to, and after, their release from prison. [Penny Abbott, School of Medicine, Western Sydney University]
- What factors encourage public-private partnerships in Vietnamese businesses? Beginning with statistical data and then moving to four case studies. [Anh Tuan, Business School, University of Technology, Sydney]
- What is the moral psychology involved in end-of-life decision making by clinicians? Beginning with a quantitative survey of surgeons, followed by qualitative interviews with palliative care physicians and nurses looking at how and why killing is distinguished from palliative care. [Charles Douglas, School of Medicine and Public Health, University of Newcastle, Australia]

These four students began with quantitative data before commencing a qualitative study. While this is one way to proceed, it is not essential. A more common way to do qualitative research is to work with qualitative data from the outset. Everything depends on how you define your research problem and whether qualitative data is appropriate to it.

READ:
COMBINING QUAL & QUANT RESEARCH

3 ARE QUALITATIVE METHODS ALWAYS APPROPRIATE?

'Qualitative research' seems to promise that we will avoid or downplay statistical techniques as well as the mechanics of the quantitative methods used in, say, survey research or epidemiology. Indeed, the qualitative/quantitative distinction seems to assume a fixed preference or predefined evaluation of what is 'good' or at least 'appropriate' (i.e. qualitative) and 'bad' or 'inappropriate' (i.e. quantitative) research when, as we all know, methods are only more or less appropriate to particular research questions.

It is worth repeating the truism that research methods should be chosen based on the specific task at hand. Amir Marvasti's personal experience with a study of juvenile offenders who were charged with adult criminal offences is a good illustration of this point. In 1999, Amir was working as a graduate research assistant on a project which used quantitative methods to isolate the factors that cause legal authorities to recommend a minor for adult judicial processing. This is how he describes his intellectual journey.

WHAT I DID: AMIR

Pushing Quantitative Research to the Limits

The data [I was working with] came from two official sources. One was a statewide database called Client Information System (CIS). The CIS data contained numerically coded information on thousands of offenders from around the state. Summarizing and analysing the numerical data was relatively easy. For example, if I wanted to know the average age of offenders who had committed a violent crime like robbery, I would write a few lines of computer syntax, submit the request, and have the report, or output, back in seconds.

However, the work was much more challenging where the local court files were concerned. To transform these documents into data suitable for statistical analysis, the researchers put together a lengthy data collection instrument. After making an appointment at the appropriate courthouse, which could be hundreds of miles away, I myself or one of my colleagues would drive to the location and peruse the dossiers in search of information that corresponded to the hundreds of variables on the data collection instrument. For example, if the minor offender had used a firearm during an offence, that would be coded as 1; a blunt weapon, such as a baseball bat, would be coded as 2; etc.

As the project proceeded, the principal investigators and I had to add more variables to capture the nuances of each case. For example, I came across a few cases that started in one jurisdiction and were transferred to another. This required the inclusion of new variables to the data collection instrument. All of us soon realized that no matter how many variables were added, many details of the case simply did not fit a precoded, standardized format. Additionally, we were faced with the problem of overlapping categories. For instance, I had difficulty recording a case in which the offender began beating his victim with a baseball bat as a 1 or a 2.

To remedy these problems, we had to supplement the numerical data about a case with a qualitative narrative or a case history to capture additional nuances. These case histories were written on a blank sheet of paper that was provided on the back of the data collection form. For example, I would write that offender X lost his father to cancer at the age of 12, and was placed in a foster home after his mother refused to care for him, and so on. Finally, the principal investigators for this project added more depth to their data by conducting in-depth interviews with a small sample of offenders. They would go to prisons, halfway houses, or other venues and interview the juvenile offenders face to face. [Amir Marvasti, USA]

As you can see from this example, methods should be our servants, not our rulers. Methods are properly used as tools when they are needed. So it would have been silly for Amir and his colleagues to turn away from the **case study** method because it seemed 'too qualitative'. It would have been equally unreasonable to exclude the statewide (CIS) data from the research because it was 'too quantitative'. So you can become much more effective as a researcher if you reject arbitrary, self-imposed categories and instead *systematically pursue knowledge about a topic wherever the data might take you.*

Any good researcher knows that your choice of method should not be predetermined. Rather you should choose a method that is appropriate to what you are trying to find out (see Punch, 1998: 244). For instance, if you want to discover how people intend to vote, then a quantitative method, like a **social survey**, may be the most appropriate choice. On the other hand, if you are concerned with exploring people's life histories or everyday behaviour, then qualitative methods may be favoured. An insistence that any research worth its salt should follow a purely quantitative logic would simply rule out the study of many interesting phenomena relating to what people actually do in their day-to-day lives, whether in homes, offices or other public and private places. This suggests a purely pragmatic argument ('horses for courses'), according to which our research problem defines the most appropriate method.

Knowing which method is best

WATCH: DAVID EXPLAINS IN PERSON

David's Top Tip 2

Never assume that qualitative methods are intrinsically superior. Indeed, a quantitative approach may sometimes be more appropriate to the research problem in which you are interested. So, in choosing a method, everything depends upon what you are trying to find out. No method of research, quantitative or qualitative, is intrinsically better than any other.

As we shall see later, research problems are not neutral. How we **frame** a research problem will, as we saw in Michelle's and Roslyn's stories, inevitably reflect a commitment (explicit or implicit) to a particular model of how the world works. And, in qualitative research, there are multiple, competing models (see Chapter 7).

What does all this mean in practice? In the final substantive section of this chapter, using some more student accounts, I look at the sort of questions you should ask yourself before embarking on a qualitative research project.

EXPLORE:
PSYCHOLOGICAL PERSPECTIVES ON QUAL & QUANT

4 SHOULD YOU USE QUALITATIVE METHODS?

It is worth reiterating that qualitative methods are not inherently superior to quantification. Everything depends on how you formulate your research problem. At the end of a four-day workshop I ran at the Helsinki School of Economics a few years ago, I recall a female Russian PhD student who said to me: 'Thank you very much for your course. I now realise that I should be using quantitative methods on my research'! I was pleased that my workshop had shown this student how to judge the appropriateness of different methods. As a consequence, she avoided wasting time barking up the wrong tree.

WHAT I DID: JOHN AND ILKA

Are Documents Only Secondary Data?

John's research topic is voluntary disclosure of environmental information. He proposes a longitudinal study of American resource companies. He will analyse what he calls 'secondary data' (hardcopy annual reports and websites for voluntary environmental disclosures (VEDs)) over the 2000–2012 fiscal years. He wants to examine any changes in disclosure levels over the fiscal years as well as change in disclosure levels in different media. He writes: 'I am keen to examine what drives US resource companies to disclose VED information in the first place. Can qualitative data alone fulfil this purpose?' [John, Accounting student, Australia].

In my response, I told John that he was quite right to be suspicious that qualitative data could tell him much about the reasons why US resource companies do or do not disclose such information. For instance, interviews with company finance managers would reveal only what they were prepared to tell outsiders rather than what actually happened when reports were being collated. A much more reliable guide would be to see which companies, at what periods, engaged in VEDs. In short, John's research topic is suited to a quantitative study. This is underlined by his reference to documents and digital material as 'secondary data'. This term reflects quantitative researchers' assumption that such texts are distant from 'what actually happened' ('primary data'). By contrast, for qualitative researchers, such materials also 'happened' and are open to lively analysis in their own terms without any need to compare them with an outside 'reality' (see my discussion of texts in Chapter 6, Section 4).

The following example shows how company documents can be examined in their own terms, using concepts drawn from qualitative research. Ilka is studying two corporate social responsibility (CSR) programmes, looking at publicly available corporate material that reports on CSR activities. The material studied may include CSR reports, annual reports, future studies and press reports related to a company's CSR activities.

Ilka's research focus is on the 'designed things' that act within CSR projects. Designed things are understood as non-human actors that participate in shaping corporate actions. Her approach derives from actor-network theory. She writes that this is an approach which 'provides descriptors for different kinds of agency exercised by actors in a network. I adopt these descriptors to identify the type of agency exercised by particular designed things within the case study CSR programmes' [Ilka, School of Design, Australia].

These two studies both analyse documents but for quite different purposes. Ilka's research depends on a close reading of corporate material informed by a distinct theory appropriate to qualitative research. By contrast, John's study leans heavily on assumptions from quantitative research and, consequently, might use a simple counting method such as **content analysis**. Neither study is better than the other. They just are different. As such, they each use data appropriate to their research problem.

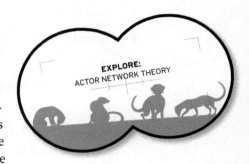

These stories show the diversity of qualitative research. The features that attract researchers to this methodology are many and so are the ways this methodology is practised. If you are unsure about whether qualitative research is appropriate to your topic, consult Table 2.1.

Table 2.1   Suitable topics for qualitative research

- Understanding social interaction in real-life situations (e.g. meetings, social media, professional consultations)
- Understanding how people perceive things or respond to situations
- Understanding processes (decision making, teaching a class, managing a business)
- Studying sensitive or complex issues which may be difficult to study in depth using quantitative research (e.g. sexuality, violence, drug use)

Source: adapted from Hennink et al. (2011: 10)

Table 2.1 shows that qualitative research is not always appropriate for every research problem. You need to think through exactly what you are trying to achieve rather than be guided by some fashion or trivial preference (perhaps you are not comfortable doing statistical calculations). Table 2.2 provides further, more practical questions to ask yourself before deciding to use qualitative methodology.

Table 2.2 Should I use qualitative research?

1 What exactly am I trying to find out? Different questions require different methods to answer them
2 What kind of focus on my topic do I want to achieve? Do I want to study this phenomenon or situation in detail? Or am I mainly interested in making standardized and systematic comparisons and in accounting for variance?
3 How have other researchers dealt with this topic? To what extent do I wish to align my project with this literature?
4 What practical considerations should sway my choice? For instance, how long might my study take and do I have the resources to study it this way? Can I get access to the single case I want to study in depth? Are quantitative samples and data readily available?
5 Will I learn more about this topic using quantitative or qualitative methods? What will be the knowledge payoff of each method?
6 What seems to work best for me? Am I committed to a particular research model which implies a particular methodology? Do I have a gut feeling about what a good piece of research looks like?

Source: adapted from Punch (1998: 244–5)

Following item 2 of Table 2.2, if you are mainly interested in making systematic comparisons in order to account for the variance in some phenomenon (e.g. crime or suicide rates), then quantitative research is indicated. Equally, as a rule of thumb, if it turns out that published research on your topic is largely quantitative (item 3), does it pay to swim against the tide? As I stress several times in this book, if you can align your work with a previous, classic study, this makes a lot of sense. The last thing you want to do is to try to reinvent the wheel!

Of course, we should not overplay the opposition between qualitative and quantitative methods. If resources allow, many research questions can be thoroughly addressed by combining different methods, using qualitative research to document the detail of, say, how people interact in one situation and using quantitative methods to identify variance (see Chapter 8). The fact that simple quantitative measures are a feature of some good qualitative research shows that the whole 'qualitative/quantitative' dichotomy is open to question.

In the context of this book, I view many such dichotomies or polarities in social science as highly dangerous. At best, they are pedagogic devices for students to obtain a first grip on a difficult field: they help us to learn the jargon. At worst, they are excuses for not thinking, which assemble groups of researchers into 'armed camps', unwilling to learn from one another.

Of course, as Table 2.2 (item 6) suggests, such armchair debates are of less relevance than the simple test of 'what works for me'. Howard Becker comments about his use of qualitative data: 'It's the kind of research I've done, but that represents a practical rather than an ideological choice. It's what I knew how to do, and found personal enjoyment in, so I kept on doing it' (1998: 6).

However, Becker adds that his 'choice' has not blinded him to the value of quantitative approaches:

> I've always been alive to the possibilities of other methods (so long as they weren't pressed on me as matters of religious conviction) and have found it particularly useful to think about what I did in terms that come from such other ways of working as survey research or mathematical modeling. (1998: 6)

Not only does it sometimes pay to think of qualitative research, as Becker suggests, in terms of quantitative frameworks, but it can also be helpful occasionally to combine qualitative and quantitative methods. As I show in Chapter 17, simple tabulations can be a useful tool for identifying **deviant cases**.

In this section, I have used students' accounts to show the importance of thinking through one's research problem before committing oneself to a choice of method. But, as I have already hinted, the situation is rather more complicated than this. In Chapter 7, we will see how theoretically defined models enter into your research strategy.

5 WRAPPING UP

There is considerable overlap between the themes discussed in this chapter. For example, as we noted, data collection, analysis and writing are virtually inseparable in qualitative research. Thus these categories are not intended to be treated as mutually exclusive; their main purpose is to show you the diversity of research experiences. If, in selecting your topic, you are pushed and pulled by different forces, you are not unique. Doing qualitative research is in many respects no different than doing everyday life: it is complex and sometimes downright chaotic. The point of this book and other advice and mentorship you receive is to help you manage this chaos and direct it into a coherent research project.

Ultimately, everything depends on the research problem you are seeking to analyse. I conclude this chapter, therefore, with a statement which shows the absurdity of pushing too far the qualitative/quantitative distinction:

> We are not faced, then, with a stark choice between words and numbers, or even between precise and imprecise data; but rather with a range from more to less precise data. Furthermore, our decisions about what level of precision is appropriate in relation to any particular claim

should depend on the nature of what we are trying to describe, on the likely accuracy of our descriptions, on our purposes, and on the resources available to us; not on ideological commitment to one methodological paradigm or another. (Hammersley, 1992: 163)

What You Need to Remember

- 'Qualitative' research involves a variety of quite different approaches.
- One common thread is the attempt to make routine features of everyday life problematic by describing what actually happens in some setting or dataset.
- This means that qualitative research is best at answering 'what' and 'how' questions. Quantitative research seeks to correlate variables usually in order to answer 'why' questions.
- If you want to begin by defining 'variables' which you seek to correlate, then quantitative research is best for you.
- Although some 'quantitative' research can be properly criticized or found insufficient, the same may be said about some 'qualitative' research.
- In these circumstances it is sensible to make pragmatic choices between research methodologies according to your research problem and model.
- Doing 'qualitative' research should offer no protection from the rigorous, critical standards that should be applied to any enterprise concerned to sort 'fact' from 'fancy'.
- Think carefully about what kinds of data are appropriate for your research topic. If it looks like your answers are to be found in correlating variables or if you want to find the causes of something, quantitative research is often your best path. Qualitative research is more suited to describing what happens without appealing to predefined variables.

Your Chapter Checklist

Working out if you should use qualitative methods

Having read this chapter, consider the following questions:

TRACK:
WHEN QUALITATIVE RESEARCH IS APPROPRIATE

1. Are you seeking to define 'variables' and then relate them?
2. Are you asking 'why' questions rather than 'what' or 'how'?
3. Are you trying to find out facts rather than understand processes or experiences?

If you answer 'yes' to any of these questions, you probably should be using quantitative methods.

Exercises

Exercise 1: Distinguish qualitative and quantitative research topics

Listed below are three examples of research topics and design:

1. Consumer motivations for content creation in online social networking exploring users' unconscious motivations in semi-structured interviews including techniques like word association and sentence completion. 24 participants will be chosen based on contribution frequency [high, medium and low] and gender. [Lucy Miller, Marketing, Macquarie University]
2. Are organizations' decisions about adopting social media for external communication more influenced by institutional pressures rather than driven by economic factors? Content analysis of four online social media followed by telephone interviews with key personnel. [Kim MacKenzie, Accounting, Queensland University of Technology]
3. The role of trust and distrust in relationships between two business organizations based on the assumption that trust is influenced by the personalities of the employees involved. Interviews with 65 pairs of individuals in contact with each other while working for different firms. [Angelos Kostis, Umeå School of Business and Economics]

Now answer the following questions:

a. Which of these topics and designs are best suited to qualitative research?
b. Which are better suited to quantitative research?
c. Suggest ways to redefine the topic and/or research design in a manner suited to qualitative research.

APPLY:
YOUR EXERCISE WORKBOOK

Exercise 2: Understand what methodology suits your research topic

*   How far are (a) qualitative and (b) quantitative methods suitable for your research topic?
*   What difference does it make to the methodology you use if you are looking for facts or 'facts'?

Exercise 3: Examine the pros and cons of mixed methods designs

Here are examples of research topics:

*   The business strategies of tuna fishermen in Vietnam. [Lan Ho, Business, Australian National University]

- Adolescents' perspectives on care practices in child welfare institutions. [Marianne Buen Sommerfeldt, Oslo and Akershus University College of Applied Sciences, Faculty of Social Sciences]
- The healthcare needs and experiences of women leaving prison. [Penny Abbott, Medicine, Western Sydney University]

What would you gain and lose by using a mixed methods research design for each of these topics?

Exercise 4: Defend your methodology choices

In relation to your own possible research topics:

- Explain why you think a qualitative approach is appropriate.
- Would quantitative methods be more appropriate? If not, why not?
- Would it make sense to combine qualitative and quantitative methods (mixed methods)? Explain your answer.

Further Reading

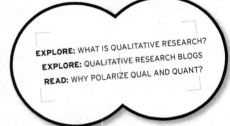

EXPLORE: WHAT IS QUALITATIVE RESEARCH?
EXPLORE: QUALITATIVE RESEARCH BLOGS
READ: WHY POLARIZE QUAL AND QUANT?

In my recent book *A Very Short, Fairly Interesting, Reasonably Cheap Book about Qualitative Research* (Sage, 2013: Chapter 1), I outline the sort of topics that I believe qualitative research is best placed to answer. Other short introductions are 'Inside qualitative research', the introduction to Clive Seale et al.'s edited book *Qualitative Research Practice* (Sage, 2004: 1–11); and my book *Interpreting Qualitative Data: Methods for Analysing Talk, Text and Interaction* (Sage, 2014: especially Chapter 1).

Discover the chapter's digital resources in your SILVERMAN FIELD GUIDE

THREE
Focusing a Research Project

Learning Outcomes

By the end of this chapter you will be able to:

- Understand the basic issues involved in developing a research project from initial ideas to data analysis.
- Appreciate the crucial links between theory and method.
- See how student researchers can work rigorously with data while following a consistent analytical approach.
- Understand how you can analyse your own impact on the field.
- Recognize the importance of keeping a research diary to note how your ideas change.

1 INTRODUCTION

Switch on your television and graze through the channels. You will undoubtedly come across a chat show in which people are talking about their rise and fall from grace. Or maybe you will find a sports channel where, more often than not, you will see not a game but interviews with players about their hopes and regrets.

We live in a world in which our yearning for people's 'experiences' is more than satisfied by the popular media and by social media such as Facebook. Indeed, very often this pursuit of the 'personal' becomes repetitive and we should resist it (Silverman, 2013: Chapter 5).

However, this is not always the case. Any book which sets out to offer information and advice about doing a piece of research without telling a few personal 'stories' would be in danger of being received as empty and unhelpful. If we can draw out appropriate implications from these stories, moving from the personal to the practical, then we will have achieved something more substantial than merely providing some kind of experiential comfort blanket.

In this spirit, this chapter is devoted to telling the stories of three of my research students. The three students have much in common apart from the fact that I supervised them for a PhD in sociology. Moira Kelly and Sally Hunt began their research many years after their first degrees. Simon Allistone began his PhD at the age of 29. All three were products of the MA in qualitative research at Goldsmiths College and had been supervised by myself on their MA dissertations.

Moira and Sally held down demanding jobs while doing their research. Moira was, in turn, a research nurse, a health promotion research manager and then a health researcher; Sally was a lecturer in nursing. Unlike Moira and Sally, Simon was able to work on his doctorate on a full-time basis thanks to a three-year grant from the British ESRC.

Their work spans a broad range of qualitative methodologies. Moira analysed interviews which she had conducted; Sally carried out an organizational **ethnography**; and Simon studied interactions at a school meeting. While all three were registered for a PhD in sociology, their substantive interests crossed into other disciplines: health studies and nursing (Moira and Sally), organization studies (Sally and Simon) and media studies and education (Simon).

However, while the three of them worked with audio-recorded data, their analytic perspectives were rather different. Sally's study of decision making by a mental health team (MHT) caring for homeless people drew on Erving Goffman's (1974) **concept** of frame. Simon based his study of a parent–teacher evening on concepts of **turn-taking** derived from **conversation analysis** (CA). In her research with surviving partners of people who had died of cancer, Moira used **narrative analysis** to study her interviews.

I realize that many of you will have different interests and backgrounds. Let me assure you at once that you will not need any special knowledge to understand what follows. The approach that my students used is, for my present purposes, of far less significance than the *trajectory* of their projects. Moreover, as I argue below, there are lessons here to be drawn for anybody who is contemplating writing a research dissertation at any level.

Perhaps more relevant than their common theoretical perspective was the different amount of time that their research took. Working full-time, Simon completed his PhD in four years. Reflecting the pressures of demanding jobs, Moira took seven years and Sally finished in ten. As already suggested, these different timespans were strongly associated with practical contingencies, more or less unrelated to technical issues of research design.

In what follows, the three tell their stories largely in their own words drawn from their research diaries. I have limited myself merely to adding some headings and asides. After each story, I suggest some more general implications. The chapter concludes with a summary in the form of a 15-point guide to completing a successful research study.

READ:
DOCTORAL STUDENT PERSPECTIVES

2 MOIRA'S RESEARCH DIARY

Beginnings

The research process began when I [Moira] took up post as research associate on a study of hospice and hospital care of people with terminal cancer directed by Clive Seale. The aim of that project was to compare hospice and hospital care for people who had died from cancer and their spouses. The project included the collection of quantitative and qualitative interview data. I had worked as a research nurse at St Christopher's Hospice (which funded the project) for four years before starting this research. I wanted both to use some of the qualitative data from the project for a PhD and to apply a theoretical approach I had learned during my MA.

In my post as hospice research nurse, I worked on a range of different topics. In one study I recruited breathless patients to a randomized controlled trial. It was this that got me interested in the (mismatched) relationship between methods of measurement used in research and the actual practices of the people being researched.

In the research trial, breathlessness was treated as a subjective symptom. However, in practice I found that nurses and doctors produced their own assessments of the patient's breathlessness, which sometimes did not correspond either with each other or with the subjective assessment of patients themselves. This problem formed the basis for my MA

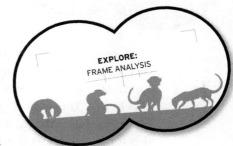

EXPLORE:
FRAME ANALYSIS

dissertation in which I applied Goffman's frame analysis (1974) to patient case note data. This study highlighted the importance of looking at *how* people do things, rather than what they say they do.

However, frame analysis only went so far in examining **members**' practices. I was drawn to the way **ethnomethodology** made it possible to identify the skills and practices ordinary people use to produce social action. The micro-analysis of social interaction seemed to me to be a valuable way of understanding some of the health issues and problems I had encountered in my experience working in clinical health settings as a psychiatric nurse and as a research nurse. Many of these problems appeared to hinge on the interactive practices and skills of the various parties involved (professional and laypeople).

Theoretical orientations

The experience of doing my MA research, together with my experience as a practitioner, policy maker and sociologist, led me to believe that social research driven by theoretical concerns (rather than by a defined social problem) can contribute to policy and practice. It can do this through developing knowledge about social issues such as experience of healthcare but without setting up a rigid definition of the problem at the beginning. This ties in with my experience as a health researcher and practitioner up to that point, where I had observed that problems often appeared to arise around attempts to measure states of health and disease through imposing particular definitions and categorizations.

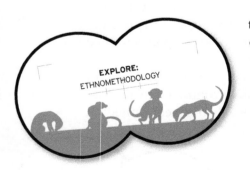

EXPLORE:
ETHNOMETHODOLOGY

There seemed to me to be value in taking a step back to get a closer look at the phenomenon. More useful outcomes may be achieved if theoretical imperatives drive the research in a direction which can offer new perspectives on social problems [see Silverman, 2013: Chapter 4]. Theoretical concerns should steer the analytic conception of the research problem, otherwise there is a danger of taking the research problem at face value, and of providing policy makers and practitioners with the answers they require, in *their* terms.

Many qualitative research studies set out clear aims and objectives at the start of a project. These may often refer to collecting and analysing data on a particular topic, such as describing the views of patients about a particular type of illness experience. The aims of ethnomethodological studies such as this one tend to be quite general, centring on the examination of some data. When analysis starts, this form of analysis throws up a whole range of possible research problems that could be examined in detail. Decisions therefore need to be made about objectives for particular pieces of analysis at each stage. Eventual objectives can be quite specific but this will follow a more general exploratory analysis to see what members are doing in the talk under examination (e.g. making assessments). Objectives therefore tend to evolve over the course of the research.

The importance of being flexible about objectives is demonstrated in the way in which the specific topics of 'cancer' and 'bereavement' were not treated as central concerns by the interviewees. I had initially used these labels in early descriptions of the study, and in presentations. However, although these accounts are about cancer, in that the 'story of the death' requested is about cancer, the interviewees do not topicalize cancer. In a similar way, as a researcher I had been referring to the data as 'accounts of bereaved spouses', giving the impression to myself and others that the analysis is about bereavement. However, the interviewees did not make bereavement relevant to their descriptions, i.e. they did not talk about their personal experience of being bereaved. This supports the need to consider the relevance of the local context in the production of meanings.

My initial intention was to explore the character of the moral accounting work members do. This contrasts with most interview studies in which the information provided by the interviewee is usually treated as data about the events and experiences described.

Ethnomethodologists view this as problematic and regard interviews as an unreliable source of information about what actually happens in the situations described. A description of healthcare produced in an interview cannot be treated as a straightforward report of that care. Treating the data as a primary source in this way can be potentially misleading even if one were to take account of such conventional issues as error and bias.

The emphasis in the first instance was on investigating *how* the interviewees (surviving spouses) are saying what they say (as members of a social world), rather than focusing on *what* they are saying, such as 'bereavement talk'. In other words this was a study not of bereaved spouses, but of social interaction. Following Baker's (2002) theoretical direction, my analysis was concerned with what kind of social world the speakers make happen in their talk and what kind of social world speakers assume so that they can speak in the way they do.

The study data

In the study directed by Clive Seale, 70 interviews were undertaken with bereaved spouses in south London. There were 35 interviews with spouses whose husband or wife had died in hospice, and 35 interviews with spouses matched by age and sex whose husband or wife had died in hospital. The **sample** was drawn from death certificates of all those who had died from cancer approximately six to nine months beforehand. These were kept at local departments of public health, and ethical committee approval was obtained from the three health authorities covered.

Each interviewee received a letter asking them to take part in the study. I called round to their house a couple of days after the letter had been sent and asked to interview them. Written informed consent was gained prior to all the interviews.

Sixty-five interviews were recorded with the consent of the respondents. The interviews started with an open-ended request, 'tell me the story of what happened'. The intention was that, for this part of the interview, there would be minimal interruption by the interviewer (MK), allowing the respondents to structure their own accounts. The response to this request, the initial 'story', constitutes the data for my PhD study. The rest of the interview followed a semi-structured format involving a series of questions.

Getting into the data: doing being reasonable

I began the analysis by reading and rereading the five interview accounts I had initially transcribed, looking for a starting point for my analysis. At this point my main interest was in the talk of the interviewees, partly because they did most of the talking. I followed Sacks's call to examine some (interview) data in terms of

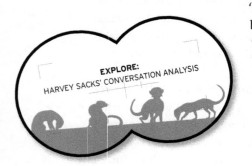

EXPLORE:
HARVEY SACKS' CONVERSATION ANALYSIS

'how it is that the thing comes off' (1992, Vol. 1: 11) but, as so much goes on in talk, a decision needed to be made as to what the 'thing' would be. Several interesting issues regarding the activities interviewees were doing in their accounts arose and appeared to warrant further exploration. These included: producing a 'reasonable' account, the use of time to locate events, the constitution of lay and medical competences, criticism, gender and emotion.

Given that there were several possible directions for the data analysis, a decision had to be made about what to look at first. In line with the (ethnomethodological) principle adopted by Baruch (1981), that a feature of all accounts is a display of moral adequacy, a key characteristic of these accounts seemed to be the way in which the interviewees construct their behaviour and that of others as reasonable or unreasonable in their descriptions. This seemed like a productive place to start. I again read and reread all the transcripts, this time extracting sections in which the spouses appeared to be presenting their behaviour and that of others as reasonable or unreasonable, systematically going through the data extracts identifying the use of pairs like husband and wife, and other categories, as well as looking for the description of activities which implied particular categories (see Silverman, 2015: 302–11).

The research process: criticism, assessments and the interview

I reread the transcriptions of the first five interview accounts, identifying instances where criticisms of health professionals were made. The health professionals referred to specifically were doctors and nurses. Identification of criticism in the accounts was not generally clear cut. Considerable identity work was carried out around criticisms. A number of different 'types' of criticism were distinguished, ranging from 'very cautious' to 'direct'. Ambiguity was used by the account-giver, with the interviewer being drawn into the production of the description as criticism. Even when the interviewee identifies their action as criticism, considerable moral work goes on regarding the roles and responsibilities of those involved, including the interviewee and interviewer.

I had initially intended to undertake separate analyses of instances of criticisms of self (by the interviewee) and of the dead spouse. However, having undertaken the analysis of criticism of health professionals, and following the ethnomethodological principles I had adopted, I decided a more theoretically consistent tack would be to conduct a closer analysis of members' practices in producing the accounts. So I took a step back in order to take a closer look.

I had identified criticism as an activity in the talk in a similar way to more traditional qualitative studies, and gone some way to describing how it was produced by interviewees through categorization work. I now wished to examine in more depth how activities such as criticism are constructed in the interview talk. This meant refocusing my analysis to look more closely at how assessment work was carried out by both parties and how the interview accounts were cooperatively produced as 'stories'.

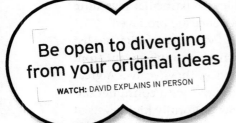

Be open to diverging from your original ideas

WATCH: DAVID EXPLAINS IN PERSON

David's Top Tip 3

In her analysis of interviews with bereaved spouses, Moira switched her focus away from the *content* of their comments about health staff *towards* an analysis of how these spouses produced criticism while being 'reasonable'. As in Moira's case, good qualitative research often abandons its initial concerns and discovers new topics in the course of data analysis.

Sampling data

I refer to the data analysed here as interviews, though the analysis is based on the first part of the interview only, up to the end of the story. These stories would constitute my data.

The detailed level of analysis involved in examining participants' practices in the talk has meant that the empirical analyses of criticism of health professionals and assessment work drew on the first five interviews only. Later analysis of the construction of the talk using CA drew on 25 interviews, with additional interviews (to the five initially analysed) being selected on the basis of emerging theory.

Decisions about the selection of the sample were not pre-set, but have been conceptually driven by the theoretical framework underpinning the research from the start (cf. Curtis et al., 2000). In order to undertake analysis that addresses the adequacy of the underlying theory described by Mitchell (1983), decisions about the sampling of data have been made during the research. This has been influenced by the two different ethnomethodological research methods which have been applied to the interview data. Analysis of communicative practices (in the interview accounts) can only be discerned in 'the fine grained detail of talk-in-interaction' (Drew, 2001: 267). I have set out to undertake the fine-grained analysis recommended by Drew and also to make comparisons across cases, using both intensive and **extensive analysis** where appropriate to my research problem.

Practical relevance

This research study set out to contribute to a body of institutional knowledge, the sociology of health and illness. The examination of how the interviews are produced has highlighted a number of analytic points regarding the status attributed to the accounts by the interviewees. They are set up as 'assessments of healthcare experience'. Setting up the accounts to be heard in this way has implications for the sociology of health and illness, and healthcare policy, in particular regarding how 'lay' or 'consumer' evaluations of healthcare experience are produced.

The increasing emphasis on the consumer in British government policy has led to a search for the best ways to find out about both what consumers want from health services and how satisfied they are with the services they receive. A great deal of this research is quantitative, but there are frustrations with consumer satisfaction questionnaires and scales, as they tend to show uniformly high levels of satisfaction (Avis et al., 1997). There has consequently been a search for different ways of evaluating satisfaction with healthcare, and an increase in qualitative research. It has been suggested that increased interest in qualitative research has, in part, been fuelled by the growing demand for research that gives consumers a voice in developing services. My study takes up the issues raised above through an ethnomethodological analysis of data initially collected as a form of lay or consumer evaluation.

Wrapping up

I have worked as a health researcher for a number of years, and this study has been the first time I have not set out with at least a fairly well-defined problem that needed a solution. This includes qualitative studies in which the goal may be to describe something about which little is known. Even in such studies, however, you do know broadly what you are required to describe. In this instance, however, I was attempting to describe something that I knew was going on but could not see at the start.

The need to refrain from introducing my own categorizations *before* producing the description of members' practices that I was aiming for has not been easy. However, I believe that the fine-grained analysis of the practices engaged in by interview participants has enabled me to contribute the new insights to the sociology of health and illness that I had hoped for at the start. What attracted me to ethnomethodology is how, in its suspension of interest in both external structural factors and assumed 'subjective' states, the skills of participants in producing social action through talk are demonstrated. This is made possible through its focus on 'describing members' viewpoints and definitions as the basis for rational actions, and for their participation in the sites of social life' (Drew, 2001: 267).

Implications of Moira's story

The beginning of Moira's story shows the value of basing a PhD thesis on a substantive area with which you are already familiar. Both her work experience and her MA research were in the health area and it made sense to stay in this familiar realm when choosing a topic for her PhD.

Her MA had shown her the uses and limitations of a particular way of conceptualizing healthcare interactions and now she wanted to shift slightly her analytic focus. But she was never in doubt of the need for such a focus in order to make sense of the data. For Moira, theory was not a piece of window-dressing to make research respectable. Instead, 'theory' represented the very practical ways in which she made sense of her data.

Moira had gathered her interview data as part of another study with different objectives. Drawing on the fortunate fact that these interviews had been audio-recorded, she was able to retranscribe them in order to address her new analytic concerns. Note that this did not mean that the previous transcripts were 'faulty'. Transcripts, like other methods of recording data (e.g. **fieldnotes**, diaries, memos), can only be judged in relation to a specific research problem and theoretical orientation.

The instant availability of her data meant that Moira, unlike many other PhD students, could begin her data analysis on day 1 of her research! As I argue in Chapter 15, such secondary analysis of existing data can offer a marvellous shortcut to completing a PhD, freeing you from the need to collect data – providing that you are not looking for excuses for delay and/or sloppy analysis.

Start analysing early

WATCH: DAVID EXPLAINS IN PERSON

David's Top Tip 4

Begin data analysis early and don't be deflected by literature reviews and the exigencies of data gathering. If you haven't got any data yourself at an early stage, try analysing someone else's data - published data, your supervisor's data, etc.

Like many qualitative researchers, Moira worked in an **inductive** way, avoiding too early categorizations of her data and setting research problems and objectives as she explored (analytically) her transcripts. As she puts it, the idea is to 'step back in order to take a closer look'. So, for instance, given her analytic orientation, it was not enough simply to report 'criticisms' of the treatment of a spouse. Instead, she wanted to understand how apparently critical comments were contexted in the co-production of 'assessments' and 'stories'.

Clearly, Moira's approach required very careful listening to the details of verbal interaction. So she focused mainly on just five out of her 65 interviews. However, this did not mean that her other interviews were completely neglected. A much larger sample of interviews was used in her chapters based on CA. In this way, her study combined intensive and extensive analysis.

Moira's research reveals that there need be no simple polarity between qualitative and quantitative research (see Chapter 2). Unlike much quantitative research, our research problems often require much more detailed analyses of small bodies of data. However, by combining intensive and extensive analysis, we can achieve understanding of a relatively large dataset and test emerging hypotheses with a fair degree of **credibility**.

Finally, Moira's story shows that theoretically driven research is far from incompatible with practical relevance. Quite the contrary! It is precisely those many, apparently atheoretical studies which have little to contribute to practical matters, simply because their authors do not have the time or the ability to stand back from their data and to think laterally. As Moira implies, her own work makes a substantial contribution to current debates regarding lay or consumer evaluation of healthcare. It also complements more 'structural' approaches in the study of health and illness with an understanding of the skills of participants involved in healthcare interactions.

3 SALLY'S RESEARCH DIARY

Getting started

When I [Sally] began this case study, I had little idea of how I might go about it. I had vague notions of exploring how diagnoses are constructed by health professionals. This was based on my past experience of having a psychiatric liaison role in a unit linked with an accident and emergency department. Looking at patient admission sheets, I was struck by the number of times I read 'schizo/ affective disorder' as the reason for admission to hospital. I concluded that such a cautious descriptor could 'cover' both patient *and* doctor for almost any clinical or legal eventuality. I also had a long-standing interest in the concept of 'illness careers'.

I anticipated that access to the field would be difficult because of the particularly sensitive ethical nature of mental health practice. I made an initial attempt at negotiating access to an inpatient area but this was not successful. A further difficulty was matching the demands of full-time teaching to the constraints of organizational shift patterns.

As with Silverman's (1987) experience of gaining access to the field of paediatric cardiology, my entry to mental health casework was a chance happening. I met up with a former colleague in a local supermarket. After I recounted my difficulty in negotiating access to an inpatient area, he invited me to meet the community team with whom he worked. I was both pleased and relieved to have been given this opportunity but I did not recognize it as advocacy at the time. Upon reflection many years later, I now appreciate that this was indeed the case.

Following two separate meetings with the team's psychiatric consultant and with the team leader (a community psychiatric nurse), I was eventually given permission to audio-record the team's weekly case meetings on the understanding that I destroy the recordings when the study concluded.

The choice of team meetings was a deliberate one. These were 'scheduled events', so I would not waste time waiting to see whether or not relevant data would appear but rather would have them to hand [see Chapter 15 of this book]. Having successfully negotiated access to the field I then became a participant–observer.

To undertake a case study of 'single homelessness' in the context of full-time employment makes heavy demands on the researcher in terms of personal resources and operational constraints. The field is so vast and the nature of subjects' lives so dispersed that I elected to observe professional caseworkers rather than service users. For practical reasons, then, I became a participant–observer at the mental health team's (MHT's) weekly case conferences.

Keeping a record

Once I had achieved access to mental health casework, my starting point was to observe and record what members were saying and doing in their meetings about clients. I audio-recorded meetings and made handwritten fieldnotes of my observations while I was recording. This enabled me to record visual data that might otherwise be lost or unavailable to me if I relied on the audio recordings alone.

A total of 15 meetings lasting approximately 75 minutes each were recorded over eight months. The first meeting was 'lost' due to problems with the recording equipment. Forty-five client stories were available overall. Of these, 13 were fully transcribed and four were partially transcribed. The shortest transcript was only three pages long. This later turned out to be a deviant case. The longest ran to 18 pages. One hour of recorded team interaction took an average of 10 hours to transcribe.

A total of 45 hours was spent on data collection overall. This included 20 hours of recording and 25 hours of **participant observation**. No selection process as such was involved in the transcribing of complete accounts. Accounts were transcribed in chronological order, which equated with the time frame of the fieldwork.

I chose to collect data in the way that I did because this was/is appropriate to the study of situated action. Audio recordings provide detailed recorded talk which fieldnotes alone cannot provide, while preparing transcripts is itself a research activity.

The act of producing the transcripts was not a straightforward matter. In the main, they were constructed according to my own common-sense reasoning as

I had no precedent for the process of transcribing. Because of this, transcripts do not always conform to accepted conventions. However, there is no perfect transcript and those I have capture sufficient detail of the MHT's practice for the kind of analysis I carried out.

The practicalities of audio-recording multiple voices in a less-than-soundproof environment exerted certain constraints. It was not possible to denote overlapping voices, for example. Nor was it possible to decipher the simultaneous secondary interactions which frequently occurred alongside the main action. I tried to transcribe what I heard as faithfully as possible using standard spelling and punctuation so that members' accounts would not appear 'unnecessarily odd' to the reader. I did not attempt to represent accented talk, and lengths of pauses were not timed exactly.

Fieldwork observation demonstrated that the talk was generally unhurried, even 'leisurely', and that it was frequently punctuated by laughter. I approximated the duration of pauses as being in the range of 1 second for the shortest, 'um', to almost 4 seconds for the longest (long pause).

With hindsight, I might use more conventional transcription devices if I were to do the transcripts again. This would save the 'creative' work of devising my own. However, as I lacked the quality of recording more commonly associated with CA, it remains a matter of debate as to whether this could have been a practical option. From a methodological perspective, I did not need the fine detail required by those working with the CA method.

Analysing my data

At the outset I made my own broad descriptive headings for each case account. These were based on the member's introduction to the case, which invoked both age and gender. An example of such a heading was: 'Fifty-year-old woman who has just been accepted by a hostel in the local area'.

I tried to make the description as 'flat' as possible, but found on later inspection that in many instances I had provided my own summary of the opening presentation. The heading was intended to be an identification device for differentiating the transcripts and for matching them to the accompanying fieldnotes. This demonstrates quite clearly that even in the role of note-taker, my recording skills as a fieldworker are influenced by my practitioner past.

I had other surprises. One heading read: 'Surveillance of a 29-year-old man in a hostel who is preoccupied with religious recordings'. Listening to the recording again and rereading fieldnotes at a later date demonstrated that the word 'surveillance' was not actually used by the narrator of that account. The heading represents my own, broad, descriptive category.

I attempted to transcribe as much as I could of what was said and to record in fieldnotes the setting in which this social activity took place. After transcribing a total of six accounts in full, I began to identify recurring instances in the raw data. These broad, analytic categories are listed, crudely, as follows:

- client vulnerability
- deviancy and common-sense reasoning
- character work
- distancing of other professionals and agencies
- bending the rules
- interchangeable roles.

'Client vulnerability' and 'deviancy' appeared to be topics of concern for MHT members. The remainder of the list was generated after noting instances of the first two categories when they emerged in the transcripts. No computer software package was used in this process. This had advantages as well as disadvantages in that the initial categories remained very flexible. For example, the last category was set aside as it served no immediate analytic purpose.

I had audio recordings, transcripts and fieldnotes, which gave me limitless opportunities to return to my original data and redefine the categories as the analysis progressed. Through such means, I was able to test out emerging hypotheses about members' common-sense reasoning generated by field-work. It was at this point that I attempted to construct a model which I later rejected because it was too rigid to explain the complexity of members' social action.

I was also able to consider deviant cases in the data which contradicted the emerging hypotheses [see Chapter 17 of this book]. One such case was an account in which the client was not directly taken on by the team.

Statistical measures were not used in the analysis overall. However, counting the number of times 'family history' was invoked in members' accounts threw new light on gender as an interpretive frame. Hammersley and Atkinson (1983) suggest that with the help of the discriminate use of numbers, quantification can be used as an aid to precision [see Chapter 17 of this book]. In *this* study, counting was used to examine a hunch.

My focus on members' activities generated initial questions about what they had to know to do their work. It also built on my original interest in diagnostic construction. It was only after the first two phases of fieldwork were complete, and I had constructed the broad categories upon which my preliminary analysis was based, that I began to examine extracts rather than whole transcripts. In this sense, my work differed from research which appears to be based on the use of 'favourable' extracts only.

Generating a research problem analytically

By using extracts in this way, I attempted to find 'the sense' of what members were saying, and what was *made* of what they were saying. I then shifted my emphasis to the discourse-based question: 'How do participants *do* things?' My desire to pose such a question derived from my reading of other ethnographic work as I strove to define my research problem.

While my early observations provided a descriptive background for my research, I still needed to focus on clear questions to ask about my data and to use these questions to shape the very act of data collection itself.

EXPLORE:
ERVING GOFFMAN'S INFLUENCE

The earliest influence on my study was Goffman's frame analysis (1974). It explores the relational dimension of meaning. For Goffman, a frame is defined by its use rather than by its content. Events are seen in terms of 'primary frameworks'. The particular frame used provides a means of interpreting the event to which it is applied. For Goffman, frames are both structural and flexible as they are susceptible to change by interacting participants. Indeed, they are highly vulnerable, being continually subject to dispute. In the event, much of my study used Goffman's concept of frame to demonstrate how understandings emerged among the MHT.

Data analysis and reading are mutually informing. In a sense, there is no end to updating one's knowledge. In this research, the literature was used as a continuing opportunity to make connections with the MHT data. For instance, half-way through the research the analysis began to lose focus. Reading Holstein's (1992) work on descriptive practice and Loseke's (1989) study of a shelter for battered women provided new knowledge about the accomplishment of social problems work. Similarly, towards the end of my research, fresh material from Kitzinger and Wilkinson (1997) helped me construct a chapter on 'gender' which arose from my reading of Holstein (1992).

Reflections on participant observation

I was now a participant–observer in a field where members were healthcare professionals like myself. Although I no longer practise directly, what effect this might have on the data is an important issue.

To suppose that *any* researcher enters a field without past experience or some pre-existing ideas is unrealistic. To suppose that their presence will not exert an influence on the data is equally unrealistic (cf. Strong, 1979: 229). In my own case, I accepted that my presence in the field would influence what I saw, but I could not predict 'how' or to what extent. In this sense, data produced by the team were a mutual production which also involved myself as researcher (cf. Emerson et al., 1995: 106).

Unlike Strong's experience of researching in paediatric settings, I cannot admit to being treated 'as part of the furniture' (1979: 229) by the team members I was observing – possibly because of my practitioner background. However, I *was* aware of feeling more accepted as the fieldwork progressed.

I was initially incorporated into the MHT's practical frame. Members were intolerant of my chosen position at the side of the room during fieldwork and 'ordered' rather than invited me to sit with them in their discussion circle even though I maintained a non-speaking role.

In the team leader's words, this was to 'close the circle'. As Peräkylä surmises about his own role as researcher, maybe this was the best way of collecting data and relating to members in the field (1989: 131). Certainly it was of practical use in that I knew I was recording data so I was left free to observe and write notes (cf. Silverman, 2011b: 277–82). However, as Hammersley warns: 'When a setting is familiar the danger of misunderstanding is especially great' (1990: 8).

I was aware that I might become too 'comfortable' with the team, but upon reflection this did not happen. Speculatively speaking, constructing a democratic atmosphere was possibly also functional to the team in that it positioned me where I could be involved and seen.

EXPLORE:
PARTICIPANT OBSERVATION

Nonetheless, the danger of 'over-rapport' with members of the team was a continuing issue for me. Despite my similar professional background to team members, like all participant–observers, I had to treat their perspectives as problematic.

Ethical considerations

Gaining ethical approval for the study was in no sense 'plain sailing'. In the early months of 1992, I put forward my proposal to the ethical committee of the trust hospital to which the team was attached. Apart from stressing the qualitative nature of my research intentions and the fact that staff, rather than clients, would be my proposed subjects, I could only state with certainty that I wished to audio-record the team's weekly case conference.

In addition, I found the form I was required to complete somewhat problematic. It conformed to the standard type for purely *clinical* research involving human subjects rather than to any proposed sociological research. Predictably, it was very 'physically' oriented.

One question asked for 'potential hazards' and the precautions I might take to meet them. The possible contravening of confidentiality was my written response to this enquiry. I undertook to use pseudonyms for the names of staff, clients and care areas throughout the research to preserve anonymity and to safeguard confidentiality.

In the event, even references to months or seasons of the year in the transcripts were changed as the work got under way. Dates of legislation were retained as were dates of fieldwork and any reference to clients' ages, as such data were necessary to the analysis. In addition, I undertook to write a report on the progress of the study for the ethical committee, should this be required at any stage of the work. I was not given permission to interview clients or to access their case records.

I guaranteed to keep all audio recordings at home under lock and key and to do all my own transcribing rather than eliciting secretarial assistance. I also promised to destroy the recordings at the end of the study. I did not expect to see or interview clients. Finally, I undertook not to proceed without the permission of all team members following a full explanation of what I proposed to do [see Chapter 10 of this book].

Several months later, I received written consent to proceed with my project from the chairman of the **ethics** committee. I also discussed my proposal with the chairman of the trust's mental health board, a practising consultant psychiatrist. He voiced no objection in principle and recommended that I contact the team's consultant and team leader to seek their individual permission, which I did.

However, being a participant–observer raises a number of ethical issues which extend beyond formal consent to the research. Before the research began, I decided that the best way to carry out participant observation, both morally and practically, was to be as open as possible with the team.

My rationale for making this decision was that this would permit me to be free to ask questions as the fieldwork progressed without creating too much suspicion. Being open would also permit audio recording of data. To a certain extent this strategy worked, although my insider knowledge of professional practice always made me conscious that what I was being offered of the team's world would be partially restricted.

I was aware that my presence in the field might affect the behaviour of those being observed, especially as the team was aware of my health professional background. I entered the field in the knowledge that a certain amount of professional self-consciousness would be inevitable, but I accepted this as a necessary 'tradeoff' in terms of access. It was a tacit assumption on my part and possibly on theirs, but on the basis of it, both I and they were able to proceed.

In this sense, my past experience as a practitioner was in no way disadvantageous to my present role as researcher. As a case study researcher, it became useful to me as a source of data.

For example, there were almost certainly times in this study when members responded to my presence in terms of what might be called 'ethical correctness'. I sensed that there were some occasions when members overtly displayed their moral adequacy as a consequence of being observed. My general *impression* was that members responded to me as a more senior member of staff, i.e. as an older, experienced professional now working in higher education. I felt that the team's display of moral adequacy in my presence was particularly marked, especially where ethical dilemmas were prominent.

Some implications of Sally's story

Research problems rarely come out of the blue. Sometimes, we may be the more or less fortunate recipient of a topic 'given' to us by a supervisor. In Sally's case, her own work experience combined with previous academic study to suggest an interesting topic. Her previous job as a nurse had underlined what she had read about illness 'careers' and the functions for staff of labelling patients and the intended and unintended consequences of such labels once applied.

Now Sally needed a setting in which to explore this issue. She made use of a chance encounter to gain access to a relevant healthcare context. The demands of her full-time work now influenced the data she sought from this setting. Like many part-time researchers, she avoided a time-consuming ethnography of everything that the MHT did, in favour of a focus upon scheduled meetings. This meant that her focus was necessarily on one side of the coin: not on how staff and clients perceived each other, but on how staff categorized their homeless clients in order to make decisions about whether (and how) to help them.

Three points emerge for beginning researchers:

- A research study can offer an opportunity to pursue a topic that intrigues you personally. Where your own experience seems to support an approach or a study that you have come across, a good research problem may be lying on your lap.
- Where access to a setting is difficult, draw upon your own contacts and experience as Sally did.
- As I argue in Chapter 8, research topics and data generally need to be narrowed down in order to be workable. Sometimes, this narrowing down will arise for quite mundane, practical reasons - for example, as in Sally's case, the amount of time you have available. Providing that you thoroughly analyse the data you have, this need not be a problem. Indeed, it can be an advantage by giving your research a direction.

As Sally argues, it was a great advantage to have audio recordings as her core data to complement her fieldnotes. Indeed, on one occasion, listening to a recording revealed a crucial error in a note.

She was satisfied that her way of transcribing her recordings was appropriate to her research topic. However, on reflection, she realized that it might have been simpler to have used an existing transcription method, like CA notation, rather than to have started from scratch (see the Appendix of this book).

This illustrates a general point to which I return several times in this book. When you are faced with a new task (e.g. finding data, coming up with a researchable problem, transcribing your data), look around for some already existing model. Nothing is gained (and a lot lost) by wasting time reinventing the wheel!

When she began to analyse her data, Sally, like Moira, worked inductively. She identified recurring instances of some activity in one meeting and then extended her search to several cases 'to examine a hunch'. Crucially, she sought contrary as well as confirming evidence to test out her hunches.

Throughout her research, Sally was aware that even the most inductive approach depends upon some theoretical orientation. In her case, Goffman's account of 'framing' gave direction to her research. However, she kept on reading other work as she analysed her data and showed a welcome readiness to modify direction as she came up with new findings and concepts.

Finally, Sally's diary discusses familiar issues in participant observation: how your own preconceptions may enter into your research; how being observed may affect people's behaviour (towards you and in relation to their own normally routine activities); and ethical issues in relation to obtaining informed consent and to what you reveal to the people you are studying. As Sally shows, it is wise to reflect on these issues but also to treat them as valuable data. Indeed, she was able to use her core concept of 'frame' to depict the MHT's categorization of herself – and thereby to understand more about how it dealt with others.

4 SIMON'S RESEARCH DIARY

Beginnings

My [Simon's] first degree was a BSc in sociology and media studies, chosen partly on account of some spurious advice I had received concerning the 'higher status' of a joint honours degree. I also felt that the media studies component meant that the course would necessarily focus on those cultural products invested with meaning by, and therefore relevant to, most people on a day-to-day basis. It is not necessary to go into explicit detail regarding the development of my thought during this time, for the purposes of this brief biographical outline. However, it is important to note that, by the end of my period of undergraduate study, I was greatly vexed by issues surrounding the tendency within the various schools of sociology towards using social structure too loosely as a way of accounting for data.

The basis for this concern can be broadly represented by examining the focus of my final-year project at City University, which took as a general theme the role of the media as 'moral entrepreneurs' (cf. Becker, 1963; also Cohen and Young, 1973; Cohen, 1980) in the creation and imposition of labels and stereotypes on a societal level. The project consisted of a comparative study of the reporting, by two contemporaneous newspapers, of two similar crime stories from the 1950s and the 1990s. Unfortunately, my experience of travelling to The British Library's Newspaper Library and reading the various original newspaper sources archived there left me with a sense of detachment from the materials I was studying. I had serious doubts as to the veracity of my own reading of the print and claims made regarding it, based mainly on the realization that I had little idea how contemporary readers may or may not have engaged with the texts.

It was in this frame of mind that I decided to broaden my knowledge of research methodologies, and gain some practical research experience in the meantime, by undertaking an MA in sociology with special reference to qualitative research at Goldsmiths College, University of London, in 1997.

Theoretical orientations

Whilst the course acquainted me with a wide range of research methodologies, it was my introduction to conversation analysis (CA) during this period that most caught my imagination. As the course began to contextualize more clearly my previous misgivings as part of the ongoing debate within sociology regarding the 'theory relative' activity of defining **social structure** (cf. Silverman, 2001), I was taken by ten Have's statement that 'CA refuses to use available "theories" of human conduct to ground or organize its arguments, or even to construct a "theory" of its own' (1998: 27).

In setting forward 'a different conception of how to theorize about social life', CA also moves away from invoking 'obvious' social structural factors when explaining social phenomena. While the concept of social structure is an important element in sociological inquiry in general, 'the problem becomes one of not allowing it to take on an analytic life of its own' (Boden and Zimmerman, 1991: 5). The way in which many sociological analyses allow social structure to 'take on a life of its own' is memorably summed up by Sacks in his analogy of society being viewed by the social sciences as a piece of machinery where much of what takes place is random, and it is worth quoting at length:

> Such a view suggests that there are a few places where, if we can find them, we will be able to attack the problem of order. If we do not find them, we will not. So we can have an image of a machine with a couple of holes in the front. It spews out some nice stuff from those holes, and at the back it spews out garbage. There is, then, a concern among social scientists for finding 'good problems', that is, those data generated by the machine which are orderly, and then attempt to construct the apparatus necessary to give those results. (1984b: 21-2)

The search for 'good problems' not only is carried out mainly in terms of reference to 'big issues' regarding large-scale institutions, but also necessarily imposes order on the phenomena being studied. Rather than search for an order based on the analyst's conception of what this order might be, CA proposes an examination of how individuals orient to (and therefore display) that order themselves: 'whatever humans can do can be examined to discover some way they do it, and that way will be stably describable. That is, we may alternatively take it that there is order at all points' (1984b: 22).

Not only did I find the movement away from fruitless theoretical debates between opposing theories refreshing, I was also impressed by the methodological focus that CA afforded. In focusing on the order found at all points within 'what humans do', CA delineated its field of study, since as Sacks pointed out, it is possible that 'detailed study of small phenomena may give an enormous understanding of the way humans do things and the kinds of objects they use to construct and order their affairs' (1984b: 24). Indeed, this focus meant that the question of social structure took on a new relevance for me, since in examining the ways in which interactional parties display their identities relative to one another, *and* how it matters to them, CA necessarily deals with the 'senses of "who they are" that connect directly to what is ordinarily meant by "social structure"' (Schegloff, 1991: 48).

Hoping to be relevant

Although the need for some theoretical formulation of what should be studied was no longer an overriding consideration, I still inclined towards research that could be said to be of practical relevance. On one level, this was due to my own lack of confidence in my ability to add anything of worth or interest to the cumulative fund of interactional knowledge that ten Have has typified as the aim of 'pure CA' (1998: 8). But it was equally due to a reaction against the ongoing dismissive view within the British media towards sociological research, claiming it is irrelevant and badly conducted.[1] Fortunately, I found that both concerns were addressed within CA.

Not only does the primacy of mundane conversation provide the 'richest available research domain' (Heritage, 1984: 240), it also 'uses the practices found in ordinary conversation as a baseline from which to analyse institutional talk' (Silverman, 2011b: 294–8). Added to this, Silverman (2013: Chapter 4), in his discussion of the contribution social science can make to wider society, highlights CA's role in offering a new perspective to participants within institutional settings. Rather than beginning 'from **normative** standards of "good" and "bad" communication', researchers should focus upon understanding the *skills* that participants deploy and the *functions* of the communication patterns that are discovered.

Finding a topic

It was with these issues in mind that I happened across the parents' evening data [at a local school]. At the time my partner was a relatively new primary school teacher, and her exposure to the realities of parents' evening led to her assertion that such meetings had not been directly addressed within her teacher-training course. This difficulty with parents' evening from the teacher's perspective chimed with further anecdotal information from my own parents, whose experience of such meetings tallied with the 'public relations exercise' view outlined by Baker and Keogh:

> [Parents' evenings] are understood and talked about as ritual or ceremonial encounters, in which teachers go through routine expressions of interest and academic diagnosis, and which parents attend in order to show their 'interest' in their children's schooling. (1995: 264)

Part of this characterization involves the view that parents' evening meetings are events in which 'nothing much was accomplished' (cf. Baker and Keogh, 1995; and above), which, as Baker and Keogh point out, 'is an invitation, if not provocation, to ethnomethodological inquiry' (1995: 265). It should equally be remembered, however, that Baker and Keogh's characterization of such meetings stems from their understanding of 'educational folklore' (1995: 264). Indeed, some parents find these occasions very helpful opportunities to review their child's academic progress. But this in itself provides further justification for examining the meetings.

Handy and Aitken, in their study of the organization of the primary school, point out that whilst there exists for all schools 'a bond between them and the families and communities they serve' (1994: 246), in practice the situation is not that simple. As they note:

Some parents are over-anxious and expect more from the school for their child than is real-istic. But sadly too many other parents abdicate once their child is at school. Teachers know that the parents whom they really want to see, to know, and to help are often the ones who never come to school. (1994: 246)

Given both this variation in parental attitudes to their children's schooling in general, and teachers' views of parents' evening meetings in particular, it is perhaps unsurprising that the assorted sections of the school community, be they teachers, parents or children, regard parents' evening in such different ways. With the question of what parents' evening 'means' being such a con-tentious one, the need to examine what goes on during them seemed to me to be particularly relevant.

Obtaining access

Having had these meetings drawn to my attention in this way, I began to con-sider their use as the basis for my dissertation. My ongoing unofficial pastoral role at my partner's school meant that I had already built up a rapport with the head teacher, so approaching him with a proposal to record some parents' evening meetings was straightforward enough. Once the process of the research was explained and agreed upon, he was happy for the recording to take place, with one stipulation: my access was restricted to the recording of only one teacher in the school, namely my partner. Not wanting to risk what rights to conduct the research I had already gained, I decided not to make any representations regard-ing the recording of any of the other Year 6 teachers. This did not unduly worry me at the time, since this restriction sat well with the time frame within which I could gather, transcribe and analyse the data for my MA dissertation. As it tran-spired, I only used a single meeting for the dissertation, leaving me (so I thought) with a surfeit of data.

Worrying about sample size

Focusing upon a single teacher has certain limitations in terms of generalizing the findings of this research to a wider population. It can be argued that the con-versational techniques utilized by the teacher in this research are unique to her, and therefore not easily extrapolated to the parents' evening practice of other teachers. Equally, the fact that the teacher in the data was a class teacher rather than a set teacher could have been an important influential factor. Perhaps set teachers do things differently in such meetings by dint of the fact that they are dealing with the specificities of their curriculum area. Furthermore, the entire format of the meetings might have been different at another stage of the academic year, even if carried out by the same teacher studied in this research. In short, various permutations in the actual accomplishment of parents' evening could be hidden by the fact that the data sample consists of a single teacher on a single parents' evening.

How, then, should this research be seen in terms of both sampling variety and external **validity**? Indeed, given the tension between the specific difficulties associated with the gathering of the data and the ideal research design outlined above, can this study say anything useful about the phenomenon that has been studied?

I believe the answer lies in seeing this research not as an attempt to provide categorical 'truths' about all parents' evenings in general, but as an attempt to raise questions about such meetings by looking at a single case in detail [see Chapter 11 of this book]. To some extent, raising questions in this way relies upon the perspective within CA that *'social practices that are possible*, that is, *possibilities of language use*, are the central objects of all conversation analytic case studies on interaction institutional settings' (Peräkylä, 2004: 297, original emphasis).

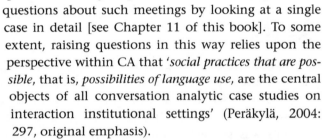

EXPLORE:
CONVERSATION ANALYSIS INTERVIEW

This element of possibility can be taken too far in terms of ascribing a certain level of universality to the findings of studies into conversational and interactional phenomena, but as Seale points out, 'readers must always make their own judgements about the relevance of findings for their own situations' (1999: 108). The corrective, he suggests, is simple: 'threats to such transferability are dealt with most adequately if details, or "thick" descriptions of the "sending" context (or the "sample"), are provided' (1999: 108). This study can therefore be seen as being exploratory rather than definitive, examining the achievement of routine by a single individual in a specific setting in such a way that further analytical possibilities are opened up.

Narrowing down my research problem

Although I subsequently came to realize the deficiencies in my MA thesis, and sought to correct them during my doctoral research, the findings of the MA (such as they were) formed the basis for my research proposal to a major British research council (the ESRC). Although the majority of the proposal focused upon CA's methodological relevance to my funding agency's thematic area of communication and learning, it did include the following research problem:

Whilst these meetings would seem to fall distinctly into the category of professional-lay interactions, with the attendant problems associated with the differential exercise of power by the
interactants, in this situation both the parents and the teacher can claim a level of 'expert'
knowledge with regard to the subject of the interaction, namely the child. The research problem to be addressed is that of what impact this dual claim to competency has upon the joint
construction of context by the parents and teacher as the two most powerful interactants.

Aside from some of the more obvious difficulties related to the unproblematic
application of concepts such as 'power' and 'claims to expert knowledge', this
research proposal conflicted with CA's stated aim that analysis should always
begin with what Psathas (1990: 45) has called 'unmotivated looking' [see Moira's
discussion in Section 2]. This is summed up by Sacks's assertion that 'when we
start out with a piece of data, the question of what we are going to end up with,
what kind of findings it will give, should not be a consideration' (1984b: 27). So,
despite the stated aims (however limited) of the research proposal, at the start
of the MPhil/PhD course I struggled to come to the data 'anew', without the
constraint of wondering where I was going to 'end up'.

Of course, the central issue of this struggle is one of discipline, not only in
terms of focusing on one or two analytic concepts at a time, but also with regard
to allowing the details of the talk to go where they will. As Sacks has pointed
out, 'it ought never to be a matter of concern to anybody who's doing a piece
of description which way it comes out, as long as it comes out some way' (1992,
Vol. 1: 472).

Discipline was imposed by moving away from the consideration of individu-
ally interesting features, framing them instead with regard to the overall structural
organization of the meetings. CA deals with and explicates 'patterns of stable,
recurrent structural features' (Heritage, 1984: 241) within talk. Through examination of the trajectory of the reportings on the child, fitted to both the search for
parental response by the teacher, and how the form of the response shaped the
unfolding trajectory, a framework for the research began to become clearer.

Some implications of Simon's story

The experience of writing an undergraduate dissertation had given Simon an
understanding of the uses and limits of a key concept: 'social structure'. Once
again, this underlines the point that true understanding comes by applying ideas
one has learned in the library to new topics.

However, being aware of the deficiencies of a concept is not sufficient. One
also needs to learn an analytic approach to data and then discover how to use it.
CA turned out to be Simon's key to the social world. Of course, ultimately such

approaches cannot be true or false but only more or less useful (see my discussion of models in Chapter 7). For Simon, the usefulness of CA seemed to be twofold. First, it gave him a clear idea of what kind of data he wanted and of how to analyse them. Second, it made personal sense to him by according with his previous research experience and also, perhaps, by being aesthetically pleasing.

Yet the appeal of theory can be double-edged. Aesthetic satisfaction can sometimes mean that you never can extricate yourself from the charms of the library to confront the external world (see my discussion of **grand theory** in Chapter 8). Simon was aware of this danger from the outset and was determined to combine his theoretical 'narrowness' with a concern for practical relevance.

At this point, like Sally, Simon had a lucky break. His partner was a primary school teacher prepared to give him access to her work. A parent–teacher evening was looming and this appeared to be a setting which was problematic to its participants and under-researched. Needing to record his data (a requirement of CA), Simon drew upon his own fortuitous association with the school and received permission from the head teacher.

However, achieving access brought its own worry. Simon was now troubled about the small size of his sample. While studying one teacher's work seemed to be enough for his MA thesis, would it be sufficient for a PhD? As it turned out, Simon came to the conclusion that a small sample will do if you have thought through its limitations and if the quality of the analysis is sufficient.

Indeed, when it came to the stage of data analysis, Simon was confronted by multiple, emergent research problems. This created an initial tension between the inductive approach he was using and his funding body's demand for an initial **hypothesis**. For a while, he could not see the wood for the trees. Fortunately, in time, an overall unifying theme became clearer as his various observations revealed a sequential structure to the parents' meetings. So Simon's thesis became organized around the trajectory of reportings of 'news' to parents by their class teacher.

5 WRAPPING UP

Obviously, there are many different stories that research students can tell about their experience, and I do not pretend that what you have read was typical or representative. Nonetheless, there are several clear messages in these stories that are worth listening to.

I set these out below as a *15-point guide*. Obviously, like any recipe, you will need to apply it to your own circumstances. Nevertheless, I believe the points below apply to *all levels* of student research from BA and MA dissertations through to the PhD.

1. *Begin in familiar territory.* If you can, work with data that is close to hand and readily accessible. For instance, if, as in Moira's case, you have data from another study which you can (re)analyse, grab the opportunity. There are no 'brownie points' to be obtained for gathering your data in difficult circumstances. Make it easy on yourself at this stage so that you can concentrate your energies on the infinitely more important task of data analysis.

2. *Find a settled theoretical orientation.* As I stress throughout this book, research is never just about techniques. All three stories refer to finding a theoretical model which made sense to the students and then could provide a settled basis for inference and data analysis. All three used a broad approach of **constructionism** focused on how an aspect of the social world is put together by participants in given settings.

3. *Narrow down your topic.* Strive to find a topic that is appropriate to your theory and data and is workable (this issue is discussed at length in Chapter 8). Later, if you wish, like Moira, Sally and Simon, you can use your research to make contributions to a substantive area (e.g. health and illness, education) and to a methodology (e.g. interview research, ethnography, CA), and to reflect upon issues of social policy.

4. *Don't try to reinvent the wheel.* In Chapter 5 I discuss what 'originality' might mean in research. For the moment, it is worth recalling that Moira used an earlier study as a model for her research and that both she and Simon used a well-established method of transcribing their recordings. So, at the outset, look at previous successful dissertations in your university library or departmental files and, where possible, focus on work directed by your supervisor.

5. *Keep writing.* Commit your ideas to paper. Don't worry how short or draft your papers are. Indeed, in some ways it makes more sense, initially at least, to submit 500-word pieces so that you can be guided in the right direction before you have expended too much time and effort.

6. *Begin data analysis early.* Don't be deflected away from early data analysis by literature reviews and the exigencies of data gathering. If you haven't got any data yourself at an early stage, try analysing someone else's data – published data, your supervisor's data, etc. (see Chapter 15).

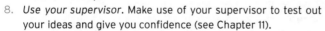

READ:
RESEARCH SUPERVISION

7. *Think critically about data.* When you start to identify a pattern in your data, don't rush to conclusions. See how robust this pattern is by working comparatively with different parts of your data (as Moira did) and by trying to identify deviant cases (like Sally).

8. *Use your supervisor.* Make use of your supervisor to test out your ideas and give you confidence (see Chapter 11).

9. *Use other resources and opportunities.* Graduate students should take every opportunity to attend relevant conferences and, better still, to give conference papers and to take appropriate training courses. Find out if there are study groups of research students working on similar topics. If not, try to establish such a real or virtual group.

10. *Do not expect a steady learning curve.* Be prepared for the sequence of highs and lows that will inevitably happen. For instance, Sally found that her early ideas about how her MHT made decisions were too simplistic, and Simon puzzled over how to integrate his apparently diverse findings. Treat setbacks as opportunities: Sally came up with a better explanatory model and Simon eventually saw an overall pattern.

11. *Keep a research diary.* Moira, Sally and Simon kept a file of their current ideas, hopes and worries. This file is an invaluable resource which, as I suggest in Chapter 23, can be used in edited form in your methodology chapter.

12. *Earmark blocks of working time.*[2] If you are researching part-time, it is crucial to find blocks of time in which you can focus solely on your research. Use this time for intensive data analysis and writing.

13. *Do not reproach yourself.* If you experience a setback, it may be best to take some time out to relax before you return to your research.

14. *Treat field relations as data.* How others treat you in the field is never just a technical matter. Like Moira and Sally, reflect upon how your interaction with your subjects is shaping your data.

15. *Understand that there is no 'perfect' model of research design.* Practical contingencies (e.g. access or the lack of it; the time you have available) are always going to affect any piece of research. Don't be afraid of working with what data you happen to have. Your examiners will not be comparing your research with some 'perfect' model, but they will expect you to have thought through the limitations of your data and your analysis (see Chapter 5).

What You Need to Remember

- It helps to begin your research in familiar territory.
- Find a settled theoretical orientation that works for you.
- Once you get a feel of your field, narrow down your topic as soon as you can.
- Don't try to reinvent the wheel; find what has worked for others and follow them.
- Keep writing.
- Begin data analysis immediately.
- Think critically about your data; don't rush to conclusions.
- Test out your ideas with your supervisor; don't worry if, in the early stages, you are often wide of the mark.
- Use other resources and opportunities inside and outside your own department.
- Don't expect a steady learning curve; no research study is without some disasters.
- Keep a research diary.
- Earmark blocks of working time to complete different activities.
- Don't reproach yourself about setbacks.
- Treat your relations within the field as data.
- Understand that there is no perfect model of research design.
- Before you finalize your research design, try out different ways of analysing relevant data in order to find a settled theoretical orientation that works for you.

NOTES

1   Although many examples could be cited, this brief quotation from an article by Will Buckley in the *Observer* newspaper of 30 May 1999 serves as a case in point: 'Here we go again. Yet more supposed research (this time from the sociology department at Edinburgh University) claiming that men are lousy parents, incapable of spending more than 15 minutes a day with their children ... Crap dads are back on the agenda because yet another bored sociologist has made a few phone calls and cobbled together some stats.'

2   Items 12 and 13 were suggested by Vicki Taylor after reading an earlier draft of this chapter.

Your Chapter Checklist

- Do you want to work with data that will take you a long time to gather and/or may be difficult to access?
- Are you unclear about which theoretical orientation (e.g. naturalism or constructionism) should guide your analysis?
- Are you delaying data analysis?
- Are you just reading but doing little writing?

If you have answered 'yes' to any of these questions, you need to think again. Discuss these matters with your supervisor and/or other students.

TRACK:
RESEARCH PRACTICE

Exercises

Exercise 1: Keep a research diary to reflect on your progress

Keep a research diary for a given period (one month for an undergraduate dissertation, three months for an MA project, at least six months for a PhD). Record:

APPLY:
YOUR EXERCISE WORKBOOK

- changes in your ideas about topic, data, theory and method
- new ideas from the literature or from lectures and talk
- meetings with your supervisor and their consequences
- life events and their consequences for your work.

At the end of your chosen period, reread your research diary and assess:

- what you have achieved in that period
- what would be required for you to do better in future
- your achievement targets for the next equivalent period
- what portions of your research diary could be used when you write up the methodology chapter of your dissertation.

Exercise 2: Understand a constructionist approach to research

All three students discussed here used a broadly constructionist approach focused on how an aspect of the social world is put together by participants.

- What specific features of one of these students' work made their research constructionist?

- How could any one of their research topics be reformulated as a naturalistic study focused on subjects' experiences?
- How could any one of their research topics be reformulated for a quantitative study?

Further Reading

The best place to look for similar research histories is in the writings of students at your own university. BA students should seek to obtain past successful undergraduate dissertations from their department. Graduate students should study MA and PhD theses in the library or available on the Internet, focusing particularly on research directed by your supervisor. If the methodology chapter does not include an autobiographical account, try to contact the author and discuss what lessons they drew from their experience.

Three books offer useful practical advice on managing a student research project: Virginia Braun and Victoria Clarke's *Successful Qualitative Research* (Sage, 2013); Renata Phelps et al.'s *Organizing and Managing Your Research: A Practical Guide for Postgraduates* (Sage, 2007); and Harriet Churchill and Teela Sanders's *Getting Your PhD: A Practical Insider's Guide* (Sage, 2007). Judith Bell's *Doing Your Research Project* (Open University Press, 2005) is a good introduction to research at the undergraduate or MA level. Estelle Phillips and Derek Pugh's *How to Get a PhD* (Open University Press, 2005) is the best British account of the practical issues involved in writing a PhD.

Discover the chapter's
digital resources in your
SILVERMAN FIELD GUIDE

CONTENTS

PART II
STARTING OUT AND PROJECT FOUNDATIONS

Part II assumes that you have overcome your initial doubts about commencing a research project and now need to deal with the nitty-gritty issues that arise when you start to design a study. Ethical issues are rightly coming much more to the fore in all research and are discussed at length in Chapter 4. Chapter 5 seeks to reassure you about the degree of originality required in a student research dissertation. Chapter 6 uses multiple student examples to discuss how to design a credible piece of research.

Many students are puzzled and even over-awed by 'theory'. Chapter 7 provides a guide to what 'theory' means in practice and how to use theoretical models to guide your research. Having thought through ethical issues and grappled with different theories, you are in a much better position to design a credible and doable research project. Chapter 8 addresses the basic question of formulating a good research question. Chapter 9 explains what is meant by 'methodology' and helps you think about how to select appropriate methods. The final chapter in Part II considers how to write a research proposal.

FOUR
Ethical Research

Learning Outcomes

By the end of this chapter you will be able to:

- Recognize the up-to-date standards required for ethical research.
- Understand why ethics matter.
- Interpret ethical guidelines in the context of actual qualitative research practice.
- Understand how research governance works.

1 INTRODUCTION

Given the many demands faced by the apprentice researcher, obtaining ethical approval for your project may seem like a further unnecessary chore. However, because qualitative research inevitably involves contact with human subjects in the 'field', ethical problems are not usually far away. Consider the following examples of ethical dilemmas in qualitative research:

- In the course of gathering data for a study of male sexuality, a doctoral student guarantees confidentiality to the men he interviews. Taking him at his word, a number of them confide that they have been involved in the sexual abuse of children. To tell or not to tell? (Adapted from *Education Guardian*, 22 August 2006)
- In a study of complementary and alternative medicine (CAM), 'no matter what we said or how we disseminated our information, the practitioners remained focused on the idea that our study would provide scientific legitimation of CAM's positive effects. Morally, we were placed in a position where we were obliged constantly to remind practitioners that the knowledge produced would not provide them with strong evidence, or even a vague hint as to whether their particular treatment actually "worked". As researchers, moreover, we found ourselves in the position of bartering, where the only thing that we could exchange for the hope and goodwill of the practitioners was our professional interest' (Baarts, 2009: 429).
- Giampietro Gobo studied 'juvenile delinquents' using lists of youths with criminal records as possible informants. 'However, the lists were furnished in exchange for my promise that I would not tell the future interviewees how I had obtained their names. The reason for this secrecy was that the youths had "paid their debt to society" and were therefore of no further concern to the social services. If they had found out that their names were still on the social workers' lists they would consider themselves branded for life. Consequently, when I contacted the youths and they asked me how I had got hold of their names, I was faced with a dilemma: tell them a lie or break my promise to the social workers? In either case, I would have breached a norm of my professional code of ethics' (Gobo, 2008: 135).
- A sociology student gains access to an inner-city gang. The gang leader asks him to decide if and how two subordinates should be punished for a minor misappropriation of drug funds. What should he do? (Venkatesh, 2008)

Although these may be extreme examples, you will be lucky if you do not come across some ethical dilemmas in the course of your research. That is why modern universities make so much fuss about protecting the dignity and safety of the research participants and the general public.

EXPLORE:
VENKATESH STUDY REVIEWS

While such concerns are widely shared among social scientists today, we should remember that this has not always been the case. Most of us are aware that the Nazis used concentration camp victims as guinea pigs in their diabolical medical experiments, but relatively few are familiar with equally egregious but lesser publicized violations of human rights under the auspices of research in democratic societies. In one of the most troubling examples of unscrupulous research, a group of 399 African–American men afflicted with syphilis unknowingly became participants in a medical experiment that lasted nearly 40 years until it was finally exposed in the early 1970s (Jones, 1981: 1–23). From the 1930s to the 1970s, the physicians assigned to these men deliberately did not treat them for their ailment, even after penicillin was developed and could have been used as a cure. Instead, the patients were secretly experimented on to examine the effects of untreated syphilis. By the time this US Public Health Service study was exposed and subsequently terminated, many of the patients whose condition had gone untreated for years had either died horribly or become severely ill.

Instances of unethical research are not limited to medical experiments. Among social scientists in the USA, a well-known example of unethical research is Laud Humphreys' *Tearoom Trade* (1970). Humphreys studied anonymous homosexual encounters in semi-public places. Specifically, he was interested in the background of men who had sex with other men in public restrooms. After positioning himself in a restroom in a city park, he gained the trust of the men who frequented it by acting as a lookout for them while they engaged in sexual activities. Humphreys secretly recorded their licence plate numbers and with the help of the police discovered who they were and where they lived. Months later, he visited the men in their homes disguised as a survey researcher. He gathered additional information about these men and their families and subsequently published his research in a book that was widely praised before questions were raised about its ethics. One of the main findings of his work was that many of the men in his study were married and of middle-class background – a discovery that was made possible through the covert invasion of the subjects' privacy.

Such flagrant abuses of research subjects in the name of science have led to the establishment of codes of research ethics. While these may vary across disciplines and national boundaries, there are a number of general principles that most researchers would agree with. Most prominent among these are:

- voluntary participation and the right to withdraw
- protection of research participants
- assessment of potential benefits and risks to participants
- respecting the privacy of participants and avoiding deceiving them
- obtaining informed consent
- avoiding harm.

READ:
APPLICATION OF ETHICAL CODES

In many countries, including the UK, your supervisor is the person who decides whether your planned research meets appropriate ethical guidelines. Many if not most universities now have research ethics committees by which all research involving human subjects must be approved. Particularly when you are seeking to obtain access to an outside organization, you will often need to comply with the demands of such an ethics committee. This tends to be mandatory when you are studying healthcare organizations.

Ideally, when you successfully obtain ethical approval for your research, you accomplish two things. First, you have benefited from the advice of at least one academic trained to detect any potential flaws in your research design that could pose a threat to the participants. The advantage of this guidance cannot be overstated. A qualitative researcher's enthusiasm and desire to become intimately familiar with a topic could blind them to the adverse consequences of their research. Your supervisor or organization's research ethics committee could alert you to problems before any inadvertent harm is done.

Second, when you assure your research participants that your study has been approved by a university and/ or medical research ethics committee, you earn their confidence that you are a trained researcher with the backing of a legitimate academic institution. This could help you establish rapport and address any reservations people might have about answering your questions or sharing their private lives with you.

2 THE STANDARDS OF ETHICAL RESEARCH

Throughout this chapter, I will offer further advice about ethical issues illustrated by many student examples. However, now is a good time to confront the 'official line'. Table 4.1 sets out the instructions regarding ethical research provided by the British ESRC. Don't despair if you find this too dense or demanding. Shortly, we will see how other graduate students have handled such matters.

3 WHY ETHICS MATTER FOR YOUR RESEARCH

I would not be surprised if many readers are overawed by Table 4.1. Indeed, it is very tempting to think that, simply by paying lip-service to these principles, one may save a lot of time for the 'real' topics of one's research.

In this section, I am not going to preach you a sermon about ethical practice. Instead, I want to show you why ethics matter in qualitative research. Then I will use a student example to show you why thinking through ethical issues properly can help you do better research.

Table 4.1   What is ethical research?

1   Research staff and subjects must be informed fully about the purpose, methods and intended possible uses of the research, what their participation in the research entails and what risks, if any, are involved.

   (a) This principle underpins the meaning of informed consent. Informed consent entails giving as much information as possible about the research so that prospective participants can make an informed decision on their possible involvement. Typically, this information should be provided in written form and signed off by the research subjects. The primary objective is to conduct research openly and without deception. Deception (i.e. research without consent) should only be used as a last resort when no other approach is possible. Consent here is not simply resolved through the formal signing of a consent document at the start of research. Instead it is continually open to revision and questioning. Highly formalised or bureaucratic ways of securing consent should be avoided in favour of fostering relationships in which ongoing ethical regard for participants is to be sustained, even after the study itself has been completed.

   (b) This emphasis on the individual can seem inappropriate or meaningless in some cultural contexts, where the individual may take less precedence than broader notions of kin or community. This may be especially so when social scientists work in developing countries.

   (c) In cases where research involves vulnerable groups such as children, older persons or adults with learning difficulties, every effort should be made to secure their informed consent. However, in cases where this is seen as impossible or where the research subjects are considered not competent to give their assent to the research, the issue of honesty and consent may need to be managed via proxies, who should be either those with a duty of care or who can provide disinterested independent approval (depending on the individual circumstances). In the case of research on children, one cannot expect parents alone to provide disinterested approval on their children's behalf. In such cases, every effort should be made to deal with consent through dialogue with both children and their parents (or legal equivalent). Again, there may be circumstances where this could jeopardise the research (again in some areas of deviance, such as research into teenage sexuality or teenage pregnancy). In such circumstances, researchers will need to regard the potential risk to the principal subjects of the research as a priority.

2   The confidentiality of information supplied by research subjects and the anonymity of respondents must be respected.

    This requires that researchers take steps to ensure that research data and its sources remain confidential unless participants have consented to their disclosure, and in this latter case ensure that plans have been made for their storage and access to them.

3   Research participants must participate in a voluntary way, free from any coercion.

    In all cases of research, researchers should inform subjects of their right to refuse to participate or withdraw from the investigation whenever and for whatever reason they wish. There should be no coercion of research subjects to participate in the research. Consent has to be freely given in order to be valid.

    This is linked to the issue of covert research and deliberate deception. Deception by definition precludes consent and should only be used in a research setting where open and transparent research is impossible, whether because of the risks it might create for the researcher or participant, or in work where consent can be secured without providing the participant with full information about the project to avoid jeopardising its performance.

(Continued)

Table 4.1   *(Continued)*

4   Harm to research participants must be avoided.

   This principle requires that social science research should be conducted in such a way that it minimises harm or risk to social groups or individuals. Participants' interests or well-being should not be damaged as a result of their participation in the research. [It is important to take account of] the way in which research is communicated, especially where material is sensitive or results could be misconstrued and subsequently used by third parties against the interests of the research participants or researchers themselves.

5   The independence and impartiality of researchers must be clear, and any conflicts of interest or partiality must be explicit.

   The research should be conducted so as to ensure the professional integrity of its design, the generation and analysis of data, and the publication of results, while the direct and indirect contributions of colleagues, collaborators and others should also be acknowledged. In addition, this principle requires that investigators ensure that there is no undeclared conflict of interest (which may be personal, academic or commercial) in their proposed work and that the relation between the sources of funding and researchers' control over results is made clear, specifically in relation to the ownership, publication and subsequent use of research data.

Source: Research Ethics Framework, ESRC, July 2005, pp. 23–5

The ethics of qualitative research

There are two reasons why ethical issues are often foregrounded in qualitative research:

- Many researchers, particularly those who follow the model of naturalism, want to know the perceptions, beliefs and feelings of people. In interviews and **focus groups**, we come into close contact with people who need to be fully informed, unharmed and guaranteed anonymity.
- Qualitative methods are often used to study *sensitive* issues such as sexuality, criminality or violence. Interviewees may be asked to revisit painful memories and communities studied ethnographically will need to trust you (Hennink et al., 2011: 63-4).

Gathering data in these kinds of ways is fraught with danger. We may be insensitive to the cultures of marginalized groups or respondents; we can put people in tense or conflict situations; and we may ask insensitive and potentially threatening questions (O'Leary, 2014: 65).

Keith Punch (2014: 43–5) gives a useful hypothetical example which reveals the complexity of ethical issues in qualitative research. Say you want to observe morning assembly in a school. You approach the head teacher. She gives permission but asks whether you propose to contact parents. She makes you aware that writing to parents is likely to elicit negative reactions. Will the head teacher's permission suffice in order to carry out the study?

Ethical awareness and the success of your project

Thinking through ethical issues is not just a moral matter. As the following example shows, if you don't properly address the issue of informed consent, your research access may sometimes disappear.

WHAT I DID: JOHN

Reactions to Suicide

I had been contacting various helplines and discussing the issue of data collection. I wanted somewhere where mental health topics and suicide were being discussed ... I contacted a number of self-help groups in the search for data. I received a great response from one in Norfolk, which was for relatives of people who had committed suicide. I had many conversations on the phone with the group's founder. [He told me] that they had agreed to me coming down and video recording one of their sessions, and they were all keen to be part of the research. I discussed discursive psychological research in great detail with him, and he liked what I was proposing.

When I got there and had set up the camera, people started to arrive. It soon became clear that they were not expecting me, had given no consent to being recorded, and did not know each other or meet regularly (one person said she had attended one session four years ago and had been phoned out of the blue and asked to attend that night). It also became clear very quickly that they were all still very much in a great deal of emotional distress and pain. I turned the camera off and decided to just sit the meeting out. The group leader then announced to the group that he had no idea what I wanted or what my research was about. It then turned very unpleasant, with one member telling me that I was making her pain worse by being there, and I felt physically threatened by another member who appeared quite angry. I cannot express how terrible I felt.

Lessons learned: I should have spoken to participants and not just the group leader before showing up with a camera to the meeting, and if I ever approach a similar group again, I would get consent forms signed before attempting any data collection. I think attending some meetings to get a feel for them before collection starts would also be the way to go. [John Moore, Social Sciences, Loughborough]

John also studied helplines available to people contemplating suicide and their families. His experience shows that one aspect of ethical practice is thinking through what your research can offer participants. By doing this, as he shows, you are more likely to obtain research access. So good ethical practice can produce better research.

WHAT I DID: JOHN

What's in It for Us?

When I started discussing data collection with MindinfoLine, it was very useful to bring along some sound-files of the ethics exchanges from another helpline where calls had been recorded for research. This helped them to decide to use a recorded message as opposed to asking each caller for individual permission, as they felt that the ethics exchanges sounded too disrupting to the calls. Most importantly, it helped to bring along examples of how similar research had been used in feedback to helplines in the past, to clearly demonstrate that the research could be beneficial to them. I also made a point of encouraging them (if they were to decide to go ahead with call recording) to give me some questions to answer for them, which they did. This feedback has been a great way to continue my relationship with the helpline staff, and I have been back once to discuss the way callers who cry during calls are supported, and will be back again to discuss callers who are unclear as to what they want from the line. [John Moore]

John's research shows how important it is to consider who may benefit from your research. So 'think about whether the research is solely for academic benefit … or whether you are conducting research to respond to a problem from the research community or for an organization working with the study community' (Hennink et al., 2011: 64).

4 ETHICAL GUIDELINES IN PRACTICE

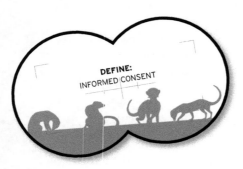

DEFINE:
INFORMED CONSENT

One could spend hours trying to decode the ESRC's list of principles set out in Table 4.1. A better learning strategy might be to consider how other graduate students have addressed ethical issues in their research. In this section, I consider what their experience can tell us about:

- obtaining consent
- research in different cultures
- research with vulnerable groups
- confidentiality.

Obtaining consent

My PhD student, Sally Hunt, sought to obtain audio recordings of a mental health team's weekly case conference. As well as completing the paperwork for an ethics committee, Sally also discussed her proposal with the chairman of the trust's mental health board, a practising consultant psychiatrist. He voiced no objection in principle and recommended that she contact the team's consultant and team leader to seek their individual permission, which she did. As Sally remarks:

> Being a participant-observer raises a number of ethical issues which extend beyond formal consent to the research. Before the research began, I decided that the best way to carry out participant observation, both morally and practically, was to be as open as possible with the team. My rationale for making this decision was that this would permit me to be free to ask questions as the fieldwork progressed without creating too much suspicion.

Sally was studying a group of professionals who needed to be properly informed. This ethical principle was even more to the fore in Charles Douglas's interviews with Australian palliative care physicians and nurses for his study of the moral psychology of end-of-life decision making. In an area fraught with both moral and legal considerations, full information needed to be provided and anonymity guaranteed.

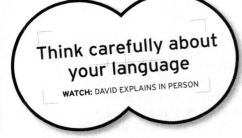

Think carefully about your language

WATCH: DAVID EXPLAINS IN PERSON

David's Top Tip 5

When preparing information sheets it is sensible to avoid terms that are potentially sensitive. For instance, in a study of obesity management in general practice medicine, the term 'weight management' was used with potential participants. In subsequent interviews it was discovered that most respondents found the terms 'obese' and 'obesity' hurtful (Barbour, 2007b: 75).

But professionals are not the only group we may want to study. When we research vulnerable people, ethical considerations should obviously be paramount. For instance, as part of a study of rehabilitation trajectories, Rikke Guldager was interviewing Danish adults with traumatic brain injuries. Rachael Dunn's PhD at Murdoch University, Western Australia, focused on a clinic treating young people with eating disorders. Like Sally, she needed approval from a participating organization and needed to adjust her proposal accordingly.

WHAT I DID: RACHAEL
Working with Ethics Committees

In the course of the ethics approval process, a number of stipulations were made by the committee concerning data collection protocols. To minimize any effect the taping of the therapy sessions might have on patients, or the therapeutic process, the participating clinicians made an informed clinical decision as to which patients to approach for consent. This potentially produced bias in which sessions were ultimately recorded, as clinicians could exclude certain patients. To minimize this, the clinicians were instructed to record a representative sample of therapeutic interactions. Patients were advised on the patient information sheet and verbally before recording commenced that they were able to withdraw their consent before, during or after the therapy sessions. Patients were also informed that withdrawal or non-participation in the study would not affect the care they received. Patients were further advised that no identifying details would be made public in the study and that the audio-tapings of therapy sessions would not be played publicly. In addition, the hospital ethics committee required a final amendment to the application, which stipulated that all original recordings and sound file copies be destroyed subsequent to the analysis phase of the study. [Rachael Dunn, Psychology, Murdoch University]

Understanding process consent

WATCH: DAVID EXPLAINS IN PERSON

David's Top Tip 6

Note that Rachael allowed participants to withdraw their consent at any time. This is known as 'process consent' and is a better way of safeguarding participants than a once-and-for-all 'informed consent'. Process consent may also imply your commitment to debrief participants afterwards. This is a common feature in focus group research where people may be allowed to talk about their contributions immediately after the event and given a contact number should they wish to talk to a researcher at a later date (see Barbour, 2007b: 82).

The information sheets you give to potential participants should be carefully constructed. Your research needs to be fully described in a way that the people concerned can understand. As noted above, it is also sensible to stress that, if consent is given, it can be withdrawn at any time.

As an example of good practice, you will find below the information sheet used by Rachael Dunn.

PATIENT INFORMATION SHEET

Project Title: Therapeutic Interaction in Anorexia Nervosa Treatment

Thank you for taking the time to read this information.

My name is Rachael Dunn and I am a PhD student at Murdoch University. The purpose of my study is to look at how language is used in therapy sessions between clinicians and adolescents diagnosed with an eating disorder. Results from this study will have the opportunity to provide new information on the role of language in the therapeutic process with patients in the area of eating disorders. It is hoped that this will enhance our understanding of what is helpful for the adolescent with anorexia nervosa.

You can help in this study by consenting to have your therapy session recorded using a digital MP3 recording device. Participation in this study is voluntary. You may withdraw your consent at any time during or after the therapy session, at which time the recording will be destroyed. No names or other information that might identify you will be used in any publication or documentation arising from the research. If you decide to withdraw from the study or do not take part, this will not in any way affect the care you receive at [named] hospital.

Being in this study will not involve any extra time for you. It will only mean that the therapy session you are already having will be recorded. After transcription, the original recordings will be stored at the hospital in a locked filing cabinet on an MP3 recording device. The tapes will be kept through the data collection and transcription parts of the study (maximum 10 months) and then they will be destroyed. Written transcripts will be made from the recording and will contain no names or details that might identify you.

A report on this study will be given to the Eating Disorders Team at the hospital and will be available for you to read. If you are willing to participate in this study, could you please complete the attached consent form. If you have any questions about this study please feel free to contact me, Rachael Dunn, on [phone number] or my supervisor [name] from the Eating Disorders Team [phone number].

Kind regards

Rachael Dunn

BA (Hons) (Psychology)

Rachael used a similar information sheet with the parents of the adolescent patients in her study. This is an excellent example of such information, which incorporates a full description of the purposes of her research, details of what will actually happen if you participate, and provision for 'process consent' as well for extra information from respected others. My only minor reservation is that the description of her research in terms of 'the role of language in the therapeutic process' may be a little bit heavy on academic jargon. Can you think of a more down-to-earth way of phrasing Rachael's topic?

Research in different cultures

What is a 'different' culture? Does this mean a different society, or can 'different' cultures be much closer to home? For instance, in the examples given at the beginning of this chapter, were the gang members and complementary medicine practitioners not members of cultures quite different from those of the researchers?

Of course, it is always wise for researchers to consider the way in which their assumptions and practices may be different from those they study. Even in the familiar medical settings studied by Sally and Rachael, they did not take for granted the way participants would understand what they were doing. In this section, however, I focus on the specific issues in studying people from another society.

Sometimes this can be a quite straightforward matter. Maddie Sandall studied the experience of international students. During her research, she interviewed 'partnership programme' students who have transferred to the UK for the final year of their degree.

WHAT I DID: MADDIE
Studying International Students

I didn't require ethics committee approval, but did create an ethics statement which I sent to each interviewee which covered issues of anonymity and confidentiality. This was particularly important as I had been seen as a member of staff in one light and then a 'fellow student' in another. I wanted them to be clear that I was in my student role for the interviews.

Other ethical considerations included ensuring I had knowledge of their cultural differences and also being clear on the questions which could have different meanings in different cultures. I also reassured the students that the research will only be read by the markers and will not in any way be fed back to their partner college or to the university.

One particularly tricky issue was when one of the students turned the interview around and started to interview me – asking me what the Western view of Asians was – I felt like I was really put on the spot and asked to generalize on behalf of all Westerners! Although I do of course have an opinion, it's quite difficult to know the 'right thing to say'. An issue I am sure the interviewees had themselves. [Maddie Sandall, Management, University of the West of England]

It is often difficult to import ethical principles from one culture and apply them without modifications to another. The experienced sociologist Catherine Riessman conducted research in villages in Kerala, South India, between 1993 and 1994. Her interest was in the meaning and management of infertility which, she remarks, was 'an invisible problem in the Indian context'. Here is a shortened account of how she describes her ethical dilemmas.

Researching Indian Villagers

My research proposal ... included procedures for obtaining informed consent from childless women. But ... the very language of Western research practice – 'obtaining' informed consent – indicates who will be in control.

The first hint of trouble happened shortly after I joined my host institution, the research unit of a small college in Kerala. [My] research assistant, Liza – a 26 year old Malayali graduate level social worker, educated in Kerala ... was surprised ... by my consent form: 'we don't do that here,' she told me gently ... I persisted, and asked her to translate into Malayalam the form I had prepared according to my University's guidelines.

Because women in Kerala are educated and literate, many informants read along as we communicated the contents of the consent form. Most women signed it. A significant number, however, were reluctant to affix their names. They were suspicious, not about interviewing or taping, but about the form. Perhaps they thought it a government document.

Reflecting now on the refusal of some women, I hear their worry. The consent form *was* a government document – an import from the West, designed to meet my University's Institutional Review Board requirement ... Signing documents in the Indian context carries a history of well-deserved suspicion: government intrusion into property rights, inheritance, marriage customs, and reproductive health. Strangers seeking information and bearing forms are not easily trusted, especially in rural villages. (Riessman, 2005: ms 8–9)

It is not always just a case of suspicion. People in non-Western cultures may regard their consent to research as a purely instrumental matter. As Anne Ryen observes:

I have frequently met expectations that I will reciprocate in one way or another in African settings ... These have been of different kinds, from expecting me to cope with local poverty and offering grants, to gift exchanges and sexual offers. (2004: 238)

In some cultures, however, it may be difficult to say 'no' to a researcher's request for access. As Ryen notes, on the basis of her research in East Africa:

For many poor Third World interviewees, local norms make it difficult to turn down a request from a visitor to be interviewed or they do not know the potential implications of participating in research. [This means that] the general ethical correctness of informed consent irrespective of the location of the field may be questionable with reference to the North–South dimension in Third World projects. (2004: 232)

Queenie Eng did her PhD research on Chinese people with diabetes living in the UK. Like Anne Ryen, she found that 'informed consent' was quite different to that imagined in Western-based research protocols.

WHAT I DID: QUEENIE

Why Do Non-Western People Give Consent?

In the UK, the rules of engagement in research are modelled along the Western ethical framework. On the other hand, the research participants are Chinese migrants whose rules of engagement are moulded by the Eastern customs and traditions.

Within the group setting, the social role of the researcher is problematic because of her position as an academic amongst participants who were largely illiterate. The reverence for and importance of education in Chinese culture is documented in literary and historical texts. In accordance with the Western framework of conducting research, participants are asked for their consent, and this is indicated by their signature on a consent form. However, the signing of a form between individuals who have verbally consented to carrying out a promise is a foreign import. Within the Chinese tradition, agreements are sealed by the 'gentleman's honour', not a signature on a piece of paper.

So, what does one do in this case? Should the researcher get the participants to sign before or after the interview? The point is, when dealing with people who come from a non-Western culture, a seemingly simple act of the signing of a consent form has cultural repercussions. Researchers need to be aware of this and know what it means for the participants as it can impact on how much information they are willing to divulge.

The participants also misunderstood the benefits they were to get out of the research. One of the reasons for participation was because some of the participants thought that they would learn something about their illness from the researcher. Despite thorough explanation at the outset of the discussion from the researcher and her assistant about the nature of the focus group discussions, misunderstanding persisted. They were angry when SE [Queenie Eng] did not accede to their demands for information on diabetes in exchange for participation in the focus groups. Arguably, the 'mutiny' was justified.

In the process of sharing their experience, both participant and researcher had to find a middle ground to satisfy the needs of both parties. [In this setting] deviation from the Western norm of conducting research is inevitable. These deviations include recruitment, obtaining consent, upholding confidentiality and anonymity, handling reciprocity and managing conflicts. [Queenie Eng (S. Eng), Medicine, Leeds]

Eng's, Ryen's and Riessman's research with non-Western people shows that obtaining consent can be far more complicated than Western ethical guidelines would suggest.

Break the rules when necessary

WATCH: DAVID EXPLAINS IN PERSON

David's Top Tip 7

As with every aspect of your research, success is not measured by passive rule following. Understand the rules but then ensure that you think through their relevance for the people and situations you wish to study. Success depends upon thoughtful, well-informed ethical practice. Sometimes this can mean deviating from rules.

Research with vulnerable groups

Issues of consent become even more complicated when you want to study vulnerable people such as children or adults with disabilities. For instance, I welcomed the idea of colleagues researching the old people's home where I do voluntary work. However, the ethical issues involved in studying people with dementia are vast and apparently intractable, particularly if you want to use video data. Families, carers and care managers will all have to be consulted. But what happens when the camera accidentally includes a resident or carer for whom you have no permission to record? Moreover, how satisfactory is it to use family permission to record intimate details of somebody's daily life?

Anne Patterson carefully attended to these issues in her PhD research on young people with learning disabilities. Her account is as follows.

WHAT I DID: ANNE
Studying People with Disabilities

In my PhD research, which studies telephone calls between family members, one of whom has a learning disability, the 'dilemma' is associated with ethics in what I think is a fairly unique way. I obtained appropriate ethics committee approval (at university level) since some of the participants were in a recognized 'vulnerable' group, and I approached three families direct, asking them to record their telephone calls with the young adults in their families who were at residential school or college and were making calls home. I gained informed consent as far as possible from all individuals involved, but it is still a concern whether it is possible to obtain 'true' informed consent or whether the motives of the research are truly understood and the individual's rights to refuse to take part are fully appreciated. Some researchers question whether individuals truly understand the research and their position within it. With this in mind, an information sheet was designed which could be read by or read to all participants. In the case of the young adults with learning disabilities the form was supplemented with extra explanation of the contents therein. It was possible then to be satisfied that the interests of these participants had been fairly served and that informed consent had been given as far as was practically possible. In order to build an even greater awareness of the purpose of the research it has been possible to show one of the young people some transcripts and allow them to listen to the recordings (much to everyone's amusement). This certainly provided a further, very practical opportunity to try to ensure that one of the young adults was aware of what was being done in the study and to understand their part in it. [Anne Patterson, Social Sciences, Loughborough]

Sometimes the complex ethical issues involved in studying potentially vulnerable groups may be redefined in terms of the research design itself. Pia Kontos applied to the research ethics board (REB) of a long-term care facility where she proposed to conduct ethnographic research on their Alzheimer's support unit. While the proposal was approved by the REB, in their letter of approval there were concerns expressed about her methodology. It was indicated that while they appreciated that there are significant differences between quantitative science and qualitative studies, they had an ethical responsibility to ensure that the residents of their facility were only subjected to research which was based on sound design. Of particular concern to the REB was that she intended to be the sole observer, which in their view carries an inherent potential for bias. In the interests of increasing her ability to obtain meaningful data, it was thus strongly recommended that she strengthen the validity of her study design by including triangulation of observations through the involvement of secondary observers. It was suggested that family members might be particularly appropriate in this role. Pia's response is shown below.

WHAT I DID: PIA

Using Your Supervisor to Support You

In response to the REB's recommendation, my thesis supervisor wrote a letter indicating that their recommendation to involve 'secondary observers' was not methodologically appropriate. She explained that verification or trustworthiness is a central topic in the qualitative research literature and that verification in the case of my thesis research would be ensured by following standard qualitative methodology criteria including: (1) the articulation of an explicit theoretical framework which informs data collection and analysis; (2) prolonged engagement in the field; (3) the production of detailed fieldnotes [**thick description**] after each engagement in the field; (4) iterative data collection and data analysis ('constant comparison method'); (5) attending to negative or disconfirming evidence; and (6) frequent debriefing with thesis committee members about the research process and development of preliminary coding categories.

This experience highlighted the importance of having qualitative researchers on REBs to ensure that qualitative studies are properly and fairly reviewed. [Pia Kontos, Department of Public Health Sciences, Toronto]

Confidentiality

Issues relating to confidentiality can usually be met straightforwardly, as the following student example shows.

WHAT I DID: ALASTAIR

Keeping Sensitive Information under Wraps

In a study of leadership, I used number-coded transcripts and all references to names of people and organizations were deleted. The names of the individuals and interested parties were changed without destroying the integrity and usefulness of the research. All written transcripts, recordings of interviews and content analysis were kept in a fireproof and secure location for long-term security. [Alastair Rylatt, Management, University of Technology, Sydney]

Next is Sally Hunt's account of how she approached this topic when making audio recordings of a mental health team's weekly case conference.

WHAT I DID: SALLY

Preserving Anonymity

I undertook to use pseudonyms for the names of staff, clients and care areas throughout the research to preserve anonymity and to safeguard confidentiality. In the event, even references to months or seasons of the year in the transcripts were changed as the work got under way. Dates of legislation were retained as were dates of fieldwork and any reference to clients' ages, as such data were necessary to the analysis. As it is not usual for a PhD thesis to be published, this further helped to maintain anonymity. In addition, I undertook to write a report on the progress of the study for the ethical committee, should this be required at any stage of the work. [I did not seek] to interview clients or to access their case records. I guaranteed to keep all audiotapes at home under lock and key and to do all my own transcribing rather than eliciting secretarial assistance. I also promised to destroy the tapes at the end of the study. [Sally Hunt, Sociology, Goldsmiths]

However, as we saw at the beginning of this chapter, confidentiality issues can be more complex. When I showed this chapter to my then Sage editor, Patrick Brindle, he remarked that, in his own PhD research, anonymity was not the choice of most of the people he interviewed.

DEFINE: CONFIDENTIALITY

WHAT I DID: PATRICK

Do People Want To Be Anonymous?

One thing that I encountered doing oral history interviewing for my PhD was that many of my interviewees did not want to be anonymized. They regarded their interview as public testimony and stated that they were looking forward to seeing their names in print in my book. When I put it to the interviewees that I would have to change their names and hide their identity they became quite upset, and one of them said that she would not have let me interview her if her identity was to be concealed.

Which made me think: who are we trying to protect? Once it was anonymized, there was nothing to stop me from tampering with the testimony knowing that there could be no comeback from the respondent. I did not, of course, but anonymization would have made it easy to do so. So a critical question for me is always: who benefits? [Patrick Brindle]

What respondents want is not the only issue regarding anonymity. Should you keep quiet when people reveal criminal offences in the course of a 'confidential' research interview? And, if you are using video data, what can you properly reveal in seminar presentations and publications? Once again, there are no easy answers. If you are faced with an apparently intractable ethical problem, consult your supervisor and read about how more experienced researchers handled such a problem. Here, as elsewhere, don't try to reinvent the wheel!

5 COMPLEX ETHICAL ISSUES

Here the waters muddy still further. In this section I deal with a number of issues which are barely mentioned in ethical guidelines such as those provided by the ESRC, namely:

- consent to observational research
- consent to Internet research
- whether there can be 'appropriate' deception
- paying participants
- the unintended consequences of good ethical practice.

Consent to observational research

Qualitative researchers sometimes encounter unique problems in obtaining ethical approval, particularly when their data depends upon observation. Indeed, a guidebook published by the US Department of Health and Human Services explicitly notes the difficulties confronting qualitative researchers where informed consent is concerned. Specifically, in a section titled 'Fieldwork' the guidebook states:

> Fieldwork, or ethnographic research, involves observation of and interaction with the persons or group being studied in the group's own environment, often for long periods of time. Since fieldwork is a research process that gains shape and substance as the study progresses, it is difficult, if not impossible, to specify detailed contents and objectives in a protocol.

> After gaining access to the fieldwork setting, the ongoing demands of scientifically and morally sound research involve gaining the approval and trust of the persons being studied. These processes, as well as the research itself, involve complex, continuing interactions between researcher and hosts that cannot be reduced to an informed consent form. Thus, while the idea of consent is not inapplicable in fieldwork, Institutional Review Boards [US ethical committees, referred to henceforth as IRBs] and researchers need to adapt prevailing notions of acceptable protocols and consent procedures to the realities of fieldwork. IRBs should keep in mind the possibility of granting a waiver of informed consent. (Penslar, 2007)

Evidently, even the US government agency in charge of defining and enforcing guidelines for dealing with human subjects is aware that qualitative researchers face unique challenges in gaining IRB approvals (it is worth noting that this guidebook was prepared by a lawyer, Robin Levin Penslar JD, the 'ORRR Program Officer', and a physician, Joan P. Porter DPA).

A case study illustrates how the student ethnographer may need to work out different forms of consent for different groups. Keith Abbott carried out doctoral (sociological) research into spiritual enlightenment at Loughborough University, and his subjects included internationally famous spiritual gurus as well as some lesser known individuals who teach about enlightenment.

WHAT I DID: KEITH

Fieldwork on Spiritual Enlightenment

I have been using audio and video recordings, and photos I have taken. I have recorded people to whom the gurus speak during short courses or fairly public events. I've taken the view that different 'subjects' require different levels of consent (so gurus have massive consent forms; people in the audience at public events being recorded anyway may not get a form at all).

When recording live events where there is an audience, I generally did not seek prior consent from all present, only the main speaker. I tried several times to catch up with people who had contributed to the event from the audience afterwards, to ask retrospective consent, but was never quick enough to intercept them and soon gave up on this as a strategy. However, such events were generally rather ostensibly recorded by the organizers anyway, sometimes unannounced and sometimes with something like the mention of a

(Continued)

(Continued)

possible podcast or CD/DVD becoming available. I took it that on such occasions all those who spoke or remained had already implicitly consented to becoming part of a worldwide spectacle and so were ethically available to my own recordings. In such cases I tried to anonymize all but the main speaker or anyone who had explicitly consented.

For small events running over several days or encounters, particularly where I was using video as well as audio recordings, I had a very short single-page consent form, different from my more elaborate 'guru form', which simply allowed course delegates the possibilities of altogether opting out of being recorded, being recorded anonymously (such as by their images being edited), or being recorded without anonymizing. There were occasions, however, where producing even the short form would have been hugely disruptive and instead I relied upon being open about my research intentions and simply asked people if they minded being audio-recorded, refraining if there seemed to be any hint of concern. [Keith Abbott, Social Sciences, Loughborough]

Although Queenie Eng's study of Chinese people living in the UK used focus groups rather than fieldwork data, she faced similar issues to Keith in deciding what counted as 'appropriate' consent.

WHAT I DID: QUEENIE
Delayed Consent with Non-Western Respondents

For people who come from a non-Western culture, a seemingly simple act of signing a con-sent form has cultural repercussions. Researchers need to be aware of this and know what it means for the participants as it can impact on how much information they are willing to divulge. The participants' attendance of the focus group meeting was construed by the researcher as a sign of consent and hence agreement to take part in the study. Therefore, it can be argued that signing the consent form would only formalize the whole interaction and put the participant into another mindset. For this reason, I delayed the signing of the consent form till towards the end of the session and did this in conjunction with the distri-bution of gift vouchers.

Thus, apparently simple protocols were difficult to adhere to. For example, the signing of consent forms which was supposed to be done before the beginning of each session was sometimes left to the last part of the interview, as the act of signing could affect the terms of engagement. Ironically, it was my moderator who reminded me that I should do what the Western protocol expects, i.e. obtain written consent before conducting the interview. As it turned out, the signature per se was not to be an issue but the verbal explanation of the consent form was. This was due to the low levels of literacy among these groups of Chinese participants. [Queenie Eng (S. Eng), Medicine, Leeds]

What Queenie calls 'the Western protocol' may be inappropriate to many field-work settings even when the participants are Western Europeans. Sally Hunt's account reveals that, faced with an ethical form based on medical research, the fieldworker needs to show considerable mental agility.

WHAT I DID: SALLY

Redefining 'Hazard'

I put forward my proposal to the ethical committee of the trust hospital to which the team was attached. I found the form I was required to complete somewhat problematic. It conformed to the standard type for purely *clinical* research involving human subjects rather than to any proposed sociological research. Predictably, it was very 'physically' oriented. One question asked for 'potential hazards' and the precautions I might take to meet them. The possible contravening of confidentiality was my written response to this enquiry. [Sally Hunt, Sociology, Goldsmiths]

Sally's experience concerning inappropriate ethical issues is very common in research involving fieldwork. If you are studying a public setting like a shopping mall, football stadium or concert, it may be impossible to obtain consent from the people you are observing. Moreover, as Giampietro Gobo (2008: 108) argues, such consent may not even be necessary because you do not interact with anyone and people know that their behaviour is open to public inspection.

DEFINE: ETHICS & NEW MEDIA

Consent to Internet research

It is sometimes assumed that the Internet is a public space where people realize that what they say can be seen by others. As David Gray (2014: 87–8) points out, Internet chatrooms and forums are full of material of potential interest to the researcher. But gathering such material raises a number of ethical dilemmas:

- Is it ethical to enter a chatroom purely for research purposes?
- Is it necessary to obtain informed consent?
- Is it sufficient simply to announce your presence and invite participants to opt out if they wish to?
- How can we protect chatroom material?

In a study of Internet sex sites, Gabriella Scaramuzzino saw these and other complex ethical issues.

WHAT I DID: GABRIELLA

Internet Sex Sites

I stayed on the Internet and I stayed there a lot, much longer than researchers had done in previous studies. I started to notice that if you observe contributors that closely you tend to get quite a lot of information about them. They do not only interact around issues that relate to prostitution, they hang out and write about many things, often personal and private stuff. How anonymous are they then? In Sweden it is also illegal to purchase sexual services but not to sell, which makes it even more [problematic]. Maybe their anonymity could be presumed in a sense. Maybe sometimes they also forget that they are interacting in a public place. People on the Internet in general tend to write private matters publicly.

To cope with these ethical dilemmas I erased all personal and sensitive information and edited pictures before they were downloaded and stored. I also noticed that some of the contributors were 'famous' in the virtual red-light district and had made themselves a name. Some of the users are not even anonymous to each other as some of them have met offline not only for sexual encounters but also socially. Therefore, I decided not to use their usernames and not to write the names of the websites included in the study. So looking at my text you cannot trace quotes made by the same user to the same person. However, the data are still there on the Internet. All posts and threads are saved in archives, like the virtual red-light district's own collective memory. Anyone can take part in the exact situations that I have done. I think that instead of dismissing unseen observation as a technique the potential harm should be weighed against the relevance of the knowledge gained. [Gabriella Scaramuzzino, Sociology, Malmö University]

Gabriella graphically demonstrates the ethical traps when you work with Internet data. The following list covers these and other dilemmas in this area:

- Many users perceive publicly accessible discourse sites as private. For example, although many online discussion groups appear to be public, members may perceive their interaction to be private and can be surprised or angered by intruding researchers. Other groups know their communication is public but nonetheless do not want to be studied.
- Anonymity is difficult to guarantee. For example, some users have a writing style that is readily identifiable in their online community, so that the researcher's use of a pseudonym does not guarantee anonymity. Also, search engines are often capable of finding statements used in published qualitative research reports. The potential harm to individuals, relationships, families and careers is not to be dismissed lightly.

- Online discussion sites can be highly transient. For example, researchers gaining access permission in June may not be studying the same population in July. Therefore, while a researcher may have gained consent from a group at one moment, this consent may not apply at later points in time.
- Vulnerable persons are difficult to identify in certain online environments. For example, age is difficult if not impossible to verify online (Markham, 2011: 122-3).

EXPLORE:
INTERNET ETHICS

Although there are no easy answers to these issues, Robert Kozinets (2010: 136–56) has provided a helpful discussion of problems and solutions when attempting what he calls 'ethical netnography'.

Appropriate deception?

Informed consent suggests that you should be entirely open with participants about the purposes of your research and that any other course involves an unacceptable degree of deception. However, such openness gives rise to two problems:

1. Revealing your true interests may influence what people say or do.
2. People may not be able to make sense of the scientific terms you use to define your research problem.

This problem arose in Charlotte Baarts's (2009) study of complementary medicine. Knowing that practitioners hoped her research would show that such medicine worked, she concealed her scepticism. She comments:

WHAT I DID: CHARLOTTE

Can we show scepticism to people we study?

With hindsight I see that I should have acknowledged and articulated my scepticism more thoroughly during my collaboration with the practitioners. I should have recognized that ethical research does not imply a comfortable sort of neutrality, and that taking a standpoint as a researcher means adopting a third position distinct from both the dominant and the marginal positions within the controversy. Had I expressed my scepticism, the practitioners might still have seen me as a potential 'convert to their cause'. Taking a

(Continued)

(Continued)

stand within the framework of highly politicized and commercialized subject matter, and making that position public, is part of conscious ethical practice, and at the same time reflects the recognition that science is both partial and political.

Taking a stand does not necessarily imply communicating everything to collaborators or participants. But it does mean that one must reflect on the part played by one's personal values and beliefs. (Baarts, 2009: 432)

These issues have been directly confronted in psychological experiments where a fully open statement of the research problem is thought to 'contaminate' the results. In these cases, a degree of deception is thought to be appropriate providing the well-being of participants and their privacy are respected. Indeed, you should never deceive people about what procedures they will undergo during your research, and always undertake to answer any questions they have both before and after the research has taken place (for further discussion of these issues, see Christians, 2005: 144–5).

Paying participants?

Sometimes it may be tempting to offer some reward to respondents who agree to be interviewed or to participate in a focus group (notice Queenie Eng's use of gift vouchers in the example on p.74). This follows the practice of many psychological studies involving students and of drug companies in certain kinds of drug trials. However, both can raise ethical issues if the reward offered tempts people to participate against their initial judgement. One way of handling this problem is to avoid advertising the payment or to omit to provide details of the payment involved (Barbour, 2007b: 80).

Unintended consequences of good ethical practice

Just as there can be no rules that cover every instance, following ethical rules can sometimes have quite unintended consequences. In Keith Abbott's research, a well-meant gesture (sharing data with participants) led to potential copyright problems.

WHAT I DID: KEITH

Consequences of Sharing Data

Legal and ethical rights and obligations relevant to researchers' own materials can also cause problems. I left some research subjects with some JPEG digital images I had taken from a personal development course I had researched as a memento and 'thank you'. All people in the data were happy for others to share their images in this way. However, some of those photographs were used in a training manual prepared by the course organizers without asking for any further permission, thus becoming part of a text intended to elaborate and teach the practices being researched. I did not anticipate such usage, and the publication in what was in effect a commercial manual prompted me to check the university's position on what was potentially an infringement of its (and possibly my) copyright in the images and a usage which demanded some consideration to its ethicality. Since in any case, ethically and under the Data Protection Act, subjects may expect to be given copies of recordings of themselves (or their works), it can be wise for researchers to give some early thought, before any such request is made and certainly before passing on research recordings, to limiting further reproduction of released materials (by for instance annotating prints or images, or only releasing low-quality or watermarked materials). If subjects are only happy if researchers share recordings fully with them, researchers may need to question whether or not such research is acceptable to them. [Keith Abbott, Social Sciences, Loughborough]

Fortunately, following ethical guidelines can unintentionally sometimes enrich the analytic breadth of a research study. Sally Hunt's efforts to achieve informed consent with her homelessness workers meant that they were prepared to allow her to audio-record as well as observe their meetings.

Keith Abbott's pursuit of materials went in the opposite direction, moving him away from recording equipment towards observation. As he puts it:

> I've had some particular 'troubles' to do with getting permission for visual recordings, and objections leading me unintentionally into ethnographic research on one particular occasion, though this made future recordings easier as I thus became something of an insider. [Keith Abbott]

A further unintended consequence for the research process arises from the fact that 'ethical practice' as a matter of concern is now widespread among many occupational groups. On some occasions, this offers a fascinating topic for the fieldworker, as Sally Hunt recognized.

WHAT I DID: SALLY

Participants Doing Ethics

There were almost certainly times in this study when members responded to my presence in terms of what might be called 'ethical correctness'. I sensed that there were some occasions when members overtly displayed their moral adequacy as a consequence of being observed. My general *impression* was that members responded to me as a more senior member of staff, i.e. as an older, experienced professional now working in higher education. I felt that the team's display of moral adequacy in my presence was particularly marked, especially where ethical dilemmas were prominent. [Sally Hunt, Sociology, Goldsmiths]

6 RESEARCH GOVERNANCE

READ:
UK ETHICS COMMITTEES

Sally's observations of nursing staff doing 'ethical correctness' reveal that 'ethics' have become much more than a matter of individual researchers seeking to employ good practice. Instead, a vast system of interlocking organizations (governmental, semi-governmental, medical and legal) now confronts the contemporary Western researcher. The way in which these organizations survey and discipline researchers is described as 'research governance'. Linnie Price gives an example of what this can mean to an experienced qualitative researcher.

WHAT I DID: LINNIE

Surveying the Researcher

As well as ethics, research governance is now a huge hassle. For our project, for which ethics approval was in place when I came in post, research governance delayed the start by four months, and we had to go cap in hand for more funding. For any contact with 'vulnerable' service users (some of ours had long-term mental illness), *every* person having contact needed an honorary contract with the local health authority *and* a Criminal Records Bureau check. In one of our sites, everyone had to have an occupational health medical with HIV test, including the principal researcher who is dean of a medical school.

The other pitfall is service user (SU) involvement. Few funding bodies will now support a project without SU involvement, which raises all sorts of other issues. Similarly, kapo-like data protection officers in health trusts can completely sabotage your ethics approved recruitment procedures. [Linnie Price, Plymouth University]

While ethical and governance requirements can play a significant role in ensuring the safety of research participants, their survey-friendly protocol may in the long run discourage more innovative research projects, especially those aimed at investigating social inequality (e.g. poverty, racism, sexism). Such studies may invariably involve some degree of risk, both for the subjects and for the organization where inequality is practised. As Nelson states:

> Of course, 'respect for persons' can hardly entail respect for every human action, but IRBs are ill equipped to negotiate the difference. Instead, they often give unquestioned allegiance to a concept that might be given more nuanced application to, say, Ku Klux Klan or Nazi Party members, who might merit humanity qualified with disapproval and who might on occasion appropriately be challenged aggressively in an interview. A historian might well wish to investigate the self-understanding of a Ku Klux Klan member and might choose to present a neutral account of the organization, but academic freedom means that the decision to do so needs to be the historian's, not that of an IRB. One consequence of an unreflective commitment to 'respect for persons' is that IRBs have great difficulty accepting research destined to be critical of its 'human subjects'. (2003: 32)

As seen in the passage above, an increasing number of US social scientists, and academics in general, are concerned about IRBs' growing 'ethics creep' (Haggerty, 2004) into their research. Initially, the social scientists responded to IRB demands with incredulity and amusement. For example, in a magazine interview, Howard Becker joked that if he was required to undergo rigorous IRB reviews, he would circumvent the bureaucracy by redefining his research as 'conceptual art' (Shea, 2000). Four years later, in response to Haggerty's 'Ethics creep: governing social science research in the name of ethics' (2004), Becker wrote:

> What began years ago as a sort of safeguard against doctors injecting cancer cells into research patients without first asking them if that was OK has turned into a serious, ambitious bureaucracy with interests to protect, a mission to promote, and a self-righteous and self-protective ideology to explain why it is all necessary ... I never had occasion to try out the idea I suggested to the reporter from Lingua Franca, of describing my work as conceptual art or performance art ... But if I did I suspect the response would be to change the rules to include art projects. (2004: 415-16)

Becker goes on to point out that some of his research on medical students, for example, could not have been conducted with the same academic rigour under the new IRB rules. His final recommendation to social scientists is: 'Start fighting this thing full time and don't give up an inch we don't have to' (2004: 416). Increasingly, UK research ethics committees are taking on the function of IRBs (see Richardson and McMullan, 2007; and, on the cost of their review, see Flynn, 2000).

Research ethics committees and North American IRBs may inadvertently block the aspirations of researchers who want to dig deeper, as it were. Moreover, in their capacity to monitor and approve research, IRBs can become a sort of 'university research police' that controls the production of knowledge. Given that IRBs are a relatively new institutional invention, it remains to be seen how they will evolve to fulfil their mission.

Figure out what ethical approval is needed

WATCH: DAVID EXPLAINS IN PERSON

David's Top Tip 8

One way of cutting through the jargon used in research governance is simply to ask yourself: what might my research question mean to possible participants? What will they be confronted with if they agree to participate? As an exercise, think about the experience of being interviewed about your future if you have early-stage dementia, or what it may be like for a homeless person to be asked about their earlier family life (Flick, 2007: 71). Although Flick's idea will help your application, you do need to be aware of the time it can take to get ethical approval, so you need to start seeking approvals in good time.

7 WRAPPING UP: MANAGING UNFOLDING ETHICAL DEMANDS

The challenge for student researchers is to package the open-ended contingencies of qualitative research in a way that convinces your supervisor and any organization you are studying that no risk is involved. Survey researchers have an easier job with this because the survey questions are designed in advance and clearly demarcate the boundaries of the project. In contrast, qualitative research moves in unpredicted directions; an informant's answers to a question may result in a line of enquiry that was not planned from the start. In the example below, Michelle Day-Miller offers advice for overcoming this sort of challenge.

WHAT I DID: MICHELLE

Planned Flexibility

The biggest problem for qualitative researchers, as I see it, is that in our data collection we have to be flexible and attuned to 'emergent data'. While qualitative researchers can dance to our particular rendition of flexible and emergent, lawyers and some quantitative researchers find this rendition lacking in rhythm (structure) and believe it is chaotic (not systematic). We need to provide structure and a systematic *outline* of what is planned and give possible outcomes of 'planned flexibility'. The phrase 'planned flexibility' is one way of handling ethical issues in qualitative research proposals. It may not be enough to inform your supervisor that you are doing qualitative research and therefore are not sure about the type of questions asked, where, and how. This applies even more to the organization you want to study. They just won't understand and agree with that line of reasoning. Instead, to the best of your ability give an outline of what shape or direction your research might take. In other words, give them something they can work with within the parameters of their institutional roles. [Michelle Day-Miller, USA]

Some research projects have to be considerably modified due to ethical constraints. For example, Michael Arter states about his PhD on a US police force:

> In the earliest planning for my research I had considered interviewing the spouses of the officers for the familial aspect of police stress. Based upon past decisions of the IRB at my institution, the plan to attempt to interview anyone other than police officers was abandoned.

Other researchers go through such a complicated ethical approval process that the experience itself becomes part of the dissertation. This was certainly the case with Sylvia Ansay, who encountered particularly stringent demands in her research on US citizens under house arrest.

WHAT I DID: SYLVIA
Which Organization Is Doing the 'Governance'?

I experienced a major hurdle that seemed to come out of nowhere. I had worked closely with the IRB administrator in writing my proposal. She assured me that we had covered all our bases and there appeared to be no problems. Approval should be automatic, she said, just a matter of waiting a couple of weeks until the board met. The process became complicated when the IRB decided that, although I was not receiving funding from the National Institute of Health (NIH), I should have NIH approval for the project. The board didn't give me any reasons for the decision; however, I filed the proposal with NIH as they required. An administrator at NIH telephoned me, surprised at the request because I was not seeking funding from them. I had no answers for her. She ended the conversation by saying the requirement raised 'red flags' which they'd have to check out. That was the first of three or four phone calls between us. (I instigated two of these in response to letters from the administrator.) The first criticized the methodology, saying they had never heard of using life stories or narrative analysis as research. It wasn't 'good science',

(Continued)

(Continued)

she said. Later, I had to explain and defend every aspect of the research point by point. In the end, their argument against approval shifted to a concern with my personal safety. They requested a conference call with my professor, during which an NIH attorney urged him not to support the in-home interviews, to consider the liability. When he could not be persuaded, they approved the project with a disclaimer that approval would not have been given if I had been applying for NIH funding. My experience with NIH became a chapter of my dissertation and has been published in *Studies in Symbolic Interaction* (Vol. 25). [Sylvia Ansay, USA]

The IRB in this case seems to have been overly protective of Sylvia and her research participants. Though she eventually secured approval for her project, it is evident that her research would have been completely stymied without the support of her dissertation chair. This sort of overprotection is especially noticeable where 'sensitive topics' or 'deviant populations' are concerned.

Consider, for example, Sara Crawley's description of the IRB mandates for her research with lesbians.

WHAT I DID: SARA

Governance Bodies Unhappy with Research on Minorities

I did have to take some pains to make the IRB comfortable with the group I was interviewing. Given that I wanted to interview 'lesbians!', the IRB was more worried about protecting confidentiality than most of my narrators. Although I was careful to respect narrators, I found most participants were very willing and expected that they might talk about lesbian experience in the lesbian groups they normally attended. For me, getting IRB approval was more about making the IRB comfortable about issues that the naturally occurring community was already comfortable discussing. [Sara Crawley, USA]

In Sara's case the IRB approval seemed to hinge around the board's comfort level with lesbians and talk of lesbianism rather than the community members' ease about discussing their lifestyles.

Eileen O'Brien, in her study of anti-racists, found that the research participants wanted to be identified by name in the research despite the IRB requirements for anonymity.

WHAT I DID: EILEEN

Breaking Confidentiality?

I was dealing with an area of activists who are pretty silenced/ignored in history – white anti-racists – and some people felt that this neglect was very calculated because it prevents whites from having visible alternative models of whiteness to follow, thereby subverting any major transformations of the dominant group in society. So I asked my advisor about it, and he said as long as I had it documented that they gave me permission to use their real names, he didn't think it would be a problem. But this issue never actually went back to IRB. I think this illustrates how qualitative research needs to be adaptable, and that following 'standard protocol' will not always work best depending on the topic and context of the data you need to obtain. [Eileen O'Brien, USA]

I conclude with Eileen's experience because it demonstrates once again that what she calls the 'standard protocol' may not always be entirely appropriate to a qualitative research study. Indeed, thoughtless rule following may blind you to unexpected ethical dilemmas.

In this context, Table 4.2 gives a jargon-free list of questions to ask yourself when you pursue informed consent.

Table 4.2   Ethical questions for researchers

- What am I expecting participants to do?
- How will I explain my research questions to participants?
- What will happen to my data (e.g. who will see any transcripts or recordings?)
- Where will I store my data?
- How can I ensure confidentiality and anonymity?
- How can I try to make my study harm-free?
- What are the communication barriers between me and my participants (e.g. culture, age, gender, impairments?)
- Have I satisfied my accountability to my university, my supervisor, my participants, any gatekeepers and the wider research community?

Source: adapted from Churchill and Sanders (2007: 48–52)

What You Need to Remember

- At every stage of the research process, from study design to data gathering to data analysis and writing your report, you need to be aware of ethical issues.
- Ethical guidelines are usually available from your university department and from the professional associations that recruit within your discipline.

- The varying social contexts of action mean that such guidelines cannot cover every situation that will arise. This means that you should always be alert to emerging ethical issues and confront them as best you can.
- At every stage of your project, from research design to communicating your findings, think through what the people you are studying may gain or lose from your research.

Your Chapter Checklist

While these may vary across disciplines and national boundaries, there are a number of general principles that most researchers would agree with. Check how far your research is in line with the following:

- voluntary participation
- protection of research participants
- assessment of potential benefits and risks to participants
- obtaining informed consent.

Exercises

Exercise 1: Create an information sheet

Draw up an information sheet for participants in your research. Now consider whether you have succeeded in the following:

- providing a clear and truthful account of your research
- avoiding jargon
- avoiding potentially sensitive terms.

Exercise 2: Apply ethical practice to your own project

Earlier in this chapter, I listed some features of good ethical practice:

- voluntary participation and the right to withdraw
- protection of research participants
- assessment of potential benefits and risks to participants
- obtaining informed consent
- not doing harm.

Assess your research proposal in terms of each of these rules. Now consider if there are any circumstances in which you might need *to bend* any of these rules.

Further Reading

Mark Israel and Iain Hay's *Research Ethics for Social Scientists* (Sage, 2006) is a valuable text-book on research ethics. Judith Green and Nicki Thorogood's *Qualitative Methods for Health Research* (Sage, 2004) provides an excellent chapter-length account of ethical issues in health research. Anne Ryen's chapter 'Ethical issues' (in C. Seale et al. (eds), *Qualitative Research Practice*, Sage, 2004) is a key source which includes fascinating material on her ethnographic research in East Africa. For more details of some fascinating case studies, see Les Back's chapter 'Politics, research and understanding' (in C. Seale et al. (eds), *Qualitative Research Practice*, Sage, 2004). For a discussion of the ethics of interviews, consult Caroline Gatrell's 'Safeguarding subjects? A reflexive reappraisal of researcher accountability in qualitative interviews' (*Qualitative Research in Organizations and Management*, 2009, 4: 110–22). For a thoughtful set of rules to diminish intrusion, look at Clifford Stake's *Qualitative Research* (Guilford, 2010: 208–9).

READ: ETHICS AND RESEARCH
READ: ETHICS AND IDENTITY

Discover the chapter's digital resources in your SILVERMAN FIELD GUIDE

FIVE
What Counts as 'Originality'?

Learning Outcomes

By the end of this chapter you will be able to:

- Know what is involved in being a professional researcher.
- Understand the basics of independent critical thought.
- Be more confident in pursuing originality.

1 INTRODUCTION

All students speculate about the standards through which they will be assessed. Many students beginning a research study crave to be 'original'. Whether the research is for a PhD, an MA or a BA dissertation, 'originality' is, for many, both a goal and a perceived critical standard which will be used by your examiners to beat you with!

Such fears are associated with a lack of knowledge about what is expected at a new, 'higher' level of your education. In this respect, we are talking about a common experience when we reach the next step on any ladder.

Many social transitions are associated with rites of passage, and educational careers are no exception. In English secondary schools, after the age of 16, one enters the sixth form, where one is expected to specialize narrowly and to become more self-reliant and less spoonfed. At my own school, boys just out of short trousers suddenly found themselves addressed by their sixth-form teacher as 'gentlemen'. We looked round the room but, weirdly, the appellation was directed at us.

The process is repeated in some form all over the world when you begin a BA at a university. Now, it seems, you are truly on your own, having to meet strange new criteria of achievement without any obvious means of support. Your time tends to be much more your own and you have to decide how much time to allocate to the library, the computer centre or – at British universities – the students' union bar.

How much worse, then, when you register to do an MA or a PhD. Suddenly, everything you could count on in the past now seems to amount to nothing. You are no longer the outstanding undergraduate but just one of many students, all of whom, presumably, achieved good first degrees. In the past, university examinations were mysteries that you had cracked. Now, although some further written examinations may await, you know that this is not how you are going to be mainly judged.

To some extent, this transition to graduate status is eased by the provision of taught courses for first-year research students, many of whom will have already taken an MA. However, a nagging doubt is still likely to torment many beginning graduate students. Are you 'up to it'? Above all, do you have the capacity to be 'original'? Or is 'originality', like so many things these days, something you can learn?

2 ORIGINALITY

Original: not derived, copied, imitated or translated from anything else; novel; creative; independent in invention. (*Chambers English Dictionary*, 1990)

Consulting a dictionary about 'originality' brings mixed blessings. You are not planning to plagiarize anybody else and so should have no problem in meeting the 'negative' definition of 'originality' given above: your dissertation is unlikely to be 'derived, copied, imitated or translated from anything else'.

But how about the 'positive' components of 'originality'? Can you be 'novel; creative; independent in invention'? Moreover, since 'imaginativeness' is linked to 'originality' by Roget's *Thesaurus*, have you the talent to be 'imaginative'?

However you answer these questions, you are going to be in trouble! Obviously, if you don't feel that your intellect is especially 'novel', 'creative', 'inventive' and 'imaginative', then you are going to worry yourself sick about whether you are up to doing a worthwhile piece of research. Conversely, if you are full of confidence about these matters, it is very likely that you are underestimating what is required to be granted these epithets.

If you doubt me, scan the book review pages in a journal in your field. My guess is that you will not find such words thrown around freely. And, remember, many of the books reviewed will be authored by established scholars, well past their own PhDs.

If the work of established scholars is not regularly judged to be 'novel', 'creative', 'inventive' or 'imaginative', what chance do you have? The answer is surprising: you have no problem.

Such epithets are rarely used by the examiners of successful PhD dissertations. Most dissertations are no more than solid and workmanlike. Indeed, it would cheapen the currency of academic description to use the vocabulary of 'originality' too frequently. Even Nobel Prize laureates never fail to cast doubt on their own supposed 'genius'. Instead, they regularly refer to the support of their research teams and to the old metaphor: 'one per cent inspiration, ninety-nine per cent perspiration' (see Mulkay, 1984).

As Phillips and Pugh point out, in the context of a PhD, 'an original contribution to knowledge' is a very shaded term: 'it does not mean an enormous breakthrough which has the subject rocking on its foundations' (1994: 34). Following Thomas Kuhn (1970), PhD research is unlikely to involve a paradigm shift in your discipline. Instead, Phillips and Pugh suggest, it demonstrates that you have a good grasp of how research is normally done in your field (i.e. that you can do what Kuhn calls 'normal science'). What does this mean in practice?

Among other things, it can mean:

> making a synthesis that hasn't been made before; using already known material but with a new interpretation, bringing new evidence to bear on an old issue ... [and] adding to knowledge in a way that hasn't been done before. (Phillips and Pugh, 1994: 61-2)

So Phillips and Pugh suggest that a PhD is less to do with 'originality' and more about displaying that you are 'a fully professional researcher' (1994: 19). In turn, this means showing:

- that you have something to say to which your peers will want to listen
- that you are 'aware of what is being discovered, argued about, written and published by your academic community across the world'. (1994: 19)

The upshot of this is that a PhD is best viewed as an apprenticeship prior to admission to a community of scholars. This implies that:

> you are not doing research in order to do research; you are doing research in order to demonstrate that you have learned how to do research to fully professional standards. (1994: 20)

Get examples from your supervisor

WATCH: DAVID EXPLAINS IN PERSON

David's Top Tip 9

If you are worried about the originality of your research project, ask your supervisor to suggest one or two journal articles which are particularly poor or unoriginal. Having read them, I predict that you will feel more confident!

3 BEING A PROFESSIONAL

'Originality' is only one of four criteria upon which examiners of the University of London PhD must report. To get a London PhD, the examiners must report:

- that the thesis is genuinely the work of the candidate
- that the thesis forms a distinct contribution to the knowledge of the subject, and affords evidence of originality by *the discovery of new facts* and/or *the exercise of independent critical power* (my emphasis)
- that the thesis is satisfactory as regards literary presentation
- that the thesis is suitable for publication ... as submitted or in abridged or modified form.

Despite the passing reference to 'originality' in the second item, all these criteria are really about professionality. We only need to concern ourselves about the second criterion: the discovery of new facts and the exercise of independent critical thought.

Considered on its own, 'the discovery of new facts' is rarely an important or even a challenging criterion in most of the social sciences. In the natural sciences, perhaps, a PhD researcher may discover a new substance or process and be applauded. But, in my experience, it is much rarer for qualitative social science PhDs to argue that they have found new 'facts'. Indeed, if they did so, they would most likely be greeted with the riposte: 'So what?'

For example, say such a dissertation claims that it has discovered that a particular group has beliefs or displays behaviours that were previously unknown. Any examiner worth their salt would then want to ask: 'Why on earth should it matter that this is the case?' In other words, what analytical or practical significance are we being asked to attach to this 'finding'?

Such a line of questioning is *not* a case of the examiner being difficult. As I argue in Chapter 7, any scientific finding is always to be assessed in relation to the theoretical perspective from which it derives and to which it may contribute.

This means that, while 'facts' are never unimportant, they derive their relevance from the theoretical perspectives from which they stem and to which they contribute. The clear implication is that 'the exercise of independent critical thought' is the major criterion through which your dissertation will be assessed.

How can you satisfy this criterion? If professionality consists in the display of independent critical thought, what is the secret of being independent, critical and professional?

4 INDEPENDENT CRITICAL THOUGHT

In fact, as is the usual case in research, there is no secret or magic process to be revealed. As Braun and Clarke suggest:

> originality is not necessarily about doing something that's 100 per cent brand spanking new; it's about generating some knowledge that might be new because of topic (a completely new area), approach (the topic has never been explored in this way) or context (the topic has never been studied in this place and time). (2013: 44)

Kathy Charmaz (2006) adds that what stands out as original depends in part on the audience. As Table 5.1 shows, writers use particular 'strategies' to convince their audiences.

Table 5.1 Strategies to claim originality

- Providing an analysis in a new area
- Offering an original treatise in an established or fading area
- Extending current ideas

Source: Charmaz (2006: 153)

In Table 5.1, note how talking about 'strategies' serves to demystify the idea of 'originality'. In such terms, 'originality' is more about persuading one's colleagues than about what is objectively discovered. As Max Travers (2006) has demonstrated, 'originality' and 'innovation' are merely claims supported by more or less effective attempts at persuasion. In this respect, we are dealing less with 'hard' scientific fact and more with marketing:

> A technique used in marketing consumer products, such as washing powder or detergent, is to place the words 'new', 'advanced' or 'improved' on the package, which will almost always increase sales, at least for a temporary period. (2006: 1)

As Charmaz points out, it may be difficult to persuade others that one has been original:

> As a field develops, the areas in which scholars claim originality narrow. In many disciplines, the days have long passed when an author could make a breakthrough by constructing a new field. (2006: 153)

In this context, Charmaz prefers to talk less about originality and more about 'making your mark' (2006: 153–4). How to make your mark when submitting a journal article is discussed below in Chapter 27 of this book.

In Chapter 3, we saw how Moira, Sally and Simon put on one side doubts about 'originality' and went about their research as solid craftspersons. Although occasionally they may have jumped out of their bath shouting 'eureka', most of the time they just plodded along, building a workmanlike analysis in the face of setbacks and opportunities.

Learn from others

WATCH: DAVID EXPLAINS IN PERSON

David's Top Tip 10

A good way to assess what counts as 'originality' in your field is to read one or two chapters by students who were successful at your degree level.

Using their experience and the work of other students I have supervised, I outline below four procedures which contribute to the successful display of 'independent critical thought':

- developing a concept and/or a methodology
- thinking critically about your approach
- building on an existing study
- being prepared to change direction.

Develop a concept and/or a methodology

Paul Acourt (1997) completed a theoretical dissertation, under my supervision, on the emergence and apparent disappearance of discussion of 'progress' in the social science literature. Armed with a well-supported argument about the analytical and practical relevance of such a concept, he was able to convince his examiners of his 'independent critical thought'.

Many social science dissertations have a more **empirical** content. Sally used Goffman's (1974) concept of frames to understand how a mental health team made decisions about what services to offer to homeless people. Moira and Simon employed the concepts and methodology that the sociologist Harvey Sacks used to study the descriptive process.

Moira applied **membership categorization device** analysis (MCDA) and conversation analysis (CA) to interviews with the partners of people who had recently died in hospital. Simon used CA to study the sequential organization of talk at parent–teacher meetings.

Twenty years earlier, Baruch (1981) had used one of these approaches (MCDA) to analyse transcripts of interviews with parents of disabled children. Like Moira and Simon, he showed the ability to work with and to advance Sacks's specialist approach. Indeed, Moira used Baruch's thesis as a baseline for her own research and showed how his analysis of interviews as 'moral tales' could be developed.

In the normal way, Moira, Simon and Geoffrey Baruch were influenced by the interests and skills of their supervisor. In my case, I had a long-standing interest in making Sacks's work more widely known (see Silverman, 1998) and four of my other successful PhD students have used the concepts and methodology of the sub-discipline Sacks founded.

Of course, social science has a broad and rich stream of concepts and methodologies and my students' work has expressed this breadth while reflecting my interests in processes of language and representation. So Kobena Mercer (1990) used some ideas from the French tradition of semiotics in his research on the speeches of an English politician, Enoch Powell. The related concepts of Foucauldian discourse analysis were used by Mary Fraser (1995) in her study of representations of children in a British nursing journal.

In all these cases, because the approach was theoretically informed, the dissertation could justifiably argue that it had contributed to conceptual development.

Think critically about your approach

As we saw in Chapter 3, your prior experience usually has an important bearing on how you approach your data. For instance, Sally was constantly aware of how her own nursing experience might be influencing how her health professionals related to her and how she might be taking for granted certain aspects of their behaviour.

Sometimes, doubts about an overall approach can have far-reaching consequences for how you think about your data. So Moira became dissatisfied with the conventional version of open-ended interviews as a potential window into people's experiences. Instead of using brief extracts from her interviews to illustrate particular categories, she started to analyse the sequential mechanisms through which her interviewees told recognizable 'stories'. Similarly, Simon was determined not to treat his parents' evenings as mere 'products' of familiar social structural variables (e.g. class and ethnicity of the parents, measured ability of the child).

Fifteen years earlier, another of my students, Gill Chapman (1987), had devised an unusual way of demonstrating her independent critical thought. Having discussed a range of possible ways of analysing her audiotapes of nurses' meetings, she decided to experiment with a wide range of concepts and methodologies. Each of the empirical chapters of her dissertation is thus both an analysis of her data and a critical evaluation of the approach used.

Build on an existing study

Don't try to reinvent the wheel! Try to find a previous study that, in some respect, mirrors your own interests and topic. Then model your own research on that study and develop some aspect of it.

Of course, with limited resources, you are unlikely to be able to offer a complete 'test' of the findings of that study. But by careful analysis of your limited data, you can reflect on its approach and conclusions in an informed way.

Sometimes a more realistic model is a previous PhD thesis. It is worth recalling that Moira used an earlier PhD that I had supervised as a model for her research. So, at the outset, look at earlier dissertations in your university library and, where possible, focus on work directed by your supervisor.

Be prepared to change direction

Both MA and PhD students tend to believe that what matters most is showing that their research has followed a logical sequence. Based on how research is sometimes reported, this structure seems to display the following sequence:

- research problem
- hypothesis
- data analysis
- conclusion.

However, anyone who has ever done any research knows that such a rigid sequence is rarely followed. Moreover, it sometimes makes sense to divert from an expected path if you come across new data or a new concept, or if your data suggests a different focus (see Chapter 15 for a discussion of how I changed paths in my research on a paediatric cardiology clinic).

So, as I argue in Chapter 26, although your examiners will look for evidence of a logical structure to your research, they will also want to see that you have been prepared to be flexible and to change direction when appropriate. After all, originality is not consonant with always following a predetermined plan.

EXPLORE:
WRITING ORIGINAL ARTICLES

5 WRAPPING UP

The message of this chapter is that a successful dissertation does not require genius. Once the task of the research student is defined in terms of the display of professional competence, then you can abandon those sessions in front of the mirror wondering whether you really look like Einstein, Keynes or Marie Curie!

In any event, you are likely to discover these things after a while through the response of your supervisor to your work. As Phillips and Pugh (1994) point out, worrying about the originality of your thought tends to be a concern only during the first few months. After this, the problem tends to disappear.

The case of a PhD examination many years ago makes this point very nicely. The thesis of the philosopher Ludwig Wittgenstein was being examined by two famous professors, Bertrand Russell and G.E. Moore. While these two had no doubt about its merits, there is some evidence that both examiners found Wittgenstein's thesis somewhat beyond them. In their report, Russell and Moore make clear that getting a PhD is different from being a genius. As they put it:

> This is a work of genius. It is also up to the standard required for a Cambridge PhD.

What You Need to Remember

Students at all levels desire to be original. However, BA and MA students can comfort themselves that even PhDs are rarely awarded for originality. In the context of a research degree, 'originality' is largely about your ability to display 'independent critical thought'. In turn, such thought can be shown by:

- developing a concept or a methodology
- thinking critically about your approach
- building on an existing study
- being prepared to change direction.

Providing your supervisor is reasonably happy with your work, don't worry about whether your research is original. If you are still troubled, read and critique a poor published paper in your field

Your Chapter Checklist

At regular intervals, check your progress in terms of the following criteria:

- developing a concept and/or a methodology
- thinking critically about your approach
- building on an existing study
- being prepared to change direction.

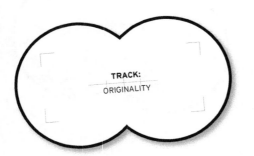

TRACK:
ORIGINALITY

Exercise

Exercise 1: Evaluate what type of originality your research project contributes

Pat Cryer has suggested that we can understand originality in research through an analogy with a travel expedition: 'the research student is the explorer and the expedition is the research programme' (1996: 145). Cryer uses the expedition analogy to suggest different senses of 'original research':

Review each kind of originality below in terms of what you think your research might contribute and decide which kind is most likely to be applicable to your work:

APPLY:
YOUR EXERCISE WORKBOOK

- originality in tools, techniques and procedures
- originality in exploring the unknown
- originality in exploring the unanticipated
- originality in use of data
- originality in outcomes
- originality in byproducts. (1996: 146-8)

You might return to this exercise at regular intervals to review any changes in how you view your research.

Further Reading

A helpful account of what counts as 'originality' in any student research is Pat Cryer's *The Research Student's Guide to Success* (Open University Press, 2006). PhD students should turn to Estelle Phillips and Derek Pugh's *How to Get a PhD* (Open University Press, 2005), which gives a realistic, supportive account of what is required to achieve a PhD.

Discover the chapter's
digital resources in your
SILVERMAN FIELD GUIDE

SIX
Research Design

Learning Outcomes

By the end of this chapter you will be able to:

- See how the way you define your research topic derives from a theoretical point of view.
- Understand what data and methods are relevant to your research topic.
- Grasp the elements of qualitative data analysis.
- See what is involved in designing a practical, achievable research study.

1 INTRODUCTION

In the first part of the book, I set out the context in which qualitative research dissertations are written. We began with a brief overview of qualitative research.

Then, in Chapter 3, we considered the lessons that could be drawn from three completed research dissertations.

Part II is concerned with the practical steps you need to take in beginning qualitative research. For many readers of this book, their own completed graduate or undergraduate dissertation is a distant, desired object. So, in this chapter, we draw upon accounts by research students at an early stage of their research. Through these accounts, we examine the analytical, methodological and practical problems that confront the beginning researcher.

In some senses, the beginning researcher has far less to prove than established scholars. If you imagine a sliding scale of levels of achievement, then journal articles, as the stock in trade of established scholars, are (or should be) the pinnacle of scholarly accomplishment. Somewhat surprisingly, books are a little further down the scale since they do not depend on the same degree of independent review. Further down the scale are also completed research dissertations which, as I suggested in Chapter 5, are properly viewed as displays of successful apprenticeship.

However, my sense of a sliding scale in research is intended simply to mark a stage of a research career; it is not a moral category. Although it is 50 years since I was at that stage, I do not look down upon the work of first-year research students. Indeed, frankly, I sometimes come across more exciting ideas in a first-year graduate workshop than in many journal articles!

What follows is by no means a representative survey of qualitative research at its early stages. Instead, the material below has been drawn from research students in my own department and in various social science and humanities departments of other universities.[1]

While the range of research covered below is limited, I hope you will eventually agree that it is not narrow. In other words, I hope and expect that readers will find at least some echo of their own ideas and interests.

In collating these presentations for this chapter, I had to decide upon an organizing principle. In particular, I had to choose whether to organize the material by topic, theory or methodology. I reasoned that grouping by topic would be lively but might appear to exclude readers working on different topics. By contrast, a theory grouping might be too abstract and, perhaps, confusing for an audience coming from a disparate range of disciplines. By taking a methodological perspective, I hope to be more inclusive by encompassing many of the methods used (and contemplated) by qualitative researchers.

DEFINE:
THEORY AND RESEARCH

The discussion below is thus organized by method, with sections on interview studies, ethnographies, textual analysis, Internet data, video and audio data, and mixed methods. However, such a focus on method is not narrowly technical. As we saw in Chapters 2 and 3, methods only acquire meaning and vitality by the way they are embedded in particular theoretical perspectives.

As in Chapter 3, I will proceed case by case, offering some comments with each example and then summarizing the points that emerge from each methodology. The chapter concludes with some suggestions about managing the early stages of research. After each topic title, I have noted the social science discipline in which the student is working as well as the student's name.

2 INTERVIEWS

Living and coping in a community of elderly people

(Information studies/sociology) [Tippi] Tippi writes about her joint research: 'We wanted to ask how the inhabitants feel about living in the community where they have lived for many years.' Her study is based upon thematic interviews with a random sample of eight elderly people from the community. As she puts it, the aim of this study 'is to [clarify] … the basic meaning of living [in this community]'.

This is how she describes her interviews: 'The elderly people were asked about their daily schedules, their attitudes to relatives, services, neighbourhood and environment, their interests and their opinions about society today compared with their earlier life experiences.'

Preliminary findings suggest two things. First, members of the community told the same kinds of life stories. Second, such people described themselves as more independent than she had thought. They described 'coping' by attempting to keep control of four issues: financial, social, health related and security.

An analytic issue potentially arises in such studies where interviews are used to elicit respondents' perceptions. How far is it appropriate to think that people attach a single meaning to their experiences? In this case, may there not be multiple meanings of living in the community, represented by what people say to the researcher, to each other, to carers, and so on (Gubrium, 1997)?

This raises the important methodological issue of whether interview responses are to be treated as giving direct access to 'experience' or as actively constructed narratives (Holstein and Gubrium, 2016; Riessman, 2016; Silverman 2017). Both positions are entirely legitimate but the position you take will need to be justified and explained.

Students' views of evaluation and feedback

(Behavioural sciences) [Laura]   Laura is examining students' responses to the assessment of their distance education essays. Her research question is: 'Does such assessment deliver the feedback that is needed and when it is needed?' Her data is derived from thematic interviews with 11 students chosen from four different localities. Her preliminary findings suggest that students want more detailed, critical feedback on their essays so that they can know what the gaps in their knowledge are and what they can do about them.

Laura describes the theoretical basis of her research as 'a **hermeneutic** method based on how researcher and subjects interpret the world and attempt to merge their horizons of meaning'. This is ambitious and its value will need to be demonstrated in the data analysis. Indeed, it might be simpler to settle on presenting her research as a descriptive study based upon a clear social problem. Either way, the issues about the status of interview data, also raised in Tippi's project, will need to be engaged.

Text processing in foreign-language classrooms

(English) [Pia]   In Finland, foreign languages are primarily taught through textbooks. Yet textbook-based learning is often defined as monotonous or boring by students. Pia's topic is whether there are different ways of doing foreign-language teaching and whether there is a conflict between them. Her broader concern is with what hinders change in classroom practices.

Her data consists of 12 interviews (half with teachers and half with students). She also has five 'think aloud' sessions in which students were asked to do an exercise from a text and think aloud at the same time.

The 'think aloud' session is an interesting idea because it attempts to relate what people say to a particular task they are doing – although it has to cope with the likelihood that people's practical skills are far more complicated than they could tell you in so many words (Garfinkel, 1967).

Pia describes her analytical approach as **discourse analysis** (DA). This implies that she is more interested in identifying different ways of talking about foreign-language reading (the constructionist approach) than in addressing the actual experiences of learning a foreign language through a textbook (the naturalist approach). Given that the latter can be seen as a social problem, there may be a mismatch between DA, which assumes, as constructionists do, that issues of social definition are paramount, and a direct address of social problems. This might suggest either dropping DA or reconceptualizing the problem.

If we are interested in what happens in the classroom, there is a further issue about the appropriateness of interview data. Should we not observe what people do there instead of asking them what they think about it? Is how we talk about schooling directly related to what happens in schooling?

The family grief and recovery process as narratives

(Psychiatry) [Katarin] Katarin is analysing interviews with couples after the loss of their baby. She is interested in how family members construct stories about their grief and recovery processes after such a loss. She has identified three discourses at work here:

- a religious discourse ('everything is clear ... I think my faith is strengthened')
- a medical discourse ('our baby did not have a chance to live, this is better, the lungs were undeveloped')
- a protest discourse ('who can decide who is allowed to live and who isn't?').

Katarin calls her work **narrative analysis**. By treating her respondents' accounts as skilfully structured stories, she gets a lively, theoretically informed grip on her data.

Only two cautions are appropriate here. First, the mere identification of different discourses in respondents' talk can lead to a simple, reductive list. At some stage, it is analytically productive to move beyond such a list in order to attempt to map the

skilful way in which such discourses are laminated on one another (see Silverman, 2006: 223–37).

Second, the assembly of narratives in interviews (or conversations) is always a two-way process. Therefore, we must treat the interviewer's questions not as (possibly distorted) gateways to the authentic account but as part of the process through which a narrative is collectively assembled (see Gubrium and Holstein, 2009: 41–53; Rapley, 2004).

Interviews: summary

Common themes have emerged from our five interview studies, which I summarize below. For the sake of simplicity, I present this summary in the form of a list of questions that you need to think about if you are planning to do an interview study.

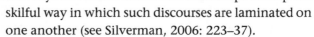

It should be apparent that here, as elsewhere, I am concerned with data *analysis* rather than the mechanics of data gathering (the latter is discussed in Chapter 14).

What status do you attach to your data?

Many interview studies are used to elicit respondents' perceptions. How far is it appropriate to think that people attach a single meaning to their experiences? May there not be multiple meanings of a situation (e.g. living in a community home) or of an activity (e.g. grieving) represented by what people say to the researcher, to each other, to carers, and so on (Gubrium, 1997)?

As mentioned earlier, this raises the important methodological issue of whether interview responses are to be treated as giving direct access to 'experience' or as actively constructed 'narratives' involving activities which themselves demand analysis (Gubrium and Holstein, 2009; Riessman, 2016; Silverman, 2014: 172–203). Both positions are entirely legitimate but the position you take will need to be justified and explained.

Is your analytic position appropriate to your practical concerns?

Some ambitious analytic positions (e.g. hermeneutics, DA) may actually cloud the issue if your aim is simply to respond to a given social problem (e.g. living and coping in a community of elderly people; students' views of evaluation and feedback). If so, it might be simpler to acknowledge that there are more complex ways of addressing your data but to settle on presenting your research as a *descriptive* study based upon a clear social problem.

Does interview data really help in addressing your topic?

If you are interested in, say, what happens in old people's homes or school classrooms, should you be using interviews as your major source of data? Think about exactly why you have settled on an interview study. Certainly, it can be relatively quick to gather interview data but not as quick as, say, extracting data from documents or the Internet. How far are you being influenced by the prominence of interviews in the media (see Atkinson and Silverman, 1997; Silverman, 2017)?

In the case of the classroom, couldn't you observe what people *do* there instead of asking them what they *think* about it? Or gather documents that routinely arise in schools (e.g. pupils' reports, mission statements, and so on)?

Of course, you may still want to do an interview study. But whatever your method you will need to justify it and show you have thought through the practical and analytical issues involved in your choice.

Are you making too large claims about your research?

It always helps to make limited claims about your own research. Grandiose claims about originality, scope or applicability to social problems are all hostages to fortune. Be careful in how you specify the claims of your approach. Show that you understand that it constitutes one way of 'slicing the cake' and that other approaches, using other forms of data, may not be directly competitive.

Proper analysis goes beyond a list

Identifying the main elements in your data according to some theoretical scheme should only be the first stage of your data analysis. By examining how these elements are linked together, you can bring out the active work of both interviewer and interviewee and, like them, say something lively and original.

We now turn to ethnographic studies that involve some element of observation. As we shall see, these kinds of studies also raise complex methodological and analytic issues.

3 ETHNOGRAPHIES

Ethnographies are based on observational work in particular social settings. The initial thrust in favour of ethnography was anthropological. Anthropologists argue

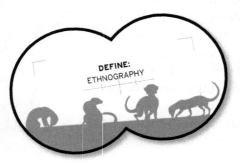

that, if one is really to understand a group of people, one must engage in an extended period of observation. Anthropological fieldwork routinely involves immersion in a culture over a period of years, based on learning the language and participating in social events with the people.

By contrast, non-anthropologists are more likely to study particular milieux or **subcultures** in their own society. We will see examples of this latter approach in the studies discussed below where activities in businesses, class-rooms, hospitals and on the Internet become objects of research observation.

Risk culture in business meetings

(Management and Economics) [Vilma Nasteckiene]   Vilma has worked in financial services and now wants to research how 'risk' is conceived and treated in business organizations. She will analyse documents and conduct interviews with managers but writes '[my] most important data are observations of meetings. My work experience will help me to collect data but further data processing is an issue for me – how to convert my tacit understanding to explicit knowledge using qualitative research'.

Vilma has grasped that data never speaks for itself and she is rightly wary of using her previous experience as a way of interpreting what she hears. To help her focus her research, I made these suggestions:

- Find an approach that allows you to focus. For example, Goffman (1974) shows how we can look at how participants 'frame' activities as appropriate to different contexts and how they move from one 'frame' to another. Alternatively, DA (Potter and Hepburn, 2008) provides a toolbox to analyse talk-in-interaction.
- Don't make the mistake of fitting everything that goes on in your meetings into your interest in 'risk'. Instead, see if, when and where 'risk' is brought into the discussion and what consequences follow. Seek to identify other topics raised and see how, if 'risk' is discussed, it fits into them.
- Be prepared to change your research topic if you discover issues other than 'risk' more relevant to meetings.
- Having established a sound analysis of meetings, think again about whether you really need to analyse documents and do interviews.

EXPLORE:
ERVING GOFFMAN

You don't have to analyse all the parts to have a whole

WATCH: DAVID EXPLAINS IN PERSON

David's Top Tip 11

Don't assume that you always need to gather multiple datasets. Often one dataset, thoroughly analysed, is a better goal. Don't make the common-sense assumption that there is a 'whole' phenomenon and that you must therefore study every aspect of it. See my discussion of **mixed methods** below.

The analysis of the communicative functions of peer interaction during small-group learning

(Education) [Caroline]   Working in small groups has become a common feature of modern education. The exact nature of such 'learning' presents a clear and apparently under-researched topic tied to a recognizable social problem. As Caroline remarks: 'The ways in which knowledge is constructed in children's verbal interactions during small-group work learning without direct teacher control have not yet been fully researched.'

Caroline has gathered data from children aged from 10 to 12 in small classroom groups working on mathematics, science and language. Her focus is on 'the socio-cognitive and interpersonal dynamics of peer interaction' using categories 'based on the communicative functions identified in the interactions'.

This is a theoretically defined topic which nonetheless might have a clear practical input. It uses a clearly defined method derived from certain forms of DA. However, Caroline's study also raises a more general issue about how a researcher goes about identifying features in the data.

Caroline's use of the passive voice in her reference to 'the communicative functions identified in the interactions' draws attention to a neglected issue in social research: that is, how does the analyst go about 'identifying features' in the data? One common answer is to claim to follow proper procedural rules. For instance, coders of data are usually trained in procedures with the aim of ensuring a uniform approach.

This is a tried and trusted method designed to improve the reliability of a research method. However, it is sensible to be conscious that **coding** is not the preserve of research scientists. In some sense, these students, like all of us, 'code' what they hear and see in the world around them. Moreover, this 'coding' has been shown to be mutual and interactive (Sacks, 1992; Silverman, 1998).

Of course, as I said earlier, the research 'cake' can be legitimately sliced in many ways. So I am not suggesting that the vast mass of researchers who treat 'coding' as purely an analyst's problem abandon their work. Instead, my minimalist suggestion is that they mention and respond to this well-established critique (for an example, see Clavarino et al., 1995).

Healthcare innovation as an organizational practice

(Organizations) [Vibeke Scheller]   Vibeke writes that: 'I study innovation processes at a Danish hospital and describe how staff, managers and patients experience innovation as changing temporal structures, i.e. duration, tempo and synchronization. My data will be field notes from observations as well as

interviewing. I am "shadowing" different professionals while making a field journal with detailed
descriptions of work practices.'

Healthcare has seen rapid change recently and
Vibeke proposes a fascinating study using the technique of 'shadowing' (Czarniawska, 2007). Below are
the questions Vibeke asked me, together with my
answers:

- How can I study innovation processes – as they happen?

Retrospective studies tell us little about how things happened in the past because
people routinely describe what has happened in the light of known outcomes (the
rewriting of history). So wait till an innovation arises and follow it through
for as long as you have time. And try to record events like meetings because fieldnotes are fallible and make it difficult to reanalyse our data.

- What can I do if the process comes to a standstill?

This is not a problem but a finding!

- What methodological approach can pay attention to spatial and temporal detail?

You mention ethnomethodology elsewhere. Its attention to the detail of everyday
practices would fit the bill. Alternatively, frame could be used.

- How can I overcome oversimplification and rationalization of the innovation process in my
  interviews?

Well spotted, because people rewrite history when you ask them about the past.
Why not stick with your observational data?

- How can I deal with conflicting agendas – especially between the staff and management group?

Once again, if you discover such conflict, treat it as a finding. Trace where, when
and how it arises and try to follow its consequences.

Analysing how radiologists work

(Information processing science) [Julia] Radiology, like many health
professions, has recently experienced a sea change of technologies, with the

conventional X-ray image being complemented by computer-based, digitalized images. As Julia points out, any new technology creates new constraints as well as new possibilities. Her focus is on such technologically mediated interaction in workplace settings.

Using video, observation and interviews, Julia has gathered data about radiological image interpretation conferences. By examining actual workplace interaction she hopes to contribute to the growing body of knowledge about human–computer interaction and to inform future technological design (see Heath, 2011; Suchman, 1987).

I hope you will agree with me that this is an exciting combination of a theoretically defined approach with clear practical relevance. However, Julia writes that she is concerned about what is missing from both her interviews and her videos. As she puts it:

> Thus far in my research it has become clear that there are aspects of work which I can't 'reach' through interviews (people can't readily articulate aspects that are so familiar to them as to be unremarkable) or through observation and interactional analysis of video-recordings (those aspects of work that are not evident in what people can actually be seen to do).

In a sophisticated way, Julia raises a problem that often troubles research students: the necessarily 'partial' character of any data source. I believe this problem is potentially huge, yet, in a practical sense, easily resolved. One simply avoids trying to find the 'whole picture'. Instead, one analyses different kinds of data separately, aware that all the kinds of data are partial.

So make do with what you have and understand that there are multiple phenomena available in any research setting. If you must go beyond any particular dataset, save that until you have completed smaller scale analyses. Worrying about the 'whole picture' at the outset is, in my view, a recipe for stalling your research (see Silverman and Gubrium, 1994).

Ethnographies: summary

Once more, I have been concerned with how you analyse your data. I deal below with three issues that have arisen above.

What is involved in coding data?

As we have seen, coders of data are usually trained in procedures with the aim of ensuring a uniform approach. Later in this book, we examine how computer-aided qualitative data analysis can help in such coding (see Chapter 16).

However, as I pointed out, it is sensible to be conscious that 'coding' is not the preserve of research scientists. All of us 'code' what we hear and see in the world around us.

One response is to make this everyday 'coding' (or 'interpretive practice') the object of enquiry. Alternatively, we can proceed in a more conventional manner but mention and respond to this well-established critique.

Is my data 'partial'?

Of course it is. But this is not a problem – unless you make the impossible claim to give 'the whole picture'. So celebrate the partiality of your data and delight in the particular phenomena that it allows you to inspect (hopefully in detail).

Is my theory appropriate?

Your theory must be appropriate to the research questions in which you are interested. Indeed, rather than being a constraint, a theory should generate a series of directions for your research.

4 TEXTS

To introduce a separate section on 'texts' can look a little artificial. After all, aren't people on the Internet constructing texts? Again, if we treat an interview as a narrative, this can mean looking for the same **textual data** as researchers working with printed material. Indeed, the mere act of transcription of an interview turns it into a written text.

In this section, I use 'text' as a device to identify data consisting of words and images which have become recorded without the intervention of a researcher (e.g. through an interview). Below I examine five studies of texts.

Analysing classroom religious textbooks

(Teacher education) [Pertti] Since 1985 Finnish schools have had a religious instruction syllabus mainly based on three textbooks deriving from the Finnish Lutheran Church. Pertti's approach treats such textbooks as a form of literary genre (see Silverman, 2011b: 75–9) which filters certain values into the school. He is examining such features as tables of contents in order to ask, 'How is otherness constructed in these texts through particular methods of classification?'

His analysis derives from Michel Foucault's (1977; 1979) discussion of the construction of subjects and disciplines.

This study benefits from a manageable body of data: three textbooks are more than enough to carry out the analysis Pertti proposes. The analysis derives from a clearly defined theoretical approach, although it may be uneconomical to work with both Foucauldian ideas and writers on literary genre. In particular, from a Foucauldian position, one would want to study education in its own right, not in terms of ideas developed to study literature (for a basic introduction to using Foucault in your research, see Kendall and Wickham, 1999).

EXPLORE:
USING FOUCAULT

The medicalization of the middle-aged female body in the twentieth century

(Sociology) [Greta]   Greta is interested in the way in which middle-aged women have become a topic for medicine and the 'psy' sciences. Like Pertti, Greta's analysis is based upon a Foucauldian discourse analytic approach, concerned with the construction of subjects within various forms of power/knowledge. Using this approach, she is able to chart how the medical gaze has moved from a biomedical model to medico-psy models and, most recently, a medico-psycho-social model.

Her data derives from the *British Medical Journal*, medical textbooks and a history of menopause clinics in the 1970s. Simple keyword analysis has proved fruitful in the early stages of her research, illustrating for instance how the clinical type of 'the chronic pelvic woman' emerged into discourse.

As Greta's research develops, like Katarin's and Moira's interview studies (discussed above), she will want to map how different discourses are laminated on each other. She will also have to decide whether to look for yet more sources of data (e.g. articles and letters on advice pages in women's magazines) or to narrow down the amount of data she has already collected.

The representation of 'crime' in local newspapers

(Sociology) [Kay]   Analysis of newspapers in the UK has usually focused on the mass circulation press and has used theoretical models deriving from either Marxism or literary studies. Kay's work is distinctive in that it uses data drawn from small, local newspapers and capitalizes on the small corpus of newspaper studies using Sacks's membership categorization analysis (see Silverman, 2014: 302–11). The research incorporates a nice comparative perspective as the two newspapers Kay is studying derive from different geographical locations: suburban London and a Northern Ireland city. The value of this comparison can be explored by examining the local categories that the newspapers use in their descriptions of crime (e.g. national and local boundaries).

Like Pertti, Kay has a manageable body of data. By limiting her data simply to two newspapers' headlines on 'crime' stories she is in a good position to say 'a lot about a little'. Like Greta, her clear analytic approach will pay off when used as more than a simple listing device in order to reveal the precise sets of relationships locally constructed in her data.

'Enterprise discourse' in higher education

(Sociology) [Neil] Neil's research is concerned with strategic development documents from a higher education college arising from recent changes in the tertiary sector. He is focusing on what he calls 'enterprise discourse' and how it constitutes the professional's conception of identity.

Like Kay, Neil's original approach derives from ethnomethodology and was based on Sacks's membership categorization analysis. However, Neil acknowledges the attraction of the Foucauldian approach and aims to recast his concerns in terms of Foucault's conception of the 'architecture of the text'.

Neil's problem is that Foucault provides no clear methodology (but see Kendall and Wickham, 1999). He is attempting to find a usable method from the 'critical linguistics' of Norman Fairclough (1995) and from **semiotics**' concern with **syntagmatic** and **paradigmatic** relations (see Silverman, 2011b: 328–35). Using these approaches, the aim is to analyse whole texts rather than a few extracts. The value of these approaches will be clearer when Neil presents an extensive piece of data analysis.

However, I feel there is less to worry about in relation to Neil's concerns that working on a single case might mean that he has too few data. As Mitchell (1983) shows, the validity of qualitative analysis depends more on the quality of the analysis than on the size of the sample. Moreover, the comparative method can be used on a single case by isolating and comparing different elements (Flyvbjerg, 2004).

Texts: summary

Limit your data

Like many other qualitative approaches, textual analysis depends upon very detailed data analysis. To make such analysis effective, it is imperative to have a limited body of data with which to work. For instance, Kay's dataset of newspaper headlines would fit onto one sheet of A4 paper! So, while it may be useful initially to explore different kinds of data (e.g. newspaper reports, scientific textbooks, magazine advice pages), this should usually only be done to establish the dataset with which you can most effectively work. Having chosen your dataset, you should limit your material further by only taking a few texts or parts of texts (e.g. headlines).

Have a clear analytic approach

READ:
DOCUMENT ANALYSIS

All the textual studies discussed above have recognized the value of working with a clearly defined approach. Even Neil, who was unsure which approach to use, was convinced that such a choice is crucial. Having chosen your approach (e.g. Foucauldian discourse analysis, Saussurian semiotics, Sacks's analysis of membership categorization), treat it as a 'toolbox' providing a set of concepts and methods to select your data and to illuminate your analysis.

Recognize that proper analysis goes beyond a list

I make no apology for repeating a point that I made above in my discussion of interview studies. It seems to me that the distinctive contribution qualitative research can make is to utilize its theoretical resources in the deep analysis of small bodies of publicly shareable data. This means that, unlike much quantitative research, we are not satisfied with a simple coding of data. Instead, we have to show how the (theoretically defined) elements identified are assembled or mutually laminated.

5 DIGITAL DATA

Since at least 1990, the Internet has been the prime site where documents are to be found. It provides a rich source of readily available data (subject to ethical constraints) which allows us to study past events as they happened through the use of net archives. As Kozinets points out:

Newsgroups, forums and other bulletin boards, blogs, mailing lists, and most other synchronous media are automatically archived. The Wayback Machine or Internet Archive captures snapshots of the Internet at certain points in time and saves them for future reference. Efficient search engines make accessible every interaction or every posting on a given topic to a specific newsgroup, or every posting by a given individual to any newsgroup. (2010: 72)

Kozinets describes such research as netnography and observes:

The analysis of existing online community conversations and other Internet discourse combines options that are both naturalistic and unobtrusive – a powerful combination that sets netnography apart from focus groups, depth interviews, surveys, experiments and in-person ethnographies. (2010: 56)

Newsgroups on the Internet

(Sociology) [Danny] Danny is concerned with how people assemble themselves as a community via the Net, without recourse to speech inflections or body language. Broader issues relate to how the Net is regulated, how it developed and what is exchanged on it. He proposes to focus on newsgroups on the Net since their messages are publicly available and offer an interesting way to look at how a 'community' is assembled and develops.

Danny's approach derives from his interest in the Internet as a possible new locus of power and, to this end, he plans to draw upon the German critical theorist Jürgen Habermas's conception of distorted communication. In this way, he will compare how people actually communicate with Habermas's normative theory.

Danny's study shows the implications of making theoretical choices. Using Habermas's concept of 'distorted communication' will give a particular thrust to his study that is very different from other kinds of theory.

Even if you decide to eschew such grand theories, that itself is a theoretical choice! In this sense, there is no escape (nor should there be) from theory. At the same time, however, there is nothing wrong with a descriptive study providing that the researcher is conscious about the choice that is being made.

Talk, text and visual communication in desktop video-conferencing environments

(English) [Erkki] Erkki is studying a one-month teaching experiment in which a university course was given on the Internet in two places in Finland and Sweden. Ideas and papers were regularly exchanged and weekly presentations and feedback sessions were held through video conferencing (Internet seminars). Recordings of the video-mediated sessions between the two centres were obtained and transcribed (see Heath, 2011).

Erkki is combining CA with ideas from Goffman (1974) about 'participation frameworks' adopted in particular settings. This setting is, of course, pretty unusual in that participants' sharing of time and space is technologically mediated. In some sessions, the camera positions were fixed. In others, the camera zoomed in and out on the participants. This is allowing Erkki to get a hold on how different use of video-conferencing technology affects interaction.

Erkki's work combines a manageable body of data and a clear theoretical approach ('participation frameworks') with a likely practical input for systems design. As she recognizes, however, it is very complex to work with video data since both transcription and analysis are more complex than is the case with audio data. Fortunately, there is a growing body of CA-inspired work on technologically mediated interaction which Erkki can use as a model (see Heath et al., 2010).

Digital technologies in the heritage and culture tourism industry

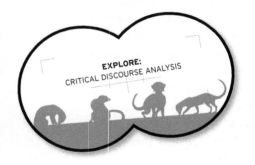

(Social science) [Helen] Helen is investigating the use of digital technologies (specifically the Internet and social media) within the heritage and culture tourism industry. She writes: 'I'm specifically looking at the Circuit of Culture and how (and why) tourism organisations, tourists and locals create and share touristic images of heritage and culture online. Data collection for this research will involve interviews with tourism organisations, online surveys of tourists and locals, as well as using digital data from websites and social media/networking sites.' Helen proposes to use critical discourse analysis (CDA) to identify various relationships in what she terms 'the Circuit of Culture'.

Helen asked me: 'Part of the data collection involves people and organisation representatives who may have an agenda when answering questions. What are some ways to handle and identify this agenda, yet still collect relevant, credible data?' Fortunately, her question has an easy answer. Her question turns on the common-sense assumption that we should go beneath appearances (what people say and do) to find an underlying reality (e.g. 'hidden agendas'). However, her chosen approach (CDA) draws upon constructionist assumptions which, by contrast, treat what people say and do as realities in their own right without any need to compare them with an assumed, external 'reality'. Consequently, whatever you discover in talk-in-interaction is a finding and, if properly analysed, is both relevant and credible.

Digital data: summary

The Internet is a marvellous site for anyone interested in how we construct our identities. As Annette Markham notes:

> As I write ... various programs on my computer and my smart phone collaborate to present a snapshot of not only my world, but also my understanding of the world. I filter news, I follow links sent by friends, and I follow random or not-so-random paths of information to build my knowledge of the world. I scan and contribute to various social networks. Each context is unique, each post authored by a slightly different version of 'me' and targeted to slightly different audiences. I'm a cook posting new recipes. I'm a photographer. I could be a methodologist, but I could also be a birdwatcher, a player of multiplayer online games, a dominatrix in an avatar-based social space, or a microcelebrity, known for my acerbic reviews of YouTube viral videos or my roles in amateur porn video. I could have a team of ghostwriters enacting my identity through Twitter if I were important enough. (2011: 121)

Subject to ethical constraints (Kozinets, 2010: 137–40, 194–6; Markham, 2011: 122–3), by looking at what people are actually doing on the Internet we might observe the following social facts:

- The text of a particular blog posting has been written and was posted.
- A certain social networking group has been formed, and certain accounts have been linked to it.
- A certain photo was uploaded to a particular photo-sharing community, and received 37 comments (Kozinets, 2010: 133).

Like old-fashioned documents, the Internet can readily provide data which is available for analysis on day 1 of a research project. However, as in all research, the data does not speak for itself. So, if you are thinking of working with Internet data, bear in mind the following constraints:

- Have you got permission to use this data?
- What analytic model will inspire your data analysis?
- How much data do you need to address your research topic effectively?
- How are you going to identify and make use of deviant cases?

6 AUDIO DATA

The four types of qualitative data discussed so far all end up in the form of some kind of text. For instance, in interviews the researchers usually work with written transcripts, and in ethnographies one often records and analyses written fieldnotes.

EXPLORE:
CONVERSATION ANALYSIS

In the same way, audios of **naturally occurring data** are usually transcribed prior to (and as part of) the analysis. The two main social science traditions which inform the analysis of transcripts of audio data are CA and DA. For an introduction to CA, see ten Have (1998); for DA, see Potter and Hepburn (2008). Both examples below involve the use of CA (a further example is found in Simon's research, discussed in Chapter 3).

Team meetings at a hospice

(Sociology) [Anthony]   While studying for his MA, Anthony started to do voluntary work at a hospice in a London suburb. Staff at the hospice were later happy to grant him access to record some of their work. He chose team meetings for two reasons. First, focusing on such data meant that he did not need to trouble patients. Second, team meetings in which patients were discussed were scheduled events, so Anthony did not have to waste time waiting for 'relevant' data to appear. Moreover, another researcher had already recorded some team meetings at the hospice and was happy to lend him her good-quality recordings.

Anthony had used conversation analytic methods for his MA dissertation and applied the Jeffersonian CA transcription method to his new data (see the Appendix to this book). He then inspected his transcripts, informed by CA's focus on the sequential organization of talk. After an initial series of discrete observations, he selected a number of sequences in which disagreements emerged and were resolved by team members.

The management of agreements and disagreements has been extensively analysed within CA through the concept of **preference organization** (Heritage, 1984: 265–9). However, Anthony now realizes that his data allowed a new twist to be given to such analyses by looking at how 'third parties' manage disagreements by others. This looks likely to be both analytically interesting and practically relevant to medical staff concerned with effective decision making.

Asymmetry in interactions between native and non-native speakers of English

(English) [Marla]   Marla is working with recorded, naturally occurring conversations in English between native speakers of English and Finnish (both informal conversations and professional/client encounters). As she notes: 'Research in pragmatics and sociolinguistics has shown that various forms of communicative trouble may arise where the linguistic and socio-cultural resources of the participants are not shared.' However, she is taking a different approach. Rather than treat asymmetries as a 'trouble', her initial idea is to examine how the participants 'use emerging asymmetries as a resource through which they can renegotiate the current context of discourse and their interpersonal relationship'.

Like much good research, this is based on a nicely counter-intuitive idea which derives from a clear theoretical perspective (CA suggests that participants can treat apparent troubles as local resources). As in Anthony's case, Marla's data, method and analytical approach are elegantly intertwined.

Audio data: summary

Choose a single concept or problem

Choosing a clear analytic approach is a help but is not everything. The danger is that you seek to apply too many findings or concepts deriving from that approach. This can make your analysis both confused and thin or a naive listing of observations consonant with each of these concepts. By narrowing down to a single issue (e.g. preference organization or troubles as a local resource), you may begin to make novel observations.

Give a problem a new twist

As the data analysis proceeds, you should aim to give your chosen concept or issue a new twist. In the studies above, we have seen this done by pursuing a counter-intuitive idea and by noting an additional feature little addressed in the literature.

Make data collection as easy as possible

There are no 'brownie points' given by most disciplines for having gathered your own data – perhaps with the exception of anthropology's expectation that most researchers will have spent their statutory year with their 'tribe'. Indeed, by choosing 'difficult' situations to gather data (because nothing 'relevant' may happen, or even because background noise may mean you have a poor-quality recording), you may condemn yourself to having less time to engage in the much more important activity of data analysis.

Marla and Anthony found practical ways of efficiently gathering data. Both chose to study scheduled encounters and Anthony was able to supplement his own data with recordings collected by somebody else. As I pointed out in Chapter 3, secondary analysis of other people's data is to be commended rather than condemned.

7 VISUAL DATA

When people interact face to face, they do not use merely verbal cues – except if they are on the telephone. Researchers who work with videos have access to many of these cues. However, as we shall see, complicated data can often mean complicated analysis!

The early interaction between a mother and a baby aged under 1 year

(Finnish) [Suzanne]   This is a study of interaction between Suzanne's own baby, Sara, and others based on 9.5 hours of videos of 22 episodes up till Sara's first birthday. Suzanne's initial interest was the age when a baby begins to imitate other people. Consequently, she is attempting to describe what she says to her baby (and how) at different ages and what linguistic elements begin to emerge in the baby's vocalizations.

Like Erkki, she is using transcription methods and analytic ideas from CA. Based on this approach, she is treating mother–baby talk as interactional (e.g. how the mother interprets the baby's utterances and behaviour in concrete situations and how she acts in response to them).

At the time of her presentation, Suzanne submitted a set of written questions, which I set out below with my answers:

- *Is one baby (my own) enough data?* For qualitative work, one case study is sufficient. Obviously, there are issues to be thought through when you are yourself a principal actor. However, from a CA point of view, the complexity of what all of us do is so great that we are unable to grasp it or indeed to change it significantly at the time.

- *Is one video camera enough, particularly as you don't always see mother and baby together?* This is not a major objection. Once you recognize that there can be no 'perfect' recording of interaction, it is always a case of making do with what you have.
- *How far can you reconstruct all aspects of the interaction between a baby and her family from 10 hours of video?* Never attempt to reconstruct everything about an interaction! Not only is this an impossible task, but it is likely to deflect you from establishing a clear focus on one manageable topic.
- *Does an analysis of interactional situations give any hints as to how the baby reciprocally interprets her mother's actions?* Who knows what baby (and mother) are thinking? CA instructs us to look at what each party does without speculating about what they are thinking.
- *Should imitations associated with gestures and expressions be analysed separately from vocal imitations?* No! Use your rich video data to examine the interweaving of talk, gesture and expression.
- *Should more approaches be used (e.g. hermeneutics)?* Don't even think about it! Once you have found an approach which suits you, stick with it. Using multiple approaches is uneconomical and likely to delay completion of your research.
- *How do we distinguish 'imitation' from other activities such as 'repetition'?* Look at how the baby's utterances are treated by the mother (e.g. praise). But be prepared to change topic. 'Imitation' may give you an early hold on the topic but detailed description may lead in different directions.

The construction of ethnic identity among Spanish immigrants in London

(Sociology) [Viviana]   Viviana's work focuses on styles of cultural consumption in relation to intergenerational differences within families of first- and second-generation immigrants. She has moved from an interview-based study to one based largely on observation and videotaping of Spanish families watching television together.

Viviana's research involves two overlapping areas: media studies and nationality. It is important for her to think through whether her main focus is on media reception or, as I think, on national identity, using the media as a case study. Again, although video data is potentially exciting material, it is notoriously difficult to analyse. Even though the analysis of interview data has all kinds of difficulties attached to it (see above), it may be more suited to her focus on ethnic identity. With a video, you have to infer identities. Through interviews, you can ask people to speak about their identity.

Viviana's work is situated in the expanding area of 'audience studies' (see Morley, 1992). Practical guidance on the methodological issues involved in studying audiences is available in Rose (2007: Chapter 9).

How 'female experience' is presented and problematized on TV

(Sociology) [Nora]   Nora's research is concerned with 'confessional' television as represented by Oprah Winfrey and other 'chat' shows. She has a particular interest in how 'psychological health' is invoked in such programmes.

She argues that most existing research focuses on audience participation in terms of issues relating to democracy and resistance. As she points out, the problem with such studies is that they simply posit general structures of power, class and gender. Instead, Nora, following Foucault, wants to problematize subjectivity. In particular, she is interested in the productivity of power in relation to what it means to be a woman; the kind of ethical agent who might adopt this subject position; and the forms of knowledge that have helped to construct it.

By its focus on media products from a Foucauldian perspective, Nora's research promises to break new ground. Her major difficulty is the lack of any detailed direction for empirical work on media products within Foucault's work. Help on this issue is provided by Kendall and Wickham (1999). Alternatively, she could review methodologies deriving from other traditions to see if there are any useful points to be derived. In particular, CA offers a detailed way of transcribing video material and is beginning to address issues of validity and reliability in relation to single case studies (see Peräkylä, 2011). Ultimately, however, she should choose the approach with which she feels most confident.

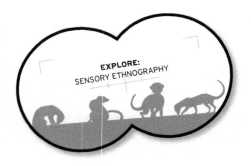

Visual data: summary

All the points made above about audio data apply here, so I limit myself to a few additional observations arising from our three video studies.

Beware of complexity

Although video data is very attractive, it is very complex to work with since both transcription and analysis are more difficult than is the case with audio data. So think very carefully about whether you need video data for your research. For instance, unlike CA, neither Foucault nor theories of identity provide a clear template for video analysis.

Keep it simple

You are not making a feature film! One video camera is fine for most purposes. When you have your data, maintain a clear focus. Never attempt to reconstruct all aspects of the interaction from the video (see Heath et al., 2010).

Think about the many kinds of visual data

Working with visual data does not necessarily mean shooting your own videos. Nora's research analyses recordings of TV programmes. Other researchers have analysed paintings and photographs or used visual cues such as family photographs as a topic for interviews (see Rose, 2007: Chapter 11).

Stick with one approach

By all means test out different ways of analysing your data, but always settle on one clear analytic approach. Draw on other approaches only for particular technical skills (e.g. in transcribing video data).

8 MIXED METHODS

Researchers are often tempted to use mixed methods. For instance, Helen's work on digital technologies in the heritage and culture tourism industry included not only digital data from websites and social media, but interviews with tourist organizations and online surveys of tourists and locals. As Table 6.1 shows, this reveals two versions of mixed methods, each with its own problems.

Table 6.1 reveals some of the problems with using mixed methods. Despite this, ethnographers often seek to combine observation with the interviewing of 'key informants'. In this section, I consider four examples of ethnographic work involving methods additional to observation.

Table 6.1   Two versions of mixed methods

Data used	Examples	Problem
Multiple qualitative data	Digital data and interviews	Why not stick with one dataset?
Qualitative and quantitative data	Social media and online surveys	Each answers different questions

Choosing mixed methods designs

WATCH: DAVID EXPLAINS IN PERSON

David's Top Tip 12

If you are doing a qualitative study, think carefully before adopting mixed methods in your research design.

1. Collecting multiple datasets may not allow time to analyse any one dataset thoroughly.
2. Quantitative data is useful for addressing 'why' questions while 'what' and 'how' questions are most suitable for qualitative research. Answers to different questions don't necessarily combine well.
3. Many qualitative models, such as constructionism, do not assume that there is a 'whole story' to be told about any phenomenon. Instead, they are satisfied with using one set of qualitative data to describe a **hyphenated phenomenon**.

Social media as strategic communication by universities

(Informatics and Media) [Daniel Lövgren]   Daniel is interested in how social media are constructed and used in the everyday activities of universities. He wants to investigate who is responsible for a university's social media, how social media use is perceived within the university and how the use and adoption of social media is 'played out' – how it is done – in the universities (in relation to norms and ideas of strategic communication, organizational context and the concerned individuals). Thus he wants to focus not just on perceptions of social media, but also on its 'doing'.

His data consists of observations, interviews and various documents (gathered at two Swedish universities). The questions he asked me and my answers are listed below:

- I have two case organizations (3 + 3 months' study) - I have some difficulties developing a strong argument for my design.

In qualitative research, we do not try to generalize about populations but about social processes. So don't worry about the apparently 'non-random' choice of cases. Your analysis of these cases will succeed if it allows you to identify credible social processes (see Chapter 13).

- How can I approach my data and structure it in the most efficient way?

Perhaps you have too many different types of data: both naturally occurring (documents and observation of events) and 'manufactured' (interviews). Do you need all this material? Why not just work with one dataset (e.g. the content of universities' social media)? In this way, you can address your interest in how social media are actually used.

- Interpretations are central in my research - from me being on the field interpreting various individuals and processes; people interpreting me as a research at their workplace; my analysis and interpretation of the gathered/generated data; to the interpretation of the final reader of the document I produce. How CAN I handle all these interpretations?

You are in danger of focusing too much on a philosophical issue which threatens us with an 'infinite regress'. Of course, qualitative research is concerned with interpretations of interpretations. But some interpretations are more credible than others (see Chapter 17 on quality issues). Treat how people interpret you in their workplace as a research topic, giving you insight into their practices (on issues of reflexivity in the field, see Buscatto, 2016).

- I really believe a constructivist approach is best suited for my research - how do I develop strong arguments in a field (media and communication) where a lot of research is of quantitative character?

Show your quantitative colleagues that you have a rich understanding of naturalistic phenomena unavailable for proper study by counting variables (e.g. how particular parts of social media work). Constructionism examines how local or 'hyphenated' phenomena are assembled *in situ*, unlike quantitative researchers, who begin with operational definitions of large-scale phenomena (e.g. a university's media profile).

The art of 'Guanxi' – the oriental network capital's role in Western European corporations' Chinese ventures

(Business) [Wenyao Zhao]   Wenyao is researching how 'Guanxi' (literally, connections), the Chinese notion of network capital, can help Western European corporations (WECs) cope with the institutional pressures they are likely to encounter when entering into the Chinese market.

Wenyao wants to examine 'how "Guanxi" can contribute to the improvement of the performance of WECs in China. Specifically, I would ask questions such as, (1) How effective is "Guanxi" as a performance booster? And (2) How these companies could exploit "Guanxi" to achieve market entry, short-term and long-term success in this market?' He will gather data on how current WECs perceive 'Guanxi', and how they build up and maintain their network capital in China using interviews and in-company observations. He asked me:

- Would this project be feasible in terms of the time required?

A good question! In-company observations are likely to be much more time consuming than interviews. Why not restrict yourself to your research question on perceptions of Guanxi? If you do this, only interviews will be needed. If you want to address your question about company networks, might this be available in how companies describe themselves on their websites?

- Would a multiple case studies method be more suitable than survey/questionnaires?

It all depends whether you believe that your research questions are best addressed through a quantitative or qualitative methodology. Your first research question (about the effectiveness of Guanxi) suggests quantitative methods. Your second question (how WECs exploit Guanxi) can probably best be answered by qualitative data. Make your choice and, to save time and to avoid possible conceptual confusion, avoid doing both.

Wenyao's research shows that you need to think through whether your research question is more appropriate to quantitative or qualitative methods. Like Wenyao, Johan is thinking of using mixed methods to study a business topic.

Small businesses' collaborative behaviour and innovation

(Business and Economics) [Johan Lidström] Johan will employ a mixed methods approach to investigate how the collaborative behaviour of small firms affects innovation performance. He writes about his research: 'A distinguishing feature is a focus on micro-foundations of strategy achieved by combining unique longitudinal Swedish data on firm behaviour and data on all individuals employed by these firms. However, this data covers only larger firms and does not address international aspects of firm's operations in greater detail. Hence, I plan to complement the quantitative part with a qualitative component that will extend the project to include new start-ups and their international initiatives.'

Johan asked me: 'how do I ensure a solid contribution with my qualitative data by itself and in combination with quantitative insights?'. I suggested:

- Studying start-ups and collaborative behaviour through qualitative data means a strict focus on real-time data deriving from what actually happens (e.g. in company meetings and/or in digital and other inter-firm communications). It tells a different story from what you can learn through statistical associations.

- This means that you should not use your quantitative data in your analysis of your qualitative case studies. If you do so, you run the risk of reducing the complexities of what happens in the field to what you already know about company behaviour. Beware of such reductionism!
- Use your concluding chapter to reflect on the implications of your findings deriving from different kinds of data.

How women experience depression

(Sociology) [Philippa]   Like Johan, Philippa began by using a quantitative survey. The question for her now is whether her research topic might be better pursued through a more qualitative methodology.

Philippa's research is concerned with how women, as user communities of psychiatry, experience depression, self and identity. Her interest in this topic arose partly from family and work experience and partly because of her curiosity about the statistics which seem to show that women are twice as likely as men to be diagnosed as 'depressives'.

Her approach derives from Foucauldian **genealogical** analysis and hence leads to a focus on how 'depression' is discursively constituted. This approach differs from feminist concerns with patriarchy and misogyny and from an **interactionism** focus on labelling by psychiatrists. The research questions that arise for her from this approach are: how do women speak of themselves as subjects who are 'depressed'? How do such women position and speak about themselves compared with 'normal' gendered subjects? And how far do we find traces of a 'pharmacological culture' in how depression is constituted and treated?

Her data is drawn from women whom she meets through her work as a counsellor. Unusually, given her approach, Philippa has opted initially at least for a questionnaire (partly this reflects her lack of confidence in interviewing women she also counsels). A pilot of this questionnaire showed a high rate of non-response. She is currently revising her questionnaire as well as planning to do some archive analysis.

Philippa is aware that there might be more fruitful research designs. In particular, the use of focus groups or of open-ended interviews based on a single request (such as 'tell me your story') might overcome the problem of using leading or incomprehensible questions. Nonetheless, her project is ambitious and she might consider working entirely with available archives in the usual Foucauldian manner.

Mixed methods: summary

Keep it simple I

Like videos, mixed methods are tempting because they seem to give you a fuller picture. However, you need to be aware that mixed sources of data mean that you will have to learn many more data analysis skills. You will need to avoid the temptation to move to another dataset when you are having difficulties in analysing one set of material.

Keep it simple II

Often the desire to use mixed methods arises because you want to get at many different aspects of a phenomenon. However, this may mean that you have not yet sufficiently narrowed down your topic. Sometimes a better approach is to treat the analysis of different kinds of data as a 'dry run' for your main study. As such, it is a useful test of the kind of data which you can most easily gather and analyse.

Keep it simple III

'Mapping' one set of data upon another is a more or less complicated task depending on your analytic framework. In particular, if you treat social reality as constructed in different ways in different contexts, then you cannot appeal to a single 'phenomenon' which all your data apparently represents.

Research design should involve careful thought rather than seeking the most immediately attractive option. However, none of the points above exclude the possibility of using mixed means of gathering data. Ultimately, everything will depend on the quality of your data analysis rather than upon the quality of your data.

Embrace the limits of your data

WATCH: DAVID EXPLAINS IN PERSON

David's Top Tip 13

Don't worry that your data might be 'partial'. Of course it is. But this is not a problem – unless you make the impossible claim to give 'the whole picture'. So celebrate the partiality of your data and delight in the particular phenomena that they allow you to inspect (hopefully in detail).

9 WRAPPING UP

In this chapter, we have examined the early stage of student research projects. The following suggestions have been made.

Define your problem

1. Research 'problems' do not arise out of a clear blue sky! Sometimes their source is a scholarly debate; sometimes it is a pressing social problem. In any event, you will need to think through the analytic basis of your way of defining your research problem. Having chosen an approach, treat it as a 'toolbox' providing a set of concepts and methods to select your data and to illuminate your analysis.

2. Your approach must be appropriate to the research questions in which you are interested. Indeed, rather than being a constraint, a theory should generate a series of directions for your research (see Chapter 7). It will influence what status you attach to your data - for instance, as a true or false representation of reality - and how you code it.

Limit your data

1. Decide which data to use by asking yourself which data is most appropriate to your research problem. For instance, are you more interested in what people are thinking or feeling or in what they are doing?

2. To make your analysis effective, it is imperative to have a limited body of data with which to work. So, while it may be useful initially to explore different kinds of data, this should usually only be done to establish the dataset with which you can most effectively work (see my further discussion of mixed methods in Chapter 8).

3. Make data collection as easy as possible. There are no 'brownie points' given by most disciplines for having gathered your own data. Indeed, by choosing 'difficult' situations to gather data (because nothing 'relevant' may happen, or even because background noise may mean you have a poor-quality recording), you may condemn yourself to having less time to engage in the much more important activity of data analysis.

4. Beware of complexity. For instance, as we have seen, although video data is very attractive, it is very complex to work with. So keep data gathering simple. Go for material that is easy to collect. Don't worry if it only gives you one 'angle' on your problem. That is a gain as well as a loss!

Go beyond a list in data analysis

1. Choosing a clear analytic approach is a help but is not everything. The danger is that you seek to apply too many findings or concepts deriving from that approach. This can make your analysis both confused and thin or a naive listing of observations consonant with each of these concepts. By narrowing down to a single issue, you may begin to make novel observations.

   Identifying the main elements in your data according to some theoretical scheme should only be the first stage of your data analysis. Go on to examine how these elements are linked together (see Chapter 15).

2. As your data analysis proceeds, you should aim to give your chosen concept or issue a new twist, perhaps by pursuing a counter-intuitive idea or by noting an additional feature little addressed in the literature.

Limit the claims you make about your research

1. It always helps to make limited claims about your own research. Grandiose claims about originality, scope or applicability to social problems are all hostages to fortune. Be careful in how you specify the claims of your approach. Show that you understand that it constitutes one way of 'slicing the cake' and that other approaches, using other forms of data, may not be directly competitive.

Understand issues of relevance

1. When you have finished, reflect upon the contribution that your research makes to contemporary scholarly debates. How does it add to knowledge or change our sense of the role of particular methods or concepts (see Chapter 25)?
2. Is your analytic position appropriate to any practical concerns you have? For instance, many contemporary social theories look at the world quite differently from respondents, policy makers or practitioners. If you use such an approach, you will need to think carefully about what you can offer such groups – although it may well turn out that you can offer them more interesting findings than rather more conventional research (see Chapters 20 and 25).

What You Need to Remember

- Define your research problem analytically.
- Limit your data.
- Demonstrate that your data analysis goes beyond a list.
- Limit the claims you make about your study.
- Think about the relevance of your research for other scholars and for 'society'.
- It is usually a good idea to stick to a small topic, to use only one dataset and to make small but credible claims about your findings.

NOTE

1   Some of these research projects derive from presentations during graduate workshops I coordinated at Goldsmiths College and at Oulu University, Finland. In the Finnish material, I have been able to draw upon research abstracts written by the students prior to the workshop. I was dependent upon my contemporary notes for the Goldsmiths' material and apologise for any inaccuracies present. For this reason, some students' names have been anonymized. Where I have been able to ask permission from students, their full names are given.

Your Chapter Checklist

In this chapter, we have examined the early stage of student research projects. The following are things you need to think about. Go through the list to check your progress.

- Have you defined your research problem analytically or simply in everyday terms?
- Have you tried to limit your data to manageable proportions?
- How can ensure that your data analysis goes beyond a list?
- How will you limit the claims you make about your study?
- What might be the relevance of your research for other scholars and for 'society'?

Exercises

Exercise 1: Examine documents for credibility and 'fact' construction

Not every document you come across in your research has to be treated as a set of true or false statements. Take any one document relevant to your topic and ask:

- How has the document been put together to make its statements seem credible?
- What can you learn from this about how the topics you are concerned with are being 'constructed' by the authors of this document?
- Where could you find other documents which might construct these 'facts' differently?

Exercise 2: Understand the different ways of gathering and analysing data

The following activity is meant to help you think through the issues raised in this chapter about the value and implications of different ways of gathering and analysing qualitative data. Go through the following steps, ideally with another student:

1. Define your research topic in no more than two sentences.
2. Explain which method you propose to use to gather data. Why that method?
3. Why would other methods not be possible or appropriate?
4. How big a data sample do you intend to collect? Could you manage with less data? Might you need more?
5. What theoretical approach (e.g. naturalist or constructionist) do you favour? How will it help or hinder you in the analysis of your data?
6. What other approaches might be appropriate or inappropriate? Why?
7. Is there anything about your theory, method and data that could be simplified to make a more effective study?

Further Reading

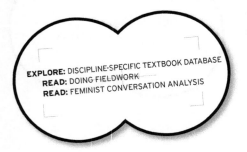

EXPLORE: DISCIPLINE-SPECIFIC TEXTBOOK DATABASE
READ: DOING FIELDWORK
READ: FEMINIST CONVERSATION ANALYSIS

An excellent practical guide to the business of writing a dissertation is Pat Cryer's *The Research Student's Guide to Success* (Open University Press, 2006). Judith Bell's *Doing Your Research Project* (Open University Press, 2005) is a much more basic treatment, mainly aimed at undergraduate dissertations. Nina Wakeford and Kris Cohen (Sage, 2008) describe how blogs can be used successfully for online research.

Discover the chapter's digital resources in your SILVERMAN FIELD GUIDE

SEVEN
Using Theories

Learning Outcomes

By the end of this chapter you will be able to:

- Know what a theory is and why it matters.
- Distinguish between a theory, a model and a concept.
- Understand the ways in which models shape your research problem.

1 INTRODUCTION

'Theory' can be a scary term. It depends on abstract thinking, which many people find somewhat challenging. Lectures, textbooks and journal articles seem to elevate 'theory' and so we worry that our research will not be respectable unless we can locate it in some theory. This seems to run against many students' desire to study a familiar social situation (e.g. learning in the classroom) or given social problem (e.g. how learning can be improved). We just want to discover some information which we hope will be relevant to society. So we ask ourselves: why should we be forced to bring in abstract theories?

The outcome is, too often, that people seek respectability by dressing up their research in theories that are incompatible with how they have formulated and studied their research topic. Unfortunately, such theoretical 'window-dressing' is all too common in qualitative research. For instance, the term **grounded theory** is frequently used to 'dress up' research which is neither grounded nor theoretical.

Such misuse of theory does not mean that we can do without it. For example, Eric Livingston (1987) asks us to imagine that we have been told to carry out some social research on city streets. Where should we begin? Some alternatives are set out in Table 7.1.

Table 7.1   Viewing a street: data possibilities

1	Official statistics (traffic flow, accidents)
2	Interviews (how people cope with rush hours)
3	Observation from a tower (viewing geometric shapes)
4	Observation/video at street level (how people queue or organize their movements)

Source: adapted from Livingston (1987: 21-7)

Believe it or not, once we have got to the stage of thinking about settings like this, we have moved deep into theoretical issues. For, as Livingston points out, each of these different ways of looking involves basic theoretical as well as methodological decisions. Very crudely, if we are attached to social theories which see the world in terms of correlations between social facts (think of demography or macroeconomics), we are most likely to consider gathering official statistics (option 1 in Table 7.1). By contrast, if we think that social meanings or perceptions are important (as in certain varieties of sociology and psychology), we may be tempted by the interview study (option 2). Or if we are anthropologists or those kinds of sociologists who want to observe and/or record what people actually do in real-life contexts, we might elect options 3 or 4. But note the very different views of people's behaviour we get from looking from on high (option 3), where people seem like ants forming geometrical shapes like wedges, or from street level (option 4), where behaviour seems much more complex.

Be aware of theory's influence

WATCH: DAVID EXPLAINS IN PERSON

David's Top Tip 14

None of the possible datasets discussed by Livingston are more *real* or more *true* than the others. For instance, people are not really more like ants or complex actors. So, in designing your research, reflect upon how your theoretical assumptions about the social world are shaping the methodology you favour.

So methodologies and research questions are inevitably theoretically informed. Even down-to-earth policy-oriented research designed to evaluate some social service will, as Livingston implies, embed itself in theoretical issues as soon as it selects a particular evaluation method (see my discussion of HIV counselling research in Chapter 9).

So we *do* need social theories to help us to address even quite basic issues in social research. Herbert Blumer quotes a famous American sociologist of the past to make just this point:

> One can see the empirical world only through some scheme or image of it. The *entire* act of scientific study is oriented and shaped by the underlying picture of the empirical world that is used. This picture sets the selection and formulation of problems, the determination of what are data, the kinds of relations sought between data, and the forms in which propositions are cast. (1969: 24-5)

READ: THEORY AND REFLEXIVITY

2 HOW THEORETICAL MODELS SHAPE RESEARCH

As we saw in Chapter 6, refining your research topic is never a purely technical activity. Many students begin with a social problem defined in common-sense terms. Some use a language of 'variables' better suited to quantitative research or confuse studying what should be with studying what 'is'. This way of defining a research topic derives from a model of science which treats 'social facts' as existing independently of the activities of both participants and researchers. By contrast, in qualitative research, we tend to study how phenomena are 'experienced' or 'constructed' in people's everyday activities. Qualitative researchers usually avoid early hypotheses and simply ask 'What is going on here?', or try out a range of concepts to see if they sensitize them to what is going on.

Choose a design that matches your topic's keywords

WATCH: DAVID EXPLAINS IN PERSON

David's Top Tip 15

Broadly speaking, if your research topic includes references to 'variables', 'factors' or 'indicators' then you should not be thinking of using a qualitative research design.

This underlines the point that how we think about our research is always shaped by our assumptions about:

- the nature of social phenomena
- the proper ways to investigate such phenomena.

Keith Punch asks us: 'Are we committed to a particular research model, which implies a particular methodology? Do [you] have a gut feeling about what a good piece of research looks like?' (1998: 245). Qualitative research designs tend to work with a relatively small number of cases. Generally speaking, qualitative researchers are prepared to sacrifice scope for detail. Moreover, even what counts as detail tends to vary between qualitative and quantitative researchers. The latter typically seek detail in certain aspects of correlations between variables. By contrast, for qualitative researchers, detail is found in the precise particulars of such matters as people's understandings and interactions in particular contexts. This is because qualitative researchers tend to use a non-positivist model of reality.

However, 'non-positivism' is a negative term which does not tell us directly about how qualitative researchers reason. As we shall now see, qualitative research is an intellectually diverse field in which researchers use many different models. In some sense, they speak different languages.

As shown in Table 7.2, models provide an overall framework for viewing reality. They inform the concepts we use to define our research problem.

Table 7.2 Three research models

Model	Assumptions	Concepts	Example	Usual Data
Positivism	Objective measurement 'Why' questions	Operational definitions Variables/social facts	Why some children are more creative than others?	Experiment
Naturalism	Subjective interpretation Meanings/ perceptions	Lived experience Definition of the situation	What is the lived experience of the creative child?	Interview
Constructionism	Reality socially constructed Active social organization	Social processes How questions	How are 'creative' children 'framed' in the classroom?	Naturalistic data

Table 7.2 reveals that qualitative research is an intellectually diverse field in which researchers use many different models. It should be stressed, however, that we should not be too rigid about what I call 'the usual method' in each model. This just indicates what tend to be the data preferences of each approach.

But bear in mind that positivists sometimes conduct interviews, naturalists regularly do ethnographies of naturalistic settings, and constructionists sometimes analyse interview data and sometimes even do experiments (Heritage et al., 2007).

Although positivism is the most common model used in quantitative research (i.e. the default option), it sits uneasily within most qualitative research designs. Take the following student example.

WHAT I DID: ANGELOS

My study's research purpose is to advance understanding on what happens within competition by looking at how trust and distrust evolve over time in a dyadic competitive relationship. My research questions are:

1. How are trust and distrust related to each other in inter-organizational relationships? (Literature review.)
2. How do the individuals' characteristics (personality, experience, position) affect the different dimensions of trust and distrust in a competitive relationship? (Quantitative study.)
3. How do the interactions between individuals from two competitive firms affect the different dimensions of trust and distrust? (Qualitative case study based upon secondary data.)
4. How do information systems (e.g. predictive analytics and cloud computing) as a means for managing competition affect the outcomes of competition? [Angelos Kostis, Business and Economics, Umeå University]

This is an example of a well-thought-out research design, based on a clear research topic, intelligent use of the literature and distinction between the use of quantitative and qualitative methods. However, there are problems in how Angelos makes use of this distinction. Quite rightly, since his Topic 2 depends upon relating variables to one another, he proposes to use quantitative methods to study it. Unfortunately, his formulation of Topic 3 as a 'qualitative case study based upon secondary data' is doubly problematic as follows:

- Operational definitions of factors like 'trust' and 'distrust' derive from a quantitative positivist model. By contrast, in qualitative research, we might want to understand whether categories like 'trust' and 'distrust' enter into employees' definition of the situation (naturalism) or how, in particular contexts such as a business meeting, versions of relationships are constructed (constructionism).
- The distinction between 'primary' data (usually statistics) and 'secondary' data (usually interviews or naturalistic data such as documents or meetings) derives from positivism. For qualitative researchers, there is no such meaningful distinction as naturalistic data actually 'happened' (documents were written, meetings were held) and so is no less 'primary' than statistics.

READ:
THEORIZING INTERVIEWS

Yet, even if we successfully distinguish the different topics which quantitative and qualitative researchers address, there is no agreed model or paradigm in qualitative research. In some sense, qualitative researchers speak different languages.

3 THE DIFFERENT LANGUAGES OF QUALITATIVE RESEARCH

At the heart of these different languages is the division between substance and process, or between *what* is being studied and *how* it is constructed. Take the topic of nudity, for example. A qualitative researcher might ask the following: *what* are the traits that characterize nudists and *what* practices are associated with being a nudist? Another researcher studying the same topic could examine *how* nudity could be made normal or routine. In 'The nudist management of respectability', Martin Weinberg (1994) explores how nudist colonies achieve the 'respectability' of the unclothed body through a set of locally defined and enforced norms like 'no body contact' and 'no accentuation of the body' (e.g. sitting with one's legs open). Weinberg's goal is to answer the question, 'How can they see their behavior as morally appropriate?' (1994: 392).

With this distinction between *how* (process of constructing reality) and *what* (reality as substantive truth), let us look further at two models of qualitative research discussed in Gubrium and Holstein's (1997) book:

* naturalism
* constructionism.

Naturalism

As a model of qualitative research, naturalism focuses on the factual characteristics of the object under study. Gubrium and Holstein cite William Whyte's *Street Corner Society* as a classic example of naturalism. In this urban ethnography from the 1940s, Whyte's goal is to describe what life is really like in an inner-city Italian neighbourhood located in Massachusetts. The observations and analysis are intended to reflect objectively *what* Whyte saw and heard in this real world of poverty. Naturalism's strength is its representational simplicity. A naturalistic ethnography is almost formulaically built around the following tasks:

- entering the setting
- establishing rapport
- recording observations with an eye towards social science concepts (e.g. social status and group dynamics)
- presenting the findings.

The major shortcoming of naturalists, according to Gubrium and Holstein, is this:

> Because they view the border [between the topic of study and the way in which it is socially constructed] as a mere *technical* hurdle that can be overcome through methodological skill and rigor, they lose sight of the border as a region where reality is constituted within representation. (1997: 106)

This criticism suggests that naturalists overlook how people create meaning in their lives. Respondents are treated as mere sources of data without any interpretive capacity of their own. In a naturalistic framework, the participants' 'interpretive practice' (Gubrium and Holstein, 1997), or how they make sense of their own world, is irrelevant.

Constructionism

The key differences between constructionism and naturalism have been well defined by Holstein and Gubrium (2008b). They state:

> Whereas naturalistic ethnography aims to delve deeply into social worlds, constructionist impulses promote a different perspective. One way of describing the difference is in terms of what we call *what* and *how* questions. Whereas the naturalistic impulse in fieldwork is typically to ask '*What* is going on?' with, and within, social reality, constructionist sensibilities provoke questions about how social realities are produced, assembled, and maintained. Rather than trying to get inside social reality, the constructionist impulse is to step back from that reality and describe *how* it is socially brought into being. While still deeply interested in *what* is going on, constructionist sensibilities also raise questions about the processes through which social realities are constructed and sustained. The analytic focus is not so much on the dynamics within social realities as it is on the construction of social realities in the first place. (2008b: 374-5)

The main features of a constructionist agenda for qualitative research are set out in Table 7.3.

The most important insight of constructionism is its emphasis on the rhetorical and constructive aspects of knowledge: that is, the realization that facts (like Angelos's study of 'trust' and 'distrust' discussed earlier) are socially constructed in

READ: CONSTRUCTIONISM

Table 7.3 A constructionist agenda

1	Look at, and listen to, the activities through which everyday actors produce the orderly, recognizable, meaningful features of their social worlds
2	Use an explicitly action orientation, focusing intently on interaction and discourse as productive of social reality
3	Maintain an abiding concern for the ordinary, everyday procedures that society's members use to make their experiences sensible, understandable, accountable and orderly
4	Retain an appreciation of naturalists' desire to describe 'what's going on', but with decided emphasis on how these whats are sustained as realities of everyday life
5	Instead of treating social facts or social worlds as either objective parameters or subjective perceptions, constructionists approach these as achievements in their own right. Both inner lives and social worlds are epiphenomenal to the constructive practices of everyday life
6	Constructionist researchers are interested in the practical activities in which persons are continually engaged, moment by moment, to construct, manage and sustain the sense that their social worlds exist as factual and objectively 'out there', apart from their own actions

Source: adapted from Holstein and Gubrium (2008b: 375)

particular contexts. In some respects this defines the constructionist model, which is concerned with the question of 'how?' that informs so much qualitative research (see Holstein and Gubrium, 2008b).

4 METHODOLOGIES

Now I must complicate matters further. While models inform the kind of questions we ask about reality, they do not in themselves define how we should conduct our research. For that we need a **methodology**. A methodology refers to the principles of reasoning we use in making choices about research design. Such choices involve consideration of appropriate *models*, cases to study, methods of data gathering, forms of data analysis, etc., in planning and executing a research study. In short, a methodology is '[a] theory of how the research proceeds' (Braun and Clarke, 2013: 333).

The relationship between models and methodologies is reciprocal: our choice of model should inform what methodology we use, and whatever methodology we do use will bring in baggage from a particular model. To illustrate this, I will discuss four kinds of methodologies deriving from constructionism:

- grounded theory
- narrative analysis
- discourse analysis
- actor-network theory.

Let me give you a taste of each approach, flavoured by student examples. Each approach is discussed later in this book.

Grounded theory (GT)

GT is firmly rooted in an assumption common to qualitative researchers: don't begin with a prior hypothesis but induce your hypotheses from close data analysis. As Charmaz and Bryant put it:

> Grounded theory is a method of qualitative inquiry in which researchers develop inductive theoretical analyses from their collected data and subsequently gather further data to check these analyses. The purpose of grounded theory is theory construction, rather than description or application of existing theories. (2011a: 292)

GT lies on the borderline between naturalism and constructionism. As Charmaz (2006) has pointed out, a constructionist will use GT in a very different way to those ethnographers who believe that their categories simply reproduce nature. In Charmaz's terms: a 'constructivist would emphasize eliciting the participant's definitions of terms, situations, and events and try to tap his or her assumptions, implicit meanings, and tacit rules. An objectivist would be concerned with obtaining information about chronology, events, settings, and behaviors' (2006: 32).

WHAT I DID: ANASTACIA

Native Indian Stories

Anastacia was studying the stories about their lives that Native Americans construct on certain websites. As she puts it: 'The aim of GT is to generate hypotheses that theoretically *describe* the constructs that arise in every sentence of the stories told. I used this approach because it made sense to take the large amount of data and describe the stories with a broad theme during my first reading. Then, I looked at the stories line by line and coded particular themes in their own words during my second reading. This allowed me to take a top down, bottom up approach to understanding hidden nuances in their stories. [Anastacia M. Schulhoff, Department of Sociology, University of Missouri-Columbia]

A defining strategy of GT is theoretical sampling. In quantitative research, we sample in order to achieve numbers that appropriately represent various demographic characteristics of the population (e.g. gender, age, health status, etc.).

By contrast, in GT, we use theoretical sampling in order to flesh out the properties of a tentative category. As Charmaz and Bryant put it:

> Theoretical sampling involves gathering new data to check hunches and to confirm that the properties of the grounded theorist's theoretical category are filled out. Researchers may also use it to define variation in a studied process or phenomenon or to establish the boundaries of a theoretical category. When these properties are saturated with data, the grounded theorist ends data collection and integrates the analysis. (2011a: 292)

Theoretical sampling helps develop GTs based on situations and concepts which are progressively widened by:

- including social situations very different from those with which one began
- linking concepts to broader theories (both substantive and formal).

CASE STUDY
Representations of Hilary Clinton

- Using GT methodology, Mary Tucker-McLaughlin and Kenneth Campbell (2012) analysed 30 television news stories or segments (approximately 3 hours of news stories) collected around important dates in Hillary Clinton's public life between the years of 1993 and 2008, which included her tenure as a First Lady, US Senator and presidential primary candidate.
- As examples of **substantive theory**, they consider what themes are represented in major network television news stories about Hillary Clinton during the most public times in her life between 1993 and 2008.
- Two primary representations emerge: Clinton as an innovator and Clinton as voiceless. Voiceless is an inherently negative representation, and although innovator is a positive theme, the news media tended to focus on representations of Clinton in negative stories.
- They also seek to contribute to the development of **formal theories** addressing the representation of female politicians seeking high political office.

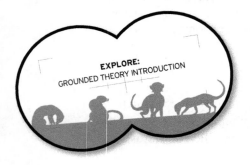

EXPLORE:
GROUNDED THEORY INTRODUCTION

Two key features of the GT approach are:

- the constant comparative method as the analyst seeks out settings which may modify or broaden the initial categories
- a continual movement between data, memos and theory so that data analysis is theoretically based and theory is grounded in data.

Narrative analysis (NA)

NA treats the accounts that people offer as *stories*. This is intended not to question the veracity of such accounts but to understand their function in particular contexts or sites. For NA, stories have the features set out in Table 7.4.

Table 7.4   Stories in NA

- Stories are constructed in concrete circumstances and in particular sites
- Stories are told with an audience in view
- Stories are eventful – they are courses of action with consequences
- Stories are always more than accounts; they are accounts that have been conveyed and stand to be reconveyed

Source: adapted from Gubrium (2010: 390–1)

WHAT I DID: METTE
Drug Dealers' Stories

The project 'A qualitative study of the heroin market' is based on 24 qualitative interviews with imprisoned offenders, 2 interviews with dealers on the outside, and 6 interviews with policemen who have followed the development of the heroin market over time. As a starting point these interviews were only meant to illuminate the organizational aspects of the heroin trade, but in meeting with the offenders and hearing their narratives, issues of self-presentation and power also became apparent and needed addressing. Some central questions: how do the heroin smugglers and dealers present themselves and their illegal activities? What explanation do they give for their illegal actions? What types of representations of normality, deviance, health and sickness are found in their narratives? [Mette Irmgard Snertingdal, Sociology, Norway]

NA suggests key questions we ask about stories:

- In what kind of a story does a narrator place herself?
- How does she position herself to the audience, and vice versa?
- How does she position characters in relation to one another, and in relation to herself?
- How does she position herself to herself, that is, make identity claims? (Bamberg, 1997, quoted by Riessman, 2011)

READ: NARRATIVE ANALYSIS

Riessman offers a number of suggestions about how we should answer these questions, and I have set these out in Table 7.5.

Table 7.5   Working with NA

- Adopt a constructionist framework and be precise in your use of an appropriate narrative vocabulary
- In analysing particular narrative segments, think about form and function – the way a segment of data is organized and why
- Don't neglect the local context in your analysis, including the questioner and listener, the setting, and the position of an utterance in the broader stream of the conversation

Source: adapted from Riessman (2011: 328-9)

Discourse analysis (DA)

Like NA, DA is quite heterogeneous and it is, therefore, difficult to arrive at a clear definition of it. Here is one authoritative version:

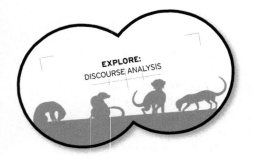

DA has an analytic commitment to studying discourse as *texts and talk in social practices* ... the focus is ... on language as ... the medium for interaction; analysis of discourse becomes, then, analysis of what people do. One theme that is particularly emphasized here is the rhetorical or argumentative organization of talk and texts; claims and versions are constructed to undermine alternatives. (Potter, 2004: 203, emphasis in original)

While GT and NA adherents include people who mix naturalist and constructionist approaches (see Charmaz, 2006), researchers who use DA tend to be quite open about their adherence to a constructionist model. As Potter and Hepburn explain:

Discursive constructionism works with two senses of construction. On the one hand, discourse is constructed in the sense that it is assembled from a range of different resources with different degrees of structural organization. Most fundamentally these are words and grammatical structures, but also broader elements such as categories, metaphors, idioms, rhetorical commonplaces and interpretative repertoires. For example, how is a description manufactured in a way that presents something that has been done as orderly and unproblematic? On the other hand, discourse is constructive in the sense that these assemblages of words, repertoires and so on put together and stabilize versions of the world, of actions and events, of mental life and furniture. For example, how does one party in a relationship counselling session construct a version that presents the breakdown of a long term relationship as primarily the responsibility of the other party, who might be the one most in need of counselling and under most pressure to change? (2008: 277)

WHAT I DID: STEVEN

Postgraduate Identities

Steven Stanley's research was concerned with the rhetorical basis of postgraduate identities. One chapter of his thesis looks at three participants who, when he interviewed them, claimed academic identities for themselves. As he writes: 'From a discourse and rhetoric perspective, the participants Ben, Fiona, and Rachel employed quite different strategies in making their academic identity claims. Each participant negotiated a different "dilemma of stake" (Silverman, 2011b: 307-9): how to claim an academic identity without coming across as a non-academic; how to create the impression that "academic" is a discredited identity while at the same time claiming that identity; and how not to claim too much or too little of an academic identity ... This chapter illustrates discursively the rhetorical nature of postgraduate identity work.' [Steven Stanley, Human Sciences, Loughborough]

Actor-network theory (ANT)

While naturalism is centrally concerned with the experiences of humans, ANT is a constructionist approach which is distinguished by its attention to the way in which *non-human actors* participate in shaping the social world. For instance, think of the way in which PCs in doctors' offices now shape what happens in a contemporary medical consultation (Heath, 2011). Or take Michel Callon's (1986) study of the politics of fishing in Newfoundland. This linked the fishermen of Saint Brieuc Bay to the scallops that supported their livelihoods – and spoke of the scallops very much as actors. Other actors or 'actants' included a group of researchers, visitors to the bay, starfish, larvae, sea currents, and so on.

This is not to say that scallops are no different to humans, 'but rather a methodological openness to how we construct agency in everyday life. We act "as if" oysters and chairs had agency, just as we act "as if" we ourselves had agency ... (for) even human agents are constructed' (Jay Gubrium, personal correspondence).

ANT has been used very productively in the analysis of documents. It shows that it is very restrictive to treat documents as simple *resources* to be used in understanding settings. By contrast, constructionists try to make documents *topics* in their own right by asking questions about how they are put together and how they function. Using ANT, Lindsay Prior argues:

> Putting an emphasis on 'topic' ... can open up a further dimension of research: the ways in which documents function in the everyday world. For when we focus on function it becomes apparent that documents serve not merely as containers of content, but as active agents in episodes of interaction and schemes of social organization. (2008: 824)

CASE STUDY
Documents and Actor-Network Theory

Prior shows 'how documents should not merely be regarded as containers for words, images, information, instructions, and so forth, but how they can influence episodes of social interaction, and schemes of social organization, and how they might enter into the analysis of such interactions and organization' (2008: 822). This way of theorizing documents allows us to treat documents in a counter-intuitive way – as actors. As Prior notes:

> The idea of conceptualizing things (non-human agents) as actors was first proposed by adherents of what is often referred to as actor-network theory or ANT (Callon, 1986; Law and Hassard, 1999). One key plank of the ANT argument is that the traditional distinction – indeed, the asymmetry – between material and human objects be not just problematized, but overturned. In the same way, it is argued that the traditional distinction between subject and object be dispensed with. So, when studying schemes of social interaction, material objects are not to be regarded as mere (passive) resources that are important only when activated by human actors, but are seen to play a part in social configurations in their own right. That is to say, material objects can be seen to instigate and direct as well as be directed (Callon and Law, 1997: 101). What is more, over and above the suggestion that non-human agents might be considered as actors, there is the notion that such actors or hybrids may be conceived as components of an actor-network. (2008: 828)

WHAT I DID: ILKA

Ilka uses ANT to study how corporate social responsibility programmes (CSR) are designed by organizations. She writes: 'In my doctoral research I mobilise theoretical concepts from ANT to inform qualitative research and design explorations that investigate the relationship between design, CSR and the public sphere. A case study approach has been chosen. The research focus is on the designed things that act within CSR projects. Designed things are understood as nonhuman actors that participate in shaping corporate actions. ANT provides descriptors for different kinds of agency exercised by actors in a network. I adopt these descriptors to identify the type of agency exercised by particular designed things within the case study of CSR programs. [Ilka, Design, UTS Business School]

By now, these multiple perspectives may have left you thoroughly confused. As a beginning researcher, you may rightly feel that the last thing you need is to sink into an intractable debate between warring camps. However, it helps if we treat this less as a war and more as a clarion call to be clear about the issues that animate our work and help define our research problem. As I argued in Chapter 6, purely theoretical debates are often less than helpful if we want to carry out effective research. The point is to work with a model and a methodology that make sense to you. The strengths and weaknesses of each will only be revealed in what you can do with it.

5 THEORIES, MODELS AND HYPOTHESES

In this section, we shall be discussing models, concepts, theories, hypotheses, methods and methodologies. In Table 7.6, I set out how each term will be used.

As we see from Table 7.6, *models* provide an overall framework for how we look at reality. In short, they tell us what reality is like, the basic elements it contains ('ontology') and what is the nature and status of knowledge ('epistemology'). In this sense, models roughly correspond to what are more grandly referred to as paradigms (see Guba and Lincoln, 1994).

Concepts are clearly specified ideas deriving from a particular model. Examples of concepts are 'social function' (deriving from functionalism), 'stimulus–response' (behaviouralism), 'definition of the situation' (interactionism) and 'the documentary method of interpretation' (ethnomethodology). Concepts offer ways of looking at the world which are essential in defining a research problem.

Theories arrange sets of concepts to define and explain some phenomenon. As Strauss and Corbin put it: 'Theory consists of plausible relationships produced among concepts and sets of concepts' (1994: 278). Without a theory,

Table 7.6   Basic research terms

Term	Meaning	Relevance
Model	An overall framework for looking at reality (e.g. positivism, constructionism)	Usefulness
Concept	An idea deriving from a given model (e.g. 'stimulus-response', 'the social construction of reality')	Usefulness
Theory	A set of concepts used to define and/or explain some phenomenon	Validity
Hypothesis	A testable proposition	Validity
Methodology	A general approach to studying research topics	Usefulness
Method	A specific research technique (e.g. interview, focus group)	Good fit with model, theory, hypothesis and methodology

Source: Silverman (2014: 53)

such phenomena as 'death', 'tribes' and 'families' cannot be understood. In this sense, without a theory there is nothing to research. So theory provides a footing for considering the world, separate from, yet about, that world. In this way, theory provides both a framework for critically understanding phenomena and a basis for considering how what is unknown might be organized (Jay Gubrium, personal correspondence).

Models versus theories

WATCH: DAVID EXPLAINS IN PERSON

David's Top Tip 16

Because models involve theoretical assumptions, models and theories are easily confused. One way of avoiding such confusion is to limit our discussion of theories to what Punch (2014: 18) calls *substantive* theory. As he puts it: 'Substantive theory [is] theory about a substantive issue or phenomenon ... [it is] content-based ... and is not concerned with methods. Theory in this sense is a set of propositions that together describe and explain the phenomenon being studied.'

By provoking ideas about the presently unknown, theories provide the impetus for research. As living entities, they are also developed and modified by good research. However, as used here, models and concepts are self-confirming in the sense that they instruct us to look at phenomena in particular ways, theories can be tested and confirmed or refuted. Theories and hypotheses exist in a reciprocal relationship. Theories can suggest hypotheses but hypotheses are often induced from data and help us to build theories (see my earlier discussion of substantive and formal theories within GT).

Examples of hypotheses, discussed in Silverman (2006), are:

- How we receive advice is linked to how advice is given.
- Responses to an illegal drug depend upon what one learns from others.
- Voting in union elections is related to non-work links between union members.

In many qualitative research studies, there is no specific hypothesis at the outset. Instead, hypotheses are produced (or induced) during the early stages of research. In any event, hypotheses can and should be tested. Therefore, we assess a hypothesis by its validity or truth.

A *methodology* refers to the choices we make about cases to study, methods of data gathering, forms of data analysis, etc., in planning and executing a research study. So our methodology defines how one will go about studying any phenomenon. In social research, methodologies may be defined very broadly (e.g. qualitative or quantitative) or more narrowly (e.g. GT or DA). Like theories, methodologies cannot be true or false, only more or less useful.

Finally, *methods* are specific research techniques. These include quantitative techniques like statistical correlations, as well as techniques like observation, interviewing and audio recording. Once again, in themselves, techniques are not true or false. They are more or less useful, depending on their fit with the theories and methodologies being used and the hypothesis being tested and/or the research topic that is selected. So, for instance, positivists may favour quantitative methods and constructionists often prefer to gather their data by observation and/or recording. But, depending upon the hypothesis being tested, positivists may sometimes use qualitative methods – for instance, in the exploratory stage of research. Equally, constructionists may sometimes use simple quantitative methods, particularly when they want to find an overall pattern in their data.

EXPLORE:
THEORY AND HYPOTHESES

The relation between models, concepts, theories, hypotheses, methodology and methods can be set out schematically as in Figure 7.1.

Reading the figure downwards, each term reflects a lower level of generality and abstraction. The arrow from 'findings' to 'hypotheses' indicates a feedback mechanism through which hypotheses are modified in the light of findings.

6 EXAMPLES

Let me now try to put flesh on the skeleton set out in Figure 7.1 through the use of some concrete examples. Imagine that we have a general interest in the gloomy topic of 'death' in society. How are we to research this topic?

Before we can even define a research problem, let alone develop a hypothesis, we need to think through some very basic issues. Assume that we are the kind of social scientist that prefers to see the world in terms of how social structures determine behaviour, following the sociologist Emile Durkheim's (1951) injunction to treat social facts as real 'things'. Such a positivist model of social life will suggest concepts that we can use in our research on death. Using such a model, we will tend to see death in terms of statistics relating to rates of death (or 'mortality'). And we will want to explain such statistics in terms of other social facts such as age or social class.

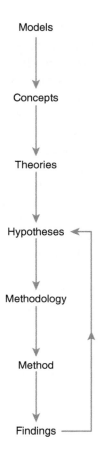

Figure 7.1   Levels of analysis

Armed with our concepts, we might then construct a theory about one or another aspect of our topic. For instance, working with our assumption that death is a social fact, determined by other social facts, we might develop a theory that the rate of early death among children, or 'infant mortality', is related to some social fact about their parents, say their social class. From this theory, it is a quick step to the hypothesis that the higher the social class of its parents, the lower the likelihood of a child dying within the first year of its life. This hypothesis is sometimes expressed as saying that there is an 'inverse' relationship between social class and infant mortality.

As already implied, a model concerned with social facts will tend to favour a quantitative methodology, using methods such as the analysis of official statistics or the application of large-scale social surveys based on apparently reliable fixed-choice questionnaires. In interpreting the findings of such research, one will need to ensure that due account is taken of factors that may be concealed in simple cor-relations. For instance, social class may be associated with quality of housing, and the latter factor (here called an **intervening variable**) may be the real cause of variations in the rates of infant mortality. This overall approach to death is set out schematically in Figure 7.2.

But there is a very different way of conceiving death as a possible research topic. For constructionists, social institutions are created and/or stabilized by the actions of participants. A central idea of this model is that how we label phe-nomena defines their character. This, in turn, is associated with the concept of

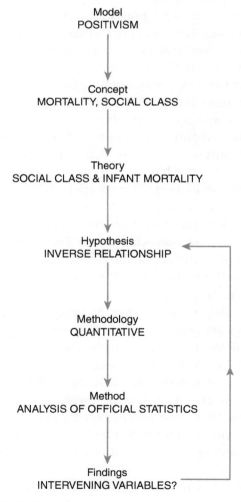

Figure 7.2   Death as a social fact

'definitions of the situation', which tells us to look for social phenomena in how meaning gets defined by people in different contexts. The overall message of this approach is that 'death' should be put in inverted commas, and hence leads to a theory in which 'death' is treated as a social construct.

Of course, this is very different from the 'social fact' model and, therefore, nicely illustrates the importance of theories in defining research problems. Its immediate drawback, however, may be that it appears to be counter-intuitive. After all, you may feel, death is surely an obvious fact. We are either dead or not dead – and, this being so, where does this leave constructionism?

Let me cite two cases which put the counter-argument. First, in 1963, after President Kennedy was shot, he was taken to a Dallas hospital with, according to contemporary accounts, half of his head shot away. My hunch is that if you or I were to arrive in a casualty department in this state, we would be given a cursory examination and then recorded as 'dead on arrival' (DOA). Precisely because they were dealing with a president, the staff had to do more than this. So they worked on Kennedy for almost an hour, demonstrating thereby that they had done their best for such an important patient (cf. Sudnow, 1968a).

Now think of contemporary debates about whether or when severely injured people should have life-support systems turned off. Once again, acts of definition constitute whether somebody is alive or dead. And note that such definitions have real effects.

Of course, such a way of looking at how death is socially constructed is just one way of theorizing this phenomenon, not intrinsically better or worse than the 'social fact' approach. But, once we adopt one or another model, it starts to have a big influence upon how our research proceeds. For instance, as we have seen, if 'dead on arrival' can be a label applied in different ways to different people, we might develop a hypothesis about how the label 'dead on arrival' is applied to different hospital patients.

Because of our model, we would then probably try to collect research data that arose in such naturally occurring (or non-research-generated) contexts as actual hospitals, using methods like observation and/or audio or video recording. Note, however, that this would not rule out the collection of quantitative data (say from hospital records). Rather, it would mean that our main body of data would probably be qualitative. Following earlier research (e.g. Dingwall and Murray, 1983; Jeffery, 1979), our findings might show how age and presumed moral status are relevant to such medical decision making as well as social class. In turn, as shown in Figure 7.3, these findings would help us to refine our initial hypothesis.

A student example on a related topic will nicely illustrate the logic of such a constructionist model. Gunhild Tøndel studied how office staff in Norwegian local authorities compiled health statistics. Here is her account.

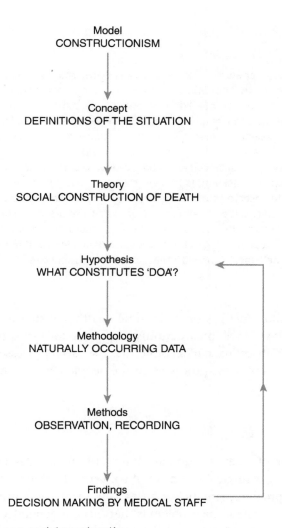

Figure 7.3   Death as a social construction

WHAT I DID: GUNHILD

Managing Health by Numbers

My project is a qualitative study of statistical practices in municipal health services. I focus on micro-level processes and take a constructivist and interactionist perspective on how statistics are constructed and produced in someone's everyday settings; how their production affects service providers who supply the data; how they are interpreted

(Continued)

(Continued)

by service users, local administrators, and politicians; and not least, what distortions thereby make their way into data during this collection, reporting, and transportation chain, and how they are accounted for when data are put to use. In other words, how statistics function as a tool of governance in these services. First and foremost I will use a statistical tool designed to measure clients' function levels and so map their needs for assistance.

I will use texts as public documents and incentive reports to gain an overview of the structural context and background framework(s) surrounding local practice. Hopefully, I will gain access to observe actors' situated production of numbers and statistical indicators within the municipalities' health service units and also the interaction between these units and the administrative bureaucracy. I will conduct interviews with data reporters (mostly health professionals) about this process and their interpretations of e.g. how this affects the 'counted ones'. [Gunhild Tøndel, Sociology, Trondheim]

Note that Gunhild's focus is on how these health statistics are put together in a particular context. As a constructionist, the issue for her is not whether such statistics are accurate or inaccurate, but rather the social processes of their production and the effects of those processes on the people who are counted.

7 WRAPPING UP

The philosopher of science Thomas Kuhn (1970) has described some social sciences as lacking a single, agreed set of concepts. In Kuhn's terms, this makes social research 'pre-paradigmatic' or at least in a state of competing paradigms. As I have already implied, the problem is that this has generated a whole series of social science courses which pose different social science approaches in terms of either/or questions.

Such courses are much appreciated by some students. They learn about the paradigmatic oppositions in question, choose A rather than B and report back, parrot fashion, all the advantages of A and the drawbacks of B. It is hardly surprising that such courses produce very little evidence that such students have ever thought about anything; even their choice of A is likely to be based on their teacher's implicit or explicit preferences. This may, in part, explain why so many undergraduate social science courses actually provide a learned incapacity to go out and do research.

Learning about rival 'armed camps' in no way allows you to confront research data. In the field, material is much more messy than the different camps would suggest. Perhaps there is something to be learned from both sides; or, more constructively, perhaps we start to ask interesting questions when we reject the polarities that such a course markets.

Even when we decide to use qualitative and/or quantitative methods, we involve ourselves in theoretical as well as methodological decisions. These decisions relate not only to how we conceptualize the world, but also to our theory of how our research subjects think about things.

But theory only becomes worthwhile when it is used to explain something. Becker (1998: 1) reports that the great founder of the **Chicago School**, Everett Hughes, responded grumpily when students asked what he thought about theory. 'Theory of what?' he would reply. For Hughes, as for me, theory without some observation to work upon is like a tractor without a field.

Theory, then, should be neither a status symbol nor an optional extra in a research study. Without theory, research is impossibly narrow. Without research, theory is mere armchair contemplation.

What You Need to Remember

Research questions are inevitably theoretically informed. So we *do* need social theories to help us to address even quite basic issues in social research. But theories need to be distinguished from models and concepts.

- *Models* provide an overall framework for how we look at reality.
- *Concepts* are clearly specified ideas deriving from a particular model.
- *Theories* arrange sets of concepts to define and explain some phenomenon.
- *Methodologies* define how one will go about studying any phenomenon.
- *Methods* are specific research techniques.

Make sure that your research questions and data analysis fit the model you are using.

Your Chapter Checklist

Check that you now understand:

- The difference between theories, models and hypotheses.
- How theoretical models shape research by working out the model you are using in your own research.
- The range of such models we can use in qualitative research and which one appeals to you and will work with your data.

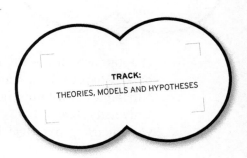

TRACK:
THEORIES, MODELS AND HYPOTHESES

Exercises

APPLY:
YOUR EXERCISE WORKBOOK

Exercise 1: Frame positivist, naturalist and constructionist research topics

Drawing on what you know so far about different models of social research, consider whether the way you have framed your research problem is primarily positivist, naturalist or constructionist. Now consider what you might gain or lose by reframing it in terms of a different model.

Exercise 2: Theorize data

Howard Becker reports that his colleague Bernard Beck responded to students seeking to theorize about their data by instructing them: 'Tell me what you've found out, but without using any of the identifying characteristics of the actual case' (1998: 126).

Becker gives the example of his own research on Chicago teachers which seemed to show that these teachers sought to improve their situation by moving to different schools rather than trying to get promoted in their present school. Using his data but forbidden to talk about 'teachers' or 'schools', how might Becker have generated an account of his research that would have satisfied Beck?

Further Reading

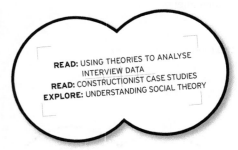

READ: USING THEORIES TO ANALYSE INTERVIEW DATA
READ: CONSTRUCTIONIST CASE STUDIES
EXPLORE: UNDERSTANDING SOCIAL THEORY

Clive Seale et al.'s edited book *Qualitative Research Practice* (Sage, 2004) contains seven chapters which show the relevance of seven contemporary theories to qualitative research (Part 2, 'Analytic Frameworks', pp. 107–213). For a comparative discussion of GT and NA see my *Interpreting Qualitative Data* (Sage, 2014: Chapter 3). Howard Becker's book *Tricks of the Trade* (University of Chicago Press, 1998) contains two chapters which are highly relevant to learning how to theorize about your data (Chapter 2 on 'Imagery' and Chapter 4 on 'Concepts'). Jay Gubrium and James Holstein's text *The New Language of Qualitative Method* (Oxford University Press, 1997) is an invaluable, thought-provoking guide to the vocabularies, investigatory styles and ways of writing of different theoretical idioms, while the same authors' edited *Handbook of Constructionist Research* (Guilford, 2008a) is a vital guide for anyone considering doing a constructionist-style research project. Martyn Hammersley's *Questioning Qualitative Inquiry: Critical Essays* (Sage, 2008) provides a lively discussion of the assumptions underlying qualitative research.

Discover the chapter's
digital resources in your
SILVERMAN FIELD GUIDE

EIGHT

Formulating a Research Question

Learning Outcomes

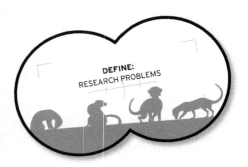

By the end of this chapter, you will be able to:

- Understand why you need a clear research topic.
- Recognize the main problems which stop you narrowing down your topic.
- Find solutions to these problems.

1 INTRODUCTION

In this chapter, I discuss the problems that you may find in defining your research topic. I then suggest some strategies you can use to overcome these problems.

Keith Punch has suggested some key characteristics of workable research topics, as given in Table 8.1.

Following Point 3, Barbara Czarniawska (2014: 1) has proposed that we often want to study a topic because it involves a new phenomenon, not studied before,

Table 8.1   Workable research questions

1   *Answerability:* we can see what data is required to answer them and how the data will be obtained
2   *Interconnectedness:* the questions are related to each other in some meaningful way, rather than being unconnected
3   *Substantively relevant:* the questions are interesting and worthwhile, so justifying the investment of research effort

Source: adapted from Punch (1998: 49)

that has aroused our curiosity. But, she asks, why has it not been studied before? Was it under some sort of taboo or was it taken for granted?

Having found the phenomenon, what do you call it? Czarniawska (2014: 2) gives the example of how organizations respond to risks and suggests three possible ways of naming your topic:

1.   The phenomenon has received a name from the people involved with it. Say organizational members refer to it as 'risk management'.
2.   You give the phenomenon a name.
3.   You baptize the phenomenon with the name of an abstract concept already known in the literature (e.g. 'the institutionalization of risk management').

As Czarniawska points out, each method for naming your phenomenon carries with it its own problems. If you follow Method 1, you are in danger of adopting the participants' point of view without studying how this fits with what they actually do when confronted by a risk and, indeed, how they may vary in defining what is 'risky'. Method 2 is alright as a first step providing you are prepared to rename your phenomenon when you know more about it. Going straight to an abstract concept (Method 3) is very risky. When you have studied your material more:

> it may turn out that there are other, better abstract concepts to theorize about what you have discovered. Why not wait for a while before you start applying abstract terms … (and) simply ask, 'what's going on here?' (Czarniawska 2014: 2)

WHAT I DID: ANGELOS

Research on Trust and Distrust in Organizations

The purpose of my study is to increase understanding of the role of trust and distrust in a dyadic competitive relationship. Trust and distrust are inherently individual-level constructs, but I believe that a firm, as a collective entity, can also have trust

(Continued)

(Continued)

(or distrust) for another firm or an individual and vice versa. I am planning to conduct interviews with individuals involved in a competitive relationship (individuals
from both firms (approx. 65 pairs)) and approach trust (and distrust) as a process
(emotion -> cognition). In my study, I argue that trust and distrust are two distinct
concepts, which are influenced by the personality of the individuals involved in such
an inter-firm relationship and the interactions between them. Finally, the way that
trust/distrust are managed (use of IT systems) affects the outcomes of competition
(for the individual, the firm, the alliance). [Angelos Kostis, School of Business and
Economics, Umeå University]

Angelos has clearly put a lot of thought into his research design. He asked me a
crucial question: 'Should I specify that I see trust as an emotion, as a cognition or
as both? How can this change the way I will collect data?' Following Czarniawska,
I advised him that he was in danger of specifying too many concepts before he
entered the field. As she suggests, why not just ask what is going on in the organi-
zation(s) studied and then see whether (and if so in what way) concepts like 'trust'
and 'distrust' are relevant?

Angelos seems to be trying to find a research topic on purely logical grounds
simply by reading the literature. By contrast, in the student stories that follow,
note that in many cases researchers come across a topic by chance, or they
begin studying a topic because the data or the research site were conveniently
available.

Using the self as a starting point

For some, direct personal experience becomes the starting point of their
research. Penny Abbott is a doctor who acts as a visiting GP in prisons and
is studying the healthcare needs and prison experiences of women leaving
prison. Similarly, Amir Marvasti's experience of being an immigrant to the
USA led him to look at homeless people (see Chapter 2). In some ways, for
Amir, homelessness became a metaphor for the immigration experience and
the struggle for belonging. In the following example, Michael Arter speaks of
how being an undercover police officer became an impetus for his study of
policing.

WHAT I DID: MICHAEL

Researching Familiar Territory

I returned to graduate school after many years in the military and law enforcement. As I became acclimated to the academic setting and my background became known to the faculty and other students, I noticed there was a lot of emphasis placed upon and inter-est in my time spent as an undercover officer. Along with much misinformation that was held by many regarding such assignments, there was an unspoken mystique and subtle respect that was accorded to me for the work I had done. I realized at that time that most individuals lacked actual knowledge about such assignments and relied on media pres-entations and sensationalized examples for their understanding about the undercover function. At the same time I was very aware of the impact undercover assignments had in my life and the lives of others with whom I had worked. I decided to adopt this topic for the research class and as I began to research the available literature, I became more entrenched in this topic as a viable venue for my dissertation. [Michael Arter, USA]

Like Michael, Simon Allistone took advantage of his own (and his partner's) work in a school to gain access for his study of parents' evenings. Another student of mine, Sally Hunt, decided to use her occupational experience to study nurses working in a mental health team. Sally's own nursing background made access to the team somewhat easier but, as we saw in Chapter 3, also influenced the team's behaviour when she was present. Sally's concern about 'contamination' of a setting is shown in the following example.

WHAT I DID: RIKKE

Studying Where I Work

I have some methodological, analytical and practical concerns, related to my impact as a researcher, in designing a study and collecting data in a field where I have clinical wisdom and knowledge (15 years of clinical experience working as a nurse at a Traumatic Brain Injury Unit). As an expert in the rehabilitation field, what should be taken into account when generating and interpreting data? How can I benefit from my clinical knowledge, besides getting easier access to patients and relatives? [Rikke Guldager, Department of Education, Aalborg University]

Rikke is rightly aware of the possible gains and losses of being an 'insider' in the setting you are studying. In this situation, my best advice is to avoid taking for granted your inside knowledge. One way to do this is to list what seems 'obvious' to insiders and then to consider what assumptions make such things obvious. Similarly, you might consider what seems 'extraordinary' or 'deviant' to insiders and then ask yourselves why this is so.

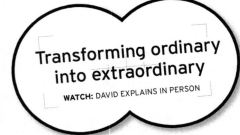

Transforming ordinary into extraordinary

WATCH: DAVID EXPLAINS IN PERSON

David's Top Tip 17

If you are an 'insider', take a look at the first chapter of my *Very Short Book* (Silverman, 2013) which discusses how to make apparently 'ordinary' phenomena 'extraordinary' and vice versa.

Social obligations

For some graduate students, selecting a topic derives from a sense of social obligation. For example, Karyn McKinney's research on how white college students construct their racial identity was motivated by her desire to expose the system of racial hierarchy in the USA. In a sense, she was morally driven to select this topic, or as she puts it, 'I was interested in the topic out of thinking about what *I should do* to effectively change the status quo.' Karyn was committed to studying race relations, and settling on a specific area within that field was a fortunate coincidence.

WHAT I DID: KARYN
Pursuing What Matters to You

Eventually, my real excitement about data was what decided me on my topic. I was teaching a class in race and ethnicity, and had asked students, as their main project for the class, to write what I referred to as a 'racial/ethnic autobiography'. In my assignment for the course, students were to go chronologically through their lives, telling their stories, focusing on situations and incidents that made them more aware of their own or other people's race or ethnicity. Basically, these papers would be first-person analyses of the development of racial and/or ethnic identity. When I got the students' papers back, I was mesmerized by reading them. I literally could not put them down. All of the students told stories that showed how racial and ethnic identity is a process, not a static characteristic. They were fascinating, to me at least. Most of my students were white, and I began to think about the new area I'd been reading in, 'whiteness studies'. [Karyn McKinney, USA]

Karyn's research agenda was not entirely planned in advance. She was simply assigning a project for a course and happened to realize the importance of the data that was pouring in; the data 'mesmerized' her. Note that her social obligations did not dictate her research entirely. To a large extent it was her fascination with the data that focused her interests.

Curiosity

Other researchers cite general curiosity as the main reason for selecting a particular topic. Essentially, they are intrigued by a facet of social life and want to learn *more* about it. Michelle Day-Miller story is illustrative of this approach.

WHAT I DID: MICHELLE

Prying with Purpose

There is a quote from Zora Neale Hurston that, for me, captures what I hope to achieve with qualitative research. She said:

> Research is formalized curiosity. It is poking and prying with purpose. It is a seeking that he who wishes may know the secrets of the world and they that dwell therein.

I have always been curious. Choosing a career as a social science researcher I assumed I could make a living asking questions and seeking answers. (In my more noble moments) I also believed that this career would enable me to make real contributions to the understanding of social behaviour and the human experience. [Michelle Day-Miller, USA]

In Michelle's story social obligations are not necessarily at the forefront of her work. A general sense of curiosity coupled with the 'noble' desire to understand others dictated her research choices. This sense of wonder about the world guided her questions and her observations.

Working as a paid researcher

As we saw in Chapter 3, Moira Kelly's interviews with bereaved relatives emerged directly out of her employment on a funded study directed by Clive Seale. Such employment fortuitously can provide access to respondents and several possible topics. This was also true in Greg Bolystein's case.

WHAT I DID: GREG
Finding a Topic from Your Job

I accepted a job as a research assistant (RA) at the local Veterans Administration Medical Center. Initially I did home interviews with veterans who recently had a stroke. Through time I became more intimately involved in the project, helping construct the initial theoretical framework with the principal investigator and my dissertation chair, who was a consultant on the study. Since I was a member of the research team on this large project it became natural for me to use the first phase of data as a basis for my dissertation research. I did not have any particular interest or knowledge in stroke recovery prior to this RA position ... Rather than being isolated in my dissertation research, I actually became integrated into a large investigative center focused on stroke rehabilitation, with my dissertation making up one component of disseminating our initial findings. [Greg Bolystein, USA]

For other researchers who received less restrictive, individual grants, the funding simply provided them with the time and resources to pursue topics of personal interest. Consider, for example, Nikitah Imani's case.

WHAT I DID: NIKITAH
Being Involved in a Scene

I became engaged by a grant-funded psychotherapy program the university was running. It targeted presumably 'dysfunctional' African-American families. Initially, without a topic, I sought merely to use ethnographic tools to describe to those external to the program what was 'taking place'. It was not long after embarking on this quest that my pursuits turned far away from merely 'test-driving' the methodology to looking at critical questions of how 'dysfunctionality', which I had taken for granted in the programmatic definitions, was being articulated, defined, redefined, and reified in the implementation phase. So it would be fair to say that the 'scene' and the associated circumstances gave me my topic which, given the methodology I had chosen, seemed an appropriate line of inquiry to follow. [Nikitah Imani, USA]

As we can see in Nikitah's example, selecting a research topic is often a complex process where personal interests, financial resources and access to data converge to shape the ideal research question.

Conclusion

The preceding student accounts reveal that the practice of qualitative research does not follow an exact, uniform model. Essentially, the lesson with selecting a topic is always to keep an eye out for researchable issues, take advantage of opportunities when they present themselves, and be flexible.

However, although chance factors are often relevant in your choice of a topic, this does not mean that anything will do. Whatever your inspiration, you will need soon to develop a well-defined and workable research question.

You may have discovered already that people are often impressed when they find out that you are 'doing research'. They may even want to know more. If you have ever been in this situation, you will know how embarrassing it can be if you are unable to explain clearly exactly what you intend to study. Such embarrassment can be multiplied a thousandfold if your interrogator is, say, a smart professor you have never met before. How are you to respond?

The answer to this question becomes easier if you recognize that there are practical as well as social reasons for having a clear research topic. Above all, such clarity can give your research focus, as shown in Table 8.2.

Table 8.2   The role of research topics

1   They organize the project and give it direction and coherence
2   They delimit the project, showing its boundaries
3   They keep the researcher focused
4   They provide a framework when you write up your research
5   They point to the methods and data that will be needed

Source: adapted from Punch (1998: 38)

In the rest of this chapter, I outline some of the challenges that you face in developing workable research questions. I then offer some provisional solutions.

2 CHALLENGES

Here are some difficulties you might face in formulating workable research questions:

- inadequate training
- unavailability of relevant data

- misleading assumptions about good research design
- misleading assumptions about qualitative research
- institutional constraints (departmental deadlines and ethical constraints)
- lack of confidence leading to over-ambitious research designs
- sticking to 'grand theory' and resisting data analysis.

Inadequate training

The undergraduate training you have received may not help much in finding a *workable* research question. Some social science programmes reward passive knowledge rather than the ability to use ideas for yourself. They often leave students better able to leap the hurdles to pass their assessments than to use their knowledge to formulate a workable research topic.

In qualitative methodology courses, this phenomenon is seen when courses encourage rote learning of critiques of quantitative research and offer minimal practice in alternative methods. By contrast, in quantitative methods courses, one tends to learn by rote the recipe knowledge which *is* of practical use in drafting a research proposal (e.g. defining variables and measures).

In this context, selecting a research topic to be studied through qualitative methods is a very risky activity. This is because it involves committing yourself to a particular course of action rather than reiterating spoonfed 'critiques'.

Graduate research training is being increasingly provided by universities. However, it is debatable whether one can learn all there is to know about qualitative research in the lecture theatre. The best sort of research training involves learning through doing, often in the form of workshops where students try out for themselves different ways of narrowing down specific research problems or analysing particular data extracts.

Unavailable data

A very nice research question may not lead anywhere simply because the data is not available to you. For instance, Jakub Galeziowski, who is doing a PhD in the Philology and History Faculty of Augsburg University, wants to do oral history interviews with Polish people fathered by German or Russian invaders during the Second World War. He writes:

> one of my main problems is how to find interviewees when there is no network of such people and the topic is taboo within society.

I responded that Jakub's problem seems intractable and suggested he might think about what material is available that would bear on the topic (e.g. newspaper reports, blogs or websites).

Jakub has a good topic but is struggling to find relevant data. By contrast, sometimes people choose a topic that is simply too broad to offer usable data. Braun and Clarke (2013) comment that students often want to research the 'influence' of the media. But this is not a good research topic because:

> it's really difficult to actually find out the sort of information that could answer this question. People aren't necessarily able to identify the influence of the media on their actions ... And even if people did and could talk about it, we wouldn't be able to claim *definitive* effects, because we'd need a quantitative design to do it. (2013: 52-3)

Better topics in this area, they suggest, would be to research how people think about certain media or how the media represent a certain issue.

Qualitative researchers often want to answer their questions by obtaining access to commercial or public organizations and are stymied when access is refused. Or they may ask questions implying the use of interviewees or focus groups who may not be easily assembled.

Fortunately, this is not so much of a problem as it appears. First, one needs to realize that one should not be limited by the common-sense assumption that the phenomenon in which you are interested has some essential 'home'. For instance, if an organization refuses you access, you can simply work with the publicly available material that it produces (e.g. company reports or press releases) and redefine your research topic accordingly.

Second, nobody should assume that you always need fresh data. Why not work with secondary qualitative data collected by data archives or, indeed, with your supervisor's own unanalysed data (see Chapter 14, Section 2 and Seale, 2011)?

Misleading assumptions about good research design

As we saw in Chapter 2, although all good research shares standards of proper practice (e.g. not rushing to conclusions, seeking contrary instances), qualitative researchers have several points of departure from their quantitative colleagues. Our skills give us excellent access to how social institutions function but less insight into the causes and consequences of such functioning.

This should have two consequences for how we think about defining a research topic. First, we tend to think more in terms of social processes, which are not easily or simply defined as 'variables'. Second, we pride ourselves on our ability to refocus our research as new and interesting phenomena start to emerge.

Punch (2014: 60) illustrates this using the example of a student interested in studying youth suicides. This suggests four possible research topics:

1.   Suicide rates among different groups
2.   Factors associated with the incidence of youth suicide
3.   How social or medical services intervene to try to limit youth suicides
4.   How young people talk about suicide.

Punch points out that Topics 1 and 2 demand a quantitative approach because they address 'why' questions and imply an investigation of statistical rates. Topics 3 and 4 are formulated in terms of 'how' questions which can be answered by qualitative data.

Unfortunately, as illustrated in the following student examples, many novice qualitative researchers tend to define their research problem using an approach much better fitted to quantitative research.

WHAT I DID: FOUR RESEARCH PROBLEMS

- What are the factors associated with the effective classroom teaching of mathematics? [Education researcher, Tanzania]
- The effectiveness of entrepreneurial education, using educational and psychological indicators. [Management student, France]
- Factors, processes and sources of inequalities in women's careers in connection with the transformation of Czech society after the fall of communism. [Sociology and geography student, Norway]
- What causes 'burnout' among female primary school teachers? [Education, Sri Lanka]

In these student examples, the language used is much more appropriate to quantitative research. In particular:

- Each uses a language of 'variables' ('factors', 'indicators').
- Each is seeking to correlate these variables.
- Each seems to be assuming that such variables ('effectiveness', 'transformation') can be defined at the outset and, in this sense, are non-problematic.
- There is a failure to consider how things like 'effectiveness' and 'transformation' come to be represented or defined in different contexts.

Here are some implications of these arguments based on models I discussed in Chapter 7:

- The common features in these statements of research topics derive from a model of science commonly used in quantitative research.
- This model, known as **positivism**, treats 'social facts' as existing independently of the activities of both participants and researchers.
- By contrast, in qualitative research, we tend to study how phenomena are 'constructed' in people's everyday activities (constructionism).
- Qualitative researchers usually avoid early hypotheses and simply ask, 'What is going on here?'

Misleading assumptions about qualitative research

How do we describe a *qualitative* research design? Interview studies which are based on a relatively small number of cases and use open-ended questions are usually treated as examples of qualitative research. However, as we have already learned, the presence or absence of numbers and rigid structures is insufficient to distinguish between qualitative and quantitative research. Much more important is how you define your research problem using a particular model of reality.

Many interview studies seek to find out how a particular group of people perceives things. By assuming that interviews can give a direct access to 'experience' (providing the research design is reliable), such qualitative researchers depend upon a naturalist model of research.

Here are some actual student examples of naturalistic ways of framing a research problem using qualitative interviews.

WHAT I DID: TIPPI, ANNIKA AND SACHIN

- How residents in a community of elderly people feel about their life. [Tippi, Information Studies and Sociology, Finland]
- How do different actors experience the implementation of labour standards in the construction industry in Chennai, India? [Annika, Sociology and Human Geography, Norway]
- Responses of patients who consult unqualified Western medical practitioners. [Sachin, Community Medicine, Sri Lanka]

These kinds of research problems exemplify a style of qualitative interviews which aims to 'get inside the heads' of particular groups of people and to tell things from their 'point of view'. Yet, as we saw in Chapter 6, how far is it appropriate to think that people attach a single meaning to their experiences?

May there not be multiple meanings of a situation (e.g. living in a community home) or of an activity (e.g. consulting an unqualified medical practitioner) represented by what people say to the researcher, to each other, to carers, and so on (Gubrium, 1997)?

This raises the important methodological issue of whether interview responses are to be treated as giving direct access to 'experience' and 'feelings' or as actively constructed 'narratives' involving activities which themselves demand analysis (Holstein and Gubrium, 1995). Both positions are entirely legitimate but the position you take will need to be justified and explained. So always think through whether qualitative interviews are appropriate to your research problem. For instance, if you are collecting facts or perceptions, would a quantitative survey make more sense?

Now let us review examples of students who use qualitative interviews to address research problems based on a constructionist model.

WHAT I DID: KATARIN, STEVEN AND SVEINUNG

- How family members construct stories about their grief and recovery processes after the death of their baby. [Katarin, Psychiatry, Finland]
- How versions of postgraduate life are discursively constructed and sustained by postgraduates in interviews about doing their PhDs. [Steven, Social Sciences, UK]
- How drug users and dealers present themselves in order to manage identity and keep self-respect during the interviews. [Sveinung, Sociology, Norway]

In these three examples, notice the use of words like 'construct' and 'manage' in the definition of the research problem. This shows how constructionist researchers want to examine the active 'work' that interviewees do in producing their answers. This is very different from positivist projects which simply seek accurate reports of experiences or feelings which are taken to lie inside people's heads.

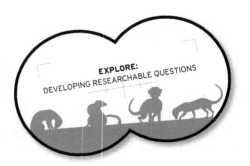

EXPLORE:
DEVELOPING RESEARCHABLE QUESTIONS

We have seen two strikingly different ways of conceptualizing your research problem which lead to contrasting ways of looking at interview data. It is worth adding that neither approach is without its own problems. Our naturalist examples may de-emphasize the multiple meanings that people attach to what they do. A constructionist way of defining a research topic overcomes that problem but lays itself open to the criticism of losing sight of important substantive issues. For instance, critics might suggest that our three studies gain theoretical sophistication at the risk of downplaying 'real' problems like 'grief' or drug use. So constructionist researchers face a real challenge in translating their findings back to social problems.

A final observation is in order. How you formulate the topic of a qualitative interview study is not just a matter of the research model you employ. You also have to ask questions that are answerable by your data. Sometimes this is merely a matter of narrowing down your topic. On other occasions, students may be tempted to use interviews to answer the wrong kind of questions.

A little while ago, I was advising some PhD students at a university in Tanzania. A politics student was interested in what seemed to be an important social issue: how water and sanitation policy had been influenced by the decentralization of Tanzanian local government since 2000. He proposed to find answers by interviewing key stakeholders.

As we learn from our quantitative colleagues, it is difficult to find out what happened in the past by asking present-day respondents. This is not because they may lie but simply because we all view the past through the lens of the present. Hence this kind of *retrospective* study is likely to offer inaccurate information.

Now can you see possible solutions? I suggested that the student could meet this difficulty in one of two ways:

- reformulate his research problem as a study of contemporary stakeholder views
- stick with the original research problem and use different, contemporary data (for instance, contrasting newspaper reports today with those in 2000).

Institutional constraints

There is great variation in the structures and facilities offered by different departments and university graduate committees. However, four problems stand out in the experience of the students I meet:

- The variable competence and interest of supervisors. Sometimes students may be allocated to supervisors with little experience of qualitative research (see Chapter 11, Section 2).
- A failure to provide hands-on training in qualitative methods or to encourage research students to work cooperatively with each other.
- An over-rigid and unrealistic version of the timing of different stages of the research process: for instance, the assumption that in year 1 you review the literature, in year 2 you collect data and in year 3 you write your thesis.

- A requirement that research students cannot proceed without a research proposal couched in terms much more appropriate to quantitative research (e.g. hypotheses, variables, etc.). This fails to take account of the emergent character of many qualitative research topics (see Cryer, 1996: 44; Punch, 2006: 37).

Over-ambitious research designs

In drafting your first research proposal, it is tempting to select a very broad topic. By including every aspect of a problem that you can think of, you hope to show the breadth of your knowledge and to impress potential supervisors.

Unfortunately, this 'kitchen sink' approach is a recipe for disaster. Unless you have the resources for a big team of researchers, depth rather than breadth is what characterizes a good research proposal. If you define your topic very widely, you will usually be unable to say anything at great depth about it.

One way to narrow down your topic is to ask yourself: 'Is it clear what data will be required to answer this research question?' As Punch says, 'If the answer is yes, we can proceed from questions to data and methods. If the answer is no, [we need] further specificity' (2014: 61).

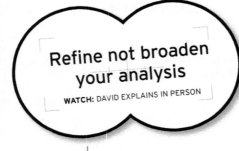

Refine not broaden your analysis

WATCH: DAVID EXPLAINS IN PERSON

David's Top Tip 18

As I tell my students, your aim should be to say 'a lot about a little (problem)'. This means avoiding the temptation to say 'a little about a lot'. Indeed, the latter path can be something of a 'cop-out'. Precisely because the topic is so wide ranging, one can flit from one aspect to another without being forced to refine and test each piece of analysis.

Grand theory

While the kitchen-sinker flits about trying this and that, the grand theorist is kept busy building theoretical empires. Stuck firmly in their armchairs, such theorists need never trifle with mere 'facts'. Instead, they may sometimes spin out cobwebs of verbiage which, as C. Wright Mills (1959) shows, can be reduced to a few sentences.

Nonetheless, a situation in which you can obtain a research degree without ever leaving your PC or your familiar university library is not to be despised. Indeed, I should be the last to criticize grand theory since my own PhD was obtained by this very method!

However, it is usually wise to assume that every 'solution' contains seeds of further problems. In the case of grand theory, these problems include:

- Can you ever get out of the library in order to write your thesis? One book will surely have a list of further 'crucial' references and so on, ad infinitum. Anybody who thinks a library PhD is a 'quick fix' would be well advised to ponder whether they have the willpower to stop reading. They would also be wise to consult a short story called 'The Library of Babel' by the Argentinian writer Jorge Luis Borges. This tells a chastening tale of scholars who believe that, if they only keep on looking, all knowledge will finally be revealed by yet another book.
- Theoretical fashions change – nowhere more so than in the social sciences. If you commit yourself to a theoretical topic, you must always be looking over your shoulder at the prospect of some change in direction in the theoretical wind from, say, Paris to an obscure location with a school of thought with which you are totally unfamiliar.

If you do grand theory, you may spend so much time constructing elegant accounts of the world that you never touch base with the ground upon which the world rests. Franz Kafka's (1961) wonderful short story 'Investigations of a Dog' creates a marvellous image of 'airdogs' (Lufthunde) who float on cushions above the ground, surveying the world from on high, yet cut off from any contact with it (so cut off that Kafka's doggy Investigator wonders how they manage to reproduce).

3 SOLUTIONS

As O'Leary (2014: 32) points out, 'without clear articulation of your (research) question, you really are travelling blind'. Good research questions:

- define an investigation
- set boundaries by showing you which new ideas are really relevant to your research
- provide direction about what sort of concepts and data are appropriate
- set a frame of reference for assessing your work by providing benchmarks. (Adapted from O'Leary, 2014: 32)

How do we reach this happy state? Readers of this book will be more interested in solutions than in critiques. In response to this, I now set out some practical strategies that may be of use to potential 'kitchen-sinkers' and 'grand theorists'. These include:

- making good use of the existing literature
- using concepts from your discipline
- finding techniques to narrow down your problem
- timing different research questions
- further suggestions for grand theorists.

Using the literature

Chris Hart (2001: 2) rightly suggests that a literature review has two uses: it gives you access to material relevant to your project, and suggests appropriate methodologies and data collection techniques. Completion of your review helps you to answer the important questions set out in Table 8.3.

Table 8.3   Questions for a literature review

1   Where does your study fit in relation to the relevant literature?
2   What is its connection to that literature?
3   How will your research move beyond what we already know?

Source: adapted from Punch (2006: 29)

Don't try to reinvent the wheel! Try to find a previous study that, in some respect, mirrors your own interests and topic. Then model your own research on that study and develop some aspect of it. Here are some examples of how my own students modelled their research on previous work.

WHAT I DID: MOIRA, SALLY AND SIMON

- In line with the (ethnomethodological) principle adopted by Baruch (1981), that a feature of all accounts is a display of moral adequacy, I was interested in the way in which the interviewees construct their behaviour and that of others as reasonable or unreasonable in their descriptions. [Moira Kelly's study of interviews with bereaved spouses]
- Much of my ethnographic study of a team dealing with homeless people used Goffman's (1974) concept of frame to demonstrate how understandings emerged among the MHT. [Sally Hunt]
- My study of parents' evenings at a primary school was informed by Baker and Keogh's observations that such evenings 'are understood and talked about as ritual or ceremonial encounters, in which teachers go through routine expressions of interest and academic diagnosis, and which parents attend in order to show their "interest" in their children's schooling' (1995: 264). [Simon Allistone]

Of course, with limited resources, you are unlikely to be able to offer a complete 'test' of the findings of that study. But by careful analysis of your limited data, you can reflect on its approach and conclusions in an informed way.

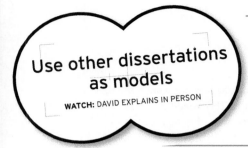

Use other dissertations as models

WATCH: DAVID EXPLAINS IN PERSON

David's Top Tip 19

My student Moira Kelly used an earlier PhD that I had supervised as a model for her research. So, at the outset, look at earlier dissertations in your university library and, where possible, focus on work directed by your supervisor.

Phillips and Pugh (1994: 49–52) suggest that one aid for the sluggish research imagination is to begin with previously proposed generalizations and then try to find their limits by postulating new conditions. For instance, in my own study of HIV-test counselling (Silverman, 1997), I became interested in the conditions under which clients were likely to demonstrate uptake of the advice that they were given in interviews with health professionals. In a study of interviews between British health visitors and first-time mothers, John Heritage and Sue Sefi (1992) had found that mothers were more likely to acknowledge the relevance of advice which was related to their expressed concerns.

Heritage and Sefi's findings gave me my initial research focus. However, I observed that time constraints in many counselling centres meant that it was very difficult for counsellors to adopt such an apparently 'client-centred' approach. My research question now changed to considering how both parties acted to prevent open disagreements while giving or receiving potentially irrelevant advice (Silverman, 1997: 154–81).

Sometimes, the previous literature or (for experienced researchers) one's own work will suggest a hypothesis crying out to be tested or a finding ripe for retesting. Where this happens, particularly where the earlier study derived from a theoretical approach to which you are sympathetic, an attempt to strike out afresh would be in danger of reinventing the wheel. Of course, as Chapter 3 shows, this does not mean that you should necessarily be stuck with your original ideas. The beauty of qualitative research is that its rich data can offer the opportunity to change focus as the ongoing analysis suggests. However, such changes of direction, like the original research proposal, do not come out of the blue but reflect the subtle interplay between theory, concepts and data.

The case study below illustrates how one research student worked to refine and narrow down her problem. Over time, Seta Waller moved from quite a broad psychological interest in the 'alcoholic' to a quite narrow but workable concern with the narrative structure of patients' accounts.

WHAT I DID: SETA

Versions of Alcoholism

When I decided to develop a PhD study, my initial interest was to find out what patients thought of their drink problem – how they conceptualized it. This would have been a quantitative study but quite different from the usual measurement of outcome studies. I therefore began designing a quantitative study enquiring into alcoholic patients' concepts of alcoholism. The sample was to be drawn from groups of alcoholics, admitted to a four-week inpatient treatment programme in the alcohol treatment unit where I was employed.

Having developed some rating scales on concepts of alcoholism, following interviews with patients, I carried out a pilot study on a small sample. Patients were asked to complete five-point rating scales consisting of statements, by indicating whether they agreed or not with each statement, responses ranging from 'agree strongly' to 'disagree strongly'.

This whole process took about eight months. However, I was feeling uncomfortable with the results of my pilot study as I tried to make sense of the data. I felt very uncertain about the attitudes and beliefs expressed in the scales; I began to question how one could consider that all patients who, for instance, stated 'agree strongly' on the rating scales, meant the same thing.

I realized that my interest lay in how patients were formulating and presenting their drinking problem and wanted to look at 'why' they were presenting in these particular ways. Adopting a qualitative approach, I was able to look at the narrative structure of patients' accounts to see how the texts were accomplished and organized. The structure of the accounts seemed to have a common chronologically organized pattern. Examination of the narratives made me realize that patients were showing their skills in presenting themselves as morally adequate individuals, as Baruch (1981) had found in his sample of parents of children with congenital illness. I also found that patients were displaying considerable insights into their problems and were emerging as well-informed individuals.

My current approach is therefore not simply an analytical shift, but another way of looking at interview data to see how they can help our understanding of alcoholic patients' versions and presentations of their problems. [Seta Waller, Sociology, Goldsmiths]

This case study illustrates how ideas derived from methodology and theory can help in specifying a research topic.

Using concepts from your discipline

If your previous education has equipped you with few research ideas of your own, comfort yourself that your predicament is not unusual and can be resolved. Treating the knowledge you have learned as a resource involves thinking about how it can sensitize you to various researchable issues as shown in the following example.

WHAT I DID: MARIANNE

Care in Child Welfare Institutions

The aim of my PhD study is to develop knowledge around adolescents' experiences with care in their everyday life in a child welfare institution. When studying the phenomenon of care the choice of theoretical perspective has a major impact on all stages of the project.

- In a realist perspective, I could assume that care is something, which *is* – a phenomenon that exists, that is tangible and constant, an objective size with specific characteristics, independent of the researcher studying it. The study will then explore the accounts and observations based on essential characteristics and definitions of the concept care. I could aim to reveal social structures in the child welfare institutions, in which care appears and how the context, the child welfare institution, interacts with care-actions. The aim could be to describe care objectively and neutral. I would see myself as a neutral researcher, and the phenomenon of interest, care, as a defined, objective phenomenon.
- In accordance with a phenomenological perspective, however, I would focus on how care appears for the adolescents in a child welfare institution, how and when the adolescents experience care. I could benefit from the expression *life-world*, and look into how the adolescents perceive and experience their everyday life in a child welfare institution.
- My choice is, however, to base my project on a social constructivist perspective, and see care not as an objective entity with specific characteristics, but as a fluid, and changeable, phenomenon. I understand care, not as something I can 'reveal', but a complex phenomenon that the social worker does, as well as adolescents' interpretations of and responses to this doing. Care is an interactive phenomenon, which exists only in interaction. The narratives of the adolescents' everyday life and experiences with relationships to the social workers will be constructed and shaped in the interview, rather than revealed by the interviewer. [Marianne Buen Sommerfeldt, Department of Social Work, Oslo and Akerhus University College]

Marianne's thoughtful recognition of how 'care' comes to take on different meanings within three analytical perspectives nicely shows how you can use concepts from your discipline to define your research topic. Rather than treat the care of adolescents in child welfare institutions as a social problem (a temptation given her own experience as a social worker in such institutions), she has produced an analytically defined research topic by making problematic certain taken-for-granted aspects of caring. This involves what I have called 'contextual sensitivity'.

In an earlier book (Silverman, 2014: 36–8), I sought to distinguish three types of sensitivity: historical, political and contextual. Most of this is self-explanatory. Historical sensitivity means that, wherever possible, one should examine the relevant historical evidence when setting up a topic to research. Political sensitivity shows the vested interests behind current media 'scares' and reveals that this way of determining our research topics is just as fallible as designing research in accordance with administrative or managerial interests. **Contextual sensitivity** is the least self-explanatory and most contentious category of the three. A longer explanation is therefore demanded. By 'contextual' sensitivity, I mean two things:

- the recognition that apparently uniform institutions like 'the family', 'a tribe' or 'science' take on a variety of meanings in different contexts
- the understanding that participants in social life actively produce a context for what they do and that social researchers should not simply import their own assumptions about what context is relevant in any situation.

Such contextual sensitivity implies that it is worthwhile to distance yourself a little from the prevailing vocabulary in the setting you want to study. For example, in medicine, there is a vocabulary of 'good communication' with patients. This vocabulary is emphasized in medical education including in-service training for physicians.

Undoubtedly, this discussion of communication is important in the study of many medical settings. However, in working out your research problem, it is worth keeping a little critical distance from it. As shown in Geraldine Leydon's study of oncology consultations, it is usually helpful to treat participants' vocabulary as a *topic* rather than as a *resource*.

WHAT I DID: GERALDINE

What Is 'Good Communication'?

Discussions of 'good' and 'bad' communication are common in the health literature in general and continue to be reported in the academic literature. In the field of oncology, *good* is routinely described as equal, facilitative, open-ended, supportive, and patient centred, and these concepts frequent policy documents and other studies in the field.

I was frustrated by the opacity of [terms] like these in practice. What, for example, might 'active listening', 'frequent clarifying and paraphrasing' sound or look like in practice? Where is the demonstration that these particular skills have positive interactional consequences? Moreover, the patients seemed to be 'missing'.

Reading conversation analytic work helped me to decide how I might distance myself from work like that above and what approach I might fruitfully take, time and data permitting. The opportunity to examine that which already occurs and, as far as possible, without thinking too much about what I or anyone else might consider to be good or bad, offered a more satisfying alternative and provided good reason for a parting of the 'methodological' ways.

Eventually, with all of these issues in mind, my PhD came to be concerned with the following: how is it that the outpatient oncology treatment consultation 'comes off' and how do participants offer and receive 'information' about cancer? [Geraldine Leydon, Sociology, Goldsmiths]

Geraldine's focus on what actually happens in certain kinds of medical consultation made use of contextual sensitivity. Rather than assume that 'medical communication' defined a single object, she preferred to study how communication worked out in a particular medical setting.

One final point. The three kinds of sensitivity we have been considering offer different, sometimes contradictory, ways of generating research topics. I follow Czarniawska (2014) in arguing that we can use too *many* concepts at the beginning of a research study. However, if we are not sensitive to *any* of these issues, then we run the risk of lapsing into a common-sense way of defining our research topics.

Finding techniques to narrow down your research topic

Do less, more thoroughly. (Wolcott, 1990: 62)

Wolcott's advice is sound. Narrowing down is often the most crucial task when drafting a research proposal. Kitchen-sinkers have so many ideas buzzing around in their heads that getting down to a focused piece of research is entirely beyond them.

Every issue seems so fascinating. Each aspect seems interconnected and each piece of reading that you do only adds further ideas (and suggests further readings). So, while you can grasp the value of making a lot out of a little, it is easier said than done. The question remains: how do you go about narrowing down your ideas?

I set out below three practical techniques which help to answer this question:

- Draw a flow chart.
- Find a puzzle.
- Look through a zoom lens.

The flow chart

Dealing with data means moving from passive reading to active analysis. If you have failed to use the early stages of your research to narrow down your topic, data analysis is going to be very difficult because 'having a large number of research questions makes it harder to see emergent links across different parts of the data base and to achieve successful integration of findings' (Miles and Huberman, 1984: 36).

To help you narrow down, it can make sense to do an early flow chart setting out your key concepts and how they might relate. Following Miles and Huberman: 'Conceptual frameworks are best done graphically, rather than in text. Having to get the entire framework on a single page is salutary' (1984: 33).

The single-page flow chart is a useful technique in writing books as well as in doing research. For instance, as I write these words, I regularly move to a second document which houses the outline of this book. This outline was continually revised as I did my preliminary reading. It is still being revised as I write each chapter.

Several attempts will usually be needed to get your flow chart into a state that will be useful to you. Miles and Huberman recommend experimenting with different ways of specifying your research focus. But their basic advice is to 'begin with a foggy research question and then try to defog it' (1984: 35).

Find a puzzle

One way to break out of the vicious circle of unending facts and theories is to put your books on one side and to ask yourself: what am I really trying to find out? More specifically, what *puzzle* am I trying to solve?

Think of research as one of many kinds of puzzle-solving among a set of activities like doing jigsaws, completing crosswords or solving crimes. Each activity will be associated with its own set of more or less unique activities (but on the parallel between the qualitative researcher and Sherlock Holmes, see Alasuutari, 1995). Jennifer Mason has argued that 'all qualitative research should be formulated around an intellectual puzzle' (1995: 6). She distinguishes three kinds of question that may generate the type of intellectual puzzle which qualitative researchers would recognize (1996: 14):

* How or why did X develop? (A developmental puzzle)
* How does X work? (A mechanical puzzle)
* What causes X or what influence does X have on Y? (A causal puzzle)

Let us consider how, following Mason, you might find a puzzle. Say you have a general interest in 'child abuse'. You might narrow down your topic by choosing among the following questions:

* How or why was 'child abuse' first recognized? (A developmental puzzle)
* How (and by whom) is 'child abuse' identified? (A mechanical puzzle)
* What are the characteristics of child abusers and abused children? What effect does child abuse have on each group? (A causal puzzle)

Once you make a list of this kind, you should see that it is impossible to solve satisfactorily all these puzzles. So which puzzle do you choose? Below are some further questions that are worth asking:

- Which puzzle most interests me?
- Which puzzle might most interest my supervisor or funding body?
- Which puzzle most relates to issues on which I already have some theoretical, substantive or practical background?
- Which puzzle would generate questions that could be answered using my own resources and with readily available data?

The zoom lens

Wolcott (1990) gives the example of one PhD student who never finished his study of classroom behaviour. A true 'kitchen-sinker', this poor student was always reading more or gathering yet more data.

Wolcott uses the analogy of a zoom lens to suggest a practical solution. Say you want to take some photographs of a holiday resort. You could find some suitably high place, say a nearby hill, and try to take a picture of the whole resort. Then, as Wolcott points out: 'if you want to take in more of the picture, you must sacrifice closeness of detail' (1990: 63).

Alternatively, you can zoom in on one small image. What you lose in breadth, you may well gain in telling detail – say a particular dish that you enjoyed or the interaction between two local people.

Now apply the zoom lens analogy to defining your own research task. Wolcott suggests 'taking some manageable "unit of one" as a focus' (1990: 69). So, if, like his student, you are interested in classroom behaviour, focus on one student, one day, one lesson or one critical event.

The beauty of this narrowing of focus is that it will produce a manageable and achievable research task. Moreover, you are not locked for ever in this close-up picture. Just like the photographer you can 'zoom in progressively closer and closer until your descriptive task is manageable, then zoom back out again to regain perspective' (1990: 69).

Following Wolcott, later on you can always attempt to broaden your generalizations through more data at different levels of 'reality'. But your initial 'zooming in' will have got you going – out of the library and into dealing with data.

Timing your research questions

Experiments, official statistics and survey data may simply be inappropriate to some of the tasks of social science. For instance, they exclude the observation of behaviour in everyday situations. Hence, while quantification may *sometimes* be useful, it can both conceal and reveal basic social processes. This has an important implication for how we should formulate research topics to be studied using qualitative methods.

Consider the problem of counting attitudes in surveys. Do we all have coherent attitudes on any topics which await the researcher's questions? And how do 'attitudes' relate to what we actually do – our practices? Or think of official statistics on cause of death compared with studies of how hospital staff (Sudnow, 1968a), pathologists and statistical clerks (Prior, 1987) attend to deaths. Note that this is *not* to argue that such statistics may be biased. Instead, it is to suggest that there are areas of social reality which such statistics cannot measure.

The main strength of qualitative research is its ability to study phenomena which are simply unavailable elsewhere. Quantitative researchers are rightly concerned to establish correlations between variables. However, while their approach can tell us a lot about inputs and outputs to some phenomenon (e.g. how national identity is correlated with voting behaviour), it has to be satisfied with a purely **operational definition** of the phenomenon and does not have the resources to describe how that phenomenon is locally constituted (see Figure 8.1). As a result, its contribution to social problems is necessarily lopsided and limited.

Figure 8.1   The missing phenomenon in quantitative research

One real strength of qualitative research is that it can use naturally occurring data to find the sequences ('how') in which participants' meanings ('what') are deployed. Having established the character of some phenomenon, it can then (but only then) move on to answer 'why' questions by examining the wider contexts in which the phenomenon arises (see Figure 8.2).

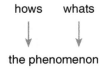

Figure 8.2   The phenomenon reappears

Figures 8.1 and 8.2 show that there are gains and losses in quantitative researchers' tendency to define phenomena at the outset through the use of operational definitions. Such definitions aid measurement but they can lose sight of the way that social phenomena become what they are in particular contexts and sequences of action. What I have called contextual sensitivity means that qualitative researchers can look at how an apparently stable phenomenon (e.g. a tribe, an organization or a family) is actually put together by its participants.

The upshot is that, in planning a qualitative study, you have to be very careful about the kinds of questions you ask. In particular:

- 'Why' questions (about causes) are usually best postponed until you have a proper understanding of the phenomenon under investigation.
- Understanding social phenomena through qualitative methods usually means trying to answer 'what' and 'how' questions.
- 'What' questions refer to the categories used by the participants in particular contexts.
- 'How' questions relate to the activities in which these categories are put to use.

Strategies for grand theorists

Reducing 'reality' to ungrounded sets of categories is an obvious potential failing of grand theorists. However, the minority of readers who feel they have the flair and temperament for theorizing will not, I suspect, be dissuaded by anything I might write. Indeed, sometimes, as I have already remarked, library-based work can be a quick way to write an acceptable thesis.

In this situation, all I can usefully do is wish you luck and offer you a couple of suggestions to speed you on your way. First, try to ignore fashions. Second, think about how some data may actually help you to theorize better. I set out these suggestions below.

Ignore fashions

Having found the corner of the intellectual garden which suits you, stick with it. Don't worry about those smart alecs who have always read a 'crucial' book by some new author; nine times out of ten, it will just distract you. Guided by your supervisor, work out the set of readings that will be your central material and stay with them. When you have written most of your thesis, you may then have the luxury of reading more widely and using that reading to reflect on the implications and limitations of your position – perhaps for your concluding chapter. Till then, don't be distracted.

Find some data

Even the most active minds can become a little stilted when confined to their armchairs. So think about examining some empirical materials of some kind. Even though these may not be central to your thesis, they may work as an aid to the sluggish imagination.

Take the case of two students in my own department who wrote 'theoretical' PhDs. Nick was interested in what he calls 'the refusal of work', which he linked to theoretical ideas about 'the ontology of desire'. Despite this highly complex theory, Nick still felt it worthwhile to gather material on the history of Autonomia – an Italian movement to refuse work – and the organization of unemployment benefit in the UK.

Jake was interested in a critique of existing theories of the community. In this context, he attempted what he described as largely a philosophical exercise. Nonetheless, to aid his thinking, he observed and interviewed homeless people, beggars and the mainstream community. Attempting what he called 'a situated phenomenology of the moral encounter', his data was intended to be only illustrative.

4 WRAPPING UP: SOME CAUTIONS
Avoid reductionism

My diagnosis of 'kitchen-sinking' and my recommendations for specifying a research problem should not be confused with attempts to reduce the complexities of the social world to a single factor. Just as doctors talk about meeting patients who make their hearts sink, there is nothing worse than when a detailed seminar on one's research is greeted by some bright spark with a version of 'that's all very interesting. But surely what you've described is all to do with power, gender, **postmodernism**, etc.'

What a nice, simple world it would be if everything reduced to one factor! For the moment, however, we should leave the pursuit of this kind of simplicity to bigots and to those theoretical physicists who are valiantly seeking a single theory of matter.

So narrowing down a research problem should not be confused with this kind of reductionism. I can only echo the arguments of the authors of a qualitative methodology textbook:

> Such reductive arguments are always distressing, given the variety and complex organization of social worlds. They reflect mentalities that cannot cope with the uncertainties and ambiguities of social research. (Coffey and Atkinson, 1996: 15)

Recognize feedback loops

Good research rarely moves smoothly from A (research topic) to B (findings). As Seta's case (discussed above) shows, alert researchers are always prepared to change their focus as they learn new things from others and from their own data.

Gabriella Scaramuzzino was studying online prostitution. Her story indicates how, in qualitative research studies, research topics are always emergent.

WHAT I DID: GABRIELLA
Online Prostitution

I started with a wide aim and questions about how the contributors interact. It did not take long before I started to feel like I was 'drowning' in empirical data: so many threads, posts and details! I wanted to give a complex picture of the virtual red-light district but I realized that I could not try to grasp and observe everything. I started to elaborate with different theories, wrote about them in my fieldnotes. Now, I am about half-way through my PhD studies and I am about to reformulate my aim and my research questions to make my study more specific and to get better guidance in my analysis. Though I am not sure if I should narrow down my research problem or broaden it. Is the Swedish red-light district interesting in itself, or is it an example of something larger? Could these findings be generalized to other online settings? [Gabriella Scaramuzzino, Sociology, Malmö University]

David Wield has called this kind of to and fro between data and topic a 'feedback loop' (2002: 42). This is how he addresses the issue of research focus in the context of such feedback:

Each stage of the research work will result in challenging a project's focus and lead to some re-evaluation. At all times, you will find that you have to maintain a careful balancing act between the desirable and the practical. Too strong a focus early on may lead to you ignoring what actually are more important issues than the ones you have chosen. Too weak a focus results in following up each side issue as it emerges and not getting anywhere! So focus needs to remain an issue as the research progresses in order to avoid the pitfall of these extremes. (2002: 42)

Recognize the theoretical saturation of categories

Seta's case, above, nicely illustrates that the categories we use to formulate our research problem are not neutral but, inevitably, theoretically saturated. In her case, the issue revolved around the status which she should attach to her interviewees' accounts. To take two extreme formulations, were these the raw experiences of alcoholics or provoked narratives in which a drinking story was constructed?

These kinds of issues have already been discussed in Chapter 6 when I examined several interview studies and will be discussed further in Chapter 15. The interdependence between research design and such analytical issues is examined in the next chapter of this book.

What You Need to Remember

Difficulties you might face in formulating workable research questions include:

* inadequate training
* unavailability of relevant data
* misleading assumptions about good research design
* misleading assumptions about qualitative research
* institutional constraints (departmental deadlines and ethical constraints)
* lack of confidence leading to over-ambitious research designs
* sticking to 'grand theory' and resisting data analysis.

These are some solutions to these difficulties:

* making good use of the existing literature
* using concepts from your discipline
* finding techniques to narrow down your problem
* timing different research questions
* strategies for grand theorists.

Don't spend too much time early on over-specifying your exact research problem. Find an interesting topic or situation and try to discover your topic(s) as you analyse your data.

Your Chapter Checklist

TRACK:
GOOD RESEARCH QUESTIONS

Zina O'Leary (2014: 42-3) suggests that good research questions have the following five features:

1. They are right for you [do they draw upon subjects and approaches that you know already; do you have the time to study them; do you have too much of an axe to grind to study them objectively?].
2. They are right for the field [why and for whom does your topic matter, e.g. to particular communities, to academic methodologists or theorist?].

3. They are well articulated [do they clearly point to the data needed and appropriate methods of research?].
4. They are doable [do you have the time, expertise and access to study them? Will you be able to get ethical clearance?].
5. They are acceptable to a potential supervisor [do they seem sensible and doable to people with more research experience than you?].

Assess your research problem in terms of these five criteria and work out how you might appropriately modify your research question.

Exercises

Exercise 1: Examine access issues and possible solutions

Take a research topic that interests you. Now consider the ways in which access to situations or informants might be a problem. Then examine how you might redefine your research topic to remove the problem of access.

APPLY:
YOUR EXERCISE WORKBOOK

Exercise 2: Visualize how your key project components relate

Draw a flow chart of no more than one page setting out your key concepts and how they relate.

Exercise 3: Form what, how and why research questions

Review your area of research interest in terms of the following questions (Mason, 1996: 14) and formulate your research problem in terms of one kind of puzzle:

- How or why did X develop? (A developmental puzzle)
- How does X work? (A mechanical puzzle)
- What causes X or what influence does X have on Y? (A causal puzzle)

Exercise 4: Rephrase your own research question

Take a research topic which interests you. Then reformulate it as:

- a 'what' question
- a 'how' question
- a 'why' question.

Exercise 5: Get to grips with the character of your research topic

Howard Becker is the author of a very useful book for research students called *Tricks of the Trade* (1998). One trick he mentions suggests the following exercise:

1. Ask your supervisor (or a fellow student who knows your work reasonably well) to offer a snap characterization of what you are trying to find out.
2. Now respond to this characterization of your work (e.g. by denying it or modifying it).

This exercise, says Becker, should help you to get a better understanding of what you *are* trying to do.

Further Reading

To help you think some more about defining your research, I recommend five basic texts: Barbara Czarniawska's *Social Science Research* (Sage, 2014); Amanda Coffey and Paul Atkinson's *Making Sense of Qualitative Data* (Sage, 1996: Chapter 2); Jennifer Mason's *Qualitative Researching* (Sage, 2002: Chapters 1 and 2); Keith Punch's *Developing Effective Research Proposals* (Sage, 2006: especially Chapter 4); and David Silverman's *Interpreting Qualitative Data: Methods for Analysing Talk, Text and Interaction* (Sage, 2011b: Chapter 2). Useful but more specialist texts are: Pertti Alasuutari's *Researching Culture* (Sage, 1995: Chapter 13); Martyn Hammersley and Paul Atkinson's *Ethnography: Principles in Practice* (Tavistock, 2007); and Anselm Strauss and Juliet Corbin's *Basics of Qualitative Research* (Sage, 2008: Chapters 1–4). Specific guidance on narrowing down a research problem is offered by Harriet Churchill and Teela Sanders's *Getting Your PhD* (Sage, 2007: 22–32), Robert Stake's *Qualitative Research* (Sage, 2010: Chapter 4) and Monique Hennink et al.'s *Qualitative Research Methods* (Sage, 2011: Chapter 3).

Discover the chapter's
digital resources in your
SILVERMAN FIELD GUIDE

NINE
Choosing a Methodology

Learning Outcomes

By the end of this chapter you will be able to:

- Understand how to choose a method appropriate to your research topic and analytic model.
- Make a rational choice about whether you want to stick to naturally occurring data.
- Decide whether you want to use mixed methods.

1 INTRODUCTION

'Methodology' can seem like a dull, technical topic. In this chapter, I aim to show you that methodological issues can lead you through lively debates which go the heart of what you are trying to achieve in your research project.

In Chapter 8, I discussed how to formulate a research question. Once you have a question, you need a research design. This involves answering several different questions:

- What do I want to know?
- Why do I want to know it?
- What type of data would best answer my research questions?
- How much data will I need?
- How will I collect and analyse my data? (Adapted from Braun and Clarke, 2013: 43)

Look toward existing methodologies for guidance

WATCH: DAVID EXPLAINS IN PERSON

David's Top Tip 20

Most students may find these issues rather daunting. But take heart! You are not starting from ground zero. There are several approaches which provide help when dealing with such issues (e.g. grounded theory, discourse analysis and narrative analysis). Try out such an approach for yourself on some data. Ask yourself:

- Does it make sense to me?
- Does it help to address my research question?
- Is a research design informed by such an approach practical and doable? (Adapted from O'Leary, 2014: 107)

As we saw in Chapter 7, decisions about methodology are always theoretically loaded. In this chapter, I provide more specific advice about the role of methodological issues in designing your research study, including the methods you use and how you propose to analyse your data. As Braun and Clarke (2013) argue, methodology is different to methods:

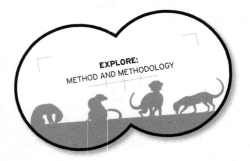

EXPLORE:
METHOD AND METHODOLOGY

Method refers to a tool or technique for collecting or analysing data ... Methodology is broader, and refers to the *framework* within which our research is conducted:

- Theories and practices for how we go about conducting our research
- A package of assumptions about what counts as research and how it is conducted, and the sorts of claims you can make about your data
- It tells us which methods are appropriate for our research and which are not.

(Hence) methodology can be understood as a *theory* of how research needs to proceed, to produce valid knowledge about the ... world. It is what *makes our research make sense*. (Adapted from Braun and Clarke, 2013: 31, their emphasis)

As Braun and Clarke note, there are many different kinds of qualitative methodologies (e.g. grounded theory, discourse analysis and narrative analysis), and this means you cannot just say you plan to use a qualitative methodology.

In this chapter, I begin by demonstrating what I mean by 'methodological' questions, illustrated by student examples. I then fill out the concept of 'research strategy' by an extended example taken from my own research. Next I discuss the contentious topic of whether naturally occurring data has a special place in qualitative research design. Finally, I examine what we mean by mixed methods and when it makes sense to use them.

2 METHODOLOGICAL QUESTIONS

We have seen that methodological questions arise when we try to ensure that our research design makes sense. Such questions may include:

- Do the data we propose to gather fit our chosen research topic?
- How many different types of data should we gather bearing in mind our research topic and the time available?
- Should we combine or compare different datasets or analyse them separately?
- What is the credible and appropriate way to record our data?
- Does our method of data analysis seem credible and appropriate to our topic?
- How far should we take account of our background knowledge in our data analysis?

These and other methodological issues are well illustrated in the questions that students ask me.

WHAT I DID: MARIA

Maria is interested in the challenges faced by people recovering from traumatic brain injury. She is collecting narratives from patients and their chosen supporters and gathering fieldnotes. She asked me:

- What is the best way to write fieldnotes in order to facilitate later analysis?
- How best to incorporate fieldnotes and narratives?
- What to consider in assessing the impact of my own background (as a medical doctor). [Maria, Medicine, UK]

When, like Maria, we ask questions about how to record and combine our data and ponder about how our own biography may enter into our data analysis, we are debating methodology. In the example below, Jakub has different types of questions.

WHAT I DID: JAKUB

Jakub wants to collect life histories from people with Polish mothers whose fathers were German or Russian soldiers who occupied Poland during the Second World War. He asked me:

- How am I to find interviewees when they don't keep in touch and the subject is taboo within Poland?
- How representative and generalizable is narrative analysis? [Jakub Galeziowski, Philology/History, Augsburg]

Jakub, like Maria, is asking himself vital methodological questions. In his case, these questions focus on the appropriateness of a method (interviewing) when it is difficult to find appropriate cases. His second question raises the crucial methodological question of the credibility of his methodology (see Chapter 17).

My final student example is taken from Veronica's research into social inclusion in the Rio Olympic Games.

WHAT I DID: VERONICA

Veronica studied the sustainable management component of Rio 2016's volunteer programme. She did some participant observation at the Olympics, gathered relevant documents and conducted semi-structured interviewees with volunteers. She asked me:

- How would you analyse the interviews, observations and documents? [Veronica Lo Presti, Management, UTS Business School]

Choosing an appropriate method of data analysis is crucial to your research strategy. Indeed, as I suggest in Chapter 15, if you can find such a method that makes sense to you and makes sense of your data, you have jumped over the most important hurdle in writing a successful research dissertation. But note that Veronica is determined to gather multiple datasets. This raises the issue of mixed methods, to be discussed towards the end of this chapter.

3 YOUR RESEARCH STRATEGY

In Chapter 7, I defined 'methodology' as 'a general approach to studying research topics'. In this sense, your choice of method should reflect an 'overall research strategy' (Mason, 1996: 19) as your methodology shapes which methods are used and how each method is used.

Four issues arise when you decide that strategy:

- making an early decision about which methods to use
- understanding the link between methods, methodologies and society
- appreciating how models shape the meaning and use of different methods
- choosing method(s) appropriate to your research topic.

An early decision?

Knowing what you want to find out leads inexorably to the question of *how* you will get that information. (Miles and Huberman, 1984: 42)

In quantitative research, it is expected that you begin by establishing a set of variables and methods (often using already existing, proven measures). However, when you are at the start of a piece of qualitative research, how far are you forced to choose between different methods?

This question is raised by Miles and Huberman (1984), who suggest that qualitative researchers have a range of options in how far they use what the authors call 'prior instrumentation' (i.e. predefined methods and measures):

- *No prior instrumentation.* Fieldwork must be open to unsuspected phenomena which may be concealed by prior instrumentation; all you really need are 'some orienting questions, some headings for observations [and] a rough and ready document analysis form' (1984: 42).
- *Considerable prior instrumentation.* If the research is not focused, you will gather superfluous data; using measures from earlier studies allows for comparability.
- *An open question.* Exploratory studies need to be far less structured than confirmatory studies; if your sample size is very small then cross-case comparison will be more limited and, therefore, the need for standardized research instruments will be less.

Miles and Huberman show that, although prior structuring of a research design is more common in quantitative studies, such structuring is worth considering in more qualitative work. For instance, in my study of HIV-test counselling (Silverman, 1997), I was able to begin with a prior hypothesis about the consequences of different kinds of advice-giving based on a recent research study which also applied CA to audio-recorded data (Heritage and Sefi, 1992).

If, as in this case, there is a previous study upon which you can base your research, a qualitative study can be highly structured. So what Miles and Huberman call 'no prior instrumentation' should not be regarded as the default option for qualitative research. An early decision about your preferred methods is often preferable.

Find inspiration from published problem-solving strategies
WATCH: DAVID EXPLAINS IN PERSON

David's Top Tip 21

Student research often works best when guided by the methodology of a previous, highly regarded, published study. You can come unstuck when you try to find your own solutions to problems already resolved by others. So don't try to reinvent the wheel (see Chapter 5 on originality).

The kind of pre-planning discussed here is helpful in sorting out your ideas early on. It is also essential for PhD students who are required at the end of their first year to make a presentation of their research plan. However, a note of caution is essential. Often the best student research studies depart most from their original plan. As Robert Stake suggests:

> Some studies are planned in great detail at the outset and some are open and developing as the study goes along. Most faculty members ... think that, for your own good, you should make a strong plan. Along the way, some of them will encourage you to stick to your plan and - as you find out more of what can be learned - other advisors will encourage you to move on to other questions or other complications and contexts. (2010: 78)

What Stake refers to as 'moving on' implies what O'Leary (2014: 117) calls an emergent methodological design. For instance, within grounded theory, at some stage we may want to re-examine existing data or to gather new data (see Charmaz, 2015). The latter occurred in my own research when, for example, in a study of oncology consultations, an unexpected possibility arose of gathering data from private consultations held by the same doctor I had observed in an NHS (state-funded) practice (Silverman, 1984; and Chapter 15, p. 339).

Your first plan isn't always the right one
WATCH: DAVID EXPLAINS IN PERSON

David's Top Tip 22

Don't feel you always need to stick rigidly to your first research plan. Once you are in the field you may become aware of exciting, unexpected data which you should follow up. Alternatively, your data analysis may suggest new questions which may suggest inspecting your existing data in new ways.

Methods are linked to methodologies

Most research methods can be used in research based on either qualitative or quantitative methodologies. This is shown in Table 9.1. The table underlines my earlier point that methods are techniques which take on a specific meaning according to the methodology in which they are used. All this means that we need to resist treating research methods as mere *techniques*.

Table 9.1 Different uses for four methods

Method	Methodology	
	Quantitative research	*Qualitative research*
Observation	Preliminary work, e.g. prior to framing questionnaire	Fundamental to understanding another culture
Textual analysis	Content analysis, i.e. counting in terms of researchers' categories	Understanding participants' categories
Interviews	'Survey research': mainly fixed-choice questions to random samples	'Open-ended' questions to small samples
Transcripts	Used infrequently to check the accuracy of interview records	Understanding the organization of talk and sometimes gaze and body movements as well

Source: Silverman (2014: 43)

To take just one example, although quantitative researchers have tried to establish quantifiable, standardized observation schedules, observation is not generally seen as a very important method of data collection in quantitative research. This is because it is difficult to conduct observational studies on large samples. Quantitative researchers also argue that observation is not a very reliable data collection method because different observers may record different observations. If used at all, observation is held to be only appropriate at a preliminary or 'exploratory' stage of research.

Conversely, observational studies have been fundamental to much qualitative research. Beginning with the pioneering case studies of non-Western societies by early anthropologists (Malinowski, 1922; Radcliffe-Brown, 1948) and continuing with the work by sociologists in Chicago prior to the Second World War (Hughes, 1984), observation has often been the chosen method to understand another culture or subculture.

But there is a broader, societal context in which methods are located and deployed. As a crude example, texts depended upon the invention of the printing press or, in the case of television or audio recordings, upon modern communication technologies.

Moreover, such activities as observation and interviewing are not unique to social researchers. For instance, as Foucault (1977) has noted, the observation of the prisoner has been at the heart of modern prison reform, while the method of questioning used in the interview reproduces many of the features of the Catholic confessional or the psycho-analytic consultation. The pervasiveness of such questioning is reflected by the centrality of the interview study in so much contemporary social research. Think, for instance, of how much interviews are a central (and popular) feature of mass media products, from 'talk shows' to 'celebrity interviews'. Perhaps we all live in what might be called an **interview society** in which interviews seem central to making sense of our lives (see Atkinson and Silverman, 1997; Silverman 2017).

This broader societal context may explain qualitative researchers' temptation to use methods such as the interview. Of course, such a link between culture and method should be an opportunity to question ourselves about our methodological preferences. However, such self-questioning (sometimes, mistakenly I think, referred to as **reflexivity**) does not itself provide a warrant for the choices we make. As I argue in Chapters 17 and 18, such a warrant depends on the robustness and credibility of our research design.

Theoretical models shape the meaning of methods

Most qualitative researchers believe that they can provide a 'deeper' understanding of social phenomena than would be obtained from purely quantitative data. However, such purportedly 'deep' understanding arises in qualitative researchers' claims to have entered and mapped very different territories such as 'inner experiences', 'language', 'narratives', 'sign systems' or 'forms of social interaction'. This means that:

> research is *never* conducted out of the blue, there is always a theory underlying data collection. It is therefore essential to make this theory explicit to indicate which theories guide your research and guided the selection of particular qualitative methods. (Hennink et al., 2011: 37, their emphasis)

Some of the claims associated with different qualitative models are set out in Table 9.2.

Table 9.2   Methods and models of qualitative research

Method	Naturalists	Constructionists
Observation	Understanding subcultures	Asking both 'what' and 'how' questions to understand how interaction is organized
Texts and documents	'Background' material	Understanding how sense is constructed
Interviews	Understanding 'experience'	Narrative or discursive construction of meaning

Each activity shown in Table 9.2 is not neutral but depends upon an implied model of how social reality works. In this table, I have simplified different approaches into just two models. Such **idioms** or models are a necessary but not sufficient warrant for a claim that any given research method has been properly used. So a purely theoretical warrant does not guarantee that a method will be appropriately used in a particular data analysis.

Choosing an appropriate method

There are no right or wrong methods. There are only methods that are appropriate to your research topic and the model with which you are working.

Let us take two contrasting examples from Chapter 6. Tippi was interested in the experience of living in a community of elderly people. Her concept of 'experience' clearly derives from a naturalist model. This makes her choice of open-ended interviews entirely appropriate. By contrast, if she were interested instead in how people interact in such a community, this constructionist topic might have suggested that she should use observational methods.

Anne's research was concerned with how a narrative changes as it is moved from book to television or radio. Her intention to observe what happens during the process of production sounds like a highly appropriate method for this topic. However, she also wanted to interview the participants to understand their motivation.

The problem here is the potential conflict within her research design between constructionist and naturalist models. If she primarily wants to understand behaviours, then the constructionist stress on observation makes most sense. By contrast, if 'experience' and 'motivation' are really her thing, then she should stick with the interview method. This argument is developed in my discussion of mixed methods later in this chapter.

Sometimes it makes sense to think laterally and to combine different methods and models. But the safest option for most apprentice researchers is to *keep it simple* and to have a straightforward fit between topic, method and model. For a discussion of the uses and limits of interview data, see Silverman (2017).

EXPLORE: INTERVIEW DATA

4 CHOOSING A METHODOLOGY: A CASE STUDY

What follows next is an extended discussion of one case. It shows how I encountered these issues in designing my study of HIV-test counselling (Silverman, 1997).

Studying counselling

The counselling study discussed here emerged out of my work as a medical sociologist. Between 1979 and 1985, I worked on data from British outpatient consultations which involved parents and children. At the same time, I also conducted a small study of adult oncology clinics, comparing National Health Service (NHS) and private consultations conducted by the same doctor. This research was reported in a number of papers (Silverman, 1981; 1983; 1984; Silverman and Bloor, 1989) and brought together in a book (Silverman, 1987). In that book, I focused on how apparently 'patient-centred' medicine can work in many different directions.

In 1987, I was given permission to sit in at a weekly clinic held at the genito-urinary department of an English inner-city hospital (Silverman, 1989). The clinic's purpose was to monitor the progress of HIV-positive patients who were taking the drug AZT (Retrovir). AZT, which seems able to slow down the rate at which the virus reproduces itself, was then at an experimental stage of its development.

Like any observational study, the aim was to gather first-hand information about social processes in a naturally occurring context. No attempt was made to interview the individuals concerned because my constructionist focus was on what they actually did in the clinic rather than on what they thought about what they did. The researcher was present in the consulting room at a side angle to both doctors and patient.

Patients' consent for the researcher's presence was obtained by the senior doctor. Given the presumed sensitivity of the occasion, tape recording was not attempted. Instead, detailed handwritten notes were kept, using a separate sheet for each consultation. The sample was small (15 male patients seen in 37 consultations over seven clinic sessions) and no claims were made about its representativeness. Because observational methods were rare in this area, the study was essentially exploratory. However, as we shall see, an attempt was made to link the findings to other social research about doctor–patient relations.

As Sontag (1979) has noted, illness is often taken as a moral or psychological metaphor. The major finding of this early study was the moral baggage attached to being HIV-positive. For instance, many patients used a buzzer to remind them to take their medication during the night. As one commented, 'It's a dead give-away. Everybody knows what you've got.'

However, despite the social climate in which HIV infection is viewed, there was considerable variation in how people presented themselves to the medical team. Four styles of 'self-presentation' (Goffman, 1959) were identified, which I called 'cool', 'anxious', 'objective' and 'theatrical' (Silverman, 1989). But there was no simple correspondence between each patient and a particular 'style' of self-presentation. Rather each way of presenting oneself was available to each patient within any one consultation, where it might have a particular social function. So the focus was on social processes rather than on psychological states.

Along the way, I also discovered how an ethos of 'positive thinking' was central to many patients' accounts and how doctors systematically concentrated on the 'bodies' rather than the 'minds' of their patients. This led on to some practical questions about the division of labour between doctors and counsellors.

About the time I was writing up this research, Kaye Wellings, who then was working for the publicly funded Health Education Authority (HEA), approached me about the possibility of extending my research to HIV counselling. Until that time, the HEA had been funding research on the effectiveness of 'safer sex' messages carried in the mass media. In the light of the explosion in the number of HIV tests in the UK in the late 1980s, Kaye thought it might be useful to take a longer look at the effectiveness of the health promotion messages being delivered in counselling people around the HIV antibody test.

I was interested in such a study for two reasons. First, it was the logical development of my study of medical interviews with AIDS patients. Second, it offered the opportunity to pursue my interest in looking at how communication between professionals and their clients worked out in practice – as opposed to the injunctions of textbooks and training manuals. Consequently, I submitted a research proposal and received funding from the HEA for 30 months beginning in late 1988.

The quantitative bias

John McLeod has reminded us that 'almost all counselling and psychotherapy research has been carried out from the discipline of psychology' (1994: 190). One consequence has been a focus on quantitative studies concerned with the attributes of individuals. This has meant that linguistic and sociological issues, such as language use and social context, have been downplayed (see Heaton, 1979).

Such a psychological focus has also had an impact on research design, leading to the dominance of experimental and/or statistical methods favoured in psychology. Of course, no research method is intrinsically better than any other; everything will depend upon one's research objectives. So it is only a question of restoring a balance between different ways of conceiving counselling research.

In designing my research proposal, I therefore needed to balance two competing objectives:

- my desire to examine how HIV counselling worked in actual counsellor-client interviews
- having to adjust to a context in which most counselling research had been informed either by a quantitative methodology or by normative assumptions about what constitutes 'good' counselling.

Designing a methodology: three familiar options

Quantitative or normative approaches suggest three obvious ways of researching counselling, all of which appear to take seriously the demands of validity and reliability. These three methodologies are set out in Table 9.3.

Table 9.3   Three familiar methodologies for counselling research

1   Measuring clients' response to counselling by means of research interviews which elicit their knowledge and reported behaviour. This would involve a longitudinal study, following a cohort of patients. The study could have either an experimental or a non-experimental design
2   Measuring clients' response to counselling by means of objective behavioural indicators. This also would involve a longitudinal study, following a cohort of patients
3   Measuring the degree of fit between actual counselling practice and certain agreed normative standards of 'good counselling'

Source: Silverman (1997: 16)

In order to underline the methodological options that arise in the early stages of research design, I review each strategy below. As I do so, we will see that each raises both methodological and analytic questions. I shall suggest that, in terms of either or both of these groups of questions, none of these three strategies is entirely satisfactory.

The research interview

As already noted, this might have either an experimental or a non-experimental design.

In the experimental design, we might randomly assign clients to two groups. In group 1 the clients are counselled, while in group 2, the **control group**, no counselling is provided. Both groups are then interviewed about their knowledge of AIDS and how they intend to protect themselves against the disease. This interview is followed up, some months later, with a further interview examining their present behaviour compared to their reported behaviour prior to the experiment.

In the non-experimental design, existing counselling procedures are evaluated by a cohort of patients. Again, we might follow up a cohort some time later.

The advantage of such research designs is that they permit large-scale studies which generate apparently 'hard' data, seemingly based on unequivocal measures. However, a number of difficulties present themselves. Of course, I know that these problems are recognized by researchers who use such research instruments. In turn, they have ingenious methods for dealing with them. Let me list a few:

1. How seriously are we to take patients' accounts of their behaviour? Isn't it likely that clients will tend to provide answers which they think the counsellors and researchers will want to hear (see McLeod, 1994: 124–6)?
2. Doesn't the experimental design ignore the *organizational* context in which healthcare is delivered (e.g. relations between physicians and other staff, tacit theories of 'good counselling', resources available, staff turnover, etc.)? Such contexts may shape the nature and effectiveness of counselling in non-laboratory situations.
3. Even if we can overcome the practical and ethical problems of not providing, say, pre-test counselling to a control group, may not the experience of being allocated to a control group affect the reliability of our measures and the validity of our findings (see McLeod, 1994: 124)?
4. Don't both studies treat subjects as 'an aggregation of disparate individuals' who have no social interaction with one another (Bryman, 1988: 39)? As such, they give us little hold on how counselling is organized as a local, step-by-step social process and, consequently, we may suspect that we are little wiser about how counselling works in practice.

The non-experimental study may have either a quantitative or a qualitative design. In the latter case, we might expect to carry out a relatively small number of open-ended interviews in order 'to enter, in an empathic way, the lived experience of the person or group being studied' (McLeod, 1994: 89).

This naturalist pursuit of 'lived experience' means that many qualitative researchers favour the open-ended interview (see Chapter 18). Unfortunately, both the 'in-depth' accounts apparently provided by the 'open-ended' interview and the apparently unequivocal measures of information retention, attitude and behaviour that we obtain via **laboratory study** or questionnaire methods have a tenuous basis in what people may be saying and doing in their everyday lives. Moreover, if our interest is in the relation of counselling to health-related behaviour, do such studies tell us how people actually talk with professionals and with each other as opposed to via responses to researchers' questions?

An example makes the point very well. At a meeting I attended in the 1990s social scientists working on AIDS expressed much concern about the difficulty of recruiting a sample of the population prepared to answer researchers' questions about their sexual behaviour. As a result, it was suggested that a subsequent meeting should be convened at which we could swap tips about how to recruit such a sample.

Now, of course, this issue of recruiting a sample is basic to survey research. And, for potentially 'delicate' matters, like the elicitation of accounts of sexual behaviour, survey researchers are quite properly concerned about finding willing respondents.

At the same time, it is generally acknowledged that the best chance of limiting the spread of HIV may be by encouraging people to discuss their sexual practices with their partners. This implies something about the limits of interview-based research in this area. Such research necessarily focuses on finding people prepared to talk about their sexuality in an interview. However, it can say nothing about how talk about sexuality is organized in 'naturally occurring' environments such as talk between partners or, indeed, talk about sexuality in the context of real-time counselling interviews.

Behavioural indicators

This method seeks to elicit behavioural measures which reliably report the effectiveness of counselling. Its advantage is that, unlike the research interview, it does not depend upon potentially unreliable client perceptions and self-reports of behaviour and behavioural change. Moreover, by eliminating a concern with the information that clients may acquire from counselling, it takes on board the research that shows that acquired knowledge does not have any direct link with behavioural change.

In relation to HIV-test counselling, it was suggested to me by a senior physician at an AIDS unit in Sweden that an appropriate behavioural indicator is seroconversion (developing antibodies to the HIV virus). Presumably, then, we would need to study a cohort of patients who test seronegative and are counselled. We could then retest them after a further period, say 12 months, to establish what proportions from different counselling centres and with different counsellors have seroconverted. In this way, it would be claimed, we could measure the effectiveness of counselling in relation to promoting safer behaviour.

As already noted, the advantage of this approach is that it generates quantitative measures of behaviour which are apparently objective. However, like the research interview, its reliability also has serious shortcomings:

1.　How do we know that the counselling alone is the variable that has produced the reported behaviour? Although we may be able to control for some gross intervening variables (like gender, age, sexual preference, drug use, etc.), it is likely that some non-measured variables may be associated with the reported behaviour (e.g. access to other sources of information, availability of condoms or clean injecting equipment, etc.).
2.　Ad hoc decisions are often made about which part of a counselling interview should be assessed. The scope extends from one whole interview (or even several interviews with the same client) down to a micro-segment of one interview. The latter approach gains precision but with a loss of context. Such context is provided by studying whole interviews but at a likely loss of precision.
3.　Even if such measures are reliable and precise, the result 'assesses only the presence or absence of a mode, and not the skilfulness with which it is delivered' (McLeod, 1994: 151).

Normative standards and outcomes

Such problems in attempts to use internal, normative standards of evaluation look even worse when viewed in the context of studies which seek to relate such measures to particular outcomes. As McLeod (1994) notes, one such study (Hill, 1989) found that only 1 per cent of variance in client responses was related to observed measures of counsellor behaviour!

The methodology chosen

It is now time to lay my cards on the table and to reveal that my research was based on a constructionist approach and used conversation analysis. CA, as we saw in the studies discussed in Chapters 3 and 6, is centrally concerned with the organization of talk, although its concern with social organization leads it to describe its subject matter as 'talk-in-interaction'.

Equally, counsellors, by definition, treat talk as a non-trivial matter. However, even if we concede the centrality of talk to social life, why should counselling researchers give priority to recording and transcribing talk? Given the usefulness of other kinds of data derived, say, from observations of behavioural change or interviews with clients, what is the special value of transcripts of tape recordings of conversation?

One way to start to discuss this question is to think about how research based upon data which arises in subjects' day-to-day activities can seek to preserve the 'phenomenon' of interactions like counselling interviews. Although such naturally occurring data is never uncontaminated (for instance, it may need to be recorded and transcribed), it usually gives us a very good clue about what participants do outside a research setting.

Conversely, in research interviews, as Heritage puts it: 'the verbal formulations of subjects are treated as an appropriate substitute for the observation of actual behaviour' (1984: 236). The temptation here is to treat respondents' formulations as reflections of some pre-existing social or psychological world.

However, even when counselling researchers contemplate tape recording actual interactions, they sometimes become easily deflected away from the counselling session itself. For instance, although McLeod calls for a study of 'the interior of therapy', he also cites favourably attempts at 'interpersonal process recall' where participants are played back the tape 'to restimulate the actual experience the person had during the session' (1994: 147). Thus, in common with many qualitative researchers, what matters for McLeod is what people think and feel rather than what they do.

However, if we follow this temptation in designing a study of counselling, then we deny something that all counsellors recognize: that talk is itself an activity. Although this is recognized in many normative versions of counselling, to base our research on such versions would be to narrow our focus to those activities which we already know about.

An alternative is to investigate how counselling interviews actually proceed without being shackled by normative standards of 'good' communication. In this way, we might discover previously unnoticed skills of both counsellors and clients as well as the communicational 'functions' of apparently 'dysfunctional' counsellor behaviour.

Summary and implications

In this section, I have used the case of a study of HIV counselling to illustrate several options that are available in designing a qualitative study. I did not want to imply that a CA study of counselling interviews is the 'one right method'. Instead, I wanted to demonstrate that choosing a particular method always has more implications than you might think. I have shown here how those implications encompass preferred analytical models, questions of reliability and validity, and, in this particular case, relevance for professional practice.

In developing my research design in this study, I took a position on two issues that need further discussion: I chose to study behaviour *in situ* (i.e. naturally occurring data); and I rejected combining multiple methods. This reflected my own preferences. Since other choices can (rightfully) be made by others, it is worth reviewing both issues.

5 NATURALLY OCCURRING DATA?

Some qualitative researchers prefer to avoid creating data through setting up particular 'artificial' research environments like interviews, experiments, focus groups or survey questionnaires. They argue that, since so much data occurs 'naturally' (i.e. without the intervention of a researcher), why not study this data and, thereby, access what people are routinely up to without, say, being asked by a researcher? To those who argue that such access can be difficult, the answer is that lateral thinking can move you into areas which *are* accessible.

For instance, I once attended a talk by a researcher who used interviews to ask couples about their sleeping habits. Now we might think that how couples negotiate the consequences of their different sleeping patterns can only be elicited by interviewing those involved. However, if indeed this is a real problem to members of society, it should appear in online blogs or elsewhere in social media. Why not try looking for actual instances first, before resorting to interviews?

Moreover, the problem with methods like interviews and (to some extent) focus groups is that the researcher has to set things up by asking questions of respondents. By contrast, as the following extended student example shows, the beauty of naturally occurring data is that it may reveal things we could never imagine.

WHAT I DID: PIERRE-NICOLAS

Studying Customer Satisfaction

Pierre-Nicolas Schwab did a business PhD at the Solvay Business School of Economics and Management, Free University of Brussels. He was interested in how small and medium enterprises (SMEs) treat customer satisfaction. By the time I met him, he had narrowed down his research question to 'How do SMEs manage complaints?' and the subquestion 'How does this differ from the way large corporations manage complaints?' He proposed initially to conduct interviews with entrepreneurs as well as observations in SMEs. I discussed his work with him during a workshop I gave in Brussels in 2011. In what follows, I show you how I responded to Pierre-Nicolas's questions over several months.

He initially wrote:

Following your workshop, I was inspired by your discussion of 'naturally occurring data' and investigated how I could tackle this research question. I was faced with two problems: nowadays firms' customer services are hotline-based to reduce costs. Although calls may be recorded, there is no way to get access to them because of privacy. I found out two alternatives:

1. To send complaint letters to selected firms belonging to both categories (SMEs and large corporations) and research how they respond to them. Would it be an acceptable method?
2. To study an online forum (with between 100 and 1000 posts per day!) dedicated to complaints in all sectors (from cell phone to travel agencies through retail and appliances). Firms which are the subject of complaints are encouraged to answer online. My aim would be to code those answers given by the firms and see how they comply with the perceived justice framework suggested in the marketing literature.

I would like to get your feedback on alternatives 1 and 2 as I'm puzzled with whether the methodologies can be seen as scientifically acceptable.

I replied that the artificial complaint letters could not mimic the complexity of everyday complaining. I strongly suggested that Pierre-Nicolas use his naturally occurring Internet material. However, as a constructionist, I was worried by his reference to 'coding'. I wrote: 'Try not to simply code what people say. The point is not to impose your categories on the data but to see when, where and how the participants use their own categories.'

Pierre-Nicolas wrote back to say that he would now choose option 2 and study the online forum. However, he was puzzled that naturally occurring data had not been used before: 'I went through an extensive literature review and could not find any empirical

(Continued)

(Continued)

research on actual answers to complaints. All researches study the effect of complaint handling on repurchase intention, loyalty etc., based on surveys.' He was also worried about the difficulty of treating the online company employee as representative of the whole firm.

My reply stated: 'Don't worry about representativeness too much. Maybe you can find comparative data elsewhere on the Internet later (e.g. in other countries or other sectors)?'

Pierre-Nicolas then wrote:

I've been searching the literature for a week now and found only a handful of papers studying organizational responses to complaints. If I pioneer the field in studying naturally occurring data, how should I point out the problems of approach 1? Why is this approach less interesting than the other one according to you?

I responded:

What is wrong with study 1 is that it invites students to write complaints when they hadn't done so in real time. Hence you invite an 'artificial' complaint. Given the fallible nature of the complaint, any response obtained is dubious too. The same applies to a lot of lab studies.

Pierre-Nicolas responded: 'I understand this is "artificial". But may I ask you, if it's so dubious, why journals accept the methodology?' My answer was that journals publish papers using this method because of the appeal of experimental methods. The logic of qualitative research is not properly understood by many academics used to quantitative methods.

Some weeks later, Pierre-Nicolas wrote:

Just wanted to give you an update and ask you one further advice. I've compiled statistics on all posts on the online forum (a list of the 297 companies, date of registration, date of first post, last post, number of posts, name of company etc.). I've started retrieving the posts and converting them in PDF to be able to code the companies' answers on Atlas.ti. I'm faced however with two methodological issues.

The forum has been open for eight years but only one company has been active over so many years. I'm therefore wondering which material I should analyse and see two options:

1.   My supervisor suggests to study only the answers published in one given month (for instance December when the pressure is at its maximum due to Christmas). Big disadvantage: my statistics show that 60% of companies have a 'lifetime' (difference between date of last post and date of first post) of less than 30 days and 80% of the 297 companies haven't had any activity in the last 12 months. By following this strategy I'll be covering only 10% of

the 297 companies, which is not very good if I want to achieve variety. Given the lifetime of <30 days, I'd prefer to analyse the material of the first 30 days of existence for each of the 297 firms. What would you go for?

2. For 99% of the companies, answers are well written and show counter-arguments, additional pieces of information etc. For one company, however, answers consist in short pieces of text giving either the status of the follow-up (like 'I'm working on it', 'will be dealt with', 'more info to come') or information related to the order itself ('tracking number XXX', 'see order YYY'). The shortness of those answers results in the company posting c.1000 answers per month! I've no particular problem working hard on this but I'm wondering how to code little pieces of information (the nature of which is very much redundant) and whether it would be acceptable, if it's worth coding, to focus on 200 or 300 instead of 1000 given the high redundancy.

I replied:

It sounds to me even 200–300 is too many cases to analyse thoroughly. Start with a small dataset as your supervisor suggests. You can then expand the sample later to test emergent hypotheses. Also, I repeat my warning about avoiding a mentality of 'coding'. That way you will be imposing your categories on the data too early. The better way to proceed is to look at longer passages to see how complaints and replies are sequentially organized.

In my debate with Pierre-Nicolas, I successfully pressed him to use naturally occurring data. However, I do not want to suggest that such data is always preferable to **researcher-provoked data** like interviews and focus groups. In particular:

EXPLORE: USING NATURALISTIC DATA
EXPLORE: BENEFITS OF NATURALISTIC DATA

- Data cannot be intrinsically unsatisfactory; it all depends on what you want to do with it.
- No data can be 'untouched by human hands' (e.g. recording equipment is sometimes present and this has to be positioned by a researcher).
- The difference between what is 'natural' and 'non-natural' should be investigated rather than used as a tacit research resource.

These are powerful arguments. However, rather than abandon my preference, I prefer to take a non-dogmatic position. This involves the following two elements:

- Everything depends on your research topic. So, as in my HIV-test research, if you want to study how counselling gets done, it may not make sense to seek retrospective accounts from clients and practitioners or to use a laboratory study.

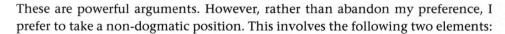

- We need to consider how far any research setting is *consequential* for our research topic. For instance in one lab study, limitations were placed on who could speak. This made the experimental setting consequential for its topic (of 'self-repair') and undercut its conclusions (Schegloff, 1991: 54). Without such limitations, the study would have been sound.

READ: NATURALISTIC DATA PROS & CONS
READ: NATURALISTIC DATA RELEVANCE

To conclude: choosing any method, based on any kind of data, can never be intrinsically right or wrong. However, as a constructionist, I am sympathetic to Jonathan Potter's (2002: 540) argument that, given the (unthought?) dominance of open-ended interviews in qualitative research, the justificatory boot might be better placed on the other foot. The question is not why should we study natural materials, but why should we not?

6 MIXED METHODS?

So far I have been assuming that you will always want to choose just one method. However, the methods presented in Table 9.2 are often combined. Mixed methods research (MMR) can take one of two forms:

- Combining quantitative and qualitative methods (e.g. a survey and open-ended interviews).
- Combining several different qualitative methods (e.g. interviews and documents).

Combining quantitative and qualitative research

This approach can go in two directions:

- Beginning with a quantitative study and going on to use qualitative data to interpret quantitative findings and/or to contextualize the behaviour under study.
- Beginning with qualitative data and then using quantitative research to try to generalize the findings to the general population (see Hennink et al., 2011: 55-8].

WHAT I DID: ROBERT, JOHAN AND KIM

- A study of the role of management training in equipping social workers with leadership skills using both quantitative data (surveys and psychometric and personality profiles) and open-ended interviews. [Robert Ford, Social Work, Sydney University]
- A study of the collaborative behaviour of small Swedish firms and its relation to innovation. The study will combine quantitative, longitudinal data on firm behaviour and all employees of these firms with a qualitative study of new start-ups. [Johan Lidström, Umeå School of Business and Economics]

- A study of factors influencing the adoption of social networking services (SNS) by Australian businesses based upon a survey of four online SNSs followed by semi-structured interviews. [Kim MacKenzie, School of Accountancy, Queensland University of Technology]

Research using these kinds of combinations is highly valued among established scholars. Many research grant givers seem to favour a study that draws upon both qualitative and quantitative data. Moreover, it seems that journal articles get more citations when they combine data this way. For instance, Richard Whittington (2003) found that a mixed methods approach was a significant positive predictor of article impact, with the mean citation count of mixed method articles being 59.13, while the mean citation count for the mono-method comparison group of articles (pairs matched by the publication year) was 37.08.

READ:
MIXED METHODS PROBLEMS

If you decide to go down this path, it is important to be clear that your research fits your theoretical model. Sharlene Hesse-Biber (2015) has noted how many positivist assumptions can creep into MMR. She quotes Lynne Giddings (2006) who notes the extent to which much MMR is conducted under the guise of a positivistic methodology – what Giddings calls 'positivism dressed in drag' (p. 200), whereby the dominant mixed methods design was confirmatory with a qualitative component playing a secondary role often in serving to triangulate research results. As Giddings notes:

> The thinking in mixed-methods rarely reflects a constructionist ... view of the world. The majority of studies use the analytic and prescriptive style of positivism, albeit with a post-positivist flavor ... A design is set in place, a protocol followed. In the main, the questions are descriptive; traditional positivist research language is used with a dusting of words from other paradigms, and the designs come up with structured descriptive results. Integration is only at the descriptive level. A qualitative aspect of the study is often 'fitted in.' The thinking is clearly positivist and pragmatic. Yet the message often received by a naïve researcher is that mixed methods combine and share 'thinking' at the paradigm level. (2006: 200)

READ:
MIXED METHODS EXAMPLE

In a sense, Giddings argues that mixed methods will only serve to strengthen the positivistic paradigm if, in fact, qualitative approaches remain just 'added and stirred' into a general 'positivistic' methodological approach (p. 202). Furthermore, if you follow my maxim, 'say a lot about a little', you should be cautious about combining quantitative and qualitative data.

Combining various qualitative methods

Many qualitative case studies combine observation with interviewing. This may be because you have several research questions or 'because you want to use different methods or sources to corroborate each other so that you are using some form of methodological triangulation' (Mason, 1996: 25).

For instance, Miles and Huberman (1984: 42) give the example of research on how police suspects are arrested and booked. You might think here of combining several methods, for example:

- interviews (with suspects, police and lawyers)
- observation (of arrests and bookings)
- collecting documents (produced by this process)
- recording (of arrests and bookings).

If you are a pure empiricist, uninterested in the theoretical bases of research design, mixed methods may look like a good idea. By having a cumulative view of data drawn from different contexts, we may, as in trigonometry, be able to triangulate the 'true' state of affairs by examining where different data intersect. In this way, some qualitative researchers believe that triangulation may improve the reliability of a single method. Take the following example of student research projects which use multiple methods.

WHAT I DID: VERONICA AND CECILIE

1. The Rio Olympics: A Catalyst for Social Inclusion?

Veronica investigated how 'social inclusion' was incorporated in the planning, organization and operation of the 2016 Olympic Games. She focused on the sustainable management component of Rio 2016's volunteer programme combining document analysis, participant observation and semi-structured interviews with volunteers. [Veronica Lo Presti, Management, UTS Business School]

2. Citizenship in a Multicultural Society

Cecilie's project asks how feminism, ethnic identity and religion are brought together in the policies of women's movements and in the daily lives of women. She will use three sets of data:

- qualitative interviews with members of selected minority and majority women's organizations in Norway
- interviews with civil servants/bureaucrats in national government departments and representatives from national political parties
- analysis of relevant policy documents: selected periodic reports to the UN, government action plans, Green and White Papers on gender equality and discrimination policy and violence against women.

She writes: 'By combining the interviews and the document analysis, my aim is to explore whether ethnic minority women's demands have been rejected and resisted or embraced and accepted by the majority women's organizations, and how the political opportunity structure works in regard to their influence on the government's policy making.' [Cecilie Thun, Sociology and Women's Studies, Oslo University]

Both Veronica and Cecilie's mixed method studies are likely to provide rich data. However, before you consider using mixed methods, I should sound two warning notes:

- Have you got the time and resources to gather and to analyse multiple datasets? Isn't there a danger that one or another of your datasets will be under-analysed?
- Have you thought through the issues involved in trying to establish the 'true' state of affairs by comparing data from different sources? In both cases, aren't documents and interview responses composed for different audiences? Does it make sense to compare them? Indeed, is there such a thing as an 'overall picture' of a phenomenon?

As I remarked in Chapter 6, 'mapping' one set of data upon another is a more or less complicated task depending on your analytic framework. In particular, if you are a constructionist and treat social reality as constructed in different ways in different contexts, then you cannot appeal to a single 'phenomenon' which all your data apparently represents (see Chapter 17).

Mason (1996: 27) gives the example of the mistaken attempt to combine (say) interview data on individuals' perceptions with DA of particular texts. The mistake arises because DA treats all accounts as socially constructed and, therefore, cannot treat interview accounts as providing a definitive version of reality.

Such triangulation of data seeks to overcome the context boundedness of our materials at the cost of analysing their sense in context. For the purposes of certain kinds of social research, particularly that based on a constructionist model, it is simply not useful to conceive of an overarching reality to which data, gathered in different contexts, approximates.

At the very least, we need to note Nigel and Jane Fielding's (1986) suggestion that the use of triangulation should operate according to ground rules:

- Always begin from a theoretical perspective or model.
- Choose methods and data which will give you an account of structure and meaning from within that perspective (e.g. by showing the structural contexts of the interactions studied).

Many theoretical perspectives in sociology and elsewhere suggest we cannot simply aggregate data in order to arrive at an overall 'truth'. This implies that we should receive with caution the clarion calls for multiple methods in areas like nursing, family medicine and elsewhere. As Hammersley and Atkinson point out: 'One should not adopt a naively "optimistic" view that the aggregation of data from different sources will unproblematically add up to produce a more complete picture' (1983: 199).

As already noted in Chapter 6, mixed methods are often adopted in the mistaken hope that they will reveal 'the whole picture'. But this 'whole picture' is an illusion which speedily leads to scrappy research based on under-analysed data and an imprecise or theoretically indigestible research problem. For instance, mixed methods may tempt novice researchers to move to another dataset when they are having difficulties in analysing one set of material. It is usually far better to celebrate the partiality of your data and delight in the particular phenomenon that it allows you to inspect (hopefully in detail).

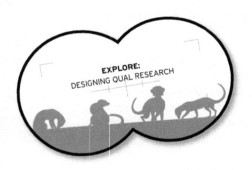

EXPLORE:
DESIGNING QUAL RESEARCH

7 WRAPPING UP

The debate about mixed methods and naturally occurring data illustrates the theoretically laden environment in which we make methodological choices. It underlines the fact that many apparently technical choices are saturated with theoretical import.

Of course, to some extent this complicates the picture when you are attempting to design a research study. However, a concern at this stage with theoretical issues also helps in at least two ways. First, it may allow you to simplify your research design as you realize that it is often misleading to attempt to research 'the whole picture'. Second, thereby, it may add theoretical consistency and even some elegance to the research design. As I remarked in Part I, often the best research says 'a lot about a little'.

What You Need to Remember

- Your choice of method should reflect both your research topic and your overall research strategy as your methodology shapes which methods are used and how each method is used.
- Although most research methods can be used in either qualitative or quantitative studies, research methods are more than mere *techniques*. Different theoretical idioms or models provide different justifications for using particular research methods.
- Methods do not just belong to social researchers. Before choosing a method, you should reflect upon the broader societal context in which this method is located and deployed.
- Think carefully before you generate data through research instruments like interviews and focus groups. Sometimes such methods may indeed be appropriate to your topic and model. Sometimes, however, you may be neglecting to study illuminating, naturally occurring data.
- Think carefully before adopting mixed methods. Many models suggest that we cannot simply aggregate data in order to arrive at an overall 'truth'. Choose simplicity and rigour rather than the often illusory search for the 'full picture'.
- Consistency is the most important feature of good research design. Your choice of data should reflect your research topic and your overall research strategy.

Your Chapter Checklist

- Think through why qualitative data is appropriate to your research topic.
- If you are using interviews or focus groups, consider why you are ruling out naturalistic data.
- List what you will gain and lose *either* by combining qualitative and quantitative data *or* by combining different kinds of qualitative data.

TRACK:
DESIGNING YOUR RESEARCH STRATEGY

Exercises

Exercise 1: Use and assess fieldnotes effectively

What I did: Maria

Maria is interested in the challenges faced by people recovering from traumatic brain injury. She is collecting narratives from patients and their chosen supporters and gathering fieldnotes. She asked me:

APPLY:
YOUR EXERCISE WORKBOOK

- What is the best way to write fieldnotes in order to facilitate later analysis?
- How best to incorporate fieldnotes and narratives?
- What to consider in assessing the impact of my own background (as a medical doctor). [Maria, Medicine, UK]

How would you answer Maria's questions?

Exercise 2: Evaluate your methods and data source options

Mason (1996: 19) notes that your choice of a methodology is likely to reflect your own biography and the knowledge and training your education has given you. As she comments: 'Whilst practical issues to do with training and skill are ... relevant in your choice of method ... they should not govern your choice' (1996: 19). She suggests instead making a list of possible research methods and data source options and thinking through why you are accepting or rejecting each one.

1. Follow Mason's suggestion about making a list of possible research methods and data source options. Explain why you are accepting or rejecting each one.
2. Answer the following questions (adapted from Mason, 1996: 20-1):

   - What data sources and methods of data generation are potentially available or appropriate?
   - What can these methods and sources feasibly tell me?
   - Which phenomena and components or properties of social 'reality' might these data sources and methods potentially help me to address?

Exercise 3: Learn what your research is telling you about data, coding and sample sizes

Review my dialogue with Pierre-Nicolas Schwab in Section 5. What methodological lessons can you learn from it for your own research? In particular, consider:

- the use of naturally occurring data
- the size of your sample
- the problems that arise from early coding of data.

Exercise 4: Play devil's advocate on your own method selection

- List the reasons why it might make sense for you to combine qualitative and quantitative methods on your research project.
- Now review the counter-argument (e.g. if you are thinking of using multiple methods, consider whether quantitative methods are appropriate to your theoretical model and whether you would have the time to do a good job by using multiple methods).

Exercise 5: Edit and simplify a research design

Holly Hasted is studying Tromso Museum in Norway while doing research at Tromso University. Her topic is knowledge production and expertise at this museum. She wants to understand how museum staff, who often come from different disciplines, transfer knowledge between each other. She is mixing different sets of qualitative data: short open-ended interviews with all 108 museum employees, multiple in-depth interviews with 15–30 informants, observation of work processes and document analysis of relevant texts. She is using constructionist grounded theory and hopes to come up with findings relevant to Museum Studies, Social Studies of Science and Organization Theory.

- Do you think her methodology fits her research design?
- Can you suggest any ways that her research could be simplified?

Further Reading

My book *A Very Short, Fairly Interesting, Reasonably Cheap Book about Qualitative Research* (Sage, 2013) discusses key issues in methodology. Many of these topics are given a different twist in Martyn Hammersley's *Questioning Qualitative Inquiry* (Sage, 2008). My edited *Qualitative Research: Theory, Method and Practice* (Sage, 2011a) provides state-of-the-art accounts by leading scholars of the uses of interviews, observations, texts, Internet data, and audio and visual data. Other useful books on methodology are: Amanda Coffey and Paul Atkinson's *Making Sense of Qualitative Data* (Sage, 1996); Jennifer Mason's *Qualitative Researching* (Sage, 2002); Pertti Alasuutari's *Researching Culture* (Sage, 1995); and my *Interpreting Qualitative Data: Methods for Analysing Talk, Text and Interaction* (Sage, 2014).

READ:
SYNTHESIZING QUAL & QUANT DATA

Discover the chapter's
digital resources in your
SILVERMAN FIELD GUIDE

TEN
Writing a Research Proposal

Learning Outcomes

By the end of this chapter you will be able to:

- Understand the key components of a qualitative research proposal.
- Recognize the importance of clarity, planning and persuasiveness in writing a proposal.
- Understand that writing of any kind must be **recipient designed** for a particular audience.
- Acknowledge that the logic of qualitative research is often quite different from quantitative studies.

1 INTRODUCTION

Before you can set out on your research, you will usually need to submit a research proposal for approval. Although this is, in one sense, a bureaucratic hurdle, it is also an opportunity for you to make sure that you are perfectly clear about the direction which you want your research to take.

Writing a research proposal allows you to clarify in your own mind that you have fully grasped the issues we have been discussing in Part II of this book. Moreover, it adds a useful discipline. Now it is not just a matter of convincing yourself but of convincing a potentially sceptical audience who will expect you to answer briefly and clearly a set of difficult questions. These questions are set out in Table 10.1.

Table 10.1   Questions answered by a research proposal

1   What? What is the purpose of my research? What am I trying to find out?
2   Who? Who do I want to speak about? Who do I plan to speak to or observe? Or will I study texts like documents or digital data?
3   How? How will the proposed research answer these questions?
4   Where? Which settings, if any, will I study?
5   When? Will my data collection and analysis fit into my time frame?
6   Why? Why is the research worth doing (and/or funding)? What will we learn and why is it worth knowing?

Source: adapted from Punch (2006: 20) and O'Leary (2014: 114)

The best way to answer these questions with brevity and clarity is to follow a standard format. Table 10.2 indicates a basic structure for a qualitative research proposal.

Table 10.2   A structure for a qualitative research proposal

1   Title
2   Abstract (further advice on titles and abstracts is found in Chapter 21)
3   Background or introduction, e.g. contemporary debates in social policy and social science
4   Statement of purpose or aims: the research question ('The intellectual problem(s) I may help solve through this research is (are) ...')
5   Review of the relevant literature (showing the importance of the project in the context of the classic or definitive pieces of research in this area)
6   Methods: description of case(s) chosen, procedures for data collection and data analysis in terms of (a) their appropriateness to your theoretical orientation and (b) how they satisfy criteria of validity and reliability (see Chapters 9 and 17)
7   Ethical issues (see Chapter 4)
8   Dissemination and policy relevance: explain how you will communicate your findings (see Chapters 20 and 27)
9   A timetable indicating the length of time to be devoted to each stage of the research
10   Limitations of your research
11   References: use a standard system like the Harvard system[1]

Source: adapted from Morse (1994: 228), Kelly (1998: 115-21) and Rudestam and Newton (1992: 18)

The proposal as a persuasive document
WATCH: DAVID EXPLAINS IN PERSON

David'sTop Tip 23

Your research proposal should convince your teachers that your research is feasible and doable and that your research design addresses your research question.

In preparing your proposal, it is worth bearing in mind the special difficulties qualitative researchers can face in achieving credibility. Particularly if you are within a university department where quantitative research is the mainstream, bear in mind that your proposal is likely to receive highly sceptical reviews.

The sceptics may make the following assumptions:

- Qualitative research is unstructured.
- The results of qualitative research are unpredictable.
- The outcome is uncertain. (Morse, 1994: 227)

Moreover, most experienced qualitative researchers will expect their potential students to be aware of such concerns and to have thought about how to respond to them. At the very least, they will want to be reassured that:

- Your research is feasible and doable.
- Your research design addresses your research question.
- Your research is worth doing.
- You can do it.
- When completed, it will produce a successful dissertation at the level of your degree (O'Leary, 2014: 107; Punch, 2006: 11).

How, then, can one convince a potential university supervisor to support your research proposal? Following the format set out in Table 10.2 should help. But how should you frame your proposal in a way likely to maximize acceptance?

The following suggestions form the rest of this chapter:

- Aim for crystal clarity.
- Plan before you write.
- Be persuasive.
- Be practical.
- Make broader links.

2 AIM FOR CRYSTAL CLARITY

The proposal should use language and terminology that is understandable to an intelligent lay person as well as to a subject expert. (Cryer, 1996: 15)

Although it is tempting to seek to display your newly acquired technical jargon, bear in mind that your proposal is likely to be read, in the first instance, by a faculty member who is not a specialist in your area of the discipline. So never be content with a proposal which can look like a stream of (perhaps undigested) theories or concepts. Always aim for clear language that describes your research in a way that non-specialists can comprehend.

As Janice Morse suggests, this means that you should resist the temptation to lapse into pure jargon: 'Because some of the reviewers will be from other disciplines, the proposal writer should assume nothing and explain everything' (1994: 227).

By explaining everything, you will have demonstrated the ability to think (and write) clearly. Not only is this the way to write a research proposal, it is also the best indicator that your research itself will be organized in a clear and logical way:

> A sloppily prepared proposal will, at best, send a message to the agency that if it funds the proposal, the research may also be sloppy. (1994: 226-7)

For instance, your objectives 'should be clear and it should be easy to decide whether they have been achieved or not' (Kelly, 1998: 117). The ways to achieve this are:

- Be concise (there is no reason why a proposal for a piece of student research should be more than 500 words, increasing to 1500 words for a PhD proposal).
- Use short, simple sentences.
- Use headings as in Table 10.2.

3 PLAN BEFORE YOU WRITE

> The writer must show that the design is the result of a series of decisions that she made because of knowledge gained from the ... literature. (Marshall and Rossman, 1989: 13)

Not only must the proposal demonstrate that it is based on an intelligent understanding of the existing literature, it also must show that you have thought about the time you will need to conduct each stage of the research from obtaining access to writing up your data analysis. So, as Sara Arber notes, your research proposal will partly be judged by how you state you are going to use your time:

> You need to adopt a systematic and logical approach to research, the key to which is the planning and management of your time. (1993: 33)

Moira Kelly (1998: 120–1, adapted here) offers an example from an interview study planned to last 32 weeks:

A research timetable

Week 2	Submit proposal to university ethical committee
Week 6	Draw up sample
Week 8	Begin interviews
Week 15	End interviews
Week 23	Complete data analysis
Week 26	First draft sent out for comments
Week 32	Submission of final report

We are not born with a natural ability to prepare research timetables! To help you plan such a timetable, seek the assistance of a trusted teacher in your department. Failing that, seek out an existing research student. With their help, make a list of all the options available in relation to your research problem, method and case(s) to be studied. Now you are in a better position to write a reasoned research proposal that explains the actual choices you have made.

4 BE PERSUASIVE

It is easy to get very wrapped up in the subject and think that, because we are convinced of the particular value of our research, others will be too. The way in which the proposal is presented can enable the reader to appreciate what you are planning to do. (Kelly, 1998: 121)

Kelly is reminding us that, in framing a research proposal, one must think first of the audience who are going to read it (and judge it). This means that it should set out to convince such readers that this is something worth supporting:

The first principle of grantsmanship is to recognize that a good proposal is an argument ... for the researcher's project. The proposal must make a case to the granting agency that the research question is interesting [and] that the study is important ... Thus the proposal must be written persuasively. (Morse, 1994: 226)

Morse is suggesting that you try to 'sell' your proposal. This means that you must recognize that the craft of selling (your proposal, yourself) is not incongruent with working in a university. 'Ivory towers' were never so isolated as the term suggests!

However, this persuasiveness must be balanced with a realistic understanding about what you can achieve within a few years as a single researcher. Like any good salesperson, do not oversell your goods!

5 BE PRACTICAL

One way to persuade non-specialists, Morse suggests, is to show the specific ways that your research can address a social problem or solve an organizational trouble (e.g. staff turnover).

Such a concern with practical problems cannot be shrugged off even if you are proposing to do a purely academic piece of research with no expectation that it will be read outside the university. Academic funding bodies are increasingly demanding practical payoffs as well as analytic insights. For instance, Kelly quotes a policy statement by the body that funds social science PhDs in the UK:

> Any lingering public perception of social science as a source of irrelevant, introverted and incoherent output is set for radical alteration ... In future, research which makes a difference to the health and wealth of the population, rather than merely supports 'ivory tower' academic excellence, will be the ESRC's priority. (1998: 112, quoting the Economic and Social Research Council)

The issue of audiences for your research is discussed further in Chapter 20. However, if what you are proposing is 'basic research', that is a study deriving from debates and concepts internal to social science, then all is not lost. You can strengthen the persuasiveness of your case by showing non-specialists why they ought to take your ideas seriously. One way to do this is to try to make broader links between your (very narrow) research proposal and wider issues.

6 MAKE BROADER LINKS

Realism need not mean that you must present your research as a narrow, anaemic exercise. Even if you cannot cover every aspect of the field yourself, you should demonstrate your understanding of the broader implications of your proposed research. One way to do that is to hint at a wider context: 'Place the problem in context to show, for instance, that "when we understand this, we will be able to work on that"' (Morse, 1994: 227).

Of course, you will be studying very few cases, or maybe only a single case. Be positive about the gains as well as the losses of this! Show how a relatively small database will enable you to conduct an in-depth analysis (see Chapters 11 and 13). And argue that your case can indicate far larger phenomena: 'The writer must show how, in examining a specific setting or group of individuals, she is studying a case of a larger phenomenon' (Marshall and Rossman, 1989: 12).

WHAT I DID: RODDY

I now offer an example of what I think is a model research proposal which is well aligned with the advice given in this chapter. After each section, I note points you can learn from it.

Roddy Walker, Department of Organization, Copenhagen Business School

Investigating the Effects of Leadership Education on the Local Practices of Day Care Institutions

Introduction to the area of research

The identification of leadership development as an essential factor in modernising public sector organisations and ensuring their efficiency has led to a massive investment in these kinds of development programmes by the Danish government, while the actual effect of such programmes on organisations has been largely unstudied. My PhD is part of a wider research project, encompassing investigations into the constitutive effects of different leadership development programmes offered to employees within the public sector. The focus of research into this area has typically fallen upon the changes occurring within individual leaders participating in development programmes and, correspondingly, the actual implications of these development programmes on the organisational level have remained largely in the background (Carroll, Levy, and Richmond 2008; Porter and McLaughlin 2006). My project aims to extend the scope of research, aiming to illuminate the travel of ideas (Czarniawska and Joerges 1995) from a specific diploma programme in leadership development, into organisational practice.

Note how Roddy provides the background to his research problem by relating it to a topic currently in the public eye (the modernization of public sector organizations).

Research Questions

* What are the constitutive effects of Metropolitan University College's diploma programme in leadership on the organisational practices of day care institutions?
* How do individual leaders translate the outcomes of their participation within this programme into local practices, and which changes in discourse, identities and practices does this precipitate?

Two very clear, researchable questions.

Choice of methodology and theoretical framework

By studying not only the intended effects of the leadership development programme, but its manifestation in the subsequent activities of leaders, the goal is to make the effects of the development programme tangible, as interconnected activities and events within networks of situated practices.

- The situated orientation and embeddedness of my project calls upon an ethno-graphically inspired approach, echoing the idea of a 'practical ethnography' (Gubrium 1988; cited in Silverman 2013, 82), with the guiding principle that more insight can be garnered by observing actions and behaviours instead of opinions and attitudes (Silverman 2017) To this end, mixed-method ethnographical research methods (Eisenhart 2001; Ybema 2009; Willis 2000; Czarniawska 2007; Borgnakke 1996), building upon participant observation, various qualitative interview forms, and the collection of relevant documents, will provide empirical material.
- This approach ultimately involves the selection of three current participants from the training programme, as case studies. This will enable the individual learning out-comes of their participation in the development programme to be established, and follow their implementation of these outcomes in their local organisational practice. This encourages theoretical divergence to enlighten different aspects and perspec-tives of the identified phenomena and the organisations within which they are at play (Eberle and Maeder 2010).

Roddy provides the methodological background to his choice of methods.

Cornerstones of my empirical approach

Participant observation: The development programme upon which the investigation is based comprises a set of 10 modules, each concluding with a spoken or written exam. I began my field studies at the end of August, following the final module of the current pro-gramme as a participant observer. As those participating are largely in full-time positions as leaders, the course is part-time, comprising six days of structured lessons, spread over three months. This module requires the participants to identify a specific organisational problem or leadership task, as the basis for their final exam project ('AP project') – mir-roring an action research approach. They must study a chosen organisational dilemma or challenge empirically, before introducing appropriate theoretical resources gained from previous modules of the education to enlighten and address the central issues at play. My observations follow a constructionist orientation (Justesen and Mik-Meyer 2012, 108) focusing on the relations between the participating actors, their doings and sayings. The interactions arising within group activities where participants collectively discuss and for-mulate their individual projects have been of particular interest, proving to be a rich source of detail in how participants bring their organisational practice into dialogues – both with one another and with the theoretical resources provided by the development programme.

Shadowing: This involves the purposive selection of individual leaders to be followed more closely as case studies, and shadowed (Czarniawska 2007) in their organisational practices on their completion of the development programme. This will primarily be recorded through field notes, but I aspire to gain recordings of specific meetings and conversations taking place in the workplace, providing the sort of naturally occurring data which can potentially support different analytical approaches, such as conversation analysis, discourse analysis and discursive psychology (Potter 2004).

(Continued)

(Continued)

Document analysis: The exam documents produced by the selected participants over the course of the 10 modules are to be viewed as artefacts produced within the practices and sense-making processes (Nicolini 2012, 7) involved in the development programme. These exam documents take the form of synopses of case-study-based projects, again bringing concrete organisational issues and problems into dialogue with the theoretical concepts and tools covered within the given module. A constructionist orientation towards document analysis, focusing on the production process (Justesen and Mik-Meyer 2012, 121), will make it possible to gain regular, qualitative 'snapshots' of the individuals' activities and development – where the texts can perceived as artefacts, and a window into practices.

Qualitative interviews: These will focus on the production of narratives in relation to particular events witnessed during the periods of observation and shadowing – an opportunity to 'to access self-reflexivity among interview subjects, leading to the telling of stories that allow us to understand and theorize the social world' (Miller and Glassner 2004). Which discourses do they draw upon in these narratives, and where do they come from? Also, as my project has an interest in revealing the identities developing from changes in practices, interviews can transform such imperceptible constructions into objects of study – by asking people directly about their identity and analysing the resulting narrative constructions.

Question: How can I provide a satisfactory qualitative response to a question based upon the measurement of an effect?

By embracing the processual nature of my study, I can use the exam documents and particularly the final exam project to guide me towards the particular phenomena and leadership tools that the individuals intend to introduce to concrete issues in their organisation (as exemplified in the previously mentioned case regarding the intended introduction of team-based performance and development reviews.) The idea of this project as a dialectical bridge between the content of the development programme and the actualities of organisational practice leads me to believe that it can be operationalised as a key data object, a textualisation of the meeting between the theory and practice of leadership. This offers a strategy to focus on how the leaders enact the chosen tools and theories derived from the development programme in their practical approach to leadership, and the eventual organisational effects arising from any changes to this. In this way I would be shadowing the leader as the carrier and translator of practices, and focusing on their enactment of the discursive and material resources made available to them during the development programme, rather than merely observing them in their role as leader.

Here Roddy identifies and responds to a criticism that may be made of his proposal: why is he using qualitative research when 'the measurement of an effect' is usually done through quantitative methods?

7 A CAUTION: MISUNDERSTANDING QUALITATIVE RESEARCH?

Up till now, by listing difficulties in writing a research proposal and then offering solutions, I may have given the impression that writing a good qualitative research proposal is a purely *technical* exercise. Unfortunately, this is not the case.

All too often, beginning researchers, aware of the low status sometimes accorded to qualitative research, try to define their research proposal in terms more appropriate to quantitative research. Many research students attending my workshops set out their research in ways which make me wonder why they have not chosen instead to do a quantitative study! For instance, they present their research plan in terms of hypotheses and variables. By contrast, in qualitative research, we often work *inductively* and generate hypotheses during the course of study. As Punch argues: 'I am against the idea that we should have hypotheses in research proposals *just for the sake of having hypotheses*. Let us use them if appropriate, and not use them if not appropriate' (2016: 56).

The most important thing is to be aware of the issues raised in Table 10.3 and to respond *appropriately*. Note how Roddy does not formulate any hypotheses in his research proposal. It takes courage to tell your department graduate committee that your only real research question is: 'What is going on here?' Faced with an implacably quantitative or positivist institution, the only safe response may be concealment, that is to knowingly use quantitative language to describe your research, telling yourself that it will be conducted quite differently. This underlines the point that all research proposals should be recipient designed for a particular audience.

However, we should not exaggerate the lack of understanding or opposition to qualitative research

Table 10.3   Problematic concepts in qualitative research proposals

Concept	Difficulty
Hypothesis	If you are working inductively, hypotheses are usually best generated in the course of data analysis. Often the most appropriate question is simply: 'What is going on here?'
Variable	Suggests measurement; in qualitative research we need to establish how participants define their activities in different contexts
Theory	In qualitative research this should include discussion of the research model used (e.g. naturalism, constructionism)
Outcomes	Cannot be known till you familiarize yourself with your data

in social science departments. I fear that, in some cases, the students who send me research proposals simply do not understand the special logic of qualitative research. If they did, they might be surprised at the reception they got from their department and be able to achieve a much more valuable end product.

8 WRAPPING UP

If you eventually submit a research proposal with the kind of logical structure I have been suggesting, you may be plagued by a horrible thought: 'Will I actually have to follow, word for word, every idea I have suggested? If things turn out differently to the way I now expect, will my supervisor insist that I follow my self-prescribed route?'

Fortunately, the answer to these kinds of questions is 'generally no'. Your research proposal should not be regarded as some kind of contract which, if approved, is legally enforceable. Every practitioner recognizes that all researchers may, at some stage, find it worthwhile to divert from an initial path. This is particularly true of qualitative research, where analysis of field data often leads in unexpected but fruitful directions (see Chapter 15). Of course, this does not mean that you may not be asked to justify any diversion. But any research proposal should not be set in stone for all time. What, then, is the point of having to write an initial proposal? Let me suggest two answers to this reasonable question.

First, having had to prepare a clear, persuasive research proposal is a wonderful discipline which will help you work out exactly what it is you want to do. As such, it can guide you in the initial stages of your research.

Second, such a proposal helps others. In particular, it allows your potential supervisors to see if you are the kind of student who is able to think critically and, just as important, to move outside their own inner world in order to work out what others may be looking for.

Don't get stuck in the details

WATCH: DAVID EXPLAINS IN PERSON

Davids' Top Tip 24

The best qualitative research often differs greatly from what it originally intends. Writing a good research proposal involves thinking about what counts as 'good' research in your field. But don't assume that you must rigidly stick to every detail afterwards.

This means that ultimately a research proposal should be regarded not as a legal contract but as a way of responding to the potential questions experienced researchers may ask about your plans. These questions are summarized in Table 10.4.

Table 10.4   Questions a research proposal must answer

1	Why should anyone be interested in my research?
2	Is the research design credible, achievable and carefully explained?
3	Is the researcher capable of doing the research?

Source: adapted from Marshall and Rossman (1989: 2)

What You Need to Remember

When preparing a research proposal, try to find answers to four questions:

1. *What?* What is the purpose of my research? What am I trying to find out?
2. *How?* How will the proposed research answer these questions?
3. *Why?* Why is the research worth doing (and/or funding)? (e.g. what will we learn and why is it worth knowing?) (Punch, 2006: 20)
4. *Which audience?* How can I design my research proposal so it will be well received by those who will read it?

NOTE

1   The Harvard system presents references in this order:

*   in the main body of your text (not in footnotes): surname of author, followed by date and page reference
*   in your references: author (with initials), date, title, place of publication, publisher and page references (for articles or chapters).

Your Chapter Checklist

Does your research proposal meet the following criteria:

*   crystal clarity
*   persuasiveness
*   is doable
*   shows how it relates to broader issues?

TRACK:
GOOD RESEARCH PROPOSALS

Exercises

Exercise 1: Draft a research proposal

Prepare a draft proposal about your research (no more than 1500 words) covering the following elements:

APPLY:
YOUR EXERCISE WORKBOOK

1   title
2   abstract
3   background or introduction
4   statement of purpose or aims
5   review of the relevant literature
6   methodology and methods (description of case(s) chosen, procedures for data collection and data analysis)
7   ethical issues
8   practical relevance
9   a timetable
10 a set of preliminary references.

Exercise 2: Defend even the vaguest of proposals

Prepare a plausible proposal about your topic which does not include hypotheses, operational definitions or a predefined number of 'cases'. How would you defend this proposal to a quantitative researcher?

Further Reading

READ:
SELLING QUAL RESEARCH TO QUANT RESEARCHERS

A research proposal is crafted according to the level of your research. MA researchers should turn to Moira Kelly's 'Research questions and proposals' (in C. Seale (ed.), *Researching Society and Culture*, Sage, 2012). At PhD level, useful references are Zina O'Leary's *Doing Your Research Project* (Sage, 2014), Pat Cryer's *The Research Student's Guide to Success* (Open University Press, 2006, Chapter 4) and Keith Punch's *Developing Effective Research Proposals* (Sage, 2016) (a much shorter version is contained in Punch's book *Introduction to Social Research*, Sage, 2005). Beyond the PhD, you should consult Janice Morse's 'Designing funded qualitative research' (in N. Denzin and Y. Lincoln (eds), *Handbook of Qualitative Research*, Sage, 2005).

Discover the chapter's digital resources in your
SILVERMAN FIELD GUIDE

CONTENTS

PART III
GETTING SUPPORT

Writing a research dissertation can be a lonely activity. In Part III, I address ways of getting support for your work. Chapter 11 discusses your relationship with your supervisor. In Chapter 12, I examine how to get feedback about your research from the wider community.

ELEVEN

Making Good Use of Your Supervisor

Learning Outcomes

By the end of this chapter you will be able to:

- Recognize the problems that can happen in supervision and know how to overcome them.
- Know what to expect from your supervisor.
- Know what your supervisor expects from you.

1 INTRODUCTION

I have supervised around 30 students who have successfully completed their PhDs. I don't know the exact number because the hard disk on my PC crashed not long ago and I lost my CV (a lesson to all of us about the need to back up files!).

I am sure that some students have been happier than others about my supervision. Equally, the enjoyment I derived from the supervision experience varied. In the best cases, the student's work would so stimulate me that I seemed to come up with lots of bright ideas and sparks would fly. On other occasions, I felt quite stupid, bereft of good ideas – maybe, I have to admit, even a little bored.

I like to think that the quality of my supervisions improved over the years as I became more experienced and also more selective about which students I chose to supervise. Towards the end of my career, I simply refused to take on anybody whom I had not supervised for their MA dissertation. That way, I could ensure that my new PhD students had already learned the way I liked (them) to work.

Now my supervisions are limited to one-off meetings during my PhD workshops in Scandinavian, French, Australian, Sri Lankan and Tanzanian universities with business, sociology, social policy, education and community medicine students. The students simply send me a brief summary of their research and a few questions which I try to answer. I hope to stimulate them but, of course, a lot will depend on whether any new ideas will work (or even be appropriate) in their home university and discipline.

In this chapter, I want to put my experience to work for you. This chapter is organized in the following sections:

- supervision horror stories (it may be good to frighten you at the start!)
- student and supervisor expectations
- early stages of supervision
- later stages of supervision
- standards of good practice.

2 SUPERVISION HORROR STORIES

The British academic and novelist Malcolm Bradbury (1988) has written about 'the three-meeting supervisor'. The first meeting is when this character informs you about which topic you will study. Three years pass before the next meeting, which happens when you deliver your dissertation. The third and final meeting takes place after a telephone call from your supervisor to tell you that he has lost your thesis!

Of course, this story has a farcical element. However, like all good farce, there is an element of truth in it. Back in the late 1960s, PhD supervision in many British universities had something of this feel about it – as my own experience as a student demonstrates.

Unfortunately, even today, all is not sweetness and light in the supervision stakes. In Table 11.1 you will find a few horror stories adapted from the 'Higher Education' section of *The Guardian*, a British newspaper.

I hope that these horror stories do not accord with even the slightest aspect of your own experience. If you are just starting out, let me reassure you that, at least at the present time, such happenings are exceptional, not least because supervisors are usually better trained and are monitored by their departments. Such stories do, however, underline an important point: when writing a dissertation, a bad outcome usually indicates bad supervision.

Later we will consider standards of good practice. But first let us consider what students and supervisors expect of each other.

Table 11.1   Supervision horror stories

- Everything that could possibly have gone wrong, has gone wrong. My supervisor was a bully and I quarrelled with him. We eventually fell out over working arrangements: I was chastised for arriving late in the mornings, though I often worked till 9 p.m. I began to suffer from anxiety and depression. I took time off, which only made matters worse
- I was within sight of finishing my PhD when my supervisor changed universities. I was isolated and left to plough on alone with my research. Not that I now saw much less of my supervisor. We had not been on speaking terms for some time and I can't even remember the last time we had a supervision
- Our department has a very high staff turnover, with most professors leaving in a year or two. I went through three supervisors, each one worse than the last. After my second supervisor left, during my third year, I got someone who knew nothing about my research area. All three supervisors have tried to steer my research towards a topic that they were personally interested in. With each change, there were miscommunications and political manoeuvring to ensure they would not be blamed for lack of progress on my part
- My supervisor encouraged me to undertake teaching responsibilities, and I ended up leading some of his courses. Off the record, he was sympathetic to my heavy teaching load, but during progress committee meetings he would blame me for too much time spent preparing lectures when I should have been concentrating on research
- My worst experience, and the one that caused me to leave the university, was a personal one. I got engaged and my supervisor said I could return home to get married if I handed in a first draft of my thesis by April. But then my supervisor changed and my next one refused to give me a leave of absence. I was told the decision was 'in my best interests'
- I told my supervisor I wanted to complain about his supervision, only to be told: 'You can make a complaint but you won't have a future in science'
- The department's idea was, if you are not brilliant, get out
- My experience has taught me that most academics have forgotten what it is like to wonder if one would ever actually do research, or to wonder just how research is done, or to not appreciate how large a contribution needs to be so as to be judged original and how one may go about doing it
- My supervisor restricted his written comments to 'super', 'well done' and 'perhaps rework this paragraph'

Source: adapted from *The Guardian* 'Higher Education', 25 September 2001, 23 October 2001, 18 March 2003

3 STUDENT AND SUPERVISOR EXPECTATIONS

Estelle Phillips chose as her PhD topic 'the PhD as a learning process'. Some of her findings are reported in Phillips and Pugh (1994). Although her data were obtained in the UK, I have no reason to think that it does not, in general terms, apply elsewhere. Table 11.2 sets out Phillips's findings about the expectations of PhD students.

All the student expectations shown in Table 11.2 seem quite reasonable to me. If you do not feel that your supervisor is meeting such expectations, it is worth raising your concerns at an early stage.

Table 11.2   Students' expectations of supervisors

- To supervise
- To read work well in advance
- To be available when needed
- To be friendly, open and supportive
- To be constructively critical
- To have a good knowledge of the student's research area
- To be interested/excited by the topic
- To help the student get a good job afterwards

Source: adapted from Phillips and Pugh (1994: Chapter 11)

More recent, detailed guidance from McCulloch (2010) about what constitutes 'effective' supervision is set out in Table 11.3.

Table 11.3   The effective supervisor

- Providing satisfactory guidance and advice during the planning of research projects
- Being responsible for monitoring the progress of the student's research programme
- Establishing and maintaining regular contact with the student and ensuring his/her accessibility to the student when s/he needs advice, by whatever means is most suitable given the student's location and mode of study
- Having input into the assessment of a student's development needs
- Providing timely, constructive and effective feedback on the student's work, including his/her overall progress within the programme
- Maintaining a balance between providing guidance and encouraging a candidate's independence
- Fostering and facilitating the candidate's development of academic skills and self-direction
- Assistance with the candidate's accessing of specialist expertise (e.g. statistics, computing, language)
- Ensuring that the student is aware of the need to exercise probity and conduct his/her research according to ethical principles, and of the implications of research misconduct
- Ensuring that the student is aware of institutional-level sources of advice, including careers guidance, health and safety legislation and equal opportunities policy
- Providing effective pastoral support and/or referring the student to other sources of such support, including student advisers (or equivalent), graduate school staff and others within the student's academic community
- Helping the student to interact with others working in the field of research, for example encouraging the student to attend relevant conferences, supporting him/her in seeking funding for such events, and where appropriate to submit conference papers and articles to refereed journals
- Maintaining the necessary supervisory expertise, including the appropriate skills to perform all of the roles satisfactorily, supported by relevant continuing professional development opportunities
- Effective arrangements made during supervisor absences

Source: adapted from McCulloch (2010)

Table 11.3 shows the many attributes that a supervisor should possess. However, you should also be aware that your supervisor will have certain expectations about you. A good guide to how the land lies in this area is found in Table 11.4.

Table 11.4   Supervisors' expectations of students

- To work independently
- To not usually submit first drafts
- To be available for 'regular' meetings
- To be honest about their progress
- To follow advice
- To be excited about their work
- To be able to surprise the supervisor
- To be fun to be with

Source: adapted from Phillips and Pugh (1994: Chapter 8)

I suspect that Table 11.4 will contain some items that you may never have thought about. But, yes, it is true that supervisors expect you to be fun to be with. Most want to be stimulated by and, indeed, to learn from their students.

Claire Maxwell has suggested some key questions to ask a prospective supervisor:

- How will you be able to support me if your area of expertise is not fully related to my own research?
- How many students have you supervised?
- How do you see your role as supervisor?
- What can I expect, e.g. likely number of supervisions in my first year? (Quoted by Churchill and Sanders, 2007: 35)

Your expectations may, of course, be quite different from your experience. I now consider how your expectations can be converted into (good) practice.

READ:
PROCESS OF SUPERVISION

EXPLORE:
WORKING WITH A SUPERVISOR

Keep records of supervisions
WATCH: DAVID EXPLAINS IN PERSON

David's Top Tip 25

Providing your supervisor is willing, it makes sense to audio-record each supervision as well as to keep written notes. This will allow you to review what was said in greater detail. It may also provide material for your methodology chapter.

4 THE EARLY STAGES

The first few months of working towards a PhD are crucial. If you fail to make a good start, it may be very difficult to retrieve the situation at a later point. Here are some points to think about:

- *Choosing a supervisor.* Ideally, you should choose someone whose approach and interests gel with your own. This may be someone whose work you have read or, better still, whose courses you have taken. Alternatively, try to get a look at completed dissertations supervised by this person. Try to avoid simply being allocated a supervisor. Also try to establish beforehand whether your potential supervisor is planning any long trips abroad or other career moves.
- *Do you need joint supervision?* Where your work covers more than one area, it can make sense to have two supervisors. However, tread warily! Not infrequently, joint supervision means that each supervisor will assume that the other is taking care of you. So make sure that there is planning so that you don't fall between the cracks.
- *Combining the PhD with being a Research Assistant or a Teaching Assistant.* Sometimes you will be expected to do some research for your supervisor or teaching within your department. If so, again make sure that there is a clear agreement about the extent of this work and the support that you can expect.
- *Getting early direction.* In the early stages, you should expect a lot of support. You should not be fobbed off with a reading list and an appointment in three months' time! Instead, you might expect weekly meetings, based on small tasks, to build your confidence and give you a sense of direction.
- *Being informed.* Right at the start of your studies, you should expect to be properly inducted with regard to your department's research training programme and to your rights and responsibilities as a student.

The following student examples show how an effective relationship with your supervisor (in the USA 'advisor') can help.

WHAT I DID: KARYN AND DARIN

Helpful Supervisors

My advisor helped in many ways. Because I had already been writing with him, he had taught me how to use qualitative data to study the sociology of race. He was supportive of my topic, once I showed him how interested I was and where it would fit into the existing research. He was always available, by phone, email, or face-to-face, to discuss the ideas I was having while analyzing the data. He read chapters as I completed them, and offered suggestions that made the project imminently better. Finally, he simply would not allow me to sabotage myself through unnecessary perfectionism. [Karyn McKinney, USA]

Though my advisor sometimes gave me feedback and advice he didn't really want to hear about my work, this was to my mind much appreciated candour and not in any way insulting or disrespectful. I didn't have any difficulties with him, and sought out his guidance as much as I could get it. We formally met perhaps every four to six weeks and once in a while informally as well. [Darin Weinberg, USA]

Amir Marvasti once heard a professor complain about a student who repeatedly bothered him with, as he put it, 'brain farts' (i.e. fleeting thoughts). Amir lost respect for that professor and his unhelpful approach toward his students, but there is a lesson to be learned here. Remember that the difference between a so-called 'brain fart' and 'insight' is timing and packaging. First, it is generally not a good idea to pour out your thoughts at the doorstep of your supervisor as they are preparing for class or trying to hurry to a meeting. Wait. Make an appointment to discuss your progress on the dissertation or invite your chair to lunch and carefully take the time to explain your ideas. Second, develop and polish your ideas before presenting them to your supervisor. While some supervisors are incredibly effective at helping you pull a string out of a mess of seemingly disconnected ideas, others lack the capacity or the inclination for this kind of 'brainstorming'. So play it safe: think before you speak.

It also helps to think about how you can use a supervision session most effectively. For instance, work out beforehand what you hope to get out of it and make sure you clarify what is expected before your next supervision (further details on this are provided by Churchill and Sanders, 2007: 183).

5 THE LATER STAGES

After the first crucial three to six months, your supervisor should gradually wean you from total dependence. As you become more confident and independent, your supervisor should encourage you to believe that you know more about your topic than they do. At these later stages, the following issues become important:

• *Shaping your writing in a professional manner.* Your supervisor should help you move your style of writing to the kind expected in the journals in your field. For instance, this may mean encouraging you to cut down the kind of tedious literature reviews you wrote as an undergraduate and to use concepts 'economically'. A few concepts (even just one) applied to your data are generally much more productive than data analysis that is all over the place.

- *Self-confidence*. To be economical in this way, you need self-confidence, and this is what your supervisor should provide. Where appropriate, you should also be told that your work is 'up to standard' for the degree you are seeking.
- *Setting deadlines*. Deadlines and targets can be a source of neurosis for students. However, without them, I guarantee you will be lost. Therefore, at the end of each supervision, you should expect to set a reasonable target and agree a date by which it can be reached.
- *Working with other students*. You should not be confined to your relationship with your supervisor. Expect to be advised about relevant conferences and websites. You will also meet other students during your research training. Find out which ones have similar topics to yours or are working with similar concepts and/or data. Then organize discussions with them. Even better, ask your supervisor to set up data sessions with other students that they are supervising (see Section 7).
- *Learning 'tricks'*. Based on a long career of supervision, the American ethnographer Howard Becker has suggested a number of useful 'tricks' that supervisors can employ for your benefit. As he puts it: 'a trick is a specific operation that shows a way around some common difficulty, suggests a procedure that solves relatively easily what would otherwise seem an intractable and persistent problem' (1998: 4). (For some of these tricks, try Exercise 2.)
- *Advising on publications*. Towards the later stages of your work, your supervisor should be a good source of advice about which journals are appropriate for submission of some of your work and about how to organize your presentation for such a setting (see Chapter 27).
- *Giving you a 'mock' viva*. Finally, it is entirely reasonable to expect PhD supervisors to provide a practice dry run for the oral examination (see Chapter 25).

Ultimately, the role of the supervisor is to help you finish your project. Sara Crawley illustrated this point by using the analogy of 'driving the bus'.

WHAT I DID: SARA

Driving the Bus

Throughout graduate school, I used a metaphor that guided my decisions and helped me organize my programme and reason through pitfalls and politically dangerous situations. The metaphor I used was 'I'm driving the bus.' I began graduate school because of personal, passionate interests and I felt it important to hold on to those ideals throughout to direct my work. The metaphor extends like this: you can get on the bus and ride along. Everyone is invited and you are welcome to get off the bus if you choose. But I'm driving and I'm determining the direction. I may let someone else navigate for a while if their expertise is helpful. But I ultimately decide where we are going with my research. [Sara Crawley, USA]

The point here is that while one can and should expect a good deal of assistance and support in graduate school, at the end the responsibility for completing the dissertation lies with the student. The casual atmosphere of some graduate programmes may give the impression that the rules of professionalism do not apply in academia. This could be a dangerous assumption. In some ways, academia is very 'corporate': there are deadlines, expectations and competition for limited resources. Accept these as the rules of the game without taking any of it too personally.

You're here to learn, not lecture

WATCH: DAVID EXPLAINS IN PERSON

David's Top Tip 26

In the haste to impress a supervisor, it is easy to come across as a 'know-it-all'. This is a deadly sin in academia, particularly at the graduate level. Once you are labelled as someone who is not educable, the doors start closing. This reaction on the part of the faculty may be justified in light of the institutional mission of academia. The academic enterprise is based on the assumption that students are there to learn, not to lecture the faculty. If you have a strong opinion about a particular issue, phrase it tentatively and, when possible, in the form of a question.

Much of the support that your supervisor can give you should be facilitated by an institutional structure within your department which encourages good practice. I conclude this chapter by discussing such practice.

6 STANDARDS OF GOOD PRACTICE

As a research student, you have a right to expect the following institutional structures. Although different formats will apply in different disciplines and countries, what follows seems to me to be a minimum requirement:

- An induction session in which research training is explained and you get to meet new and existing research students.
- A graduate committee with an identified and accessible chairperson.
- A handbook of expected practice for the supervision and training of research students. This handbook should set out training requirements and the rights and responsibilities of research students. It should also explain what to do if you want to change supervisors or if you have a problem that you cannot sort out between you.
- Written memos to be agreed after each supervision.
- Annual reports agreed between supervisor and student. These to be submitted for review by the graduate committee of your department.

7 BEYOND THE SUPERVISION

None of the above is meant to suggest that you should expect to be spoonfed by your supervisor. Good supervision is not just about the transmission of knowledge but involves *enabling* the student to work successfully. As Susan Danby and Alison Lee put it:

> Doctoral pedagogy is not so much [about] what an educator 'transmits' but what they 'enable' by 'setting up a critical exchange' between the student and the discipline, field or domain of the research. (2012: 6)

Part of that enablement is encouraging you to work collaboratively with other research students either within your institution or by virtual contact. Ideally, this should be with someone who is working upon similar data to you and also using the same body of concepts. It can begin by offering mutual assistance to improve transcription of recorded data. That can then lead naturally to making new observations about what is present in your data.

Finally, just as many people doubt they have the ability to complete a PhD, a minority feel that it is all a piece of cake. In our contemporary digital age, this minority will need to learn to resist the temptation to believe that all knowledge can be immediately obtained by searching the Net. As Nicholas Carr puts it:

> The Net's interactivity gives us powerful new tools for finding information, expressing ourselves and conversing with others. It also turns us into lab rats constantly pressing levers to get tiny pellets of social or intellectual nourishment. (2010: 117)

A great deal will always depend upon your willingness to complete the hard, detailed work that a PhD dissertation demands.

8 WRAPPING UP

The number of students registered for courses involving a research dissertation has increased hugely over the past few decades. One good consequence of this has been that supervision has increasingly become recognized as a professional skill which requires proper training and monitoring.

Of course, getting a PhD, or even an MA, should never be achieved via any methods resembling factory mass production. I hope that there will always be a place for inspiration and lateral thinking. But such features of intellectual achievement should not be a substitute for an institutional structure that offers proper student support and guidance. Let us hope that Bradbury's three-meeting supervisor is a thing of the past!

What You Need to Remember

- Some students have terrible experiences of supervision. By understanding what produced these 'horror stories', you can try to avoid them happening in your case.
- It is not unreasonable to have a set of clear expectations about the support and advice which your supervisor can offer (and to know what to do if these expectations are not met).
- Supervisors have a set of expectations about you too. Know what they are and try to meet them.
- Your department should have structures of training and of monitoring supervision which offer you the support you need.

Your Chapter Checklist

- Discuss with your supervisor what they expect of you.
- Ask to record supervisions.
- Ask for a written note of what came out of each supervision.

TRACK:
EFFECTIVE SUPERVISIONS

Exercises

Exercise 1: Assess your relationship with your supervisor

If you are beginning your research, ask your supervisor for a meeting to review the contents of Tables 11.3 and 11.4. Check whether these features fit your supervisor's view of your relationship.

APPLY:
YOUR EXERCISE WORKBOOK

Exercise 2: Work with your supervisor to understand your project

Here are a few activities which you might ask your supervisor to think about doing with you (adapted from Becker, 1998):

1. Offering a snap characterization of your work which you can, if you wish, deny and thereby be helped to get a better understanding of what you are doing.
2. Challenging any generalization that you come up with by asking 'Or else what?' You will then probably find that something you thought impossible (about your topic) happens all the time.

3.   Cutting through purely theoretical characterizations of your work by giving you a limited task which asks you to begin from one situation or datum and then to theorize through it.

Further Reading

Howard S. Becker's book *Tricks of the Trade* (University of Chicago Press, 1998) is a beautifully written account of a lifetime of helping research students to think critically. It is appropriate for both MA and PhD students. For PhD students, Estelle Phillips and Derek Pugh's *How to Get a PhD* (Open University Press, 2005) is a gold mine of practical advice. Another useful guide is Harriet Churchill and Teela Sanders's *Getting Your PhD* (Sage, 2007: especially Chapter 15).

Discover the chapter's
digital resources in your
SILVERMAN FIELD GUIDE

TWELVE
Getting Feedback

Learning Outcomes

By the end of this chapter you will be able to:

- Understand the importance of feedback on your work.
- Recognize and organize opportunities for feedback.
- Understand the nature and importance of shaping your work with an audience in mind.

1 INTRODUCTION

Analysing research data and writing up our findings are never solitary activities – although this is certainly how they can seem as we labour in front of our PC screen in the small hours. In practice, researching involves entering a series of social relationships. These include supervisor with supervisee; student with student; student with members of the wider academic community; and student researcher with research subjects in the field.

As we saw in the previous chapter, such relationships need not just be viewed as potential or real sources of 'trouble'. Instead, they can and should be treated as important sources of insight into how well we are practising our research skills. Effective feedback is an essential resource for effective research. As two psychologists have put it:

> Adults learn best in situations where they can practise and receive feedback, in a controlled, non-threatening environment. So a good principle to aim for is: no procedure, technique, skill, etc., which is relevant for your thesis project should be exercised by you there for the first time. (Phillips and Pugh, 1994: 52)

Non-threatening feedback can also work if your writing seems to have dried up. 'Writer's block' is something we all experience from time to time. So don't despair. If you can't face feedback, I have found that a complete break for a week or two usually works (for more discussion of writer's block, including solutions, see Ward, 2002: 96–100).

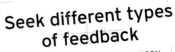

Seek different types of feedback

WATCH: DAVID EXPLAINS IN PERSON

David's Top Tip 27

Effective feedback is essential for good research. Seek feedback not just from your supervisor but from other students and from conference audiences.

In this chapter, I will discuss three means of obtaining feedback on your research:

*   writing draft papers
*   giving oral presentations
*   reporting back to the people you study.

2 WRITING

Delivering papers on agreed topics at regular intervals to your supervisor is the standard university method of working towards a final piece of assessed research. Constructive feedback from your supervisor can encourage you to scale new heights. By contrast, where that feedback is minimal or even destructive, your whole enterprise may be threatened.

So, if your supervisor is very critical of a paper you have submitted, you should expect to be told how you can improve your work and to be offered practical suggestions rather than woolly generalities. For instance, being told to think 'more critically' or to 'be more rigorous' is unlikely to be helpful. By contrast, specific advice about a new topic or a different way of pursuing one of your existing topics should give you some useful impetus (see Chapter 11).

But your supervisor is not the only person who can give you useful feedback on your work. Your fellow students, particularly those working in similar areas, should be delighted to provide feedback. In return, they will learn about related work and have the opportunity to test their ideas out on you.

Sometimes you will need to take the initiative to form such a student support group. Sometimes, as I do with my own research students, your supervisor will organize workshops for students working on similar topics or using similar methods to present and discuss their data. In either case, you will gain the opportunity to test out preliminary ideas in a non-threatening environment.

Writing for your peers or speaking to them is wonderful practice at getting the correct level for your thesis. The great temptation in writing up what may be your first piece of serious research is to try to achieve an exalted level of technical language in order to impress your supervisor. Unfortunately, this attempt often leads to clumsy jargon which clouds your real line of argument and confuses your readers.

In discussing writing a thesis, Wolcott wisely addresses this issue of the level at which you write:

> Write for your peers. Pitch the level of discussion to an audience of readers who do not know what you are talking about. Write your dissertation with fellow graduate students in mind, not your learned committee members. Address your subsequent studies to the many who do not know, not the few who do. (1990: 47)

Contrary to appearances, Wolcott's injunction 'write for your peers' is not a cop-out. For many researchers, the most difficult thing to do is to write with such clarity that their work can be understood and enjoyed by non-specialists. Indeed, for some researchers, the hardest thing to grasp is that writing should always be tailored for as big an audience as possible. This means thinking about what that audience may know already and expect from you. Naturally, the same applies to oral presentations.

Writing can also include creating your own website. This helps to give your work a public profile and make contact with research participants or other stakeholders (see Phelps et al., 2007: 123–5).

3 SPEAKING

You should take every opportunity to present your research at any setting that arises from an informal meeting of fellow students, to interested laypeople, to a scientific conference in your field. Watch out for 'calls for papers' and regularly inspect the sites where they are posted. However, when you give your talk, everything may go terribly wrong.

Paul Edwards (2004) has described something that we have all experienced. He calls it: 'the awful academic talk'. The features of this talk are familiar to anyone who has attended an academic conference or a university seminar:

> The speaker approaches the head of the room and sits down at the table. (You can't see him/her through the heads in front of you.) S/he begins to read from a paper, speaking in a soft monotone. (You can hardly hear. Soon you're nodding off.) Sentences are long, complex, and filled with jargon. The speaker emphasizes complicated details. (You rapidly lose the thread of the talk.) With five minutes left in the session, the speaker suddenly looks at his/her watch. S/he announces – in apparent surprise – that s/he'll have to omit the most important points because time is running out. S/he shuffles papers, becoming flustered and confused. (You do too, if you're still awake.) S/he drones on. Fifteen minutes after the scheduled end of the talk, the host reminds the speaker to finish for the third time. The speaker trails off inconclusively and asks for questions. (Thin, polite applause finally rouses you from dreamland.) (2004: 1)

This chapter aims to help you to avoid presenting this kind of awful, soporific talk. But first we need to know what lies behind such poor presentations. Stupidity is rarely the reason. Poor presenters are unlikely to be stupid. Instead, as Edwards suggests, we need to find an answer to the puzzle of 'why … otherwise brilliant people give such soporific talks' (2004: 1). Edwards comes up with two good answers to this question:

- fear: reading a paper seems to offer you a suit of armour which can conceal your stage fright
- academic culture, which erroneously equates oral presentations with 'giving a paper'.

A solution is to tailor what you say for your audience. However, even then, you may make the wrong judgement about what your audience expects or wants.

Consider your audience

WATCH: DAVID EXPLAINS IN PERSON

David's Top Tip 28

Before you give a talk, try to learn what kinds of things will be relevant to your audience. Try to attend other researchers' talks and see what kind of things get good responses from listeners.

Early on in my academic career, I was invited to talk about my research at a seminar at another university. I had already grasped the need to tailor my remarks to a particular audience and so had prepared two different talks on my research.

One was highly specialist, the other was non-technical. Unfortunately, on that day, I had misjudged my audience and brought with me what turned out to be the 'wrong' talk. Faced with a heavyweight group of specialists, I was insufficiently experienced to improvise and was forced to present the 'Mickey Mouse' version of my research!

I still cringe when I think of this experience. However, although I failed embarrassingly on this occasion, I had at least been partially correct in my method: I had attempted to prepare a talk with an audience in mind (see Cryer, 1996: 133).

When you speak, tailor what you say for your audience. Just as we design our ordinary conversation for particular recipients (children, colleagues, etc.), so recipient design should always go into your oral presentations. As Gary Marx comments:

> Try to remember who you are talking to, and the differential stake you and your audience have in your topic. Gear your talk to your audience. (1997: 107)

Following Marx, you will clearly want to give different kinds of talks to experts in your field, to participants in your research, and to general but non-specialist academic audiences. For each audience, you should choose a particular focus (e.g. theory, method, substance) and an appropriate vocabulary (see Strauss and Corbin, 1990: 226–9). Table 12.1 is a useful guide about how to prepare your work for different audiences.

Table 12.1   Speaking to an audience

1	Get to know the audience and what they are interested in (find out who is likely to attend; listen to how they respond to earlier speakers)
2	Reconnoitre the facilities (arrive early, check your slides will display correctly and see if you will need a microphone)
3	Give yourself a limited ambition (decide on the most important point you want to convey and stick to it)
4	Rehearse your talk before you deliver it
5	Reflect on your natural speaking speed and think whether you need to slow down or speed up

Source: adapted from Collins (2012), Braun and Clarke (2013) and Gray (2014)

However, such recipient design is insufficient. Many have had the experience of speakers who only have time to get through a small part of their material or who overrun and then use up the time for questions. Good time management is a quality possessed by effective speakers. If you think you will not have the confidence to improvise to beat the clock, then it is wise to try out your talk beforehand with a watch nearby.

The usual experience is that it takes far longer to get through your material than you expect. So take the minimum of material in one file and, if necessary, bring a 'comfort blanket' of additional material in another file to use in the unlikely event that you need it. Bear in mind the wise advice below if time runs out:

> If you find that you are running out of time, do not speed up. The best approach is normally to abort the presentation of your findings ... and move straight to your conclusion. (Watts and White, 2000: 445)

Finally, never read out a talk (2000: 444). I know that having your full script is a source of comfort. As Marx puts it:

> The fact that you get only one chance with a live audience may engender anxiety and the written word is a safety net. But it has a pre-determined, even stultifying quality, which denies the fluid and interactive nature of live presentations. (1997: 107)

But think back to all those boring talks you have attended in which the speaker had his head buried in his script. Do you really want to inflict that on your audience? More positively: 'You will never know what verbal riffs lie buried in your consciousness if you always cling to the security of the page' (1997: 107). Instead, try to present your points through uncluttered visual aids (PowerPoint slides, overhead projector transparencies). Where you need to provide extensive material (e.g. long transcripts or tables), then distribute handouts.

Try to present your points through effective, uncluttered visual aids. Take on board the following wise suggestions about PowerPoint slides (adapted from Edwards, 2004: 2):

- Keep each slide concise (six lines of text as a maximum).
- If you need more space, use more slides.
- Reveal each point on a slide in turn as you speak about it.
- Pictures or other images help keep your audience interested.
- Don't talk to the screen.
- Have a paper version of your talk in front of you.
- Don't just read out slides but illustrate with interesting examples.

Table 12.2   Good and bad presentation techniques

Usually better	Usually worse
Talk	Read
Stand	Sit
Move	Stand still
Vary voice pitch	Speak in a monotone
Speak loudly and clearly towards the audience	Mumble facing downwards
Make eye contact with the audience	Stare at the podium
Focus on main arguments	Get lost in details
Use visual aids: outlines, pictures, graphs	Have no visual aids
Finish the talk within the time limit (corollary: rehearse the talk)	Run over time (don't practise)
Summarize the main arguments at beginning and end	Fail to provide a conclusion
Notice your audience and respond to their needs	Ignore audience behaviour

Source: Edwards (2004: 2)

Table 12.2 summarizes much of what I have been saying so far.

Above all, try to grab your audience's attention at the outset. There are many tactics you can use at the start of your talk:

- Begin with a puzzle, as in a detective novel.
- Start with an interesting data extract.
- Start with a personal anecdote about how you became interested in your topic.
- If you are not the first speaker, try to relate what you have to say to what has gone before.
- Tell an apposite witty story (but only if this comes naturally!).

Finally, remember that both you and your audience need to get something out of your talk. Avoid the temptation just to give talks based on finished chapters approved by your supervisor. If the chapter is really finished, what will you gain from audience feedback? A much better strategy is to send such a chapter to a journal (see Chapter 27).

Instead, try to use early work or working papers. Here the responses of your audience may well help you to see a way ahead. As Watts and White suggest:

in giving ... conference papers from your project ... present incomplete work. In this way, you can seek guidance from your audience and receive stimulus for thinking about the next stage of your work ... In your paper you can direct the discussion towards particular issues on which you would like other people's opinions by drawing attention to them. (2000: 443)

4 THE ART OF PRESENTING RESEARCH

You will have gathered already that, in my view, even the most astounding research can sound dull if not properly presented. Unfortunately, this does not mean that poor research can be overlooked if you are a witty and effective speaker because you will eventually be found out! But effective presentation of good research should be your aim.

To flesh out the bare bones of my argument, I have taken extracts from my reports on presentations by research students completing their first year in my own department. Naturally, to protect the innocent, I have given these students false names.

Each student was allowed up to 15 minutes to make a presentation to their fellow students on their progress during their first year and their plans for further work. A further 10–15 minutes were allowed for questions.

Just as we tend to preface 'bad' news by 'good' news when giving information in everyday life, let me begin by some reports of 'good' practice. Below are some extracts from my reports.

Good practice

- Pat's talk was lively and clear, making good use of slides. She responded well to questions. This was a well-focused presentation, lively and interesting. The handouts were helpful and the video data were fascinating.
- Derek gave a lively and relatively clear talk, making good use of his slides. He spoke with some humour, gave an 'agenda' to his audience and explained the difficulties of his project.
- This was highly professional with good use of slides and handouts. Mary used her limited time well, managing to accommodate her talk to the 15 minutes available. Her answers to questions were most effective, giving me the impression that she is already in control of her topic.
- This was a well-focused presentation, lively and interesting. Sasha's answers to questions were good. Overall, I felt this was an excellent presentation based upon a piece of highly professional research. My views seem to be shared by the students present, one of whom remarked that she hoped her own work would be up to this standard in a year or two's time. Congratulations are due to Sasha and her supervisor.
- This was a well-focused presentation, lively and interesting and improvised rather than read. The audience's attention was held throughout. Ray's answers to questions were thoughtful and helpful. In particular, he was able to establish a dialogue with students from a range of backgrounds and was at home responding to theoretical and practical issues. I especially liked Ray's attempt to derive methodological issues from the data analysis. There were time problems from which Ray will have learned something. Overall, I felt this was an excellent presentation based upon a piece of highly professional research.

Summary

The following qualities impressed me in these presentations:

- liveliness
- not reading out a prepared text
- recipient design for the audience
- clarity
- effective visual aids
- humour
- explaining your agenda
- not minimizing difficulties
- good time management
- good response to questions.

Now for the 'bad' news!

Bad practice

- John was hampered by lack of preparation. His extempore presentation may have confused the audience by introducing too many topics and using too many examples which were not fully explained. His habit of turning his back on the audience to address the (empty) blackboard was unfortunate and, I am afraid, added to the impression of a non-user-friendly talk. This is disappointing given John's breadth of reading and excellent understanding. I think the only solution is to work harder on trying to relate his concerns to the interests and knowledge of particular audiences.
- This was an interesting presentation. However, Bruce made things a little difficult for his audience by offering no initial agenda, by not using visual aids and by having only one copy of some data extracts. He also ran into time problems which better planning could have obviated. This presentation will have given him the opportunity in future talks to think through his objectives and to offer more user-friendly methods.
- This was probably too specialized for a mixed audience, although Larry responded clearly to questions. The talk blossomed when Larry departed from his script and gave a concrete example which brought to life the abstract concepts he was using. I strongly suggest that, in future, for such an audience, he uses more visual aids and then talks around them, using such helpful examples.

Summary

The following qualities concerned me in this group of presentations:

- lack of preparation
- too much material
- not looking at the audience
- lack of recipient design
- no agenda
- no visual aids
- poor time planning.

Most presentations fell between these extremes. I will conclude with some 'mixed' examples.

Mixed practice

- Maurice gave a clear presentation using handouts and slides. His delivery was good and appropriately recipient designed. My only suggestion is that he should try to put less material on each slide.
- Stan had taken the trouble to prepare handouts. However, it was disappointing that, perhaps because of time limitations, he did not have time to analyse the data provided. I would also have preferred him not to read out a paper. It is important to practise the art of talking using only a few props, like overheads, if you want to keep the audience's attention. Nonetheless, Stan's talk was well organized and timed and he offered interesting responses to questions, showing a pleasing ability to admit when he was unsure about a point.

- As in an earlier talk, this was very professional, combining good slides with helpful illustrations from video and audiotape. My only suggestion is that it might be helpful to give more guidance to the audience about the issues to look for before offering data.
- Mary gave a confident, well-prepared talk based on a handout. She responded well to questions. My only suggestion is that, in future, she works more on integrating any handout with her talk so that her audience are not confused about what they should be attending to at any one time.
- Yoko had thoughtfully prepared overheads but these were not as clearly related to her talk as they might have been. Although it is always very difficult to speak in one's second language, it is difficult to keep the audience's attention when a paper is read. In my view, it is worth Yoko practising at giving presentations simply by talking around her slides. One way to do this would be to focus on the nice examples of texts and images that she presented and to pull out her analytic and methodological points from them rather than to attempt to read a rather abstract paper.
- Julia gave an engaging, lively presentation which held her audience throughout. I liked her explanation of the personal reasons behind her research and admired her ability to speak without notes. Her slides were useful. Some minor suggestions for future talks: remember to avoid turning away from the audience to look at the screen; think about using other information sources as well as slides (handouts of definitions would have been useful); try out a talk beforehand so as to avoid time problems.
- This was an interesting talk which carefully explained the issues involved for a non-specialist audience. Jane's account of how her interest in the topic 'coalesced' was very useful as were her slides (although, in future, she should note that these can be most effectively used by covering up parts of each slide until she gets on to them). She ran into some time difficulties and this is also something to watch in future. Overall, a good account of a fascinating topic.
- Luigi made a good attempt to explain a difficult topic to a non-specialist audience. I particularly liked his account of his intellectual and personal background. In future, he will need to pay more attention to explaining his concepts and to time constraints.

Summary

The following were the 'good' and 'bad' news about these presentations:

- using visual aids but these are poorly prepared
- well organized but reading out a prepared text
- giving examples of data but not explaining what to look for
- using handouts but not integrating them in the talk
- explaining the background but not explaining the concepts used
- using visual aids but turning away to look at them or having too much material on the screen.

Good and bad presentations

Take your oral presentations as seriously as you do your writing. Speak to your audience with clarity, logic, vigor, and examples that will grab them. (Marx, 1997: 107)

In Table 12.3 I set out what we have learnt about making an effective oral presentation of your research.

Table 12.3   Giving a talk: problems and solutions

Problem	Solution
Losing your audience	Recipient design
Overrunning	Don't prepare too much material
Boring your audience	Use visual aids: don't read out a talk

Giving a talk is one way of networking, allowing you to make links with people both inside and outside your own department or university (see Churchill and Sanders, 2007: 95–104).

5 FEEDBACK FROM THE PEOPLE YOU STUDY

> The bottom line for practitioners is always, 'So what?' A qualitative researcher's efforts to convey nonjudgmental objectivity is likely to be perceived instead as a typical academic cop-out. (Wolcott, 1990: 59)

Not least among the people who can offer you feedback are the persons you have studied. Let me give you an example from my research on HIV-test counselling (Silverman, 1997). In order to address practitioners' 'So what?' questions, I held many workshops for AIDS counsellors – including many who had not participated in the study. To give some idea of the extent of this 'feedback', I ran four workshops on the research for counsellors in London (two at hospitals, one at Goldsmiths College and one at The Royal Society of Medicine), as well as three workshops in Australian centres, three in Trinidad and Tobago, and one each in the USA, Finland and Sweden. In addition, each participating centre was given a detailed report of our findings.

At these workshops, we did not shelter behind a posture of scientific neutrality. But neither did we seek to instruct counsellors about their presumed 'failings'. Instead, we spoke about the ways in which our data showed that all communication formats and techniques had mixed consequences. We then invited our audience to discuss, in the light of their own priorities and resources, the implications for their practice. Moreover, when asked, we were not afraid to suggest possible practical options.

In my judgement, these meetings were successful, not least because our detailed transcripts showed features of counselling of which the practitioners themselves were often unaware. Often such features revealed how these people were cleverer than they had realized in following their own theoretical precepts and achieving their desired goals.

However, less experienced researchers may be more hesitant to offer feedback to practitioners and organizations. In this case, Wolcott (1990) offers the three ideas set out in Table 12.4.

Table 12.4   Giving feedback to service providers

1   Ask for the kind of additional information required for you to make a recommendation (e.g. what exactly is the organization trying to accomplish?)
2   Identify seeming paradoxes in the pursuit of goals (e.g. doctors who encourage their patients to communicate and to make choices may be the most autocratic)
3   Identify alternatives to current practices and offer to assess these

Source: Wolcott (1990: 60)

Of course, not all qualitative research is concerned with service providers such as organizations or professional practitioners. What kind of feedback is possible when you are studying non-work-related activities?

It is important that you try to offer feedback to all parties that are under study. So, if your target is, say, the activities of counsellors or doctors, then you have not finished your task without offering some degree of feedback to their clients or patients. One way to do this is to utilize already existing networks, for example patients' or community groups. So during my work on paediatric consultations I spoke to parents' groups at heart and diabetic clinics. For instance, I used my clinic data to show mothers of diabetic adolescents that their feelings of inadequacy were common and probably inevitable given the guilt-provoking character of diabetic control and the usual rebelliousness of teenagers.

Where it is difficult to identify such community groups, you may well find that participants in a study welcome receiving their own transcript of relevant data. For instance, a transcript of their own medical interview may work as a useful reminder of what the doctor said. And a transcript of a life-history interview may give a respondent a tangible autobiographical record.

Obviously, you can learn from such feedback to participants. But it is not always the case that respondent validation does really validate your findings (see Chapter 17, Section 2).

6 WRAPPING UP

Why does feedback matter? There are two reasons why student researchers write papers and give talks:

- to pass some internal assessment
- to get feedback on their work.

Unfortunately, in our assessment-obsessed university culture, students tend to forget that feedback from peers and advanced scholars serves both normative and instrumental ends.

In a normative sense, offering material for feedback recognizes the community of scholars to which scientific work aspires. Instrumentally, such feedback will undoubtedly help improve your thesis. If you have long-term academic ambitions, it will also help you to improve your teaching skills and, perhaps, to plant the seeds of future journal articles!

So never think of this as 'mere' presentation or the 'boring' bit that has to be got through in order to get your degree. If we cannot use our research to engage others in dialogue, maybe we are in the wrong business!

What You Need to Remember

Effective feedback is an essential resource for effective research. This chapter has discussed three means of obtaining feedback on your research:

- by writing draft papers
- by giving oral presentations
- by setting up online discussion groups with other researchers.

Writing should always be tailored for as big an audience as possible, and this means thinking about what that audience may know already and expect from you. So get feedback from fellow students as well as your supervisor and think about setting up your own website.

Attempt to give a talk on your research before you write a final version for your thesis. In this talk, avoid losing your audience (recipient design your presentation); set a time limit and never overrun; and use visual aids to avoid boring your audience.

Your Chapter Checklist

- Have you tried to find fellow students working in the area of your research?
- Have you looked for appropriate conferences to attend?
- Have you presented a paper on your research?
- What have you learnt about how to improve your research and how to do better presentations?

TRACK:
GETTING GOOD FEEDBACK

Exercises

Exercise 1: Build an external support network for your project

This exercise is meant to help you find support outside your university.

APPLY:
YOUR EXERCISE WORKBOOK

- Type your research topic into an Internet search engine.
- Find out other research students working on similar topics.
- Get in touch with them and offer to review their data or papers in return for help with your own work.
- Think about setting up an online discussion group where you post news about your research and details of any useful readings and conferences.

Exercise 2: Explore how published research targets cater to certain audiences

Select two articles in your area of research from two different journals or books. Work out the audience(s) at which the journal or book is aimed by reading the journal's 'instructions to contributors' or a book's introductory editorial chapter. Then go through the steps below:

1. In what way does each article attempt to reach its appropriate audience(s)?
2. How successful is it in doing so?
3. How could it be improved to appeal more to its target audience(s)?

Exercise 3: Practice explaining your research to an audience

Get invited to give a talk on your research and make sure that somebody attends who is prepared to give you good feedback. Plan the talk to reach the audience (e.g. students, staff, laypeople or a mixture). Having given your talk, ask the attending person for feedback on the success of your talk. Then consider how you could have improved the talk to appeal more to its target audience.

Further Reading

Harry Wolcott's little book *Writing Up Qualitative Research* (Sage, 2009) covers feedback as well as many other practical matters. Pat Cryer's *The Research Student's Guide to Success* (Open University Press, 2006: Chapter 13), David Gray's *Doing*

Research in the Real World (Sage, 2014: 659–78) and Doug Watts and Paul White's chapter 'Presentation skills' in Dawn Burton's edited book *Research Training for Social Scientists* (Sage, 2000: 437–55) discuss giving presentations on your work. Renata Phelps et al.'s *Organizing and Managing Your Research* (Sage, 2007: 263–8) provides very useful advice on using software in your presentations. Gary Marx's paper 'Of methods and manners for aspiring sociologists: 37 moral imperatives' (*The American Sociologist*, Spring 1997: 102–25) is a lively and extremely helpful guide for the apprentice researcher.

EXPLORE: GUIDE TO GOOD PRESENTATIONS
EXPLORE: PRESENTATION TIPS

Discover the chapter's digital resources in your
SILVERMAN FIELD GUIDE

CONTENTS

PART IV
COLLECTING AND ANALYSING YOUR DATA

Part IV moves you on to issues in data collection and analysis. Beginning researchers often worry about whether they have enough data. So Chapter 13 answers the question: how many cases do you need? In Chapter 14, I outline what is involved in collecting interview and fieldwork data. Chapter 15 discusses how to develop your data analysis by working early with datasets. The next two chapters in this part of the book consider the use of computer-aided qualitative data analysis and validity and reliability. Chapter 18 shows you how to apply what you have learned in Part III to evaluate qualitative research. Finally, Chapter 19 serves as a short summary of Parts I to III.

THIRTEEN
How Many Cases Do You Need?

Learning Outcomes

By the end of this chapter you will be able to:

- Understand what a case study is.
- Know the main types of case study.
- Recognize the theoretical basis of case study research.
- Understand how to generalize from a single case.

1 INTRODUCTION

I concluded Chapter 9 with my favourite research maxim: 'say a lot about a little'. If you take me seriously, you will have every chance of producing a thorough, analytically interesting research study. However, at least three nagging doubts may well remain. I list them below together with some soothing words about each:

- *My case may not be important.* Here you are worried that the case you are studying may be seen by others as 'trivial' or 'not a real problem'. The famous ethnographer Howard Becker remarks that such criticisms have been made of his own work on several occasions. As he puts it: 'Just as some people think tragedy is more important than comedy ... some problems are seen as inherently serious and worthy of grownup attention, others as trivial, flyspecks on the wall-paper of life ... mere exotica' (1998: 92). There is a very good response to this kind of complaint: that is, what seems to be important is usually governed by little more than current fashions; who knows what might become important? Apparently trivial cases may, through good analysis, turn out to have far-reaching implications.

- *I can only study the (part of the) case to which I have access.* This is a more serious issue. When we are studying an organization, we are dependent on the whims of **gatekeepers**. Such people will usually seek to limit what we can study, assuring us that, if we need to know more, they can

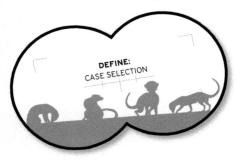

tell us about it (1998: 90). How do we get round this problem? Becker suggests two answers: first, 'doubt everything anyone in power tells you'; second, 'look for other opinions' (1998: 91). Like Mel Dalton (1959), in his classic study of middle managers, case study researchers should systematically attempt to assess the likely linkages between opinions, activities and interests.

- *I have so little data, just one case.* This worries many beginning researchers. As we shall see below, even in qualitative research it is important to consider what kind of generalizations can be made from a single case.

2 WHAT IS A CASE STUDY?

This question has a relatively simple answer. As Punch puts it:

> The basic idea is that one case (or perhaps a small number of cases) will be studied in detail, using whatever methods seem appropriate. While there may be a variety of specific purposes and research questions, the general objective is to develop as full an understanding of that case as possible. (1998: 150)

There is, of course, an endless variety of possible 'cases'. Business researchers tend to treat each organization as a 'case' and, given their focus on business organizations, usually use the term 'case study research' as a synonym for qualitative research. If, like Becker, you are interested in occupations, cases to study may range from dancehall musicians to student physicians. By contrast, if you are interested in childhood, a case may be a single child, a classroom or clinic, or a charity concerned with the welfare of children. So, as Stake suggests: 'A case may be simple or complex ... [but] it is one among others. In any given study, we will concentrate on the one' (2000: 436).

All this is purely descriptive. Table 13.1 identifies three analytic features of case study research.

Table 13.1   Case study research

1	Each case has boundaries which must be identified at an early stage of the research (e.g. if you are studying a school, whether this includes classroom behaviour, staff meetings, parent-teacher meetings, etc.)
2	Each case will be a case of something in which the researcher is interested. So the unit of analysis must be defined at the outset in order to clarify the research strategy
3	Case studies seek to preserve the wholeness and integrity of the case. However, in order to achieve some focus, a limited research problem must be established that is geared to specific features of the case

Source: adapted from Punch (1998: 153)

Stake (2000: 437–8) has identified three different types of case study:

1. The *intrinsic case study* where 'this case is of interest ... in all its particularity and ordinariness'. In the intrinsic case study, according to Stake, no attempt is made to generalize beyond the single case or even to build theories.
2. The *instrumental case study* in which a case is examined mainly to provide insight into an issue or to revise a generalization. Although the case selected is studied in depth, the main focus is on something else.
3. The *collective case study* where a number of cases are studied in order to investigate some general phenomenon.

The idea of a purely intrinsic case study is resisted by many qualitative researchers. If all you aim to do is simply to 'describe a case', you may rightly get the response: 'So what?' Such scepticism arises from the following concerns:

- Description is a tricky activity which is inevitably theoretically laden (if you doubt this, you might look back at Table 7.1).
- To call something a 'case' implies that it is a case of 'something', so we can only understand the distinctiveness of a case by making theoretical assumptions about what is typical for a certain population.
- Given how behaviour varies in different contexts, we need to understand how any one setting may be different from others (see Gobo, 2008: 97-8).

In this context, most supervisors of student qualitative research would expect your study of a case to be based upon some concept(s) which are developed as a result of your study. For examples of concept development through case study research, see Chapter 3.

Furthermore, empirical issues arise in case studies just as much as theoretical concerns. It is reasonable to ask what knowledge your case study has produced.

If you are to answer this question, you must consider the degree of **generalizability** of your research. As Mason puts it:

> I do not think qualitative researchers should be satisfied with producing explanations which are idiosyncratic or particular to the limited empirical parameters of their study ... Qualitative research should [therefore] produce explanations which are *generalizable* in some way, or which have a wider resonance. (1996: 6)

So description of a case for description's sake (the intrinsic case study) is a weak position. Quite rightly, the problem of 'representativeness' is a perennial worry of many qualitative or case study researchers. Take a look at these student examples (with my answers in italics):

- Rikke is studying the rehabilitation of patients with traumatic brain injury and asks: 'Can my finding be transferred to other settings and patient groups?'
  Raise this question in your concluding chapter; only further research can tell us whether the processes you have observed recur with other patient groups and other settings.
- Martijn is studying how multinational organizations respond to the campaigns of voluntary organizations and asks: 'How many case studies should I ideally aim to use?'
  Unlike quantitative research, there is no formula available to decide how many cases to use. Instead, see what you can find in a single organization and only then decide which, if any, further organizations you need to study.
- Neil is interviewing planning officials about how they take account of local concerns. He asks: 'How can I respond to criticisms that if I'd interviewed a different bunch of people, I might have come up with different conclusions?'
  In qualitative research, we are not trying to generalize to populations but to identify social processes. If we wanted to talk about populations, we should do a quantitative survey.
- Daniel is looking at how public sector organizations use social media and asks: 'I am studying two organizations and have some difficulties developing a strong argument for my selection of cases'.
  Which organizations we study is usually due to chance factors like access. Stick with what you have and see what you can discover in those settings.

Are you generalizing or identifying?

WATCH: DAVID EXPLAINS IN PERSON

David's Top Tip 29

We often worry about generalizing because we are asking the wrong sort of questions. If you want to answer a 'why' question, you usually should design a quantitative study. By contrast, if you want to ask 'what?' or 'how?', then qualitative research is appropriate. In this case, you are seeking to identify a social process and *not* generalizing to a population.

My answers are expanded in the rest of this chapter which will be devoted to the issue of generalizability in case study research.

3 THE QUANTITATIVE MODEL OF GENERALIZATION

Generalizability is a standard aim in quantitative research and is normally achieved by statistical sampling procedures. Such sampling has two functions. First, it allows you to feel confident about the representativeness of your sample: 'If the population characteristics are known, the degree of representativeness of a sample can be checked' (Arber, 1993: 70). Second, such representativeness allows you to make broader inferences: 'The purpose of sampling is usually to study a representative subsection of a precisely defined population in order to make inferences about the whole population' (1993: 38).

Such sampling procedures are, however, usually unavailable in qualitative research. In such studies, our data is often derived from one or more cases and it is unlikely that these cases will have been selected on a random basis. Very often a case will be chosen simply because it allows access. This gives rise to a problem, familiar to users of quantitative methods: 'How do we know … how representative case study findings are of all members of the population from which the case was selected?' (Bryman, 1988: 88).

Gobo has neatly summed up these concerns:

> Even though qualitative methods are now recognized in the methodological literature, they are still regarded with skepticism by some methodologists, mainly those with statistical training. One reason for this skepticism concerns whether qualitative research results can be generalized, which is doubted not only because they are derived from only a few cases, but also because even where a larger number is studied these are generally selected without observing the rigorous criteria of statistical sampling theory. (2007: 193)

As a consequence, students doing qualitative research sometimes try to sample whole populations or, where this is impractical, try to construct random samples. Two student examples are provided below. As you will see, rather than making your study more generalizable, adopting this kind of defensive posture can create further problems for the qualitative researcher.

WHAT I DID: TWO SRI LANKAN STUDENTS

Using Large or Random Samples

In one interview study of unqualified medical practitioners, one province district was selected and included 10 (out of 14) practitioners who gave their consent and 350 of their patients.

A second study of 'burnout' among female primary school teachers used a sample of 15 teachers who were randomly selected from the participants of a much larger, quantitative, prevalence study.

Both studies, modelled on quantitative research design, create further difficulties:

- Can detailed qualitative methods of analysis be fully used if you do 350 interviews? Apart from anything else, will you have time to transcribe your data properly? Data gathering may be so time consuming that you have little time for data analysis.
- In the second example, do you really need a fully random selection of cases in order to do credible qualitative research? Should we reject a case just because it is the only one to which we have access even if it looks highly illuminating?

Ultimately, the question 'How many cases do I need?' depends upon your research problem and purposive sampling may be appropriate.

How can we escape this defensive posture with its unintended side effects? The first thing to realize is that the logic of random sampling may not work in qualitative research or may simply be inappropriate. The reasons for this are set out in Table 13.2.

Table 13.2   The problematic use of probability samples in social research

- The difficulty of finding sampling frames (lists of population) for certain population subsets when these frames are often not available. The majority of studies on particular segments of the population cannot make use of population lists: consider studies on blue-collar workers, the unemployed, homeworkers, artists, immigrants, housewives, pensioners, football supporters, members of political movements, charity workers, elderly people living alone, and so on
- The phenomenon of non-response: account must be taken of the gap (which varies according to the research project) between the initial sample (all the individuals about whom we want to collect information) and the final sample (the cases about which we have been able to obtain information); the two sets may correspond, but usually some of the subjects in the first sample are not surveyed
- Representativeness and generalizability are not two sides of the same coin: the former is a property of the sample, while the latter concerns the findings of research

Source: adapted from Gobo (2007: 194)

4 THE RATIONALE OF CASE STUDY DESIGN

The logic of case study design is *not* modelled on how quantitative researchers select samples. Five issues are relevant here. In case study research:

- We generalize to theoretical propositions, not to populations.
- We sample social relations, not individuals.

- We can test theories by choosing extreme or deviant cases.
- We can choose new cases during our research, confident that this is not problematic but expected and useful.
- We stop gathering more cases, when we repeatedly find the same answers ('data saturation').

I will now review each argument.

Theoretical generalizations

In qualitative research, our choice of cases should always be theoretically guided. This means that our selection of cases is not based on statistical grounds but derived from a particular theory which we seek to test. As Robert Yin argues:

> case studies, like experiments, are generalizable to theoretical propositions and not to populations or universes. In this sense, the case study, like the experiment, does not represent a 'sample', and, *in doing a case study, your goal will be to expand and generalize theories (analytic generalization) and not to enumerate frequencies (statistical generalization).* (2009: 15, my emphasis)

Take my study of HIV-test counselling, discussed in Chapter 9, Section 4. This study was based on the theoretical tradition of conversation analysis (CA). So, although I tried to include counselling centres from different countries and with a varying mix of professional expertise, I was not trying to count how many counsellors or clients engaged in particular activities. Instead, my sample was designed to test previous CA-based generalizations about professional–client communication. Gobo (2007: 204) calls this kind of theoretically based reasoning deductive inference.

Sampling social relations, not individuals

Quantitative surveys usually sample individuals. In most social science research, we are more concerned with situations. This means that our research design is quite different. As Clive Seale puts it:

> many textbooks assume that when one is going to do a research study one always wants to sample 'people' (rather than, say, documents). Students should realise that all kinds of phenomena can be studied for social research purposes (e.g. building design, music lyrics, websites, small ads etc.). (Personal correspondence)

Gobo underlines Seale's point:

> The [qualitative] researcher should focus his/her investigation on interactive units (such as social relationships, encounters, organizations), not only because social processes are more easily detectable and observable, but also because these units allow more direct and deeper analysis of the characteristics observed. (2007: 203-4)

Choosing extreme or deviant cases

'One rationale for a single case is when it represents the *critical case* in testing a well-formulated theory' (Yin, 2009: 47). This allows us to make generalizations similar to statistical inferences but without employing probability criteria. Gobo offers the following example of the value of choosing an extreme case to test a theoretically based generalization:

> We can choose two elementary schools where, from press reports, previous studies, interviews or personal experiences, we know we can find two extreme situations: in the first school there are severe difficulties of integration between pupils of natives and immigrant parents, while in the second there are virtually none. We can also pick three schools: the first with severe integration difficulties; the second with average difficulties; and the third with rare ones … If, in these optimal conditions, the consequences foreseen by the theory do not ensue, it is extremely unlikely that the theory will work in all those empirical cases where those requirements are more weakly present. Hence the theory is falsified, and its inadequacy can be legitimately generalized … Moreover, the legitimacy of the generalization (of the scant explanatory capacity of the theory just falsified) depends not only on the cogency of the rhetorical argument but also on the strength of the connections established between theory and observations. (2007: 204-5)

Changing cases during research

Later on in this book (Chapter 15, Section 3) I discuss how, in my research on a medical clinic treating children with congenital heart disease, a chance finding about what happened to children with Down's syndrome in the clinic led me to seek further cases of consultations with such children. As Gobo puts it:

> It is … necessary to approach the entire question of sampling sequentially, and it would be misleading to plan the whole strategy beforehand. In order to achieve representativeness, the sampling plan must be set in *dialogue* with field incidents, contingencies, and discoveries … When the researcher has formulated hypotheses, s/he restarts sampling in order to collect cases systematically relating to each hypothesis, and seeking to make his/her analysis consistent. (2007: 207-8)

Gobo's comments have important consequences for qualitative research design. They mean that any research proposal should recognize that the number and nature of cases studied must be provisional. One cannot know fully how many or which cases to study until the data analysis is quite advanced. Mario Luis Small makes exactly this point:

> In a case model, the number of units (cases) is unknown until the study is completed; the collection of units is, by design, not representative ... The first unit or case yields a set of findings and a set of questions that inform the next case. If the study is conducted properly, the very last case examined will provide very little new or surprising information. The objective is saturation. (2009: 25)

Data saturation

Grounded theory resolves the question of how much data you need by instructing you to stop gathering more data when you keep finding the same things. Describing data saturation, Czarniawska suggests: 'When your field material (interviews, observations, documents collected) becomes repetitive, it is time to stop' (2014: 145).

5 CASE STUDY RESEARCH IN PRACTICE

In Section 4, we were concerned with the theoretical underpinnings of case study research. I now want to move on to how this works out in practice. What are the implications for case study design?

To answer this question, I will outline three ways of proceeding:

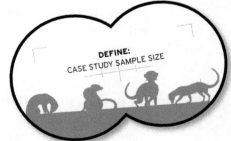

- purposive sampling guided by time and resources
- theoretical sampling
- working with a single case, using an analytic model which assumes that generalizability is present in the existence of *any* case.

Purposive sampling

Before we can contemplate comparing our case with others, we need to have selected our case. Are there any grounds other than convenience or accessibility to guide us in this selection?

Purposive sampling allows us to choose a case because it illustrates some feature or process in which we are interested. However, this does not provide a simple approval to any case we happen to choose. Rather, purposive sampling demands that we think critically about the parameters of the population we are studying and choose our sample case carefully on this basis. As Denzin and Lincoln put it:

'Many qualitative researchers employ ... purposive, and not random, sampling methods. They seek out groups, settings and individuals where ... the processes being studied are most likely to occur' (1994: 202).

WHAT I DID: ANASTACIA

Purposive Sampling in a Study of Native Americans

I first hoped to gain approval from a local tribe so I could conduct interviews on narrative identity. However, this proved too difficult. As established, Native Americans are an invisible group, in that they are not widely visible in general populations and are therefore difficult for researchers to contact. Additionally, Native American tribal groups who are located on reservations are sovereign nations. Therefore, they will not participate in scientific research without tribal government approval. For this thesis, I decided to make use of several untapped Internet resources provided by storytellers from a wide variety of tribal affiliations. I chose to look for online groups that were constructing a Native American identity through the processes of storytelling. Initially, I found a total of eight websites. I decided upon two affiliated websites that provide audio recordings and transcripts of their stories. The other six websites were not chosen because the stories featured were not directly told by Native Americans. [Anastacia M. Schulhoff, Department of Sociology, University of Missouri-Columbia]

With many more resources than Anastacia, Stake (2000: 446–7) gives the example of a study of interactive displays in children's museums. He assumes that you only have resources to study four such museums. How should you proceed? He suggests setting up a typology, which would establish a matrix of museum types as in Table 13.3. His typology yields six cases which could be increased further by, say, distinguishing between museums located in small and big cities – bringing the cases up to 12. Which cases should you select?

Table 13.3   A typology of children's museums

Programme type	Type of museum		
	Art	Science	History
Exhibitory	1	2	3
Participative	4	5	6

Source: adapted from Stake (2000: 446-7)

You will be constrained by two main factors. First, there may not be examples to fit every cell. Second, your resources will not allow you to research every existing unit. So you have to make a practical decision. For instance, if you can cover only two cases, do you choose two participatory museums in different locations or in different subjects? Or do you compare such a museum with a more conventional exhibit-based museum?

As a student researcher, your limited time and resources will usually determine how you settle these questions. However, the very fact that you have asked yourself these questions will satisfy most examiners.

Take the case of the mathematics teacher I met in Tanzania who was trying to design a qualitative study to discover what made maths lessons 'effective'. We came up with two factors that might be important here:

- the teaching style used (loosely 'traditional' or 'non-traditional')
- background features (school resources, staff turnover, parental support) which were likely to make maths lessons more or less 'effective'.

This suggested a simple 2 × 2 purposive sample as set out in Table 13.4. The simplicity of the research design set out in the table made for a study that showed the necessary critical thinking about the research problem and was achievable within the constraints of time and resources.

Table 13.4   A typology of mathematics lessons

	Teaching methods	
Background	Traditional	Non-traditional
Favourable	1	2
Unfavourable	3	4

However, in thinking through issues of sampling, we are following our quantitative colleagues. Before reading on, think what this student might gain from using a qualitative perspective on each of his 'cells'.

My answer to this question arises from the way in which the analytical models we use in qualitative research allow us to problematize matters that our quantitative colleagues may be compelled to take for granted or to settle prior to the commencement of research. In the context of this study, although our sample will be based upon prior assumptions, we can problematize:

- whether the categories 'traditional' and 'non-traditional' do justice to the variety of lessons we observe in the classroom
- what 'effective' education looks like in different contexts, so that we can go beyond scoring examination performance in each cell to considering how 'effectiveness' may be used as a rhetoric in settings as diverse as parent-teacher meetings, teacher promotion reviews and government documents.

In both cases, the beauty of qualitative research design is that it allows us to put 'scare marks' around apparently 'objective' concepts such as 'effectiveness'.

This shows that how you set up your typology and make your choice between cases should be grounded in the theoretical apparatus you are using. Sampling in qualitative research is neither statistical nor purely personal: it is, or should be, theoretically grounded.

Theoretical sampling

Theoretical sampling and purposive sampling are often treated as synonyms. Indeed, the only difference between the two procedures applies when the 'purpose' behind 'purposive' sampling is not theoretically defined.

Following what I previously suggested (p.267), Bryman argues that qualitative research follows a theoretical, rather than a statistical, logic: 'The issue should be couched in terms of the generalizability of cases to *theoretical* propositions rather than to *populations* or universes' (1988: 90, my emphasis).[1]

The nature of this link between sampling and theory is set out by Mason:

> theoretical sampling means selecting groups or categories to study on the basis of their relevance to your research questions, your theoretical position ... and most importantly the explanation or account which you are developing. Theoretical sampling is concerned with constructing a sample ... which is meaningful theoretically, because it builds in certain characteristics or criteria which help to develop and test your theory and explanation. (1996: 93-4)

Theoretical sampling has three features, which I discuss below:

1. Choosing cases in terms of your theory.
2. Choosing 'deviant' cases.
3. Changing the size of your sample during the research.

Choosing cases in terms of your theory

Mason writes about 'the wider universe of social explanations in relation to which you have constructed your research questions' (1996: 85). This theoretically defined universe 'will make some sampling choices more sensible and meaningful than others'. Mason describes choosing a kind of sample which can represent a wider population. Here we select a sample of particular 'processes, types, categories or examples which are relevant to or appear within the wider universe' (1996: 92). She suggests that examples of these would include single units such as 'an organization, a location, a document ... [or] a conversation'.

Mason gives the example of a discourse analysis of gender relations as discourses which construct subjects of gender relations. In this approach, as she puts it, 'You are … unlikely to perceive the social world in terms of a large set of gender relations from which you can simply draw a representative sample of people by gender' (1996: 85).

So in qualitative research the relevant or 'sampleable' units are often seen as theoretically defined. This means that it is inappropriate to sample populations by such attributes as 'gender', 'ethnicity' or even age because how such attributes are routinely defined is itself the *topic* of your research.

As an example of theoretically defined sampling, Bryman uses Glaser and Strauss's discussion of 'awareness contexts' in relation to dying in hospital:

> The issue of whether the particular hospital studied is 'typical' is not the critical issue; what is important is whether the experiences of dying patients are typical of the broad class of phenomena … to which the theory refers. Subsequent research would then focus on the validity of the proposition in other milieux (e.g. doctors' surgeries). (1988: 91)

We can understand better the theoretical logic behind choice of a sample in a further example of a study of police work. Say you are interested in the arrest and booking of suspects (see Miles and Huberman, 1984: 37–8). You are now confronted with a series of choices which relate to:

- the particular setting to be studied
- the elements or processes on which you will focus
- how you might generalize further.

Let us look at each of these in turn.

- *Settings*. In independent, unfunded research, you are likely to choose any setting which, while demonstrating the phenomenon in which you are interested, is accessible and will provide appropriate data reasonably readily and quickly. In a police study, this might well lead you to study the police station rather than a squad car, the scene of the crime, the suspect's residence or hangout. In the police station, at the very least, you will keep warm and dry, you will be safe and you can expect several arrests and bookings on any visit. However, so far you are being guided by quite practical influences.
- *The research focus*. In focusing your research, you necessarily are making a theoretically guided choice. By opting to focus on particular individuals, events or processes, you are electing particular theoretical frameworks. For instance, a focus on differential behaviour between police officers and suspects with different characteristics may draw on some version of the structural determinants of action. Conversely, a focus on how laws are interpreted in practice (cf. Sudnow, 1968b) may derive from a concern with the creative power of common-sense interpretive procedures.
- *Generalizing further*. When wedded to other studies which share your theoretical orientation, your research on a single police station may provide enough data to develop all the generalizations you want about, say, how common-sense reasoning works. However, if you have a more 'structural' bent, it may now be necessary to widen your sample in two ways: first, to add more observations of arrests in this police station; and second, to compare it with other stations, perhaps in a range of areas.

In all these cases, the sample is not random but theoretical. It is 'designed to provide a close-up, detailed or meticulous view of particular units which may constitute … cases which are relevant to or appear within the wider universe' (Mason, 1996: 92).

As Charmaz argues, this kind of 'theoretical sampling directs you where to go' (2006: 100) when you need to make further generalizations from the cases you have already selected.

Choosing 'deviant' cases

Mason notes that you must overcome any tendency to select a case which is likely to support your argument. Instead, it makes sense to seek out negative instances as defined by the theory with which you are working. For instance, in a study of the forces that may make trade unions undemocratic, Seymour Lipset et al. (1962) deliberately chose to study a US printing union. Because this union had unusually strong democratic institutions, it constituted a vital deviant case compared with most American unions of the period. Lipset et al.'s union was also deviant in terms of a highly respected theory which postulated an irresistible tendency towards 'oligarchy' in all formal organizations.

So Lipset et al. chose a deviant case because it offered a crucial test of a theory. As our understanding of social processes improves, we are increasingly able to choose cases on such theoretical grounds.

Expect the unexpected

WATCH: DAVID EXPLAINS IN PERSON

David's Top Tip 30

When designing your research, it is useful to contemplate the kind of experiences or situations that you initially think are most unlikely. One of Howard Becker's 'tricks of the trade' is: 'Just to insist that nothing that can be imagined is impossible, so we should look for the most unlikely things that we can think of and incorporate their existence, or the possibility of their existence, into our thinking' (1998: 85-6).

Changing the size of your sample during the research

So far we have been discussing theoretical sampling as an issue at the *start* of a research study. However, we can also apply such sampling during the course of a piece of research. Indeed, one of the strengths of qualitative research design is that it often allows for far greater (theoretically informed) flexibility than do most quantitative research designs. As Mason puts it:

> Theoretical or purposive sampling is a set of procedures where the researcher manipulates their analysis, theory, and sampling activities *interactively* during the research process, to a much greater extent than in statistical sampling. (1996: 100)

Such flexibility may be appropriate in the following cases:

- As new factors emerge you may want to increase your sample in order to say more about them (for instance, a gatekeeper has given you an explanation that you doubt on principle).
- You may want to focus on a small part of your sample in the early stages, using the wider sample for later tests of emerging generalizations.
- Unexpected generalizations in the course of data analysis lead you to seek out new deviant cases.

Alasuutari has described this process using the analogy of an hourglass:

> A narrow case-analysis is broadened ... through the search for contrary and parallel cases, into an example of a broader entity. Thus the research process advances, in its final stages, towards a discussion of broader entities. We end up on the bottom of the hourglass. (1995: 156)

Alasuutari (1995: 155) illustrates this hourglass metaphor through his own study of the social consequences of Finnish urbanization in the 1970s. He chose local pubs as a site to observe these effects and eventually focused upon male 'regulars'. This led to a second study even more narrowly focused on a group where drinking was heavier and where many of the men were divorced. As he puts it: 'Ethnographic research of this kind is not so much generalization as extrapolation ... the results are related to broader entities' (1995: 155).

Generalizability is present in a single case

The third and final way of thinking about how we generalize in qualitative research is far more radical than our earlier alternatives. According to this approach, since the basic structures of social order are to be found anywhere, it does not matter where we begin our research. Look at *any* case and you will find the same order.

For this linguistically inspired approach, the possibility something exists is enough. As Peräkylä suggests:

> Social practices that are possible, i.e., *possibilities of language use*, are the central objects of all conversation analytical case studies on interaction in particular institutional settings. The possibility of various practices can be considered generalizable even if the practices are not actualized in similar ways across different settings. (2011: 375)

Peräkylä illustrates his argument by the example of his own study of AIDS counselling in a London teaching hospital (Peräkylä, 1995). This study focused on specific questioning practices used by counsellors and their clients. As he puts it:

> As possibilities, the practices that I analyzed are very likely to be generalizable. There is no reason to think that they could not be made possible by any competent member of (at least any Western) society. In this sense, this study produced generalizable results. The results were not generalizable as descriptions of what other counsellors or other professionals do with their clients; but they were generalizable as descriptions of what any counsellor or other professional, with his or her clients, *can* do, given that he or she has the same array of interactional competencies as the participants of the AIDS counselling sessions have. (2011: 376)

As the most cogent proponent of this view once put it: 'tap into whomsoever, wheresoever and we get much the same things' (Sacks, 1984b: 22).

Sacks had a strategy of working with any data that crossed his path. This clearly conflicts both with the standard approach of quantitative social scientists, who usually work with random samples from particular populations, and with the common defensiveness of their qualitative brethren about the representativeness of the cases that they study.

Sacks's lack of defensiveness on this issue stems from his argument about the obvious pervasiveness of the social forms (or what he calls the 'machinery') with which he is concerned. For example, Sacks notes the ability of a child to learn a culture from very limited contacts, and of the sociolinguist Whorf to build a Navajo grammar from talking to just one person (Sacks, 1992, Vol. 1: 485).

For Sacks, the pervasiveness of structures which these examples suggest carries the implication that it does not matter what data you select. As he argues:

> Now if one figures that that's the way things are ... then it really wouldn't matter very much what it is you look at - if you look at it carefully enough. And you may well find that you [have] got an enormous generalizability because things are so arranged that you *could* get them; given that for a member encountering a very limited environment, he has to be able to do that, and things are so arranged as to permit him to. (1992, Vol. 1: 485)

However, apprentice researchers have to be very cautious about simply parroting Sacks's 'solution' to the problem of the generalizability of research findings. This solution is really only appropriate to the most basic research on social order guided by theoretically sophisticated positions like Sacks's own conversation analytic approach (or, perhaps, French **structuralism**).

If you are interested in this sort of research, you should now attempt Exercise 3.

6 WRAPPING UP

In this chapter, I have set out various strategies which you can use to defend your research against the charge that it 'merely' depends upon a single case. Indeed, as Giampietro Gobo has pointed out, there is a danger of confusing quantitative researchers' concept of a 'case' with qualitative researchers' pursuit of instances. As he puts it:

The term 'case' is used ambiguously in ethnographic research. In surveys and discursive interviews, the cases correspond to the number of persons interviewed (the sample), who are usually interviewed only once. Indeed, it is rather rare for several interviews to be conducted with the same person (during a single piece of research). Hence statistical calculations and analyses of the interview texts are performed on cases.

Ethnographic research is very different. What is usually referred to as the 'case' (the organization or the group studied) is in fact the setting. The cases are instead the hundreds of instances (pertaining to rituals, ceremonials and routines) that the researcher observes, or the dozens of individuals that he or she meets *dozens of times* during his or her presence in the field. The researcher is not interested in the organization (or the group) *per se* but rather in the behaviours which take place within it. Consequently, in order not to create confusion with the other methodologies, it would be better in ethnographic research to abandon the term 'case' and replace it with that of 'instance'. (Personal correspondence)

Gobo's argument that qualitative research really deals with 'instances' rather than 'cases' takes much of the heat out of this discussion. It suggests three key points:

- Identifying an organization as a 'case' is only satisfactory within quantitative research.
- In qualitative research, by contrast, we discover 'cases' of particular phenomena *within* a single organization (e.g. how decision making or organizational identities are 'framed').
- This means that we often discover such cases in our research and this gives us guidance as to what other cases we need to study (within the organization or in other organizations).

The overall message of this chapter is that there is usually no need to be defensive about the claims of qualitative research. As Becker argues:

Sampling is a major problem for any kind of research. We can't study every case of whatever we're interested in, nor should we want to. Every scientific enterprise tries to find out something that will apply to *everything* of a certain kind by studying *a few examples*, the results of the study being, as we say, 'generalizable' to all members of that class of stuff. We need the sample to persuade people that we know something about the whole class. (1998: 67)

Following Becker, sampling is not a simple matter even for quantitative researchers. Indeed, as we have seen, the relative flexibility of qualitative research can improve the generalizability of our findings by allowing us to include new cases after initial findings are established.

Appreciate the benefits of small-scale research
WATCH: DAVID EXPLAINS IN PERSON

David's Top Tip 31

Try not to be defensive if your data is limited to one or two 'cases'. Instead, seek to understand the logic behind such an approach and work out what you can gain by intensive analysis of limited but rich data.

The crucial issue here seems to be thinking through one's theoretical priorities. Providing that you have done that and can demonstrate a research design driven by those priorities, nobody should have cause for complaint.

So the secret seems to be to substitute theoretical cogency for the statistical language of quantitative research. In this sense, as Alasuutari (1995) has suggested, perhaps 'generalizability' is the wrong word to describe what we attempt to achieve in qualitative research. As he puts it:

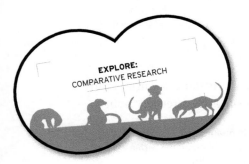

EXPLORE:
COMPARATIVE RESEARCH

> Generalization is … [a] word … that should be reserved for surveys only. What can be analyzed instead is how the researcher demonstrates that the analysis relates to things beyond the material at hand … *extrapolation* better captures the typical procedure in qualitative research. (1995: 156-7)

One way of resisting a defensive posture about the claims we can make from qualitative data is to replace 'case' with 'instance' and 'generalization' with 'extrapolation'.

What You Need to Remember

There are four answers to the question of how we can generalize from qualitative data:

- Abandoning the idea that a 'case' is always identical to a single organization.
- Avoiding asking 'why' and instead asking 'what' and/or 'how'.
- Looking for 'instances' of social processes and seeking to generalize about them.
- Talking about 'extrapolation' rather than 'generalization'.

You should try to aim towards analytic generalization in doing case studies, and you should avoid thinking in such confusing terms as 'the sample of cases' or the 'small sample of cases', as if a single case study were like a single respondent in a survey or a single subject in an experiment (Yin, 2009: 39).

NOTE

1   As Clive Seale (personal correspondence) has pointed out, theoretical sampling may have more to do with generating theories than with empirical generalization. I take up Seale's point at the end of this chapter in relation to Alasuutari's argument that the idea of empirical generalization 'should be reserved for surveys only' (1995: 156).

Your Chapter Checklist

- Are you able to work out the logic behind the number of cases you are studying?
- Can you explain how you are able to generalize from the cases you studied?
- What are you trying to generalize about (populations or social processes)?
- What social processes have you discovered?

TRACK:
LOGIC OF CASE STUDY RESEARCH

Exercises

Exercise 1: Defend arguments and explain the value of data

- Go to the links just before Section 4.
- Assess whether Flyvbjerg or Ruddin has the better of this argument.
- How would you explain the value of your data to a sceptical quantitative researcher?

APPLY:
YOUR EXERCISE WORKBOOK

Exercise 2: Work with a single case

Assume that you are studying a single case. On what basis do you think you might generalize from your findings? Distinguish your possible empirical contribution from any potential development of concepts.

Exercise 3: Create a typology of potential cases

Imagine that you have the resources to study four cases of the phenomenon in which you are interested. Following my discussion of Stake (Table 13.3), draw up a typology to indicate the universe of cases potentially available. This typology should include between six and twelve possible cases.

   Now explain why you propose to select your four cases in terms of the logic of purposive sampling.

Exercise 4: Understand how theory can justify a small dataset

Using conversation analysis, Harvey Sacks has argued: 'tap into whomsoever, wheresoever and we get much the same things' (1984b: 22). Consider how far your own theoretical model might allow you to use Sacks's argument to justify working with a very small dataset.

Further Reading

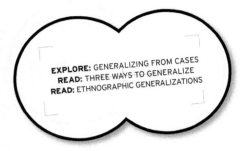

EXPLORE: GENERALIZING FROM CASES
READ: THREE WAYS TO GENERALIZE
READ: ETHNOGRAPHIC GENERALIZATIONS

Clive Seale et al.'s edited book *Qualitative Research Practice* (Sage, 2004: 420–72) contains three very useful chapters on case studies by Flyvbjerg, Gobo and Emerson. Gobo's chapter 'Re-conceptualizing generalization: old issues in a new frame' (in Pertti Alasuutari (ed.), *Social Research Methods*, Sage, 2007: 193–213) is another useful source. The most thorough book on this topic is Clive Seale's *The Quality of Qualitative Research* (Sage, 1999). For other chapter-length treatments of this topic, see Kathy Charmaz's excellent *Constructing Grounded Theory: A Practical Guide through Qualitative Analysis* (Sage, 2006: 96–122). Other useful discussions are: Jennifer Mason's *Qualitative Researching* (Sage, 2002); Pertti Alasuutari's *Researching Culture* (Sage, 1995, Chapter 12); and Howard Becker's *Tricks of the Trade* (University of Chicago Press, 1998: Chapter 3). Robert Stake's chapter 'Case studies' is a good account of the conventional qualitative methods position on generalizability (in N. Denzin and Y. Lincoln (eds), *Handbook of Qualitative Research*, Sage, 2005: 435–54); and Anssi Peräkylä's chapter 'Validity in qualitative research' is an excellent, more specialist treatment (in D. Silverman (ed.), *Qualitative Research*, Sage, 2016: 413–28).

Discover the chapter's
digital resources in your
SILVERMAN FIELD GUIDE

FOURTEEN
Collecting Your Data

Learning Outcomes

By the end of this chapter you will be able to:

- Recognize the key questions involved in collecting different kinds of qualitative data.
- Know about how to answer each of these questions.
- Understand that such questions and answers are shaped by the theoretical model that you are using.

Most qualitative studies are based on asking respondents questions or making observations in the field. In this chapter, I will walk you through many of the practical problems involved in collecting and recording such data. I will also discuss issues that arise in setting up focus groups as well as the collection of Internet data.

As I will show, collecting data is much more than a technical matter. Following Chapter 7, I will demonstrate that how you conceive and resolve practical research problems is always shaped by your model of how the social world works.

1 COLLECTING INTERVIEW DATA

In some respects, doing an interview is the most natural thing in the world. After all, a fair proportion of what appears on the Internet, television, radio and in newspapers consists of interviews. And these interviews seem not to have a predetermined pattern (as in survey research) but to be fairly free-flowing and open-ended (as in qualitative research). It is hardly surprising, then, that most student researchers identify qualitative research with the open-ended interview. For we all know what an interview looks like and have no difficulty in interviewing or being interviewed.

If you have had any experience of interview research, you will realize that things are not quite so straightforward as this might suggest, although maybe not quite so bad as the following example from an American sociology student attempting to gather interview data in Bangladesh.

WHAT I DID: ROSLYN
The Game of Field Research

Lately, when something good, bad, expected, and unexpected happens in the field, I imagine a giant board game spread out before me. I am the culturally awkward pawn on the board, trying to get from point A, the beginning, to point B, the finish line.

At point A I have no interviews done. At point B I have roughly 35 interviews finished and on their way to translation.

I have approximately 60 days to move from point A to point B. But, like all board games, the deck is full of challenges and surprises and you never know what you're going to draw next. Here is how the board game goes.

You have arrived at the field site. Set your timer to 34 days and draw a card. The 'Waiting on Bureaucracy' card. Your in-country ethical review has not communicated with your home institution IRB office. Because they operate in different time zones, you must strategically email each of them and remind them of the communication delay. LOSE 1 DAY. Next up, the 'IT Failure' card. You have ethical review approval but the translated documents are turned to nonsensical gibberish on your laptop because you lack the appropriate foreign-language font. LOSE 1 DAY. 'The Techie' card. You overcome your IT problems by placing the Bangla documents on your assistant's laptop through email. Once she makes the edits you use a pen drive to transfer the documents to a computer in the lab that has Adobe Professional and Bangla, but no Internet. You convert everything to PDF and save it back to the pen drive and transfer all documents back to your laptop for emailing to the IRB. GAIN 2 DAYS. You successfully locate your first respondent. MOVE FORWARD 1 SPACE. Your second respondent is out of town visiting relatives and will be back in two weeks. LOSE A TURN. You have drawn the 'Lights Out' card. You take your interview questionnaire to the photocopy centre in town, but because the power goes out for the rest of the day, they don't get any copies made. You must return to pick them up the next morning. LOSE HALF A DAY. Play the 'Throwing Money at the Problem' card. Realizing you are short on time, you hire a speedboat to take you to the far villages for your next set of interviews. Your research assistant is thrilled by the chance to ride in a speedboat and is happy all day. MOVE AHEAD 3 SPACES. 'Social Butterfly' card. You accepted too many invitations from people wanting to feed you. LOSE 2 DAYS. A respondent who lives far away happens to be visiting nearby your guest house. MOVE AHEAD 1 SPACE. Due to the annual core donor visit, the guesthouse asks you to move all of your crap into a new room. LOSE HALF A DAY. Due to a broken toilet, the guesthouse asks you to move again. LOSE HALF A DAY. Your voice recorder runs out of battery during an interview. LOSE A TURN. You counter with the 'Think Outside the Box' card. You remember your camera can take video so you solve the problem by pointing the camera at a wall and recording the interview. MOVE AHEAD 1 SPACE. And so it goes until you painstakingly work your way up to 30-some interviews, racing against the calendar and everything else life hands you. So far, we have finished 18 interviews. [Roslyn Fraser, Sociology, University of Missouri-Columbia]

Roslyn's horror story is shocking and most readers of this book, particularly if their field data is being collected closer to home, will not experience all her difficulties. In this section, I will discuss how you can manage the troubles that will arise by thinking through:

- how you define your research problem
- how many interviews you need
- the interview protocol
- recording and transcribing interviews
- whether you really need mixed methods.

Defining your research problem

How do we describe a *qualitative* research design? Interview studies which are based on a relatively small number of cases and use open-ended questions are usually treated as examples of qualitative research. However, as we have already learned, the presence or absence of numbers and rigid structures is insufficient to distinguish between qualitative and quantitative research. Much more important is how you define your research problem using a particular model of reality.

Many interview studies seek to find out how a particular group of people perceives things. As we saw in Chapter 7, by assuming that interviews can give a direct access to 'experience' (providing the research design is reliable), such qualitative researchers depend upon a naturalist model of research shared by quantitative interviewers, such as survey researchers.

Here are some actual student examples of naturalist ways of framing a research problem using qualitative interviews.

WHAT I DID: TIPPI, SANATH, MARTINA, ANNIKA AND SACHIN

- How residents in a community of elderly people feel about their life. [Tippi, Information Studies and Sociology, Finland]
- Job satisfaction and occupational 'burnout' among female primary school teachers. [Sanath, Community Medicine, Sri Lanka]
- The factors and contexts of gender discrimination and how they combine to affect opportunities and circumstances and choices, and how these are reflected in the realization of life and employment trajectories. [Martina, Sociology and Human Geography, Czech Republic]
- How do different actors experience the implementation of labour standards in the construction industry in Chennai, India? [Annika, Sociology and Human Geography, Norway]
- Responses of patients who consult unqualified Western medical practitioners. [Sachin, Community Medicine, Sri Lanka]

These kinds of research problems exemplify a style of qualitative interviews which aims to 'get inside the heads' of particular groups of people and to tell things from their 'point of view'. Yet, as we saw in Chapter 6, how far is it appropriate to think that people attach a single meaning to their experiences? May not multiple meanings of a situation (e.g. living in a community home) or of an activity (e.g. consulting an unqualified medical practitioner) be represented by what people say to the researcher, to each other, to carers, and so on (Gubrium, 1997)?

This raises the important methodological issue of whether interview responses are to be treated as giving direct access to 'experience' and 'feelings' or as actively constructed 'narratives' involving activities which themselves demand analysis (Holstein and Gubrium, 1995). Both positions, naturalist and constructionist, are entirely legitimate, but the stance you take will need to be justified and explained.

Let your research question guide your method

WATCH: DAVID EXPLAINS IN PERSON

David's Top Tip 32

Always think through whether qualitative interviews are appropriate to your research problem. For instance, if you are collecting facts or perceptions, would a quantitative survey make more sense?

A final observation is in order. How you formulate the topic of a qualitative interview study is not just a matter of the research model you employ. You also have to ask questions that are answerable by your data. Sometimes this is merely a matter of narrowing down your topic (see Chapter 6). On other occasions, students may be tempted to use interviews to answer the wrong kind of questions.

A little while ago, I was advising some PhD students at a university in Tanzania. A politics student was interested in what seemed to be an important social issue: how water and sanitation policy had been influenced by the decentralization of Tanzanian local government since 2000. He proposed to find answers by interviewing key stakeholders.

Can you see what the problem is with this approach?

As we learn from our quantitative colleagues, it is difficult to find out what happened in the past by asking present-day respondents. This is not because they may lie but simply because we all view the past through the lens of the present. Hence this kind of *retrospective* study is likely to offer inaccurate information.

Now can you see possible solutions? I suggested that the student could meet this difficulty in one of two ways:

- reformulate his research problem as a study of *contemporary* stakeholder views
- stick with the original research problem and use different, contemporary data (for instance, contrasting newspaper reports today with those in 2000).

How many interviews do I need?

This question is very common among beginning research students. Remembering what they have been taught on quantitative methods courses, they are terrified that they may be torn to shreds for not having enough data.

Ultimately, the question 'How many cases do I need?' depends upon your research problem. As we saw in Chapter 13, many qualitative researchers use purposive sampling to choose a case because it illustrates some feature or process in which we are interested. This does not provide a simple approval for any case we happen to choose. Rather, purposive sampling demands that we think critically about the parameters of the population we are studying and choose our sample case carefully on this basis.

Here are some examples of students who used purposive sampling to find people to interview.

WHAT I DID: STEVEN, SVEINUNG, KAMALA, ANDERS AND SELMA

- A study of 16 students which contained samples of doctoral postgraduates and young lecturers who were registered as PhD candidates in different departments (psychology and social science) in universities in two UK regions. [Steven, Social Sciences, UK]
- Using observation of street drug scenes to recruit 60 young people composed of 40 adolescent street dwellers picked up in the area around an 'open drug scene' and 20 street cannabis dealers aged 15-30 selling at a more dispersed drug scene. [Sveinung, Sociology, Norway]
- A study of care providers of children whose mothers work overseas. Some of the care providers were the fathers of children while the others were their grandparents, aunts and other relatives, and a sample of 20 care providers was selected to represent these different categories. [Kamala, Community Medicine, Sri Lanka]
- Studying the local understanding of 'cultural landscapes' (biophysical) and the processes behind different landscape changes using 16 informants found in the Norwegian agricultural registry, grouped according to work, sex and age in a balanced manner. [Anders, Geography, Norway]
- A study of work/family balance among a segment of professionals in high-commitment occupations where confrontations between care and career might be expected to be accentuated. Based on a sample of 43 semi-structured, in-depth interviews collected in 2005-7 with female (26) and male (17) white, heterosexual, lawyers (29) and consultants/managers (14) in the process of establishing different work/life adaptations. Informants were recruited formally through firms, and informally through different (non-related) social networks. [Selma, Sociology, Norway]

These examples show you can select your interviewees purposively based on the groups which your research problem addresses. In addition, as in the final example ('work/family balance'), it can be helpful to use a 'snowball sample', using the social networks of one or two initial informants. In an MSc study of the experience of international students at a UK university, Maddie Sandall used email addresses to contact people. She then asked her respondents if they could persuade any of their friends to encourage them to come along for interview.

However, if, as in the following example, you are collecting your data far from home, there may be little prospect of gathering further data.

WHAT I DID: ROSLYN

Child Gender Preference in Rural Bangladesh

Now that I am home I occasionally feel powerless. It is not uncommon for me to be working through a transcript and become completely furious with myself for not probing a certain way or following up on an aspect of the participant's life. But my hands are tied because I can't go back. It is a lesson in forgiveness and accept-ance. I have to recognize my data limitations over and over during analysis and then forgive myself when I don't have the data necessary to delve a little deeper into a specific respondent's case. On the other hand, there is a lot that I can say from my data and I am finding that 80 interviews provide an overwhelming amount of information. I have a lot to say on the data I do have, and it isn't productive to become obsessed with the data I don't have. [Roslyn Fraser, Sociology, University of Missouri–Columbia]

In Roslyn's situation, her decisions in the field about how many interviews to conduct and what questions to ask were crucial. There was no going back.

What questions should I ask?

Survey researchers use a predefined, fixed set of questions which are often derived from pre-tested measures used in other studies. This set of questions is usually known as a *research protocol*. When you have large samples and wish to use statistical tests of significance, fixing your questions can help to increase the reliability of your findings.

Some qualitative researchers follow quantitative researchers by sticking to a pre-prepared, structured set of questions. For instance, a Sri Lankan PhD student used the following detailed interview guide in his study of the coping mechanisms of women subject to domestic violence.

WHAT I DID: RAVI

- Tell me about your visit today, why did you come, who advised you to come?
  [about services]
- How did the problems start (tell me from the beginning)?
  [create timeline]
- Tell me about you and your family. Where did you live before marriage?
  [family background, community]
- Was there physical (sexual) abuse/violence?
  [specify]
- Were the children involved?
  [children abused, coping]

(Continued)

(Continued)

- What did you do about the problem (why/why not)?
  [coping strategies, cultural factors]
- What is the reason for the problem (in your opinion/others/family)?
  [perspective, opinions and influence]
- What would you like to see happening?
  [expectations, knowledge]
- How can we help you?
  [anything additional?]

[Ravi, Community Medicine, Sri Lanka]

If you have ever tried to conduct a research interview, you will know that such guidelines, while helpful, only take you so far. As one student comments:

> Although the schedules include complete questions for the interviewees to answer, it was not the aim of the interviewing procedure to read these out verbatim. Throughout the interviews I adopted an in-depth semi-structured or 'conversational' interviewing style. The general aim was to encourage the respondents to speak personally and at length about their lives as doctoral students, while at the same time covering the issues which I was interested in as a researcher. There was a constant balance to be struck therefore between what was interesting to me and what was interesting to them, and as such the interviewer–interviewee relationship veered between impersonality and rapport. [Steven Stanley, Social Sciences, UK]

The kinds of problems to which Steven alludes are illustrated by the following questions raised by research students.

WHAT I DID: ANNIKA, MARTA AND SELMA

Research students' questions on interviewing:

- In the interviews I need to ask many direct questions in order to get specific information about working conditions, how institutions function, etc. However, in order to get information on matters I have not thought of beforehand, it is important also to ask more open questions which encourage the informants to reflect more freely. I find it a bit challenging how to formulate such questions, and would appreciate any input in this regard. [Labour standards in developing countries, using the construction industry in the city of Chennai, South India, as a case. Annika, Sociology and Human Geography, Norway]

- How can I try to make the interviews more open-ended (though based on an interview guide)? [Transnationalism, integration and the Norwegian policy environment: remittance practices and integration among Pakistanis in Norway. Marta, Human Geography, Norway]
- I would appreciate a lot of input from you on issues important to discuss when interviewing elites. With some of the informants I was hardly able to get beyond a definition of the interview situation, more similar to a pitch or 'beauty contest' of the informant as a professional or his/her company than a research interview ... compared to informants in my previous work (teachers and students), these elite interviewees generally seemed much less comfortable - and/or acquainted - with conversation frames focusing on their own - or even others' - difficult experiences. [Selma, Sociology, Norway]

The highly intelligent questions posed by these three students ask how to make interviews more open-ended. However, as the last student recognizes, much depends upon the kind of people you are interviewing. When you interview 'up', you may find elite members unhappy about 'opening up' about themselves.

Beware of your influence on the interviewee

WATCH: DAVID EXPLAINS IN PERSON

David's Top Tip 33

Don't think of the role of the interviewer as just asking questions. Consider the variety of your other actions (e.g. saying 'hmm, mm', reformulating a question, agreeing and remaining silent). Always assess how these influence what an interviewee says.

So there are no recipes for successful open-ended interviews. But there are ways of proceeding which give you more hope of success. In the rest of this section, I will discuss:

- avoiding posing your research question directly to the participants
- piloting your interview schedule.

Don't ask your research question directly

Thoughtless researchers sometimes present their main research question directly to the respondents themselves. This causes two problems. First, as is well known in quantitative surveys, if respondents are made fully aware of your research interest, this can affect their responses. Second, it can lead to lazy research in which careful data analysis is simply replaced by reporting back what people have told you.

As Clive Seale (personal correspondence) has pointed out:

> This is a very common problem in all kinds of studies, but particularly ones where people mistakenly use a qualitative design to answer a question better suited to an experimental or quasi-experimental design. People decide, say, that they are going to see if TV violence encourages violent behaviour. Instead of doing a survey of what people watch on TV and a parallel survey of their tendency to violence, and then seeing whether there is a correlation (hoping that there are no spurious reasons for such a correlation of course), they just select a group of people and ask them (more or less), 'Do you think TV watching causes violence?'

WHAT I DID: VIBEKE

Vibeke was studying healthcare innovation at a Danish hospital. She shadowed various hospital staff and also interviewed them afterwards. She suggests three ways of avoiding being over-directive in doing an interview:

- I try to restrain myself from taking over the conversation by primarily using 'non-verbal responses' and suppressing the need for 'filling out the awkward silences'.
- Towards the end of the interview, I sometimes ask the interviewee about specific events that I witnessed together with him or her when I was shadowing.
- I am inspired in my interviewing by Nicolini's idea about 'the interview to the double' (Nicolini, 2013: 225). I ask the interviewees to instruct 'a double' on how to do their job or how to perform a well-organized patient trajectory. The purpose is to get some ideas about how they experience (getting things done) in their hospital practice. [Vibeke Scheller, Department of Organization, Copenhagen Business School]

Pilot your interview schedule

It is often sensible to try out different styles of questioning prior to your main study. This kind of *piloting* is a feature of most kinds of good research – both qualitative and quantitative.

In the following example, a Finnish PhD student of marketing talks about how she used a pilot study to learn from her early mistakes.

WHAT I DID: EMMA
Going Wrong and Putting It Right

In some interviews I participated a bit too enthusiastically, sometimes because the topic at hand was interesting, sometimes – especially at the beginning – because of the imagined need to reassure them about my knowledge of the themes discussed, or because I was too nervous to tolerate any silence. Before starting the interviews, I was confident about my ability to listen, but seeing the first transcripts and listening to the tapes was a shock. For example:

E: How have you ended up here?
I: I have only been here two years …
E: As an assistant?
I: … senior assistant …
E: So, you are senior …
I: Now I'm an assistant again, and I don't know about the future … It is like this in the academia.
E: That's correct. How long ago, you've graduated from here, haven't you?
I: Yes, I graduated in 19XX and I'm finishing the doctoral thesis this year …
E: You are in a hurry, so to speak!
I: Well, I don't know, if you do research full-time, so you should come up with something as well. There's not much else to do …

I did not allow this interviewee to start his own narrative, but kept on interrupting him. However, as my confidence grew and my knowledge of the subject increased, I started to relax and let people talk at their own pace. I also learned to be careful with leading questions or the use of words with strong connotations – terms like 'career' or 'to drift'. Although many respondents told me that they had 'drifted' into academia, I should never have asked one interviewee: 'How did you drift into this profession?' However, I never repeated that mistake. [Emma, Sociology, Finland]

A British student concurs with Emma about the advantages of pilot interviews.

WHAT I DID: STEVEN
The Advantages of a Pilot Study

At the beginning of the first year of my PhD I carried out two pilot interviews with fellow PhD students who were studying at the same university as myself. These initial pilot interviews served several different functions:

- They allowed me to practise interviewing. Although I had used the method of interviewing for my first degree, I did not have much experience of carrying out in-depth interview discussions. In this sense the first few interviews served as useful practices, as I gradually changed my interviewing style.

(Continued)

(Continued)

- [They helped me] to find out whether I was going to get interesting and substantial data from my participants. They generally seemed to appreciate the opportunity to speak openly about their dilemmas in the presence of a fellow student. Indeed, this was mentioned in the letter of introduction sent out to potential doctoral student participants.
- [They] ... were helpful in developing interview schedules for the interviews subsequently carried out with doctoral postgraduates at institutions other than my own. [Steven Stanley, Social Sciences, UK]

However, Steven adds that his constructionist approach limits the advantages of piloting. As he points out:

This 'improvement' in my capability as an interviewer did not necessarily equate with 'improved' data. When I carried out my first interview I was relatively inexperienced and tended to ask awkward questions of my participant. This generated some interesting data. However, as I became more experienced, my subsequent interviews tended to be somewhat less interesting.

The differences in constructionist models

WATCH: DAVID EXPLAINS IN PERSON

David's Top Tip 34

Steven's and Emma's successful piloting of their interviews shows there are ways to improve your interviewing skills. However, one caution is in order. Protocol design is less important if you are using a constructionist model and are, therefore, interested in how interviewers and interviewees co-construct a version of 'reality'. In this approach, questions and answers are made a topic as well as a resource (see Rapley, 2004).

Recording and transcribing interviews

READ:
IDENTITY WORK IN INTERVIEWING

It goes without saying that your interviews should always be recorded. With improved technologies and a growing recognition of the advantages of being able to play back interviews, the old days of pen and paper recording are long gone! Here is Steven's account of how he recorded and transcribed his interviews with PhD students.

WHAT I DID: STEVEN

Recording and Transcribing Interviews

Initial transcripts were made of all the interviews with doctoral students, at first recording only the words which were said by the interviewer and the respondents. These early verbatim transcripts were organized around topics and themes going across the interviews, such as doctoral postgraduate identity work, descriptions of the supervisory relationship, and stories of publishing from doctoral theses. When, after repeated reading, particular extracts were chosen for detailed discursive analysis, they were then retranscribed using a simplified and modified version of the notation developed by Jefferson (1984) for conversation analysis [see the Appendix of this book]. This system captured not only what doctoral students said about their identities and experiences, but also how they said it. [Steven Stanley, Social Sciences, UK]

The issue of transcription is important in at least two ways. First, transcribing takes a great deal of your time. The danger is that after having spent ages defining your research problem, finding your interviewees and piloting your interview protocol, you then lose yourself in transcription. The end product is that you have very little time to analyse your data when, as I stress throughout this book, this is the crucial part of writing a dissertation.

However, my second point is that transcription quality should not be neglected. Too many dissertations, not to mention publications, fail to show sufficient detail in their extracts from interview data, sometimes excluding the researcher's question which provoked a particular answer as well as the 'hm, hms' and other sound particles which can be crucial in guiding an interviewee in a particular direction (see Rapley, 2004).

I have three suggestions to deal with these problems:

- Be comforted by the fact that there is no 'best' method for transcribing interviews, so transcribe in a way that is appropriate to your research problem and theoretical model (for instance, constructionists will need more detailed methods of transcription than positivists or naturalists).
- Again, don't try to reinvent the wheel: use a standard set of transcription symbols (see the Appendix of this book for a version that constructionists like Steven Stanley tend to use).
- Don't try to transcribe all your interviews at once: select a few to be transcribed in detail, analyse these, and then decide how many and which other interviews need detailed transcription.

Do I need mixed methods?

Whatever research method you use, it is tempting to seek out more data using other methods. Sometimes, this can be a good use of time. For instance, in her MSc study of the experience of international students, Maddie Sandall found that a broader comparison would overcome the limitations of her handful of interviews. As she puts it:

> Although the data I have gathered had been quite rich and interesting, I felt that more was needed, therefore this has been backed up by a largely quantitative survey of students in Malaysia.

Similarly, Wenyao Zhao, a management student at EMU–Lyon, proposed to study how social networks between Chinese managers (the art of 'Guanxi') could contribute to the performance of Western European corporations working in China. He proposed to combine in-company observations with interviews but, sensibly, he was worried about how much time would be taken by using these mixed methods.

You may recall my earlier advice to students contemplating the use of mixed methods: 'Keep it simple'! Sometimes, multiple methods seem to offer little more than a 'comfort blanket' to give you the feeling that, whatever the deficiencies of your research, you have, at least, covered your research topic from many angles.

If your principal data is interviews, there are at least three reasons to be wary of venturing beyond the data:

- Ironically, multiple datasets, assembled through different methods, can encourage laziness: as soon as you have a problem analysing one dataset, you tend to switch to another (thereby resolving nothing).
- Using mixed methods can involve you in intractable problems about where the 'truth' lies. As I argue later in this book, this kind of **triangulation** is highly problematic.
- Is there a unitary phenomenon 'out there' which you need to study? Positivists and naturalists tend to think there is, but constructionists prefer to talk about the hyphenated phenomenon (e.g. the family-as-narrated-to-an-interviewer, the family-as-displayed-on-a-photograph, the family-as-reported-in-a-newspaper-story, etc.).

However, we should not throw the baby out with the bathwater. Let me try to answer a student question on the use of mixed methods. In a study of remittance practices and integration among Pakistanis in Norway, a student asks:

> How can I combine data from interviews with data from other conversations and observations in a good way in a study which is mainly interview based? [Marta, Human Geography, Norway]

My answer is straightforward and in two parts:

- Keep things simple by using non-interview data as a guide to conducting your interviews. For instance, in her study of the balance between work and family among female professionals, Selma preceded her interviews by participant observation of five female informants for one work day each.
- When you have completed the analysis of your interviews, collect further data which may help put your findings into a wider context. For instance, in a PhD study based on interviews with Sri Lankan women subject to domestic violence, the final phase of the research involved an evaluation of an existing hospital-based intervention programme for abused women in a provincial hospital using case profiles and interviews with care givers. [Ravi]

2 COLLECTING FOCUS GROUP DATA

Focus groups as a research method originated in the work of the Bureau of Applied Social Research at Columbia University in the 1940s. The sociologist Paul Lazarsfeld was conducting commercial market research on audience responses to soap operas. The US government requested the Bureau to assess the impact of its wartime radio propaganda and Lazarsfeld asked another famous sociologist, Robert Merton, to join the project. Until then,

EXPLORE:
FOCUS GROUPS IN ACTION

focus group members had simply responded to what they heard by pressing buttons to express approval or disapproval. At Merton's suggestion, the groups were now given questions about the broadcasts and asked to discuss them among themselves (Bloor et al., 2001: 1–2).

Since then, focus groups have continued to be a key tool in commercial market research. For instance, an episode of the fourth television series of *Mad Men* shows a focus group on skincare products being held in a Madison Avenue advertising agency in 1964.

This is an example of a commercial focus group aimed at getting responses to a product. Notice how the focus group leader asks a series of very pointed questions. In academic research, it is usually better to avoid direct questioning as this may make it clear what kind of responses you want. Instead, you can offer a stimulus to discussion (e.g. a photograph) and allow the discussion to develop without your intervention.

EXPLORE:
OPEN-ENDED FOCUS GROUPS

WHAT I DID: KAMALA

Using a Focus Group to Pilot an Interview Study

Setting up a focus group prior to interviews can help to clarify the issues which you wish to raise.

Prior to interviews with carers of Sri Lankan children whose mothers worked overseas, I identified the schools which the children attended. Subsequently, teachers in these schools who teach the target children were invited to take part in focus group discussions. The difficulties and problems of the children at school were identified through these focus group discussions. [Kamala, Community Medicine, Sri Lanka]

Sometimes focus groups are used as a standalone way of gathering qualitative data and do not precede interviews. For example, Sara writes about how she used her existing rapport with the lesbian community to collect data for her research on gender roles among lesbians.

WHAT I DID: SARA

Studying a Familiar Community

I had chosen to study lesbians, an identity that I hold myself. I was already familiar with the local community and knew where to access narrators. I found focus groups particularly easy to organize because I was looking for 'naturally occurring' settings (in the sense that I did not arrange them, but participants would be there regardless of my research). So for focus groups I approached pre-existing groups and simply asked to be their topic for the evening. As a result, I not only intervened less as a researcher in creating the groups, but also needed to expend little energy organizing places, time, participants, etc. [Sara Crawley, USA]

Through studying members of her own community, Sara's example provided neat solutions to two problems that arise in collecting focus group data:

- accessing people to engage in a focus group discussion
- trying not to 'lead' the discussion.

In most cases, however, the focus group researcher is an 'outsider'. The kinds of problems this can generate are suggested by the following examples.

WHAT I DID: AMY AND ELEANOR
How Should I Run a Focus Group?

- I am concerned with the social dimensions of environmental management and the organization of stakeholders within institutions managing natural resources. Some of my data will be gathered through a focus group organized during my fieldwork in Papua New Guinea. I would be interested in tips on moderating focus groups or using a facilitator in working with often marginalized populations. [Amy Louise Bott, Management, University of Technology, Sydney]
- I am studying the social construction of climate change. Data will be generated in climate 'conversation cafés' that I will set up with existing community groups in Sydney. The 'cafés' are like focus groups but involve dialogue and exploration rather than answering set questions. Do you have any recommendations on running the cafés? [Eleanor Glenn, Institute for Sustainable Futures, UTS]

Before we can answer Amy and Eleanor's questions, we need to know more about the fundamentals of focus group research. Sue Wilkinson has described focus group methodology when used in social science research as 'deceptively simple' (2011: 168). The following points have been adapted from Wilkinson (2011) and Bloor et al. (2001) to show ways of collecting qualitative data:

- Recruiting a small group of people (often between six and eight) who usually share a particular characteristic (e.g. mothers of children under 2; sufferers of a particular illness).
- Encouraging an informal group discussion (or discussions) 'focused' around a particular topic or set of issues. This could be, for example, young women sharing experiences of dieting, single parents evaluating childcare facilities, or fitness instructors comparing and contrasting training regimes.
- The discussion is usually based on the use of a schedule of questions. This is sometimes followed by use of some kind of stimulus material (visual or otherwise) for discussion. A wide range of more structured 'exercises', including ranking, rating, card sorting or use of vignettes, is sometimes used.
- Although focus groups are sometimes referred to as 'group interviews', the moderator does not ask questions of each focus group participant in turn but, rather, facilitates group discussion, actively encouraging group members to interact with each other.
- Focus groups may be reconvened at a later date (a 'longitudinal' design) or a series of focus groups may be held, using the outcome of an earlier focus group to specify the subjects under discussion.
- Typically, the discussion is recorded, the data transcribed and then analysed using conventional techniques for qualitative data, most commonly content or thematic analysis. However, as Wilkinson (2011) has shown, constructionist approaches such as discourse analysis and conversation analysis can fruitfully be used on focus group data.

As the final point shows, more than purely technical questions arise when you gather data. This is demonstrated by Eleanor's framing of her research problem within a constructionist model (i.e. 'the social construction of climate change'). Conceived this way, is focus group data really appropriate? Why not think about the everyday contexts in which 'climate change' is topicalized (e.g. blogs on the Internet, media reports, company statements, etc.) and study these kinds of naturally occurring data?

I now move on to collecting observational data in ethnographic fieldwork. As you will see, many similar issues arise, for example sampling and recording.

3 COLLECTING ETHNOGRAPHIC DATA

In this section, I will be discussing the issues that arise if you are working in the field gathering ethnographic data. Although such fieldwork can use interviews, it always involves observation and recording.

Student researchers face four difficult issues when doing fieldwork:

- access
- narrowing down the research problem
- deciding whether one case is enough
- recording observations.

I discuss these questions below. Each question will lead on to suggestions for possible 'solutions' and several case studies will be used for illustration.

Gaining access

Textbooks (e.g. Gobo, 2008: 118–33; Hornsby-Smith, 1993: 53; Walsh, 1998: 224–5) usually distinguish between two kinds of research setting:

- 'closed' or 'private' settings (organizations, deviant groups) where access is controlled by gatekeepers
- 'open' or 'public' settings (e.g. vulnerable minorities, public records or settings) where access is freely available but not always without difficulty, either practical (e.g. finding a role for the researcher in a public setting) or ethical (e.g. whether we should be intruding upon vulnerable minorities).

Depending on the contingencies of the setting (and the research problem chosen), two kinds of research access may be obtained:

- 'covert' access without subjects' knowledge
- 'overt' access based on informing subjects and getting their agreement, often through gatekeepers.

Covert access, particularly to 'closed' settings, raises difficult ethical issues, discussed in Chapter 10. However, we should not assume that 'covert' access always involves possible offence. For instance, on a course I used to teach, students were asked to observe people exchanging glances in an everyday setting (see Sacks, 1992, Vol. 1: 81–94). Providing the students are reasonably sensitive about this and refrain from staring at others, I do not envisage any problems arising.

However, in other cases, covert observation can lead to severe ethical problems as well as physical danger to the researcher. For instance, Nigel Fielding (1982) obtained permission to research a far right British political party but still felt it necessary to supplement official access with covert observation (see also Back, 2004).

Student researchers more commonly seek to obtain *overt* access to field settings. What does this involve?

In Chapter 3, we saw how my students Sally Hunt and Simon Allistone sought access for fieldwork. Sally was interested in how mental health professionals define patient diagnoses. As she recognized, observing mental health practice involves highly sensitive ethical issues and her early attempt to gain access to an inpatient setting was unsuccessful. Then what she describes as a 'chance happening' occurred:

> I met up with a former colleague in a local supermarket. After I recounted my difficulty in negotiating access to an inpatient area, he invited me to meet the community team with whom he worked ... Following two separate meetings with the team's psychiatric consultant and with the team leader (a community psychiatric nurse), I was eventually given permission to audio-record the team's weekly case meetings on the understanding that I destroy the tapes when the study concluded. [Sally Hunt, Sociology, Goldsmiths]

Simon's access for his MA research was even easier. He already had contacts at a primary school (children aged 5–11 years) where his partner was a teacher. As he puts it:

> At the time my partner was a relatively new primary school teacher, and her exposure to the realities of parents' evening led to her assertion that such meetings had not been directly addressed within her teacher-training course ... My ongoing unofficial pastoral role at my partner's school meant that I had already built up a rapport with the head teacher, so approaching him with a proposal to record some parents' evening meetings was straightforward enough. Once the process of the research was explained and agreed upon, he was happy for the recording to take place, with one stipulation: my access was restricted to the recording of only one teacher in the school, namely my partner. [Simon Allistone, Sociology, Goldsmiths]

These experiences show that it is not uncommon for qualitative researchers to use their existing relationships and contacts for their research. For instance, in his research on undercover police officers, Michael drew upon his existing contacts for fieldwork access:

> I capitalized on my prior law enforcement experience to gain access to the departments from which I collected data. Some of the agencies I contacted were personally known to me and others had individuals who worked there who knew me from my time in law enforcement. [Michael Arter, USA]

The lesson from these three accounts is that, if you are contemplating fieldwork, it simplifies access if you draw upon your existing circle of contacts. Trying to enter new fields is likely to involve time-consuming negotiations and may end in failure, particularly if you want to research an ethically sensitive area. In the example below (also given in Chapter 4, where the ethical aspects are discussed), John tells what he himself describes as 'a horror story' in his attempt to study suicide helplines.

WHAT I DID: JOHN

Entering New Fields: A Horror Story

[My story is] positive in part, but essentially a horror story in places. I contacted a number of self-help groups in the search for data. I received a great response from one in Norfolk, which was for relatives of people who had committed suicide. I had many conversations on the phone with the group's founder, who had told me that they met regularly, were all good friends, and had even been recorded for part of a TV show before, and he would tell them about my research. He came back to me saying that they had agreed to me coming down and video recording one of their sessions, and they were all keen to be part of the research. I discussed discursive psychological research in great detail with him, and he liked what I was proposing.

When I got there and had set up the camera, people started to arrive. It soon became clear that they were not expecting me, had given no consent to being recorded, and did not know each other or meet regularly (one person said she had attended one session four years ago and had been phoned out of the blue and asked to attend that night). It also became clear very quickly that they were all still very much in a great deal of emotional distress and pain. I turned the camera off and decided to just sit the meeting out. The group leader then announced to the group that he had no idea what I wanted or what my research was about. It then turned very unpleasant, with one member telling me that I was making her pain worse by being there, and I felt physically threatened by another member who appeared quite angry. I cannot express how terrible I felt.

Lessons learned: I should have spoken to participants and not just the group leader before showing up with a camera to the meeting, and if I ever approach a similar group again, I would get consent forms signed before attempting any data collection. I think attending some meetings to get a feel for them before collection starts would also be the way to go. [John Moore, Social Sciences, Loughborough]

In his concluding paragraph, John offers some very useful suggestions to novice researchers. It is dangerous to assume that consent from one person is sufficient, and it helps for others to get to know you before you begin to gather your data. The impression you give may be very important in deciding whether you get overt access:

> Whether or not people have knowledge of social research, they are often more concerned with what kind of *person* the researcher is than with the research itself. They will try to gauge how far he or she can be trusted, what he or she might be able to offer as an acquaintance or a friend, and perhaps also how easily he or she could be manipulated or exploited. (Hammersley and Atkinson, 1983: 78)

Given these kinds of issues of trust, there are a number of ways that help field-work students to secure and maintain access:

- *Impression management* related to the 'fronts' that we present to others (see Goffman, 1959). It involves avoiding giving an impression that might pose an obstacle to access, while more posi-tively conveying an impression appropriate to the situation (see Hammersley and Atkinson, 1983: 78-88). For instance, I have failed to gain access, despite initial expressions of interest, to two settings. In a paediatric clinic in the early 1980s, a very conservatively dressed physician, spot-ting my leather jacket, said I was being 'disrespectful to his patients' and threw me out! Fifteen years before that, as a novice researcher, I let slip over lunch that I was thinking of moving from the UK to North America when I had completed my PhD. This attitude was apparently viewed as improperly 'instrumental' by my host organization and the promised access was subsequently refused. The implication of the latter incident is that there is no 'time out' in field relations and that the most apparently informal occasions are times when you will often be judged.
- *Obtaining bottom-up access* can sometimes be forgotten at great cost. For instance, in the early 1970s, the access granted by the head of personnel at a large local government organization was put in danger by the fact that I had not explained my aims properly to his subordinates. This underlines the point that access should not be regarded as a once-and-for-all situation.
- *Being non-judgemental* is often a key to acceptance in many settings including informal subcul-tures and practitioners of a particular trade or profession. While the tendencies of **relativism** of many social sciences may allow the researcher sincerely to profess non-judgementality on particu-lar groups' values and practices, this is not always the case when you are studying certain forms of professional practice. Indeed for researchers who think they know something about 'professional dominance' or even just basic communication skills, it is very easy to appear judgemental.
- *Offering feedback* because some research subjects will actually want your judgements - provid-ing they are of an 'acceptable' kind. For instance, public or business organizations will expect some 'payoff' from giving you access.

Narrowing down

Let us assume you obtain access to the field. Suddenly, vast amounts of possible data flow around your ears and eyes. Yet, as I argue in Chapter 6, narrowing down your topic and data is essential if you are to complete a successful dissertation. How are you to do this?

Sometimes, quite pragmatic considerations become relevant. Sally Hunt chose to record the meetings of a mental health team because:

> To undertake a case study of 'single homelessness' in the context of full-time employment makes heavy demands on the researcher in terms of personal resources and operational constraints. The field is so vast and the nature of subjects' lives so dispersed that I elected to observe professional caseworkers rather than service users. For practical reasons, then, I became a participant-observer at the mental health team's (MHT's) weekly case conferences ... These were 'scheduled events', so I would not waste time waiting to see whether or not relevant data would appear but rather would have them to hand.

Having decided what she would observe, Sally decided to narrow down her research topic using a constructionist model which involved an ethnomethodological focus on members' knowledge and an ethnographic attention to frames. As she puts it, this focus provided her with a set of questions:

> My focus on members' activities generated initial questions about what they had to know to do their work. It also built on my original interest in diagnostic construction ... I attempted to find 'the sense' of what members were saying, and what was *made* of what they were saying. I then shifted my emphasis to the discourse-based question: 'How do participants *do* things?' My desire to pose such a question derived from my reading of other ethnographic work as I strove to define my research problem.

Like Sally, Simon narrowed down his research using the literature and models with which he was familiar. His focus was on what was 'routine' and apparently 'obvious' about parent–teacher meetings. He comments:

> the view that parents' evening meetings are events in which 'nothing much was accomplished' ... as Baker and Keogh point out, 'is an invitation, if not provocation, to ethnomethodological inquiry' (1995: 265) ... [So I attempted] what Psathas (1990: 45) has called 'unmotivated looking'. This is summed up by Sacks's assertion that 'when we start out with a piece of data, the question of what we are going to end up with, what kind of findings it will give, should not be a consideration' (1984b: 27).

Piera decided early on that her classroom research would focus on what the ethnomethodological and CA literature calls 'instruction sequences' (see Mehan, 1979). Her task was to discover whether such sequences are the most representative way of describing classroom interaction. With such a clearly defined topic, Piera's worries shifted to how she should narrow down her data.

WHAT I DID: PIERA

Narrowing Down When Data Are 'Extremely Available'

Paradoxically, the less you have troubles in having access to data, the more you risk being paralysed, worrying about whether your own choice in selecting how much/what/where to record might influence the findings of the research and be detrimental to their reliability. The decisions I faced were just the very basic ones for an absolute beginner: (1) ... that goes on in classrooms, what should be recorded; (2) which year group is the ... resentative, or should all year groups be recorded; (3) for how long the recording should ... (4) how many different classes; (5) how many teachers; (6) would the topic matter; and if so (7) would some lessons be excluded, and why etc.? I had no limits as to which and how many groups I was allowed to record. However, a selection was necessary and it was decided on the two third-year groups, each consisting of 25 children all of the same age (8-9). The choice was made on several grounds: first, I was not interested in a longitudinal perspective; second, presumably in the first two year groups the activities and interaction would have been about learning the school routines and discipline management, mostly; third, it is exactly during the third year of primary school that specific disciplines are introduced to the children for the first time. [Piera Margutti, Sociology, York]

Piera's experience shows that having a clear research topic by no means solves the problem of narrowing down so that you can do a piece of manageable student research. Once you have defined your topic, you must rigorously examine the relevance to your research of all the settings to which you have access. Following Piera's example, you need to choose the setting which will most obviously fit your topic and the previous research literature and findings.

Is one case enough?

There is something more we can learn from Piera's experience. Her account reveals that even a single case, like a school, contains infinite possibilities for comparison.

However, it is important to be balanced about the claims you make about your fieldwork when it uses material from a single setting. In his study of one teacher's meetings with parents, Simon acknowledges the limitations of his research but concludes with a theoretical justification.

WHAT I DID: SIMON
Single Cases and Generalizations

Focusing upon a single teacher has certain limitations in terms of generalizing the findings of this research to a wider population. It can be argued that the conversational techniques utilized by the teacher in this research are unique to her, and therefore not easily extrapolated

(Continued)

(Continued)

to the parents' evening practice of other teachers. Equally, the fact that the teacher in the data was a class teacher rather than a set teacher could have been an important influential factor. Perhaps set teachers do things differently in such meetings by dint of the fact that they are dealing with the specificities of their curriculum area. Furthermore, the entire format of the meetings might have been different at another stage of the academic year, even if carried out by the same teacher studied in this research. In short, various permutations in the actual accomplishment of parents' evening could be hidden by the fact that the data sample consists of a single teacher on a single parents' evening.

How, then, should this research be seen in terms of both sampling variety and external validity? Indeed, given the tension between the specific difficulties associated with the gathering of the data and the ideal research design outlined above, can this study say anything useful about the phenomenon that has been studied?

I believe the answer lies in seeing this research not as an attempt to provide categorical 'truths' about all parents' evenings in general, but as an attempt to raise questions about such meetings by looking at a single case in detail. To some extent, raising questions in this way relies upon the perspective within CA that '*social practices that are possible*, that is, *possibilities of language use*, are the central objects of all conversation analytic case studies on interaction in institutional settings' (Peräkylä, 2004: 297, original emphasis). [Simon Allistone, Sociology, Goldsmiths]

The language of 'possibilities' which Simon uses is more or less specific to CA. However, whatever model you use, you need not feel overly self-conscious when your fieldwork is based on a single case. Three simple ways of managing this concern are available:

- Be open about the limitations of your study.
- Show how your narrowing down even within a single setting has been rigorously conducted.
- Emphasize that qualitative researchers treat single cases as crucial in attempting to *refute* initial hypotheses. Flyvbjerg (2004) reminds us of Popper's suggestion that the observation of a single black swan would be sufficient to falsify the generalization that all swans are white. As a consequence: 'Falsification is one of the most rigorous tests to which a scientific proposition can be subjected: if just one observation does not fit with the proposition it is considered not valid generally and must therefore be either revised or rejected ... The case study is well suited for identifying "black swans" because of its in-depth approach: what appears to be "white" often turns out on closer examination to be "black"' (Flyvbjerg, 2004: 424).

Recording your observations

Recordings of naturally occurring interaction allow you to return to your data in its original form as often as you wish. The problem with fieldnotes is that you are stuck with the form in which you made them at the time and that your readers will only have access to how you recorded events.

There are two partial solutions to this problem: following strict conventions in writing fieldnotes; and adhering to a consistent theoretical orientation. The issue of fieldnote conventions will be discussed in Chapter 15. In this chapter, I discuss an observational research study which began from a well-defined theory.

In the early 1980s, I obtained access to a number of clinics treating cancer patients in a British NHS hospital. Following Strong's (1979) account of the 'ceremonial order of the clinic', I was interested in how doctors and patients presented themselves to each other. For instance, Strong had noted that NHS doctors would adhere to the rule 'politeness is all' and rarely criticize patients to their faces.

While at the hospital, I noticed that one of the doctors regularly seemed to 'go missing' after his morning clinics. My curiosity aroused, I made enquiries. I discovered that most afternoons he was conducting his 'private' practice at consulting rooms in a salubrious area of London's West End.

Nothing ventured, nothing gained, so I tried asking this doctor if I could 'sit in' on his private practice. To my great surprise, he consented on condition that I did not tape record. I happily agreed, even though this meant that my data was reduced to (what I saw as) relatively unreliable fieldnotes.

Obviously, in making fieldnotes, one is not simply recording data but also analysing it. The categories you use will inevitably be theoretically saturated – whether or not you realize it! Given my interest in Strong's use of Goffman's (1974) concept of framing, I tried to note down the activities through which the participants managed their identities. For instance, I noted how long the doctor and patient spent on social 'small talk' and how subsequent appointments were arranged.

However, if the researcher is physically present, two different kinds of issues should never be neglected:

- what you can see (as well as hear)
- how you are behaving and how you are being treated.

What you can see

Both NHS clinics were held in functional rooms, with unadorned white walls, no carpets and simple furniture (a small desk, one substantial chair for the doctor, and a number of stacking chairs for patients, families and students). As in most NHS hospitals, heating pipes and radiators were very obtrusive.

To enter the consulting rooms of the private clinic is to enter a different world. The main room has the air of an elegant study, perhaps not unlike the kind of room in a private house where a wealthy patient might have been visited by an eighteenth-century doctor. The walls are tastefully decorated and adorned with prints and paintings. The floor has a fine carpet. The furniture is reproduction antique and includes a large, leather-topped desk, several comfortable armchairs, a sofa, a low table covered with coffee table books and magazines, and a bookcase which holds ivory figures as well as medical texts. Plants are placed on several surfaces and the room is lit by an elegant central light and a table lamp. To add an executive touch, there are three phones on the desk, as well as a pen in a holder.

This room establishes an air of privacy as well as luxury. At the NHS clinics, patients are nearly always examined in curtained-off areas. Here, however, the examination couch is in a separate room which can only be entered through the consulting room. Although more functional than the latter, it is nonetheless carpeted and kept at a high temperature to keep patients warm. Even the doctor himself may knock before entering this examination room while the patient is dressing or undressing.

How you are being treated

The emphasis on privacy in British 'private' medicine creates a special problem for the researcher. While at the NHS clinics I sheltered happily behind a name-tag; at the private clinic my presence was always explained, if ambiguously ('Dr Silverman is sitting in with me today if that's all right'). Although identified and accepted by the patient, I remained uncomfortable in my role in this setting. Its air of quiet seclusion made me feel like an intruder.

Like the doctor, I found myself dressing formally and would always stand up and shake hands with the patient. I could no longer merge into the background as at the NHS clinics. I regularly experienced a sense of intruding on some private ceremony.

My impression was that the private clinic encouraged a more 'personalized' service and allowed patients to orchestrate their care, control the agenda, and obtain some 'territorial' control of the setting. In my discussion of the data, like Strong, I cite extracts from consultations to support these points, while referring to deviant cases and to the continuum of forms found in the NHS clinics.

My interest in how observers are treated in medical settings is nicely demonstrated in Peräkylä's (1989) study of a hospital ward for terminally ill people. Peräkylä shows how staff use a 'psychological' frame to define themselves as objective surveyors of the emotional reactions of such patients. The psychological frame is a powerful means of resolving the identity disturbances found in other frames; when a patient resists practical or medical framing, staff can explain this in terms of the patient's psychological state.

However, the psychological frame also turns out to be highly relevant to understanding the staff's response to Peräkylä himself. By seeing him as a researcher principally interested in patients' feelings, the staff had a ready-made explanation of his presence to give to patients and also were able to guess which of their own activities might need explaining to him.

Like Peräkylä, by examining my own involvement in the 'framing' of the interaction, and using my eyes as well as my ears, I had kick-started my analysis. However, were there other ways in which I could systematically compare the two NHS clinics with the private clinic? In Chapter 15, I discuss some simple quantitative measures I used in order to respond to this problem.

As already noted, I relied on fieldnotes in this study because I was refused permission to record. Obviously, recording (audio or visual) is the preferred option since it gives you the opportunity to replay data uncontaminated by your assumptions at the time of the recording.

In her PhD on mental health casework, Sally Hunt gathered audio recordings of team meetings which were supplemented by contemporary fieldnotes. As I recommended earlier in this chapter, she began by transcribing only a few meetings. This allowed her to begin early data analysis and to guide which (parts of) other recordings should be transcribed. A basic technical problem for all forms of recording is where you place your equipment. As Sally discovered, the location of microphones can lead to too much background noise. In collecting video recordings of physiotherapy treatment sessions within the British health services, Ruth had to come up with original solutions to obtain the sound and images she needed.

WHAT I DID: RUTH
Coping with Recording 'Troubles'

I encountered a number of troubles, and worked out various solutions as a result. Sound was a challenge, since treatments go on in curtained-off areas of large rooms or gyms. After trying several mics, I found that I could best capture the local sound by fitting the therapist with a tiepin (sometimes called a Lavalier) microphone, attached to a transmitter. The receiver was also a challenge: small models are now available (particularly those designed especially for camcorders by Sennheiser), but mine was rather bulky, and I attached it to the camera's tripod using the rubberized band material (Thera-Band®) that physiotherapists often use in treatment activities. When recording, I turned on the sound and the camera as soon as the therapist went to greet the patient and bring them to the treatment area, and tried to avoid turning off until the final goodbyes; this maximized the capture of the interaction. [Ruth Parry, Social Sciences, Loughborough]

Ruth's story shows that, however well prepared you are, unforeseen contingencies will arise when you first try to make recordings. As Menisha implies, it may turn out that quite basic things go wrong.

WHAT I DID: MENISHA

Getting the Basics Right

Just after starting my PhD I went to my first setting for data collection, a fire service control room, to film the staff at work. I remembered to take all the right equipment – camcorder, microphone, tripod and power supply – and set it up correctly. Whilst I was pleased at the time that everything was running smoothly, I was horrified to discover afterwards that in the four hours that I had been 'recording', only one and half hours had recorded. My camera angle was also a bit dubious, as a few times, instead of capturing the correct angle, where participants were gathering around a desk to solve a problem, I was filming a desk and its empty chair – not the most stimulating subjects for analysis. From personal experience, what advice would I have to offer? As well as ensuring that you have camera angles set up carefully, and that microphones are positioned so you can hear the participants on play-back, there are simpler things to remember. Ensure you know how to set up equipment, such as how the camera fits on the tripod, and understand the features of the camera you will use. Charge batteries and, before recording, ensure you have checked the recording time of the tape, so that it does not run out mid filming. Planning and preparation are essential. Finally, go into an environment with an open mind; things might not be as you expect, but this is not necessarily a bad thing. [Menisha, Management, UK]

Make technology work for you

WATCH: DAVID EXPLAINS IN PERSON

David's Top Tip 35

Make use of the technologies you already possess. Maddie Sandall's interviews with international students for her MSc were recorded using a digital recorder. She adds that these recordings were then 'converted to MP3 and downloaded to my iPod to allow easy transcription from the comfort of my sofa!'

Menisha and Ruth's experiences show the complicated issues that arise when you are trying to produce images and sound relevant to your research problem. The clear implication is that you should pre-test the effectiveness of your recordings before you gather your main data. And, of course, even when you have obtained your recordings, you still have to sort out adequate methods of transcription (on collecting video data, see Heath et al., 2010: Chapter 3).

However, I would not want to conclude this chapter on a note of despair. As in Piera's research on a primary school classroom, technical issues in recording naturally occurring interaction can sometimes be readily resolved.

WHAT I DID: PIERA
Simple Problems, Simple Solutions

Deciding where to place the cameras was clear from the beginning. In fact, it is rather typical of the Italian school system that each year group is assigned to a classroom that actually 'belongs' to the group for the whole school year. Here students do most of their learning activities, except for gymnastics and foreign-language classes. In each classroom, one teacher and 25 students had fixed positions most of the time: one facing the others in parallel rows of seats. In order to capture both sides, it was necessary to place two cameras facing each other. The cameras I used at the time (2000) worked with cassettes lasting 45 minutes, with the disadvantage of having to enter the classroom frequently in order to replace the cassette in each camera - a great disturbance for the ongoing activity. The problem was resolved by connecting the cameras with video recorders operating with VHS cassettes. In this way, four-hour recording without interruption was granted. The cassettes were replaced at the routine and natural interruptions of the school days, while the children were having their lunch in another room and at the end of the school day. It was possible to gather data without the participants seeing me. Furthermore, everything that happened in the classroom was recorded. I believe that now digital cameras have their own hard disk, long sessions of talk can be recorded without difficulties. [Piera Margutti, Sociology, York]

4 COLLECTING INTERNET DATA

It bends reality considerably to imply that ethnography is today the main method of qualitative research and that observational material is the main data source. In a way this is hardly surprising given the plethora of materials that invite our attention. These extend beyond what we can observe with our own eyes to what we can hear and see on recordings, what we can read in paper documents and electronically download on the Internet, and what we can derive by asking questions in interviews or by providing various stimuli to focus groups.

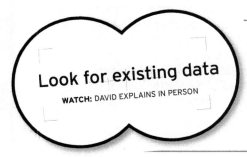

Look for existing data

WATCH: DAVID EXPLAINS IN PERSON

David's Top Tip 36

Before you set out to gather new data using research instruments (such as interviews or focus groups), consider whether the kind of material you need is available on the Internet. If it is, not only will you save a lot of time but your data will be naturally occurring.

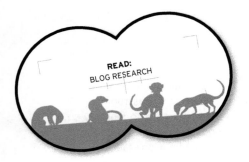

It is now commonplace to remark that communication is increasingly mediated by information technology. Originally, telephone calls were a great impetus to research. Somehow, without visual cues, people managed to communicate with each other. Researchers investigated how we create an orderly structure here with stable expectations of the rights and obligations of, for instance, 'caller' and 'called' (see Schegloff, 1968).

More recently, with the expansion of social networking, the Internet has become a crucial medium of largely text-based communication. Subject to ethically appropriate access, this has opened up a whole new field for ethnographic investigation of textual data including homepages, chatrooms and email correspondence.

The following student example brilliantly evokes the advantages of working with Internet data.

WHAT I DID: GABRIELLA
Virtual Red-Light Districts

I have experienced the empirical data on the Internet to be extremely accessible. I can easily do observations, copy and paste and download the interaction and communication that take place in the virtual red-light district like it was already transcribed and use this material in my fieldnotes. A special program called 'Snagit' helps me to take pictures of what is on the computer screen. I can therefore also gather a range of visual material like photographs, video clips, avatars, banners and use it as empirical data.

So, I think it is easy to gather a lot of empirical data on the Internet, sometimes too much, because it is so easily accessible. My experience, though, is that it is not as easy to get an ethnographic understanding online. I carry my research field in my iPhone and it is easy to go online and offline. For how long do I have to be there? When is it enough? I have been observing the red-light district off and on for three years. In the beginning I spent a lot of time on the field setting, now I only visit now and then. It took me some time to realize for example that some of the users who contributed the most in the virtual red-light district, especially about being a real 'punter', did not really purchase sexual services. I found it fascinating! Initially, I had planned to go on and complement my observations with interviews. After a while I decided to stay on the Internet, the interaction and communication were interesting in themselves, and I decided that the amount of data that I had gathered was more than enough for a thesis. My final reflection on this matter is that I needed to stay as long as it took to go beyond the mere text and content analysis and start to see the interaction behind. [Gabriella Scaramuzzino, Sociology, Malmö University]

Gabriella reveals what Internet data can offer the qualitative researcher:

- access to a setting where interviews or observations would be very difficult and ethically fraught
- the availability of recording techniques like Snagit to store Internet data.

Interestingly enough, Gabriella found her Internet data so rich that she abandoned her original idea of supplementing it with interviews.

EXPLORE:
DIGITAL RECORDINGS

5 WRAPPING UP

In this chapter, we have reviewed many of the practical problems that can arise in collecting, recording and transcribing qualitative data. In most cases, I have shown that there are straightforward solutions to these problems.

However, as I have emphasized throughout, doing qualitative research is not quite like following a cookbook. To produce a worthwhile study depends upon first sorting out what features of the social world attract your interest. And this, in turn, depends upon working with a consistent model of social reality.

What You Need to Remember

Collecting data is never just a technical matter. Data collection must be organized in terms of answering a specific research question which itself is shaped by a particular analytical model of the social world.

Whatever type of data you collect, you should consider *both* the technical issues of accessing your data *and* what your chosen research model tells you about how to recognize 'good' data.

Your Chapter Checklist

1. If you are gathering interview data, you need to think through the following issues:

   - How many interviews are sufficient?
   - Do I need some kind of interview schedule?
   - Do I need to pilot my interviews?
   - How do I propose to transcribe my data?
   - Should I use other sources of data?

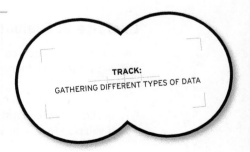

TRACK:
GATHERING DIFFERENT TYPES OF DATA

2. If you are collecting observational data, you need to consider:

    - how you are going to obtain access (and the implications of such access)
    - how your initial observations may help you to narrow down your research problem
    - how you should record your observations
    - whether one 'case' is enough.

3. If you are collecting focus group data, you need to assess:

    - whether you should study a group with whom you are already familiar
    - how to intervene effectively in focus group discussions
    - how well focus group data fit your theoretical model.

4. If you are collecting Internet data, you need to assess:

    - how much data you need
    - effective means of recording data
    - whether you need to supplement Internet data with other material (e.g. interviews).

Exercises

Exercise 1: Avoid problems with asking about past events

APPLY:
YOUR EXERCISE WORKBOOK

Arne Petersen (PhD student, Denmark) was interested in how people in the Faroe Islands responded to the sudden discovery of oil there in the 1990s. As he puts it: 'in May 2015 I conducted nine semi-structured interviews with top management and local politicians involved in the oil industry and tried to sense the locals' take on the oil industry. I had a set of questions which were to support my intensive interviewing, but what I really wanted to achieve was an in-depth understanding of the interviewees' interpretation of the organization and the history of the oil industry'.

- What problems arise in asking interviewees about past events?
- How could Arne modify his research topic to take account of these problems?

Exercise 2: Evaluate interview guidelines

The following research on burnout among Sri Lankan female primary school teachers includes a detailed interview guide.

- What advantages and disadvantages do you see in this guide in the context of a qualitative research study?
- If you plan to do interview research, what sort of guide (if any) will you use? Why?

Interviewer guide

1. Socio-demographic factors of the teacher:

    - Age
    - Ethnicity
    - Religion
    - Marital status
    - Husband's occupation
    - Number of children
    - Family income
    - Place of residence: district, urban or rural
    - Distance of school
    - Method of travel to school

2. Capacity and experience of the teachers:

    - Highest educational qualification
    - Total experience in teaching
    - Number of years in current school
    - Grade of the class

3. Satisfaction:

    - Are you satisfied with your job?
    - If yes, what more than anything do you feel leads to this job satisfaction?
    - If no, what more than anything do you feel prevents you from being satisfied with your job?

4. Satisfaction regarding factors in the classroom:

    - Number of children
    - Space, ventilation, temperature
    - Teaching materials

5. Satisfaction regarding student interaction:

    - Students' achievements
    - Students' behaviour

6. Satisfaction regarding cooperation from colleagues and superiors:

    - Colleagues
    - Superiors

[Sunil, Sri Lanka]

Exercise 3: Explore the role of the researcher in interviewing

Make an audio recording of one interview. Then review how your contribution is presenting a version of your identity. Consider how this might affect your interviewee's responses.

Exercise 4: Plan for fieldwork observations

If you are planning to do some fieldwork observations, write a short research plan covering the following issues:

- How will I obtain access to the field (and why are access negotiations important ethically and as a source of data)?
- How can I use my fieldwork to narrow down my research topic?
- Am I going to use one or more settings? Will one 'case' be enough?
- How do I plan to record my observations?

Exercise 5: Assess uses of interview data

Here are two examples of student research projects related to the Internet.

1. A study of consumer motivations for content creation in online social networking sites. [Lucy Miller, Macquarie University]
2. The impacts of rural Internet centres on quality of life in rural areas of Malaysia. [Marhaini Mohd Noor, University of South Queensland]

Both studies propose to gather data by interviews with users of appropriate sites. Consider:

- What sort of data from the Internet itself might answer these students' questions?
- What are the gains and losses of supplementing such data by interviews, focus groups and/or onsite observations?

Further Reading

Steinar Kvale's *Doing Interviews* (Sage, 2007: 33–66) is a great source of practical advice on conducting interviews. If you are considering using interviews to access narratives, I recommend Jay Gubrium and James Holstein's *Analyzing Narrative Reality* (Sage, 2009) and Catherine Riessman's *Narrative Methods for the Human Sciences* (Sage, 2008). Barbara Czarniawska's *Shadowing and Other Techniques for Doing Fieldwork in Modern Societies* (Liber, 2007) is a gold mine of insightful advice on collecting fieldwork data. There is a plethora of advice on the methodological and procedural choices entailed in setting up and conducting a focus group: see, for example, Michael Bloor et al.'s *Focus Groups in Social Research* (Sage, 2001) and Rosaline Barbour's *Doing Focus Groups* (Sage, 2007a). Sue Wilkinson's 'Analysing focus group data' (in D. Silverman (ed.), *Qualitative Research: Theory, Method and Practice*, Sage, 2016) provides a valuable discussion of the theoretical and epistemological choices entailed in analysing and interpreting focus group data. Robert Kozinets's book *Netnography* (Sage, 2010) is an invaluable resource if you want to study Internet data.

READ: RECRUITING SUBJECTS
READ: CREDIBLE FOCUS GROUP RESEARCH
READ: RECORDING FIELD NOTES
READ: RECORDING & TRANSCRIPTION

Discover the chapter's digital resources in your SILVERMAN FIELD GUIDE

FIFTEEN
Developing Data Analysis

Learning Outcomes

By the end of this chapter you will be able to:

- Kick-start your data analysis.
- Work systematically with interviews, observational data, audio recordings or visual images.
- Recognize the useful role that theoretical models play in shaping your research.

Understanding which type of analysis would work best for you
WATCH: DAVID EXPLAINS IN PERSON

David's Top Tip 37

This chapter shows you ways to begin data analysis very early on. Early data analysis will allow you to assess which methods of data analysis make most sense to you and work best for your data corpus.

1 INTRODUCTION

After their first year of PhD research, people have varying degrees of certainty about the future. As Coffey and Atkinson (1996) put it, the end of year 1 sees two kinds of researchers. The uncertain ones feel they are drowning in data and ask: 'I've collected all these data, now what should I do?' The other, more confident, researchers state: 'I've collected all my data, now I'm going to analyse them and write them up.'

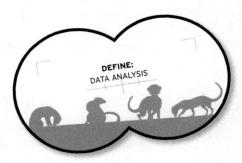

The temptation might be to find merit in both positions. After all, self-questioning and self-confidence both seem to be worthy qualities in a researcher. In fact, *neither* position is satisfactory and both reflect a more or less wasted first year of research:

> Both positions imply a woeful lack of appreciation of what is and can be meant by analysis ... [Such analysis] is a *pervasive* activity throughout the life of a research project. Analysis is not simply one of the later stages of research, to be followed by an equally separate phase of 'writing up results'. (Coffey and Atkinson, 1996: 10–11, my emphasis)

Research designs which devote the first year solely to a literature review and/or data gathering may look excellent on paper. Indeed, they may be just the thing in quantitative studies more concerned with implementing pre-designed 'measures' rather than employing a theoretical imagination. But in most qualitative research, unless you are analysing data more or less from day 1 you will always have to play 'catch-up'.

'All very well,' you might respond, 'but where on earth am I going to get my data from on day 1? Whether I'm doing an MA or a PhD, surely most of my early work will involve getting access to some research site or set of respondents and then, if successful, gathering my data. How is it going to be possible to start data analysis so quickly?'

In the rest of this chapter, I show you how to kick-start your data analysis very early on. I then discuss ways to begin data analysis on many different kinds of qualitative data: interviews, fieldnotes, transcripts of conversation and visual data.

2 KICK-STARTING DATA ANALYSIS

As already noted, you might well ask: 'Where am I going to get my data on day 1?' For both MA and PhD students, there are five very practical, complementary solutions to this puzzle:

- Analyse data already in the public sphere.
- Beg or borrow other people's data.
- Seek advice from your supervisor.

- Analyse your own data as you gather them.
- Ask key questions about your data.

I briefly discuss each strategy below.

Analyse data already in the public sphere

Some types of naturally occurring materials are already waiting for you. Think of blogs, social media, company statements and newspapers available on the Internet. Now select a few sites which covered a particular story (e.g. Princess Diana's death, the O.J. Simpson trial, Donald Trump's presidency or the financial crash of 2008). Then there are those rare qualitative studies which reproduce large portions of data, making them available for your own reanalysis, perhaps following up different questions from those originally asked.

Even if you intend, in due course, to gather your own data, these materials are immediately available. As such, they provide a marvellous opportunity to refine your methods and to get a feel of the joys (and torments) of 'hands-on' data analysis.

Of course, you still lack a research problem and a method of analysis, and you will need to think long and hard about both. But you have your data, so go to it!

Beg or borrow other people's data

Perhaps your research interests cannot be accommodated by data in the public sphere. If so, it is always worth making enquiries in your department about relevant data that other people may be willing to share with you.

Your supervisor is an obvious person to turn to. Having agreed to supervise you, and thereby acknowledged a common research interest, it is probable that your supervisor will have already gathered data that may be relevant to your project. Don't be shy to ask if you might have access to it. This was exactly the strategy that my student Vicki Taylor followed. I was delighted to pass on my counselling audio files to her so she could explore a research problem which was different to mine.

Of course, there may be ethical or other reasons why such access is not always possible. But most supervisors will be delighted, perhaps even flattered, if you are interested in their own data. After all, your research may lead to new ideas which will help them in their own work.

If your supervisor cannot deliver the goods, explore your various peer groups. Fellow research students in your department, perhaps two or three years into their research, may, like your supervisor, welcome passing on some of their own data. If not, explore the Internet to see if there are others working on your topic.

Secondary data websites are now up and running. So, before you think of gathering your own data, explore what is already available (for a discussion of the uses and limits of secondary qualitative data, see Seale, 2011).

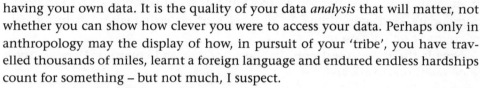

Above all, you must remember that, in most disciplines, no 'brownie points' are usually given for having your own data. It is the quality of your data *analysis* that will matter, not whether you can show how clever you were to access your data. Perhaps only in anthropology may the display of how, in pursuit of your 'tribe', you have travelled thousands of miles, learnt a foreign language and endured endless hardships count for something – but not much, I suspect.

Even if you feel happier to have your own data, remember that this does not exclude the first two strategies. In the early stages, analysing other people's data or public data may still give you the impetus you need for research 'lift-off' when you are ready to analyse your own materials.

Seek advice from your supervisor

As an undergraduate, your main face-to-face contact with a faculty member may have been when you submitted a term paper or, occasionally, when you got some feedback after such a submission. However, this model of a student–staff relationship is totally inappropriate when you are doing your own research. Supervisors are there to offer support when you most need it (see Chapter 11). If you feel that you are 'drowning in data', that is a prime time to ask for help.

One way supervisors can help you gain focus is to suggest a small and hence achievable task. Two examples of such tasks from Howard Becker and Harry Wolcott are given below:

- Offering a snap characterization of what seems to be happening in your data and asking you to respond to it. It really doesn't matter how wide of the mark this idea is if it can get you to start working with your data (Becker, 1998).
- Asking you to take 'some manageable *unit of one* as a focus' (Wolcott, 1990: 69; discussed at greater length in Chapter 6 of this book). In this way, instead of confronting your data as one large, threatening mass, you can narrow down and achieve a focus on one topic, one activity or one day (or one minute).

These kinds of task should help you overcome the kind of mental blocks we all too readily erect for ourselves when first confronting data. If we are set a small task, we are more likely to succeed and to gain confidence. Moreover, through such small tasks, we can start to see subtleties in our data which may be hidden if we ask big questions at the outset. As Becker (1998) reminds us, don't over-theorize early on in data analysis. Instead, begin from a situation or a datum and then build theories out of this limited material.

Analyse your own data as you gather them

Data analysis should not only happen after all your data has been safely gathered. If you only have one interview or recording or set of fieldnotes, go to it! Where appropriate, start transcribing. In all cases, start reviewing your data in the light of your research questions.

Now is the time to test out methods, findings and concepts. Here are some good questions to ask yourself:

- Do I feel comfortable with my preferred method of data analysis (e.g. grounded theory, narrative, conversation or discourse analysis)?
- Is my method of data analysis suggesting interesting questions?
- Is it giving me a strong grip on my data that looks like it might generate interesting generalizations?
- Do previous research findings seem to apply to my data? If not, why not? If so, how can I use my data to develop these findings?
- How do particular concepts from my preferred model of social research apply to my data? Which concepts work best and hence look likely to be most productive?

WHAT I DID: MARIANNE
Studying the Care of Adolescents

Marianne Buen Sommerfeldt (Oslo) is studying a child welfare institution. She realized early on that what counts as 'care' in her research is not obvious but depends upon her preferred model of social research. As she writes:

When studying the phenomenon of care the choice of theoretical perspective has a major impact on all stages of the project:

1. In a *realist* perspective, I could assume that care is something, which *is*. A phenomenon that exists, that is tangible and constant, an objective size with specific characteristics, independent of the researcher studying it. I could aim to reveal social structures in the child welfare institutions, in which care appears and how the context, the child welfare institution, interacts with care-actions. The aim could be to describe care objectively and neutral.

I would see myself as a neutral researcher, and the phenomenon of interest, care, as a defined, objective phenomenon.

2. In accordance with a *phenomenological* perspective, however, I would focus on how care appears for the adolescents in a child welfare institution, how and when the adolescents experience care. I could benefit from the expression 'life-world', and look into how the adolescents perceive and experience their everyday life in a child welfare institution. It would be the experience of care that was my object of analysis, from the adolescents' own perspectives. I would then aim to get thick descriptions of care experiences. The adolescents would be my 'vessels-of-answers' and repositories of reflections, opinions and experiences (Holstein and Gubrium, 2016).

3. My choice is, however, to base my project on a *constructionist* perspective, and see care not as an objective entity with specific characteristics, but as fluid, and changeable phenomenon. I understand care, not as something I can 'reveal', but a complex phenomenon that the social worker does, as well as adolescents' interpretations of and responses to this doing. Care is an interactive phenomenon, which exists only in interaction. Care is not a static phenomenon that appears in a coherent way in different contexts, but is created in the specific encounter, where a range of conditions can affect the doing of care. Care emerges in the interaction and is shaped by both the caregiver and the care receiver. Also, the adolescents' experiences with care and their reflections upon their relationship to the professionals is not readily stored in their consciousness, but rather I see the interview as an opportunity where the adolescents and I will actively construct the information (cf. Holstein and Gubrium, 2016).

Marianne concludes:

Care as a term is highly used in discourses on everyday family practices, laden by cultural meaning, and therefore often understood as a term with an obvious content, that doesn't need any explanation. A constructionist perspective however challenges the non-questioned meanings of the concept that could be taken for granted, and forces me in the research process to openly look for other forms, definitions, understandings of the phenomenon.

Finding out which theoretical perspective works best for you cannot be properly answered from the armchair or drawing board. No matter how elegant your original research proposal, its application to your first batch of data is always salutary. In most qualitative research, sticking with your original research design can be a sign of inadequate data analysis rather than demonstrating a welcome consistency.

None of this will you know until you begin analysing your data. Of course, this will mean committing yourself to writing up your analysis at a very early stage. As

Wolcott argues: 'You cannot begin writing early enough' (1990: 20). Even a 200-word shot at data analysis will give your supervisor something to go on. And even if your understandable initial hesitancy means that you are not 'off and running', at least you will have started.

PRACTICE:
ANALYSING INTERVIEW DATA

Ask key questions about your data

Of course, what is a 'key' question will depend upon your research topic and your preferred model of qualitative research. Models and methods are never right or wrong; they are only more or less useful. Only by trying out different approaches can you tell if they work for you.

Table 15.1 offers tips on beginning qualitative data analysis. The table shows that there are few if any 'free-floating' key questions.

Table 15.1   Beginning data analysis

1	Try out different theoretical approaches (e.g. naturalism and constructionism) and various methods of data analysis (e.g. grounded theory, narrative analysis and discourse analysis) and see what works for you (and for your data)
2	Avoid too early hypotheses and try to see where your analysis is leading in order to establish a hypothesis
3	Don't look for telling examples which support your hypotheses, but analyse your data thoroughly and fairly to test your hypotheses rigorously
4	Initially, focus on a small part of your data and analyse it intensively; there will be time later to test out your findings on your dataset as a whole (extensive analysis)
5	Try to focus on sequences (of talk, written material or interaction)

Source: adapted from Silverman (2011b: 58)

WHAT I DID: GABRIELLA
Studying a Virtual Red-Light District

Despite point 3 in Table 15.1, a typical but mistaken strategy in early data analysis is to focus upon unusual or even extraordinary stories or incidents. Looking back on her early attempts at data analysis, Gabriella now recognizes this error.

When I look back in my fieldnotes I can see that in the beginning of my observations I gathered a lot of data and I wrote very detailed fieldnotes but I mainly saw conversations and interactions that in some ways 'stood out'. I observed the interaction and communication between people who purchase and sell sexual services and at first I was very caught up in the content of the interaction as they tended to discuss matters that were very interesting to me. I could not really go beyond this and see the interaction in itself and the 'ordinary things' in the virtual red-light district. Maybe it is a little bit ironic, but it was first when I did a user and content analysis of the virtual red-light district and spent an entire month on the field setting that I actually could see the interaction and not just the content. [Gabriella Scaramuzzino, Sociology, Malmö University]

As Gabriella recognizes, the point is to understand the interaction, not what 'stands out' in the surface content. This is because:

- Extraordinary incidents may not help you properly understand what is 'routine' in the context you are studying.
- Qualitative research is at its most powerful in exploring things which are everyday and taken for granted (see Silverman, 2013: Chapter 1).

In order to get going fruitfully, the following list has worked with my own students and the questions are worth posing about your own research:

- What are the main units in my data and how do they relate to one another? Remember that no meaning resides in a single unit and so everything depends on how your units fit together. This is an issue of *articulation*.
- Which categories are actually used by the people you are studying? Remember that, unlike quantitative researchers, we do not want to begin with our own categories at the outset but to understand participants' categories. This is an issue of *definition*.
- What are the contexts and consequences of your subjects' use of categories? Remember that it is rarely right to ask 'why' questions before you have identified the local phenomena involved. This is an issue of *hows* and *whats*.
- How do my difficulties in the field over, say, access and how I am defined by my research subjects provide me with further research topics? Remember that the beauty of qualitative research is that it offers the potential for us to topicalize such difficulties rather than just treat them as methodological constraints. This is an issue of the creative use of *troubles*.

However, a checklist of 'suggestions' can appear somewhat anaemic and without substance. Let me illustrate these general points with an account of how data analysis developed in one qualitative study. The beauty of qualitative research is that it gives you access to the nitty-gritty reality of everyday life viewed through a new analytic lens. Through the example that follows, you will learn how to take advantage of that access in order to focus and then refocus your data analysis.

3 A CASE STUDY

EXPLORE:
ANALYSING ETHNOGRAPHIC DATA

In the early 1980s (see Silverman, 1987: Chapters 1–6) I directed a group of researchers studying a paediatric cardiology (child heart) unit. Much of our data derived from tape recordings of an outpatient clinic that was held every Wednesday.

It was not a coincidence that we decided to focus on this clinic rather than upon, say, interaction on the wards. Pragmatically, we knew that the clinic, as a scheduled and focused event, lasting between two and four hours and tied to particular outcomes, would be likely to give us a body of good-quality data. By contrast, on the ward, audio recording would be much more intrusive and produce audio files of poorer quality because of multiple conversations and background noise. Even if these technical problems could be overcome, the (apparently) unfocused character of ward life meant that it would be far harder to see order than in the outpatient clinic. For instance, unlike the latter, there would be no obvious repetitive structures like scheduled meetings by appointment, physical examinations and announcements of diagnosis and prognosis.

Of course, this does not mean that a researcher should never study apparently unfocused encounters – from the hospital ward to the street corner. But it does mean that, if you do, you must be prepared for long vigils and apparently unpromising data before researchable ideas start to gel.

At our hospital clinic, we became interested in how decisions (or 'disposals') were organized and announced. It seemed likely that the doctor's way of announcing decisions was systematically related not only to clinical factors (like the child's heart condition) but to social factors (such as what parents would be told at various stages of treatment). For instance, at a first outpatients' consultation, doctors would not normally announce to parents the discovery of a major heart abnormality and the necessity for life-threatening surgery. Instead, they would suggest the need for more tests and only hint that major surgery might be needed. They would also collaborate with parents who produced examples of their child's apparent 'wellness'. This step-by-step method of information giving was avoided in only two cases. If a child was diagnosed as 'healthy' by the cardiologist, the doctor would give all the information in one go and would engage in what we called a 'search and destroy' operation, based on eliciting any remaining worries of the parent(s) and proving that they were mistaken.

In the case of a group of children with the additional disability of Down's syndrome, as well as suspected cardiac disease, the doctor would present all the clinical information at one sitting, avoiding a step-by-step method. Moreover, atypically, the doctor would allow parents to make the choice about further treatment, while encouraging them to dwell on non-clinical matters like their child's 'enjoyment of life' or friendly personality.

We then narrowed our focus to examine how doctors talked to parents about the decision to have a small diagnostic test on their children. In most cases, the doctor would say something like:

> What we propose to do, if you agree, is a small test.

No parent disagreed with an offer which appeared to be purely formal – like the formal right (never exercised) of the Queen not to sign legislation passed by the British Parliament. For children with Down's syndrome, however, the parents' right to choose was far from formal. The doctor would say things to them like the following:

> I think what we would do now depends a little bit on parents' feelings.
>
> Now it depends a little bit on what you think.
>
> It depends very much on your own personal views as to whether we should proceed.

Moreover, these consultations were longer and apparently more democratic than elsewhere. A view of the patient in a family context was encouraged and parents were given every opportunity to voice their concerns and to participate in decision making.

In this subsample, unlike the larger sample, when given a real choice, parents refused the test – with only one exception. Yet this served to reinforce rather than to challenge the medical policy in the unit concerned. This policy was to discourage surgery, all things being equal, on such children. So the democratic form co-existed with (and was indeed sustained by) the maintenance of an autocratic policy.

The research thus discovered the mechanics whereby a particular medical policy was enacted. The availability of tape recordings of large numbers of consultations, together with a research method that sought to develop hypotheses inductively, meant that we were able to develop our data analysis by discovering a phenomenon for which we had not originally been looking.

The lessons to be drawn from this study are summarized in Table 15.2.

Table 15.2   Four ways to develop data analysis

- Focus on data which is of high quality and easiest to collect (audio recordings of clinics)
- Look at one process within this data (how medical 'disposals' are organized)
- Narrow down to one part of that process (announcing a small diagnostic test)
- Compare different subsamples of the population (children with Down's syndrome and the rest)

So much for general issues. We will now see how you can kick-start data analysis in the context of using four different kinds of data:

- interviews
- fieldnotes
- audio files of naturally occurring talk
- visual images.

4 INTERVIEWS

In Chapters 3 and 14, I examined the various ways that researchers can read sense into answers that respondents give to open-ended interviews. The most popular approach is to treat respondents' answers as describing some external reality (e.g. facts, events) or internal experience (e.g. feelings, meanings). Following this approach, it is appropriate to build into the research design various devices to ensure the accuracy of your interpretation. So you can check the accuracy of what your respondents tell you by other observations (see Chapter 17 on the method of triangulation). And you can treat such measures as inter-coder agreement (see Chapter 17) and computer-assisted qualitative data programs (see Chapter 16) as a means of securing a fit between your interpretations and some external reality. Containing elements of positivism (facts) and **romanticism**'s interest in 'experience', we can call this a naturalist approach to interview data.

EXPLORE: NARRATIVE ANALYSIS

As Clive Seale has pointed out (personal correspondence), 'naturalism' is here used in the sense of the literary genre whose aim is to describe the 'gritty' reality of people's lives. In this approach, typical of tabloid journalism, 'confessional' stories are gathered and presented to the reader as new 'facts' about personalities. This form of naturalism has had much influence on qualitative research (see Atkinson and Silverman, 1997).

The alternative constructionist approach treats interview data as accessing various stories or narratives through which people describe their world (see Gubrium and Holstein, 2009; Riessman, 2008). This approach claims that, by abandoning the attempt to treat respondents' accounts as potentially 'true' pictures of 'reality', we open up for analysis the culturally rich methods through which interviewers and interviewees, in concert, generate plausible accounts of the world. Although this second approach may use similar measures to achieve 'quality control' (e.g. group data sessions to ensure agreement about the researchers' reading of a transcript), these measures are used in pursuit of a different, 'narrated' reality in which the 'situated', or locally produced, nature of accounts is to the fore.

I am aware that many readers of this volume will favour the former, naturalist approach. At the same time, I do not want to neglect the latter, constructionist approach – particularly as it is closer to my own theoretical orientation. Fortunately, there are examples available which show how you can kick-start a piece of interview research using both these approaches. In this student example, thematic analysis, a naturalist version of content analysis, was combined with grounded theory and the constructionist approach of narrative analysis.

WHAT I DID: ANASTACIA

Native American Storytelling

I used thematic analysis and grounded theory (GT) approaches because Native American storytellers use abstract ideas and concepts in their stories. If I did not use this approach, I believe many of the meanings and subtleties in their stories would have been lost. To put it simply, the aim of thematic analysis is to make sense out of a large amount of qualitative data by simply looking at data as a whole and counting how many times a descriptive pattern arises in the stories. The aim of GT is to generate hypotheses that theoretically *describe* the constructs that arise in every sentence of the stories told. I use this approach because it made sense to take the large amount of data and describe the stories with a broad theme during my first reading. Then, I looked at the stories line by line and coded particular themes in their own words during my second reading. This allowed me to take a top down, bottom up approach to understanding hidden nuances in their stories. I used narrative analysis on the final reading of these stories because it enables me to locate any temporal sequencing that is occurring in the stories and to present my findings in story form. [Anastacia M. Schulhoff, Department of Sociology, University of Missouri-Columbia]

Anastacia was able to work with different models by using them at different stages of her research. However, when you are beginning a research project, it is not always clear how you should analyse your data. At this stage, clarity about your answers to analytical questions (about what kind of a model you are using) can help sort out apparently intractable questions about data analysis. Look at this next student example.

WHAT I DID: CECILIE
Citizenship and Feminism

My PhD asks how feminism, ethnic identity and religion are brought together in the policies of women's movements and in the daily lives of women. I have started to conduct interviews with women who are active in women's organizations. I do two interviews with each: one primarily about the organization's work (women's issues, relations with other organizations and political work), and one more 'personal' about the person's everyday life, including questions about citizenship (identity, belonging, participation in different areas of society and so on).

The issues overlap, but when the person is representing the organization my impression is that some of them are afraid that they will say something 'wrong' on behalf of the organization and they want to say what's considered to be 'politically correct'. My question is related to ways to handle the interview material when the people I'm interviewing are speaking with 'several voices'. [Cecilie Thun, Women's Studies and Gender, Oslo University]

Cecilie's question emerges from a well-designed project which is right on the cusp between naturalist and constructionist approaches to interview data. Viewed from a naturalist (factual) perspective, people 'speaking with several voices' is a problem in need of a technical solution. For instance, you might ask the 'same' question in several different ways or compare what respondents say with what they do.

By contrast, constructionists argue that 'identity' is never a fixed entity lying somewhere inside people's heads. We present different aspects of ourselves in different contexts. So, rather than eliminate multiple voices, we need to examine what voices people use, how they use them and with what consequences. In other words, constructionists assume that interview participants actively create meaning. This lies behind Holstein and Gubrium's idea of 'the active interview':

Construed as active, the subject behind the respondent not only holds facts and details of experience, but, in the very process of offering them up for response, constructively adds to, takes away from, and transforms the facts and details. The respondent can hardly 'spoil' what he or she is, in effect, subjectively creating. (1995: 117)

In a project on the quality of care and quality of life of nursing home residents, Gubrium (1993) noted how residents adopted varying 'standpoints':

> In speaking of the quality of care, for example, nursing home residents, as interview respondents, not only offer substantive thoughts and feelings pertinent to the topic under consideration, but simultaneously and continuously monitor who they are in relation to the person questioning them. For example, prefacing her remarks about the quality of life in her facility with the statement 'speaking as a woman', a nursing home resident informs the interviewer that she is to be heard as a woman, not as someone else – not a mere resident, cancer patient, or abandoned mother. (In Holstein and Gubrium, 1995: 122)

Viewed in this light, the constructionist answer to Cecilie's question is threefold:

- Treat the 'several voices' you have identified as a *finding* rather than a problem.
- Delineate the range of voices that your respondents use ('what' questions).
- Examine how these voices are articulated in relation to each other and the interactional contexts in which this happens ('how' questions).

EXPLORE:
THE ACTIVE INTERVIEW

In what Holstein and Gubrium call 'the active interview', 'Data can be analyzed to show the dynamic interrelatedness of the whats and the hows' (1995: 127).

Being aware of your active narration

WATCH: DAVID EXPLAINS IN PERSON

David's Top Tip 38

Holstein and Gubrium (1995: 33–4) cite tell-tale phrases which respondents use to signal shifts in roles: for example, 'speaking as a mother now'; 'thinking like a woman'; 'wearing my professional hat'; 'if I were in his shoes'; and 'now that you ask'. When analysing your interview data, look for prefaces of this kind and try to identify the range of subject positions your respondents invoke.

Note that this approach is a useful antidote to the assumption that people have a single identity waiting to be discovered by the interviewer. By contrast, it reveals that we are active narrators who weave skilful, appropriately located, stories.

Two further Norwegian student projects follow this focus on the 'whats' and 'hows' of interview accounts. We first came across Sveinung Sandberg's research on the street drug scene in Chapter 8. Here is how he describes the 'self-presentations' of users and dealers.

WHAT I DID: SVEINUNG

Street Drug Narratives

The topics of my research are street drug scenes, illegal drug dealing and drug consumption, violence, ethnicity, and hip-hop culture. The data are observation (partly participatory) over a two-year period and interviews with 60 young people. Of these, 40 were adolescent street dwellers picked up in the area around an 'open drug scene' (Plata/Skippergata). The rest were street cannabis dealers aged 15–30 selling at a more dispersed drug scene (Akerselva), all ethnic minorities.

It is often emphasized that qualitative interviews are social situations where data are constructed as a result of the interaction between the interviewer and the interviewed. In this paper I wish to discuss how qualitative interviews can be analysed as social situations, struggles for power, and self-presentation. The paper presents six strategic self-presentations my research participants use in order to manage identity and keep self-respect during the interviews: (a) 'I'm a nice guy'; (b) 'It was my own choice'; (c) excuses/sad tales/neutralization; (d) emphasizing similarity between interviewer and research participant; (e) posing as gangsters; (f) exaggerating in order to get attention. [Sveinung Sandberg, Sociology, Oslo]

In a related project, Mette has examined the narratives produced about drug dealing within the prison system.

WHAT I DID: METTE

Drug Narratives and the Penal System

The project 'A qualitative study of the heroin market' is based on 24 qualitative interviews with imprisoned offenders, 2 interviews with dealers on the outside, and 6 interviews with policemen who have followed the development of the heroin market over time. As a starting point these interviews were only meant to illuminate the organizational aspects of the heroin trade, but in meeting with the offenders and hearing their narratives, issues of self-presentation and power also became apparent and needed addressing. Some central questions: How do the heroin smugglers and dealers present themselves and their illegal activities? What explanation do they give for their illegal actions? What types of representations of normality, deviance, health and sickness are found in their narratives? [Mette Irmgard Snertingdal, Sociology, Norway]

Topics like 'self-presentation' and multiple 'voices' are a very nice way to kick-start constructionist interview research. But a problem remains. Issues like drug use, the penal system and citizenship are important substantive and political topics.

If we treat our respondents' accounts only as 'self-presentations' or 'narratives', aren't we losing sight of such broader issues?

Fortunately, both Mette and Sveinung are very much aware of these issues. Mette asks:

> Do the offenders create their narratives in meeting with different institutionalized practices? How does the practice of criminal law shape the narratives of the offenders? And how freely do the offenders create their narratives, and in what way should perspectives of power be integrated in the analyses of the heroin smugglers' and dealers' narratives?

And Sveinung observes:

> An important argument in the discussion will be that analysing self-presentations is more important than methodological reservations; it is crucial in order to understand the social world of the research participants.

Put in other terms, although Sveinung and Mette begin with 'what' and 'how' questions, they want to go beyond such questions in order to ask 'why?' Or, as Sveinung tellingly puts it: 'What can lies tell us about life?'

By moving from 'what' and 'how' to 'why' questions, constructionist interviewers seek to understand the varied contexts out of which we 'draw from experience' to convey accounts of who and what we are. A telling example is provided in an anecdote about one of Jay Gubrium's doctoral students (Gubrium and Holstein, 2002: 21–2). The student interviewed pharmacists who had engaged in substance abuse. His aim was to understand how those who 'should know better' accounted for what had happened to them. As

it turned out, what these pharmacists said closely fitted the familiar recovery rubrics of self-help groups. (Indeed, many had attended groups like Alcoholics Anonymous and Narcotics Anonymous.) So in what sense were these accounts the pharmacists' 'own' stories? As Gubrium pointed out, don't these stories 'belong' not only to individuals but to particular organizational discourses which are merely 'voiced' here?

5 FIELDNOTES

We now move on to ethnographic studies based on observation and fieldnotes. In Chapter 14, we considered the nitty-gritty questions involved in gathering field data. Now we need to see how we can kick-start the analysis of such data. The following areas will be discussed:

- why detail is important
- expanding fieldnotes in order to develop your sense of what is going on
- thinking about what you are seeing as well as hearing
- examining how interactions and events are articulated or put together
- progressive focusing
- the relevance of simple counting techniques
- the limits of coding observational data.

Why detail is important

> Field researchers seek to get close to others in order to understand their way of life. To preserve and convey that closeness, they must describe situations and events of interest in detail. (Emerson et al., 1995: 14)

By preserving the details of interaction, you are in a better position to analyse the issues set out in Table 15.3.

Like any set of animating questions, the kinds of issues set out in Table 15.3 reflect a particular model of the social world. As in my study of heart clinics, Emerson et al. assume a constructionist or ethnomethodological model in which the meaning of events is not transparent but is actively constructed by the participants (members).

Table 15.3   Functions of detailed fieldnotes

- To identify and follow processes in witnessed events
- To understand how members themselves characterize and describe particular activities, events and groups
- To convey members' explanations for when, why or how particular things happen and, thereby, to elicit members' theories of the causes of particular happenings
- To identify the practical concerns, conditions and constraints that people confront and deal with in their everyday lives and actions

Source: adapted from Emerson et al. (1995)

Two methodological imperatives flow from this model:

- a concern with what participants take to be *routine* or obvious.
- a recognition that what is routine is best established through watching and listening to what people do rather than asking them directly.

Unlike much ethnographic fieldwork, the interview is not regarded as a major research tool. Instead:

> the distinctive procedure is to observe and record naturally occurring talk and interaction ... [while] it may be useful or essential to interview members about the use and meaning of specific local terms and phrases ... the researcher's deeper concern lies in the actual, situated use of those terms in ordinary interaction. (1995: 140)

Such a concern with what participants take to be ordinary and unexceptional gives a clear focus to making and analysing fieldnotes. Data analysis can then develop through asking the sort of questions set out in Table 15.4.

Table 15.4   Six initial questions for fieldnote analysis

1	What are people doing? What are they trying to accomplish?
2	How exactly do they do this? What specific means and/or strategies do they use?
3	How do members talk about, characterize and understand what is going on?
4	What assumptions are they making?
5	What do I see going on here? What did I learn from these notes?
6	Why did I include them?

Source: Emerson et al. (1995: 146)

The questions in Table 15.4 will help you address the nagging problem that you are simply imposing your interpretation upon your data (the issue of validity). The following example shows how one student, working with Internet data, had a telling answer to such concerns.

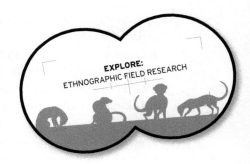

EXPLORE: ETHNOGRAPHIC FIELD RESEARCH

WHAT I DID: GABRIELLA

Interpretation of a Virtual Red-Light District

Throughout the text I try to show deviant examples to demonstrate the complexity in the virtual red-light district but also to make my data analysis more credible.

Ethnographers like me, who (only) use naturally occurring data on the Internet, have been criticized as some scholars argue that it is too much interpretation going on, only observing, no physical bodies present and no interviews face-to-face. My experience is, however, that on the Internet, bodies, body language and emotions are reproduced in textual exchanges and there are a lot of 'interactional clues' which I can look for and use to interpret the interaction and communication. I mean that the contributors use emoticons, acronyms, capitals, dots, pictures, etc., when they interact. To make my data analysis credible I also plan to discuss and show how I interpret situations, and how many different interactional clues actually are used in textual exchanges. The Internet is hence not a totally disembodied space. [Gabriella Scaramuzzino, Sociology, Malmö University]

Expanded fieldnotes

> Fieldwork is so fascinating and coding usually so energy-absorbing, that you can get preoccupied and overwhelmed with the flood of particulars – the poignant quote, the appealing personality of a key informant. You forget to *think*, to make deeper and more general sense of what is happening, to begin to explain it in a conceptually coherent way. (Miles and Huberman, 1984: 69)

In order to make 'deeper and more general sense of what is happening', Spradley (1979) suggests that observers keep four separate sets of notes:

1. Short notes made at the time.
2. Expanded notes made as soon as possible after each field session.
3. A fieldwork journal to record problems and ideas that arise during each stage of fieldwork.
4. A provisional running record of analysis and interpretation (discussed by Kirk and Miller, 1986: 53).

Spradley's suggestions help to systematize fieldnotes and thus improve their reliability (see Chapter 15). Like Spradley, Miles and Huberman (1984) offer systematic ways of expanding what gets recorded in fieldnotes. They suggest writing 'contact summary sheets' or extended memos after each observation (1984: 50–1, 69–71). An example of how to use a contact summary sheet to encourage analytic thinking is set out in Table 15.5.

Table 15.5 Questions for contact summary sheets

- What people, events or situations were involved?
- What were the main themes or issues in the contact?
- Which research questions did the contact bear most centrally on?
- What new hypotheses, speculations or guesses about the field situations were suggested by the contact?
- Where should the fieldworker place most energy during the next contact, and what sorts of information should be sought?

Source: Miles and Huberman (1984: 50)

Miles and Huberman (1984: 51, adapted here) suggest five reasons why such contact sheets are valuable:

1. To guide planning for the next contact.
2. To suggest new or revised codes.
3. To coordinate several fieldworkers' work.
4. To serve as a reminder of the contact at a later stage.
5. To serve as the basis for data analysis.

How we record data is important because it is directly linked to the quality of data analysis. In this sense, fieldnotes and contact sheets are, of course, only means to an end: developing the analysis.

Using your eyes

In a study of the social organization of a restaurant, W.F. Whyte (1949) reaped rich rewards by using his eyes to observe the spatial organization of activities. More recently, in a study of interaction in hospital wards, Anssi Peräkylä (personal correspondence) notes how spatial arrangements differentiate groups of people. There are the wards and patient rooms, which staff may enter anytime they need to. Then there are patient lounges and the like, which are a kind of public space. Both areas are quite different from areas like the nurses' room and doctors' offices, where patients enter only by invitation. Finally, if there is a staff coffee room, you never see a patient there.

As Peräkylä points out, one way to produce different categories of human beings in a hospital is the allocation of space according to categories. At the same time, this allocation is reproduced in the activities of the participants. For instance, the perceptive observer might note the demeanour of patients as they approach the nurses' room. Even if the door is open, they may stand outside and just put their heads round the door. In doing so, they mark out that they are encroaching on foreign territory.

Unfortunately, we have all become a little reluctant to use our eyes as well as our ears when doing observational work. However, there are exceptions. Gerry Stimson has noted how 'photographs and diagrams are virtually absent from sociological journals, and rare in sociological books' (1986: 641). He then discusses a room set out for hearings of a disciplinary organization responsible for British doctors. The Professional Conduct Committee of the General Medical Council sits in a high-ceilinged, oak-panelled room reached by an imposing staircase. There are stained-glass windows, picturing 16 crests and a woman in a classical Greek pose. As Stimson comments:

> This is a room in which serious matters are discussed: the room has a presence that is forced on our consciousness ... speech is formal, carefully spoken and a matter for the public record. Visitors in the gallery speak only, if at all, in hushed whispers, for their speech is not part of the proceedings. (1986: 643-4)

In such a room, as Stimson suggests, even without anything needing to be said, we know that what goes on must be taken seriously. Stimson aptly contrasts this room with a McDonald's hamburger restaurant:

> Consider the decorations and materials - plastic, paper, vinyl and polystyrene, and the bright primary colours. [Everything] signifies transience. This temporary character is further articulated in the casual dress of customers, the institutionally casualised dress of staff and the seating that is constructed to make lengthy stays uncomfortable. (1986: 649-50)

Stimson and Peräkylä show that ethnographers who fail to use their eyes as well as their ears are neglecting a crucial source of data. This lesson is most readily learnt if you imagine a sighted person being forced to make sense of the world while blindfolded!

The articulation of different elements

> The move from coding to interpretation is a crucial one ... Interpretation involves the transcendence of 'factual' data and cautious analysis of what is to be made of them. (Coffey and Atkinson, 1996: 46)

As Miles and Huberman (1984) point out, qualitative data comes in the form of words rather than numbers. The issue, then, is how we move from these words to data analysis. They suggest that data analysis consists of 'three concurrent flows of activity: data reduction, data display and conclusion drawing/verification' (1984: 21):

- *Data reduction* 'refers to the process of selecting, focusing, simplifying, abstracting, and transforming ... "raw" data'. Data reduction involves making decisions about which data chunks will provide your initial focus.
- *Data display is* 'an organized assembly of information that permits conclusion drawing and action taking'. It involves assembling your data into displays such as matrices, graphs, networks and charts which clarify the main direction (and missing links) of your analysis.
- *Conclusion drawing means* 'beginning to decide what things mean, noting regularities, patterns, explanations, possible configurations, causal flows and propositions'.
- *Verification* means testing our provisional conclusions for 'their plausibility, their sturdiness, their "confirmability" – that is, their validity' (1984: 21, 22).

Miles and Huberman demonstrate that in field studies, unlike much quantitative research, we are not satisfied with a simple coding of data. As I argued in Chapter 3, this means that qualitative researchers have to show how the (theoretically defined) elements that they have identified are articulated or mutually laminated. The distinctive contribution qualitative research can make is by utilizing its theoretical resources in the deep analysis of usually small bodies of publicly shareable data.

This means that coding your data according to some theoretical scheme should only be the first stage of your data analysis. You will then need to go on to examine how these elements are linked together. At this second stage, lateral thinking can help. For instance, you can attempt to give your chosen concept or issue a new twist, perhaps by pursuing a counter-intuitive idea or by noting an additional feature little addressed in the literature.

In any event, as I show below, one way of achieving better data analysis is by a steadily more narrow focus.

Progressive focusing in fieldwork

We only come to look at things in certain ways because we have adopted, either tacitly or explicitly, certain ways of seeing. This means that, in observational research, data collection, hypothesis construction and theory building are not three separate things but are interwoven with one another.

This process is well described by using an analogy with a funnel:

> Ethnographic research has a characteristic 'funnel' structure, being progressively focused over its course. Progressive focusing has two analytically distinct components. First, over time the research problem is developed or transformed, and eventually its scope is clarified and delimited and its internal structure explored. In this sense, it is frequently only over the course of the research that one discovers what the research is really 'about', and it is not uncommon for it to turn out to be about something quite remote from the initially foreshadowed problems. (Hammersley and Atkinson, 1983: 175)

Atkinson (1992) gives an example of such a redefinition of a research problem. Many years after completing his PhD, Atkinson returned to his original fieldnotes on medical education. He shows how the original data can be reread in a quite different way. Atkinson's earlier method had been to fragment his fieldnotes into relatively small segments, each with its own category. For instance, a surgeon's description of post-operative complications to a surgical team was originally categorized under such headings as 'unpredictability', 'uncertainty', 'patient career' and 'trajectory'. When Atkinson returns to the description, it becomes an overall narrative which sets up an enigma ('unexpected complications') that is resolved in the form of a 'moral tale' ('beware, unexpected things can always happen'). Viewed in this way, the surgeon's story becomes a text with many resemblances to a fairy tale!

Two studies of British medical clinics that I carried out in the 1980s also nicely illustrate Hammersley and Atkinson's funnel. As I showed above, my observation of a paediatric cardiology unit moved unpredictably in the direction of an analysis of disposal decisions with a small group of children with Down's syndrome. Similarly, my research on cancer clinics, discussed in Chapter 14, unexpectedly led into a comparison of fee-for-service and state-provided medicine (Silverman, 1981; 1987).

These two cases had three features in common:

1.   The switch of focus – through the 'funnel' – as a more defined topic arose.
2.   The use of the comparative method as an invaluable tool of theory building and testing.
3.   The generation of topics with a scope outside the substantive area of the research. Thus the 'ceremonial orders' found in the cancer clinics are not confined to medicine, while the 'democratic' decision making found with the children with Down's syndrome had unexpected effects of power with a significance far beyond medical encounters.

As I have noted elsewhere (Silverman, 2014), working this way parallels Barney Glaser and Anselm Strauss's (1967) famous account of grounded theory. A simplified model of this involves three stages:

- an initial attempt to develop categories which illuminate the data
- an attempt to 'saturate' these categories with many appropriate cases in order to demonstrate their relevance
- the development of these categories into more general analytic frameworks with relevance outside the setting.

EXPLORE:
GROUNDED THEORY

Glaser and Strauss use their research on death and dying as an example. They show how they developed the category of 'awareness contexts' to refer to the kinds of situations in which people were informed of their likely fate. The category was then saturated and finally related to non-medical settings where people learn about how others define them (e.g. schools).

'Grounded theory' has been criticized for its failure to acknowledge implicit theories which guide work at an early stage. It is also clearer about the generation of theories than about their testing. Used unintelligently, it can also degenerate into a fairly empty building of categories or into a mere smokescreen used to legitimize purely empiricist research (see my critique of four qualitative studies in Chapter 18; also see Bryman, 1988: 83–7). At best, 'grounded theory' offers an approximation of the creative activity of theory building found in good observational work, compared with the dire abstracted **empiricism** present in the most wooden statistical studies.

The following example shows how one student attempted such theorizing about her data.

WHAT I DID: GABRIELLA

Theorizing a Virtual Red-Light District

I started with a wide aim and questions about how the contributors interact. I did not take long before I started to feel like I was 'drowning' in empirical data: so many threads, posts and details! I wanted to give a complex picture of the virtual red-light district but I realized that I could not try to grasp and observe everything. I started to elaborate with different theories, wrote about them in my fieldnotes. Now, I am about half-way through my PhD studies (have been on parental leave with two children) and I am about to reformulate my aim and my research questions to make my study more specific and to get better guidance in my analysis. Though, I am not sure if I should narrow down my research problem or broaden it. Is the Swedish red-light district interesting in itself, or is it an example of something larger? Could these findings be generalized to other online settings? [Gabriella Scaramuzzino, Sociology, Malmö University]

Quantification should not be seen as the enemy of good field research. In the following section, I discuss one example of how simple tabulations were used to test an emergent hypothesis in the study of cancer clinics.

Using tabulations in testing fieldwork hypotheses

In the cancer study, I used a coding form which enabled me to collate a number of crude measures of doctor and patient interactions (Silverman, 1984). The aim was to demonstrate that the qualitative analysis was reasonably representative of the data as a whole. Occasionally, the figures revealed that the reality was not in line with my overall impressions. Consequently, the analysis was tightened and the characterizations of clinic behaviour were specified more carefully.

The crude quantitative data I had recorded did not allow any real test of the major thrust of this argument. Nonetheless, the data did offer a summary measure of the characteristics of the total sample which allowed closer specification of features of private and NHS clinics. In order to illustrate this, let me briefly show you the kind of quantitative data I gathered on topics like consultation length, patient participation and the scope of the consultation.

My overall impression was that private consultations lasted considerably longer than those held in the NHS clinics. When examined, the data indeed did show that the former were almost twice as long as the latter (20 minutes as against 11 minutes) and that the difference was statistically highly significant. However, I recalled that, for special reasons, one of the NHS clinics had abnormally short consultations. I felt a fairer comparison of consultations in the two sectors should exclude this clinic and should only compare consultations taken by a single doctor in both sectors. This subsample of cases revealed that the difference in length between NHS and private consultations was now reduced to an average of under 3 minutes. This was still statistically significant, although the significance was reduced. Finally, however, if I compared only *new* patients seen by the same doctor, NHS patients got 4 minutes more on average: 34 minutes as against 30 minutes in the private clinic. This last finding was not suspected and had interesting implications for the overall assessment of the individual's costs and benefits from 'going private'. It is possible, for instance, that the tighter scheduling of appointments at the private clinic may limit the amount of time that can be given to new patients.

As a further aid to comparative analysis, I measured patient participation in the form of questions and unelicited statements. Once again, a highly significant difference was found: on this measure, private patients participated much more in the consultation. However, once more taking only patients seen by the same doctor, the difference between the clinics became very small and was *not* significant. Finally, no significant difference was found in the degree to which non-medical matters (e.g. patient's work or home circumstances) were discussed in the clinics.

These quantitative data were a useful check on over-enthusiastic claims about the degree of difference between the NHS and private clinics. However, as I argued in Chapter 14, my major concern was with the 'ceremonial order' of the three clinics. I had amassed a considerable number of exchanges in which doctors and patients appeared to behave in the private clinic in a manner deviant from what we know about NHS hospital consultations. The question was: would the quantitative data offer any support to my observations?

The answer was, to some extent, positive. Two quantitative measures were helpful in relation to the ceremonial order. One dealt with the extent to which the doctor fixed treatment or attendance at the patient's convenience. The second measured whether patients or doctor engaged in polite small talk with one another about their personal or professional lives. (I called this 'social elicitation'.) As Table 15.6 shows, both these measures revealed significant differences, in the expected direction, according to the mode of payment.

Table 15.6   Private and NHS clinics: ceremonial orders

	Private clinic (n = 42)	NHS clinics (n = 104)
	(% in all such clinics)	(% in all such clinics)
Treatment or attendance fixed at patients' convenience	15 (36%)	10 (10%)
Social elicitation	25 (60%)	31 (30%)

Source: adapted from Silverman (2001: 243)

Now, of course, such data could not offer proof of my claims about the different interactional forms. However, coupled with the qualitative data, they provided strong evidence of the direction of difference, as well as giving me a simple measure of the sample as a whole, which contexted the few extracts of talk I was able to use. I do not deny that counting can be as arbitrary as qualitative interpretation of a few fragments of data. However, providing researchers resist the temptation to try to count everything, and base their analysis on sound concepts linked to actors' own methods of ordering the world, then each type of data can inform the analysis of the other.

PRACTICE: SYNTHESIZING ETHNOGRAPHIC DATA

In Chapter 17, I return to the role of counting as an aid to validity in qualitative research. In the case of observational studies, such counting will often be based on the prior coding of fieldnotes. I now, therefore, turn to the issues that arise in such coding.

Limits in coding fieldnotes

The tabulations used in the cancer study derived from:

> that well-established style of work whereby the data are inspected for categories and instances. It is an approach that disaggregates the text (notes or transcripts) into a series of fragments, which are then regrouped under a series of thematic headings. (Atkinson, 1992: 455)

Such coding by thematic headings has been supported by computer-aided qualitative data analysis systems as discussed in Chapter 16. In larger projects, the reliability of coding is also buttressed by training coders of data in procedures which aim to ensure a uniform approach.

However, there remain two problems with coding fieldnotes. The first, and more obvious, problem is that every way of seeing is also a way of not seeing. As Atkinson points out, one of the disadvantages of coding schemes is that, because they are based upon a given set of categories, they furnish 'a powerful conceptual grid' (1992: 459) from which it is difficult to escape. While this 'grid' is very helpful in organizing the data analysis, it also deflects attention away from uncategorized activities. Therefore, as Clive Seale (personal correspondence) has noted:

> a good coding scheme would reflect a search for 'uncategorized activities' so that they could be accounted for, in a manner similar to searching for deviant cases.

The second, less obvious, problem is that, as I pointed out in Chapter 6, 'coding' is not the preserve of research scientists. All of us 'code' what we hear and see in the world around us. This is what Garfinkel (1967) and Sacks (1992) mean when they say that societal members, like social scientists, make the world observable and reportable.

Put at its simplest, this suggests that researchers must be very careful how they use categories. For instance, Sacks quotes from two linguists who appear to have no problem in characterizing particular (invented) utterances as 'simple', 'complex', 'casual' or 'ceremonial'. For Sacks, such rapid characterizations of data assume 'that we can know that [such categories are accurate] without an analysis of what it is [members] are doing' (1992, Vol. 1: 429).

How should we respond to Sacks's radical critique of ethnography? The first point is not to panic! Sacks offers a challenge to conventional observational work of which everybody should be aware. In particular, Sacks's lecture 'On doing "being ordinary"' (1992, Vol. 2: 215–21; 1984a) is essential reading for every fieldworker.

However, awareness does not mean that everybody has to follow Sacks's radical path. So one response is to state something like 'thanks but no thanks'. For instance, grounded theory is an equally respectable (and much more popular) way of theorizing (about) fieldwork.

To this effective but essentially defensive manoeuvre, we can add two more ambitious responses. First, we can seek to integrate Sacks's questions about 'how' the social world is constituted with more conventional ethnographic questions about the 'whats' and 'whys' of social life (Gubrium and Holstein, 1997). Or, second, as I describe below, we can make this everyday 'coding' (or 'interpretive practice') the object of enquiry by asking 'how' questions about talk-in-interaction.

6 TRANSCRIPTS

The two main social science traditions which inform the analysis of transcripts of audio files are conversation analysis (CA) and discourse analysis (DA). For an introduction to CA, see ten Have (1998; 2007); for DA, see Potter and Wetherell (1987) and Potter (2016).

In this book we are, of course, more concerned with the practicalities of doing qualitative research. In the rest of this chapter I will, therefore, deal with two practical issues:

- the advantages of working with audio files and transcripts
- the elements of how to do analysis of such audio files.

Why work with audio files?

> [The] kind of phenomena I deal with are always transcriptions of actual occurrences in their actual sequence. (Sacks, 1984b: 25)

The earlier ethnographers had generally relied on recording their observations through fieldnotes. Why did Sacks prefer to use an audio recorder?

Sacks's answer is that we cannot rely on our recollections of conversations. Certainly, depending on our memory, we can usually summarize what different people said. But it is simply impossible to remember (or even to note at the time) such matters as pauses, overlaps, inbreaths and the like.

Now whether you think these kinds of things are important will depend upon what you can show with or without them. Indeed, you may not even be convinced that conversation itself is a particularly interesting topic. But, at least by studying audio files of conversations, you are able to focus on the 'actual details' of one aspect of social life. As Sacks put it:

> My research is about conversation only in this incidental way, that we can get the actual happenings on tape and transcribe them more or less, and therefore have something to begin with. If you can't deal with the actual detail of actual events then you can't have a science of social life. (1992, Vol. 2: 26)

Audio files and transcripts also offer more than just 'something to begin with'. In the first place, they are a public record, available to the scientific community, in a way that fieldnotes are not. Second, they can be replayed, transcriptions can be improved, and analyses can take off on a different tack unlimited by the original transcript. As Sacks told his students:

> I started to play around with tape recorded conversations, for the single virtue that I could replay them; that I could type them out somewhat, and study them extendedly, who knew how long it might take … It wasn't from any large interest in language, or from some theoretical formulation of what should be studied, but simply by virtue of that; I could get my hands on it, and I could study it again and again. And also, consequentially, others could look at what I had studied, and make of it what they could, if they wanted to disagree with me. (1992, Vol. 1: 622)

A third advantage of detailed transcripts is that, if you want to, you can inspect sequences of utterances without being limited to the extracts chosen by the first researcher. For it is within these sequences, rather than in single turns of talk, that we make sense of conversation. As Sacks points out:

> having available for any given utterance other utterances around it, is extremely important for determining what was said. If you have available only the snatch of talk that you're now transcribing, you're in tough shape for determining what it is. (1992, Vol. 1: 729)

It should not be assumed that the preparation of transcripts is simply a technical detail prior to the main business of the analysis. The convenience of transcripts for presentational purposes is no more than an added bonus.

EXPLORE:
HOW TO TRANSCRIBE

As Max Atkinson and John Heritage (1984) point out, the production and use of transcripts are essentially 'research activities'. They involve close, repeated listenings to recordings which often reveal previously unnoted recurring features of the organization of talk. Such listenings can most fruitfully be done in group data sessions. As described by Paul ten Have (1998), work in such groups usually begins by listening to an extract from a tape with a draft transcript and agreeing upon improvements to the transcript. Then:

> the participants are invited to proffer some observations on the data, to select an episode which they find 'interesting' for whatever reason, and formulate their understanding or puzzlement, regarding that episode. Then anyone can come in to react to these remarks, offering alternatives, raising doubts, or whatever. (1998: 124)

EXPLORE: CONVERSATION ANALYSIS RESOURCES
EXPLORE: DISCOURSE ANALYSIS RESOURCES

However, as ten Have makes clear, such group data sessions should be rather more than an anarchic free-for-all:

> participants are, on the one hand, *free* to bring in anything they like, but, on the other hand, *required* to ground their observations in the data at hand, although they may also support them with reference to their own data-based findings or those published in the literature. (1998: 24)

Analysing audio files

There is a strongly inductive bent to the kind of research that ten Have and Sacks describe. As we have seen, this means that any research claims need to be identified in precise analyses of detailed transcripts. It is therefore necessary to avoid premature theory construction and the 'idealization' of research materials which use only general, non-detailed characterizations.

Heritage sums up these assumptions as follows:

> Specifically, analysis is strongly 'data-driven' – developed from phenomena which are in various ways evidenced in the data of interaction. Correspondingly, there is a strong bias against *a priori* speculation about the orientations and motives of speakers and in favour of detailed examination of conversationalists' actual actions. Thus the empirical conduct of speakers is treated as the central resource out of which analysis may develop. (1984: 243)

In practice, Heritage adds, this means that it must be demonstrated that the regularities described can be shown to be produced by the participants and attended to by them as grounds for their own inferences and actions. Further, deviant cases, in which such regularities are absent, must be identified and analysed.

However, the way in which CA obtains its results is rather different from how we might intuitively try to analyse talk. It may be helpful, therefore, if I conclude this section by offering a crude set of prescriptions about how to do CA. Table 15.7 summarizes how to do CA, and Table 15.8 sets out things to avoid when doing CA.

Table 15.7   How to do CA

1	Always try to identify sequences of related talk
2	Try to examine how speakers take on certain roles or identities through their talk (e.g. questioner–answerer or client–professional)
3	Look for particular outcomes in the talk (e.g. a request for clarification, a repair, laughter) and work backwards to trace the trajectory through which a particular outcome was produced

Source: Silverman (2011b: 299)

Table 15.8   Common errors in doing CA

1	Explaining a turn at talk by reference to the speaker's intentions
2	Explaining a turn at talk by reference to a speaker's role or status (e.g. as a doctor or as a man or woman)
3	Trying to make sense of a single line of transcript or utterance in isolation from the surrounding talk

Source: Silverman (2011b: 299)

If we follow these rules, the analysis of conversations does not require exceptional skills. As Schegloff puts it, in his introduction to Sacks's collected lectures, all we need to do is to:

PRACTICE:
CONVERSATIONAL DATA

> begin with some observations, then find the problem for which these observations could serve as ... the solution. (Schegloff in Sacks, 1992, Vol. 1: xlviii)

This means that doing the kind of systematic data analysis that CA demands is not an impossibly difficult activity. As Sacks once pointed out, in doing CA we are only reminding ourselves about things we already know:

> I take it that lots of the results I offer, people can see for themselves. And they needn't be afraid to. And they needn't figure that the results are wrong because they can see them ...

[It is] as if we found a new plant. It may have been a plant in your garden, but now you see it's different than something else. And you can look at it to see how it's different, and whether it's different in the way that somebody has said. (1992, Vol. 1: 488)

7 VISUAL DATA

Visual data comprises a very broad category which can encompass anything from videos to photographs to naturally occurring observational data like those discussed earlier in the chapter (p.335), and to such aspects of our environment as street signs and advertisements (see Emmison and Smith, 2000).

To simplify matters for the beginning researcher, I will examine four ways in which visual data can be gathered and analysed:

- allowing people to produce their own images using content analysis
- studying pet photographs and videoing how people interact with their pets using grounded theory
- using family photographs in interviews and analysing the narratives produced
- workplace studies using conversation analysis to see how sequences of interaction get put together.

Content analysis

Mike Sharples et al. (2003) had the interesting idea of studying the kinds of photographs made by children. One hundred and eighty children of three different ages (7, 11 and 15) were given single-use cameras and asked to use them in any way they pleased over a weekend. Over 4300 photographs were generated by this means.

Data analysis took off through using a form of content analysis which produced a kind of 'radar screen … a two-dimensional scatterplot showing the principal axes of variability' (2003: 311). This data was set up in this way in order to answer some early, key research questions:

- What is the content of each photograph?
- Are the people or objects shown posed?
- Who are the people shown?
- How does each of these features vary by the age of the photographer?

The analysis showed significant variation by the age of the child. For instance, 7-year-old children were more likely to take photographs of toys and other possessions. They also took more photographs of their home and family. By contrast, the 11-year-olds concentrated on outdoor and/or animal photographs (usually their pets), while the 15-year-olds mainly took photographs of their friends, usually of the same sex and often in 'informal and striking poses' (2003: 316–17).

This study shows that an apparently simple count of such apparently basic features can raise a number of interesting issues (for a discussion of the nature and limits of content analysis, see Marvasti, 2004). In this case, the researchers sought to pursue these issues by qualitative interviews with their child photographers.

This study took off by beginning with descriptive questions of 'what?' and 'how?'. This generated 'why' questions which they later sought to answer through interviews with subjects. The interviews also allowed the comparison of the categories that the researchers used with those used by the children themselves.

Grounded theory

Kryzysztof Konecki (2005) used photographs to study various aspects of direct contacts between domestic animals and people. He was interested in the ways in which owners represented their relations with the animals by means of gestures and 'choreographic' arrangement of the bodies and objects. The research aimed at finding the cultural framework which would be useful in categorizing oneself through photographic representation.

Konecki used grounded theory to generate a set of workable categories and a set of hypotheses to be tested. This is how he describes this coding in the context of a further study reported shortly:

> Open coding in the methodology of grounded theory means ascribing labels to his data. The labels should usually have a conceptual character, shifting the researcher from direct description ... Some of the labels become categories, which later become saturated with qualities, that is conceptual elements, which have their empirical references (that is references to actual events, situations, interactions, gestures, etc.). (Konecki, 2008)

Konecki's analysis of the photographs showed that hugging and touching animals is mainly depicted with children and women. By contrast: 'Men usually keep the animals on the leash or firmly in their hands in order to, practically, create an opportunity to take the photograph, which consequently, from the social perspective, represents men in a dominating social position' (2005: 163–4).

In the later paper, Konecki (2008) assembled video recordings of human–animal interactions. Sixty video clips were recorded by means of a portable camera. The clips were transcribed and then analysed by means of grounded theory. The recordings were gathered in order to show typical everyday situations of interaction between humans and animals in their households. The context of the recording was also described thoroughly and the basic ethnographic information was provided, such as *who*, *where*, *when* and *why* regarding the particular animal or owner.

Among the activities that Konecki identified were: talking with animals, ascribing intentionality to them, playing, greeting, feeding and touching. He found that touching is a vital part of displaying close contact with family pets. He distinguished four kinds of touching shown in his videos:

EXPLORE: ANALYSING VISUAL DATA

- touching characterized by positive affection (showing feelings or support)
- entertaining touching (showing playful anger or attachment)
- controlling touching (showing compliance)
- ritual touching (showing greetings or farewells).

Narratives

An interview is a way of gathering researcher-provoked data. As such, interviewers must be aware of the extent to which they are imposing their own categories on respondents. One way of limiting such imposition is to find a stimulus or topic which is relevant to the people being studied. Photographs can be such a stimulus. For instance, Neil Jenkings et al. (2008) asked 16 military personnel each to choose 10 photos that best represented their experience of military life. Each person was then interviewed and their accounts of the photos were used to analyse how military identity is represented.

For most of us, family photographs are even more important than photographs of our working life. Moreover, talking about these photos to others is quite a common activity. Gillian Rose (2007) discusses interviews she conducted with women about their family photos. This is how she describes how she began analysis:

> I transcribed the interviews and then worked with them, working outwards from what I was told about the things that were done with photos, and gradually finding recurring themes and taken-for-granted assumptions which I felt were the meanings of the photos in this phase of their existence. (2007: 230-1)

However, these photos did not constitute the only visual data that was relevant. It also mattered what her women did with their photos (e.g. which photos were selected or emphasized and then displayed to her in particular ways). So Rose kept fieldnotes about what the women in her study were doing as they talked or remained silent, and noted what she did in response.

Working with both interviews and fieldnotes, she discovered 'the way in which these photos helped to produce a relation of "togetherness"' (2007: 231). This involved:

- choosing photos showing family members together
- pointing out how photo frames or albums were presents from family members
- arranging photos in groups to show family links (e.g. children and other relatives)
- discussing which photos had been given to or received from other family members.

Conversation analysis using video data

We first came across conversation analysis (CA) in Chapter 2 when I discussed the research of several of my students. It is a method which involves recording naturally occurring situations, transcribing them in great detail using standardized conventions (see the Appendix) and analysing sequences of interaction in order to see how the participants produce various outcomes.

Until 1980, most CA was carried out using audio recordings and this meant that the outcomes identified derived from the participants' conversation (e.g. an invitation preface or an acceptance of a piece of advice). More recently, however, the emergence of digital camcorders, in combination with the editing and playback possibilities of desktop computers, mean that video is likely to become as straightforward for social scientists to use in their research as photographs. The cutting-edge research now being done involves looking at workplace settings in order to document the tacit procedures and forms of common-sense reasoning involved in the performance of tasks (see Heath and Luff, 2000).

Ruth Parry collected video recordings of physiotherapy treatment sessions within British NHS settings during her PhD using Transana software to support her analysis of video data. She notes that 'the Transana database should not be set up until you have carefully thought through and set up a consistent labelling and indexing system: the program creates links to your stored videos and you don't want to be reorganizing your filing system once you have started making links. Transana allows for the kind of ethnographic note taking or 'logging' that is useful in the first watch-through of data. It also

EXPLORE:
TRANSCRIPTION USING TRANSANA

facilitates transcribing, whether verbatim or the full Jeffersonian style. It allows collection of and keywording of multiple clips and extracts'. [Ruth Parry, Social Sciences, Loughborough]

Analyse your data in small pieces

WATCH: DAVID EXPLAINS IN PERSON

David's Top Tip 39

Focus on a small part of your data and analyse it intensively; there will be time later to test out your findings on your dataset as a whole (what I call extensive analysis).

In the following account of her work, Ruth adds that video data analysis is helped by purposive sampling and group data sessions.

WHAT I DID: RUTH

Analysing Videos

Given the vast amounts of data contained in videos, the key thing for me has been learning how to purposefully sample from within the data so as to allow detailed analysis of a smaller amount, upon the basis of a sound selection strategy. This also works back to design issues: once access has been managed, it is easy to collect a good deal of video data pretty quickly, and though it is sometimes heartbreaking to realize how many of one's data one has not examined in detail, having this big 'bank' allows for appropriate selection and 'natural experiments'.

One other note on data analysis. Like everyone, I bring a certain perspective to my analysis. One element of this perspective is my past as a clinical physiotherapist. I find that joint data analysis sessions are a very useful way of helping balance this perspective with others. I have found that non-clinicians attending these sessions tend to 'take the perspective of', or at least primarily focus their attention upon, patients, whereas sometimes my attention tends to be skewed towards therapists and their practices. I think it is important to note that the non-clinicians don't have a neutral position themselves. [Ruth Parry, Research Fellow, Nottingham University]

8 WRAPPING UP

We have seen how data analysis can be developed during and after data collection. However, as I have implied throughout, good data analysis is never just a matter of using the right methods or techniques but is always based on theorizing about data using a consistent model of social reality. This commitment to theorizing about data makes the best qualitative research far superior to the stilted empiricism of the worst kind of quantitative research. However, theorization without methodological rigour is a dangerous brew. In Chapter 16, we consider how computer software can aid qualitative research. Then, in Chapter 17, the issues of validity and reliability are discussed.

What You Need to Remember

To analyse data, try to answer the following questions:

1. *'What' and 'how' questions.* Avoid the temptation to rush to explanations of your data. Don't begin with 'why' questions. Instead ask yourself 'what' verbal and behavioural and contextual resources are being used here, and look for the detail of 'how' they are being used (and with what consequences).
2. *Chronology.* Look at the timing of people's behaviour or their use of time in their accounts. Alternatively, gather data over time in order to look at processes of change. If appropriate, try searching out historical evidence which may at least suggest how your research problem came into being.
3. *Context.* How is your data contextualized in particular organizational settings, social processes or sets of experiences? For instance, as the Norwegian students' work shows, answering an interviewer's question may be different from engaging in the activity which is the topic of the interview. Therefore, think about how there may be many versions of your phenomenon.
4. *Comparison.* Always try to compare your data with other relevant data. Even if you cannot find a comparative case, try to find ways of dividing your data into different sets and compare each. Remember that the comparative method is the basic scientific method.
5. *Implications.* When you are reporting your research, think about how what you have discovered may relate to broader issues than your original research topic. In this way, a very narrow topic (e.g. self-presentation by drug dealers) may be related to much broader social processes (e.g. how crime is defined and treated).
6. *Lateral thinking.* Don't erect strong boundaries between concepts but explore the relations between apparently diverse models, theories and methodologies. Celebrate anomaly.

You can develop your data analysis by:

- working with data which is easy to collect and is reliable
- focusing on one process within this data
- narrowing down to one part of that process
- comparing different subsamples of the population concerned.

Your Chapter Checklist

When you analyse your data, you should attempt to:

TRACK:
ANALYSING DATA

1. Focus on one process within this data. Now narrow down your focus to one part of that process. Survey your data in terms of this narrow focus. What can you now find?
2. Compare different subsamples of your data in terms of a single category or process. What does this show?
3. Decide what features of your data may properly be counted and tabulate instances of a particular category. What does this tabulation indicate? Identify 'deviant' cases and explain what you will do with them.
4. Attempt to develop your categories into more general analytic frameworks with relevance outside the setting you are studying.

Exercises

Exercise 1: Brainstorm sources of existing secondary data

This gives you the opportunity to think about relevant datasets to which you may have early access.

1. Review relevant data already in the public sphere, for instance on the media (from newspapers to television and radio to the Internet). Select a dataset and begin to analyse it (you may use the datasets provided online in this book).
2. Ask your supervisor and/or fellow students about any relevant data that they might have which you could borrow either as a preliminary exercise or possibly to develop long-term collaboration. Do a brief analysis of some of the data.

Exercise 2: Ask questions of your own data right after obtaining it

This gives you an opportunity to analyse your own data as soon as you obtain it.

APPLY:
YOUR EXERCISE WORKBOOK

1. Which questions does your preferred method of data analysis suggest? What interesting generalizations can you start to pull out of your data?
2. Do previous research findings seem to apply to your data? If not, why not? If so, how can you use your data to develop these findings?
3. How do particular concepts from your preferred model of social research apply to your data? Which concepts work best and hence look likely to be most productive?

Further Reading

Chapter 3 of my recent book *A Very Short, Fairly Interesting, Reasonably Cheap Book about Qualitative Research* (Sage, 2013) examines how you can develop data analysis by examining sequences of data. For a useful treatment of coding observational data, see Robert Emerson et al.'s *Writing Ethnographic Fieldnotes* (University of Chicago Press, 1995). Martyn Hammersley and Paul Atkinson's *Ethnography: Principles in Practice* (Tavistock, 2007: Chapters 8, 9) offers a classic discussion of how to analyse ethnographic data. A development of some of these ideas can be found in Martyn Hammersley's book *Questioning Qualitative Inquiry* (Sage, 2008). The best treatment of grounded theory is Kathy Charmaz's *Constructing Grounded Theory* (Sage, 2015). For a series of highly relevant case studies illustrating what is involved in analysing fieldwork data, visit: www.sagepub.co.uk/gobo (Chapters 9 and 10). Sacks's work on conversation analysis is discussed in my book *Harvey Sacks: Social Science and Conversation Analysis* (Polity, 1998). The case studies of the cancer and heart clinics discussed

READ: BUILDING GROUNDED THEORIES
READ: USING NARRATIVE INQUIRY
READ: USING VISUAL DATA

here are found in my book *Communication and Medical Practice* (Sage, 1987: Chapters 6, 7). The analysis of visual data can be very complicated and, in some hands, can be so over-theorized that one feels that the theoretical tail is leading the empirical dog! Gillian Rose in *Visual Methodologies* (Sage, 2007) provides a useful guide to data analysis of visual images which, while not short of theory, provides practical advice on the analysis itself. For a supurb guide to working with video data, see Heath et al. *Video in Qualitative Research* (Sage, 2010).

Discover the chapter's
digital resources in your
SILVERMAN FIELD GUIDE

SIXTEEN

Using Computers to Analyse Qualitative Data

Clive Seale

Learning Outcomes

By the end of this chapter you will be able to:

- Understand the strengths and limitations of computer-assisted qualitative data analysis (QDA) using QDA software tools.
- Recognize the key features of some of the main QDA software products.
- Find the details of QDA software tools on the Internet and evaluate their usefulness for your research project.

Using software to help analyse qualitative materials is now very common. Many software tools are available, the most well-known of which is probably NVivo. In this chapter I will show you how QDA software can be helpful in supporting the kind of qualitative data analysis discussed in the previous two chapters – while also pointing out its limitations. Software tools usually have certain core features that get used again and again, together with some extra things for more specialized use.

Think of your word-processing software as an example: most of the time you use its core features to input text, format it a bit and perhaps print it out or send it to someone. Maybe you have used 'track changes' to record changes made to a document. But how often have you used a specialized function like 'macros' in Word? Most use of QDA software follows this kind of pattern.

I will first focus on the core features, widely used by qualitative researchers since specialized software was introduced from the early 1980s onwards. Then I will discuss a growing new approach to the analysis of text: software-assisted text mining or text analytics, which requires a different kind of software. I can't hope to cover all of the things you can do with all of the different products in a short chapter like this though. For that, read Silver and Lewins (2014), a book-length treatment of the subject by two experienced QDA software teachers.

Although I will name particular products and show you some screenshots, I will not review all the available QDA tools, or seek to describe the finer details of how particular types work. That would mean this chapter would soon be out of date, since software developers continue to release new versions with extra features. The websites given in the text will give you access to information about the latest software versions. Like most things in research, you learn best when you have a specific project in mind, and have time to explore how various available techniques might benefit what you want to do.

1 A NOTE ON LEARNING TO USE QDA SOFTWARE

But first, some advice about how to overcome barriers that put some people off QDA software. These barriers are:

- discovering the software does not do your analysis for you
- finding the whole thing too complicated and time consuming.

The first of these is encouraged by the fact that the 'A' in QDA stands for 'Analysis'. It is crucial to recognize that these tools do not do your analytic thinking for you, but support it by organizing your data so that you can inspect it from viewpoints that would otherwise be unavailable to you. It would be more accurate to call these products QDM (Qualitative Data Management) software. The tools allow you to organize and inspect data, and record your own thoughts about it, in ways that would be very time consuming, perhaps even impossible, with manual methods. But you have to have some analytic purpose, some methodological skills, quite separate from the software, in order to know what kinds of viewpoint you want to conjure up. So, to overcome barriers:

- get clear about the separation between software procedures and analytic procedures
- work on developing some analytic skills before you start finding out how software might help you apply them
- work on learning the software before using it on a real project.

This is related to the second barrier, whose underlying cause is biting off more than you can chew. Why do people do this? It is because the software appears to promise rapid progress through a technological fix, but makes people upset when they can't swallow the oversized mouthful they have taken. The following case study shows what can happen if you do this.

CASE STUDY
Biting off More than You Can Chew

Katie MacMillan (2005) wanted to carry out a 'trial' of three software tools – MAXQDA, NVivo and Qualrus – to see if they were suitable for her discourse analysis of some news stories. She had not used QDA software before and she had heard it wasn't much use for discourse analysis.

Her first problem was her frustration at the data preparation stage: she believed she would have to separate all 2000 news stories, downloaded in a single file from a news archive, into 2000 separate files, before importing it into the software. Unlike more experienced researchers, she was unable to discover a way of doing this without highlighting each article and pasting it into each of 2000 separate files.

She then wanted to search for a particular phrase in her documents ('smoking gun') and believed she needed to use a Boolean search to do this, rather than a simple search for all instances of that phrase. Her computer crashed.

Giving up on this, she then read all the articles on screen and coded the instances of 'smoking gun' manually. She added more codes to indicate things like who said 'smoking gun', but then discovered this was pointless since her discourse analysis did not require that knowledge, and instead required her to know how the phrase was used. She was tired of reading and coding at this point, so she decided it was not worth coding again to identify the different ways in which the phrase 'smoking gun' was used. She justified her reluctance (in spite of having gone ahead with the earlier coding exercise) on the grounds that coding itself was incompatible with discourse analysis, which treats every instance of a thing as unique rather than sharing general characteristics.

She concluded that use of QDA software was too time consuming and took her away from actually doing her analysis.

The solution to Katie's problem is clearly to take bite-sized chunks. First, she should have learned perhaps just one of the three tools in order to find out how to do things with it before starting her analysis. She should have consulted a more experienced

(Continued)

(Continued)

researcher to find out how to prepare her data more economically (some QDA software will automatically split a file of news stories into separate story files). She should have followed her own advice ('the researcher should be in charge of the analysis') and figured out what procedures would be helpful according to her analytic purpose, rather than feeling she had to implement a procedure, such as coding who said 'smoking gun', just because the procedure existed, without first assessing whether it would be relevant.

Learn your method and software separately

WATCH: DAVID EXPLAINS IN PERSON

David's Top tip 40

Trying to learn both a method and a new bit of software at the same time is likely to overload you, so first try to get some practical experience of your chosen analytic method using manual methods. Then take time out from your research project to learn how to use the software tool.

2 WHAT QDA SOFTWARE CAN DO FOR YOU

In this section of the chapter I will describe the core features of some popular QDA software products, listed below.

GO ONLINE: ATLAS.TI
GO ONLINE: HYPERRESEARCH
GO ONLINE: MAXQDA

POPULAR QDA SOFTWARE TOOLS

ATLAS.ti	www.atlasti.com
HyperRESEARCH	www.researchware.com/products/hyper research.html
MAXQDA	www.maxqda.com
NVivo	www.qsrinternational.com
QDA Miner	https://provalisresearch.com
Transana	www.transana.com

To use this type of software, a 'project' is normally created, representing the particular research project that you are working on. In this project are, first, the raw materials associated with the project. These may be, for example, transcripts of interviews or other types of text such as documents, sound or video files. Increasingly, QDA software allows social media data – Twitter feeds and Facebook data, for example – and sources such as web pages, the contents of emails, pdfs or spreadsheets, to be

imported as well. Transana was originally developed for the analysis of video material and is probably the best tool for this type of material, although most of the other software products in the list above enable still and moving images to be incorporated into a project.

Mainstream QDA software allows you to see these materials and to search through them for particular features, for example a particular word or phrase, or a photograph illustrating a particular theme. Each instance of a word or phrase can usually be inspected in its context.

Additionally, and this is perhaps the most commonly used core feature, since QDA software was originally developed to support thematic qualitative content analysis of various sorts, such software allows you to code segments of data (e.g. bits of text or moments in a video) according to some conceptual scheme. It is important to realize that codes can refer to content, or to form. For example, if you are doing some kind of qualitative content analysis you may be interested in whether something being said in a transcript is about this or that topic (a content code). On the other hand, you may be interested in whether the thing being said is a question or an answer (perhaps you are a conversation analyst), or a particular type of turning point in a narrative, such as a complicating factor in a story, or a denouement (if you are a narrative analyst), or, if you are a discourse analyst, a phrase which designates some class of person as 'other'. In all of those cases, you are looking at form rather than content. Codes can refer to all kinds of things and are simply devices for marking chunks of material so that they can be retrieved at some later point.

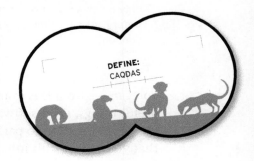

You can then search for and retrieve coded segments. Together, this is known as the 'code-and-retrieve' element of such software. You can usually search according to rules involving Boolean logic (e.g. 'show me all instances where people talking about topic A are *also* talking about topic B' or 'show me all instances where people who talk about topic A are *not also* talking about topic B'). Retrieved material can normally be outputted in a way that can be easily copied and pasted into a word processor.

WHAT I DID: HANNAH
Coding a Project for Thematic Content

I used NVivo software during a project exploring UK media coverage of financial incentives to encourage healthy behaviour. This was eventually published (Parke et al., 2011). To understand the types of arguments used in the print media coverage of health incentives, I performed a thematic content analysis on the data. Using a sample of articles, I developed a coding scheme to identify the arguments for and against health incentives which were contained in the media. The finalized codes were then applied to all articles using the software.

When working with large volumes of data NVivo can be invaluable in helping to organize sources. In this project I identified 210 media articles for inclusion. NVivo allowed me to label and categorize these articles according to the health problem targeted (such as weight control, smoking cessation and health-promoting behaviour in pregnancy). This was essential as I wanted to compare the media coverage of incentive schemes targeted at these different client groups. These comparisons were greatly facilitated by NVivo; I was able to organize the data according to the client group targeted whilst applying the same set of codes across all data.

During coding NVivo allows more than one code to be applied to any section of text. The various display settings mean that not all codes need to be displayed at the same time. I found this facility to be very helpful, especially when working with densely coded sections of text where confusion may have otherwise arisen.

Once articles had been coded, I could view all of the text coded to a particular node. This feature was invaluable in aiding comparison and allowed me to perform a richer and more detailed analysis. Display setting within NVivo also allowed me to see coded material within its original context. This was very useful when I had coded only a narrow section of text, where its meaning could get lost if not viewed in its wider context. [Hannah, Public Health and Primary Care, Queen Mary, University of London]

You can see from this example that the software allowed Hannah to do a lot of useful things. QDA software such as NVivo will normally allow you to attach bits of information to particular files, or parts of files, contained in a project so that you can use this information in searches. Let us say, for example, that you have interviewed 20 men and 20 women of different ages. To each interview transcript you can attach information about the gender and age of each interviewee. You can then do searches on subsets of the data (e.g. 'show me every time men interrupted women and then show me times when women interrupted women'). This allows you to perform comparative analysis. Hannah, for example, could compare what newspapers had to say about incentive schemes to get people to lose weight with other schemes that aimed to help pregnant women eat more healthy foods. She found the weight loss stories contained more stigmatizing messages, reflecting negative stereotypes about overweight people.

Very frequently such software will also support you in writing analytic notes or 'memos' that allow your emerging ideas about your research materials to be recorded in appropriate places. Additionally, most of this sort of software supports the export and import of quantitative information about the project, so that your work can be integrated with statistical or spreadsheet software if that is what you prefer. Some packages will allow you to draw diagrams that give a visual display of relationships between coding categories, thus supporting the development of theoretical models grounded in data analysis.

Quite a few of these features are shown in Figures 16.1 and 16.2, showing NVivo software. The first one shows some retrievals of text coded as being about 'care' in a study of people's experiences of cancer. On the right you can see what NVivo software calls 'coding stripes', these being other codes which this researcher has applied to the retrieved extracts. If needed, the researcher could do a further retrieval from within this collection, perhaps asking to see the bits coded as being both 'care' and 'GPs' (General Practitioners, or family doctors). They could then perhaps compare this with what people said about 'care' when they were referring to other kinds of doctor, enabling a comparison of care delivered by the two types of doctor.

Look at the next image now (Figure 16.2). This comes from an early version of NVivo software. It is from a project which I did, involving the analysis of newspaper articles (Seale, 2002a). I focused on what newspapers had to say about the personal stories of people with cancer. Quite often people were in the news because they had written a book about their cancer experiences, and pretty often this was a book about breast cancer rather than some other kind of cancer, so gender was involved in the book-writing phenomenon. These books either were by people who were already 'celebrities' or made people into celebrities of a sort. They followed a very common pattern: the person found that having cancer made them review and re-evaluate their life. Cancer was experienced as a struggle at all kinds of level. Eventually, the person felt they had been transformed by the experience, so they wrote a book to tell people about it all. The diagram in NVivo helped me organize these thoughts. Using the software I could click on one of the buttons in the picture and retrieve all of the text which I had coded as 'struggles', 'celebrity', and so on.

Figure 16.1 Coding with NVivo (version 11.0)

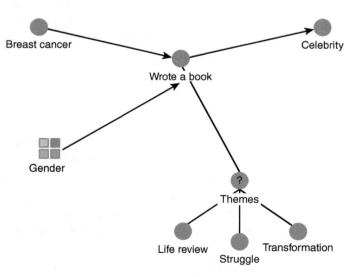

Figure 16.2 Writing a book about cancer experiences: use of an early version of the NVivo modeler (NVivo version 2.0)

Space out software lessons

WATCH: DAVID EXPLAINS IN PERSON

David's Top Tip 41

Learn the software procedures in bite-sized chunks. You aren't going to come away on the first day with a full repertoire of software skills.

3 ADVANTAGES OF QDA SOFTWARE

I have found that there are three main advantages of QDA software:

1. Speed at handling large volumes of data.
2. Improvement of rigour and transparency.
3. Facilitation of team research.

Speed

This advantage is most obvious when you are faced with a large amount of qualitative data, wanting to sort it into categories or coded segments which may then be filed and retrieved easily. The speed at which software can carry out sorting procedures on large volumes of electronically entered data is remarkable. This saves time and effort which might otherwise be expended on boring clerical work, perhaps involving mounds of photocopied paper, colour coded, sorted into piles on the floor, cut up, pasted, and so on. In turn, this gives you more time to think about the meaning of data, providing rapid feedback on the results of particular analytic ideas so that you can formulate new ones. QDA then becomes more devoted to creative and intellectual tasks, and less immersed in routine.

But don't imagine everything about QDA software is faster than manual methods. Here is Hannah again:

> It should not be assumed that using a piece of software will be a time-saving device in data analysis. This was my first experience of using NVivo, and it was important that adequate time to familiarise myself with the software was factored into the research process. Additionally, uploading data to NVivo can be a time intensive process as the version of NVivo I was using meant that all data had first to be saved in a format compatible with NVivo. [Hannah, Public Health and Primary Care, Queen Mary, University of London]

Later versions of NVivo have got better at accepting lots of different file formats, but you should always expect to find glitches like this that could slow things down. In addition, developing a coding scheme and applying it to your materials – if that is how you want to work – take just as much time with a computer as they do with bits of paper and coloured pens. You still have to think through your codes, read all of your materials and apply the coding scheme to them. It is just that once you have done that, searching through the project is infinitely faster than it would be when using pieces of paper.

Having said that, in the initial stages of analysis, the rapidity with which QDA software can help you identify patterns in large volumes of text can be useful. Fisher (1997) gives an example from a project involving 244 interviews with children, parents and social workers about local authority childcare procedures. The data had been analysed previously using manual methods. Fisher's analysis was done in order to assess the contribution which different QDA software products could make. He searched for the word 'discipline' in the interviews and found that different family members appeared to have different meanings for the word, a feature that had been missed in the original manual analysis. This led to some creative thinking about what could have led to this and what it might mean for childcare issues. In turn, this thinking led to the development of ideas for coding segments of text. Fisher likens this sort of pattern searching to an aerial view of a landscape. Patterns can sometimes be seen from the air which, at ground level, appear to be merely random features. You will see more elaborate applications of this kind of pattern searching described later on this chapter.

Rigour and transparency

A lot of QDA – particularly the sort that depends on a particular analytic 'knack' or attitude, as can be the case for discourse analysis – depends on the use of procedures which are not normally very explicit. Using QDA software can be an uncomfortable experience if you are used to skating over the rationale for your methodological decisions, as the software tends to make things visible – both to you and to others. If you use a coding scheme it is more difficult to select bits of text that support your argument and to ignore ones that contradict it, since you may have to show that you have applied the codes to all of the data. You may even start to worry about whether your coding categories are ones that another person would apply to the data in the same way, start reading accounts of why qualitative researchers really shouldn't be worrying about this and end up not knowing what to believe. These mental struggles can in themselves be tiring when you are trying both to make progress with your analysis and to learn a new bit of software, which is why I advised earlier to take things in bite-sized chunks.

Michelle Salmona and Dan Kaczynski (2016), two experienced teachers of QDA software, report that many people encountering one of these tools for the first time think it is largely a question of learning a new bit of technology, but then discover that they are also being asked to make a lot of purely methodological decisions as they face up to new questions the technology is forcing them to answer. They add:

> As the researcher builds an audit trail throughout the inquiry they are able to make the messy process of decisions and choices more transparent to themselves and to others ... [This] enhances credibility and promotes transparency. (Salmona and Kaczynski, 2016)

All of this means that QDA software helps you demonstrate that your conclusions are based on rigorous analysis.

'Rigour', of course, can mean a lot of different things, but one version of rigour can involve counting the number of times things occur, as well as demonstrating that you have searched for negative instances by examining the whole corpus of data rather than selecting only anecdotes supporting your interpretation.

QDA software helps with this, since it makes the combination of qualitative and quantitative analysis easier. First, things can be counted very rapidly, even exported to spreadsheets and subjected to statistical analysis if you want to go that far. These may be individual words or phrases, or coded segments of text. I can give an example of this from my own work.

EXAMPLE FROM MY WORK
Counting in Qualitative Research

I used QDA software to code interviews with 163 people who had known elderly people living alone in private households in the year before their deaths (Seale, 1996). I wanted to show what the speakers had said about the elderly people's attitudes to receiving help from others, and I wrote in the final report:

> It was very common for the people living on their own to be described either as not seeking help for problems that they had (65 instances covering 48 people), or as refusing help when offered (144 instances in 83 people). Accounts of this often stressed that this reflected on the character of the person involved, although other associations were also made. In particular, 33 speakers gave 44 instances where they stressed the independence which this indicated:
>
> [She] never really talked about her problems, was very independent.
>
> [She] was just one of those independent people who would struggle on. She wouldn't ask on her own.
>
> She used to shout at me because I was doing things for her. She didn't like to be helped. She was very independent.
>
> Being 'self sufficient', 'would not be beaten', and being said to 'hate to give in' were associated with resisting help. (Seale, 1996: 34)

As you can imagine, the 163 interviews generated a large amount of text. Because I had read through each interview, marking segments of text with a code called Help to indicate when speakers had discussed the topic of the elderly person's attitude to help, which I had then entered on the computer, I was able to generate a listing of all these coded segments. Reading through this, I was able to code these into subcategories, distinguishing segments describing elderly people not seeking help in spite of problems, instances where a refusal of help was described, and, within this, those segments that involved explicit reflections on the character of the person. A code called Indep marked segments where independence was mentioned. For all these things, the QDA software which I was using allowed me to generate counts, some of which can be seen in the text above. I could then select illustrative quotations that gave good, typical examples of the things I was talking about.

If I had wanted to take this analysis further, I could have asked the computer to show me quotations about women separately from men, or to compare what neighbours as opposed to adult children said about the elderly person's attitude to help. Such an analysis might have been done as part of a more general investigation of the effect of gender on the experience of living alone towards the end of life, or as a part of an investigation into kinship obligations in contemporary society. The computer would have generated lists of quotations separately, which might then have been subjected to more detailed scrutiny (e.g. how women discuss 'independence' compared with men) but would also have enabled these to be counted. Such counts help readers see how widespread phenomena are, guarding against excessive emphasis on rare things that might have suited the arguments I preferred.

Team research

One view of a team approach to data analysis is to celebrate the fact that many different minds can explore many different interpretations of data. Another view is to emphasize how convergence on a single point adds authority to the analysis. There is probably some happy medium to this: team research not only can ensure that data is thoroughly explored from all points of view, particularly when developing analytic categories, but can also provide reassurance that consistent, reliable interpretations underlie the final analysis.

Several QDA software tools allow different researchers access to a project. NVivo allows this in real time, so that several researchers may be working on a project simultaneously, rather than having to wait until one has finished before another can start contributing. Christian Bröer et al. (2016) describe how this can work, using web-based software they designed themselves. At a meeting of anthropologists in Amsterdam they tried it out, asking people to stroll through the streets making notes and taking photos of things they felt were indicators of 'diversity'.

These were then uploaded into the software, which then enabled participants to comment on interpretations of the images and observations, so that these were refined and resulted in a limited, agreed list of definitions.

These researchers were concerned to demonstrate how many minds helped increase the range of interpretations available to the project, but also meant that these could be debated so that they were refined and a degree of consensus reached. For this latter reason, Bröer et al. argue that concerns about reliability are less relevant.

So does it matter that different researchers faced with the same material would interpret it in different ways? There are a lot of arguments both ways about this, but many people nowadays conclude that it is better if some level of independent agreement between researchers can be demonstrated. Otherwise, critics are likely to say 'Well it's just your point of view that is being expressed here', and will dismiss your findings. QDA software, where it supports team research, can help here.

I worked on a project with Carol Rivas, another researcher, coding transcripts of meetings between nurses and patients to talk about diabetes care. We used NVivo for this, and independently coded samples of transcripts, comparing our coding to see if we overlapped (NVivo calculates a kappa statistic to enable a numerical measure of agreement). After some months in which we often found we had to revise our definitions of coding categories so that better agreement between us could be achieved, we finally achieved a respectable kappa level. This meant our results could be published in a medical journal (Seale et al., 2013). Medical journal editors do not, in general, have patience for philosophical justifications for different researchers coming up with different interpretations of the same data extract.

Unfortunately we could not afford to buy a version of NVivo software that enables different researchers to work on the same saved project at the same time. Instead, we had to merge our work after each of us had done more coding. This proved pretty awkward at times, especially when some students joined us for a while. Here is Carol, reflecting on that experience.

EXAMPLE FROM CAROL AND CLIVE'S PROJECT

The main purpose of using NVivo was to code data into a broad brushstroke coding frame that could be shared amongst the team to generate further analyses. We were limited, for practical reasons, to using the single-user version to share the project between team members. This was not always ideal. If there were errors in the content, we had to coordinate their correction; team members had to stop working on the project and wait for a new 'master' project as otherwise we would no longer be able to merge projects. This led to

(Continued)

(Continued)

particular problems when two students joined the team, as their schedules meant they had to keep working on the version they had. When we wanted to develop papers from their work their coding had to be re-entered into our latest master copy of the project.

The software enabled us to manage a large amount of data and to produce summary data in the form of matrices. It also enabled us to group bits of the data in different ways with relatively little effort, to suit the varying interests of the different team members. It has also resulted in something that we can carry on working with, and transfer to other users in such a way that they can see clearly what we have done and carry on with further analyses without a difficult handover.

4 TEXT ANALYTICS

The 'code-and-retrieve' approach support by mainstream QDA software products requires the researcher to inspect all of the original materials being analysed and to assign codes to bits of those materials. The availability of very large amounts of electronic material, 'big data' if you like, means that such detailed inspection and coding can be very time consuming. Text analytics (sometimes called text mining) can help you exploit the opportunities made available by very large collections of text in a reasonably economical way.

Text mining is an approach normally thought of as an extension of content analysis, and therefore a quantitative method. In fact, the results of text mining are very similar to those of qualitative thematic analysis involving coding (probably the most widespread form of 'qualitative' analysis) and I have found you can present them in ways that are compatible with the needs of journals that publish qualitative research. In addition, there are varieties of text mining within the sub-discipline of corpus linguistics (to which text mining is related) that have been successfully used to support critical discourse analysis (Baker, 2006; Mautner, 2013). There is no logical reason why the approach might not be combined with grounded theorizing, though I am not aware of any examples of this. The approach may be unsuited to conversation analysis or narrative analysis.

I'll start with a fairly simple approach to text analytics which can be called keyword analysis, before moving on to more sophisticated software associated with QDA Miner software.

Keyword analysis

Keyword analysis, adapting software developed in the discipline of linguistics, is a method that allows you to analyse very large amounts of text without losing touch with focusing on small amounts of the material in considerable depth. It is a good way to identify sections of text in large collections that is likely to repay more detailed scrutiny and perhaps then more conventional methods of qualitative analysis.

WordSmith Tools (www.lexically.net/wordsmith) is the leading software here, although AntConc (www.antlab.sci.waseda.ac.jp/antconc_index.html), a free tool, also enables many of the procedures used in keyword analysis. This type of software does not support a 'code-and-retrieve' approach but instead works with 'wordlists.' A wordlist is a list of all the words that occur in a given group of texts, sorted by frequency of occurrence or by alphabetical order. If you then compare the words that occur more frequently in one collection of text than in another collection (comparative keyword analysis, described in Seale and Charteris-Black, 2010) you can often find things that you wouldn't have noticed by simply reading the texts. Here is an example.

EXAMPLE FROM CLIVE'S PROJECT INVESTIGATING GENDER AND THE LANGUAGE OF CANCER

Seale et al. (2006) report the first stage of a study comparing the words used by men and women with cancer when interviewed about their experiences. Once imported into the software (97 interviews comprising about 730,000 transcribed words) it took about five minutes to discover the following: men with prostate cancer used the following words significantly more frequently than women with breast cancer:

> wife, he, men, man, chap, male, his, chaps, guy

On the other hand, women with breast cancer used the following words more frequently than men with prostate cancer:

> I, she, husband, her, you, women, my, people, mum, sister, everybody, me, children, mother, friends, woman, lady, dad, she'd, daughter, she's, yourself, myself, sisters, I'd, auntie, ladies, who've, someone, somebody, your

This suggested women's experience of illness incorporates consideration of a wider range of people than men's. We therefore then focused further analysis on the bits of text where interviewees referred to other people to compare what it was that men and women said about them.

You can see that the keyword analysis is not itself a full qualitative analysis but is a quick snapshot or 'aerial view' of a large volume of text that precedes a more detailed look at particular features. This is reminiscent of Fisher's (1997) use of the word search facility in a mainstream QDA tool, described earlier in this chapter, which he used to identify how 'discipline' was talked about. WordSmith Tools allows you to inspect each instance of a word in its context, allowing the disambiguation of single words being used to convey multiple meanings (e.g. 'bank' can refer to a river bank or a financial bank).

Using dictionaries

QDA Miner supports a conventional code-and-retrieve approach but, with the add-on module Wordstat, allows a sophisticated combination of text analytics with qualitative data analysis. First, let's deal with the idea of a dictionary.

In keyword analysis, words that belong to a theme (such as the 'people words' described in the last example) are placed together, using the same kind of rationale as you might do when coding segments of text. Thus, the words 'I', 'she', 'husband', 'her', etc., are 'coded' as 'people words'. A code of this sort can be understood to be the same as a dictionary category.

There are ready-made content analysis dictionaries that you can buy if you like, and you can apply them to text to detect things like sentiments such as anger or love. They rely on counting words that the dictionary maker has concluded 'belong' to the dictionary categories 'love', 'anger' or whatever.

It is much better, though, to make your own dictionary, having disambiguated the words you want to place in your dictionary categories. Otherwise, a word that someone else thinks might indicate 'love' could actually be used to mean something else in the particular collection of texts you are analysing. In addition, if you make the dictionary yourself the categories are the ones you think are important for your project, rather than those someone else has dreamed up.

In fact, it helps if dictionary categories contain short phrases rather than single words, since these are less subject to the problem of ambiguous meaning.

Wordstat supports the creation of user-defined dictionaries, including both single words and phrases, and thus enables themes to be tracked over different documents. This can, for example, enable trends over time to be analysed, or documents produced by different groups of people to be compared to see what is emphasised and what is ignored by each group.

It also enables linkages with QDA Miner so that (for example) paragraphs containing particular themes can be identified, inspected and codes attached to them for later retrieval. In fact, QDA Miner can use artificial intelligence to retrieve segments that seem similar to a segment that you have coded under a theme. If you agree, you can assign the segment to that theme. You can also carry out a dictionary analysis in Wordstat solely on segments of text you have coded as belonging to a theme in QDAMINER. This capacity to interact between coding and text mining means the combined software is very powerful for certain kinds of analysis.

Figure 16.3 shows a 'correspondence analysis' in Wordstat. This was part of a project comparing interviews done with doctors and nurses in Belgium, the Netherlands and the UK concerning the use of sedative drugs with terminally ill patients (Seale et al., 2015; Seymour et al., 2014). The numbers represent the three countries, with the UK being allocated the number 1. You can see that the Netherlands and Belgium (2 and 3) are at the opposite end of the image from the UK. The words are in fact dictionary categories and the closer each one is to a number, the more likely it is that interviewees from that country will have used words belonging to that dictionary category.

You can see, for example, that being 'unable to continue', 'saying goodbye' and 'starting sedation' are close to Belgium and the Netherlands. This is because, in those countries, doctors were more likely to say they gave large doses of sedation and ensured that patients did not wake up again before they died. Sometimes, they even stopped fluid and nutrition to ensure the patient died. This is because they saw palliative sedation as an alternative to euthanasia, something that is legal in both those countries, but illegal in the UK, where doctors and nurses had a very different rationale for their actions.

Dictionary categories in Wordstat correspondence analysis output can be clicked on to reveal the underlying segments of text that contribute to each category, enabling typical quotes to be selected for a final report.

5 WRAPPING UP

In this chapter I have introduced you to some of the basic features of QDA software, emphasizing how useful such software can be when storing, coding, searching and retrieving bits of qualitative data. I have also noted some commonly experienced barriers to its uptake and ways of overcoming these, including the need to take things gradually when learning to incorporate a piece of software into your own research practice.

I have stressed the time-saving element of this, as well as other advantages, such as the way in which software obliges you to be explicit about the methodological procedures you use in your analysis. I have pointed out that different approaches to qualitative data analysis may mean some software products are better than others for a particular purpose, and that you need to be careful in choosing which procedures to implement within QDA software if they are to be relevant to your purpose. I have also introduced the topic of text mining or text analytics, an approach that can help you make the most of the increased availability of very large quantities of material for analysis, which qualitative researchers ought not to miss out on.

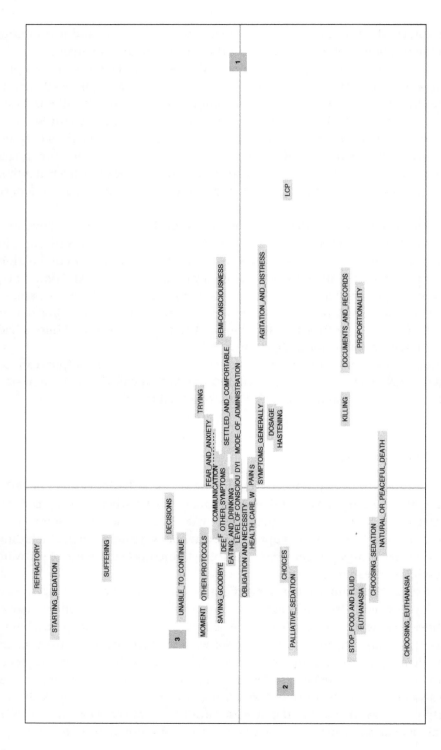

Figure 16.3 Correspondence analysis in Wordstat

As a result I hope that you will feel able to use QDA software confidently and for your own ends, rather than have it dictate an analytic strategy to you. There are many such software products available and, if you find that a particular one does not support what you want to do, the odds are that another product will contain something more useful if you look hard enough.

What You Need to Remember

- Specialized computer software (QDA software) can speed up the routine tasks of sorting and searching through large quantities of qualitative data. This frees up time for analytic thought.
- Such software promotes rigour and transparency about methodological decisions.
- Coding, searching and retrieving are basic and much used features of most QDA software.
- Text mining, or text analytics, with QDA software, enables qualitative researchers to analyse 'big data'.
- QDA software does not do the thinking for you. You need to be in charge of that.

Your Chapter Checklist

- Do you understand the strengths and limitations of computer-assisted qualitative data analysis (QDA) and QDA software tools?
- Can you recognize the key features of some of the main QDA software products?
- Can you evaluate their usefulness for your research project?

TRACK:
RELEVANCE OF CAQDAS TO YOUR PROJECT

Exercises

Exercise 1: Get to know different QDA software packages

Download a demonstration version of one of these software products. Demonstration versions will usually contain sample datasets to use in learning the features of the software.

ATLAS.ti   www.atlasti.com

HyperRESEARCH   www.researchware.com/products/hyperresearch.html

APPLY:
YOUR EXERCISE WORKBOOK

MAXQDA	www.maxqda.com
NVivo	www.qsrinternational.com
QDA Miner	https://provalisresearch.com
Transana	www.transana.com

You could also try out WordSmith Tools or, for free, get a copy of AntConc.

WordSmith Tools	www.lexically.net/wordsmith
AntConc	www.antlab.sci.waseda.ac.jp/antconc_index.html

When you have spent some time getting to know the software and what it can do, jot down answers to the following questions:

1. How could I use this software to save time on my research project?
2. How could I use this software to improve the rigour of my study?
3. How could I use this software to develop the theoretical aspects of my study?
4. What are the limitations and disadvantages of using this software for my study? Would another product overcome these, or should I opt for a 'manual' approach?

Exercise 2: Evaluate the code-and-retrieve approach

This will help you evaluate the relative merits of a code-and-retrieve approach to qualitative thematic analysis and text mining using dictionary software.

The following two articles report data analyses that were carried out concurrently on the same data, using two different methods: coding and retrieval (Seymour et al., 2014) and a dictionary-based analysis using Wordstat (Seale et al., 2015). Here are the references in full:

Seymour, J., Rietjens, J., Bruinsma, S., Deliens, L., Sterckx, S., Mortier, F., Brown, J., Mathers, N. and van der Heide, A. on behalf of the UNBIASED consortium (2014) 'Using continuous sedation until death for cancer patients: a qualitative interview study of physicians' and nurses' practice in three European countries'. *Palliative Medicine*, 29 (1), 48–59.

Seale, C., Raus, K., Bruinsma, S., van der Heide, A., Sterckx, S., Mortier, F., Payne, S., Mathers, N. and Rietjens, J. on behalf of the UNBIASED consortium (2015) 'The language of sedation in end-of-life care: the ethical reasoning of care providers in three countries'. *Health: An interdisciplinary Journal*, 19 (4), 339–54.

Examine these articles and make a list of all the findings the authors report. Which ones are reported by one but not the other? Which analysis is the more convincing?

Exercise 3: Explore coding without the use of QDA software

Select a published qualitative research project that you already know quite well, which was done without the use of QDA software. It could, for example, be an early 'classic' study of Chicago School ethnography, or a well-known study relevant to your research topic. Examine the way in which the researcher appears to have collected and analysed the data and answer the following questions:

1. How might QDA software have been used to aid data collection in this study?
2. How might QDA software have been used to develop a coding scheme in this study?
3. How might the use of QDA software have improved the quality and rigour of data reporting in this study?
4. What other questions might have been asked of the data in the study, and could QDA software have helped in answering these?

Further Reading

Christina Silver and Ann Lewins' *Using Software in Qualitative Research* (Sage, 2014) is an excellent guide to QDA software. Patricia Bazeley and Kriste Jackson (Sage, 2013) provide a guide to using NVivo and Susanne Friese (Sage, 2014) a guide to using ATLAS.ti. The websites listed in the text contain plentiful advice and training and self-help tutorials on the subject, as well as links to books and articles.

READ THE RESEARCH: USING CAQDAS
READ THE RESEARCH: CAQDAS ON INTERVIEW DATA
READ THE RESEARCH: CAQDAS ON SPORT DATA

Discover the chapter's digital resources in your
SILVERMAN FIELD GUIDE

SEVENTEEN
Quality in Qualitative Research

Learning Outcomes

By the end of this chapter you will be able to:

- Understand the concepts of validity and reliability.
- Incorporate into your research design a number of methods for improving validity and reliability.
- Design and generate research sensitive to quality issues.

1 INTRODUCTION

EXPLORE:
RESEARCH QUALITY

This is the first of two chapters which deal with quality considerations. In this chapter, I will attempt a diagnosis of the problem and suggest some practical solutions for you to use in your own research. In Chapter 18, I suggest how you can apply quality rules to evaluate research publications.

Quality has been a continuing theme of this book. Deciding to do qualitative research is not a soft option. Such research demands theoretical sophistication and methodological rigour.

Just because we do not use complicated statistical tests or do much counting, this does not mean that we can wallow in comforting hot baths of 'empathic' or 'authentic' discussions with respondents. After all, if this is the limit of our ambitions, can we do better than a talk show presenter?

Why does 'quality' matter, and what does 'quality' mean? To get a feel of the issues involved, let us begin with how students frame these matters.

EXPLORE:
QUAL RESEARCH CREDIBILITY

WHAT I DID: MARIANNE AND DANIEL

Just My Interpretation?

In an ethnographic study of adolescents in care homes, Marianne wonders how she can deal with the criticism that her findings derive from her own perspectives and values as an experienced social worker. As she puts it: 'How can I manage and reflect upon my participation in the observations and interviews and its impact on what I find?' [Marianne Sommerfeldt, Social Work, Oslo University]

Daniel is carrying out ethnographic research on the use of social media by senior administrative staff in two Swedish universities. Like Marianne, he wonders how objective he can be. In his own words, 'Interpretations are central in my research – from me being in the field interpreting various individuals and processes; people interpreting me as a researcher at their workplace and my analysis of the data ... How CAN I handle all these interpretations?' [Daniel Lovgren, Informatics and Media, Uppsala University, his emphasis]

The traditional way of handling these valid concerns about how we interpret data is to let the reader know about your past experiences and possible biases so that they can judge the degree of objectivity of your findings. More recently, people have questioned any claim to a purely 'objective' position. Rather than make such a claim, it is far better to treat 'interpretation' as not just a researcher's problem but to understand how the people you are studying are interpreting each other's behaviour.

It follows that the best path is to study how identities are constituted in relations in the field. So Marianne and Daniel should study how they and their research subjects co-construct versions of who they are during the course of research interviews and organizational practice. In this way, we redefine 'interpretation' as no longer a question of the validity of our knowledge but as an everyday, practical activity.

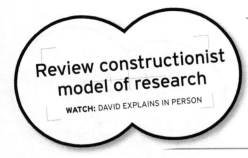

Review constructionist model of research

WATCH: DAVID EXPLAINS IN PERSON

David's Top Tip 42

The approach recommended here derives from a constructionist model of social research. If you are puzzled about how to study interpretation in the manner just suggested, return to Chapter 7 where constructionism is defined and compared with other analytic models

As we saw in Chapter 13, many students are less worried by global issues of 'interpretation' than about the small number of cases that they are able to study. Maddie Sandall's research for her MSc was based on interviews with foreign students who had transferred to the UK for the final year of their degree. Having gathered her data, she worried about her sample as follows.

WHAT I DID: MADDIE

Do I Need More Data?

The request for interviewees generated a relatively small response rate, possibly due to the characteristics of the students required for the sample, or it could have been due to the numerous coursework assignments due in during that term. Although the data I have gathered had been quite rich and interesting, I felt that more was needed, therefore this has been backed up by a largely quantitative survey of students in Malaysia. [Maddie Sandall, Management, University of the West of England]

In a focus group study of Chinese people with diabetes living in the UK, Queenie Eng had similar concerns. Like Maddie, she worried about the representativeness of her respondents. Unlike Maddie, she did not gather more data but spent time explaining the rationale behind the composition of her focus group.

WHAT I DID: QUEENIE

Representativeness Again

It is extremely important that findings obtained with convenience samples are critically evaluated against the following questions:

Q1: What types of people were systematically excluded from the sample, and why? The following individuals were excluded from the study:

- Students, asylum seekers and refugees were excluded because of their limited length of stay and the lack of fixed abode in the UK.
- Non-Chinese-language speakers were excluded because the study is focused on Chinese people and the researcher cannot communicate fluently in other non-Chinese languages.
- Those with cognitive impairment were excluded because of potential inability to articulate thoughts and feelings effectively.

Q2: What types of people were over-represented in the sample?

- Given the nature of diabetes, where males are more predisposed than women, proportionately more men were involved in Phase 2 of the study. [Queenie Eng (S. Eng), Medicine, Leeds]

As I noted in Chapter 13, given the small numbers of people or situations with which qualitative research is concerned, many students worry about the representativeness of their case studies. Yet there are two straightforward solutions to this worry:

- an emphasis on the value of even a single case since, like a black swan, it can test a general rule (Flyvbjerg, 2004: 421)
- as Queenie Eng shows, the choice of a purposive sample based on logical grounds.

Representativeness is not the only quality issue that troubles students. Many have doubts about the extent to which respondents' answers really relate to what they do outside the interview (see Hammersley, 2008: 89–100). In the 2016 UK referendum that led to Brexit, there were suspicions that people were concealing racist feelings behind slogans like 'controlling immigration'. Similarly, in an interview study of perceptions of race in New Zealand, Farida Tilbury was concerned about whether she could take at face value her respondents' expressions of non-racist sentiments.

WHAT I DID: FARIDA

Truth or Rhetoric?

Speakers about race relations use a number of rhetorical devices to convince and to manage the impression they make when giving accounts of their views. One device is to claim a personal relationship with members of the group one goes on to criticize,

(Continued)

(Continued)

producing the oft-heard justification, 'Some of my best friends are Maori ... but ....' The purpose of this research was to determine the influence such friendships *actually* have on identity and attitudes. When a friendship is reported by a respondent, is it possible to tell whether a respondent is using their 'friendship' as a rhetorical device, or whether they are reporting a genuine friendship? When is a friend a friend, and not a rhetorical device? Basically, if respondents were reporting close friendships which did not exist, how can the data be taken as valid? A person may have reported two good friendships across ethnic boundaries, but if they reported these purely for impression management reasons, the relationship between attitudes reported and friendships is going to be misleading. This is a special case of the more general question – how are accounts related to 'reality'? [Farida Tilbury, Sociology, Murdoch University]

Farida nicely illustrates a dilemma about validity common to interview researchers. There are two ways of responding to this dilemma:

- insisting on a more detailed analysis of the data in order to sort 'fact' from 'fiction' (the positivist solution)
- changing the focus away from the 'facts' of racism towards the rhetoric of racism (the constructionist solution).

Although Farida's use of discourse analysis led towards the second response, she also made use of a more positivist solution, as the extract below illustrates.

WHAT I DID: FARIDA

Sorting 'Fact' from 'Fiction'

[Because] there was inevitably a degree of impression management influencing the choice of friendships reported by the participants ... it was necessary to analyse the entire interviews much more closely to try to glean whether these friendships had a strong influence on respondents' views, taking note of how frequently they were used as warrants for particular views, and how often other influences were mentioned, the manner in which they were referred to, the nature of the story told, the tone of surrounding comments, and noting the ways they were used as examples to support certain attitudes. It became easier to tell whether friendships reported were simply credentials or justifications, or were genuine close friendships, from the ways that they were talked about. [Farida Tilbury]

Irrespective of the theoretical model that lies behind your research problem, the kind of in-depth analysis that Farida uses here is an essential way to achieve valid findings. Later I will refer to this approach as 'comprehensive data treatment'.

Once again mobilizing a positivist model, in the following extract Farida worries about the reliability of her chosen 'research instrument' – the open-ended interview.

WHAT I DID: FARIDA

The Reliability of Open-Ended Questions

Perhaps their extreme open-endedness left respondents a little unsure how to respond, or with less time to consider their response [to my questions]. For example, if the interviewer merely says 'affirmative action', respondents may not have time to consider their response, not know where to start, or not understand the concept. On the other hand, if the issue were framed in terms of a longer question, such as, 'Some people have argued that special quotas for Maori or other disadvantaged groups are a good idea in order to give them access to jobs or educational opportunities that they might not otherwise have access to. Do you have any views on affirmative action programmes such as this?', respondents would have a clear explanation of the topic and time to collect their thoughts and consider their answer. I still feel that the longer format tends to lead respondents to answer in particular ways, and so prefer the format used, but it is interesting to consider the effect of this approach on the forms of respondents' expressions. [Farida Tilbury]

A logical way of testing whether different question formats produce different answers, as Farida suspects, is to pre-test questions before the main research starts. A more constructionist solution is to examine long sequences of talk to examine how interviewer and interviewee co-assemble particular versions of 'reality' (see Rapley, 2011). As I suggested earlier in this chapter, this is to transform the issue of 'interpretation' from a researcher's problem into a research topic by studying how different identities are constructed or performed.

Whatever your theoretical model, it is good practice to address how your relationship with the people in your study might affect your findings. In ethnographic studies, using participant observation, the researcher–researched relation has been a

READ:
CONTRADICTORY DATA

continuing interest. Ben Heaven's ethnography of the conduct of a randomized controlled trial (RCT) is a case in point.

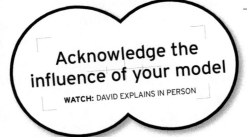

Acknowledge the influence of your model

WATCH: DAVID EXPLAINS IN PERSON

David's Top Tip 43

Apparent 'contradictions' in your data depend on the model you are employing. For constructionists, such contradictions may reflect the different discourses that are being used by participants.

WHAT I DID: BEN
Studying a Team Carrying Out a Medical Trial

A key difficulty I experienced in my interpretation of the data was a sense of loyalty to the trial team. I was exposed to the daily frustrations of these researchers, and sometimes participated in their struggle to make the trial work. It was difficult at times therefore to question their actions or perspectives.

My mind raced with the uses to which I could apply certain quotes: in paper titles, conclusions to conference presentations and formal reports. However, I was also mindful that I was amongst colleagues and friends, and that such statements were typically made out of frustration. The dilemma was: should they be reported, and if so how?

To address the dilemma of utilizing inflammatory statements in the thesis, I employed a single, relatively risky strategy. The risk in this sense stemmed from an increased opportunity for censorship. *When an inflammatory action or statement was recorded I discussed my interpretation of the event with the actor in question.* [Ben Heaven, Health Studies, Newcastle]

Ben's thoughtful account of his research raises several ethical problems about what you owe to the people you study (discussed in Chapter 4). However, it also addresses two important quality issues:

- going 'native' (i.e. being so personally involved with the people you are studying that it is difficult to be objective)
- anecdotal use of data extracts (like spectacular quotes from participants) out of context.

Ben offers two solutions to the problem of anecdotalism. First, he takes his interpretations back to the people concerned. This method, known as **respondent validation**, is discussed later in this chapter. Second, instead of choosing a few spectacular data extracts, he elects to situate 'perspectives in their broader contexts ... explicitly acknowledging the trajectories preceding them'. Like Farida's work, this is another excellent example of 'comprehensive data treatment'.

All of the student examples used here employ what Seale has called 'methodological awareness':

> Methodological awareness involves a commitment to showing as much as possible ... the procedures and evidence that have led to particular conclusions, always open to the possibility that conclusions may need to be revised in the light of new evidence. (1999: x)

It follows that unless you can show your audience the procedures you used to ensure that your methods were reliable and your conclusions valid, there is little point in aiming to submit a research dissertation. Having good intentions, or the correct political attitude, is unfortunately never the point. Short of reliable methods and valid conclusions, research descends into a bedlam where the only battles that are won are by those who shout the loudest.

READ: GENERALIZATION IN QUAL RESEARCH
READ: ETHNOGRAPHIC DATA CREDIBILITY

In Chapter 11, I was able to be reassuring about the scientific status of case studies based upon small amounts of data. However, I am less tempted to assure qualitative researchers that they need not be concerned about the reliability of their methods or the quality of their interpretations. The reader has only to refer to Chapter 18 to see that my concerns about these matters extend to some published research.

But first it is important to be clear about the relevant terms: validity and reliability. For simplicity, I will work with the two straightforward definitions set out in Table 17.1.

Table 17.1   Validity and reliability

Validity

By validity, I mean truth: interpreted as the extent to which an account accurately represents the social phenomena to which it refers (Hammersley, 1990: 57)

Reliability

Reliability refers to the degree of consistency with which instances are assigned to the same category by different observers or by the same observer on different occasions (Hammersley, 1992: 67)

Using examples of actual research studies, I review below the pitfalls and opportunities that the demands of validity and reliability create for the novice researcher. Let me begin with validity.

2 VALIDITY

'Validity' refers to the credibility of our interpretations. As Peräkylä puts it:

> The validity of research concerns the interpretation of observations: whether or not the inferences that the researcher makes are supported by the data, and sensible in relation to earlier research. (2011: 365)

Catherine Riessman is an exponent of the constructionist approach known as narrative analysis. However, she insists that her students treat their reports as more than just a story. As she puts it:

> Is the investigator's interpretation of data (stories told in field interviews, for example) persuasive and plausible, reasonable and convincing? Every reader has had the experience of encountering a piece of research and thinking 'but of course …' even when the argument an author was making was counterintuitive. Persuasiveness is strengthened when the investigator's theoretical claims are supported with evidence from informants' accounts, negative cases are included, and alternative interpretations considered. The strategy forces investigators to document their claims for readers who weren't present to witness stories as they unfolded, or beside the investigator who tried to make sense of them. (Personal correspondence)

Behind Riessman's demands is a doubt about the validity of an explanation where the researcher has clearly made no attempt to deal with contrary cases or to locate an example in a broader context (as Ben and Farida do). Or sometimes, the requirement of journal editors for shorter and shorter articles and the word limits attached to university courses mean that the researcher is reluctantly led only to use 'telling' examples.

Of course, such challenges to validity are not confined to qualitative research. The same sort of problems can happen in the natural sciences. The demands of journal editors and university courses are little different in most fields. Nor is the temptation to exclude contrary cases unique to qualitative research. Moreover, the large research teams that sometimes collaborate in the natural sciences can unexpectedly threaten the credibility of findings. For instance, laboratory assistants have been shown to select 'perfect' slides for their professor's important lecture, while putting on one side the slides about which awkward questions might be asked (see Lynch, 1984).

It also should not be assumed that quantitative researchers have a simple solution to the question of validity. As Fielding and Fielding point out, some interpretation takes place even when using apparently 'hard' quantitative measures:

> ultimately all methods of data collection are analysed 'qualitatively', in so far as the act of analysis is an interpretation, and therefore of necessity a selective rendering. Whether the data collected are quantifiable or qualitative, the issue of the *warrant* for their inferences must be confronted. (1986: 12, my emphasis)

So, as you prepare your qualitative study, you should not be overly defensive. Quantitative researchers have no 'golden key' to validity.

Nonetheless, qualitative researchers, with their in-depth access to single cases, have to overcome a special temptation. How are they to convince themselves (and their audience) that their 'findings' are genuinely based on critical investigation of all their data and do not depend on a few well-chosen 'examples'? This is sometimes known as the problem of **anecdotalism**.

As Mehan (1979) notes, the very strength of ethnographic field studies – its ability to give rich descriptions of social settings – can also be its weakness. Mehan identifies three such weaknesses:

1. Conventional field studies tend to have an anecdotal quality. Research reports include a few *exemplary* instances of the behavior that the researcher has culled from field notes.
2. Researchers seldom provide the criteria or grounds for including certain instances and not others. As a result, it is difficult to determine the typicality or *representativeness* of instances and findings generated from them.
3. Research reports presented in tabular form do not preserve the materials upon which the analysis was conducted. As the researcher abstracts data from raw materials to produce summarized findings, the original form of the materials is *lost*. Therefore, it is impossible to entertain alternative interpretations of the same materials. (1979: 15, my emphasis)

Some years later, this problem was succinctly expressed by Bryman:

> There is a tendency towards an anecdotal approach to the use of data in relation to conclusions or explanations in qualitative research. Brief conversations, snippets from unstructured interviews ... are used to provide evidence of a particular contention. There are grounds for disquiet in that the representativeness or generality of these fragments is rarely addressed. (1988: 77)

Let me use one more student example to show how a proper degree of 'methodological awareness' can help you overcome anecdotalism and improve the validity of your findings. Alan Quirk's dissertation examined how mental health professionals made decisions about the 'careers' of mental patients (from being compulsorily admitted, or 'sectioned', to their hospital stay and discharge). Below you will find his discussion of how he improved the validity of his findings using three interrelated studies. In this long example, look out for Alan's discussion of:

- following the trajectory of patients' careers (longitudinal design, i.e. over time)
- examining negative instances rather than rushing to early conclusions
- triangulating different methods to address a particular topic
- using simple tabulations of the frequency of certain phenomena
- employing member validation to check his findings.

WHAT I DID: ALAN

Striving for Validity

Combining the findings from my three studies means I am able to comment not only on how people are admitted onto an acute psychiatric ward – both under mental health legislation and voluntarily (two of the audio-taped outpatient consultations resulted in an informal admission) – but also what happens to them when they get there. Further, in the Prescribing Decisions Project I observed some people's first outpatient appointment after their discharge from hospital. This offers some insight into people's experiences after a stay in hospital, as do the follow-up interviews undertaken with discharged patients for the MHA study. In short, the observations presented in this thesis span events leading up to, during, and after hospital admission. To my knowledge this is the first combined observational study to encompass all of these aspects of psychiatric practice. [Alan goes on to explain how he has attempted to improve the validity of his findings:]

- All three studies have been undertaken in a *spirit of grounded theorizing*, with attempts made to search and account for negative instances.
- Various methods of *triangulation* have been used. In the two ethnographic studies various types of evidence were collected before concluding that a thing is true, and in the Prescribing Decisions Project, the CA research complemented our interview study. It did so because, while the analysis of consultation transcripts revealed activities that psychiatrists failed to mention in research interviews (e.g. what patients do to construct safe conversational environments in which to discuss non-compliance), the interviews helped one-off psychiatric consultations to be understood in the context of the unfolding doctor–patient relationship in which they take place.
- *Simple counts* of well-defined phenomena have been included in the findings chapters where appropriate. This is aimed at increasing the credibility of claims and guarding against accusations of anecdotalism that can be levelled at certain qualitative studies.
- *Respondent validation* techniques were used. [Alan Quirk, Human Sciences, Brunel University]

Alan's use of multiple methods and settings was ambitious and well beyond the range of most PhD (let alone MA) research. Nevertheless, his high degree of 'methodological awareness' and resistance to 'anecdotalism' is something to which we can all aspire.

Now let us look more closely at some of the strategies that Alan uses. *Triangulation* refers to the attempt to get a 'true' fix on a situation by combining different ways of looking at it (method triangulation) or different findings (data triangulation). In Chapter 6, I showed some of the difficulties that novice researchers can get into by attempting such triangulation. In Chapter 9, I discussed in more detail the analytical limitations of this approach.

Broadly, using a constructionist model is simply not compatible with the assumption that 'true' fixes on 'reality' can be obtained separately from particular ways of looking at it. Of course, this does not mean that you should not use different datasets or deploy different methods. The problem only arises when you use such multiplicity as a way of settling validity questions.

Respondent validation suggests that we should go back to the subjects with our tentative results and refine them in the light of our subjects' reactions (Reason and Rowan, 1981).

Some writers are very gung-ho about the use of feedback as a validation exercise. For instance, Peter Reason and John Rowan (1981) criticize researchers who are fearful of 'contaminating their data with the experience of the subject'. On the contrary, they argue, good research goes back to the subjects with the tentative results, and refines them in the light of the subjects' reactions.

This is just what Michael Bloor (1978; 1983) attempted in his research on doctors' decision making. Bloor (1978) discusses three procedures which attempt respondent validation:

1. The researcher seeks to predict members' classifications in actual situations of their use (see Frake, 1964).
2. The researcher prepares hypothetical cases and predicts respondents' responses to them (again see Frake, 1964).
3. The researcher provides respondents with a research report and records their reactions to it.

In his study of doctors' decision making in tonsillectomy cases, Bloor used method 3. However, he had reservations about his surgeons' reactions to his report. It was not clear that they were very interested in findings that were not focused on their day-to-day concerns. Bloor's worries have been very effectively taken up by Fielding and Fielding (1986) (respondent validation is also criticized by Bryman, 1988: 78–9). The Fieldings concede that subjects being studied may have additional knowledge, especially about the context of their actions. However, they conclude:

> there is no reason to assume that members have privileged status as commentators on their actions ... such feedback cannot be taken as direct validation or refutation of the observer's inferences. Rather such processes of so-called 'validation' should be treated as yet another source of data and insight. (1986: 43)

I can only add that, if feedback is a highly problematic way of validating research, this does not mean that it should be ignored as a way of maintaining contact with subjects in the field. However, this issue should not be confused with the validation of research findings.

As Bloor points out, the problematic research status of this activity need not mean that attempts at respondent validation have *no* value. They do generate fur-

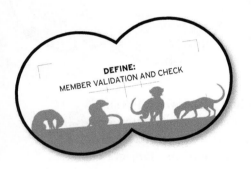

DEFINE:
MEMBER VALIDATION AND CHECK

ther data which, while not validating the research report, often suggests interesting paths for further analysis (Bloor, 1983: 172).

Of course, this leaves on one side the ethics, politics and practicalities of the researcher's relation with subjects in the field (see Chapters 4 and 14). Nonetheless, these latter issues should not be confused with the validation of research findings.

If triangulation and respondent validation are fallible paths to validity, what more satisfactory methods remain? I discuss below five interrelated ways of thinking critically about qualitative data analysis in order to aim at more valid findings. These are:

- the refutability principle
- the constant comparative method
- comprehensive data treatment
- deviant case analysis
- using appropriate tabulations.

The refutability principle

One solution to the problem of anecdotalism is simply for qualitative researchers to seek to refute their initial assumptions about their data in order to achieve objectivity. As Kirk and Miller argue:

> The assumptions underlying the search for objectivity are simple. There is a world of empirical reality out there. The way we perceive and understand that world is largely up to us, but the world does not tolerate all understandings of it equally. (1986: 11)

Even if we do not employ Kirk and Miller's positivist language, we need to recognize that 'the world does not tolerate all understandings of it equally'. This means that we must overcome the temptation to jump to easy conclusions just because there is some evidence that seems to lead in an interesting direction. Instead, we must subject this evidence to every possible test.

The critical method implied here is close to what Karl Popper (1959) calls 'critical rationalism'. This demands that we must seek to falsify or refute assumed relations between phenomena. Then, only if we cannot refute the existence of a certain relationship are we in a position to speak about 'objective' knowledge. Even then, however, our knowledge is always provisional, subject to a subsequent study which may come up with disconfirming evidence. Popper puts it this way:

> What characterizes the empirical method is its manner of exposing to falsification, in every conceivable way, the system to be tested. Its aim is not to save the lives of untenable systems but, on the contrary, to select the one which is by comparison the fittest, by exposing them all to the fiercest struggle for survival. (1959: 42)

Of course, qualitative researchers are not alone in taking Popper's critical method seriously. One way in which quantitative researchers attempt to satisfy Popper's demand for attempts at 'falsification' is by carefully excluding spurious correlations.

To do this, the survey researcher may seek to introduce new variables to produce a form of 'multivariate analysis' which can offer significant, non-spurious correlations (see Mehan, 1979: 21). Through such an attempt to avoid spurious correlations, quantitative social scientists can provide a practical demonstration of their orientation to the spirit of critical enquiry that Popper advocates.

How can qualitative researchers satisfy Popper's criterion? The remaining four methods suggest an interrelated way of thinking critically during data analysis.

The constant comparative method

Comparison has always been the backbone, acknowledged or not, of good sociological thinking. Finding two or more things that are alike in some important way yet differ in other ways; looking for the further differences that create those you first noticed; looking for the deeper processes these surface differences embody: these operations create sociological knowledge of the world and give us the more abstract theories that tell us what to look for the next time out (Becker, 2010: 1).

The comparative method means that the qualitative researcher should always attempt to find another case through which to test out a provisional hypothesis. In an early study of the changing perspectives of medical students during their training, Becker and Geer (1960) found that they could test their emerging hypothesis about the influence of career stages upon perceptions by comparing different groups at one time and also comparing one cohort of students with another over the course of training. For instance, it could only be claimed with confidence that beginning medical students tended to be idealists if several cohorts of first-year students all shared this perspective.

Similarly, when I was studying what happened to children with Down's syndrome in a heart hospital, I tested out my findings with tape recordings of consultations from the same clinic involving children without the congenital abnormality (Silverman, 1981). And, of course, my attempt to analyse the ceremonial order of private medical practice (Silverman, 1984) was highly dependent on comparative data on public clinics.

However, beginning researchers are unlikely to have the resources to study different cases. Yet this does not mean that comparison is impossible. The constant comparative method involves simply inspecting and comparing all the data fragments that arise in a single case (Charmaz, 2006: 178–80; Glaser and Strauss, 1967).

While such a method may seem attractive, beginning researchers may worry about two practical difficulties involved in implementing it. First, they may lack the resources to assemble all their data in an analysable form. For instance, transcribing a whole dataset may be impossibly time consuming – as well as diverting you from data analysis! Second, how are you to compare data when you may have not yet generated a provisional hypothesis or even an initial set of categories?

Fortunately, these objections can be readily overcome. In practice, it usually makes sense to begin analysis on a relatively small part of your data. Then, having generated a set of categories, you can test out emerging hypotheses by steadily expanding your data corpus. This point has been clearly made by Peräkylä using the example of studies based on tape-recorded data:

> There is a limit to how much data a single researcher or a research team can transcribe and analyse. But on the other hand, a large database has definite advantages … a large portion of the data can be kept as a resource that is used only when the analysis has progressed so far

that the phenomena under study have been specified. At that later stage, short sections from the data in reserve can be transcribed, and thereby, the full variation of the phenomenon can be observed. (2004: 288)

I employed this constant comparative method, moving from small to larger datasets, in my study of AIDS counselling (Silverman, 1997). For example, having isolated an instance of how a client resisted a counsellor's advice, I trawled through my data to obtain a larger sample of cases where advice resistance was present.

However, the constant comparative method, because it involves a repeated to and fro between different parts of your data, implies something much bigger. All parts of your data must, at some point, be inspected and analysed. This is part of what is meant by 'comprehensive data treatment'.

Comprehensive data treatment

ten Have notes the complaint that in CA, as in other kinds of research:

findings ... are based on a subjectively selected, and probably biased, 'sample' of cases that happen to fit the analytic argument. (1998: 135)

This complaint, which amounts to a charge of anecdotalism, can be addressed by what ten Have, following Mehan (1979), calls 'comprehensive data treatment'. This comprehensiveness arises because, in qualitative research, 'all cases of data ... [are] incorporated in the analysis' (1979: 21).

Such comprehensiveness goes beyond what is normally demanded in many quantitative methods. For instance, in survey research one is usually satisfied by achieving significant, non-spurious, correlations. So, if nearly all your data supports your hypothesis, your job is largely done.

By contrast, in qualitative research, working with smaller datasets open to repeated inspection, one should not be satisfied until one's generalization is able to apply to every single gobbet of relevant data collected.

The outcome is a generalization which can be every bit as valid as a statistical correlation. As Mehan puts it: 'The result is an integrated, precise model that comprehensively describes a specific phenomena [*sic*], instead of a simple correlational statement about antecedent and consequent conditions' (1979: 21).

Comprehensive data treatment implies actively seeking out and addressing anomalies or deviant cases. Again Mehan makes the point:

The method begins with a small batch of data. A provisional analytic scheme is generated. The scheme is then compared to other data, and modifications [are] made in the scheme as necessary. The provisional analytic scheme is constantly confronted by 'negative' or 'discrepant' cases until the researcher has derived a small set of recursive rules that incorporate all the data in the analysis. (1979: 21; see also Becker, 1998: 211-12)

Deviant case analysis

What is important in depicting anomalies precisely? If you cannot do it, that shows you do not know your way around the concepts. (Wittgenstein, 1980: 72e)

In quantitative research you turn to deviant cases in two circumstances:

*   when the existing variables will not produce sufficiently high statistical correlations
*   when good correlations are found but you suspect these might be 'spurious'.

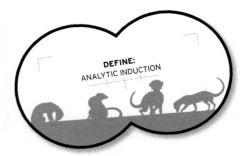

DEFINE:
ANALYTIC INDUCTION

By contrast, the qualitative researcher should not be satisfied by explanations which appear to explain nearly all the variance in their data. Instead, as I have already argued, in qualitative research, every piece of data has to be used until it can be accounted for.

Explaining every deviant case in your data is also known as **analytic induction**.

WHAT I DID: GABRIELLA
Deviant Cases in Internet Data

Ethnographers like me, who (only) use naturally occurring data on the Internet, have been criticized as some scholars argue that it is too much interpretation going on, only observing, no physical bodies present and no interviews face-to-face. My experience is, however, that on the Internet, bodies, body language and emotions are reproduced in textual exchanges and there are a lot of 'interactional clues' which I can look for and use to interpret the interaction and communication. I mean that the contributors use emoticons, acronyms, capitals, dots, pictures, etc., when they interact. Throughout the text I try to show deviant examples to demonstrate the complexity in the virtual red-light district but also to make my data analysis more credible. [Gabriella Scaramuzzino, Sociology, Malmö University]

Rapley (2011) calls such deviant cases 'exceptions'. He notes that, in the early stages of research, before you have a clear grip on analysing your data, every case looks like an exception. By contrast, once you have a sense of what is going on, it is difficult not to see every case as an instance of the same thing. So exceptions become far less visible. As he puts it:

> At this point, when you do notice something that does not really fit what has gone before, it can really start to stand out, and in rarer cases it can become vital for your argument, as it can either make you re-think your ideas or illuminate and strengthen your thinking.
>
> At these later stages, exceptions really take three forms. These are what are known as the negative or deviant case (see Peräkylä, 2011) where the issue or case does not fit your current understanding of the phenomena. They take three forms:
>
> • Those that, despite being different, *actually support your finding*, as people themselves understand them and orientate to them as 'exceptions to the rule' and in so doing show you the 'rule'.
> • Those that, through their difference, *mean you need to re-evaluate or change* your labelling or ideas.
> • Those that are different for *very specific, idiosyncratic and contingent reasons* that neither support your findings nor mean you need to re-evaluate your ideas. (2011: 287)

In the following case study, Clive Seale examined exceptions – deviant case analysis – with the aim of a comprehensive data treatment.

CASE STUDY
Being Present at a Relative's Death

This case is drawn from an interview study of reports by relatives about family members who had died alone (Seale, 1996; discussed in Seale, 1999: 79-80).

Most relatives reported that a relative dying alone was an unwelcome event and that they would have wanted to be present at the death if they had been able. Seale argued that such accounts worked to display a relative's moral adequacy.

However, in a small minority of cases, people said they had not wanted to be present at such a death. Rather than treat these examples as statistically insignificant, Seale examined them in greater detail to see if his overall argument needed to be modified.

(Continued)

(Continued)

In all these deviant cases, it turned out that respondents offered legitimations for their position. For instance, in one case, a son said that his father's dementia meant that he would have been 'oblivious' if his son had been present. In another case, a husband referred to his own potential distress at being present at the death of his wife. He also added that it 'didn't make any difference as she was in a coma' (1999: 79).

Seale concluded that, in his five deviant cases, respondents did not depart from displays of moral adequacy but:

> successfully demonstrated their moral adequacy by alternative means. In doing this, they showed an orientation towards the event [i.e. not being present at the death of a loved one] as deviant from normal behaviour, requiring explanation, so strengthening the general case that accompaniment of dying people is perceived as a generally desirable social norm. (1999: 80)

Seale shows how the identification and further analysis of deviant cases can strengthen the validity of research. As implied here, it is important to underline the fact that such identification needs to stem from a theoretical approach to the data. Seale's work derived from a way of treating interview responses as moral narratives. My own research was based upon an ethnographic interest in the 'ceremonial order' of the clinic (Strong, 1979).

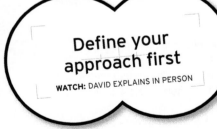

Define your approach first

WATCH: DAVID EXPLAINS IN PERSON

David's Top Tip 44

Pieces of data are never intrinsically 'deviant' but rather become so in relation to particular hypotheses generated from a particular model and method of data analysis. This theoretically defined approach to analysis should also properly apply to the compilation and inspection of data in tabulated form.

Using appropriate tabulations

By our pragmatic view, qualitative research does imply a commitment to field activities. It does not imply a commitment to innumeracy. (Kirk and Miller, 1986: 10)

It is usually a mistake to count simply for the sake of counting. Without a theoretical rationale behind the tabulated categories, counting only gives a spurious validity to research.

For instance, in the observation of classroom behaviour, Mehan suggests that many kinds of quantification have only limited value:

> the quantitative approach to classroom observation is useful for certain purposes, namely, for providing the frequency of teacher talk by comparison with student talk ... However, this approach minimizes the contribution of students, neglects the inter-relationship of verbal to non-verbal behavior, obscures the contingent nature of interaction, and ignores the (often multiple) functions of language. (1979: 14)

READ:
COUNTING IN QUAL RESEARCH

I do not attempt here to defend quantitative or positivistic research per se. I am not concerned with research designs which centre on quantitative methods and/or are indifferent to how participants construct order. Instead, I want to try to demonstrate some uses of quantification in research which is qualitative and interpretive in design. As the following case study shows, results from quantitative surveys can reveal a phenomenon which qualitative research can explain.

CASE STUDY

Explaining Prescribing Errors

A very nice example of how simple tabulations can improve the quality of data analysis is provided by Ross Koppel et al. (2003). Their earlier ethnographic research had revealed that hospital computer-based ordering systems were often associated with errors when doctors prescribed patients' medications. A quantitative survey now showed that over 75 per cent of doctors had used the computer system incorrectly.

It turned out that the computer display tended to convey a false sense of accuracy to many doctors. For example, by focusing solely on the electronic medication chart, doctors would tend to miss crucial paper stickers attached to the hardcopy casenotes. Various features of the computer software also seemed to be associated with these errors. For instance, the display on the screen would show amounts of a medication appropriate for warehousing needs and purchasing decisions. Yet this level might be clinically inappropriate. In addition, it was possible for a doctor

(Continued)

(Continued)

to add a new medication without cancelling an existing prescription for something very similar.

Koppel et al.'s survey increased the validity and generalizability of their qualitative study. Using both sets of data, they were able to argue more convincingly about how the computer software could be improved.

Koppel et al. used survey data as an impetus to credible qualitative research. By contrast, Heritage et al. (2007) followed up their findings in a qualitative study of general practice consultations with a quantitative experimental study.

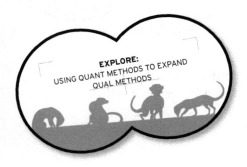

An alternative approach is to count members' own categories as used in naturally occurring places. For instance, in my analysis of cardiac consultations with children with Down's syndrome (see Chapter 15), I constructed a table, based on a comparison of Down's and non-Down's consultations, showing the different forms of the doctor's questions to parents and the parents' answers. This tabulation showed a strong tendency with children with Down's syndrome for both the doctor and parents to avoid using the word 'well' about the child, and this absence of reference to 'wellness' proved to be crucial to understanding the subsequent shape of the clinic consultation. So there is no reason why qualitative researchers should not, where appropriate, use quantitative measures.

David's Top Tip 45

Simple counting techniques, theoretically derived and ideally based on members' own categories, can offer a means to survey the whole corpus of data ordinarily lost in intensive, qualitative research. Instead of taking the researcher's word for it, the reader has a chance to gain a sense of the flavour of the data as a whole. In turn, researchers are able to test and to revise their generalizations, removing nagging doubts about the accuracy of their impressions about the data.

3 RELIABILITY

Counting based on members' own categories in the context of comprehensive data treatment is possible because, in principle, the quality of data should be high in qualitative research. By contrast, although quantitative researchers try to claim reliability by using pre-tested measures and scales, they can end up with highly unreliable tabulations. This is not because survey research questions are ambiguously worded, but rather because asking and answering any question can never be separated by mutual interpretations which are inherently local and non-standardizable (see Antaki and Rapley, 1996).

By contrast to tabulated figures from survey research interviews, tapes and transcripts are open to further inspection by both researchers and readers. However, this opportunity is not always present in qualitative research. There are many observational studies where the reader has to depend on the researcher's depiction of what was going on. Indeed, perhaps the extended immersion in the 'field', typical of much qualitative research, leads to a certain preciousness about the validity and reliability of the researcher's own interpretation of 'their' tribe or set of interview respondents.

As Bryman notes about such studies:

> field notes or extended transcripts are rarely available; these would be very helpful in order to allow the reader to formulate his or her own hunches about the perspective of the people who have been studied. (1988: 77)

By implication, Bryman is calling for what Seale (1999) calls **low-inference descriptors**. Although, as Seale notes, no act of observation can be free from the underlying assumptions that guide it (see Chapter 2 of this book), detailed data presentations which make minimal inferences are always preferable to researchers' presentation of their own (high-inference) summaries of their data.

Low-inference descriptors involve 'recording observations in terms that are as concrete as possible, including verbatim accounts of what people say ... rather than researchers' reconstructions of the general sense of what a person said' (1999: 148). I would add that low-inference description also means providing the reader with long data extracts which include, for instance, the question preceding a respondent's comments as well as the interviewer's **continuers** (e.g. 'mm hmm'), which encourage a respondent to enlarge a comment (see Rapley, 2004).

Earlier in this book, I have discussed two ways of strengthening the reliability of field data: fieldnote conventions (see Chapter 14) and inter-coder agreement. In the remaining part of this chapter, I will concretize this discussion of reliability by looking at an example of how reliability was addressed in the context of one piece of student research. I will then examine practical issues of reliability in a study which worked with tapes and transcripts of naturally occurring interaction.

Anne Patterson's dissertation was concerned with the meaning of disability to family members. As this extract shows, rather than ask family members to talk about the 'disability experience', she studied whether and how 'disability' entered into ordinary situations (like talking on the telephone).

WHAT I DID: ANNE

Reliability and Research on Family Life

Much disability research relies on anecdotal accounts of life experiences of being in a family which contains someone with a learning disability, and a whole body of research continues to be derived from such experts by experience. In this study the researcher does not set out, as an outsider, to collect reflexive accounts of life experiences, but rather examines how family moments (chatting on the phone) are lived 'here and now' with the researcher as an intrinsic part. It provides for a non-filtered, viewable-by-all set of data from which to draw insights and conclusions.

In a conversation analytic approach, researchers work with audio or video recordings, which means that the recordings and the transcripts they give rise to represent a source of data that is detailed, accurate and available for public scrutiny. Of course the quality of recording and of transcription can be variable, but as technology improves so can quality of recordings, and transcription can benefit from input from other analysts in data sessions. Such was the approach taken in this current study; data were collected via digital recorders and transcripts were the subject of discussion and review with and by fellow analysts. Thus reliability in this study is built through factors that are intrinsic in CA methodology and through meticulous attention to issues of recording and transcription. [Anne Patterson, Social Sciences, Loughborough]

Anne's account offers an instructive way to manage reliability issues by thinking through the extent to which different types of data allow you to address your research problem and then record and transcribe your data using an analytically informed method.

As the following case study shows, when people's activities are tape-recorded and transcribed, the reliability of the interpretation of transcripts may be gravely weakened by a failure to transcribe apparently trivial, but often crucial, pauses and overlaps.

CASE STUDY

The Reliability of Transcripts

A study of medical consultations was concerned to establish whether cancer patients had understood that their condition was fatal. In this study (Clavarino et al., 1995), we attempted to examine the basis upon which interpretive judgements were made about the content of a series of audio-taped doctor-patient interviews between three oncologists and their newly referred cancer patients. It was during this interview that the patients were supposedly informed that their cancer was incurable.

Two independent transcriptions were performed. In the first, an attempt was made to transcribe the talk 'verbatim' (i.e. without grammatical or other 'tidying up'). Using the first transcription, three independent coders, who had been trained to be consistent, coded the same material. Inter-coder reliability was then estimated. Inconsistencies among the coders may have reflected some ambiguity in the data, some overlap between coding categories, or simple coding errors.

The second transcription was informed by the analytic ideas and transcription symbols of CA. This provided additional information on how the parties organized their talk and, we believe, represents a more objective, more comprehensive and therefore more reliable recording of the data because of the level of detail given by this method.

By drawing upon the transcription symbols and concepts of CA, we sought to reveal subtle features in the talk, showing how both doctor and patients produced and received hearable ambiguities in the patient's prognosis. This involved a shift of focus from coders' readings to how participants demonstrably monitor each other's talk. Once we pay attention to such detail, judgements can be made that are more convincingly valid. Inevitably, this leads to a resolution of the problem of inter-coder reliability.

For instance, when researchers first listened to tapes of relevant hospital consultations, they sometimes felt that there was no evidence that the patients had picked up their doctors' often guarded statements about their prognosis. However, when the tapes were retranscribed, it was demonstrated that patients used very soft utterances (like 'yes' or more usually 'mm') to mark that they were taking up this information. Equally, doctors would monitor patients' silences and rephrase their prognosis statements.

4 WRAPPING UP

Some social researchers argue that a concern for the reliability and validity of observations arises only within the quantitative research tradition. Because what they call the 'positivist' position sees no difference between the natural and social worlds, reliable and valid measures of social life are only needed by such 'positivists'. Conversely, it is argued, once we treat social reality as always in flux, then it makes no sense to worry about whether our research instruments measure accurately (e.g. Marshall and Rossman, 1989).

Such a position would rule out any systematic research since it implies that we cannot assume any stable properties in the social world. However, if we concede the possible existence of such properties, why shouldn't other work replicate these properties?

As Kirk and Miller argue about reliability:

Qualitative researchers can no longer afford to beg the issue of reliability. While the forte of field research will always lie in its capability to sort out the validity of propositions, its results will (reasonably) go ignored minus attention to reliability. For reliability to be calculated, it is incumbent on the scientific investigator to document his or her procedure. (1986: 72)

Of course, exactly the same point may be made about the claims to validity, or truth status, of qualitative research studies. So, to underline the point with which this chapter began, unless you can show your audience the procedures you used to ensure that your methods were reliable and your conclusions valid, there is little point in aiming to conclude a research dissertation.

What You Need to Remember

Validity is another word for truth. We cannot say that the claims of a research study are valid when:

- Only a few exemplary instances are reported.
- The criteria or grounds for including certain instances and not others are not provided.
- The original form of the materials is unavailable.

Five ways of thinking critically about qualitative data analysis in order to aim at more valid findings were discussed:

- the refutability principle
- the constant comparative method
- comprehensive data treatment
- deviant case analysis
- using appropriate tabulations.

Reliability refers to the degree of consistency with which instances are assigned to the same category by different observers or by the same observer on different occasions. For reliability to be calculated, it is incumbent on the scientific investigator to document the procedure and to demonstrate that categories have been used consistently.

Whatever your breadth of data and however good your knowledge of the literature, your research will be inadequate unless it is credible. At the very least, this means you must not jump to conclusions but carefully sift your data.

TRACK:
QUAL RESEARCH VALIDITY & RELIABILITY

Your Chapter Checklist

- How can you make your research valid?
- How can you ensure that your data is reliable?
- How would you defend your research if somebody asked you to assess its credibility?

Exercises

Exercise 1: Achieve credibility in your data analysis

- List the ways in which you can make your data analysis credible.
- In the context of your own research project, what is the single best way of achieving credibility?

APPLY:
YOUR EXERCISE WORKBOOK

Exercise 2: Achieve validity in your data analysis

This is an exercise designed to help you think about the validity of your data analysis. It is best attempted when you have already written at least one substantial paper on your findings.

1. Choose any paper you have written on your data.
2. Explain on what grounds you chose those particular data extracts to report.
3. To what extent can you claim that this data was 'typical' or 'representative'?
4. To what extent have you investigated and reported 'deviant' cases?

Exercise 3: Explore the benefits and limits of your data

This exercise is meant to accustom you to the advantages and limitations of simple tabulations.

1. Select one dataset from your data corpus (e.g. a particular collection of interviews, observations or transcripts).
2. Count whatever seems to be countable in this data according to your theoretical orientation.
3. Assess what this quantitative data tells you about social life in this setting (e.g. what associations you can establish).
4. Identify deviant cases (i.e. items that do not support the associations that you have established). How might you further analyse these deviant cases, using either quantitative or qualitative techniques? What light might that throw on the associations which you have identified?

Exercise 4: Explain how your analysis gives the reader access to your data

The following is a quotation from Barry Glassner and Julia Loughlin about how they handled the issue of reliability in a study of adolescent drug users:

> In more positivistic research designs, coder reliability is assessed in terms of agreement among coders. In qualitative research one is unconcerned with

standardizing interpretation of data. Rather, our goal in developing this complex cataloguing and retrieval system has been *to retain good access to the words of the subjects*, without relying upon the memory of interviewers or data analysts. (1987: 27, my emphasis)

Now write a short piece (say 1000 words) explaining how your own data analysis provides the reader with good access to your original dataset. Check out this piece with your supervisor and other students. If they think it works, you may be able to use it as part of your final methodology chapter.

Further Reading

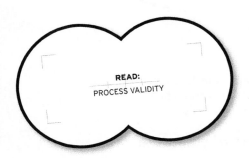

READ:
PROCESS VALIDITY

Clive Seale's book *The Quality of Qualitative Research* (Sage, 1999) offers an excellent overall treatment of the issues discussed in this chapter. Chapter-length discussions of quality are to be found in Anssi Peräkylä's 'Validity in qualitative research' (in D. Silverman (ed.), *Qualitative Research*, Sage, 2016: 413–28) and Victoria Braun and Virginia Clarke's *Successful Qualitative Research* (Sage, 2013: Chapter 12) Kathy Charmaz's *Constructing Grounded Theory* (Sage, 2015) is a thoughtful discussion of how credibility can be achieved in a constructivist version of grounded theory. Martyn Hammersley's book *Questioning Qualitative Inquiry* (Sage, 2008) has several chapters dealing with credibility issues. For a detailed discussion of deviant case analysis or analytic induction, see Howard Becker's *Tricks of the Trade* (University of Chicago Press, 1998: 197–212). Joseph Maxwell's 'Using numbers in qualitative research' (*Qualitative Inquiry*, 2010, 16 (6): 475–82) presents both the advantages of integrating quantitative information in qualitative data collection, analysis and reporting, and the potential problems created by such uses and how these can be dealt with. It also addresses the definition of mixed methods research, arguing that the use of numbers by itself doesn't make a study 'mixed methods'.

Discover the chapter's digital resources in your SILVERMAN FIELD GUIDE

EIGHTEEN
Evaluating Qualitative Research

Learning Outcomes

By the end of this chapter you will be able to:

- Understand the key questions to ask about published qualitative research studies.
- Apply agreed criteria to evaluate the quality of research carried out by yourself or by other people.

1 INTRODUCTION

In Chapter 17, we examined various strategies which can help to improve the quality of your research design and data analysis. Knowledge of such strategies also gives you a powerful set of tools through which to evaluate other people's research. Such evaluation skills are crucial in writing effective literature reviews (see Chapter 22). They will also stand you in good stead in preparing papers for publication (see Chapter 27) and in hallmarking your dissertation as the work of a truly professional researcher (see Chapter 5).

In this chapter, I will review evaluation criteria for qualitative research, using multiple case studies to illustrate what these criteria mean in practice.

In considering such criteria, we must first establish what is different about qualitative research. In Table 18.1, I set out one such attempt to establish what is unique about our kind of research.

Table 18.1   Distinguishing features of qualitative research

- Qualitative research is embedded in a research tradition and makes explicit reference to the theoretical, methodological and topic-related literature
- Qualitative research makes explicit its links to social science perspectives such as positivism, naturalism and constructionism
- Qualitative research selects methods of data collection and analysis that are appropriate for the issue under study as well as for the particular theoretical framework
- Qualitative research clarifies its methods of data collection and analysis to the point of enabling intersubjective agreement
- Depending on the particular theory and methods used, qualitative research can involve an 'emic' perspective (i.e. a culture-specific account; an account meaningful to actors themselves) as well as an 'etic' perspective (i.e. an account of the observer, which can be used for comparing different accounts)

However, any unique features of qualitative research do not free it from the standards of evaluating any piece of scientific work. I start from the assumption that all social science should base itself on a form of enquiry that is self-critical. This means that, if we wish to establish criteria for evaluating qualitative research, we will need to understand the similar issues faced by any systematic attempt at description and explanation, whether quantitative or qualitative. Table 18.2 makes this case in detail.

Table 18.2   Why qualitative research must respect scientific standards

- Including the subjective or 'native' point of view does not necessarily discharge researchers from the task of developing and defending their own interpretation, which may or may not correspond to that of the research subjects
- Qualitative research positions itself within a social science framework. In so doing, it inevitably creates a distance between researchers and their research subjects. Subjects' everyday concepts constitute the object of the research, but must not be adopted uncritically as analytical research tools
- Therefore, complete congruence between the perspectives of the researcher and the research subjects cannot in itself be an indicator of the quality of the analysis
- Qualitative research is contextualized. In other words, information on the research context is provided. The scope of its results beyond this context must be discussed
- Qualitative research is conducted within an ethical framework

Source: Tables 18.1 and 18.2 are adapted from the Swiss Academy of Humanities and Social Sciences (n.d.), unpublished paper.

Be critical in judging arguments

WATCH: DAVID EXPLAINS IN PERSON

David's Top Tip 46

When you read a research article, always assess whether it convinces you. One sound criterion to use is whether the author identifies and evaluates deviant cases rather than just offering examples which support her analysis.

2 TWO GUIDES FOR EVALUATING RESEARCH

Researchers are not the only people concerned about the quality of published research. Governments and smaller public and private organizations are currently inundated by research reports that seem to have a bearing on policy. How can they assess the quality of such reports?

EXPLORE: RESEARCH QUALITY

Table 18.3   Criteria for assessing qualitative research

Appraisal quality indicators	Questions
Appropriate research design?	Convincing argument for different features of research design?
Reliable data?	Recording methods? Fieldnote or transcription conventions?
Clear theoretical assumptions?	Discussion of models employed?
Adequate documentation of research?	Discussion of strengths and weaknesses of process? Data and methods? Documentation of changes made to the research design?
How credible are the findings?	Are the findings supported by data? Clarity of links between data, interpretations and conclusions?
Can the findings be generalized?	Evidence for wider inference?

Source: adapted from Spencer et al. (2003: 9–15)

A very detailed list of evaluative criteria has been devised by a team of researchers commissioned by the British Cabinet Office (Spencer et al., 2003). An adapted version of these criteria is set out in Table 18.3.

Another useful set of evaluation criteria is provided in Table 18.4. Like Table 18.3, it can be employed when you are evaluating research publications. It also, of course, suggests a number of tricky questions that you should address in your own work!

Table 18.4   Criteria for the evaluation of research

- Are the methods of research appropriate to the nature of the question being asked?
- Is the connection to an existing body of knowledge or theory clear?
- Are there clear accounts of the criteria used for the selection of cases for study, and of the data collection and analysis?
- Does the sensitivity of the methods match the needs of the research question? Were the data collection and record keeping systematic?
- Is reference made to accepted procedures for analysis?
- How systematic is the analysis?
- Is there adequate discussion of how themes, concepts and categories were derived from the data?
- Is there adequate discussion of the evidence for and against the researcher's arguments?
- Is a clear distinction made between the data and their interpretation?

Source: adapted from criteria agreed and adopted by the British Sociological Association Medical Sociology Group, September 1996

3 FOUR QUALITY CRITERIA

READ:
QUALITY CRITERIA

While Tables 18.3 and 18.4 set out a very rigorous set of criteria, they focus on purely methodological issues. By now you will be aware that, in this book, I have been arguing for a more broadly based set of criteria for evaluating qualitative research which weds methodological, theoretical and practical issues. To simplify matters, I limit the discussion to the four aspects of quality set out in Table 18.5.

Table 18.5   Four criteria for assessing research quality

- How far can we demonstrate that our research has mobilized the conceptual apparatus of our social science disciplines and, thereby, helped to build useful social theories?
- How far can our data, methods and findings satisfy the criteria of reliability and validity or, put more crudely, counter the cynic who comments 'Sez you'?
- To what extent do our preferred research methods reflect careful weighing of the alternatives or simple responses to time and resource constraints – or even an unthinking adoption of the current fashions?
- How can valid, reliable and conceptually defined qualitative studies contribute to practice and policy by revealing something new to practitioners, clients and/or policy makers?

Using classic case studies, I will now illustrate each of the four quality criteria set out in Table 18.5. My case studies are taken from sociology and anthropology. For a fascinating attempt to apply these criteria to media studies, see Martin Barker (2003).

Building useful theories

My case study here is Mary Douglas's (1975) work on a Central African tribe, the Lele. Douglas notes that people in most cultures find certain things anomalous. For us, it may be a celebrity who refuses to 'reveal all', rejecting invitations to talk shows and eschewing public performances. For the Lele, it was an animal that seemed to be anomalous.

An anteater, called a pangolin by Western zoology, was seen by the Lele to combine apparently opposite characteristics. The Lele were puzzled by how this pangolin seemed to have some human features: for instance, it tended to have only one offspring at a time. Moreover, while most animals were either land or water creatures, it was both.

Douglas noted how most cultures tend to reject anomalous entities. Since anomaly seems to cast doubt on how we classify the world, it would appear to be dangerous to take it too seriously. However, the Lele are an exception. They celebrate their anomalous pangolin and this suggests that there may be no *universal* propensity to frown upon anomaly.

Douglas moves from this observation to an examination of the forms of social organization which may encourage different responses to perceived anomalies. In particular, she argues convincingly that successful exchange across borders with other groups may be associated with favourable responses to entities which match such border crossing. Since successful relations with other groups may not be all that common, it is hardly surprising that, in many cultures, anomaly is not tolerated.

Building on an ethnography of an obscure tribe, Douglas has developed an important theory about the relation between cultural categories and social organization. In doing so, she reveals how a simple qualitative case study can build social theory.

Using a self-critical approach

Mel Dalton (1959) carried out an early case study of an American factory. He was particularly interested in eliciting the perspectives of middle managers.

He reports that he was very pleased that, in the early stages of his research, he was approached by several managers prepared to tell him their stories. However, he then started to reflect on what these early informants shared in common and compared it with the background information he could gather on other managers.

It turned out that the keen informants tended to be managers whose position and prospects within the firm were the most marginal. In brief, they were keen to talk to Dalton because nobody else wanted to hear their stories!

Dalton used this insight to study the resources which gave different managers leverage at the firm. He began to see that power worked through a clique structure in which groups of managers with similar access to resources used collective tactics to oppose (or bring about) particular changes which favoured their own clique.

Dalton's study reveals the benefits of a self-critical approach. Rather than treat the accounts of willing informants as 'inside dope' on what was really going on at the firm, Dalton reflected on their motivation and, as a consequence, obtained a much broader understanding of the links between control over resources and managers' behaviour. In doing so, like Mary Douglas, he made a theoretical contribution (in Dalton's case, a theory about how cliques work within management).

A similar self-critical spirit is also present in good student research. In the following case study of psychiatric consultations, notice how Alan Quirk seeks to demonstrate why the reader should take his findings seriously.

WHAT I DID: ALAN
Achieving Credibility

Trust in the findings presented in this thesis will hopefully have been enhanced in a number of ways. First, all three studies have been undertaken in a *spirit of grounded theorizing*, with attempts made to search and account for negative instances. Second, various methods of *triangulation* have been used. In the two ethnographic studies, various types of evidence were collected before concluding that a thing is true; and in the Prescribing Decisions Project, the CA research complemented our interview study. It did so because, while the analysis of consultation transcripts revealed activities that psychiatrists failed to mention in research interviews, the interviews helped one-off psychiatric consultations to be understood in the context of the unfolding doctor–patient relationship in which they take place. Third, *simple counts* of well-defined phenomena have been included in the findings chapters where appropriate. This is aimed at increasing the credibility of claims and guarding against accusations of anecdotalism that can be levelled at certain qualitative studies. And fourth, *member validation* techniques were used. [Alan Quirk, Human Sciences, Brunel University]

Notice how Alan uses four strategies to increase the credibility of his findings. While questions can legitimately be raised about the utility of some of these strategies (e.g. triangulation and member validation), the reader is left in no doubt that this is a self-critical piece of research.

Thinking about appropriate research methods

Like Douglas, Michael Moerman is an anthropologist interested in how a people categorized its world. Moerman (1974) studied the Lue tribe of northern Thailand.

First Moerman learnt the local language and then started to interview Lue people. Like many Western ethnographers, he was interested in how his people saw themselves and how they distinguished themselves from other peoples. As a result of his interviews, Moerman assembled a set of traits which seemed to describe the Lue.

At this stage, like Dalton and Alan Quirk, he thought critically about the status of his data. Put in its simplest terms, what does it mean when you answer the questions of a visiting ethnographer? Imagine someone coming to your town and asking you to identify your 'group'. You could certainly do it, but it would be an unusual activity of self-reflection. Surely most of the time we manage to live our lives without unduly worrying about our identities? As Moerman put it:

> To the extent that answering an ethnographer's question is an unusual situation for natives, one cannot reason from a native's answer to his *normal* categories or ascriptions. (1974: 66, my emphasis)

Moerman now started to see that perhaps he had been asking the wrong kind of questions. He had been using interviews to answer the question: 'Who are the Lue?' But a more interesting question was when, if at all, the people being studied actually invoke ethnic identities.

So Moerman changed his research question to: 'When are the Lue?' This meant abandoning interviews and using observation and audio recording of the people in question engaged in 'ordinary' events like going to market. In such naturally occurring contexts, one could observe when (and with what consequences) people living in these Thai villages actually invoked ethnic identification labels.

By thinking critically about the relation between his research methods and research problems, Moerman rightly moved away from a conventional ethnographic research design.

Making a practical contribution

Unlike the three earlier studies, Lucy Suchman (1987) gathered data through a VCR. However, like Moerman, her method was entirely appropriate to her research problem.

Suchman was interested in the highly practical issue of how people use photo-copying machines. Her video recordings revealed that most people's behaviour bore little relation to the user's manual provided by the manufacturer. This was seen most clearly in the troubles that many users had in effectively responding when an order to the machine had produced an unexpected response and the user wanted to abort or repair an activity in which the machine had engaged. People's behaviour could exhibit a variety of actions which from the user's per-spective turned out to be ineffective. However, from a design point of view, the machine was acting quite properly.

Suchman's study has clear practical implications. It suggests the construc-tive role of users' troubles in system design. As she notes, based on this kind of research, expert systems may seek not to eliminate users' errors but 'to make them accessible to the user, and therefore instructive' (1987: 184).

Having cited a number of classic studies, I now want to present a more critical evaluation of some more recent research. As before, however, my evaluation will be based on the four criteria set out in Table 18.5.

4 APPLYING QUALITY CRITERIA

READ:
EVIDENCE-BASED HEALTHCARE RESEARCH

For convenience, I have simply selected three arti-cles reporting research studies in the last two 1996 issues of the US journal *Qualitative Health Research* (*QHR*). The Editor of *QHR*, Janice Morse, has a nurs-ing background and many of its contributors are in university nursing departments. This nursing focus distinguishes *QHR* from other journals like *Sociology of Health & Illness* and *Social Science & Medicine*, although its explicit concern with practice has a parallel with *Social Sciences in Health*.

The contents of these papers can, therefore, only offer a taste of the kind of work that counts as qualitative health research, let alone qualitative research in general. Furthermore, such a 'taste' does not allow inspection of the deviant cases that I recommend below as a feature of good research practice. However, these papers allow me to develop a coherent focus with implications which extend well beyond health research. In Section 5, I develop the argument with a critique of an interview study of women's drinking behaviour.

Women's process of recovery from depression

Rita Schreiber (1996) describes an interview study with a snowball sample of 21 women who identified themselves as having recovered from depression. She sets out to establish an account of the depression experience which, she claims, is 'grounded in the real world of the participant' (1996: 471). This 'real world', we are told, contains six 'phases' of '(re)defining the self', each with between three and five 'properties' or 'dimensions'.

Schreiber's discussion of her methodology shows some concern for the quality of her research. Like many researchers with an academic appointment in nursing, she holds up Glaser and Strauss's (1967) account of grounded theory as a *sine qua non* of good qualitative research. Indeed, three of the four papers I am considering here mentioned grounded theory at some point – usually as a central reference.

Following the logic of grounded theory, Schreiber searched her data for subjects' categories and only stopped when her analysis became 'saturated' because no new information about the emerging theory was forthcoming (1996: 472). These findings were then fed back to the participants and revised accordingly.

However, in my view, a number of problems remain with what we are told about this research, and I set these out in the following.

This was a retrospective study. This problem is recognized by the researcher, who comments that the first phase ('My Self Before') 'is only seen upon reflection' (1996: 474). Such recognition might have led her to abandon her claim to access the depression experience.[1] But instead Schreiber is satisfied with the rather glib assertion that 'there is merit in hearing the women's understandings of the people they were at the time' (1996: 474). What merit, we might ask? Moreover, despite the fragile status of her data, she has no hesitation in setting out to search for external causes of these accounts (1996: 489).

Schreiber presents extracts from her data. But, in place of analysis, we are simply presented with a common-sense précis of what each respondent said followed by an apparently arbitrary label. This gives the paper an anecdotal feel and makes this reviewer wonder why one needs social science skills to write this kind of report.

Of course, it is not difficult to find instances that fit a given set of categories. Despite this the paper does not report deviant cases, although such reporting and subsequent analysis are a central feature of grounded theory.

I am uncertain from where Schreiber is claiming her categories (phases and dimensions) derive. It is unclear whether these are the women's categories ('the recovery process was described by the women in this study as ...'; 1996: 473) or the researcher's. If the latter, the author gives no hint of the relevant social science theories from which her categories might derive (e.g. a theory of self-definition). If the former, then one wonders at the lack of analytic nerve which treats research as simply reporting what respondents tell you (see my comments in Chapter 6 on 'going beyond a list'; and see Gilbert and Mulkay, 1983).

Urban healers

Joan Engebretson (1996) reports a participant observation and interview study of three groups of healers who 'heal' through the laying on of hands. She locates her findings in terms of three 'dimensions' (setting, interaction and cognitive process) and finds, unsurprisingly, that such healing differed from biomedicine on each of these dimensions.

Although she mentions no explicit theory and, unlike Schreiber, has no explicit quality controls, Engebretson does strengthen the reliability of her account by detailed ethnographic description. Through it, we learn about the setting, how healing was organized and how the sessions were opened and closed. All of this description has at least the potential to suggest practical relevance. However, three problems remain with the observational data presented:

- No data extracts are given (presumably what occurred was not taped, and for some reason the researcher's fieldnotes are not made available). This means that the reader has no basis to contest the researcher's account.
- No mention is made of the system used for recording fieldnotes and its impact on the reliability of her data (see Chapter 17).
- As in Schreiber's study, the account of the data is presented just as a simple description. Without a discussion of the analytic basis for the researcher's account, her report once more can only have a journalistic status.[2]

Again, like Schreiber, Engebretson groups her interview respondents' accounts into a number of categories (in this case, physical sensations, emotional experiences and visual images). But there is nothing to suggest that these are anything but ad hoc labels without a clear analytical basis (see the discussion in Chapter 16 of using categories in QDA). Again the chosen extracts simply illustrate her argument and no deviant cases are provided or explored.

Quality care in the hospital

Vera Irurita (1996) describes semi-structured interviews with a sample of 10 patients (one to two weeks after discharge) and 10 nurses from the same hospital wards. Respondents were asked about what they saw as the nature and causes of 'quality care'.

According to the author, patients saw themselves as 'vulnerable' and described what they and the nurses did to preserve patient 'integrity'. Nurses described the time and resource constraints which limited them in providing such care.

Like Schreiber, Irurita locates her research within the approach of grounded theory, particularly through her attempt at the constant comparative method.

Like many interview researchers, she reports the use of a qualitative computer program (in her case Ethnograph). Moreover, she argues that an important quality control was the separation of the studies of nurses and patients and because theory was built as 'an ongoing process' (1996: 346).

Nonetheless, in my view, three serious quality problems remain:

- Is 'quality care' a normative or a participants' category? Irurita's account of her research findings is unclear about this but her abstract implies that she accepts a normative category without question.[3]
- No analytic basis behind the researcher's selection of categories is given. For example, 'preserving integrity' is presented as a simple description of what respondents said and not, for instance, in relation to Goffman's (1961) account of identity in total institutions. Hence the findings appear, once more, to be journalistic.
- The interview protocol is not provided and, unlike Schreiber, no extracts from the interviews are given. Hence the reader is in no position to know how 'quality care' was investigated, or how the researchers analysed data.

5 DEVELOPING THE CRITIQUE

In reviewing these three papers, you may feel that I have been making rather an ad hoc series of criticisms applied to research only in the field of health and illness. I now want to develop my argument quite briefly and then illustrate it with an interview study concerned with leisure activities.

My critique is based on assumption that interviews like any other kind of research data are *active* occasions:

> Researchers should no longer be content simply to catalogue what respondents say in an interview. The challenge of framing the interview as a thoroughly active process is to carefully consider what is said in relation to how, where, when, and by whom narratives are conveyed, and to what end. (Holstein and Gubrium, 2016: 79)

Holstein and Gubrium's stress on the 'where' and 'when' of narratives is crucial. So it is never enough just to note a particular element of an interviewee's account without asking: 'What is this doing here?' Unfortunately, the vast majority of interview research seems quite content to list features of what interviewees say and ignore positioning. Often analysis seems to consist of going through an interview transcript looking for quotations that relate to your research topic and then grouping them together.

Data *analysis* is always the name of the game. Unless you can show that your data analysis is soundly based and thorough, all the effort you put into accessing and collecting your data will have come to naught. In quantitative research, numbers talk.

With few numbers, qualitative researchers appear to rely on examples or instances to support their analysis. Hence research reports routinely display data extracts which serve as telling instances of some claimed phenomenon. The use of a thin evidential base rightly provokes the charge of (possible) anecdotalism (i.e. choosing just those extracts which support your argument).

One further example of an interview study will make my point. Laura Sheard (2011) was interested in the much discussed topic of female drinking and the dangers to which women were exposed when they went out to drink at night. She interviewed 40 women in the north of England about how they used spaces in the night-time economy and consumed alcohol.

This raises the issue of why one should prefer interview data. Sheard responds in this way:

> This method was chosen instead of other qualitative methods such as focus groups or participant observation as it was felt to be the greatest way of 'mining' the richness and depth needed for a topic of this contextual, sensitive and individualistic nature. (2011: 623)

What does mining look like in practice? We can answer this question by looking at Sheard's report. Here is an extract:

> Being alone and in alcohol-centred spaces was discussed by many women. Some would never go into a pub by themselves, even if they were meeting others. One woman would intentionally arrive 15 minutes late when meeting friends to avoid having to be in a pub or bar by herself. (2011: 624)

Now consider the similarities between what Sheard says here and what a journalist might write about such interviews. In both cases, I suggest, you simply describe what people tell you that bears on the topic in which you are interested. For both journalists and many qualitative interviewers, what people tell you is treated as a (more or less accurate) report on people's perceptions of your topic. And instances of what they say can be offered in support of your interpretation.

Here is one example. Sheard observes that: 'A few of the older women interviewed believed their dislike or avoidance of being alone in a pub was related to age and generational differences' (2011: 624). She cites the following interview extract in support of her observation:

Interviewer: Would you ever tend to use spaces like pubs or bars or alcohol-centred spaces?
Participant: I do go out to the pub but only with my husband. I've never been in a pub without somebody with us. I've never walked in on my own. I've never had a reason to. If I was meeting somebody it was always outside and then we would all go in.
Interviewer: Why is that?
Participant: I don't know. Maybe it's my age and thinking that women shouldn't go in the pub by themselves ... Like I said I've been in with my husband and my daughter but not on my own. A lot of lasses do now though, don't they? (Marie, 47 years, cleaner)

There are two points of note about this extract. First, this transcript lacks indicators of the pauses, overlaps and stressed sounds that are part of everyday speech. So we lose some degree of contact with how the participants made sense of each other's talk.

Second, the information that Sheard provides in brackets is deeply problematic. People can identify themselves by many more characteristics than name, age and occupation (e.g. marital status, sexual preference, leisure tastes, etc.). So, in choosing the set of identifiers used here, Sheard is guiding her readers to a particular set of interpretations. This deflects attention from the actual categories that speakers themselves use.

Moreover, like so many qualitative interviewers, Sheard simply restates part of what her interviewee says using the participant's own terms (e.g. 'age') mixed with social science categories (e.g. 'generational differences'). She simply does not attend to the way in which we shape our answers in terms of the question asked and in relation to how the questioner has been identified (in this case, as a researcher).

Indeed, there may be something even more subtle going on in this extract. Notice how the Interviewer's first question can be heard as asking for a 'description'. When this answer is finished, she might have asked for another description. But instead she asks, 'Why is that?'

In everyday conversation, unlike courts of law, assessments of insurance claims or classrooms, descriptions often routinely suffice and are not challenged. To ask, as here, 'Why is that?' can thus be heard as a *challenge* to account for your behaviour. And, interestingly enough, her interviewee responds *defensively* in the following ways:

- beginning with 'I don't know' and then 'maybe'
- appealing to her age as a warrant for her account
- implying that her behaviour may be old fashioned ('A lot of lasses do now though, don't they?')
- inviting agreement to this assertion ('don't they?').

So, by 'mining' her interviews for apposite extracts, Sheard, like so many interviewers, loses sight of how sequence is consequential for what we say and do. But, to her credit, in this extract, she has at least provided her readers with a relatively long extract which includes the interviewer's questions.

READ:
ANALYSING INTERVIEW DATA

6 ACHIEVING QUALITY

Obviously, from my own perspective, I have found many defects, as well as some good points, in these examples of qualitative research. Table 18.6 summarizes my criticisms.

You may now be asking yourself: is my criticism of these studies too harsh? After all, these were published papers. Have I raised the bar too high for student researchers?

Table 18.6   Some defects in selected qualitative studies

They tend to be atheoretical

Categories are usually participants' own or are ad hoc and commonsensical, e.g. journalistic

Normative concepts are sometimes accepted unproblematically

They use unreliable data

Only tidied-up data extracts are given: no interviewers' questions, no indication of how far a particular answer had to be extracted from a respondent, e.g. after a pause or a monosyllabic initial response

Data extracts are sometimes replaced by researchers' 'summaries'

The analysis can be of doubtful validity

No deviant cases

Some accounts are retrospective

Let me reassure you that it is perfectly possible to combine credibility and theoretical sensitivity within a student dissertation. Anne Patterson's research on disability, like the studies we have been discussing, was in the health area. However, in the case study that follows (partly introduced in Chapter 17), notice how she combines theoretical awareness with an attempt to convince the reader of the credibility of her data and findings.

WHAT I DID: ANNE

From 'Life Experience' to Reliable Data

Much disability research relies on anecdotal accounts of life experiences of being in a family which contains someone with a learning disability, and a whole body of research continues to be derived from such experts by experience. In this study the researcher does not set out, as an outsider, to collect reflexive accounts of life experiences, but rather examines how family moments (chatting on the phone) are lived 'here and now' with the researcher as an intrinsic part. It provides for a non-filtered, viewable-by-all set of data from which to draw insights and conclusions.

It was also possible to be sure that the researcher-participant could not influence any phenomena-to-be-found through some very practical means. Most of the calls in the dataset in question were recorded well before preliminary analysis even began and thus well before any phenomenon was mooted. The subset of calls used in the first round of observation did not include those which involved the researcher-participant, so the noticings which form the basis of this study were present initially in calls which did not include the researcher-participant. There were also three other participants involved in the calls, each of which engaged in the interactional 'actions' that have become the main subject of the study. Thus the researcher was able to ensure that the phenomenon observed could not also have been one that was produced by her own involvement. A further way of ensuring this was by regular data sessions with other analysts who independently made similar observations. [Anne Patterson, Social Sciences, Loughborough]

Consider how Anne systematically demonstrates the steps that she has taken to ensure that her data is reliable and her analysis is valid.

Be reliable

WATCH: DAVID EXPLAINS IN PERSON

David's Top Tip 47

The model of research you use is your own choice and the only credibility issue is whether you use it consistently. So Anne's work is not necessarily better than the studies reviewed earlier because, unlike them, she uses a constructionist model. When your research is evaluated, the issue is: how reliable is your data and how valid are your interpretations?

7 FOUR QUALITY ISSUES REVISITED

Having given these examples of the failings (and successes) of several qualitative research studies, in the rest of this chapter I will make some positive proposals about each of the four 'quality' issues identified in Table 18.5.

Analytic depth

How far can we demonstrate that our research has mobilized the conceptual apparatus of our social science disciplines and, thereby, helped to build useful social theories?

A continuing theme of my critiques above was that these researchers tended to describe their data in terms of sets of categories which either reproduced participants' categories or put a common-sense gloss upon them. Although it is arguable that this is a proper first-stage procedure within grounded theory, Glaser and Strauss (1967) and Charmaz (2006) make clear that such description cannot itself build theories. To do so, we need to move beyond ad hoc labels and redefine our data within a well-articulated analytic scheme.

As I argue in Chapter 7, a theory is best understood as a set of concepts used to define and/or explain some phenomenon. A criterion for adopting a theory is its usefulness.

Some classical studies illustrate this sense of theory in sociology and anthropology:

- Using an interactionist theory concerned with 'labelling', awareness of dying is related to a set of 'awareness contexts' (Glaser and Strauss, 1968).
- Using a structuralist theory of the nature of binary oppositions, an African tribe's favourable response to an anteater is used to build a theory about the relation between perceived 'anomalies' and the experience of crossing boundaries (Douglas, 1975).
- Using a discourse analytic theory of the active use of language, scientists' accounts of their work are shown to function in local contexts (Gilbert and Mulkay, 1983).
- Using an ethnomethodological theory of accounting practices, the 'cause' of 'suicide' is to be found in the common-sense judgements of coroners (Atkinson, 1978).

Without the active employment of these and other theories, we are bound to lapse into ad hoc use of common-sense interpretations and may, like Irurita's (1996) appeal to the label 'quality care', even smuggle normative concepts into our data analysis. However, like many other people researching issues that affect our daily lives, health researchers may have two particular difficulties in thinking theoretically. First, their preference for the study of 'people' rather than, say, variables may lead to the pursuit of a kind of 'empathy' which does not permit sufficient distance. Second, if you research an area like health or drinking behaviour, which generate so many pressing social problems, it may sometimes be difficult to look beyond what your common-sense knowledge tells you about the 'meaning' of social situations.

How, then, can we aid our sluggish imaginations to think theoretically about data? In Chapter 6, I discussed how social science theory building can benefit from three types of sensitivity: historical, political and contextual.

I shall return to the question of whether such theoretically guided research can have a greater practical relevance as well as building a better social science. For the moment, I will turn to my second 'quality' issue.

Why should we believe qualitative research?

How far can our data, methods and findings satisfy the criteria of reliability and validity or, put more crudely, counter the cynic who comments 'Sez you'?

If we argue for the pre-eminence of analytic issues in research, the implication might follow that the sole requirement for any research study is analytic integrity. This would mean that the validity of a piece of qualitative research could be settled simply by asserting its pristine, theoretical roots.

Along these lines, it is sometimes suggested that the assessment of the quality of qualitative data should transcend the conventional methodological approaches. The quality of qualitative research, it is argued:

> cannot be determined by following prescribed formulas. Rather its quality lies in the power of its language to display a picture of the world in which we discover something about ourselves and our common humanity. (Buchanan, 1992: 133)

If David Buchanan is saying that the main question in field research is the quality of the analysis rather than the recruitment of the sample or, say, the format of the interview, then I would agree (see Table 18.1). However, Buchanan's opposition to 'prescribed formulas' can amount to something which goes beyond the Swiss Sociological Association's statements in Tables 18.1 and 18.2 and might be called 'methodological anarchy' (see Clavarino et al., 1995).

How far do you want to go with such anarchism? First, does it make sense to argue that all knowledge and feelings are of equal weight and value? Even in everyday life, we readily sort 'fact' from 'fancy'. Why, therefore, should science be any different? Second, methodological anarchy offers a clearly negative message to research funding agencies: that is, don't fund qualitative research because even its proponents have given up claims to reliability and validity. Moreover, in such an environment, can we wonder that qualitative research's potential audiences (e.g. the medical professions, corporations, trade unions) take its 'findings' less than seriously?

In Chapters 13 and 17, I examined in detail methods for improving the validity, reliability and generalizability of qualitative research. I now turn to my third 'quality' issue.

Only interviews?

To what extent do our preferred research methods reflect careful weighing of the alternatives or simple responses to time and resource constraints – or even an unthinking adoption of the current fashions?

In 1996, while writing a paper for a methodology conference, I did a crude survey of recently published research-based articles which used qualitative methods. In my own sub-speciality, the sociology of health, the preference for the open-ended interview was overwhelming. Table 18.7 is based on articles in *QHR*.

The results in the table are consistent with the four non-randomly selected health research articles discussed above, all of which used interviews as their sole (or main) method. The skewing towards qualitative interviews in *QHR* probably reflects the fact, already noted, that many of the authors are in nursing, where the open-ended interview is regarded as both an appropriate research technique and a preferred model of communicating with the patient.

Table 18.7   Type of research method (*Qualitative Health Research*)

	Articles (n = 91)	
	Number	% of total
Qualitative interviews	65	71
Other methods	26	29

Source: qualitative data articles in *Qualitative Health Research*, 1991–6

Of course, we should not make too much of findings based on such a tiny and perhaps unrepresentative dataset. Nonetheless, Table 18.7 may not be strikingly out of line with the preference for interview-based qualitative research found in the articles published in the more mainstream journals.

To test out this hypothesis, I turned to the journal of the British Sociological Association called *Sociology*. My findings are set out in Table 18.8. The table shows a preference for the use of the interview method in qualitative papers published in *Sociology*. Although the proportion is only 55:45, given that the category 'other methods' lumps together every other non-interview-based qualitative method, the interview method clearly predominates as the single most preferred method.

Table 18.8   Type of research method (*Sociology*)

	Articles (n = 49)	
	Number	% of total
Qualitative interviews	27	55
Other methods	22	45

Source: qualitative data articles in *Sociology*, 1991–6

Other social sciences may vary in the extent of use made of the interview method. Anthropologists, for instance, may pay relatively more attention to observational methods (but see my discussion above of the study by Moerman, 1974). However, I suspect that the choice of the open-ended interview as the gold standard of qualitative research is pretty widely spread.

For example, information systems (IS) is a discipline which studies the human consequences of information technology. In preparing a talk to an IS conference,

I surveyed the methodologies chosen in research articles published in a number of recent IS journals. Of the six qualitative research articles, five were derived from interviews. More recently, I assembled the research papers published in 2008–9 in the journal *Qualitative Research in Organizations and Management*. Of 18 research articles, 16 used interviews, 1 used focus groups and 1 was based on documents.

The almost Pavlovian tendency of qualitative researchers to identify research design with interviews has blinkered them to the possible gains of other kinds of data. For it is thoroughly mistaken to assume that the sole topic for qualitative research is 'people'. As noted in Chapter 13, Clive Seale (personal correspondence) seeks to contest this common supposition:

> I find that, in order to counteract the tendency towards wanting to do interviews, it helps to repeatedly make the point that many textbooks assume that when one is going to do a research study one always wants to sample 'people' (rather than, say, documents). This helps [students] realise that all kinds of phenomena can be studied for social research purposes (e.g. building design, music lyrics, websites, small ads etc.) and it is then obvious that interviews aren't the only thing to do.

EXPLORE:
INTERVIEW DATA LIMITS

Even when the choice of interviews is thought through (for instance, interviews undoubtedly give you far more rapid results than observation which, when done properly, can take months or years), many research reports offer journalistic 'commentaries' or merely reproduce what respondents say rather than provide detailed data analysis.

Such a situation suggests that we need to look twice at the unthinking identification of the open-ended interview as the gold standard of qualitative research (see my discussion of naturally occurring data in Chapter 9). Note that this is not to reject each and every interview study. I merely suggest that the choice of any research instrument needs to be defended and that the pursuit of people's 'experience' by no means constitutes an adequate defence for the use of the open-ended interview (for further discussion of interviews, see Silverman, 2014: 165–204; 2017). I now turn to my final 'quality' point.

Research and practitioners

How can valid, reliable and conceptually defined qualitative studies contribute to practice and policy by revealing something new to practitioners, clients and/or policy makers?

Research instruments like interviews, focus groups and questionnaires, which ask respondents to provide facts, attitudes or experiences, have an important part to play in areas like health which affect us all. In particular, they can give policy makers a reasonable sense of how, at one moment in time, their clients are responding to a particular service. Moreover, unlike observational or conversation analytic studies, interview studies can be completed relatively quickly and, in this sense, can give rapid 'answers'.

Unfortunately, as I have already suggested, some qualitative interview studies may lack the analytic imagination to provide anything more than anecdotal 'insights'. When there are also legitimate doubts about the rigour of the data analysis, then, I suggest, policy makers and practitioners should doubt the quality of the 'answers' such research provides.

One response might be to return to purely quantitative research, given the serious attention it usually pays to issues of reliability and validity. Indeed, if the only alternative were *impressionistic* qualitative research, I would certainly always back quantitative studies such as well-designed questionnaires or randomized controlled trials.

However, this is not the only alternative. As already suggested, both the 'in-depth' accounts apparently provided by the 'open-ended' interview and the seemingly unequivocal measures of information retention, attitude and behaviour that we obtain via laboratory or questionnaire methods have a tenuous basis in what people may be saying and doing in everyday health contexts. The following case study shows the contribution that well-conducted qualitative research can make to practice and policy.

CASE STUDY

People with Disabilities on the Boston Buses

In 2004, University of Pennsylvania sociologist Ross Koppel was asked by the Greater Boston Legal Services (GBLS) to determine the incidence of abuses to people with disabilities who attempted to use the area's bus system. The Massachusetts Bay Transportation Authority (MBTA) had a long and undistinguished history of mistreating persons with disabilities (e.g. people in wheelchairs, with walkers or with canes, and the frail elderly).

Stories of driver abuse to people with disabilities (PWDs) were rampant. Drivers were hostile, assistive equipment was erroneously declared broken by drivers, and PWDs were passed by – all in violation of the Americans with Disabilities Act and US Department of Transportation regulations. People in wheelchairs would be left in the middle of streets, in traffic, or far from curb cuts; 300 pound wheelchairs were often not secured to the bus, creating a 'missile hazard'.

GBLS had been in a legal battle with the MBTA for five years, costing both sides millions of dollars. GBLS's problem was that all of the reports were anecdotal, and anecdotes were insufficient to prove a court case. Also, everyone knew the disabled community was angry at the bus system. Their anger mitigated the value of their depositions about mistreatment and ride failures.

This is where Koppel's sociological skills came in. He said:

My first idea was to use observers with hidden cameras on buses. This was a lousy idea for three reasons: One, this was not cost effective, as there are insufficient numbers of PWDs riding buses. Two, there are a few routes with many PWDs on them, for example, routes that passed by hospitals or rehab centers, but the study had to represent the 'system,' not just a few routes; and three, there was some quirky WWI-era law seemingly outlawing taking photographs on buses.

Koppel quickly understood that he had to assemble a group of testers – PWDs in wheelchairs, with canes, or using walkers – who he would send throughout the bus system with a scientifically designed sampling method. Moreover, because the disabled community would not accept faux-disabled, those testers needed to be genuinely disabled. Also, knowing that the court would not believe reports by PWDs themselves, he realized each tester would have to be accompanied by a trained observer with no prior involvement in these cases.

The project hired 20 teams of PWDs paired with observers, trained them on Koppel's eight-page observation schedule, and sent them to pre-selected spots throughout the bus system. Each team measured about 120 aspects of the ride, including, for example, measures of pulling to the curb and positioning the bus so a lift or ramp can be used; operating of the lift, ramp and kneeler; helping the PWD reach the safety area; securing a wheelchair to the bus (there are straps built into the floor), or helping a frail elderly passenger to a seat.

Koppel's team collected almost a thousand observations of PWDs using buses. In his final report – several hundred pages in length – he combined the parenthetical comments from the observers with the quantitative data from the observation forms. The team found MBTA bus services for people with disabilities evidenced pervasive patterns of non-compliance in most areas of operation. While drivers generally sought to accommodate people with disabilities, the ratios of (reported) failed equipment, seemingly untrained drivers, and refusals of service were high. Barriers to public transit use were everywhere.

Koppel anticipated the transit system would continue its legal battle and would hire a battery of statisticians, engineers, etc., to refute his findings. But that's not what happened. The transit system's leaders and their lawyers read the report, and to Koppel's shock they called it 'the most definitive study of transportation for the disabled ever conducted'. Then they capitulated entirely, and they put up the funds to fix it: one-third of a billion dollars to buy new buses and to hire managers to oversee the programmes for PWDs. The court-approved agreement also involved new driver training programmes and, critically, monitoring (Koppel, 2009).

(Continued)

(Continued)

Koppel says he sees this research as an example of the power of social research when applied to real problems. Koppel, who both takes public transportation and jogs daily, added:

> We are all getting older and we are all just one slip away from needing a little help. A bus that can extend a ramp or lower its front step is a reasonable accommodation. If sociological methods can help ensure transit systems comply with the laws, then this is an especially rewarding application of our discipline. (Personal correspondence)

A further bonus of studying communication *in situ* is that both findings and raw data can be valuable resources in training practitioners. Although the researcher cannot tell practitioners how they should behave, understanding the intended and unintended consequences of actions can provide the basis for a fruitful dialogue.

8 WRAPPING UP

The ability to evaluate published research is a key skill which will help you to locate gaps in the field which can inspire your own research and to write your literature review (see Chapter 22). In this chapter, I have critically assessed four published qualitative research articles using four criteria of 'quality'.

I am aware that many readers will feel that I have raised the bar too high for student researchers. So let me make clear the limits of my argument.

I am *not* suggesting that you should be so consumed by 'quality' issues that you become paralysed or lose the excitement of your encounters with the 'field'. As Geraldine Leydon comments in her PhD:

> To be sure, in choosing one route, other just as feasible and reasonable routes were ruled out. So in choosing a way, certain critiques become all the more apparent. As well as criticisms from external sources, those engaged in the business of qualitative enquiry have become evermore self-conscious and reflective about their own shortcomings. This general tendency towards a more self-critical line on the representation of data, and claims that can be made of those data, can become unhelpful when taken to their extreme. There is, as Gubrium and Holstein (1997) argue, a danger of empirical analysis being threatened or overwhelmed by 'procedural self-consciousness'. A more pragmatic line of being aware of and attempting to confine the limitations is a more realistic approach. Striving for perfection can only promise 'methodological paralysis'. [Geraldine Leydon, Sociology, Goldsmiths]

Like Geraldine, I acknowledge the danger that constant self-criticism can lead to 'methodological paralysis'. So don't take self-criticism too far. But also don't become so involved with your subject that you lose your critical senses.

What You Need to Remember

Good-quality research satisfies the following criteria:

- It thinks theoretically through and with data.
- It develops empirically sound, reliable and valid findings.
- It uses methods which are demonstrably appropriate to the research problem.
- Where possible, it contributes to practice and policy.

When you read published qualitative research, consider whether the author(s) provide sufficient evidence for you to believe that their findings are credible.

NOTES

1   Abandoning the claim that interview accounts directly represent 'experience' need not be disastrous to interview research, as I show elsewhere (Silverman, 2017). As Gubrium and Holstein (1997) point out, we can say analytically and practically interesting things about interviews analysed as locally structured narrative forms.
2   This is not to criticize journalism which, at its best, can be highly illuminating. It is simply intended to distinguish between journalism and social science.
3   Note that how 'quality care' gets defined is not treated as problematic in the following sentence: 'The delivery of quality care, although acknowledged as being vital to health care systems, is a complex, poorly understood phenomenon' (Irurita, 1996: 331).

Your Chapter Checklist

Assess your research in terms of the following criteria:

- Does it demonstrate use of the conceptual apparatus of your social science discipline and has it helped to build useful social theories?
- How far can your data, methods and findings satisfy the criteria of reliability and validity or, put more crudely, counter the cynic who comments 'Sez you'?

TRACK:
EVALUATING RESEARCH

- To what extent do your preferred research methods reflect careful weighing of the alternatives or simple responses to time and resource constraints – or even an unthinking adoption of the current fashions?
- How does it contribute to practice and policy by revealing something new to practitioners, clients and/or policy makers?

Exercise

Exercise 1: Apply and determine quality criteria

Select a qualitative research study in your own area. Now go through the following steps:

1. Review the study in terms of the quality criteria set out in Table 18.5 (if you prefer, you may use the criteria in Table 18.3 or Table 18.4).
2. If the study fails to satisfy all these criteria, consider how it could have been improved to satisfy them.
3. Consider to what extent these criteria are appropriate to your area. Are there additional or different criteria which you would choose?

Further Reading

State-of-the-art accounts of qualitative research which fit the criteria discussed in this chapter are to be found in David Silverman's (ed.) *Qualitative Research: Theory, Method and Practice* (Sage, 2016). Clive Seale's 'Quality issues in qualitative inquiry' (*Qualitative Social Work*, 2002, 1 (1): 97–110) is a good summary of the debate about how we should evaluate qualitative research. Martin Barker's paper 'Assessing the "quality" in qualitative research: the case of text–audience relations' (*European Journal of Communication* 2003, 18 (3): 315–35) applies the criteria set out in Table 18.5 to research in cultural studies. Good treatments of theoretically inspired but rigorous qualitative research are: Pertti Alasuutari's *Researching Culture: Qualitative Method and Cultural Studies* (Sage, 1995); Jennifer Mason's *Qualitative Researching* (Sage, 2002); Amanda Coffey and Paul Atkinson's *Making Sense of Qualitative Data* (Sage, 1996); and Kathy Charmaz's *Constructing Grounded Theory* (Sage, 2015).

Discover the chapter's
digital resources in your
SILVERMAN FIELD GUIDE

NINETEEN
Effective Qualitative Research

Learning Outcome

This chapter offers an opportunity to revise the main themes of Parts I to IV of this book.

1 INTRODUCTION

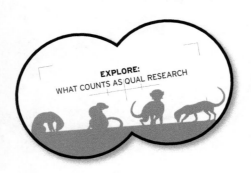

EXPLORE:
WHAT COUNTS AS QUAL RESEARCH

In this chapter, I want to pull together the different threads that have run through this book. Throughout, I have encouraged you to distinguish relatively easy activities from the really tough ones and to concentrate your efforts on the latter. For instance, writing a literature review should be relatively easy for any graduate student (see Chapter 22). Equally, obtaining your data does not need to be too difficult if you follow some of my suggestions in Chapter 14.

By contrast, the really tough issues tend to concern data analysis. This area has been discussed in detail in Part IV. In this short chapter, I want to provide a snapshot of the issues involved in the form of five rules to encourage effective qualitative research. Here are the rules:

- Keep it simple.
- Do not assume that we are only concerned with subjective experience.
- Take advantage of using qualitative data.
- Avoid drowning in data.
- Avoid 'journalistic' questions and answers.

I will now review each rule in turn. But first, a warning: none of us can escape our intellectual biography. I have been influenced in more ways than I can realize by my training and experience as (one kind of) a sociologist. Therefore, if any of my rules look a little odd in the light of your own discipline, please discuss it further with your supervisor. Even if you differ, at least you will have a point of departure!

2 KEEP IT SIMPLE

Keep it simple

WATCH: DAVID EXPLAINS IN PERSON

David's Top Tip 48

Student research projects should not be over-complicated. Try to minimize the cases you study and the range of methods you use. The best research says a lot about a little.

In Chapter 6, I identified a 'kitchen sink' mentality. Kitchen-sinkers attempt to study very broad problems, using many concepts and methods as well as large sets of data. Unfortunately, such a wide-ranging approach is unlikely to impress examiners and often will prevent you finishing your study.

In doing student research, simplicity is not a drawback but a necessity. Here are some ways to keep it simple:

- Narrow down your research problem (Chapter 8 offers a number of ways to do this).
- Use one model only (e.g. positivist, naturalist or constructionist).
- Use concepts which fit your model.
- Avoid mixed methods or, if you must use them, make sure they fit your model and research problem.
- Analyse a small dataset (you can always add comparative data later - if you have time).
- Recognize that the comparative method can be used within a small dataset.

3 DO NOT ASSUME THAT WE ARE ONLY CONCERNED WITH SUBJECTIVE EXPERIENCE

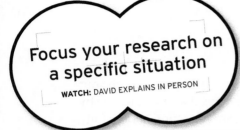

Focus your research on a specific situation

WATCH: DAVID EXPLAINS IN PERSON

David's Top Tip 49

Qualitative research should not just be concerned with 'subjective experience' as evidenced in interviews. Think about designing a research project to study what people actually do in particular situations – for example in a classroom or on an online blog.

Many people are attracted to qualitative research because they assume that it offers them a special opportunity to peer into the human psyche. For them, qualitative research is always about how people perceive the world, their emotions and 'lived experience'. Indeed, in a sense they are right. The interview study is common in much contemporary social research. For instance, when I reviewed one qualitative journal, I found that 16 out of 18 research papers used interview data (see Chapter 18). One possible reason for this may not derive from methodological considerations. Think, for instance, of how much interviews are a central (and popular) feature of mass media products, from 'talk shows' to 'celebrity interviews'. The method of questioning used in the interview reproduces many of the features of the Catholic confessional or the psycho-analytic consultation. Perhaps we all live in what might be called an 'interview society' in which interviews seem central to making sense of our lives (Atkinson and Silverman, 1997; Silverman 2017). It is then hardly surprising that so many beginning researchers assume that qualitative research is only about 'experience' and that the optimum method is the interview.

We need to stand back from such common-sense assumptions about 'experience'. Constructionists do not assume that experience is necessarily located inside people's heads. Sacks (1992) has shown how storytellers prefer to display some kind of 'first-hand' involvement in the events they describe. Indeed, people are only entitled to have experiences in regard to events that they have observed and/or which affect them directly. For instance, in telephone calls, events like earthquakes are usually introduced in terms of how we survived them, and become newsworthy less in terms of when they happened and more in relation to when we last talked – our 'conversational time' (1992, Vol. 2: 564).

In this way, Sacks notes, we seek to turn events into experiences or 'something for us' (1992, Vol. 2: 563). What Sacks says about storytelling is taken up by narrative analysis (Riessman, 2016), discourse analysis (Potter, 2016) and conversation analysis (Heritage, 2016).

These approaches show that telling someone our experiences is not just about emptying out the contents of our head but about organizing a tale told to a proper recipient by an authorized teller. In this sense, experiences are 'carefully regulated sorts of things' (Sacks, 1992, Vol. 1: 248). For instance, Peräkylä and Silverman (1991) have shown how, in family therapy clinics, spouses respond to questions about their partner's current concerns. Through talk and gaze, both spouses and partners make it clear who 'owns' the 'experience' being described.

So, while it is perfectly all right to use interviews, you need to be aware of lively alternative ways of gathering data. Why not study naturally occurring situations such as face-to-face behaviour or interactions on the Internet? Why not work with visual data or documents? Why assume that what people (say they) think is more interesting than what they actually do?

4 TAKE ADVANTAGE OF USING QUALITATIVE DATA

In Chapter 13, I noted that many research students attending my workshops set out their research in ways which make me wonder why they have not chosen instead to do a quantitative study! For instance, they format their research plan in terms of hypotheses and variables. By contrast, in qualitative research, we often work *inductively* and generate and test hypotheses during the course of study. This means that phenomena such as participants' accounts and actions should not be predefined. Instead, your research proposal should make it clear that these are the sort of things you hope to discover *after you have entered the field*.

Of course, it takes courage to tell your department graduate committee that your only real research question is: 'What is going on here?' However, this does *not* mean that your research proposal need be a blank sheet of paper! You should describe what you know about the setting you intend to study, outline the data you intend to gather and discuss how you intend to analyse your data. You should also demonstrate the way your thinking about methods has been shaped by theoretical models (e.g. naturalism, constructionism) and how your proposed analysis will employ one of the existing qualitative models (e.g. grounded theory, narrative analysis or discourse analysis). It is also useful to discuss a previous study which has inspired you.

Sometimes students elect to use qualitative methods because (they feel) they are not very good at statistics. This is not unreasonable (assuming they are right). However, qualitative methods are not appropriate for every research problem. In Chapter 2, I reviewed a number of student research projects which could more effectively be researched using quantitative rather than qualitative methods. The former approach could focus on the relation between a set of variables, and employ reliable, standardized operational definitions of the variables studied. It could also work effectively with large datasets to establish correlations between these variables.

I showed how it is possible to transform such projects into workable qualitative research studies, for instance by avoiding the language of 'variables' and studying whether participants themselves use concepts like 'effectiveness', when and how they do so, and with what local consequences. These are interesting research issues but they take us on a very different path to that envisaged by the original formulation of the research problem.

Considerations of this nature suggest that, if we want to do qualitative research, there are a set of strategies to *avoid*:

- Beginning with variables that you wish to relate.
- Beginning with problems that are already defined by members of society (e.g. social or administrative problems).
- Making assumptions about where things take place (e.g. is 'efficiency' a state of mind, a set of behaviours or a common-sense category employed in many different ways?).
- Searching for explanations: 'why' questions are usually best answered by quantitative methods.
- Working with normative assumptions (e.g. what is 'effective' communication?) and with prior versions of policy outputs.

However, we do not need to be entirely negative. Taking advantage of qualitative data means using some or all of the following strategies:

- Asking 'how', 'what' and 'when' and delaying (or avoiding) 'why' questions.
- Wherever possible (and it usually is possible) working with naturalistic data (see Chapter 9).
- Studying the categories actually employed by participants (and when and how they are used – and with what effect).
- Studying what is unremarkable, the routine and the 'ordinary'.
- Recognizing the interconnectedness of categories and of activities so that we always study how each is laminated upon another (see Chapter 6).

5 AVOID DROWNING IN DATA

A continuing argument of this book is that, if you delay your data analysis until your final year of study, you are courting disaster. By contrast, I have suggested the following:

- Start data analysis from day 1; if you have no data, then work with other people's data or use other publicly available material (e.g. texts of all kinds; see Chapter 15).
- Begin with the intensive analysis of a small amount of data. Seek to generate hypotheses which you can test when you have more data.
- One case is usually enough, providing you use internal comparisons (see Chapter 13); delay other cases and then try to sample theoretically.

- Keep to small targets; recognize that the student researcher is usually an apprentice and that learning from your mistakes is a key to success.
- Write above your PC the following motto: 'The point of qualitative research is to say a lot about a little'!

6 AVOID JOURNALISM

Journalism is a trade which, like any other, has good and bad features. In suggesting that you should avoid journalism, I do not mean to disparage what journalists do; I simply wish to underline that qualitative research should not be the same thing as journalism.

Given the daily nature of most newspapers, journalists tend to focus on unusual, out of the ordinary events which often involve 'celebrities'. When they describe public rather than private issues, the journalistic focus, quite understandably, is on social problems as generally conceived (e.g. the economy, health policy, international relations).

My message to student researchers is: let journalists get on with what they do best. Your job is somewhat different. Now is the time to display the skills which you have learnt through years of training. As an apprentice qualitative researcher, your research will differ from most journalism in the following ways:

- You will formulate a problem in an analytic manner; for example, you will not begin from a social problem but will often seek to study something that is quite unremarkable, even 'obvious' to participants.
- Your data analysis will not rely on identifying gripping or spectacular stories; instead it will reveal the various ways in which apparently 'obvious' phenomena are put together.
- You will not rush to conclusions even when you have some compelling instances; instead, you will carefully sift all the evidence, actively seeking out deviant cases.
- You will employ the analytical resources of your discipline, working with your data in the context of a coherent model and set of concepts.
- You will unashamedly theorize about situations and events, but this will not serve as mere window-dressing (see Chapters 7 and 18); instead you will theorize with your data and build new theories.

7 WRAPPING UP

This book has been written to offer you practical ways to cope with some of the doubts that affect most novice qualitative researchers. Apart from what I can offer, I suggest that you turn to your fellow students. If you do so, I guarantee that nearly all of them will have been through many of the same doubts about their research and their capacity to do it.

If you remain worried that you do not have enough data, my message has been that you probably have too much! If you believe that your work is not particularly original, I ask: 'Whose is?' Just turning to some of the more pedestrian journal articles in your field should convince you of my argument.

As I suggest in Chapter 5, success in student qualitative research can be achieved by demonstrating that you are a 'professional'. We all know that professions contain people with varying capacities. So the bar you face is really quite low. However, I hope you will aspire to something higher!

What You Need to Remember

Effective qualitative research can be undertaken on the basis of following these five rules:

- Keep it simple.
- Do not assume that we are only concerned with subjective experience.
- Take advantage of using qualitative data.
- Avoid drowning in data.
- Avoid 'journalistic' questions and answers.

Think critically and use concepts from your discipline to avoid journalistic questions and answers.

TRACK:
REVIEW YOUR RESEARCH

Your Chapter Checklist

Review your research. How far does it follow my five rules? If it does not, explain why, using other authors who take different positions to myself.

Exercise

Exercise 1: Apply the rules for effective qualitative research

Select any qualitative research report in your field. Now proceed as follows:

1. Apply to it the five rules discussed in this chapter.
2. Consider how well the report measures up in relation to each rule.
3. How could the research be improved?
4. Do any of the rules need to be modified or overturned in the light of your example?

Further Reading

In my book *A Very Short, Fairly Interesting, Reasonably Cheap Book about Qualitative Research* (Sage, 2013), I expand on many of the themes contained in this chapter. Another relevant source is my book *Interpreting Qualitative Data* (Sage, 2014: Chapter 15).

Discover the chapter's digital resources in your SILVERMAN FIELD GUIDE

CONTENTS

PART V
WRITING UP YOUR RESEARCH

Alasuutari describes writing a thesis as rather like learning to ride a bicycle through gradually adjusting your balance: 'Writing is first and foremost analyzing, revising and polishing the text. The idea that one can produce ready-made text right away is just about as senseless as the cyclist who has never had to restore his or her balance' (1995: 178).

Alasuutari reminds us that 'writing up' should never be something left to the end of your research. Instead, writing should be a continuous process, with you learning as you go from your supervisor, your peers and your own mistakes.

In the following five chapters, we will examine how this writing up can be accomplished efficiently if rarely painlessly. The chapters address the following topics: communicating with different audiences; how to begin your research report; how to write an effective literature review and your methodology; how to structure your data chapters; and what to put in your concluding chapter.

TWENTY
Audiences

Learning Outcomes

By the end of this chapter you will be able to:

- Recognize the range of different audiences for social science research.
- Know what is involved in tailoring your work to meet audience expectations.

Long ago, when PhDs were rarer, young researchers barely looked beyond university ivory towers. How times have changed! Getting a PhD by no means guarantees an academic post or indeed any other kind of job. And even experienced researchers know that good 'pure' research is often, by itself, insufficient to secure a grant. Increasingly, funding bodies want to know how your proposed research will contribute to society and demand identification of such 'outputs'.

In this situation, beginning researchers need to think about how to position their research in a broader context. Some universities realize that research training is incomplete if you lack the skills to transmit your findings to broader audiences. As one weekly magazine noted:

> The organisations that pay for research have realised that many PhDs find it tough to transfer their skills into the job market. Writing lab reports, giving academic presentations and conducting

six-month literature reviews can be surprisingly unhelpful in a world where technical knowledge has to be assimilated quickly and presented simply to a wide audience. Some universities are now offering their PhD students training in soft skills such as communication and teamwork that may be useful in the labour market. In Britain a four-year NewRoute PhD claims to develop just such skills in graduates. (*The Economist*, 16 December 2010)

1 INTRODUCTION

As I suggest in Chapter 27, getting published is all about designing your writing for a particular audience. In this spirit, Zina O'Leary suggests that writing is 'an exercise in communication … The ultimate goal is to explain, illuminate and share your research with others. You need your readers to understand your research journey and appreciate its consequences' (2014: 326).

Table 20.1 suggests some questions you need to ask yourself in order to communicate better with your readers.

Table 20.1 shows how we can attempt to tailor our writing for the likely priorities of our audience. As Coffey and Atkinson put it:

Table 20.1   Engaging audiences

1	Who am I writing for? Is it just academics or is it also policy makers, managers, practitioners or community activists?
2	What do they know? The challenge is to add value to what they know without losing them in the process
3	What are their expectations? Your examiners will expect you to show thoughtful engagement with relevant literature and a coherent methodology which avoids inconsistencies. Practitioners may fear that you will be ignorant of the constraints under which they work so you will need to demonstrate that you understand these and are not an uninformed do-gooder

Source: adapted from O'Leary (2014: 327)

Reading is an active process, and no text can have a completely fixed meaning … when we write - and hence inscribe certain preferred interpretations in our books, dissertations and papers - we do so with an implied audience of readers. (1996: 118)

In this sense, fellow academics are only one of several potential audiences, including policy makers, practitioners and laypeople. Each group will only want to hear about your work if it relates to their needs. These four audiences and their likely expectations are set out in Table 20.2.

Table 20.2   Audiences and their expectations

Audience	Expectation
Academic colleagues	Theoretical, factual or methodological insights
Policy makers	Practical information relevant to current policy issues
Practitioners	A theoretical framework for understanding clients better; factual information; practical suggestions for better procedures; reform of existing practices
Lay audiences	New facts; ideas for reform of current practices or policies; guidelines for how to manage better or get better service from practitioners or institutions; assurances that others share their own experience of particular problems in life

Source: adapted from Strauss and Corbin (1990: 242-3)

The expectations of academic audiences about both written work and oral presentations have already been discussed at length in this book. Indeed, the range of other audiences shown in Table 20.2 may tend to induce despair about the amount of work required to meet their separate expectations and needs. However, there is a simple, easy-to-follow message: good communication requires focus and yet more focus.

The trick is to combine a recognition of the expectations and needs of such audiences with our own active shaping of our materials. The good news is that a little practice may make you adept at working the same material in a range of different ways. In this context, Marx's concept of 'leverage' is very useful. As he puts it:

> Try to leverage your work. The sociological equivalent of a bases-loaded homerun is to take material prepared for a class lecture, deliver it at a professional meeting, publish it in a refereed journal, have it reprinted in an edited collection, use it in a book you write, publish foreign versions and a more popular version and have the work inform a documentary. (1997: 115)

Marx reminds us of the range of audiences that await the qualitative researcher. In the rest of this chapter, I consider the three non-academic audiences listed in Table 20.2: policy makers, practitioners and lay audiences. How do you fashion what Marx calls 'a popular version' for such audiences?

2 THE POLICY-MAKING AUDIENCE

The idea that social research might influence public policy provides an inspiration for many young social scientists. In most English-speaking countries, the sad truth is that things have never worked in this way.

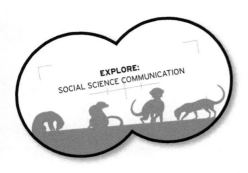

Qualitative research has rarely had much appeal to civil servants and administrators geared to focus on numbers and the 'bottom line'. The one possible exception, Goffman's (1961) account of the dehumanizing consequences of 'total institutions' in his book *Asylums* appears merely to have legitimated the cost-cutting frenzy known as 'community care'.

Moreover, it is arguable that number-crunching researchers have fared little better. As Roger Hadley (1987: 100) has pointed out, 'not being heard' is the common experience of Anglo-American social researchers who attempt to influence public policy. Among the reasons for this, Hadley suggests, is that:

> Research is often commissioned to buy time in the face of public scandal or criticism. This means that: 'the customer's motives for commissioning a research project may not necessarily be directly related to an interest in the topic concerned'. (1987: 101)

The time lag between commissioning a study and receiving a report may mean that the customer's interests have shifted. Academic researchers who produce unpalatable conclusions can be written off as 'unrealistic' (1987: 102).

Of course, fashions change. At the time of writing, there is some evidence that public bodies may be starting to take qualitative research more seriously. Focus groups in particular seem to be 'the flavour of the month' – mainly, I think, because they are relatively cheap and quick and give nice 'sound bites' for politicians and advertisers. However, such changes in fashion do little to affect the natural tendency of policy makers to redefine the meaning of research 'findings'.

I should also add that we often don't help ourselves when we want to influence policy makers. Our communication failures include:

- putting more effort into collecting data than into analysing its implications
- not being prepared to context what we say in current policy debates, while being ready to tell people things they don't want to hear
- not thinking through new or innovative approaches to policy problems based on our research (see Duncan, 2005: 11).

However, as Bloor (2011; 2016) has noted, the policy community is not the sole audience for social research.

3 THE PRACTITIONER AUDIENCE

The real opportunities for social research influence lie closer to the coalface than they do to head office ... the real opportunities for influence lie in relations with practitioners, not with the managers of practice. (Bloor, 2011: 410)

READ:
APPLYING PRACTICE-BASED RESEARCH

Taking the example of the sociology of health and illness, Bloor argues that practitioners rather than policy makers are the most reliable and eager audience for social research:

Sociologists who have conducted research on sociological aspects of health and medicine ... have long been aware that there is a role for sociologists as participants in debates on public policy, but that there are also other audiences for social research, notably audiences of patients and practitioners (clinicians, nurses and other professionals). (2004: 307)

Bloor suggests that qualitative social researchers have a twofold advantage in influencing practitioners. First, they can build upon their research relationships with practitioners in order to discuss practical implications. As he puts it:

In respect of practitioners who are research subjects, qualitative researchers can call upon their pre-existing research relationships with their research subjects as a resource for ensuring an attentive and even sympathetic response to their research findings. A close personal and working relationship, based on lengthy social contact and built up over weeks and months, is likely to ensure that, not only will practitioner research subjects have a particular interest in the findings (because of the identity of the researcher as much as a particular interest in the research topic), but also practitioner research subjects may be willing to devote an unusual amount of time and effort to discussions of the findings. (2004: 320-1)

Second, even if you have no research relationship with the data, the detail and transparency of some qualitative data have an appeal to many practitioners:

The qualitative researcher has the advantage that the research methods allow rich descriptions of everyday practice which allow practitioner audiences imaginatively to juxtapose their own everyday practices with the research description. There is therefore an opportunity for practitioners to make evaluative judgments about their own practices and experiment with the adoption of new approaches described in the research findings. (2004: 321)

Bloor's argument resonates with my own experience with AIDS counsellors. Like most practitioners, counsellors will be suspicious that outside researchers intend to be judgemental. It helps to reassure them that you do not believe in any normative, decontextualized theory of *good* communication. For further discussion of how to approach such practitioner audiences, see Silverman (2013: Chapter 4).

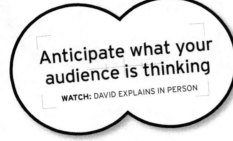

David's Top Tip 50

Think about the expectations of different audiences. For example, your examiners will expect you to show thoughtful engagement with relevant literature and a coherent methodology which avoids inconsistencies. Practitioners may fear that you will be ignorant of the constraints under which they work so you will need to demonstrate that you understand these and are not an uninformed do-gooder.

4 THE LAY AUDIENCE

There are at least four reasons why qualitative researchers may become involved in reporting back to lay audiences:

1. To answer questions asked by your respondents.
2. To 'check' provisional findings.
3. To provide 'feedback' to organizations and relevant groups.
4. To provide information for the media.

Points 1 and 2 have been considered in Chapter 12. Feedback to lay audiences is usually set up because of your own desire to 'give something back' to the general public. The format should vary according to whether your audience are members of an established organization or simply a group of people with similar interests or concerns.

As an example, following my own research on hospital clinics for children, I gave a talk to the parents' association at one of the hospitals I had studied. In this talk, following Table 20.2, I discussed new facts from my research about doctor–parent communication. I also examined the implications of my findings for reform of current hospital practices. Subsequently, I was invited to write a short piece on my research for the newsletter of a British organization called the Patients' Association. In this article, I covered much the same ground as well as adding guidelines for how to manage better or get better service from hospitals that treat sick children. Finally, I spoke at a meeting of parents of children with diabetes. My aim here was to stress what my research had revealed about the painful dilemmas experienced by such parents. In this way, I sought to assure them that others share their own experience and that there is no need for them to reproach themselves.

It is most unlikely, however, that you will be able to reach a general audience through the mass media. Nearly all social science goes unreported by such media. Needless to say, this is even truer of student research.

However, perhaps your research has provided you with a story that you want to tell to the general public. How should you go about this?

Perhaps a journalist will approach you after a talk you have given. More likely, a media contact will begin after you have studied the kind of topics covered by broadcast programmes and by particular journalists and approached the 'right' person.

For example, when my book on communication in hospital clinics was published (Silverman, 1987), I rang the medical correspondent of a national newspaper. He was very interested in some of my findings and, by the next day, I had a reporter at my house.

At this point, I panicked! I started to worry that the reporter might sensationalize my research and, thereby, upset the medical staff who had supported it. To try to avoid this, I got the reporter to agree for me to record her interview and for me to have a sight of her copy before it was published.

My cautiousness had an unforeseen and unfortunate consequence. The 'story' that followed ended up being so bland that it was never printed.

This experience highlights the dilemma that researchers have in seeking to get their work more widely known. The cautious way in which researchers are taught to write about their findings runs up against the media's need to pull in audiences with sensational stories. So it is always a question of balance between the media's sense of what is 'newsworthy' and your own desire for an accurate, unsensationalized account of your research.

Calculating a 'fog index'
WATCH: DAVID EXPLAINS IN PERSON

David's Top Tip 51

Green and Thorogood (2014) suggest it is worth calculating a 'Fog Index' when you try to write for non-specialists. You calculate this by:

- working out the average number of words in each sentence
- adding the percentage of words of three or more syllables to this
- multiplying by 0.4.

Then 'as a rule of thumb, if the result of the Fog Index is more than 12, general readers may find the text difficult' (2014: 227-8).

5 WRAPPING UP

It is appropriate that, to begin a section on writing up your research, we reflect on our 'audiences'. Too often, qualitative research is written up in an intellectual and social vacuum in which one writes for just oneself or, at best, for one's supervisor. Sometimes, this partial approach can succeed in getting you the degree you require. More frequently, in the absence of actual or imagined audiences, it will lead to writer's block and consequent failure to complete.

In the final analysis, if you want to succeed in your research and beyond, you will have to be responsive to the various audiences who might be prepared to listen to what you have to say. As in so many other aspects of life, people who complain about the 'cruel world' are often the very people who disdain the occasionally difficult but generally rewarding business of listening to what others are saying.

What You Need to Remember

Communication should always be designed for a particular audience:

- Academic colleagues will expect theoretical, factual or methodological insight.
- Policy makers will want practical information relevant to current policy issues.
- Practitioners will expect a theoretical framework for understanding clients better; factual information; practical suggestions for better procedures; reform of existing practices.
- The general public want new facts; ideas for reform of current practices or policies; guidelines for how to manage better or get better service from practitioners or institutions; and assurances that others share their own experience of particular problems in life.

If you want to communicate effectively, you must focus upon your audience's concerns and recipient design your output accordingly.

Incorporate your audience's concerns

WATCH: DAVID EXPLAINS IN PERSON

David's Top Tip 52

Recipient design is about shaping our actions to those around us. If you want to communicate effectively, you must focus upon your audience's concerns and recipient design your output accordingly.

Before you write anything, work out the audience you want to read your work and tailor your writing accordingly.

Your Chapter Checklist

- Before you start to write about your research, work out the audience at whom you are aiming.
- What might be the interest of your research to policy makers, practitioners or managers, and the general public?

TRACK:
ADDRESSING DIFFERENT AUDIENCES

Exercise

Exercise 1: Modify your writing style to suit different audiences

Refer back to Gary Marx's comments about 'leveraging' your work. Now take any chapter of your dissertation and outline how you might write it up for as many as possible of the following audiences:

APPLY:
YOUR EXERCISE WORKBOOK

1. a specialist academic journal
2. a non-specialist social science audience
3. policy makers
4. practitioners
5. the general public.

If you have time, try out these different versions with their intended audiences.

Further Reading

For an extended discussion of how qualitative research can communicate with a range of audiences, see my *Very Short Book* (2013: Chapter 4). Anselm Strauss and Juliet Corbin's *Basics of Qualitative Research* (Sage, 2008: Chapter 13) covers both written and oral presentations of your research for different audiences. Gary Marx's paper 'Of methods and manners for aspiring sociologists: 37 moral imperatives' (*The American Sociologist*, 1997: Spring, 102–25) is a lively and extremely helpful guide for the apprentice

READ:
PRACTITIONER WORKSHOPS

researcher desiring to make links with a range of audiences. Roger Hadley's chapter 'Publish and be ignored: proselytise and be damned' in G.C. Wenger (ed.) *The Research Relationship: Practice and Politics in Social Policy Research* (Allen & Unwin, 1987: 98–110) is a good account of the pitfalls of trying to reach a policy audience. Practitioner audiences are very well discussed in Michael Bloor's chapter 'Addressing social problems through qualitative research' in D. Silverman (ed.) *Qualitative Research: Theory, Method and Practice* (Sage, 2016: 15–30).

Discover the chapter's
digital resources in your
SILVERMAN FIELD GUIDE

TWENTY ONE
The First Few Pages

Learning Outcomes

By the end of this chapter you will be able to:

- Recognize why the first few pages of your thesis are very important.
- Construct a title, an abstract, keywords, a table of contents and an introduction which are appropriate, informative and attention grabbing.

1 INTRODUCTION

Nearly all dissertations begin with five elements:

- a title
- an abstract
- keywords
- a table of contents
- an introduction.

If you follow my advice and devote most attention to your data analysis chapters, then you may tend to treat these beginnings as routine matters, speedily disposed of. However, the impression you create at the start of your dissertation is very important and the writing of the first few pages should never be regarded as 'busy work' (i.e. as a triviality).

In this short chapter, I offer some practical advice about each of these beginning sections of your dissertation.

2 THE TITLE

EXPLORE:
GOOD TITLES

In the early stages, you will probably be asked to give a short title to your research for administrative purposes. You will almost certainly change this title before long, so do not attach too much importance to it. However, as Wolcott (1990: 70–1) suggests, it is a good idea to be thinking about an effective final title and to keep notes about your ideas in your research diary.

Titles should catch the readers' attention while properly informing them about the main focus of your research. My own preference is for a two-part title: a snappy main title, often using a present participle to indicate activity, followed by a more descriptive sub-title. For illustration, two of my books were entitled:

> *Reading Castaneda: A Prologue to the Social Sciences*
>
> *Interpreting Qualitative Data: Methods for Analysing Talk, Text and Interaction*

Among my papers, you will find the following titles:

> 'Describing sexual activities in HIV counselling: the co-operative management of the moral order'
>
> 'Unfixing the subject: viewing "Bad Timing"'
>
> 'Policing the lying patient: surveillance and self-regulation in consultations with adolescent diabetics'

Of course, using a present participle in the main title is merely my preference, intended to stress the *active* nature of my research as well as the fact that I study people's *activities*. Nor do I always follow my own rule. For instance, my 1997 book on AIDS counselling was entitled *Discourses of Counselling: HIV Counselling as Social Interaction*.

But titles do matter and need careful thought, as any marketing person will tell you. So give this matter thought and discuss it with your supervisor.

Revise your title

WATCH: DAVID EXPLAINS IN PERSON

David's Top Tip 53

In the early stages of your research, you will probably be asked to give a short title to your research for administrative purposes. You will almost certainly change this title before long, so do not attach too much importance to it. Later on, it is a good idea to be thinking about an effective final title and to keep notes about your ideas in your research diary.

3 THE ABSTRACT

This should succinctly cover the following:

* your research problem
* why that problem is important and worth studying
* your data and methods
* your main findings
* their implications in the light of other research.

There is usually a word limit for abstracts (100 words is common). So, as Punch points out: 'abstract writing is the skill of saying as much as possible in as few words as possible' (1998: 276). Within the word limitations, try to make your abstract as lively and informative as possible.

WHAT I DID: ADEL

The Abstract

Adel Al-Taitoon (2005), Information Systems, LSE

Title: Making Sense of Mobile ICT-Enabled Trading in Fast Moving Financial Markets as Volatility-Control Ambivalence: Case Study on the Organization of Off-Premises Foreign Exchange at a Middle-East Bank

Abstract: This research study is concerned with the organization of mobile work. The changes towards increased physical separation and the wide adoption of mobile

(Continued)

(Continued)

technology are likely to entail fundamental changes to the organization of work. The de-contextualization and mobilization of social activities magnify the complexity of organizing remote working. When the context of mobile interaction and ICT-enabled remote working is a highly volatile environment which involves instantaneous decision making and spontaneous acts within institutionalized systems of control, then researchers are presented with added complexities that require careful analysis. Thus, embarking on theoretical endeavours to build an understanding of mobility and the organization of mobile work in highly fluid and dynamic environments should not be underestimated.

This study explores how mobile ICT-enabled remote working is organized. Inspired by emerging theoretical developments on mobile interaction and motivated by the researcher's self-interest in social, technological and economic issues concerning the financial market, the research aims to make sense of the distinct mobility of foreign exchange traders. The use of mobile computing technologies in foreign exchange trading represents a mode of remote working in a highly dynamic and fluid environment. The study, specifically, examined the influence of market volatility and corporate control on the organization of mobile ICT-enabled off-premises trading. To achieve this objective, I have undertaken empirical case study research at a large banking organization in the Middle East.

I have adopted Weick's theory of 'organizing as sensemaking' which offers a conceptual framework that consists of ecological change and three sensemaking processes (i.e. enactment, selection and retention) together with feedback loops. The findings of this study are, therefore, based on employing Weick's framework as an analytical lens. Furthermore, drawing upon Weick's conception of ambivalence and loose coupling, I have argued that the existence of volatility-control sensemaking entails organizing mobile foreign exchange as loosely coupled mobility. The market volatility represents not only the fluctuation of exchange rates but also the equivocality that characterizes the foreign exchange environment. To cope with such volatility, equivocality and uncertainty, financial institutions adopt systems of control that, in turn, influence the traders' interaction. This ambivalence of volatility and control entails an optimal compromise. In this study, I have argued that this optimal compromise is achieved by adopting loosely coupled organization of mobile work to satisfy the simultaneous effects of volatility and control as two antithetical factors.

This student example shows what you can learn from reading the abstracts of other dissertations in your area. It is worth trying out drafts on other students to see if they find your abstract clear and pithy – think of movie trailers! Know what your audience are likely to be most interested in and 'emphasize your problem and content, not your fieldwork techniques' (Wolcott, 1990: 81). Wolcott nicely sums up what makes a good abstract:

> An abstract can offer a valuable opportunity to inform a wide audience, to capture potential readers, and to expand your own interactive professional network. Whether others will pursue their reading may depend largely on their assessment of your abstract, including its style. (1990: 81)

Test – and re-test! –
your abstract

WATCH: DAVID EXPLAINS IN PERSON

David's Top Tip 54

Read the abstracts of other dissertations in your area. Try out drafts on other students to see if they find your abstract clear and pithy – think of movie trailers! Know what your audience is likely to be most interested in and emphasize your problem and content, not your fieldwork techniques.

4 KEYWORDS

Many PhD theses are supposed to list keywords. In half a dozen words, you should try to list the main areas of interest of your research. In this way, potential readers can quickly assess whether it is worth reading your work.

The following student examples indicate the kind of keywords that fit particular research topics.

WHAT I DID: EMMA AND CAROLINE

Keywords

Emma Doyle, The University of Edinburgh

Title: Calling NHS 24: An Exploration of Illness Behaviour amongst Patients Using the Service

NHS 24 receives over 1.5 million calls per year and over 750,000 hits to its website. The service is likely to be transforming aspects of illness behaviour as options for patients increase and they interact in different ways with service providers. This project aims to explore illness behaviour amongst patients using NHS 24 for self-limiting conditions.

Keywords: NHS 24; unscheduled care; health and illness behaviour; self-limiting conditions; popular and professional sectors of healthcare

Caroline King, The University of Edinburgh

Title: Health for All Children: How Professionals and Parents Experience the Implementation of Hall 4

The project is a qualitative study exploring the implementation of Hall 4 (the current policy on child health surveillance) in Lothian, from the perspectives of health professionals and parents.

Keywords: children and young people; health services; parents and parenting

5 THE TABLE OF CONTENTS

You may think this is a very trivial matter. Not so! A scrappy or uninformative table or list of contents (or, worse still, none at all) will create a terrible impression.

In order to be user-friendly, recipient design this table to achieve two ends:

1.   To demonstrate that you are a logical thinker, able to write a dissertation with a transparently clear organization.
2.   To allow your readers to see this at once, to find their way easily between different parts of the dissertation and to pinpoint matters in which they have most interest.

One useful device which helps to achieve these two things is to use a double numbering system. So, for instance, the chapter containing the review of the literature might be listed as:

CHAPTER 3: REVIEW OF THE LITERATURE

3.1   The background studies
3.2   The core readings
3.3   The study closest to my own

Of course, this is only an illustration. More detailed discussion of what a literature review should contain is provided in the next chapter of this volume.

6 THE INTRODUCTION

Anne Murcott (1997: 1) says that the point of an introduction is to answer the question: 'What is this thesis about?' She suggests that you answer this question in four ways by explaining:

- why you have chosen this topic rather than any other (e.g. either because it has been neglected or because it is much discussed but not properly or fully)
- why this topic interests you
- the kind of research approach or academic discipline you will utilize
- your research questions or problems.

Like this chapter, there is no reason why your introduction should be any longer than two or three pages, particularly if your methodology chapter covers the natural history of your research (see Chapter 23). The role of the introduction, like your abstract, is to orientate your readers. This is best done clearly and succinctly.

7 WRAPPING UP

The impression you create at the start of your dissertation is very important. Your title should catch the readers' attention while properly informing them about the main focus of your research.

An abstract should describe your research problem; why that problem is important and worth studying; your data and methods; your main findings; and the implications of your findings in the light of other research.

Your table of contents should allow your readers to find their way easily between different parts of the dissertation and to pinpoint matters in which they have most interest. Your introduction should explain why you have chosen this topic rather than any other; why this topic interests you; the kind of research approach or academic discipline you will utilize; and your research questions or problems.

What You Need to Remember

- The first few pages of your thesis are very important.
- Your title, abstract, keywords, table of contents and introduction should be appropriate, informative and attention grabbing.

Put time and effort into choosing your title and table of contents.

Your Chapter Checklist

- Can you work out a title that will grab a reader's attention?
- Can you design an abstract, keywords, table of contents and introduction that are appropriate and informative?

Exercises

Exercise 1: Form your best title and abstract

This is an exercise to encourage you to find a good title and abstract for your dissertation.

APPLY:
YOUR EXERCISE WORKBOOK

1. Make a list of three or four possible titles for your dissertation. Try to make the main title intriguing and the subtitle descriptive.
2. Now reverse the order, putting the subtitle first. Which works best? Why?
3. Try out your titles on students working in similar areas or using similar methods or data. Which do they think works best? Why?
4. Now try out two different abstracts in the same way.

Exercise 2: Assess an abstract in terms of clarity, content and compelling arguments

Assess the following PhD abstract:

* Is it clear and pithy?
* Does it sufficiently emphasize the research problem?
* Is it likely to attract potential readers?

Peter Lenney, Marketing, Lancaster, 2006

Title: In Search of Marketing Management

Abstract: This empirical study attempts to craft a richer description, and deeper understanding, of the work of managers in marketing than that elaborated in the managerial work literature and within the marketing management discourse. Perspectives on both the character of the 'content' and 'conduct' of marketing manager work are sought. Several marketing managers, operating in diverse commercial contexts, were interviewed and observed. The field research deployed an array of longitudinal methodologies including programmes of diary-stimulated interviews, work shadowing, participant self-observation, and action research. A description of managerial work is developed that rests at an 'ontic level' between that of classical/'Fayolian' management theory and the conceptualizations generated through the empirical study of managerial work. The developed model characterizes the 'substance' of managerial conduct as the 'shaping and sustaining of commitments'. The model, based on a metaphorical temporal rope, elaborates the various interweaving strands and threads of what is argued to be the quintessence of managerial behaviour, the forms and characteristics of organizational commitments, the character of their crafting and conducing, and the properties of the so-emerged commitment webs.

   The 'content' of the subject managers' work is elaborated through the concept of endeavour portfolios, and the inherently political, weak-situation/ wicked-problem character of their endeavours is illuminated. The 'rhetorical technology' of the marketing discourse is found to permeate the content of the subject managers' endeavours, and provide adequate labels for the strands and threads of their endeavours. However, outside of their use in the staging of truth effects, the processual prescriptions of the marketing discourse are not evident in their daily work. The marketing management discourse is found not to speak to the milieu or substance of the subject managers' marketing management. This 'substance' rests in their pursuit of innovative reconciliations for the complex of contradictions that confronts them.

Exercise 3: Get feedback on your introduction

Show the introduction to your dissertation to a range of fellow students. Encourage them to tell you whether they feel tempted to read more. If not, why not? If so, why?
Now use their response to revise your introduction.

Further Reading

Harry Wolcott's *Writing Up Qualitative Research* (Sage, 2009, Chapters 2, 3) has an excellent discussion of how to present student dissertations. Chapter 15 of Zina O'Leary's *Doing Your Research Project* (Sage, 2014) has some good tips on writing up. A further useful source is Pat Cryer's *The Research Student's Guide to Success* (Open University Press, 2006).

Discover the chapter's
digital resources in your
SILVERMAN FIELD GUIDE

TWENTY TWO
The Literature Review Chapter

Learning Outcomes

By the end of this chapter you will be able to:

- Keep usable records of your reading.
- Distinguish between research literature and theoretical literature
- Understand what a literature review should contain.
- Know the principles underlying a good literature review.
- Think about when is the most appropriate time to write a literature chapter.
- Consider the alternatives to having such a chapter.

In this chapter, I will make some practical suggestions about what a literature review should contain. Somewhat controversially, I will also question whether you really need a separate chapter dealing with the literature and what might replace it.

A good discussion of the literature in your area presupposes sensible recording of what you read. So I now ask: 'What is the best way to record your reading?'

Save your literature review for last

WATCH: DAVID EXPLAINS IN PERSON

David's Top Tip 55

The best time to write a literature review is at *the end* of your research. By then, you will be aware of which literature is crucial to your argument. So, if you are required to present a literature review early on, keep it simple and be prepared to replace it later.

1 RECORDING YOUR READING

By the time you begin a research degree, it is likely that you will have learned the habit of keeping your reading notes in a word-processed file, organized in terms of (emerging) topics. I stress 'reading notes' because it is important from the start that you do *not* simply collate books or photocopies of articles for 'later' reading but read as you go. Equally, your notes should not just consist of chunks of written or scanned extracts from the original sources but should represent your ideas on the *relevance* of what you are reading for your (emerging) research problem. Table 22.1 offers suggestions for sensible note-taking.

Table 22.1   Reading and note-taking

1	Never pick up and put down an article without doing something with it
2	Highlight key points, write notes in the margins and write summaries elsewhere
3	Transfer notes and summaries to where you will use them in your dissertation
4	Ensure that each note will stand alone without your needing to go back to the original

Source: adapted from Phelps et al. (2007: 175-6)

Table 22.1 makes it clear that you should always read *critically*. Don't just copy chunks of material. Strauss and Corbin (1990: 50–3, adapted here) suggest that the existing literature can be used for five purposes in qualitative research:

1. *To stimulate theoretical sensitivity*, 'providing concepts and relationships that [can be] checked out against (your) actual data'.
2. *To provide secondary sources of data* to be used for initial trial runs of your own concepts and topics.
3. To stimulate questions during data gathering and data analysis.
4. *To direct theoretical sampling* to 'give you ideas about where you might go to uncover phenomena important to the development of your theory'.
5. *To be used as supplementary validation* to explain why your findings support or differ from the existing literature.

Following Strauss and Corbin, you should always approach any publication or website with a set of questions, for instance:

- What are the relevant findings?
- What are the relevant methodologies?
- What are the relevant theories?
- What are the relevant hypotheses?
- What are the relevant samples?
- What is the relevance to how I now see my research problem?
- What possible new directions for my research are implied?.

It goes without saying that you should use a consistent system for referencing authors and other details of the material you are reading. The Harvard method of referencing is usually the system chosen. In your main text, this involves entering an author's surname, followed by date of publication and any page reference, as follows: 'Abrams (1984: 2); Agar (1986: 84)'. By using this method, you can save footnotes for substantial asides rather than for (boring) references. Detailed references are then appended in a bibliography in a form such as the following:

Baker, P. (2006) *Using Corpora in Discourse Analysis*. London: Continuum.

Bazeley, P. and Jackson, K. (2013) *Qualitative Data Analysis with NVivo*. London: Sage.

Bröer, C., Moerman, G., Wester, J.C., Malamud, R.L., Schmidt, L., Stoopendaal, A., Kruiderink, N., Hansen, C. and Sjølie, H. (2016) 'Open online research: developing software and method for collaborative interpretation'. *Forum: Qualitative Research*, 17 (3), Art. 2.

When you come to write your literature review chapter, ideally towards the end of your research, you will have all the relevant material on file. But, just as important, you will also have a record of your changing thoughts about the literature and its relevance to your emerging research topic.

2 RESEARCH LITERATURE AND THEORETICAL LITERATURE

At the outset it is obviously important to focus on literature relevant to your project. However, there are different meanings of such relevance. Punch makes an important distinction between empirical research literature and theoretical literature:

Empirical research literature: reveals 'what previous empirical evidence is there about this question, and what (it) tells us about this question i.e. what is known – and not known – about this question'.

Theoretical literature: 'includes relevant concepts and theories that contain ideas and information relevant to the topic'. (2014: 95)

Put another way, your research literature shows the reader what facts we already have about your chosen topic and what is unclear or unknown. The theoretical literature is far broader and covers the research models (e.g. naturalism or constructionism), concepts and methodologies which have been used to uncover those facts.

Both sets of literature need to be considered. However, the balance between them will vary from thesis to thesis and needs to be carefully thought through.

You don't need to create a new method to be successful

WATCH: DAVID EXPLAINS IN PERSON

David's Top Tip 56

Don't try to reinvent the wheel. So, if you are sensibly using an *existing* methodology or research model e.g. Grounded Theory, Constructionism etc, don't spend time explaining and defending it. There are plenty of textbooks that do that and your Examiners are likely to be familiar with your research model and favourable towards it.

3 WRITING YOUR LITERATURE REVIEW

There are four common misconceptions about the literature review chapter:

- It is done just to display that 'you know the area'.
- It is easier to do than your data analysis chapters.
- It is boring to read (and to write).
- It is best 'got out of the way' at the start of your research.

EXPLORE: LIT REVIEW PROBLEMS

Later in this chapter, all these assertions will be questioned. By contrast I will argue that a literature review:

- should combine knowledge with critical thought
- involves hard work but can be exciting to read
- should mainly be written after you have completed your data analysis.

I will begin, however, by trying to answer some practical questions about writing a literature review. What should it contain? How should you prepare? Where will you find what you need to read? How should you read?

4 PRACTICAL QUESTIONS

What should a literature review contain?

In part, a literature review should be used to display your scholarly skills and credentials. In this sense, you should use it:

EXPLORE:
GOOD LIT REVIEWS

To demonstrate skills in library searching; to show command of the subject area and understanding of the problem; to justify the research topic, design and methodology. (Hart, 1998: 13)

Such justification also means, as I remarked in Chapter 3, that any literature review connected with a piece of research has as much to do with the issue of generalizability as with displaying your academic credentials. This involves addressing the questions set out in Table 22.2.

Table 22.2   Contents of a literature review

- What do we already know about the topic?
- What do you have to say critically about what is already known?
- Has anyone else ever done anything exactly the same?
- Has anyone else done anything that is related?
- Where does your work fit in with what has gone before?
- Why is your research worth doing in the light of what has already been done?

Source: adapted from Murcott (1997)

However, Table 22.2 should not give you the impression that writing a literature review means simply listing a set of *facts*. Charmaz (2006) has shown how writing such a review always stems from a particular position that you take in your research. As she puts it:

> Do you envision an objective scholar who labors over the materials to present an impartial analysis? Although scholars may don a cloak of objectivity, research and writing are inherently ideological activities. The literature review and theoretical frameworks are ideological sites in which you claim, locate, evaluate, and defend your position.
>
> The [literature review] should contain much more than summaries. Instead, show why you favor certain arguments, what evidence you accept and reject, and how you arrived at considered decisions. What do you need to take into account? How do you go about it? (2006: 163)

Table 22.3 underlines what Charmaz calls the *ideological* nature of such reviews. As she puts it:

> The literature review can serve as an opportunity to set the stage for what you do in subsequent sections or chapters ... *Assess and critique* the literature from this vantage point. Make your literature review do more than merely list, summarize, and synthesize key works. (2006: 166)

Above all, a literature review should read as a *dialogue* with other researchers. Once you start to see your literature review as dialogic rather than a mere replication

Table 22.3   The purposes of a literature review

- To demonstrate your grasp of the specific field
- To show your skill in identifying and discussing the most significant ideas and findings
- To specify who did what, when, and why and how they did it
- To evaluate the earlier studies
- To explain points of convergence and divergence between your study and earlier studies
- To reveal gaps in extant knowledge and state how your research answers them
- To position your study
- To clarify its contribution
- To permit you to make claims later in the thesis

Source: adapted from Charmaz (2006: 168)

of other people's writing, you are going in the right direction. Conceived as an answer to a set of questions, your reading can immediately become more directed and your writing more engaging and relevant.

Preparing a literature search

As Hart (2001: 24) points out, it helps to do some preliminary thinking about what you are doing before you begin the search itself. Below are some issues to think about (drawn from Hart, 2001: 24):

- What discipline(s) relate to my main topic?
- How can I focus my topic to make my search more precise?
- What are the main indexes and abstracts relevant to my topic?
- What means of recording will be most efficient for many tasks such as cross-referencing? (Hart points out that index cards are useful.)

Where will I find the literature?

Once you are prepared, it is time to review the many potential sources of information about what literature you need to read and where to find it:

- your supervisor
- the subject librarian in your university library
- bibliographies in the literature you read
- online searches
- the Social Sciences Citation Index
- newsgroups on the Internet
- your fellow students (past and present).

Excellent discussions of using the Web for literature searches are provided by Phelps et al. (2007: 129–65) and Ó Dochartaigh (2007).

In literature searches, there is no need to worry about admitting your lack of knowledge. Indeed, the American sociologist Gary Marx recommends taking 'short cuts': 'learn how to use computer searches, encyclopedias, review articles. Ask experts for help' (1997: 106).

Once you start looking, you will speedily find that you have a problem not with too little literature but with too much! Getting away from the books and towards your data is a leap that most of us need to make as early as possible. As Marx cautions: 'Don't become a bibliophile unless it suits you' (1997: 106). Or, more pointedly, 'know when enough is enough' (Phelps et al., 2007: 176).

There's so much: how will I find the time?

Before you panic, you need to remember that you would not have reached this stage of your academic career without learning the tricks of the reading trade. These tricks go beyond the skills of speed reading (although these help); your aim is usually to 'fillet' a publication in terms of your own agenda (not the author's!). Again, Marx makes the point well:

> Sample! Learn how to read by skimming, attending to the first and last sentence, paragraph or chapter. Read conclusions first, then decide if you want the rest. Most social science books probably shouldn't be books; they have only a few main (or at least original) ideas. (1997: 106)

If these are some answers to the usual 'nuts and bolts' questions, we still need to tackle the underlying principles behind a literature review. As my earlier discussion of 'misconceptions' suggested, these principles are not always obvious or clear cut.

5 PRINCIPLES

This is how a valuable book on the topic defines a literature review:

EXPLORE:
WRITING A LIT REVIEW

> The selection of available documents (both published and unpublished) on the topic, which contain information, ideas, data and evidence written from a particular standpoint to fulfil certain aims or express certain views on the nature of the topic and how it is to be investigated, and the effective evaluation of these documents in relation to the research being proposed. (Hart, 1998: 13)

Hart's term 'effective evaluation' means, I believe, attending to the following principles.

Show respect for the literature

Your single-minded pursuit of your (ideally) narrow research topic should not lead you to show disrespect for earlier research or to disconnect your work from the wider debate in which it figures. Your dissertation will be assessed in terms of its scholarship, and being 'scholarly' means showing 'respect' as well as striking out on your own. In Marx's words:

> Even producers of literature must know the literature, and a major criterion for evaluating work is whether or not it is put in a context of prior scholarship. We are not only creators of new knowledge, but protectors and transmitters of old knowledge. Our inheritance is the astounding richness of the work of prior scholars. Beyond that, one has a strategic interest in the peer reciprocity inherent in the citing system. (1997: 106)

Be focused and critical

Respect can only get you so far. Scholarship also means advancing knowledge – although the level of the advance required will vary according to the degree at which you are aiming. Such advance involves a strict focus and a critical perspective on what you read:

> After some initial groveling, know what you are looking for. Approach the literature with questions and remember that your goal is to advance it, not simply to marvel at its wonders. Seek an appropriate balance between appreciation and advancement of the literature. (Marx, 1997: 106)

Avoid mere description

Any academic has horror stories of literature reviews which were tediously and irrelevantly descriptive. Kjell Rudestam and Rae Newton characterize well such failing reviews:

> [They consist of] a laundry list of previous studies, with sentences or paragraphs beginning with the words, 'Smith found ...', 'Jones concluded ...', 'Anderson stated ...', and so on. (1992: 46)

In this vein, Marx recommends avoiding writing 'a literature summary without an incisive critique that will help your peers to view the world differently' (1997: 106). Instead, you need to focus on those studies that are relevant for defining *your* research problem. By the end of the literature review:

> the reader should be able to conclude that, 'Yes, of course, this is the exact study that needs to be done at this time to move knowledge in this field a little further along.' (Rudestam and Newton, 1992: 47)

This entails giving different amounts of attention to what you read according to how central it is to your topic. Background literature can just be described in a sentence. By contrast, the most relevant studies 'need to be critiqued rather than reported' (1992: 49). Such critique can focus on failings of theory or method (see Chapter 18).

Write up after your other chapters

The common version of a student research trajectory suggests that a major early aim is to complete a literature review. This version is supported in the 'time checklist' provided by the British Research Councils (1996) for PhD students. This includes the following recommendation: 'First year ... student to complete a literature survey.' Elsewhere the same publication gives less dogmatic advice:

> In some subjects a *literature survey* forms an important starting portion of the work, and this should be carried out in the early stages. Before the end of the first year, the student should have a good idea of relevant work carried out by others, but it will be necessary to keep up with new literature throughout the period, so that the thesis takes account of the latest developments in its subject area.

This more considered advice hints at the problems of completing your literature review at an early stage. These problems may include:

- Completing the literature survey in year 1 and writing it up can mean a lot of wasted effort. Until you have done your data analysis, you do not know what stuff will be relevant.
- You may be tempted to regard the literature review as a relatively easy task. Since it tests skills you have already learned in your undergraduate career, it may become potential 'busy work'. If so, it will only delay getting down to the data analysis on which you should be judged.
- As I asked in Chapter 8, can you ever get out of the library in order to write your thesis? One book will surely have a list of further 'crucial' references and so on, ad infinitum. Anybody who thinks a library PhD is a 'quick fix' would be well advised to ponder whether they have the will-power to stop reading.

These considerations mean that the bulk of your reading is usually best done in and around your data collection and analysis. In the end, this will save you the time involved in drafting your literature review chapter before you can know which literature will be most relevant to your treatment of your topic. It will also force you out of the library. As Marx comments: 'searching the literature must not become an end in itself or a convenient way to avoid the blank page' (1997: 106).

So: read as you do the analyses. By all means write notes on your reading, but don't attempt to write your literature review chapter early on in your research.

However, as researchers, we should be critical and innovative. In this regard, how far is the literature review chapter simply an unthought relic of an out-of-date version of scholarship? Do you need such a chapter?

EXPLORE: RELIABLE LIT REVIEWS

6 DO YOU NEED A LITERATURE REVIEW CHAPTER?

The major unorthodox figure here is the American ethnographer Harry Wolcott. Wolcott (1990) argues that student researchers often mistakenly assume a need to defend qualitative research in general as well as the particular approach or method they are using. But, as he suggests, after a century of qualitative research (and several decades of more specific qualitative approaches):

> There is no longer a call for each researcher to discover and defend [qualitative methods] anew, nor a need to provide an exhaustive review of the literature about such standard procedures as participant observation or interviewing. Instead of having to describe and defend qualitative approaches, as we once felt obligated to do, it is often difficult to say anything new or startling about them. Neophyte researchers who only recently have experienced these approaches first-hand need to recognize that their audiences probably do not share a comparable sense of excitement about hearing them described once again. (1990: 26)

Wolcott also points to some positive gains of avoiding the statutory review chapter. As he puts it:

> I expect my students to know the relevant literature, but I do not want them to lump (dump?) it all into a chapter that remains unconnected to the rest of the study. I want them to draw upon the literature selectively and appropriately as needed in the telling of their story. (1990: 17)

This means that you can bring in appropriate literature as you need it, not in a separate chapter but in the course of your data analysis:

> Ordinarily this calls for introducing related research toward the end of a study rather than at the beginning, except for the necessary 'nesting' of the problem in the introduction. (1990: 17)

In the following example, you can see how one of my students followed Wolcott's suggestions. Instead of a separate literature review chapter, Geraldine 'nested' relevant literature in her data chapters and in an early chapter setting out the 'natural history' of her research.

WHAT I DID: GERALDINE

Telling My Research Story

A step-by-step appraisal of the broad literature read during the course of study carried a risk of providing an unnecessarily protracted read. In place of the conventional literature review chapter, I opted to tell the *story* of the research and in so doing describe some of the literature that left an impression on me – *good* and *bad* – and which encouraged me to ask the questions that I eventually came to ask. To impose a structured description of *my literature* retrospectively would have failed to capture adequately a more 'honest' and oftentimes-chaotic journey toward achieving a coherent topic and analytic approach, and in being able to nest the problem in an apposite literature.

As well as situating the research in a broader context, I attempt to situate myself as an audience of the literature and explain how my reading of 'it' led to the work reported on the following pages. In so doing, the constraints or limitations imposed by alternative analytic approaches are raised. The resulting critique is intended not to attack the utility of work already undertaken in the broad research domain of cancer, information and communication, but to demonstrate my rationale for choosing one way over another.

In providing a natural history chapter in place of a literature review, the insights and influences of other literatures are still drawn on at relevant points. Moreover, in line with a qualitative approach to data analysis, reference to the literature occurs throughout the data chapters to augment and illuminate the points conveyed. In short, the thesis engages with relevant literatures throughout, and not in a single chapter. [Geraldine Leydon, Sociology, Goldsmiths]

Geraldine's approach, which follows Wolcott's unorthodox suggestions, is, no doubt, too radical for most students (and their supervisors!). Nevertheless, even if you decide to write the conventional literature review chapter, what Wolcott has to say is a salutary reminder that, in writing a research dissertation, you should cite other literature only in order to connect your narrow research topic to the directly relevant concerns of the broader research community. Making wider links should properly be left to your concluding chapter (see Chapter 25).

7 WRAPPING UP

In this chapter, I have argued that a literature review should combine knowledge with critical thought. It should involve hard work but be exciting to read and should mainly be written *after* you have completed your data analysis.

What You Need to Remember

A literature review should contain answers to the following questions:

- What do we already know about the topic?
- What do you have to say critically about what is already known?
- Has anyone else ever done anything exactly the same?
- Has anyone else done anything that is related?
- Where does your work fit in with what has gone before?
- Why is your research worth doing in the light of what has already been done?

Avoid writing your literature review too early – you will be in the best position to work out which literature is relevant after you have written up your findings.

Your Chapter Checklist

- Does your literature contain an argument or does it just list a set of writings?
- Does it explain the rationale for your research?
- Have you (rightly) delayed writing it up or are you writing it too early?

TRACK:
LITERATURE REVIEW PROGRESS

Exercises

Exercise 1: Achieve balance between empirical and theoretical literature

- Read the literature review chapters of a couple of recently successful dissertations in your department and assess their balance between discussion of empirical and theoretical literature
- Using that information, try out different ways of handling that balance in your first draft.

APPLY:
YOUR EXERCISE WORKBOOK

Exercise 2: Use existing literature to help your own research

This exercise gives you an opportunity to test out your skills in using the existing literature to help you in your own research. It emphasizes that we should never read such literature without having formulated some prior set of questions.

Select what you regard as the two or three most relevant pieces of literature. Now:

1. Make notes on each, attempting to use each one to answer the questions found in Table 22.2.
2. Incorporate these notes in a short literature review chapter which only refers to these two or three works.
3. Discuss this review with your supervisor.

Exercise 3: Evaluate your use of references

When you complete each data analysis chapter, look back over the literature you have discussed. Now ask yourself these questions:

1. Is there sufficient discussion of each reference to render further discussion (in a literature review chapter) redundant?
2. If not, practise writing about these references in a way that adds to how you have described them in your data analysis chapters. You may use Table 22.2 as a guide.

Further Reading

The essential book on this topic is Chris Hart's *Doing a Literature Review: Releasing the Social Science Imagination* (Sage, 1998). This covers in detail all the issues discussed in this brief chapter as well as addressing the different requirements of literature reviews for BA, MA and PhD dissertations. Hart's later book *Doing a Literature Search* (Sage, 2001) is a helpful guide to planning and executing a literature search. Good chapter-length discussions are to be found in Keith Punch's *Introduction to Social Research* (Sage, 2014: Chapter 6) and Zina O'Leary's *Doing Your Research Project* (Sage, 2014: Chapter 6). For short, lively discussions see Harry Wolcott's *Writing Up Qualitative Research* (Sage, 2009) and Gary Marx's paper 'Of methods and manners for aspiring sociologists: 37 moral imperatives' (*The American Sociologist*, 1997: 102–25). On keeping a record of your reading, see Renata Phelps et al.'s *Organizing and Managing Your Research: A Practical Guide for Postgraduates* (Sage, 2007: 128–49); Anselm Strauss and Juliet Corbin's *Basics of Qualitative Research* (Sage, 2008: Chapter 4); Kathy Charmaz's *Constructing Grounded Theory* (Sage, 2006: 163–8); and Pat Cryer's *The Research Student's Guide to Success* (Open University Press, 2006).

Discover the chapter's
digital resources in your
SILVERMAN FIELD GUIDE

TWENTY THREE
The Methodology Chapter

Learning Outcomes

By the end of this chapter you will be able to:

- Recognize what is involved in writing a methodology chapter which transparently documents the research process.
- Understand the key questions which this chapter must answer.
- Consider the nature and advantages of writing this chapter in a 'natural history' format.

1 INTRODUCTION

We can distinguish three different kinds of student dissertation: theoretical, methodological and empirical. Each of these demands different discussion of 'methods':

- *Theoretical.* Here you claim to develop some theoretical insights by means of a critical review of a body of literature. In the theoretical dissertation, your methodology chapter will need to discuss your rationale for selecting your corpus of literature and any illustrative examples. It will also need to show how you have attempted to produce a systematic analysis (e.g. by considering the arguments for positions that you reject).

EXPLORE:
METHODOLOGY CHAPTER WRITING

- *Methodological.* Here you are mainly concerned to develop a method (e.g. focus groups or textual analysis) or to compare and contrast the use of several different methods. Here the whole thesis may be devoted to methodological matters, and so a separate chapter called 'methodology' may be redundant or simply devoted to explaining why you have chosen certain methods to compare and/or which data you choose to use for this exercise.
- *Empirical.* In this, the most common form of research report or dissertation, you will analyse some body of data. Here you will be expected to show that you understand the strengths and weaknesses of your research strategy, design and methods.

This chapter focuses on empirically based research reports. It argues for openness and clarity about what actually happened during your research. It suggests that a bland account in the passive voice is an entirely inappropriate format for your methodology chapter.

Qualitative researchers are often interested in the narratives or stories that people tell one another (and researchers). Indeed, our data analysis chapters tell (structured) stories about our data. It is only natural, then, that our readers should expect to be told how we gathered our data, what data we ended up with, and how we analysed it.

This is why all research reports seem to have a methodology chapter, or at least a section devoted to 'data and methods'. Within that rubric, however, as I show later in this chapter, there are many different (non-bland) formats we can use to give an account of our data and methods. First, however, we need to clear the ground about the issues you need to cover in your methods chapter.

Use an active voice
WATCH: DAVID EXPLAINS IN PERSON

David's Top Tip 57

Good methodology chapters describe how the research was actually done and highlight the challenges you faced, the changes in your research ideas and what you learnt from it. Therefore try to avoid writing in the passive voice and trying to kid your examiners that everything went as planned.

2 WHAT SHOULD THE METHODOLOGY CHAPTER CONTAIN?

In a quantitative study, there is a simple answer to this question. You will have a chapter usually entitled 'Data and Methods'. As Table 23.1 shows, this chapter will typically contain four elements.

Table 23.1   The methods chapter in a quantitative thesis

1   Subjects studied
2   Research instruments used
3   Procedures used in applying these instruments to these subjects
4   Statistical analysis

Source: adapted from Rudestam and Newton (1992: 61)

The straightforward character of a quantitative methods chapter unfortunately does not spill over into qualitative research reports. At first sight, this simply is a matter of different language. So, in reporting qualitative studies, typically we do not talk about 'statistical analysis' or 'research instruments'. These linguistic differences also reflect broader practical and theoretical differences between quantitative and qualitative research. More particularly, in writing up qualitative research, we need to recognize:

- the (contested) theoretical underpinnings of methodologies
- the (often) contingent nature of the data chosen
- the (likely) non-random character of cases studied
- the reasons why the research took the path it did (both analytic and chance factors).

Each of these four features raises issues which should not be concealed or generate guilt. Your research training courses and your reading should have made you aware of the theories on which your methods rest. So the rule here, in writing your methods chapter, is simply: spell out your theoretical assumptions.

Here is an example of how this can be done via an extract from Steven Stanley's PhD, which used discourse analysis on interviews with other research students.

WHAT I DID: STEVEN

The Theoretical Assumptions of Methodologies

Within qualitative, discursive and critical approaches to psychology it is generally acknowledged that methodological issues cannot be separated from theoretical assumptions. [This] chapter constitutes both a presentation of 'what happened' in this study, as well as a discussion of the particular issues surrounding method in discursive psychology and in studies of doctoral education. Each section will include descriptive details of how the study was developed and conducted, as well as a discussion of the associated theoretical issues. The aim is not to provide an exhaustive and complete account of the various methodological issues relating to the topics under discussion, but rather to highlight some of the central issues involved in adopting a discursive approach to the study of doctoral education, and to show how the presentation and practice of 'method' is inherently bound up with theoretical assumptions. [Steven Stanley, Human Sciences, Loughborough]

Notice how Steven is seeking an alternative to presenting a methodology chapter as a purely descriptive account of 'what happened'. Instead, he documents the way in which his chosen theoretical approach (discourse analysis) shaped the way he studied his topic.

However, 'theory' alone does not totally determine the course of your research. Everybody realizes that contingent events related to personal interest, access, or even simply being in the right (wrong) place at the right (wrong) time, often determine which data you are able to work upon. So, when you write your methods chapter, be straightforward: *spell out the (sometimes contingent) factors that made you choose to work with your particular data.*

Finally, everybody knows that qualitative researchers can work fruitfully with very small bodies of data that have not been randomly assembled. If this is the case, *explain how you can still generalize from your analysis.* For example, in Chapter 13, I discussed five different but positive answers to this question of how we can obtain generalizability:

- combining qualitative research with quantitative measures of populations
- purposive sampling guided by time and resources
- theoretical sampling
- generalizing to theoretical propositions (not to populations)
- using an analytic model which assumes that generalizability is present in the existence of any case.

So, when writing your methodology chapter, avoid over-defensiveness. Many great researchers will have used similar methods with few qualms. So draw from their strength.

On the other hand, self-confidence should not mean lack of appropriate self-criticism. Your literature review chapter will already have considered other studies in terms of 'the strengths and limitations of different research designs and techniques of data collection, handling and analysis' (Murcott, 1997: 2). Treat your methodology chapter in the same way – as a set of cautious answers to questions that another researcher might have asked you about your work (e.g. 'Why did you use these methods?', 'How did you come to these conclusions?').

Spencer et al. (2003) argue that this documentation process requires transparency about your methods. In other words, you should anticipate and answer reasonable questions about your research. Table 23.2 sets out the issues involved here.

Table 23.2   How to document your research transparently

- Give an honest account of the conduct of the research
- Provide full descriptions of what was actually done in regard to choosing your case(s) to study, choosing your method(s), collecting and analysing data
- Explain and justify each of your decisions
- Discuss the strengths and weaknesses of what you did
- Be open about what helped you and held you back

Source: adapted from Spencer et al. (2003: 76)

Another way of putting these kinds of matters has been suggested by Murcott. Table 23.3 shows how we can use our methods chapter to answer a set of questions.

Table 23.3   Questions for a qualitative methods chapter

1	How did you go about your research?
2	What overall strategy did you adopt, and why?
3	What design and techniques did you use?
4	Why these and not others?

Source: Murcott (1997)

To answer the questions will usually mean describing the following:

- the data you have studied
- how you obtained this data (e.g. issues of access and consent)
- what claims you are making about the data (e.g. as representative of some population or as a single case study)
- the methods you have used to gather the data
- why you have chosen these methods
- how you have analysed your data
- the advantages and limitations of using your method of data analysis.

3 A NATURAL HISTORY CHAPTER?

To answer Murcott's four questions in Table 23.3, in the context of my elaborations above, may now look to be a pretty tall order, particularly if you feel you have to devote a long section to each of these issues.

However, the methodology chapter of a qualitative study can be a much more lively, interesting affair than this suggests. In this context, there are three issues to bear in mind. First, a highly formal chapter can be dull to read as well as to write. Many is the time I have ploughed through a desperately boring methodology chapter, usually written in the passive voice. I often get the feeling that the chapter is there for purely formal purposes. In the words of a British song about why soldiers were fighting a war, 'because we're here, because we're here, because we're here'! In such cases, I can hardly wait to get on to the (more lively) heart of the study.

Second, 'methodology' has a more flexible meaning in qualitative research than in its quantitative sister. In Chapter 9, I defined 'methodology' as 'a general approach to studying research topics'. As such, your readers will be more interested in a methodological discussion in which you explain the actual course of your decision making rather than a series of blunt assertions in the passive voice (e.g. 'the method chosen was …').

Third, a research study submitted for a university degree, even up to the PhD level, is principally evaluated in terms of how far you can demonstrate that you have the makings of a competent researcher. Hence your examiners will be interested to know something about the history of your research, including your response to the various difficulties and dead ends that we all experience.

David's Top Tip 58

From day one of your research, keep a diary to record your ideas at the time and the challenges you perceive. A research diary will be an invaluable resource when you later write your methodology chapter.

As Alasuutari argues, false leads and dead ends are just as worth reporting as the method eventually chosen:

> It is precisely for this reason that taking 'fieldnotes' about the development of one's thinking is needed ... The text can be like a detective story, where one presents these 'false leads' until they are revealed to be dead-ends. (1995: 192)

Alasuutari's version of the history of research as a 'detective story' is incompatible with a formal methodology chapter in the passive voice. Instead of a formal, impersonal chapter, one offers the reader 'fieldnotes about the developments of one's thinking'. One way to do this is to rename the 'methodology' chapter 'The Natural History of My Research'.

In Chapter 3, we saw how some of my research students used their field diaries to write lively natural histories. These informed the reader about, among other things:

- the personal context of their research topic
- the reasons for their research design
- how they developed their research through trial and error
- the methodological lessons they learned.

Examples of how these topics can be treated in your 'natural history' chapter are set out in Table 23.4.

Table 23.4   Topics for a natural history chapter

The personal context

By the end of my period of undergraduate study, I was greatly vexed by issues surrounding the tendency within the various schools of sociology towards using 'social structure' too loosely as a way of accounting for data. [Simon]

The micro-analysis of social interaction seemed to me to be a valuable way of understanding some of the health issues and problems I had encountered in my experience working in clinical health settings as a psychiatric nurse and as a research nurse. Many of these problems appeared to hinge on the interactive practices and skills of the various parties involved. [Moira]

As with Silverman's (1987) experience of gaining access to the field of paediatric cardiology, my entry to the field of mental health casework was a chance happening. I met up with a former colleague in a local supermarket. After I recounted my difficulty in negotiating access to an inpatient area, he invited me to meet the community team with whom he worked. [Sally]

Reasons for research design

I chose to collect data in the way that I did because it was appropriate to the study of situated action. Audiotapes provide detailed recorded talk which fieldnotes alone cannot provide, while preparing transcripts is itself a research activity. [Sally]

Many qualitative research studies set out clear aims and objectives at the start of a project. These may often refer to collecting and analysing data on a particular topic, such as describing the views of patients about a particular type of illness experience. The aims of ethnomethodological studies such as this one tend to be quite general, centring on the examination of some data. Decisions therefore need to be made about objectives for particular pieces of analysis at each stage. [Moira]

Developing through trial and error

I had initially intended to undertake separate analyses of instances of criticisms of self and of the dead spouse. However, I decided a more constructive tack would be to conduct a closer analysis of members' practices in producing the accounts. This would involve taking a step back in order to take a closer look. [Moira]

To undertake a case study of 'single homelessness' in the context of full-time employment makes heavy demands on the researcher in terms of personal resources and operational constraints. The field is so vast and the nature of subjects' lives so dispersed that I elected to observe professional caseworkers rather than service users. For practical reasons then, I became a participant–observer at weekly case conferences. [Sally]

Methodological lessons I have learned

I was attempting to describe something that I knew was going on but could not see at the start. The need to refrain from introducing my own categorizations before producing the description of members' practices that I was aiming for has not been easy. However, I believe that the fine-grained analysis of the practices adopted by interview participants has enabled me to contribute new insights to the sociology of health and illness. [Moira]

With hindsight, I might use more conventional transcription devices if I were to do the transcripts again. This would save the 'creative' work of devising my own. [Sally]

How, then, should this research be seen in terms of both sampling variety and external validity? I believe the answer lies in seeing this research not as an attempt to provide categorical 'truths' about all parents' evenings in general, but as an attempt to raise questions about such meetings by looking at a single case in detail. This study can therefore be seen as being exploratory rather than definitive, examining the achievement of routine by a single individual in a specific setting in such a way that further analytical possibilities are opened up. [Simon]

As these student comments show, the more informal 'natural history' style of methodology chapter that I recommend should not be taken to mean that 'anything goes'. On the contrary, by asking readers to engage with your thinking in process, they are in a far better position to assess the degree to which you were self-critical. Moreover, an autobiographical style is only appropriate to the extent that it allows you to address properly the kind of crucial methodological issues and questions set out in Tables 23.2 and 23.3. Clearly, your readers will not want to hear needlessly and endlessly about how your personal life impinged upon the process of obtaining your degree!

Gubrium has clearly set out the dangers of what he calls 'self-referential writing':

> My concern with self-referential writing isn't meant to denigrate. Rather, mine are words of caution to students not to take writing of this kind too far lest the subject matter in question not be addressed. (Of course, the subject matter might be 'itself,' in which case we're back to square one, but I don't figure that this should be the main focus of an empirical science.) By self-referential writing, I mean writing that refers mainly or exclusively to what you thought or did, or went through, in working up the empirical material that supports your account. [I am particularly concerned about] the kind of writing that refers to the personal experience of the researcher, emphasizing either his or her thoughts and feelings over the course of a project or the development of his or her interpersonal relations with research participants.

This definitely has a place especially in the social and behavioral sciences, and now also in social studies of science. The bad habit is that it too can eclipse writing about the subject matter in view. I know that the subject matter can be the experience of the researcher, but what I'm concerned with here is the emphasis this can take in the final written product. If you do aim to feature your place in a project in writing, in particular yourself and your relation with others, then write about how that relates to broader issues of personal and interpersonal experience in the circumstances. (2009)

4 WRAPPING UP

Some universities (like some academic journals) still have a pretty fixed idea of what a methodology chapter (or section) should contain. Therefore, it is probably worth discussing with your teachers whether a 'natural history' format is appropriate to describe the methodology that you have chosen. But even if you do not write your chapter in this way, you will still gain by keeping dated fieldnotes about the trajectory of your project.

However, if you do write a 'natural history' chapter, it is much more likely that you will avoid boring your readers (and yourself). It is also more likely that you will overcome the common problem of failing to explicate to the reader what is now 'obvious' to you. As Alasuutari puts it: 'Researchers always become more or less blind to their texts and thoughts, so that they do not notice that they have failed in spelling out certain premises or starting points without which an outsider has a hard time

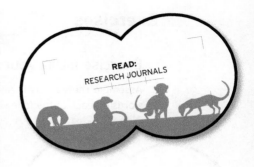

understanding the text' (1995: 192). A 'natural history' chapter, based on contemporary fieldnotes, will be more likely to make your readers 'insiders' and to avoid your being an 'outsider' in relation to your own text.

What You Need to Remember

All research reports have a methodology chapter, or at least a section devoted to 'data and methods'. In it, you will be expected to show that you understand the rationale and the strengths and weaknesses of your research strategy, design and methods.

In this chapter you should explain:

- your theoretical assumptions
- the factors that made you choose to work with your particular data
- how you can generalize from your analysis.

A highly formal methodology chapter can be dull to read as well as to write. Instead, it is often right to offer the reader fieldnotes about the developments of one's thinking called 'The Natural History of My Research'.

Your Chapter Checklist

- Have you avoided using the passive voice?
- Have you explained the actual progress of your research - the pitfalls, what you have learned and how you might have done things differently?
- Are you keeping a research journal/natural history diary?

Exercises

Exercise 1: Use your memos as a jumping off point for reflection

Assemble the various memos you have written during your research. Now write 500 words on each of the following topics related to your research:

APPLY:
YOUR EXERCISE WORKBOOK

1. The main things that have helped you finish and the main things that have held you back
2. What you have learned about your research topic.
3. How you have improved your knowledge of (a) methodology and (b) theory.
4. What lessons your research has for other students at your level.

Note: if you have not finished your research yet, do Chapter 2, Exercise 1 instead.

Exercise 2: Evaluate the benefits of a research journal

- What have your learned from Cate Watson's experience of keeping a research journal (above)?
- How could you incorporate such a journal in your methodology chapter?

Further Reading

EXPLORE:
METHODOLOGY CHAPTER ADVICE

Helpful comments on writing a methodology chapter are to be found in Pertti Alasuutari's *Researching Culture: Qualitative Method and Cultural Studies* (Sage, 1995: Chapters 13 and 14) and Amir Marvasti's chapter 'Three aspects of writing qualitative research: practice, genre and audience' in D. Silverman (ed.), *Qualitative Research* (Sage, 2011: 383–96).

Discover the chapter's digital resources in your SILVERMAN FIELD GUIDE

TWENTY FOUR
The Data Chapters

Learning Outcomes

By the end of this chapter you will be able to:

- Plan the overall structure of your thesis.
- Recognize and choose between different stories you can tell about your research.
- Work out how to present data effectively.
- Appreciate the importance of writing in a clear and persuasive manner.

1 INTRODUCTION

As we have already seen, many supervisors and funding bodies suggest that doing a research study falls into three equal phases. These phases are commonly defined as:

- reviewing the literature
- gathering your data
- analysing your data.

Faced with this convention, it may be necessary to restate the obvious. Assuming that you are writing an empirically based study, your data analysis chapters are (or should be) the key basis on which your dissertation will be judged. Unlike coursework essays, where knowledge of the literature and an ability to analyse it critically will stand you in good stead, dissertations that involve research are worth nothing without good data analysis.

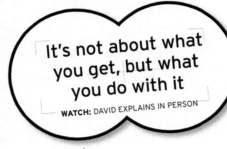

David's Top Tip 59

There are usually no 'brownie points' awarded for successfully gathering your data. Whether or not such data gathering involves discomfort, danger or the need to learn another language is, ultimately, neither here nor there. In the final assessment, everything comes down to what you do with your data. Hence your data chapters are the crucial part of your dissertation.

This situation implies two clear messages:

- You cannot begin too early in your data analysis.
- When you write up data, you need to develop the skills to present your analysis clearly and cogently to your readers.

This is why, as Jay Gubrium (personal correspondence) has commented, students need advice on the actual writing up of their data analysis. They need to understand 'what to say first, next, where to place things, how to introduce extracts and what to say in relation to them, how to draw conclusions'. In this chapter, I offer advice addressed to the issues that Gubrium raises.

It will be useful at once to make a distinction between how you write up your analysis of particular sets of data and how you craft your overall argument. Alasuutari (1995) calls the former area the 'microstructure' of a thesis and the latter its 'macrostructure'. This is how he explains the difference between the two levels:

The difference between the two could be compared to different dimensions of the architecture of a house. At the macrolevel one thinks how the rooms and different activities are placed in relation to each other, whereas at the microlevel one considers the furnishing and interior decoration of different rooms. (1995: 179)

This is a helpful distinction because, as Alasuutari suggests, different issues arise in relation to the organization of individual chapters (the microstructure) and the overall organization of your thesis (the macrostructure). In the rest of this chapter, I will consider each structure separately and then go on to explain how to make a final check that everything is in place before you tighten up the structure (Wolcott, 1990: 47).

2 THE MACROSTRUCTURE

The macrostructure is how the investigation proceeds from one chapter to another so that it forms a logical and sound whole. (Alasuutari, 1995: 179)

Let your findings inform your writing

WATCH: DAVID EXPLAINS IN PERSON

David's Top Tip 60

Don't think of your data chapters as a *report* on your findings. This assumes that you can know everything that you want to say *before* you write. Instead, begin writing up early in order to work out exactly what you want to say and how you want to say it. This means that you should assume that your data chapters will go through several drafts (see O'Leary, 2014: 329; Punch, 2014: 342-4).

How do you ensure that your data analysis chapters form 'a logical and sound whole'? I discuss below two answers to this question:

- Plan your table of contents at an early stage and continually revise it.
- In the final write-up, decide the form of the 'story' you want to tell about your research.

EXPLORE: WRITING UP DATA

Early planning of table of contents

Plan what you may put into your data chapters as early as you can and then keep revising your list. As Wolcott suggests, projecting a table of contents provides for:

an orderly progression, a clear identification of major points and subordinate ones, and an overview ... to assess whether the structure I have designed accommodates the data to be presented and provides an appropriate sequence for the presentation. (1990: 18)

By such early planning of the structure of your thesis you can help to clarify your research design and identify upcoming problems:

> Insurmountable problems in finding a sound macrostructure may be a sign of weaknesses in the research design: problems which have to be sorted out first. (Alasuutari, 1995: 179)

Alasuutari gives the example of a set of chapters which veer unpredictably between different themes – a good indication of an unclear research design. This means that, if you have difficulty in working out your table of contents, then you are exhibiting symptoms of a confused research design.

To show you how tables of contents can be projected, I set out below examples from two of my research students: Sally Hunt and Kay Fensom. In each case, these research students started to project a table of contents at an early stage.

WHAT I DID: SALLY AND KAY
Table of Contents

Sally Hunt

Title: Producing Single Homelessness: Descriptive Practice in Community Mental Casework

Sally gathered audio recordings of case conferences of a community health team seeking to house mentally ill, homeless people. Her work, which was discussed in Chapter 3, is ethnographic in focus. The following is her draft table of contents, prepared while she was still writing her data chapters:

1	Introduction: aims of the study
2	Natural history of the research
3	Literature used in the analysis
4-6	The ethnographic context
7	Constructing the case
8	Constructing the client
9	Gender as an interpretive framework
10	Constructing the mental health team
11	Conclusion: limitations and implications

In the final version of her thesis, Sally reorganized most of it into two parts: an introduction (which included Chapters 1-3) and the data analysis (Chapters 7-10). Sally recognized that her projected chapters on the ethnographic context were peripheral to her main argument. So her draft Chapters 4-6 were vastly shortened and incorporated into her introduction.

Kay Fensom

Title: Locating Newsworthiness in Newspaper Headlines: Reading Inference and 'Motive'

Kay analysed crime stories in local newspapers in London and Northern Ireland. To do this, she used Harvey Sacks's membership categorization device (MCD) analysis. The following are her early ideas about the organization of her thesis:

1 Natural history: stages, directions and influences
2 Theoretical framework
3 The media, 'newsworthiness' and the activity of reading
4-7 Data chapters (each on a separate crime headline)
8 Dealing with critiques of MCD analysis
9 Conclusions: what has the analysis achieved?

By the time Kay submitted her PhD, she had one extra data chapter. She now felt that two of her draft chapters were based on literature reviews which were not distinctively original. So Chapters 3 and 8 disappeared from the final version of her thesis, although parts of each were used elsewhere. Kay's title also changed to: 'Crime, Locality and Morality: Membership Categorization and "Newsworthiness" in Local Newspapers'. This improved title nicely reflected (what had turned out to be) Kay's key concepts and database.

Sally and Kay's redrafting carries three important implications about how you should think about the structure of your thesis:

- Work out the main message and findings your data chapters should contain.
- Ensure that the structure of your thesis underlines that message.
- Strip out or minimize draft chapters that are peripheral to your argument.

Deleting or shortening chapters over which you have toiled requires a degree of ruthlessness on your part. Seek the guidance of your supervisor about whether such chapters might find a better home in, say, a conference paper or journal article (see Chapter 27).

Don't tell the whole story

WATCH: DAVID EXPLAINS IN PERSON

David's Top Tip 61

When planning the topics of your data chapters, do not assume that you must tell the 'whole story'. There is no 'whole story', there is only the story that you want to tell. So be ruthless about what you include, using the rule: include only those data chapters that work really well.

More than a year before Sally and Kay finished their dissertations, they were already planning a draft table of contents. Planning is important because your research dissertation will probably be the longest piece of writing you have ever done. BA or MA research essays are commonly 10,000 words and PhDs are usually between 70,000 and 100,000 words. However, it is important not to focus upon your own difficulties in writing at this length, for I guarantee that in nearly every case you will find you have too *little* space.

Instead, think of how the reader needs a guide to follow a long story. Provide that guide at the start and repeat it, as appropriate, in every chapter (see Alasuutari, 1995: 180). This will mean giving regular 'signposts' to help the reader understand what you are going to do (or have done) and how these components relate to your overall theme. It also means planning the form of the 'story' you wish to tell.

Planning your story

There are at least three models to choose from in working out the macrostructure of your thesis:

- the hypothesis story
- the analytic story
- the mystery story.

Each is discussed briefly below.[1]

The hypothesis story

This is how many journals require you to organize your paper. It follows a standard three-part way of writing up research reports derived from quantitative studies:

1. State your hypotheses.
2. Test them.
3. Discuss the implications.

As Alasuutari (1995: 181) points out, there are two reasons why you are unlikely to want to use this model for writing up your qualitative dissertation:

- You may well be proceeding inductively, developing and testing hypotheses in the course of your data analysis. If so, then clearly you cannot state a prior hypothesis.
- There are reasons to be suspicious of the hypothesis story because, even in quantitative studies, it often represents not the 'actual' logic of the research but a reconstructed logic fitted to how your cross-tabulations of variables actually worked out (see Alasuutari, 1995: 181-3).

The analytic story

The hypothesis story usually demands a passive voice format (e.g. 'it was hypothesized that …' or 'the findings were …') which can be difficult to write and still more painful to read! Telling an analytic story is a more conversational way of writing. It involves deciding 'the main analytic story line that you wish to tell' (Strauss and Corbin, 1990: 200). As Strauss and Corbin put it:

> think intently about the analytic logic that informs the story. Every research monograph, indeed every research paper, will have such a logic ... In a sense the entire thesis or monograph will represent a spelling out of this analytic story. (1990: 230)

To write this story, you need to ask yourself questions like:

- What are the key concepts that I have used in this study?
- How do my 'findings' shed light on these concepts and, through them, on the substantive topics I studied?
- What, therefore, has become of my original research problem and the literature regarding it?

Rather than hope that the reader will eventually find out these matters, telling an analytic story lays everything out on a plate at the outset.

There is much to be said for this model, for it helps the reader, who can settle back knowing what they will find in the rest of your thesis. Some readers, however, may actually want to be surprised. Such surprises can be planned rather than the mere outcome of sloppy design. This is where the mystery story comes in.

The mystery story

Alasuutari (1995) refers to an approach to writing that 'proceeds by pointing out mysteries and by gradually developing questions and answers'. In this approach, one:

> starts directly from empirical examples, develops the questions by discussing them, and gradually leads the reader to interpretations of the material and to more general implications of the results. (1995: 183)

An effective way of telling a mystery story is as follows:

- Begin with a piece of data.
- Show why it puzzled you.
- Gradually unveil how you solved the puzzle.

CASE STUDY

For example, in my HIV-test counselling research (Silverman, 1997), I found many examples of clients failing to respond to a piece of advice with anything more than a response token (e.g. 'mm hmm'). We know this sometimes happens but, when it does, it usually

(Continued)

(Continued)

creates some turbulence in the talk that follows. Advice-givers tend to expect some kind of uptake. However, I found no such turbulence in my data following such non-uptake [PUZZLE]. I went back to the data and discovered that most counsellors were formatting their advice in a highly specific, non-personal way. So, instead of saying, 'I suggest that you do X', they tended to say, 'In this clinic, we usually advise people to do X' [RELEVANT FINDING]. This meant that they were formatting their advice in an ambiguous way so that it could be heard not as personal advice but merely as information about the advice given to everybody at the clinic [RELEVANT IMPLICATION]. Unlike advice, it is not expected that we need to respond to information with a strong uptake. This means that counsellors need not worry when they get only a minimal uptake of their advice [SOLUTION OF PUZZLE].

Beginning one's data analysis in the form of a mystery story has at least two advantages. First, it may well capture your readers' attention as, like the readers of detective stories, they want to stay with you in order to find 'whodunnit'. Second, it more accurately mirrors the inductive form of much qualitative research where findings (and even topics) are only gradually revealed.

Set against this, you must remember that writing a mystery story requires many craft skills. Should you fail, you will certainly lose your readers' interest. So, in practice, many writers of good qualitative disser-

EXPLORE:
TELLING A STORY

tations follow Strauss and Corbin's idea of telling an analytic story to lead the readers through the data analysis chapters.

In a sense, whichever story form you choose can be safely left to personal choice. More important is whether you are telling *some* coherent story. For, despite their differences, all three models share one important feature in common: they give the study focus and point. This means that the structure of your thesis should only rarely flow from the chronological order in which you happened to find out things. As Cryer puts it: 'the final version of the thesis should be written, with hindsight, knowing where one has been' (1996: 178).

Discussing the order in which you discovered things is a story which is only appropriate for a natural history chapter (see Chapter 23). If the overall structure of your thesis just reflects the order in which you discovered things, then your examiners are unlikely to praise you for your verisimilitude. They are much more likely to criticize you for being too lazy to work out a coherent structure for your argument.

As Alasuutari puts it, returning to the motif of a 'mystery story':

> A good investigation is indeed like a murder mystery in that it does not contain much irrelevant text: themes or details that have nothing to do with the solution revealed in the end ... One could talk about the economy principle of a study: everything included must be related and tied in with the argumentation developed and presented in the investigation. (1995: 186)

READ:
REVISING DATA CHAPTERS

3 THE MICROSTRUCTURE

With a clear macrostructure, you are well set up to write well-organized and well-argued data chapters. Whether it is a matter of setting out an overall argument (the macrostructure) or developing an analysis of a particular topic (the microstructure), you should always write in a way that helps the reader. As Jay Gubrium (personal communication) notes, this is not always something that comes easily to inexperienced researchers:

> many students don't take their readers into account; they don't know how to 'teach' their readers what they should be reading into the empirical material present. Many just throw stuff into the text and expect the reader to get the point.

Thinking about your reader(s) turns out to be an excellent way of answering perennial problems that arise when you first write up a qualitative study. For instance, you may ask yourself: 'How much depth is needed in my data analysis? How much is enough?' Strauss and Corbin suggest a good way of answering such questions:

EXPLORE:
WRITING UP QUALITATIVE DATA

> The answer is first that you must know what your main analytic message will be. Then you must give enough conceptual detail to convey this to readers. The actual form of your central chapters should be consonant with the analytic message and its components. (1990: 232-3)

So the answer to these questions is found in how you have depicted the main message of your thesis (the macrostructure). The point here is: know your message and stick to it!

Normally, each data analysis chapter will have three sections:

- an introduction in which you explain what you are going to do in advance
- the main section in which you work through your data in terms of what you have already said
- a conclusion in which you summarize what you have shown and connect to the next chapter.

I set out below some suggestions for writing each of these sections with an audience in mind.

Introduction

Never spring anything on your readers. Even if you have decided to tell a mystery story (see above), your audience should always know what the mystery is about and what kind of 'clues' they should be looking for. As Becker has cautioned:

> Many social scientists ... think they are actually doing a good thing by beginning evasively. They reveal items of evidence one at a time, like clues in a detective story, expecting readers to keep everything straight until they produce the dramatic concluding paragraph ... I often suggest to these would-be Conan Doyles that they simply put their last triumphant paragraph first, telling readers where the argument is going and what all this material will finally demonstrate. (1986: 51-2)

So, at the outset, preface each data analysis chapter with an explanation of how its topic relates to your thesis as a whole and how the chapter will be organized. As a broad rule, no subheading should ever appear in a chapter without its having received a prior explanation of its nature and logical place in your argument.

Along these lines, Cryer suggests four components of a good introduction to a chapter. These are set out in Table 24.1.

Table 24.1   Components of a data chapter introduction

1	Scene-setting for the chapter, i.e. explaining the general area(s) that the chapter considers
2	Locating the gap in knowledge which the chapter addresses
3	Explaining how the chapter fills that gap
4	Providing a brief overview of what is in the chapter

Source: adapted from Cryer (1996: 182)

Main section

Now that your readers know the areas that this chapter will discuss, it is important that you initially pull apart these areas and discuss each one separately. The golden rule for writing data analysis is:

- Make one point at a time.

So, if you find yourself veering off in another direction, cut out the offending material and put it in another section. Sometimes this will mean returning to the same data but from a different perspective. Sometimes it will mean getting rid of some data altogether.

Your readers will find life much easier if they are not distracted by too many different arguments. And it is also much more likely that you will be able to recognize holes in your argument if it is stripped to the bone.

If you are making just one point at a time, it is, of course, crucial that your readers should immediately grasp what that point is. Therefore, a second rule is:

- 'Top and tail' each data extract.

This means writing a sentence or two before every extract to context it in your argument. This way your readers will know what to look for while they read it.

Follow that up with a more detailed analysis of the extract in terms of the single point you are using it to make. If the extract is inconclusive, then admit to it. So, a third rule is:

- Always show that you understand the limitations of both your data and your analysis of it.

For your readers to be able to follow your analysis, they will need to be able to locate the extract(s) to which you are referring and where to find the relevant part of that extract. So a fourth rule is:

- Always number your extracts.

One effective way to do this is to give each extract two identifying numbers: the first will be the chapter number in which it appears, and the second the order in which it is placed in the chapter. So the first data extract in Chapter 3 of your thesis should be numbered Extract 3.1.

Line numbers should also be used for any extracts over two lines in length. In this way, for instance, you can refer to Extract 3.1, lines 5–7, without having to reprint the passage.

A fifth rule is:

- Convince the reader.

Not only must your readers be able to see why you interpreted your data in the way you did, but also they must be convinced by your interpretation. As Murcott suggests: 'the basis for saying that the data say "x" rather than "y" has to be made apparent' (1997: 2). Murcott suggests that the way to display that your analysis has this kind of critical component is to 'discuss candidate interpretations and make the case for judging, and so discarding, alternatives as inferior or inadequate' (1997: 2).[2]

Conclusion

When you reach the end of a tight piece of data analysis, you may feel that nothing further needs to be done. Not so! You owe it to your readers to tie the whole chapter together again. Not only will this remind them of what you (and they) have learnt in the preceding pages, but it will also prepare them for the chapter(s) to follow. Table 24.2 sets out what the conclusion of a data chapter might contain.

Table 24.2   Components of a data chapter conclusion

1	Explain what the chapter has done
2	Describe the new questions the chapter has identified
3	Explain where these questions will be addressed (e.g. in the next chapter or in the overall conclusions)

Source: adapted from Cryer (1996: 183)

It is worth remembering that it is unlikely that you will achieve a well-argued, reader-friendly thesis at one go. I conclude this chapter, therefore, with some suggestions about moving to a final draft or what Wolcott calls 'tightening up' (1990: 47).

4 TIGHTENING UP

Make sure all parts are properly in place before tightening. (Directions for assembling a new wheelbarrow, reported by Wolcott, 1990: 47)

READ:
WRITING UP CHAOTIC DATA

Wolcott's analogy of assembling a wheelbarrow reminds us that no subtle change of detail will work if the macrostructure of your thesis is not properly in place. As he puts it:

Before you start tightening, take a look at how the whole thing is coming together. Do you have everything you need? (And do you need everything you have? Remember, you're only supposed to be tightening up that wheelbarrow, not filling it!) (1990: 48)

You are likely to be too close to your work to tell easily whether everything is properly in place. As Cryer suggests, the author of a thesis 'will know it inside and out and back to front. So the link between its components may be clear to you, while not being as clear to those who have met your work only recently' (1996: 186).

There are two ways of giving yourself the critical distance necessary to see whether all the parts of your thesis are in place. First, if time allows, put it to one side for a while. Wolcott notes:

> I do a better job of strengthening the interpretation, spotting discrepancies and repetitions, locating irregularities in sequence or logic, and discovering overworked words, phrases, and patterns after periods of benign neglect. (1990: 52)

Locating what Wolcott calls 'irregularities' can mean deleting particular points to which you may have become attached but which detract from your overall argument (Clive Seale, personal correspondence).

A second strategy to obtain distance is to give a talk on your research during the writing-up stage or to find 'someone new to your work who will listen to you explaining it or will read the draft thesis and tell you where they have trouble following' (Cryer, 1996: 186).

Once the macrostructure is in place, it is time to tighten up the microstructure. Among the things to look at here are:

- unclear or infelicitous language
- over-large claims about your data or analysis
- needless repetition
- insufficient detail (see Wolcott, 1990: 49–50).

When you have done all of these things, you must recognize that the tightening-up period is nearly over. Certainly, you can ask yourself: 'Have I really got the last details in? Got them right?' (Strauss and Corbin, 1990: 235).

To check this out, you can ask your supervisor and/or fellow students to have one final read and then respond to their comments. But remember: the revision process is potentially endless! The real cop-out is not submitting a less than perfect thesis but being stuck in a process of endless revisions:

> Part of an increasing maturity as a research-writer is to understand that no manuscript is ever finished. (1990: 235)

Just as parents eventually realize that their children have become adults and will leave home, now is the time to make the break with your manuscript. Like 'empty nest' parents, you should be ready to strike out in new directions. But first you must 'let go'.

5 WRAPPING UP

Your data analysis chapters are (or should be) the key basis on which your dissertation will be judged. However, different issues arise in relation to the organization of individual chapters (the microstructure) and the overall organization of your thesis (the macrostructure).

Good overall organization is based upon planning your table of contents at an early stage and continually revising it. You also need to decide the form of the 'story' you want to tell about your research and structure your data chapters accordingly. Each data chapter should have a microstructure based on three sections: an introduction in which you explain what you are going to do in advance; the main section in which you work through your data in terms of what you have already said; and, finally, a conclusion in which you summarize what you have shown and connect to the next chapter.

What You Need to Remember

- Work out what main message and findings you want your data chapters to contain.
- Ensure that the structure of your thesis underlines that message.
- Strip out or minimize draft chapters that are peripheral to your argument.
- Avoid telling your story in the order which you found things out or wrote them up. The secret of a successful data chapter is that it transforms what happened to you into a convincing account of what your data shows.

NOTES

1   As we shall see, the ideas of the hypothesis story and the mystery story derive from Alasuutari (1995).
2   See Chapter 17 for a discussion of these issues in terms of 'validity' and 'reliability' and Chapter 15 for an explanation of how diagrams and charts may illustrate your rigorous thinking. On this latter point, see also Mason (1996: 131–3) and Strauss and Corbin (1990: 131–7).

TRACK:
WRITING DATA PROGRESS

Your Chapter Checklist

As you write up your data, check this list:

- Make one point at a time.
- Context each data extract in your argument.
- Show that you understand the limitations of your analysis.

- Always number your data extracts.
- Realize that the reader will need to be convinced and that what is obvious to you will not always be so clear to others.

Exercises

Exercise 1: See what structure works best for your data analysis

Try organizing your data analysis into two chapters. Don't do this arbitrarily but find a logical approach. Now try reordering this material into five shorter chapters with a different logic. Consider which format works best and why.

APPLY:
YOUR EXERCISE WORKBOOK

Exercise 2: Break your data analysis into manageable pieces

Select a coherent piece of your data analysis which might become a chapter. Give the chapter a title that fits what you are trying to do there. Using Tables 24.1 and 24.2, now:

1. Write an introduction for this chapter.
2. Write a conclusion.
3. Add in your data analysis and show the whole chapter to a colleague. Ask them whether your introduction and conclusion helped them to see what you were getting at. If so, why? If not, why not?
4. Now revise the text and repeat the process.

Further Reading

Harry Wolcott's *Writing Up Qualitative Research* (Sage, 2009) is a marvellous account of how to write up data. Useful shorter treatments are: Pat Cryer's *The Research Student's Guide to Success* (Open University Press, 2006: Chapter 23); and Pertti Alasuutari's *Researching Culture: Qualitative Method and Cultural Studies* (Sage, 1995: Chapter 14). For useful chapter-length accounts of writing, consult Tim Rapley's 'Some pragmatics of qualitative data

EXPLORE:
GOOD SOCIAL SCIENCE WRITING TIPS

analysis' and Amir Marvasti's 'Writing qualitative research: practice, genre and audience' (both in D. Silverman (ed.), *Qualitative Research*, 4th edition,

Sage, 2016: 331–46 and 429–46). For versions of writing data chapters from within grounded theory, try Kathy Charmaz's ideas on memo-writing and 'clustering' in her book *Constructing Grounded Theory* (Sage, 2006: Chapter 7) or Anselm Strauss and Juliet Corbin's *Basics of Qualitative Research* (Sage, 2008: Chapter 13).

Discover the chapter's digital resources in your
SILVERMAN FIELD GUIDE

TWENTY FIVE
The Concluding Chapter

Learning Outcomes

By the end of this chapter you will be able to:

• Understand why a concluding chapter is necessary in a research report.
• See what this chapter should contain.
• Think about the theoretical implications of your research.
• Work out which audiences you are addressing and how you can shape your chapter accordingly.
• Recognize that writing a concluding chapter can be fun.

1 INTRODUCTION

In the previous chapter, I concluded with the recommendation to 'let go'. However, since all research reports (including dissertations) seem to end with a set of 'conclusions', you cannot finally let go until your concluding chapter is written.

Having cycled painfully to the top of the hill, you may experience the great temptation to relax and freewheel down to the finish. In practice, such relaxation of effort is reflected in the all too common 'summaries' found in the concluding chapter of dissertations.

Although summaries are often quite useful devices at the end of data analysis chapters, I suggest that you should *never* write a summary as your concluding chapter. If your readers need a summary at this point, then your 'macrostructure' (Alasuutari's concept discussed in Chapter 24) is not in place. If it is in place, then what you have said should already be crystal clear. So resist the temptations of a final downhill freewheel.

But does this mean that you may not even need a concluding chapter? Can't your thesis stop after you have finished your data analysis?

Think of a musical example. Classical symphonies typically end with a fast movement marked 'allegro' or 'presto'. Rather than a mere recapitulation of earlier themes, they take them up and develop them still more. As such, they seem designed to provide listeners with some of the most stimulating material in the composition.

So your concluding chapter is, indeed, necessary. But it should function to *stimulate* your readers by demonstrating how your research has stimulated you.

This chapter begins by showing you the interesting and liberating functions of a concluding chapter. It then provides some practical suggestions about what this

concluding chapter should contain and reviews the balance between confessing to your errors and proclaiming your achievements. I go on to show how your concluding chapter should reconnect your data analysis to the basic analytic questions that have inspired you and should think through what your research can offer to a range of different audiences. Finally, I demonstrate why writing your concluding chapter can be fun.

2 THE CONCLUDING CHAPTER AS MUTUAL STIMULATION

Your concluding chapter should be stimulating for you to write. If this is the case, it is likely to stimulate your readers. Part of that stimulation arises in linking the particularities of your own research back to the more general issues that arise within (your part) of your discipline. As the authors of the standard British text on PhDs comment:

> You are not doing some research for its own sake; you are doing it in order to demonstrate that you are a fully professional researcher, with a good grasp of what is happening in your field and capable of evaluating the impact of new contributions to it - your own as well as others. (Phillips and Pugh, 1994: 60)

Your contribution is what you must set out to demonstrate in your concluding chapter: 'It is here that you underline the significance [to your discipline] of your analysis, point out the limitations in your material, suggest what new work is appropriate, and so on' (1994: 59).

Phillips and Pugh's remarks suggest part of the answer to the practical question: 'What exactly should your concluding chapter contain?'

3 WHAT EXACTLY SHOULD YOUR CONCLUDING CHAPTER CONTAIN?

> In the most general terms it [your concluding chapter] is a discussion as to why and in what way ... the theory that you started with [is] now different as a result of your research work. Thus your successors (who include, of course, yourself) now face a different situation when determining what their research work should be since they now have to take account of your work. (Phillips and Pugh, 1994: 59-60)

A helpful way of looking at this is in terms of Murcott's question: 'What does the candidate want the reader to make of all this?' (1997: 3). As Table 25.1 shows, the concluding chapter offers you the opportunity to give your own twist to the wider implications of your research. Such implications must, of course, reflect your own critical sense of what is good and not so good in your own research. Always remember: unless you define your own sense of the limitations (and implications) of your work, your readers will do it for you!

WATCH:
DAVID EXPLAINS IN PERSON

Table 25.1   Suggested contents for your final chapter

- The relation between the work done, the original research questions, previous work discussed in the literature review chapter, and any new work appearing since the study began
- Some answer to the classic examiner's question, 'If you were doing this study all over again, is there anything you would do differently? Why so?'; that is, the lessons to be learned from the conduct of the study
- Any implications for policy and practice
- Further research that might follow from your findings, methods or concepts

Source: adapted from Murcott (1997: 3)

The example that follows shows how Rachael Dunn's dissertation (on therapeutic interaction in anorexia nervosa (AN) treatment) dealt with two of the issues in Table 25.1: the limitations of her research and recommendations for further research.

WHAT I DID: RACHAEL

Extract from a Concluding Chapter

Thesis limitations

This thesis has looked at *some* of the functions of the interactional practices identified in the analysis. Without question, any number of theses could have potentially been written about each analytic insight produced, and infinite alternative analytic directions could have been pursued in the data. Overall, the focus of the analysis could only be very narrow, and in the end I endeavoured to take a direction that had potential for clinical relevance. Furthermore, my own interpretations, analytic categories and institutional identities were not *imposed* onto the data corpus; instead, the analysis relied on the speakers' own orientations to elements and structures of the interactions.

This thesis also did not directly address the issue of high dropout rates, reported in AN populations. While it can speculate on the link between certain interactional practices being representative of therapeutic engagement, it cannot make a direct association between engagement in therapy and reduced dropout rates (as discussed in the following section).

Future research

Though it is not a basis for this study, it could be proposed that increased engagement in therapy may be correlated with improved rates on external outcome measures, such as number of hospital admissions, as well as internal measures of AN symptomatology ... Future studies could associate the presence or absence of certain interactional practices with specific treatment outcomes such as therapeutic withdrawal rates [and] could also study certain interactional circumstances in which therapeutic approaches in AN treatment such as individual or family-based therapies are more effective, as called for in the literature. [Rachael Dunn, Psychology, Murdoch University, my emphasis]

Notice how Rachael combines reflections on the limitations of her research with a discussion of how she addressed them. This shows that you can go too far in focusing solely on the limitations of your work. Research reports should not just be confessions! In the next section, I discuss the balance between owning up to where you feel you went wrong and blowing your own trumpet about your achievements.

4 CONFESSIONS AND TRUMPETS

As Wolcott (1990) notes, in assessing your thesis, your examiners will recognize that chance happenings as well as your research design have limited (as well as improved) your research. Be upfront about these matters. So, in your concluding chapter, write:

> a broad disclaimer in which [you] make quite clear [your] recognition of all the limitations of the study (e.g. that it occurred in a particular place, at a particular time, and under particular circumstances; that certain factors render the study atypical; that limited generalization is warranted; etc.). (1990: 30)

However, what Wolcott calls 'this litany of limitations' should be coupled with a stress on what you believe you have achieved. So, as in life, be realistic but don't undersell yourself! This can be in the form of:

> a conservative closing statement that reviews succinctly what has been attempted, what has been learned, and what new questions have been raised. (1990: 56)

Wolcott's helpful suggestion is, in my view, somewhat undermined by his use of the adjective 'conservative'. Beware of employing so much caution that you bore the reader! If you can effectively show why you have been stimulated, then you are much more likely to stimulate your audience.

Stimulation requires an active imagination. And, in science, it is theory which feeds the imagination.

Theory has been extensively discussed in the first three parts of this volume. Here I want to suggest a practical sense of theorizing which can help in writing an effective concluding chapter.

5 THEORIZING AS THINKING THROUGH DATA

An imaginative conclusion will move on from the careful description and analysis of your earlier chapters to a stimulating but critical view of the overall implications of your research. Without this, your research may amount to no more than a set of descriptions of data achieved by some mechanical use of a method.

Since much qualitative research works inductively, generating and testing hypotheses during data analysis, your concluding chapter is often the best place to present theoretical linkages and speculations. As Alasuutari comments, in qualitative data analysis:

> One preferably starts directly from empirical examples, develops the questions by discussing them, and gradually leads the reader into interpretations of the material and to more general implications of the results. If one feels like discussing and constructing them, the best position for grand theoretical models is in the *final page*. (1995: 183, my emphasis)

Grounded theory is a term used to describe a way of inducing theoretically based generalizations from qualitative data. However, it is crucial that, if grounded theory is your 'thing', you use it imaginatively rather than as a label to dress up a largely pedestrian study (see Charmaz, 2015).

As I argue in Chapter 18, some grounded theory studies fall short of imagination. This possibility is recognized in a leading text on grounded theory:

> It is entirely possible to complete a grounded theory study, or any study, yet not produce findings that are significant. If the researcher simply follows the grounded theory procedures/ canons without imagination or insight into what the data are reflecting – because he or she fails to see what they are really saying except in terms of trivial or well-known phenomena – then the published findings can be judged as failing on this criterion [i.e. of being significant]. (Strauss and Corbin, 1990: 256)

The concluding chapter is likely to be the place where your examiners will discover whether your theoretical pretensions are, as implied by Strauss and Corbin, merely mechanical. But, if theory must never be mere window-dressing, this does not mean that theory is ultimately more important than research. Theory without data is empty; data without theory says nothing.

This reciprocal relationship between theory and data is well captured by Coffey and Atkinson:

> Data are there to think with and to think about ... We should bring to them the full range of intellectual resources, derived from theoretical perspectives, substantive traditions, research literature and other sources ... [this means] that methods of data collection and data analysis do not make sense when treated in an intellectual vacuum and divorced from more general and fundamental disciplinary frameworks. (1996: 153)

The problem is that you may become so immersed in your highly specific research topic that you are ill-prepared to step back and to think about what Coffey and Atkinson call 'more general and fundamental disciplinary frameworks'. You can give your research this broader perspective by forcing yourself to think about how what you have discovered may relate to broader issues than your original research topic. In this way, a very narrow topic may be related to much broader social processes. As we saw in Chapter 18, this was how Mary Douglas's anthropological study of an African tribe took us from a very narrow issue (how the Lele perceive the pangolin) to a very broad social process (how societies respond to anomalous entities).

In this way, argue Coffey and Atkinson, 'qualitative data, analyzed with close attention to detail, understood in terms of their internal patterns and forms, should be used to develop theoretical ideas about social processes and cultural forms that have relevance *beyond these data themselves*' (1996: 163, my emphasis).

6 WRITING FOR AUDIENCES

A continuing message of this book is that, like any form of writing, writing a research report should always be framed for particular audiences. Drawing on this insight, many of my PhD students have organized their concluding chapters in terms of the different audiences who might be interested in their research.

Take the case of Moira Kelly's research on how her respondents describe the death of a spouse (discussed in Chapter 3). Her concluding chapter describes what her findings imply for four different audiences: methodologists, theorists, people with a substantive interest in the sociology of health and illness, and health policy makers.

One useful exercise to get you thinking about how to proceed in this way is simply to list all the possible audiences for your research. When I used this exercise with students doing business PhDs at the Helsinki School of Economics, the following audiences were noted:

- disciplinary (e.g. management, organization studies, marketing)
- methodological (e.g. case study researchers, interviewers)
- practitioners (e.g. managers, entrepreneurs, marketers)
- the general public (e.g. clients, consumers, politicians).

Such a list of your likely audiences should give you a good idea of how you could structure an effective concluding chapter. But don't just guess what will most interest your audiences! Show your findings to groups drawn from each audience and find out what is relevant to them (see Chapter 20 for further discussion of audiences for research).

7 WHY YOUR CONCLUDING CHAPTER CAN BE FUN

It may surprise you to think that writing your concluding chapter can be fun. Having struggled to reach the end of your data chapters, you may already be exhausted and tempted to try to get away with a short concluding summary. After all, you feel, what more can you add?

I have good news for you! Until your concluding chapter, you have had to be highly disciplined. Not only have you had to stick to the point, but you also (I hope) have had to stick closely to your data. Your only respite has been your footnotes. Used properly, footnotes are the place for asides and barbed comments (never the place for references).

But, if footnotes can be fun, so can your concluding chapter. For this is the place where caution temporarily should go out of the window and lateral thinking should rule. Here is the place to make broader links, eschewing the narrow focus found in the rest of your thesis. Here 'off-the-wall' comments ('from left field' as they say in baseball) are not only allowable but welcome. As Table 25.2 shows, here is a space for you to reveal your true colours – providing that you recognize that such self-expression has always to be recipient designed for an audience.

Table 25.2   How to make your concluding chapter fun

1	Making broader links (e.g. showing how a study of business meetings in just one company has implications for theories about how decisions are made)
2	Making 'off-the-wall' comments (e.g. considering the similarities and differences between talk in business meetings and family gatherings; speculating about the difference between online and offline talk)

8 WRAPPING UP

Let me make an obvious point: when you have finished your concluding chapter, it is time to submit your thesis. Yes I know research reports can always be improved, and the beauty of word processing is that the mechanical aspects of revision are quite simple, but how long do you want to stay a student? Providing your supervisor is supportive, isn't it better to submit right now? Even if your examiners require changes, at least your rewrites will have a pragmatic focus.

Being a perfectionist sounds like a nice identity. As Becker has commented:

> Getting it out the door is not the only thing people value. A lot of important work in a lot of fields has been done with little regard for whether it ever got out the door. Scholars and artists, especially, believe that if they wait long enough they may find a more comprehensive and logical way to say what they think. (1986: 123)

However, Becker also makes us aware that rewriting can be the alibi for the persistent waverer. By contrast, he tells us:

> I like to get it out the door. Although I like to rewrite and tinker with organization and wording, I soon either put work aside as not ready to be written or get it into a form to go out the door. (1986: 124)

After a long period of study, do you really want to 'put work aside'? Follow your supervisor's advice (providing they are not a ditherer!) and get your work 'out the door'!

What You Need to Remember

You should *never* write a summary as your concluding chapter. Instead, your concluding chapter must help the reader to decide what to make of your dissertation. This should explain:

- the relation between the work done, the original research questions, previous work discussed in the literature review chapter, and any new work appearing since the study began
- anything you would do differently now
- implications for policy and practice
- further research that might follow from your findings, methods or concepts
- the limitations of your own study.

Your concluding chapter is an opportunity to make wider links from your research. It should be stimulating to read (and to write).

Your Chapter Checklist

Ensure that your concluding chapter can stimulate your readers by:

- showing how theories and recently published research have helped you think through your data
- addressing each of the audiences who might be interested in your work.

TRACK:
GOOD CONCLUDING CHAPTERS

Exercises

Exercise 1: Start compiling discussion points for your conclusion chapter

Get into the habit of keeping files on each of the issues below (taken from Table 25.1):

- the relation between your present work and your original research questions
- anything you would do differently now
- implications for policy and practice
- further research that might follow from your findings, methods or concepts
- the limitations of your own study.

APPLY:
YOUR EXERCISE WORKBOOK

At regular intervals, attempt to write a summary of what you can currently say about each of these issues.

Exercise 2: Use existing articles to support your conclusions

As this chapter has argued:

> Data are there to think with and to think about ... [this means] that methods of data collection and data analysis do not make sense when treated in an intellectual vacuum and divorced from more general and fundamental disciplinary frameworks. (Coffey and Atkinson, 1996: 153)

Find one or two recent journal articles which you think are important and show why they are relevant to your conclusions.

Exercise 3: Determine audiences for your research

Make a list of the different audiences who might be interested in your research (e.g. disciplinary, methodological, practitioners, general public).

Now work out how you could write a concluding chapter which framed the contribution of your research for each of these audiences.

Further Reading

EXPLORE:
CONCLUDING CHAPTER ADVICE

Estelle Phillips and Derek Pugh's *How To Get a PhD* (Open University Press, 2005: Chapter 6) is the best British account of the practical issues involved in concluding a research dissertation. On using theory to develop your conclusions, see: Tim Rapley's 'Some pragmatics of qualitative data analysis' (in D. Silverman (ed.), *Qualitative Research*, 4th edition, Sage, 2016: 331–46); Kathy Charmaz's *Constructing Grounded Theory* (Sage, 2006: Chapter 6); Pertti Alasuutari's *Researching Culture: Qualitative Method and Cultural Studies* (Sage, 1995: Chapter 13); Jennifer Mason's *Qualitative Researching* (Sage, 2002: Chapter 7); and Amanda Coffey and Paul Atkinson's *Making Sense of Qualitative Data* (Sage, 1996, Chapter 6)

Discover the chapter's digital resources in your
SILVERMAN FIELD GUIDE

CONTENTS

PART VI
MAKING THE MOST OF YOUR RESEARCH

The two chapters in Part VI consider the aftermath of a finished research project. Depending on the level of your work and the practices of your university, this may involve an oral examination, the possibility of getting a publication and, perhaps, getting a job. Whatever its level, a good research report is always for particular audiences.

TWENTY SIX
Surviving an Oral Examination

Learning Outcomes

By the end of this chapter you will be able to:

- Be reassured that truly horrific PhD orals are very rare.
- Take practical steps to prepare for your oral.
- Know how to function effectively at the oral.

1 INTRODUCTION

When you have finished a BA or an MA thesis, your task is done. Your research paper will now be marked but its grading will be out of your hands. However, if you are working for a PhD, one further task may await you – your oral examination or 'viva'. Here you will be expected to 'defend' your dissertation, and your performance will have an impact on the outcome. For instance, in the UK, your dissertation may pass but you may be required to retake your viva if your performance is weak.

How this viva is conducted will vary between different universities and countries. In the UK, a specialist external examiner will be appointed from outside your university and will take the lead in questioning you. Further questions will come from an internal examiner who may be rather less of a specialist in your area.

In other countries, many more academics may be able to question you. In the Nordic countries, for instance, an 'opponent' will be appointed from outside your university to interrogate you. The viva will be a public affair with members of the audience able to ask questions.

In Scandinavia, your faculty committee are usually passive observers of the dialogue between opponent and candidate. By contrast, in North America, you will face a faculty committee, all of whom may ask you questions. The character of this dialogue can vary considerably, as an American text points out:

> The defense ranges from a congenial ritual in which the student publicly presents his or her findings to an assemblage of receptive 'colleagues', to a more excruciating examination of the quality of the dissertation and grilling of the candidate by an unsympathetic faculty committee. (Rudestam and Newton, 1992: 142)

To use Rudestam and Newton's word, what can a 'grilling' look like? In this chapter, I set out to prepare you for a PhD oral examination, reviewing the mechanics of the oral and its possible outcomes (including the subsequent revisions to your thesis that your examiners may require).

This chapter seeks to offer sensible reassurance. As I will later demonstrate, the viva is not usually quite as awful as you may suspect. However, to prepare you for the worst, I begin with some 'horror' stories.

2 VIVA HORROR STORIES

One student reported a common fear about an impending viva: 'When I went into that room, I was scared – what if they ask me something I do not know, what if they said: this a PhD, you have got to be joking?' Such fears are normal; terrible experiences are much rarer. Rowena Murray (2003: 2) provides four examples of pretty nasty vivas:

- a nine-hour viva
- aggressive examiners who seem to want to break down the candidate
- the candidate forgetting everything she knew ('blank mind syndrome')
- examiner(s) deciding that you have made a serious error – but this is based on a misunderstanding about what you have said and you don't have the confidence to correct them.

I have a horror story of my own to add. Back in the 1960s, I felt confident about submitting my thesis because of the praise it had received from my PhD supervisors.

I was totally unprepared when the external examiner was very critical of what I had written. Indeed, I later learned that it was only my strong defence at the viva that saved me from being failed! Fortunately, the external gave me several pages of suggestions and I managed to put together a revised version which was passed 12 months later.

By now, you may be thoroughly scared. But take comfort. Supervision is much better monitored nowadays and is usually much more effective than the example of the three-meeting supervisor described in Chapter 11. There are also a number of practical steps you can take beforehand to prepare for your examination.

3 PREPARING FOR YOUR ORAL

Examiners need time to read your dissertation. They also have busy diaries. So you will probably have from one to three months between submission of your dissertation and your oral examination. How should you spend this time?

EXPLORE:
TEN VIVA SURVIVAL TIPS

In the immediate weeks after submission, with the viva some way away, you deserve some time off after your exertions – although a break is usually an unavailable luxury to students in full-time employment. However, as your viva approaches, some preparation is very useful. This preparation can take a number of forms, as set out in Table 26.1.

Table 26.1   Preparing for a PhD oral examination

- Revise your thesis, particularly the concluding chapter
- Prepare a list of points you want to get across
- Be ready to explain and to defend any changes to your original research question
- Read up recent work in your field
- Find out about your external and internal examiners' work
- Practise with others in a mock viva

Phillips and Pugh (1994) suggest that summarizing in a sentence each page of your finished thesis can be a very effective way of revising your thesis so that you will be fully in touch with it on the big day. You should then use this summary as a basis for deciding which points you want to try to get across at the examination.

WATCH:
DAVID EXPLAINS IN PERSON

Now is a good time to research your examiners' own work. Reading their latest papers may well inform you about the likely slant of their questions and, perhaps, allow you to look for any links between your work and theirs – although you should first consult your supervisor about whether this is appropriate. Finally, try to find some fellow students or some friendly faculty members prepared to simulate an oral examination.

4 DOING THE ORAL

Remember that, as a result of your research, you are now a specialist. This probably means that you now know more about your topic than your examiners. As Rudestam and Newton put it:

EXPLORE: ORAL EXAM TIPS
EXPLORE: VIVA RESOURCES
EXPLORE: SURVIVING A VIVA

In the best of cases, the oral defense is an opportunity to think about and articulate the implications of your study [for] your own discipline and to be challenged by your committee to claim your right to sit among them as an acknowledged expert in your field of study. (1992: 142)

Being 'an acknowledged expert' is not a licence to wallow in jargon. On the contrary, part of one's expertise is the ability to explain your work in a straightforward way and to make links with the work of others.

So, at the viva, be ready to summarize your main research problem, the contribution of your research and how you would do anything differently. Remember that the oral examination is not a test of memory. So you will be allowed to refer to the text of your thesis as necessary.

In order to add more substance to these points, in Section 7 I have given some details of a Swedish PhD dissertation that I examined a few years ago. While the questions I asked, as opponent, were of course tied to that particular dissertation, I believe that they can give you some flavour of the kind of concerns, both specific and general, that examiners raise at PhD vivas.

As Clive Seale (personal correspondence) has pointed out, the skills you need at an oral examination are not dissimilar to those you need at a job interview. In both situations, it helps to be fairly assertive while respecting the knowledge and experience of your interviewer. Table 26.2 offers some tips for your oral along these lines.

Table 26.2 Tips for the oral examination

- Always say if you have not understood a question; if so, ask for more clarification
- Avoid one-word or one-sentence answers even if the question is a 'closed' one. Use the questions as opportunities to get your point across by making links between the questions and the things you want to say
- Avoid overlong answers which drift far from the original question
- After a sentence or two, ask if you are on the right track and if your examiners want to know more
- Refer to the list of points you want to get across when your examiners ask whether there is anything they have not covered
- Ask your supervisor to make notes of questions and answers. This will be of considerable use if you have to revise your thesis and/or intend to publish any of it

Source: adapted in part from Clive Seale (personal correspondence)

5 OUTCOMES

In most British universities, the possible outcomes of a PhD viva are as follows (see also Phillips and Pugh, 1994: 142–5):

- the immediate award of the PhD – often subject to certain minor corrections or amendments
- the requirement that you put right some weaknesses identified in writing by the examiners (the 'yes, but …' result, as Phillips and Pugh put it) and a given time period (up to two years) to do this
- a pass on the dissertation but a fail on the viva, with an opportunity to resit the latter after a period of up to a year
- the judgement that your dissertation is inadequate, and the examiners cannot see any way in which it can be successfully revised but offer you the lower award of an MPhil degree
- an outright fail with no possibility of resubmission and no offer of any lower degree.

Despite your worst fears, an outright fail is rare. This is less to do with the goodwill of your examiners than with the fact that your supervisors are unlikely to recommend submission unless they believe that your work has a reasonable chance of passing – although the recent punitive policy of the British ESRC towards departments whose funded students take more than four years to submit may change this.

WATCH:
DAVID EXPLAINS IN PERSON

Ask for publishing
advice

WATCH: DAVID EXPLAINS IN PERSON

David's Top Tip 62

If you are passed, remember to ask for advice about what parts of your thesis might be publishable, how you should revise or shorten them, and which journals might be the best place to submit them. Now go out and celebrate!

6 REVISING YOUR THESIS AFTER THE ORAL

In the UK, it is common practice for examiners to require some rewriting of your thesis before they will pass it. After discussion with your supervisor, they will allow you a certain period to undertake such revision – normally between 6 and 18 months.

Following Clive Seale (personal correspondence), I suggest some tips to follow when you are revising a thesis for re-examination:

- Make a list of the main criticisms.
- Make sure your revisions address all of these criticisms.
- Resubmit your thesis together with a separate sheet of paper identifying what you understand the criticisms to have been, how you have addressed them, and the page numbers where this has been done.

7 A CASE STUDY

An example of an actual PhD oral may be helpful. Vesa Leppanen completed his thesis at the Department of Sociology at Lund University in Sweden. I was appointed his opponent because Vesa's work was related to mine analytically (we both use conversation analysis, CA) and substantively (we both had studied communication between healthcare professionals and patients).

A brief summary of the dissertation

Vesa had researched encounters between Swedish district nurses and their elderly patients. These encounters may take place in the patient's home or at a clinic. Their primary clinical purpose is to perform routine tasks like measuring blood pressure or giving injections. Naturally, in the course of these encounters, other matters arise – from the patient raising a problem to the nurse giving advice. A sample of 32 consultations provided just over 10 hours of videotaped and transcribed nurse–patient interaction, half at primary care centres, half in patients' homes. Standard CA notation was used on the audio. Non-verbal activities were reported by descriptions placed immediately above the place in the transcript where they occurred.

Four principal topics were studied:

- how tests and treatments were discussed
- patients' presentations of their concerns
- how nurses delivered test results to patients
- advice-giving about health behaviours.

The dissertation concluded with a summary of the research findings, a practical recommendation that such data is highly appropriate in training nurses (and many other practitioners) and some general implications for future research. Its call for the study of apparently non-problematic research settings and data is a useful reminder that, when studying the world around us, we should seek to discover the extraordinary in the ordinary (Silverman, 2013: Chapter 1).

EXPLORE:
DISSERTATION PUBLICATION

My questions

- What do you see as the main contribution of your research?
- Would you do anything differently now?
- Chapter 4 on tests and treatments reads as very 'descriptive' based on one extended case. Would you agree? How could it be improved?
- On p. 88, you explain that this chapter serves as a background to the other three data chapters. But can you say anything more, for example do you ever meet resistance to tests? Do nurses ever have to work at getting permission?

Several detailed questions on the data analysis follow. Now come some more general points:

- Your data are equally drawn from home and clinic. Why did you decide not to systematically compare these different environments? Don't clinic and home provide very different resources? [I mention one of my past PhDs, by Maura Hunt, who had looked at the problems that community nurses may face in beginning their work in the patient's home, as well as the work of Anssi Peräkylä on doctors' use of X-rays and scans in the clinic to 'prove' diagnoses to patients.]
- Your use of the video material. The only detailed treatment is on pp. 213-18 where you use the video to show how the nurse underlines advice by abandoning other tasks, gazing

at the patient and waving a pill bottle. Why is there relatively little use of the video data elsewhere? [I discuss various possible uses of the video data that might have strengthened the dissertation.]

- Have you ever given feedback to the nurses you studied? If not, why not?
- Your only practical conclusion is about the relevance of this kind of detailed research for professional training. I entirely agree about this, but isn't there more that you can say?
- Your discussion of the analytic implications of your research is not very specific. How does your work advance other well-known [named] studies and findings?

My concluding remarks

This is a fascinating, detailed and orderly study of great analytic interest. I learned a lot from reading it. It is also an exemplary case from which nurses and beginning researchers could learn a great deal about the value of the analytic mentality of CA.

The highlights for me were:

1. Various parts of Chapter 5. First, the most detailed treatment on institutional data about the positioning and functioning of the question: 'How are you?' Second, the discussion about how patients achieve recipiency for the statement of their concerns.
2. Parts of Chapter 7. In particular, nurses finding the right position to deliver advice.
3. An unusually lively methods (or procedures) chapter. This provides a nice natural history of your research and a lovely account of the ethnographic work that preceded it.
4. Throughout, I liked your non-partisan spirit and open-mindedness, particularly towards the judicious combination of CA and ethnography (e.g. p. 44).

Of course, as you show, bad news is usually delayed. So, in this case too. But I really have only two reservations. The first is your somewhat limited use of your video data. The second is your underplaying of the practical relevance of your research.

But, in the context of such a well-crafted dissertation, these are quibbles. I eagerly encourage you to turn parts of your thesis into journal articles. In particular:

- Your excellent summary and critique of much nursing research (pp. 21-7) is highly relevant in a field riddled by crude positivism and **emotionalism.**
- Your account of patients' skills in positioning their statement of their concerns is highly original and publishable (pp. 110-28). Perhaps it could be combined with your comparison (pp. 130-1) with Jefferson on everyday trouble-telling, or perhaps the latter could be a separate article.
- Parts of Chapter 7 where you compare your findings with other [named] research on advice-giving and advice-reception are also highly publishable.

The outcome

I am pleased to say Vesa was awarded his PhD by his local committee. When I last heard, Dr Leppanen had a teaching position at a Swedish university and his supervisor, Professor Ann-Mari Sellerberg, had obtained a substantial research grant for the two of them to study telephone counselling by community nurses.

General implications

1. My two first questions are pretty standard for PhD vivas, namely: 'What do you see as the main contribution of your research?' and 'Would you do anything differently now?' It pays to prepare your answers to such questions!
2. Prepare for constructive criticism of your analysis, for example 'Chapter 4 on tests and treatments reads as very "descriptive" based on one extended case. Would you agree?' This is a nice example of a question where a one-word answer would have been inappropriate. The right strategy here might be to agree in part but point to counter-evidence elsewhere.
3. Prepare to defend your methods and selection of cases, for example 'Your data are equally drawn from home and clinic. Why did you decide not to systematically compare these different environments?' If possible, explain the advantages of not making such a comparison.
4. Be ready to discuss further the contribution of your research to your discipline and (where relevant) to practitioners and policy makers.
5. Expect your examiners to offer advice about which parts of your thesis may be publishable (see my concluding remarks).

8 WRAPPING UP

Although the prospect of a PhD oral is intimidating, horror stories are actually quite rare. Use your revision period to prepare a list of points you want to get across at the examination. Now is also the time to find out about your examiners' own published work. In addition, try to get some practice with others in a mock viva.

At the oral examination, always say if you have not understood a question and, if so, ask for more clarification. Avoid one-word or one-sentence answers even if the question is a 'closed' one. Use the questions as opportunities to get your point across by making links between the questions and the things you want to say. But avoid overlong answers which drift far from the original question. Finally, refer to the list of points you want to get across when your examiners ask whether there is anything they have not covered.

It is also a good idea to ask your supervisor to make notes of questions and answers. This will be of considerable use if you have to revise your thesis and/or intend to publish any of it.

What You Need to Remember

There are many ways to prepare for your oral. You can:

- Revise your thesis, particularly the concluding chapter.
- Prepare a list of points you want to get across and ask your examiners if you are on the right track.
- Be ready to explain and to defend any changes to your original research question.
- Read up recent work in your field.
- Find out about your external and internal examiners' work.
- Practise with others in a mock viva.
- Go online to find advice or discussion groups.

At the oral itself:

- Always say if you have not understood a question; if so, ask for more clarification.
- Avoid one-word or one-sentence answers even if the question is a 'closed' one. Use the questions as opportunities to get your point across by making links between the questions and the things you want to say.
- Avoid overlong answers which drift far from the original question.
- Ask if you are on the right track and if your examiners want to know more.

TRACK:
GOOD PRACTICE FOR ORALS

Your Chapter Checklist

- Prepare for the viva by reading the latest research in your field (including publications by your examiners) and listing the points you wish to get across.
- Practise the viva with your supervisor or other research students.

Exercises

APPLY:
YOUR EXERCISE WORKBOOK

Exercise 1: Get to know your examiners through their own works

To find out about your examiners' own published work, read at least one book or journal article by each of them. As you read, make notes about the following points:

1. What model of social research (see Chapter 7) is being used? How far does it differ from or complement your own? What useful lessons can you learn from these differences or similarities?

2. Are there any theoretical developments, methodological innovations or substantive findings that relate to your own work? If so, how can you bring these out in the oral? If not, how can you demonstrate respect for the examiners' approach while standing up for your own?

3. Examine the writing style in this material. How different is it from your own? What can you learn from these differences (or similarities)? For example, do these simply reflect the differing demands of (say) a scholarly journal and a research dissertation, or are there basic differences of temperament and outlook?

Exercise 2: Conduct a mock oral examination

When you have completed your revision, ask your supervisor or a couple of your fellow students who are familiar with your research to give you a mock oral examination. Following Table 26.2 and using your prepared list of points that you want to get across, try out your skills in answering their questions.

Further Reading

The most useful guides to preparing for oral examinations are: Pat Cryer's *The Research Student's Guide to Success* (Open University Press, 2006: Chapter 24); Estelle Phillips and Derek Pugh's *How To Get a PhD* (Open University Press, 2005: Chapter 10); and Harriet Churchill and Teela Sanders' *Getting Your PhD* (Sage, 2007: Chapter 10).

EXPLORE:
DISSERTATION VIVA

Discover the chapter's digital resources in your
SILVERMAN FIELD GUIDE

TWENTY SEVEN
Getting Published

Learning Outcomes

By the end of this chapter you will be able to:

- Recognize the realistic publishing opportunities for your work.
- Think about the appropriate place to submit your research.
- Work out how to turn your research into something more appropriate for a journal.
- Understand how journal editors and reviewers make decisions about which papers to publish.
- Treat a decision of 'revise' and 'resubmit' as a golden opportunity.

1 INTRODUCTION

When you have finished your research study, you usually want its readership to extend beyond your supervisor and examiners. Don't expect that any more than a handful of people will borrow it from your university library. So, if you want your work to be disseminated, you must publish it.

Publishing your research is work. It will take a good deal of effort, time and patience. It may take you well over a year to publish a manuscript in a refereed journal. The revisions may at times become tedious and far less exciting than the data collection and writing of initial drafts. Reviewers and editors may ask you to change your work significantly and, by the end, your original idea from the first draft may be barely recognizable in the published manuscript. Why then, you might ask, should anyone subject themselves to this process?

The simple answer is that you don't have to publish. Most MA dissertations never go beyond their examiners. Moreover, a considerable number of PhD students complete their dissertations and never publish anything. However, you have to realize the consequences of this choice. Without publications, your job opportunities will most likely be limited.

The discouraging news is that, in these competitive times, it is unlikely that an MA or even a PhD will get you a university post. Certainly, a good reference from your supervisor and other examiners will help. And any teaching experience you have gained is also a plus mark if you are seeking a regular academic post. However, if you have not yet made it into print, faced with people with PhDs and several publications, you may not even make it onto the shortlist – at least at prestigious institutions.

Obviously, your desire to publish is only the first part of the battle. In what follows, I discuss five key practical matters:

- the backstage politics of publishing
- the strategic choices available to you
- understanding the kinds of paper that appeal to the editors of academic journals
- preparing for and dealing with reviewers' comments
- knowing how to write an effective journal article.

2 THE BACKSTAGE POLITICS OF PUBLISHING

In an ideal world, the peer-refereed system of publishing would allow for scholarly writing to be judged purely on the basis of its merits. And for the most part, that is precisely what happens. Yet it would be naive not to acknowledge the presence of other extraneous influences in the world of publishing. A good discussion of such factors is offered in Frank E. Hagan's *Essentials of Research Methods in Criminal Justice and Criminology* (2005: 10–11). Hagan reviews three fascinating, but somewhat disheartening, articles that point to the backstage politics of publishing. The first is Robert Merton's (1968) essay on 'The Matthew effect in science'. Merton's use of the term was inspired by the following biblical passage: 'For unto everyone that hath shall be given, and he shall have abundance: but from him that hath not shall be taken away that which he hath' (Matthew 13:11–12).

In the context of publishing, the Matthew effect implies that previously published authors, especially those who do not challenge canonical views of their discipline, are more likely to be published again. In Merton's words:

> The Matthew effect consists in the accruing of greater increments of recognition for particular scientific contributions to scientists of considerable repute and the withholding of such recognition from scientists who have not yet made their mark. (1968: 58)

Hagan notes that the Matthew effect was tested by Michael Mahoney (1977), who asked 75 reviewers of a psychology journal to evaluate five different versions of a fictitious article. The five versions (a) supported pure behaviourism, (b) negated behaviourism, (c) offered no findings, and (d) and (e) reported mixed results. Of the five versions, the one that agreed with the basic tenets of behaviourism (i.e. did not challenge an established doctrine) was accepted by all the assigned reviewers. On the other hand, the version challenging behaviourism was rejected and highly criticized for its methodology. According to Hagan, in a similar study by Douglas Peters and Stephen Ceci (1982), the researchers took 12 previously published articles and resubmitted them to the same journals where they had appeared two years earlier. The titles were changed and the names of the authors and their universities were altered, the latter being done to reflect less prestigious institutions. Three of the resubmissions were recognized, but eight of the remaining nine were rejected. While the Peters and Ceci study itself was published, one of the authors nearly lost tenure because of it (Hagan, 2005: 10).

Though such events may be isolated and your work may very well be judged on its own merits, practicality and realism dictate that novice authors maintain their associations with their senior mentors to the extent possible. Specifically, it is good practice to establish your publication record by co-authoring papers with a senior scholar in your field. Eventually, your work will be recognized by editors on its own terms, but until then, try to bask in someone else's reflected glory.

Similarly, institutional affiliation seems to play a role in reviewers' evaluations. Therefore, if you are likely to acquire a job in an institution that is less prestigious than the one from which you will receive your PhD, try to earn your first few publications while you are still at your PhD university. That way, you can use that institution's name for your journal submission.

Such backstage politics is underlined by the possible vested interests of reviewers. Along these lines, Marvasti (2016) has proposed a worrying typology of the various orientations of reviewers set out in Table 27.1.

However, realism about the varying motives of reviewers should not slip into cynicism. Reviewing for journals is a thankless, unrewarded task. Marvasti's

Table 27.1   The different orientations of reviewers

- *Editor impressers:* their comments tend to be directed more at the journal editor than the authors. These reviewers write detailed (sometimes irrelevant) reviews with the hope of being invited to contribute their own manuscript to the journal
- *Ego bruisers:* these reviewers seem to receive pleasure from attacking the competition in their field. They have elevated their insulting and backhanded comments to an art form (one can almost hear them giggling at their own handiwork in between the lines)
- *Ego bruised:* these reviewers are primarily concerned with the critique of their own work or that someone neglected to cite them. Their comments sometimes include direct references to their own articles
- *Shoddy:* these folks (usually well-established scholars in their field) do not really read the papers they are asked to comment on. Their reviews contain comments so brief and perfunctory as if to suggest to the editor, 'Don't bother me with this kind of submission again'
- *Helpful:* this is the ideal reviewer. They actually read the papers carefully and provide specific suggestions for improving them

Source: Marvasti (2016: 438)

comments should be balanced by the following observations by the editorial team of the academic journal *Sociology of Health & Illness* (2009):

> We continue to rely heavily on the hard work and excellent support to ourselves and to authors from our referees. We are always impressed and grateful for the level of commitment shown by so many of our referees, whose reports are consistently rated by us and by authors as being of high quality. One example of a type of author response to an 'accept' decision which we often see is as follows:
>
> 'Thanks for the great news! ... the anonymous referees have helped make my paper much stronger at every stage of the reviewing process and I'm delighted that it will appear in a forthcoming issue of your journal.'
>
> But on occasion, too, we have received similar messages from authors of papers which we have rejected, thanking us and our referees for the feedback which the refereeing process has provided. When you referee a paper for us, then, you are doing more than just helping us make a decision: you are making a valuable contribution to the academic standards in our field.

3 STRATEGIC CHOICES

There are three sets of issues here: the medium of publication (usually a book or journal article), the particular outlet chosen (publisher or journal) and the kinds of material that obtain publication. Each of these issues is discussed below.

Books

You may have plans to publish your PhD as a book. But don't count on it! PhDs can be written for a tiny audience – effectively composed of your supervisor, committee or examiners. Before a publisher will even consider publication, they will usually want to know how you plan to revise your thesis to reach a wider audience.

The other thing is that contemporary publishers are not actually standing in line to publish (even revised) PhDs. Unless you can find a kind university press, you will discover that publishers are driven by the commercial need to find books that will sell upwards of 5000 copies. And the sad fact is that even a good research monograph will be unlikely to sell more than 1000 – an amount that probably will mean that its publisher will actually lose money.

It was this situation that, over a quarter of a century ago, made Wolcott (1990) write about how difficult it can be to get your PhD published in entirety. Almost decades later, things are still tougher. Most social science publishers will now only rarely publish research monographs – even by established scholars. So, for most researchers, the answer is to be realistic! Pick out a promising data chapter and rewrite it for a journal.

Choosing a journal

The moral of this story is to plan ahead. So, if your supervisor likes, say, one of your data chapters, discuss with them whether it might not be worth sending it to a journal.

However, not any journal will do. Think twice before sending your paper to a journal that is not specifically devoted to qualitative research or does not welcome research with a small number of cases. Otherwise you may get the kind of negative response illustrated in the following student example.

WHAT I DID: PRIYA
Small Sample Size

It can be challenging to manage credibility issues and publish research if one has a small sample size. For instance, I did a study that explored the effect of hair loss on women's identity work and attitudes towards appearance by conducting over 25 face-to-face and email interviews with women who had hair loss for a variety of reasons (cancer, alopecia, etc.). I had to be extremely creative in recruiting participants because of the sensitive nature of the topic. Since this topic has received little sociological attention, I decided to write a manuscript that focused on the experiences of women with alopecia that had a sample size of eight women. I felt quite comfortable in having such a small sample size since data saturation was present. I submitted the manuscript to several well-known journals that published articles on qualitative research and it was rejected by each one due to its small sample size, despite the paucity of sociological research on this topic. In this case, the empirical value of the research topic could not successfully outweigh the sample size. [Priya Dua, Sociology, University of Missouri–Columbia]

Priya's experience shows that it is important to find the journal which is likely to be most sympathetic to what you have to say because its audience share your interests and its editorial policy is favourable to your kind of ideas and/or data. The following questions may help you to think about what is the right journal for your paper:

- What kinds of articles has it recently published?
- How formal is its academic style? Does this suit you?:
- Which kind of research model is favoured? Is it the one you have used? (Adapted from Gray, 2014: 644)

For example, qualitative researchers should be cautious about journals that expect papers to be written in the standard form of introduction, methods, results and discussion. As Alasuutari (1995: 180–1) points out, this format is likely to be inappropriate to non-quantitative, inductive studies. However, you need to bear in mind that journals that mainly publish quantitative research may sometimes have attractive statistics on impact factors. Table 27.2 indicates what editors of one such journal (*Academy of Management Journal*), where only about one in ten of its contents are based on qualitative research, are looking for when they review qualitative papers.

Table 27.2   Making qualitative research acceptable

1	To bring the reader closer to the phenomenon being studied
2	To engage others in a scholarly conversation by showing how your approach or findings suggest a new direction
3	To show the evidence for your conclusions by describing the who, what, where, when and how the researcher moved from the raw data to their conclusions
4	To juxtapose new theory with existing theory

Source: adapted from Bansal and Corley (2011)

The contents of Table 27.2 are encouraging. These editors add three other comments which fit how qualitative research is presented in this book:

- They argue that you do not need large datasets in a qualitative paper. Instead, in-depth analysis of a few critical incidents can reveal that you are deeply engaging with some phenomenon.
- They encourage qualitative papers which go beyond quantitative findings rather than just being a preface to quantitative research.
- They encourage qualitative papers written in the first person.

So there is no reason to exclude quantitative journals from consideration. However, your most obvious port of call for publication may be qualitative

journals. But bear in mind that such journals do not always have the same policy about legitimate approaches and/or adequate datasets. For instance, a paper submitted by one of my students to a qualitative journal was unexpectedly turned down on the grounds that 'it did not have a big enough dataset'.

So find the right journal. Seek guidance from established academics and look at recent editions of journals they mention. Look out for statements of policy printed in most journals, and note changes of editor and of editorial policy.

Here is one example of a policy statement from *Sociology of Health & Illness* (2009) (*SHI*):

> A word of warning ... any authors who submit to the journal would do well to study its existing content, and work on their own submission so that it conforms to the kind of article that we specialise in. For example, it is wise to use the words 'sociology' or 'sociological' somewhere! We receive too many submissions that appear to be written for other kinds of journals, and we are then unable to send these for review.

Other issues to think about when choosing a journal are its ranking or impact and how speedily it makes decisions about submitted papers. Many journals publish statistics about these matters. For instance, in 2009, the website of *SHI* gave the following information:

- two-year impact factor: 1.845
- five-year impact factor: 2.899
- ranked sixth out of 99 world sociology journals
- average submission to final decision: 54 days.

Responding to editors' decisions

Once you have submitted, don't be discouraged by a rejection. Most journal articles are rejected or returned with a request for substantial revision. So treat the outcome as a learning experience. As Marvasti puts it:

> Most journal articles are rejected or returned with a request for substantial revision from the reviewers whose comments are returned to the author along with a letter from the editor. If the editor's letter contains the phrase 'revise-and-resubmit', especially when

preceded by 'strongly encourage you to', that is very good news. In revising the paper, authors are advised to give special attention to the reviewer comments that were echoed by the editor. In other words, one may ignore some of the reviewers' comments, but it would be a huge mistake to set aside the editor's suggestions. (2011: 391)

Be prepared for challenging comments, and don't expect others to be surprised by requests for revision ('They said what?', Churchill and Sanders, 2007: 90). Wendy Hulko's attempts to publish her dissertation (which used grounded theory) are documented next.

EXPLORE:
ARTICLE REJECTION RECOVERY

WHAT I DID: WENDY

Sometimes Numbers Matter

I used grounded theory methodology for my doctoral research on the relationships between the experiences of older people with dementia and the intersections of 'race', class, ethnicity and gender. My estimated sample size was 12 older people with dementia and their significant others and, through theoretical sampling, I planned to ensure that participants ranged from multiply marginalized to multiply privileged on the basis of their class, gender, 'race' and ethnicity.

Believing that I had achieved theoretical saturation, I stopped recruiting participants once I had a diverse sample of eight older people with dementia, with whom I had spent a considerable amount of time over the course of three individual interviews (person with dementia), two to three group observation sessions (person with dementia, his/her significant others, other members of his/her social world), and one joint focus group (persons with dementia and their significant others). Nevertheless, the sample size became the big issue when it came to publishing my research. I could not understand the amount of attention being placed on the small n when this was clearly a qualitative study that had met the trustworthiness criteria – the standards for judging qualitative research. In the end, I realized that focusing on the eight older people with dementia with whom I had spent more than 75 hours over a nine-month period of data collection and data analysis was not doing my study sufficient justice, as far as editors and peer reviewers were concerned. I felt that I needed to count the number of data collection points (43), include the more than 50 additional people who participated in the study through the participant observation sessions (and signed consent forms and/or photo release forms), and then distinguish between my primary sample of 8 and my secondary sample of 50+. In a sense, this meant playing the numbers game and representing the

(Continued)

(Continued)

research differently than I had in my theoretically complex and methodologically dense PhD thesis. However, I did manage to find a way to do so that was honest and did not misrepresent the qualitative nature of the study; for example, I presented the findings (categories or themes) in a purely qualitative fashion (see Hulko, 2009), so as to avoid producing a 'quasi-quantitative' representation of qualitative research. [Wendy Hulko, Public Health Sciences, Toronto]

Like Priya, Wendy was trapped in what she calls 'the numbers game'. However, Wendy refused to be discouraged after her paper was initially rejected. She eventually realized that, in return for a submission, you are very likely to get a set of (often detailed) referees' comments upon which you can base a revised submission.

Trust the referees

WATCH: DAVID EXPLAINS IN PERSON

David's Top Tip 63

Treat referees' comments as gold dust. However biased you might think they are, they inform you, in practical detail, of the external audience outside (what may be) your cosy relationship with your supervisor. So now you can see what might be required to make your way in the academic world. If your resubmission is not much better received, you probably have only yourself to blame.

Recognizing the format for a journal article

Above all, bear in mind that journal articles (usually around 6000 words) are often much shorter than data chapters from a PhD. This can make things very difficult for you since, in a shorter space, you must fill in your audience about the overall orientation of your research. So, in writing a journal article, you must, at one and the same time, be highly focused but also provide a proper context.

Easier said than done! How do you write a paper that is likely to be published? And how do you cope with such strict word limits? Don't you need more rather than fewer words to explain the context of your research?

Question-based titles yield more citations

WATCH: DAVID EXPLAINS IN PERSON

David's Top Tip 64

Think about having a question as your title. Ben Goldacre reports a study that showed papers with questions in their title got downloaded more frequently ('Bad Science', *Guardian*, 15 October 2011)

There are five quick solutions to these dilemmas (further advice is provided by Phelps et al., 2007: 276):

- Select a topic which will be the most intriguing to readers of this journal.
- Ensure that this topic can be handled with a limited number of data extracts.
- Provide the appropriate context for your work: for instance, your audience will not need to be reminded about the basic assumptions of research in their area.
- Stick rigidly to the point throughout.
- If necessary, offer further data on a website.

The rest of this chapter will expand upon this advice. Later I will discuss how to focus a journal article within the required word length. Such focus, of course, requires that you have a good sense of what journal editors are looking for. So now I will look in more detail at the criteria used by academic journals to make their decisions.

4 WHAT JOURNALS ARE LOOKING FOR

The policy of academic journals may vary by their focus, discipline or audience. As I have already noted, many quantitatively oriented journals expect their articles to have a standard format which assumes that all research has an initial hypothesis and that some form of random sampling will be employed. Equally, journals that seek to appeal to practitioners and other non-specialists will be particularly interested in looking for papers that set out to have this wider appeal.

Despite this degree of variation, my experience suggests that there are several criteria that recur in referees' comments in the kind of qualitative journals to which you might submit a paper. These criteria are set out in Table 27.3.

Table 27.3 indicates what to do if you want your submitted piece to have a reasonable chance of success. It, therefore, implies a series of 'don'ts':

Table 27.3   Evaluation of qualitative articles

1	Goodness of fit between the model chosen and what is actually delivered
2	Internal coherence
3	Showing something 'new' when compared with past work
4	Speaking to the interests of the journal's target audience
5	Clear presentation

Source: adapted from Loseke and Cahill (2004)

- Don't cite models or approaches if they are mere window-dressing.
- Don't vary the format; announce a clear structure at the start and stick to it.
- Don't forget that your paper should contribute to an ongoing conversation of scholars in your area.
- Don't waste space defending approaches already familiar to readers of the journal.

Balance your arguments with existing stances

WATCH: DAVID EXPLAINS IN PERSON

David's Top Tip 65

Your paper cannot be original unless it demonstrates what it does better than earlier work. So refer to the crucial publications in your area. However, don't spend so much time reviewing the literature that you have little space for your own arguments. This is always a matter of *balance*.

5 REVIEWERS' COMMENTS

As well as these general points, it is also useful to have advance warning of the specific kind of criticisms that reviewers make about the submissions they see. Since other people may be quite sensitive about showing you the critical reviews they have received, I have set out below extracts from some of my (usually anonymous) reviews during the past few years. Naturally, I've tried to delete any phrases that might identify the paper or the author. No doubt I am still going to make myself very unpopular by giving these examples!

To help you follow these comments, I have grouped them as 'good news' and 'bad news'. Each section contains portions of comments about many papers.

Good news

- A fascinating topic with some nice data.
- This is an interesting paper, using theoretically generated analysis on a practically relevant topic.
- This paper deals with an important issue. As presently written, it is highly accessible to practitioners and patients.
- The paper is based on an apparently well-transcribed piece of data.

- The data chosen are very manageable.
- This is a carefully done study and brings out some important practical issues.
- This is a highly ambitious methodological paper. Its claim to originality, I take it, is that several different methods can be combined to shed more light on a text than any one alone. There is considerable insight in the way in which these methods are used.
- This paper discusses some potentially interesting data. It uses an approach which, I presume, will be relatively unfamiliar to readers of the journal. Quite correctly, therefore, the author(s) take up a fair bit of space explaining the approach used.

Bad news

I have grouped these 'bad news' comments under several headings.

Over-ambition

- I think it currently tries to do too much.
- Unfortunately, the abstract promises much more than is ever delivered.
- So many issues are raised that it is difficult for any to be developed properly. Each would make a separate paper. Given so many issues, it is not surprising that the data analysis is rather thin and not really linked to the literature review.

Over-generality

- The broad-brush approach adopted here I found frustrating. There is no attempt to ground the argument in a piece of data.

Unanalytic

- For the most part, the observations on the data strike me as commonsensical. To develop this paper further, much more use needs to be made of the vast literature on this subject based on material of this kind.
- The final sentence of the abstract is trite and unnewsworthy.
- The abstract sets the tone for the paper. It lacks theoretical and methodological orientation and is purely descriptive.
- Although a literature review is attempted, it appears to have provided very few analytic insights because the data themselves are simply organized and explained by categories deriving from the subjects.
- The analysis of data only begins more than halfway through the paper and is very thin.
- It hardly analyses its data at all and should be rejected.
- The paper works by assertion. For instance, it simply isn't always the case that [X follows Y].
- Unfortunately, the data analysis is very thin indeed, barely rising above descriptions which are sometimes banal.

Inconsistency

- Methodologically, the approach does not fit the issues that the author wants to address.

Methodological failings

- I found the citation of 'cases' less than convincing. While space constraints always limit the number of data extracts one can use, the paper fails to give any sense that deviant cases were analysed and that prior assumptions were in any way tested by the data.
- Unfortunately, the research design and data analysis are deeply conventional (and, in my view, flawed) and the critique of [a particular approach] is misplaced.

Lack of originality

- The paper discusses a contentious methodological issue. It is also an issue that has been discussed in a mountain of publications over the last 10 years. Therefore, it is particularly hard to say anything fresh about the topic.

Lack of clarity

- I am unclear about the relevance of the approach used; the presence of several traditional assumptions which sit uneasily with it; and the issue of practical relevance.
- I don't understand the first sentence of the abstract.

Lack of recipient design

- The section on theory is, I feel, inappropriate. Readers who know about this already will be bored, and readers who do not will not want to cope with a theoretical discussion before they get to the data. Much better, then, to introduce the required elements of theory in the course of the data analysis.
- You may lose your international audience by going straight into issues relating to one small country.

I hope that my present readers will not be intimidated by these comments. Do treat them as providing guidance about practices best avoided. However, I try never to be merely negative. Below are some suggestions I have made to authors and one from another reviewer.

Suggestions

- I would like the paper to be revised to become sharper in focus and to take account of other relevant work.
- You need an introduction setting out the *general* themes. Then an early data extract would whet the reader's appetite.
- I suggest that you submit your revised draft to a native English speaker. Currently, there are multiple infelicities.
- If space allowed, the analysis would also benefit from comparison with one more case.
- The present conclusion combines analytic *descriptions* of the findings and practical recommendations. Instead, I would like to see the practical conclusions separated and the paper's analytic *contribution* clarified.

- I understand that word limits cast severe constraints on the amount of data shown. However, I think that your argument would be more effective if rather more data were shown. One way to do this would be to offer some simple tabulation of all your cases to see if they fit what you say about your four extracts. Another possibility would be to locate and analyse one extract where misunderstandings appeared to occur.
- I would like to see a more developed theoretical framing of the paper. The one it has now is quite general, which makes it difficult to give a clear contribution. With a good framing, I believe your empirical study can make a good contribution and I therefore wish you the best luck with the work of crafting your paper. (Other reviewer)

It may be the case that my own reviewing methods are idiosyncratic and even unfair. If so, I hope you never come across me as a reviewer! However, every reviewer is likely to attend to the word limits of the journal. I now turn to the art of writing a short journal article.

6 HOW TO WRITE A SHORT JOURNAL ARTICLE

As already noted, most journals nowadays cap papers at around 6000 words. Yet no doubt you want to context your research – and you have so much data and so many findings. How can you present your research in such a small frame?

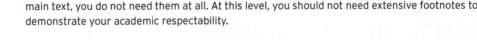
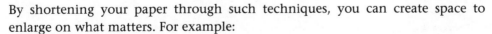

EXPLORE: SUBMITTING JOURNAL ARTICLES

There are three ways to shorten a paper:

- Stick rigidly to the point (e.g. one topic, one case, one theory, one model, one method).
- If you are working within an existing approach or model, don't waste time defending it (reinventing the wheel).
- Consider whether you need all your footnotes. Surely if they are not worthy of being in your main text, you do not need them at all. At this level, you should not need extensive footnotes to demonstrate your academic respectability.

By shortening your paper through such techniques, you can create space to enlarge on what matters. For example:

- focusing on a topic that will intrigue readers of this journal (e.g. one relating to a recent debate)
- demonstrating credibility by combining intensive and extensive methods (e.g. short data extracts and simple tabulations)
- writing a conclusion that displays lateral thinking, for instance by relating your substantive account to a broader area.

Finally, if your paper is still too long, consider splitting it up into different topics appropriate for several journals. Working the same material in a number of different ways is what Marx (1997) has called **leverage**.

7 WRAPPING UP

Publications are good for academic careers. They also can provide an outlet for your key data chapters as well as for beloved draft chapters that you decided were too peripheral to be included in the final version of your thesis.

Getting published depends upon making a number of strategic choices (e.g. book or journal article; which journal to select). There are several ways of improving your chance of getting your paper accepted by a journal. First, 'decide on what you wish to focus. What is your theoretical story?' (Strauss and Corbin, 1990: 246). Second, you need to ask yourself:

> Do I need this detail in order to maximize the clarity of the analytic discussion, and/or to achieve maximum substantive understanding? (1990: 247)

Remember that your audience are both bigger than and very different from the small audience for your thesis. So ruthlessly strip out inappropriate references and material and recontext your work. As Wolcott (1990: 51) puts it, when writing a journal article, 'dedissertationalize' your work. Don't expect to get your paper accepted as it is. Make use of the referees' comments as helpful encouragements to rewrite a better article.

Finally, you should try to write a compelling argument. Jay Gubrium (personal communication) has suggested that much qualitative data is 'inherently' interesting. Take advantage of this and use the interest that the reader may have in your material to your advantage. Tease, entice and puzzle your readers.

What You Need to Remember

There are at least six ways of improving your chances of getting a paper accepted by a journal:

- Find a focus.
- Avoid too much detail.
- Redefine your audience.
- Expect an initial rejection and make use of referees' comments in a second submission.
- Make a compelling case.
- Don't be discouraged by journal referees' critical comments – treat them as gold dust.

Your Chapter Checklist

- Have you read the recent issues of the journal to which you are submitting?
- Have you avoided polishing your article too much prior to submission?
- Are you prepared for rejection or being asked to resubmit?
- When resubmitting have you listed how your revised paper meets the editor's suggestions?

TRACK:
GETTING PUBLISHED

Exercises

Exercise 1: Review papers from journals which might be interested in your research

1. Find two different academic journals that might be interested in your research.
2. Review recent papers in each journal in order to establish themes in which the journals are interested and styles of presenting research.
3. Recipient design your research findings for each journal.

APPLY:
YOUR EXERCISE WORKBOOK

Exercise 2: Practice being a referee

Nigel Gilbert (2008a) suggests choosing a journal article written by someone else and writing a review of it as if you were the referee. If you need guidance on what to look for, use some of the 'good news' and 'bad news' lines of approach found in this chapter.

Now ask your supervisor to read your review. Use the feedback you get to:

1. Think critically about how you might publish your own work.
2. Invite your supervisor to ask book review editors to send books to you for review in journals (this is one way to get a first step on the publications ladder!).

Further Reading

Useful sources are: Donna Loseke and Spenser Cahill's chapter 'Publishing qualitative manuscripts' in C. Seale et al. (eds) *Qualitative Research Practice* (Sage, 2004); Harry Wolcott's little book *Writing Up Qualitative Research* (Sage, 2009: Chapter 7); and Nigel Gilbert's chapter 'Writing about social research' in N. Gilbert (ed.) *Researching Social*

EXPLORE: EFFECTIVE ARTICLE PRESENTATION
EXPLORE: IMPROVING PUBLISHING CHANCES
EXPLORE: PUBLISHING SUCCESSFULLY

Life (Sage, 2008b: Chapter 21). Amir Marvasti's chapter 'Writing qualitative research: practice genre and audience' in D. Silverman (ed.) *Qualitative Research* (Sage, 2016: 439–42) gives some useful advice about online publishing. If your area is management, one journal recently published guidelines for submitted qualitative papers: 'The coming of age for qualitative research: embracing the diversity of qualitative methods', *Academy of Management Journal*, 2011, 54 (2), 233–7.

Discover the chapter's
digital resources in your
SILVERMAN FIELD GUIDE

Appendix: Transcription Symbols

[ ]	Brackets: onset and offset of overlapping talk
=	Equals sign: no gap between two utterances
(0.0)	Timed pause: silence measured in seconds and tenths of seconds
(.)	A pause of less than 0.2 seconds
.	Period (stop): falling or terminal intonation
,	Comma: level intonation
?	Question mark: rising intonation
↑	Rise in pitch
↓	Fall in pitch
-	A dash at the end of a word: an abrupt cutoff
<	Immediately following talk is 'jump started', i.e. starts with a rush
><	Faster-paced talk than the surrounding talk
< >	Slower-paced talk than the surrounding talk
____	Underlining: some form of stress, audible in pitch or amplitude
:	Colon(s): prolongation of the immediately preceding sound
° °	Degree signs surrounding a passage of talk: talk with lower volume than the surrounding talk
.hh	A row of h's prefixed by a dot: an inbreath
hh	A row of h's without a dot: an outbreath
WORD	Capital letters: utterance, or part thereof, that is spoken much louder than the surrounding talk

(word)	Utterance or part of it in parentheses: uncertainty on the transcriber's part, but a likely possibility
( )	Empty parentheses: something is being said, but no hearing can be achieved
(( ))	Double parentheses: transcriber's descriptions of events, rather than representations of them.

Source: adapted by A. Peräkylä from Atkinson and Heritage (1984)

Glossary

Analytic induction   The equivalent to the statistical testing of quantitative associations to see if they are greater than might be expected at random (random error). Using AI, the researcher examines a case, and, where appropriate, redefines the phenomenon and reformulates a hypothesis until a universal relationship is shown.

Anecdotalism   Found where research reports appear to tell entertaining stories or anecdotes but fail to convince the reader of their scientific credibility.

CAQDAS   Computer-Assisted Qualitative Data Analysis Software.

Case study   Research based on the study of a limited number of naturally occurring settings.

Chicago School   A form of sociological ethnography usually assumed to originate in the 1920s when students at the University of Chicago were instructed to put down their theory textbooks and to get out onto the streets of their city and use their eyes and ears. It led to a series of studies of the social organization of the city and of the daily life of various occupational groups.

Coding   Putting data into theoretically defined categories in order to analyse them.

Cognitive anthropology   Attempts to understand the structures that organize how people perceive the world. This leads to the production of ethnographies, or conceptually derived descriptions, of whole cultures, focused on how people communicate.

Concepts   Clearly specified ideas deriving from a particular *model*.

Constructionism   A model which encourages researchers to focus upon how phenomena come to be what they are through the close study of interaction in different contexts. It is opposed to *naturalism*.

Content analysis   Involves establishing categories and systematic linkages between them, and then counting the number of instances when those categories are used in a particular item of text.

Contextual sensitivity   Involves the recognition that apparently uniform social institutions (e.g. 'tribes', 'families', 'crime') take on different meanings in different contexts.

Continuer   An utterance which signals to a listener that what they have just said has been understood and that they should now continue (see *conversation analysis*).

Control group   A group not given some stimulus provided to another group; a control group is used for comparative purposes.

Conversation analysis   A qualitative approach based on an attempt to describe people's methods for producing orderly talk-in-interaction. It derives from the work of Sacks (1992).

Credibility   The extent to which any research claim has been shown to be based on evidence.

Culture   A common set of beliefs, values and behaviours.

Deviant case   In qualitative research, analysis which involves testing provisional hypotheses by 'negative' or 'discrepant' cases until all the data can be incorporated in your explanation.

Discourse analysis   The study of 'the way versions of the world, of society, events, and inner psychological worlds are produced in discourse' (Potter, 2004: 202).

Emotionalism   A model of social research in which the primary issue is to generate data which gives an authentic insight into people's experiences. Emotionalists tend to favour open-ended interviews (see Gubrium and Holstein, 1997).

Empirical   Based on evidence through observation or experiment.

Empiricism   An approach which believes that evidence about the world does not depend upon *models* or *concepts* (see *positivism*).

Ethics   Guidelines or principles relating to good professional practice.

Ethnography   Puts together two different words: 'ethno' means 'folk', while 'graph' derives from 'writing'. Ethnography refers, then, to social science writing about particular folks.

Ethnomethodology   The study of folk – or members' – methods. It seeks to describe the methods that persons use in doing social life. Ethnomethodology is not a methodology but a theoretical model.

Extensive analysis   Searching through your whole dataset to test hypotheses generated by analysis of one or two cases.

Field   The setting or place where *ethnographic* research takes place.

Fieldnotes   Records of observations and speech fragments arising from the field.

Focus groups   Group discussions usually based upon stimuli (topics, visual aids) provided by the researcher.

Formal theories   Theories which relate findings from one setting to many situations or settings (see Glaser and Strauss, 1967).

Frame   Using the metaphor of a picture frame, Goffman (1974) applies this term to reference how people treat what is currently relevant and irrelevant. Such treatment defines the frame through which a setting is constituted.

Gatekeeper   Someone who is able to grant or refuse access to the *field*.

Genealogical   Following Foucault (1977; 1979), the study of the ways in which discourses have been structured at different historical points.

Generalizability   The extent to which a finding in one setting can be applied more generally.

Grand theory   A term used by Mills (1959) to describe highly abstract speculation which has little or no use in research.

Grounded theory   A theory which involves three stages: an initial attempt to develop categories which illuminate the data; an attempt to 'saturate' these categories with many appropriate cases in order to demonstrate their relevance; and the attempt to develop these categories into more general analytic frameworks with relevance outside the setting.

Hermeneutics   An approach concerned with interpretation (originally derived from the study of biblical texts).

Hyphenated phenomena   A concept which refers to the way in which apparently stable social phenomena (a 'tribe' or a 'family') take on different meanings in different contexts. Thus a-family-as-seen-by-the-oldest-child takes on a different meaning than a-family-as-seen-by-the-youngest (see *constructionism*).

Hypothesis   A testable proposition often based on an educated guess.

Idiom   A term used by Gubrium and Holstein (1997) to describe a set of analytical preferences for particular concepts, styles of research and ways of writing (see *model*).

Inductive   Based on the study of particular cases rather than just derived from a theory.

Interactionism   A theory, commonly used in qualitative sociological research, which assumes that our behaviour and perceptions derive from processes of interaction with other people.

Intervening variable   A *variable* which is influenced by a prior factor and goes on to influence another. Commonly used in quantitative research to work out which statistical association may be spurious.

Interview society   A term used by Atkinson and Silverman (1997) to point out the ways in which interviews have become a central medium for understanding who we are.

Laboratory study   A method used in quantitative research in which subjects are placed in an artificial environment and their responses to various stimuli are measured.

Leverage   Used by Marx (1997) to describe ways of finding multiple publishing outlets for one piece of research.

Low-inference descriptors   Recording observations 'in terms that are as concrete as possible, including verbatim accounts of what people say, for example, rather than researchers' reconstructions of the general sense of what a person said, which would allow researchers' personal perspectives to influence the reporting' (Seale, 1999: 148) (see *reliability*).

Member   Used by Garfinkel (1967) to refer to participants in society. It is a shorthand term for 'collectivity member' (see *ethnomethodology*).

Membership categorization device   A collection of categories (e.g. baby, Mummy, Daddy = family; male, female = gender) and some rules about how to apply these categories.

Methodology   Refers to the choices we make about appropriate *models*, cases to study, methods of data gathering, forms of data analysis, etc., in planning and executing a research study.

Methods   Specific research techniques. These include quantitative techniques, like statistical correlations, as well as techniques like observation, interviewing and audio recording.

Mixed methods   Usually means combining quantitative and qualitative research. Can also mean using two or more qualitative datasets gathered through different methods (e.g. interviews and observation) (see *triangulation*).

Model   Provides an overall framework for how we look at reality (e.g. positivism, naturalism and constructionism). Models tell us what reality is like and the basic elements it contains ('ontology') and what are the nature and status of knowledge ('epistemology'). See also *idiom*.

Narrative analysis   The study of the organization of stories (e.g. beginning, middle and end; plots and characters) that makes stories meaningful or coherent in a form appropriate to the needs of a particular occasion.

Naturalism   A model of research which seeks to minimize presuppositions in order to witness subjects' worlds in their own terms (Gubrium and Holstein, 1997).

Naturally occurring data   Data which derives from situations which exist independently of the researcher's intervention.

Normative   Pertaining to a norm or value; prescriptive.

Operational definition   Working definition which allows the measurement of some *variable* within quantitative research.

Paradigm   A conceptual framework (see *model*).

Paradigmatic   A term used in structuralism to indicate a polar set of *concepts* or activities where the presence of one denies the existence of the other (e.g. a red traffic light).

Participant observation   A method that assumes that, in order to understand the world 'first hand', you must participate yourself rather than just observe at a distance. This method was championed by the early anthropologists but is shared by some ethnographers.

Positivism   A model of the research process which treats 'social facts' as existing independently of the activities of both participants and researchers. For positivists, the aim is to generate data which is valid and reliable, independently of the research setting.

Postmodernism   A contemporary approach which questions or seeks to deconstruct both accepted concepts (e.g. the 'subject' and the 'field') and scientific method. Postmodernism is both an analytical model and a way of describing contemporary society as a pastiche of insecure and changing elements.

Preference organization   A concept derived from *conversation analysis* which suggests that recipients of actions recognize a preference for what they should do next.

Recipient designed   Work that is designed for a particular audience (the term derives from *conversation analysis* where it is used to describe how all actions are implicitly designed in this way).

Reflexivity   A term deriving from *ethnomethodology* where it is used to describe the self-organizing character of all interaction so that any action provides for its own context. Mistakenly used to refer to self-questioning by a researcher.

Relativism   A value position where we resist taking a position because we believe that, since everything is relative to its particular context, it should not be criticized.

Reliability   'The degree of consistency with which instances are assigned to the same category by different observers or by the same observer on different occasions' (Hammersley, 1992: 67) (see *validity*).

Researcher-provoked (data)   Data which is actively created and, therefore, would not exist apart from the researcher's intervention (e.g. interviews, focus groups).

Respondent validation   Involves taking one's findings back to the subjects being studied. Where these people verify one's findings, it is argued, one can be more confident of their validity.

Rewriting of history   A term used by Garfinkel (1967) to refer to the way in which any account retrospectively finds reasons for any past event.

Romanticism   An approach taken from nineteenth-century thought in which authenticity is attached to personal experiences (see *emotionalism*).

Sample, sampling   A statistical procedure for finding cases to study. Sampling has two functions: it allows you to feel confident about the representativeness of your sample, and such representativeness allows you to make broader inferences.

Semiotics   The study of signs (from speech, to fashion, to Morse code).

Social structure   A term used in sociology and anthropology to describe the institutional arrangements of a particular society or group (e.g. family and class structures).

Social survey   A quantitative method involving the study of large numbers of people, often through the use of questionnaires.

Structuralism   A *model* used in anthropology which aims to show how single cases relate to general social forms. Structural anthropologists draw upon French social and linguistic theory of the early twentieth century, notably Ferdinand de Saussure and Emile Durkheim. They view behaviour as the expression of a 'society' which works as a 'hidden hand' constraining and forming human action.

Subculture   A set of beliefs, values and behaviours shared by a particular group.

Substantive theory A theory about a particular situation or group. Can be used to develop *formal theory*.

Syntagmatic A term used within *semiotics* to denote the order in which related elements occur (e.g. how colours follow one another in traffic lights).

Textual data Documents and/or images which have become recorded without the intervention of a researcher (e.g. through an interview).

Theories Ideas which arrange sets of concepts to define and explain some phenomenon.

Thick description A term from anthropology and *ethnography* used to describe research reports which analyse the multiple levels of meaning in any situation (see Geertz, 1973).

Triangulation The comparison of different kinds of data (e.g. quantitative and qualitative) and different methods (e.g. observation and interviews) to see whether they corroborate one another.

Turn-taking The sequential organization of speech acts (see *conversation analysis*).

Validity 'The extent to which an account accurately represents the social phenomena to which it refers' (Hammersley, 1990: 57). Researchers respond to validity concerns by describing 'the warrant for their inferences' (Fielding and Fielding, 1986: 12) (see *reliability*).

Variables Factors which are isolated from one another in order to measure their relationship; usually described in quantitative research.

References

Acourt, P. (1997) 'Progress, utopia and intellectual practice: arguments for the resurrection of the future'. Unpublished PhD thesis, University of London, Goldsmiths College.

Alasuutari, P. (1995) *Researching Culture: Qualitative Method and Cultural Studies*. London: Sage.

Antaki, C. and Rapley, M. (1996) '"Quality of life" talk: the liberal paradox of psychological testing'. *Discourse and Society*, 7 (3), 293–316.

Arber, S. (1993) 'The research process'. In N. Gilbert (ed.), *Researching Social Life* (pp. 62–80). London: Sage.

Atkinson, J.M. (1978) *Discovering Suicide*. London: Macmillan.

Atkinson, J.M. and Heritage, J.C. (eds) (1984) *Structures of Social Action*. Cambridge: Cambridge University Press.

Atkinson, P. (1992) 'The ethnography of a medical setting: reading, writing and rhetoric'. *Qualitative Health Research*, 2 (4), 451–74.

Atkinson, P. and Silverman, D. (1997) 'Kundera's immortality: the interview society and the invention of self'. *Qualitative Inquiry*, 3 (3), 324–45.

Avis, M., Bond, M. and Arthur, A. (1997) 'Questioning patient satisfaction: an empirical investigation in two outpatient clinics'. *Social Science and Medicine*, 44 (1), 85–92.

Baarts, C. (2009) 'Stuck in the middle: research ethics caught between science and politics'. *Qualitative Research*, 9, 423–39.

Back, L. (2004) 'Politics, research and understanding'. In C. Seale, G. Gobo, J.F. Gubrium and D. Silverman (eds), *Qualitative Research Practice* (pp. 261–75). London: Sage.

Baker, C. (2002) 'Ethnomethodological analysis of interviews'. In J. Gubrium and J. Holstein (eds), *Handbook of Interview Research* (pp. 777–96). Thousand Oaks, CA: Sage.

Baker, C. and Keogh, J. (1995) 'Accounting for achievement in parent–teacher interviews', *Human Studies*, 18 (2/3), 263–300.

Baker, P. (2006) *Using Corpora in Discourse Analysis*. London: Continuum.

Bamberg, M. (1997) 'A constructivist approach to narrative development'. In M. Bamberg (ed.), *Narrative Development: Six Approaches* (pp. 89–132). Mahwah, NJ: Erlbaum.

Bansal, P. and Corley, K. (2011) 'From the editors: the coming of age for qualitative research. Embracing the diversity of qualitative methods'. *Academy of Management Journal*, 54 (2), 233–7.

Barbour, R. (2007a) *Doing Focus Groups*. London: Sage.

Barbour, R. (2007b) *Introducing Qualitative Research*. London: Sage.

Barker, M. (2003) 'Assessing the "quality" in qualitative research: the case of text–audience relations'. *European Journal of Communication*, 18 (3), 315–35.

Baruch, G. (1981) 'Moral tales: parents' stories of encounters with the health profession'. *Sociology of Health & Illness*, 3 (3), 275–96.

Bazeley, P. and Jackson, K. (2013) *Qualitative Data Analysis with NVivo*. London: Sage.

Becker, H. (1963) *Outsiders: Studies in the Sociology of Deviance*. New York: Free Press.

Becker, H. (1986) *Writing for Social Scientists*. Chicago: University of Chicago Press.

Becker, H. (1998) *Tricks of the Trade: How to Think about Your Research While Doing It*. Chicago: University of Chicago Press.

Becker, H. (2004) 'Comment on Kevin D. Haggerty, "Ethics creep: governing social science research in the name of ethics"'. *Qualitative Sociology*, 27 (4), 415–16.

Becker, H. (2010) 'The art of comparison: lessons from the master, Everett C. Hughes'. *Sociologica*, 2/2010 (online). http://www.sociologica.mulino.it/journal/article/index/Article/Journal:ARTICLE:423.

Becker, H. and Geer, B. (1960) 'Participant observation: the analysis of qualitative field data'. In R. Adams and J. Preiss (eds), *Human Organization Research: Field Relation and Techniques*. Homewood, IL: Dorsey.

Bell, J. (2005) *Doing Your Research Project*, 4th edn. Buckingham: Open University Press.

Bloor, M. (1978) 'On the analysis of observational data: a discussion of the worth and uses of inductive techniques and respondent validation'. *Sociology*, 12 (3), 545–57.

Bloor, M. (1983) 'Notes on member validation'. In R. Emerson (ed.), *Contemporary Field Research: A Collection of Readings*. Boston, MA: Little, Brown.

Bloor, M. (2004) 'Addressing social problems through qualitative research'. In D. Silverman (ed.), *Qualitative Research: Theory, Method and Practice*, 2nd edn (pp. 304–23). London: Sage.

Bloor, M. (2011) 'Addressing social problems through qualitative research'. In D. Silverman (ed.), *Qualitative Research: Theory, Method and Practice*, 3rd edn (pp. 399–415). London: Sage.

Bloor, M., Frankland, J., Thomas, M. and Robson, K. (2001) *Focus Groups in Social Research*. London: Sage.

Blumer, H. (1969) *Symbolic Interactionism*. Englewood Cliffs, NJ: Prentice Hall.

Boden, D. and Zimmerman, D.H. (eds) (1991) *Talk and Social Structure: Studies in Ethnomethodology and Conversation Analysis* (pp. 44–71). Cambridge: Polity.

Borgnakke, K. (1996) 'Pædagogisk Feltforskning Og Procesanalytisk Kortlægning – En Forskningsberetning' (Educational Field Research and Process Analytical Mapping – A Research Report). Unpublished PhD thesis, Danmarks Lærerhøjskole.

Bradbury, M. (1988) *Unsent Letters*. London: André Deutsch.

Braun, V. and Clarke, V. (2013) *Successful Qualitative Research*. London: Sage.

British Research Councils (1996) *Priorities News*, Spring. Swindon: ESRC.

Bröer, C., Moerman, G., Wester, J.C., Malamud, R.L., Schmidt, L., Stoopendaal, A., Kruiderink, N., Hansen, C. and Sjølie, H. (2016) 'Open online research: developing software and method for collaborative interpretation'. *Forum: Qualitative Research*, 17 (3), Art. 2. www.qualitative-research.net/index.php/fqs/article/view/2388

Bryman, A. (1988) *Quantity and Quality in Social Research*. London: Unwin Hyman.

Buchanan, D.R. (1992) 'An uneasy alliance: combining qualitative and quantitative research methods'. *Health Education & Behavior*, 19 (1), 117–35.

Burton, D. (ed.) (2000) *Research Training for Social Scientists*. London: Sage.

Buscatto, M. (2016) 'Practising reflexivity in ethnography'. In D. Silverman (ed.), *Qualitative Research*, 4th edn (pp. 137–52). London: Sage.

Callon, M. (1986) 'Some elements of a sociology of translation: domestication of the scallops and the fishermen of Saint Brieuc Bay'. In J. Law (ed.), *Power, Action and Belief: A New Sociology of Knowledge? Sociological Review Monograph* (pp. 32, 196–233). London: Routledge & Kegan Paul.

Callon, M. and Law, J. (1997) 'After the individual in society: lessons on collectivity from science, technology and society'. *Canadian Journal of Sociology*, 22 (2): 165–82.

Carr, N. (2010) *The Shallows: How the Internet is Changing the Way We Think, Read and Remember*. London: Atlantic Books.

Carroll, B., Levy, L. and Richmond, D. (2008) 'Leadership as practice: challenging the competency paradigm'. *Leadership*, 4 (4), 363–79.

Chapman, G. (1987) 'Talk, text and discourse: nurses' talk in a therapeutic community'. Unpublished PhD thesis, University of London, Goldsmiths College.

Charmaz, K. (2006) *Constructing Grounded Theory: A Practical Guide through Qualitative Analysis*. London: Sage.

Charmaz, K. (2015) *Constructing Grounded Theory: A Practical Guide through Qualitative Analysis*, 2nd edn. London: Sage.

Charmaz, K. and Bryant, A. (2011a) 'Grounded theory and credibility'. In D. Silverman (ed.), *Qualitative Research: Theory, Method and Practice*, 3rd edn (pp. 291–309). London: Sage.

Christians, C. (2005) 'Ethics and politics in qualitative research'. In N. Denzin and Y. Lincoln (eds), *Handbook of Qualitative Research*, 3rd edn (pp. 139–64). Thousand Oaks, CA: Sage.

Churchill, H. and Sanders, T. (2007) *Getting Your PhD: A Practical Insider's Guide*. London: Sage.

Clavarino, A., Najman, J. and Silverman, D. (1995) 'Assessing the quality of qualitative data'. *Qualitative Inquiry*, 1 (2), 223–42.

Coffey, A. and Atkinson, P. (1996) *Making Sense of Qualitative Data*. London: Sage.

Cohen, S. (1980) *Folk Devils and Moral Panics: The Creation of the Mods and Rockers*. Oxford: Martin Robertson.

Cohen, S. and Young, J. (1973) *The Manufacture of News*. London: Constable.

Collins, P. (2012) *The Art of Speeches and Presentations*. New York: Wiley.

Cryer, P. (1996) *The Research Student's Guide to Success*. Buckingham: Open University Press.

Cryer, P. (2006) *The Research Student's Guide to Success*, 3rd edn. Buckingham: Open University Press.

Curtis, S., Gesler, W., Smith, G. and Washburn, S. (2000) 'Approaches to sampling and case selection in qualitative research: examples in the geography of health'. *Social Science and Medicine*, 50, 1000–14.

Czarniawska, B. (2007) *Shadowing, and Other Techniques for Doing Fieldwork in Modern Societies*. Liber; Copenhagen Business School Press; Universitetsforlaget.

Czarniawska, B. (2014) *Social Science Research*. Sage: London.

Czarniawska, B. and Joerges, B. (1995) *Travels of Ideas: Organizational Change as Translation*. Berlin: WZB, Forschungsschwerpunkt Technik, Arbeit, Umwelt.

Dalton, M. (1959) *Men Who Manage*. New York: Wiley.

Danby, S. and Lee, A. (2012) 'Framing doctoral pedagogy as design and action'. In A. Lee and S. Danby (eds), *Reshaping Doctoral Education* (pp. 3–11). Abingdon: Routledge.

Denzin, N. and Lincoln, Y. (eds) (1994) *Handbook of Qualitative Research*. Thousand Oaks, CA: Sage.

Denzin, N. and Lincoln, Y. (eds) (2005) *Handbook of Qualitative Research*, 3rd edn. London: Sage.

Dingwall, R. and Murray, T. (1983) 'Categorization in accident departments: "good" patients, "bad" patients and children'. *Sociology of Health & Illness*, 5 (12), 121–48.

Douglas, M. (1975) 'Self-evidence'. In M. Douglas, *Implicit Meanings* (pp. 276–318). London: Routledge.

Drew, P. (2001) 'Spotlight on the patient'. *Text*, 21 (1/2), 261–8.

Duncan, S. (2005) 'Towards evidence-inspired policy-making'. *Social Sciences*, 61, 10–11.

Durkheim, E. (1951) *Suicide*. New York: Free Press.

Eberle, T.S. and Maeder, C. (2010) 'Organizational Ethnography'. In D. Silverman (ed.) *Qualitative Research*, 3rd edn. (pp. 53–73). London: Sage.

Edwards, P.N. (2004) 'How to give an academic talk'. Online at: pne.people.si.umich.edu/PDF/howtotalk.pdf.

Eisenhart, M. (2001) 'Educational ethnography past, present, and future: ideas to think with'. *Educational Researcher*, 30 (8), 16–27.

Emerson, R.M., Fretz, R.I. and Shaw, L.L. (1995) *Writing Ethnographic Fieldnotes*. Chicago: University of Chicago Press.

Emmison, M. and Smith, P. (2000) *Researching the Visual*. London: Sage.

Engebretson, J. (1996) 'Urban healers: an experiential description of American healing touch groups'. *Qualitative Health Research*, 6 (4), 526–41.

Eriksson, P. and Kovalainen, A. (2016) *Qualitative Methods in Business Research*, 2nd edn. London: Sage.

Fairclough, N. (1995) *Critical Discourse Analysis: The Critical Study of Language*. London: Longman.

Fielding, N. (1982) 'Observational research on the National Front'. In M. Bulmer (ed.), *Social Research Ethics: An Examination of the Merits of Covert Participant Observation*. London: Macmillan.

Fielding, N. and Fielding, J. (1986) *Linking Data*. London: Sage.

Fisher, M. (1997) *Qualitative Computing: Using Software for Qualitative Data Analysis*. Aldershot: Ashgate.

Flick, U. (2007) *Designing Qualitative Research*. London: Sage.

Flynn, E. (2000) *Issues in Health Care Ethics*. Englewood Cliffs, NJ: Prentice-Hall.

Flyvbjerg, B. (2004) 'Five misunderstandings about case-study research'. In C. Seale, G. Gobo, J. Gubrium and D. Silverman (eds), *Qualitative Research Practice* (pp. 420–34). London: Sage.

Foucault, M. (1977) *Discipline and Punish*. Harmondsworth: Penguin.

Foucault, M. (1979) *The History of Sexuality*, Vol. 1. Harmondsworth: Penguin.

Frake, C. (1964) 'Notes on queries in ethnography'. *American Anthropologist*, 66, 132–45.

Fraser, M. (1995) 'The history of the child: 1905–1989'. Unpublished PhD thesis, University of London, Goldsmiths College.

Freebody, P. (2003) *Qualitative Research in Education*. London: Sage.

Friese, S. (2014) *Qualitative Data Analysis with ATLAS.ti*. London: Sage.

Garfinkel, H. (1967) *Studies in Ethnomethodology*. Oxford: Polity.

Gatrell, C. (2009) 'Safeguarding subjects? A reflexive reappraisal of researcher accountability in qualitative interviews'. *Qualitative Research in Organizations and Management*, 4 (2), 110–22.

Geertz, C. (1973) *The Interpretation of Cultures*. London: Fontana.

Giddings, L.S. (2006) 'Mixed-methods research: positivism dressed in drag?'. *Journal of Research in Nursing*, 11, 195–203.

Gilbert, N. (2008a) 'Writing about social research'. In N. Gilbert (ed.), *Researching Social Life*, 3rd edn (pp. 328–44). London: Sage.

Gilbert, N. (ed.) (2008b) *Researching Social Life*, 3rd edn. London: Sage.

Gilbert, N. and Mulkay, M. (1983) 'In search of the action'. In N. Gilbert and P. Abell (eds), *Accounts and Action*. Aldershot: Gower.

Glaser, B. and Strauss, A. (1967) *The Discovery of Grounded Theory*. Chicago: Aldine.

Glaser, B. and Strauss, A. (1968) *Time for Dying*. Chicago: Aldine.

Glassner, B. and Loughlin, J. (1987) *Drugs in Adolescent Worlds: Burnouts to Straights*. New York: St Martin's.

Gobo, G. (2007) 'Re-conceptualizing generalization: old issues in a new frame'. In
P. Alasuutari (ed.), *Social Research Methods* (pp. 193–213). London: Sage.

Gobo, G. (2008) *Doing Ethnography*. London: Sage.

Goffman, E. (1959) *The Presentation of Self in Everyday Life*. New York: Doubleday
Anchor.

Goffman, E. (1961) *Asylums*. New York: Doubleday Anchor.

Goffman, E. (1974) *Frame Analysis*. New York: Harper and Row.

Gray, D.E. (2014) *Doing Research in the Real World*, 3rd edn. London: Sage.

Green, J. and Thorogood, N. (2014) *Qualitative Methods for Health Research*, 3rd
edn. London: Sage.

Guba, E. and Lincoln, Y. (1994) 'Competing paradigms in qualitative research'. In
N. Denzin and Y. Lincoln (eds), *Handbook of Qualitative Research* (pp. 105–17).
Thousand Oaks, CA: Sage.

Gubrium, J.F. (1988) *Analyzing Field Reality*. Newbury Park, CA: Sage.

Gubrium, J. (1993) *Living and Dying at Murray Manor*. New York: St Martin's.

Gubrium, J. (1997) *Living and Dying at Murray Manor*. Charlottesville, VA: University
Press of Virginia.

Gubrium, J. (2009) 'Curbing self-referential writing'. Retrieved 13 March 2012
from www.dur.ac.uk/writingacrossboundaries/writingonwriting/jaygubrium.

Gubrium, J. (2010) 'A turn to narrative practice'. *Narrative Inquiry*, 20 (2),
387–91.

Gubrium, J. and Holstein, J. (1997) *The New Language of Qualitative Method*. New
York: Oxford University Press.

Gubrium, J. and Holstein, J. (eds) (2002) *Handbook of Interview Research*. Thousand
Oaks, CA: Sage.

Gubrium, J. and Holstein, J. (eds) (2008) *Handbook of Constructionist Research*. New
York: Guilford.

Gubrium, J. and Holstein, J. (2009) *Analyzing Narrative Reality*. Thousand Oaks, CA:
Sage.

Hadley, R. (1987) 'Publish and be ignored: proselytise and be damned'. In G.C.
Wenger (ed.), *The Research Relationship: Practice and Politics in Social Policy
Research* (pp. 98–110). London: Allen & Unwin.

Hagan, F.E. (2005) *Essentials of Research Methods in Criminal Justice and Criminology*.
Englewood Cliffs, NJ: Prentice Hall

Haggerty, K.D. (2004) 'Ethics creep: governing social science research in the name
of ethics'. *Qualitative Sociology*, 27 (4), 391–414.

Hammersley, M. (1990) *Reading Ethnographic Research: A Critical Guide*. London:
Longmans.

Hammersley, M. (1992) *What's Wrong with Ethnography? Methodological Explorations*.
London: Routledge.

Hammersley, M. (2008) *Questioning Qualitative Inquiry: Critical Essays*. London:
Sage.

Hammersley, M. and Atkinson, P. (1983) *Ethnography: Principles in Practice*.
London: Tavistock.

Hammersley, M. and Atkinson, P. (2007) *Ethnography: Principles in Practice*, 3rd edn. London: Tavistock.

Handy, C. and Aitken, A. (1994) 'The organisation of the primary school'. In A. Pollard and J. Bourne (eds), *Teaching and Learning in the Primary School* (pp. 239–49). London: Routledge.

Hart, C. (1998) *Doing a Literature Review: Releasing the Social Science Imagination*. London: Sage.

Hart, C. (2001) *Doing a Literature Search*. London: Sage.

Heath, C. (2011) 'Embodied action: video and the analysis of social interaction'. In D. Silverman (ed.), *Qualitative Research: Theory, Method and Practice*, 3rd edn (pp. 250–69). London: Sage.

Heath, C., Hindmarsh, J. and Luff, P. (2010) *Video in Qualitative Research*. London: Sage.

Heath, C. and Luff, P. (2000) *Technology in Action*. Cambridge: Cambridge University Press.

Heaton, J.M. (1979) 'Theory in psychotherapy'. In N. Bolton (ed.), *Philosophical Problems in Psychology* (pp. 179–98). London: Methuen.

Hennink, M., Hutter, I. and Bailey, A. (2011) *Qualitative Research Methods*. London: Sage.

Heritage, J. (1984) *Garfinkel and Ethnomethodology*. Cambridge: Polity.

Heritage, J. (2016) 'Conversation analysis: practices and methods'. In D. Silverman (ed.) *Qualitative Research: Theory, Method and Practice*, 3rd edn (pp. 207–24). London: Sage.

Heritage, J., Robinson, R., Elliott, M., Beckett, M. and Wilkes, M. (2007) 'Reducing patients' unmet concerns in primary care: the difference one word can make'. *Journal of General Internal Medicine*, 22 (10), 1429–33.

Heritage, J. and Sefi, S. (1992) 'Dilemmas of advice: aspects of the delivery and reception of advice in interactions between health visitors and first time mothers'. In P. Drew and J. Heritage (eds), *Talk at Work* (pp. 359–417). Cambridge: Cambridge University Press.

Hesse-Biber, C. (2015) 'Mixed methods research: the "thing-ness" problem'. *Qualitative Health Research*, 25 (6), 775–88.

Hill, C.E. (1989) *Therapist Techniques and Client Outcomes*. London: Sage.

Holstein, J.A. (1992) 'Producing people: descriptive practice in human service work'. *Current Research on Occupations and Professions*, 7, 23–9.

Holstein, J. and Gubrium, J. (1995) *The Active Interview*. Thousand Oaks, CA: Sage.

Holstein, J. and Gubrium, J. (eds) (2008a) *Handbook of Constructionist Research*. New York: Guilford.

Holstein, J. and Gubrium, J. (2008b) 'Constructionist impulses in ethnographic fieldwork'. In J. Holstein and J. Gubrium (eds), *Handbook of Constructionist Research* (pp. 373–95). New York: Guilford.

Holstein, J. and Gubrium, J. (2016) 'Narrative practice and the active interview'. In D. Silverman (ed.), *Qualitative Research*, 4th edn (pp. 67–82). London: Sage.

Hornsby-Smith, M. (1993) 'Gaining access'. In N. Gilbert (ed.), *Researching Social Life* (pp. 52–67). London: Sage.

Hughes, E.C. (1984) *The Sociological Eye*. New Brunswick, NJ: Transaction.

Hulko, W. (2009) 'From "not a big deal" to "hellish": experiences of older people with dementia'. *Journal of Aging Studies*, 23 (3), 131–44.

Humphreys, L. (1970) *Tearoom Trade: Impersonal Sex in Public Places*. Chicago: Aldine.

Irurita, V. (1996) 'Hidden dimensions revealed: progressive grounded theory study of quality care in the hospital'. *Qualitative Health Research*, 6 (3), 331–49.

Israel, M. and Hay, I. (2006) *Research Ethics for Social Scientists*. London: Sage.

Järviluoma, H., Moisala, P. and Vilkko, A. (2004) *Gender and Qualitative Methods*. London: Sage.

Jefferson, G. (1984) 'On stepwise transition from talk about a trouble to inappropriately next-positioned matters'. In J.M. Atkinson and J.C. Heritage (eds), *Structures of Social Action: Studies of Conversation Analysis* (pp. 191–222). Cambridge: Cambridge University Press.

Jeffery, R. (1979) 'Normal rubbish: deviant patients in casualty departments'. *Sociology of Health & Illness*, 1 (1), 90–107.

Jenkings, K.N., Woodward, R. and Winter, T. (2008) 'The emergent production of analysis in photo elicitation: pictures of military identity'. *Forum: Qualitative Social Research*, 9 (3), Art. 3. www.qualitative-research.net/index.php/fqs/article/view/1169

Jones, J.H. (1981) *Bad Blood*. New York: Free Press.

Justesen, L. and Mik-Meyer, N. (2012) *Qualitative Research Methods in Organisation Studies*. Copenhagen: Hans Reitzels Forlag.

Kafka, F. (1961) 'Investigations of a dog'. In *Metamorphosis and Other Stories*. Harmondsworth: Penguin.

Kelly, M. (1998) 'Writing a research proposal'. In C. Seale (ed.), *Researching Society and Culture* (pp. 111–22). London: Sage.

Kelly, M. (2012) 'Research questions and proposals'. In C. Seale (ed.), *Researching Society and Culture*, 3rd edn. London: Sage.

Kendall, G. and Wickham, G. (1999) *Using Foucault's Methods*. London: Sage.

Kirk, J. and Miller, M. (1986) *Reliability and Validity in Qualitative Research*. London: Sage.

Kitzinger, C. and Wilkinson, S. (1997) 'Validating women's experience? Dilemmas in feminist research'. *Feminism & Psychology*, 7 (4), 566–74.

Konecki, K. (2005) 'Wizualne wyobrazenia. Główne strategie badawcze w socjologii wizualnej a metodologia teorii ugruntowanej'. *Przegląd Socjologii Jakosciowej*, I (1), Pobrany Miesiac 10, Rok 2007.

Konecki, K. (2008) 'Touching and gesture exchange as an element of emotional bond construction: application of visual sociology in the research on interaction between humans and animals'. *FQS Forum: Qualitative Research*, 9 (3), Art. 33. www.qualitativesociologyreview.org/PL/Volume1/PSJ_1_1_Konecki.pdf.

Koppel, R. (2009) 'Reprise of a battle won: sociologist monitors Boston Transit System's treatment of the disabled'. *Footnotes*, 37 (2). www.asanet.org/sites/default/files/savvy/footnotes/feb09/ps.html.

Koppel, R., Cohen, A. and Abaluck, B. (2003) 'Physicians' perceptions of medication error using differing research methods'. Paper presented at the meeting of the European Sociological Association (Qualitative Methods Group), Murcia, Spain.

Kozinets, R.V. (2010) *Netnography: Doing Ethnographic Research Online*. London: Sage.

Kuhn, T.S. (1970) *The Structure of Scientific Revolutions*, 2nd edn. Chicago: University of Chicago Press.

Kvale, S. (2007) *Doing Interviews*. London: Sage.

Law, J. and Hassard, J. (eds) (1999) *Actor-Network Theory and After*. Oxford: Blackwell.

Lipset, S.M., Trow, M. and Coleman, J. (1962) *Union Democracy*. Garden City, NY: Anchor Doubleday.

Livingston, E. (1987) *Making Sense of Ethnomethodology*. London: Routledge.

Loseke, D. (1989) 'Creating clients: social problems work in a shelter for battered women'. *Perspectives on Social Problems*, 1, 173–93.

Loseke, D. and Cahill, S. (2004) 'Publishing qualitative manuscripts: lessons learned'. In C. Seale, G. Gobo, J.F. Gubrium and D. Silverman (eds), *Qualitative Research Practice* (pp. 576–91). London: Sage.

Lynch, M. (1984) *Art and Artifact in Laboratory Science*. London: Routledge.

MacMillan, K. (2005) 'More than just coding? Evaluating CAQDAS in a discourse analysis of news texts'. *FQS Forum: Qualitative Research*, 6(3), Art. 25. www.qualitative-research.net/index.php/fqs/article/view/28.

Mahoney, M.J. (1977) 'Publication prejudices: an experimental study of confirmatory bias in the peer review system'. *Cognitive Therapy and Research*, 1, 161–75.

Malinowski, B. (1922) *Argonauts of the Western Pacific*. London: Routledge.

Markham, A. (2011) 'Internet research'. In D. Silverman (ed.), *Qualitative Research: Theory, Method and Practice*, 3rd edn (pp. 111–28). London: Sage.

Marshall, C. and Rossman, G. (1989) *Designing Qualitative Research*. London: Sage.

Marvasti, A. (2004) *Qualitative Research in Sociology*. Thousand Oaks, CA: Sage.

Marvasti, A. (2011) 'Three aspects of writing qualitative research: practice, genre and audience'. In D. Silverman (ed.), *Qualitative Research: Theory, Method and Practice*, 3rd edn (pp. 383–96). London: Sage.

Marvasti, A. (2016) 'Writing qualitative research: practice, genre and audience'. In D. Silverman (ed.), *Qualitative Research: Theory, Method and Practice*, 4th edn (pp. 429–44). London: Sage.

Marx, G. (1997) 'Of methods and manners for aspiring sociologists: 37 moral imperatives'. *The American Sociologist*, Spring, 102–25.

Mason, J. (1996) *Qualitative Researching*. London: Sage.

Mason, J. (2002) *Qualitative Researching*, 2nd edn. London: Sage.

Mautner, G. (2013) 'Checks and balances: how corpus linguistics can contribute to CDA'. In R. Wodak and M. Meyer (eds), *Methods of Critical Discourse Studies* (pp. 154–79). London, Sage.

Maxwell, J.A. (2010) 'Using numbers in qualitative research'. *Qualitative Inquiry*, 16 (6), 475–82.

McCulloch, A. (2010) 'Excellence in doctoral supervision: competing models of what constitutes good supervision'. In M. Kiley (ed.), *Proceedings 9th Quality in Postgraduate Research Conference: Educating Researchers for the 21st Century* (pp. 175–86), 13–15 April, Adelaide.

McLeod, J. (1994) *Doing Counselling Research*. London: Sage.

Mehan, H. (1979) *Learning Lessons: Social Organization in the Classroom*. Cambridge, MA: Harvard University Press.

Mercer, K. (1990) 'Powellism as a political discourse'. Unpublished PhD thesis, University of London, Goldsmiths College.

Merton, R.K. (1968) 'The Matthew effect in science'. *Science*, 159, 56–63.

Miles, M. and Huberman, A. (1984) *Qualitative Data Analysis*. London: Sage.

Miller, M. and Glassner, B. (2004) 'The "inside" and the "outside": finding realities in interviews'. In D. Silverman (ed.), *Qualitative Research: Theory, Method and Practice* (pp. 125–39). London: Sage.

Mills, C.W. (1959) *The Sociological Imagination*. New York: Oxford University Press.

Mitchell, J.C. (1983) 'Case and situational analysis'. *Sociological Review*, 31 (2), 187–211.

Moerman, M. (1974) 'Accomplishing ethnicity'. In R. Turner (ed.), *Ethnomethodology* (pp. 34–68). Harmondsworth: Penguin.

Moisander, J. and Valtonen, A. (2006) *Qualitative Marketing Research: A Cultural Approach*. London: Sage.

Morley, D. (1992) *Television, Audiences and Cultural Studies*. London: Routledge.

Morse, J.M. (1994) 'Designing funded qualitative research'. In N. Denzin and Y. Lincoln (eds), *Handbook of Qualitative Research* (pp. 220–35). Thousand Oaks, CA: Sage.

Mulkay, M. (1984) 'The ultimate compliment: a sociological analysis of ceremonial discourse'. *Sociology*, 18, 531–49.

Murcott, A. (1997) 'The PhD: some informal notes'. Unpublished paper, School of Health and Social Care, South Bank University, London.

Murray, R. (2003) 'Survive your viva'. *Guardian Education*, 16 September.

Myers, M. and Avison, D. (2002) *Qualitative Research in Information Systems*. London: Sage.

Nelson, C. (2003) 'Can E.T. phone home? The brave new world of university surveillance'. *Academe*, 89, 30–5.

Nicolini, D. (2012) *Practice Theory, Work, and Organization: An Introduction* (HB). Oxford: Oxford University Press.

Nicolini, D. (2013) *Practice Theory, Work and Organization: An Introduction* (PB). Oxford: Oxford University Press.

Ó Dochartaigh, N. (2007) *Internet Research Skills*. London: Sage.

O'Leary, Z. (2014) *Doing Your Research Project*, 2nd edn. London: Sage.

Parke, H., Ashcroft, R., Brown, R., Marteau, T.M. and Seale, C. (2011) 'Financial incentives to encourage healthy behaviour: an analysis of UK media coverage'. *Health Expectations*. DOI 10.1111/j.1369–7625.2011.00719.x.

Penslar, R.L. (2007) *IRB Guidebook*. University of Illinois: Chicago. https://research. uic.edu/sites/default/files/0855.pdf.

Peräkylä, A. (1989) 'Appealing to the experience of the patient in the care of the dying'. *Sociology of Health & Illness*, 11 (2), 117–34.

Peräkylä, A. (1995) *AIDS Counselling*. Cambridge: Cambridge University Press.

Peräkylä, A. (2004) 'Reliability and validity in research based upon transcripts'. In D. Silverman (ed.), *Qualitative Research: Theory, Method and Practice*, 2nd edn (pp. 282–303). London: Sage.

Peräkylä, A. (2011) 'Validity in research on naturally occurring social interaction'. In D. Silverman (ed.), *Qualitative Research: Theory, Method and Practice*, 3rd edn (pp. 365–82). London: Sage.

Peräkylä, A. and Silverman, D. (1991) 'Owning experience: describing the experience of others'. *Text*, 11 (3), 441–80.

Peters, D.P. and Ceci, S.J. (1982) 'Peer-review practices of psychological journals: the fate of published articles, submitted again'. *Behavioral and Brain Sciences*, 5 (2), 187–95.

Phelps, R., Fisher, K. and Ellis, A. (2007) *Organizing and Managing Your Research: A Practical Guide for Postgraduates*. London: Sage.

Phillips, E. and Pugh, D. (1994) *How to Get a PhD*, 2nd edn. Buckingham: Open University Press.

Phillips, E. and Pugh, D. (2005) *How to Get a PhD*, 4th edn. Buckingham: Open University Press.

Popper, K. (1959) *The Logic of Scientific Discovery*. New York: Basic Books.

Porter, L.W. and McLaughlin, G.B. (2006) 'Leadership and the organizational context: like the weather?'. *Leadership Quarterly*, 17 (6), 559–76.

Potter, J. (2002) 'Two kinds of natural'. *Discourse Studies*, 4 (4), 539–42.

Potter, J. (2004) 'Discourse analysis as a way of analysing naturally occurring talk'. In D. Silverman (ed.), *Qualitative Research: Theory, Method and Practice*, 2nd edn (pp. 200–21). London: Sage.

Potter, J. (2016) 'Discursive psychology and the study of naturally occurring talk'. In D. Silverman (ed.), *Qualitative Research: Theory, Method and Practice*, 2nd edn (pp. 189–206). London: Sage.

Potter, J. and Hepburn, A. (2008) 'Discursive constructionism'. In J. Holstein and J. Gubrium (eds), *Handbook of Constructionist Research* (pp. 275–93). New York: Guilford.

Potter, J. and Wetherell, M. (1987) *Discourse and Social Psychology: Beyond Attitudes and Behaviour*. London: Sage.

Prior, L. (1987) 'Policing the dead: a sociology of the mortuary'. *Sociology*, 21(3), 355–76.

Prior, L. (2008) 'Repositioning documents in social research'. *Sociology*, 42 (5), 821–36.

Psathas, G. (1990) *Interaction Competence*. Washington, DC: University Press of America.

Punch, K. (1998) *Introduction to Social Research: Quantitative and Qualitative Approaches*. London: Sage.

Punch, K. (2005) *Introduction to Social Research: Quantitative and Qualitative Approaches*, 2nd edn. London: Sage.

Punch, K. (2006) *Developing Effective Research Proposals*, 2nd edn. London: Sage.

Punch, K. (2014) *Introduction to Social Research: Quantitative and Qualitative Approaches*, 3rd edn. London: Sage.

Punch, K. (2016) *Developing Effective Research Proposals*, 3rd edn. London: Sage.

Radcliffe-Brown, A.R. (1948) *The Andaman Islanders*. Glencoe, IL: Free Press.

Rapley, T. (2004) 'Interviews'. In C. Seale, G. Gobo, J.F. Gubrium and D. Silverman (eds), *Qualitative Research Practice* (pp. 15–33). London: Sage.

Rapley, T. (2011) 'Some pragmatics of qualitative data analysis'. In D. Silverman (ed.), *Qualitative Research: Theory, Method and Practice*, 3rd edn (pp. 273–90). London: Sage.

Reason, P. and Rowan, J. (1981) *Human Inquiry: A Sourcebook of New Paradigm Research*. Chichester: Wiley.

Richardson, S. and McMullan, M. (2007) 'Research Ethics in the UK: What can Sociology Learn from Health?' *Sociology*, 41(6), 1115–32.

Riessman, C. (2005) 'Exporting ethics: a narrative about narrative research in South India'. *Health*, special issue on Informed Consent, Ethics and Narrative, 9 (4), 473–90.

Riessman, C.K. (2008) *Narrative Methods for the Human Sciences*. Thousand Oaks, CA: Sage.

Riessman, C.K. (2011) 'What's different about narrative inquiry? Cases, categories and contexts'. In D. Silverman (ed.), *Qualitative Research: Theory, Method and Practice*, 3rd edn (pp. 310–30). London: Sage.

Riessman, C.K. (2016) 'What's different about narrative inquiry? Cases, categories and contexts'. In D. Silverman (ed.), *Qualitative Research: Theory, Method and Practice*, 4th edn (pp. 363–78). London: Sage.

Rose, G. (2007) *Visual Methodologies*. London: Sage.

Rudestam, K. and Newton, R. (1992) *Surviving your Dissertation*. Newbury Park, CA: Sage.

Ryen, A. (2004) 'Ethical issues'. In C. Seale, G. Gobo, J.F. Gubrium and D. Silverman (eds), *Qualitative Research Practice* (pp. 230–47). London: Sage.

Sacks, H. (1984a) 'On doing "being ordinary"'. In J.M. Atkinson and J. Heritage (eds), *Structures of Social Action: Studies in Conversation Analysis* (pp. 513–29). Cambridge: Cambridge University Press.

Sacks, H. (1984b) 'Notes on methodology'. In J.M. Atkinson and J. Heritage (eds), *Structures of Social Action: Studies in Conversation Analysis* (pp. 21–7). Cambridge: Cambridge University Press.

Sacks, H. (1992) *Lectures on Conversation*, Vols 1–2. Oxford: Blackwell.

Salmona, M. and Kaczynski, D. (2016) 'Don't blame the software: using qualitative data analysis software successfully in doctoral research', *FQS Forum: Qualitative Social Research,* 17 (11), Art.11. www.qualitative-research.net/index.php/fqs/article/view/2505.

Saukko, P. (2003) *Doing Research in Cultural Studies*. London: Sage.

Schegloff, E.A. (1968) 'Sequencings in conversational openings'. *American Anthropologist*, 70, 1075–95.

Schegloff, E. (1991) 'Reflections on talk and social structure'. In D. Boden and D. Zimmerman (eds), *Talk and Social Structure: Studies in Ethnomethodology and Conversation Analysis* (pp. 44–70). Cambridge: Polity.

Schreiber, R. (1996) '(Re)defining my self: women's process of recovery from depression'. *Qualitative Health Research*, 6 (4), 469–91.

Seale, C. (1996) 'Living alone towards the end of life'. *Ageing & Society*, 16, 75–91.

Seale, C. (1999) *The Quality of Qualitative Research*. London: Sage.

Seale C. (2002a) 'Cancer heroics: a study of news reports with particular reference to gender'. *Sociology*, 36 (1), 107–26.

Seale, C. (2002b) 'Quality issues in qualitative inquiry'. *Qualitative Social Work*, 1 (1), 97–110.

Seale, C. (2011) 'Secondary analysis of qualitative data'. In D. Silverman (ed.), *Qualitative Research: Theory, Method and Practice*, 3rd edn (pp. 347–64). London: Sage.

Seale, C. (ed.) (2012) *Researching Society and Culture*, 3rd edn. London: Sage.

Seale, C. and Charteris-Black, J. (2010) 'Keyword analysis: a new tool for qualitative research'. In I.L. Bourgeault, R. DeVries and R. Dingwall (eds), *The SAGE Handbook of Qualitative Methods in Health Research*. London: Sage.

Seale, C., Charteris-Black, J. and Ziebland, S. (2006) 'Gender, cancer experience and internet use: a comparative keyword analysis of interviews and online cancer support groups'. *Social Science & Medicine*, 62 (10), 2577–90.

Seale, C., Gobo, G., Gubrium, J.F. and Silverman, D. (eds) (2004) *Qualitative Research Practice*. London: Sage.

Seale, C., Raus, K., Bruinsma, S., van der Heide, A., Sterckx, S., Mortier, F., Payne, S., Mathers, N. and Rietjens, J. on behalf of the UNBIASED consortium (2015) 'The language of sedation in end-of-life care: the ethical reasoning of care providers in three countries'. *Health: An Interdisciplinary Journal*, 19 (4), 339–54.

Seale, C., Rivas, C.A. and Kelly, M.J. (2013) 'The challenge of communication in interpreted consultations in diabetes care'. *British Journal of General Practice*, 63 (607), e125–33.

Seymour, J., Rietjens, J., Bruinsma, S., Deliens, L., Sterckx, S., Mortier, F., Brown, J., Mathers, N. and van der Heide, A. on behalf of the UNBIASED consortium (2014) 'Using continuous sedation until death for cancer patients: a qualitative interview study of physicians' and nurses' practice in three European countries'. *Palliative Medicine*, 29 (1), 48–59.

Sharples, M., Davison, L., Thomas, G. and Rudman, P. (2003) 'Children as photographers: an analysis of children's photographic behaviour and intentions at three age levels'. *Visual Communication*, 2 (3), 303–30.

Shaw, I. and Gould, N. (2002) *Qualitative Research in Social Work*. London: Sage.

Shea, C. (2000) 'Don't talk to humans: the crackdown on social science research'. *Lingua Franca*, 10 (6).

Sheard, L. (2011) 'Anything could have happened': Women, the night-time economy, alcohol and drink spiking' *Sociology* 49 (4), 619–33.

Silver, C. and Lewins, A. (2014) *Using Software in Qualitative Research*. London: Sage.

Silverman, D. (1968a) 'Clerical ideologies: a research note'. *British Journal of Sociology*, XIX (3), 326–33.

Silverman, D. (1968b) 'Formal organizations or industrial sociology: towards a social action analysis of organizations'. *Sociology*, 2, 221–38.

Silverman, D. (1970) *The Theory of Organizations*. London: Heinemann Educational.

Silverman, D. (1981) 'The child as a social object: Down's syndrome children in a paediatric cardiology clinic'. *Sociology of Health & Illness*, 3 (3), 254–74.

Silverman, D. (1983) 'The clinical subject: adolescents in a cleft palate clinic'. *Sociology of Health & Illness*, 5 (3), 253–74.

Silverman, D. (1984) 'Going private: ceremonial forms in a private oncology clinic'. *Sociology*, 18, 191–202.

Silverman, D. (1987) *Communication and Medical Practice: Social Relations in the Clinic*. London: Sage.

Silverman, D. (1989) 'Making sense of a precipice: constituting identity in an HIV clinic'. In P. Aggleton, G. Hart and P. Davies (eds), *AIDS: Social Representations, Social Practices*. Abingdon: RoutledgeFalmer.

Silverman, D. (1997) *Discourses of Counselling: HIV Counselling as Social Interaction*. London: Sage.

Silverman, D. (1998) *Harvey Sacks: Social Science and Conversation Analysis*. Cambridge: Polity.

Silverman, D. (2001) *Interpreting Qualitative Data: Methods for Analysing Text, Talk and Interaction*, 2nd edn. London: Sage.

Silverman, D. (2006) *Interpreting Qualitative Data: Methods for Analysing Text, Talk and Interaction*, 3rd edn. London: Sage.

Silverman, D. (ed.) (2011a) *Qualitative Research: Theory, Method and Practice*, 3rd edn. London: Sage.

Silverman, D. (2011b) *Interpreting Qualitative Data: Methods for Analysing Talk, Text and Interaction*, 4th edn. London: Sage.

Silverman, D. (2013) *A Very Short, Fairly Interesting, Reasonably Cheap Book about Qualitative Research*, 2nd edn. London: Sage.

Silverman, D. (2014) *Interpreting Qualitative Data: Methods for Analysing Talk, Text and Interaction*, 5th edn. London: Sage.

Silverman, D. (2016) *Qualitative Research: Theory, Method and Practice*, 4th edn. London: Sage.

Silverman, D. (2017) 'How was it for you? The interview society and the irresistible rise of the [poorly analyzed] interview. *Qualitative Research*, 17 (2), 144–58.

Silverman, D. and Bloor, M. (1989) 'Patient-centred medicine: some sociological observations on its constitution, penetration and cultural assonance'. In G.L. Albrecht (ed.), *Advances in Medical Sociology* (pp. 3–26). Greenwich, CT: JAI Press.

Silverman, D. and Gubrium, J. (1994) 'Competing strategies for analyzing the contexts of social interaction'. *Sociological Inquiry*, 64 (2), 179–98.

Small, M.L. (2009) '"How many cases do I need?" On science and the logic of case selection in field-based research'. *Ethnography*, 10 (1), 5–38.

Sociology of Health & Illness (2009) Letter from the Editor. e-news@wiley.com, 11 September.

Sontag, S. (1979) *Illness as Metaphor*. Harmondsworth: Penguin.

Spencer, L., Ritchie, J., Lewis, J. and Dillon, J. (2003) *Quality in Qualitative Evaluation: A Framework for Assessing Research Evidence*. London: Government Chief Social Researcher's Office.

Spradley, J.P. (1979) *The Ethnographic Interview*. New York: Holt, Rinehart and Winston.

Stake, R. (2000) 'Case studies'. In N. Denzin and Y. Lincoln (eds), *Handbook of Qualitative Research*, 2nd edn (pp. 435–54). Thousand Oaks, CA: Sage.

Stake, R. (2010) *Qualitative Research*. New York: Guilford.

Stimson, G. (1986) 'Place and space in sociological fieldwork'. *Sociological Review*, 34 (3), 641–56.

Strauss, A. and Corbin, J. (1990) *Basics of Qualitative Research*. Newbury Park, CA: Sage.

Strauss, A. and Corbin, J. (1994) 'Grounded theory methodology: an overview'. In N. Denzin and Y. Lincoln (eds), *Handbook of Qualitative Research* (pp. 262–72). Thousand Oaks, CA: Sage.

Strauss, A. and Corbin, J. (2008) *Basics of Qualitative Research*, 3rd edn. London: Sage.

Strong, P. (1979) *The Ceremonial Order of the Clinic*. London: Routledge.

Suchman, L. (1987) *Plans and Situated Actions: The Problem of Human–Machine Communication*. Cambridge: Cambridge University Press.

Sudnow, D. (1968a) *Passing On: The Social Organization of Dying*. Englewood Cliffs, NJ: Prentice Hall.

Sudnow, D. (1968b) 'Normal crimes'. In E. Rubington and M. Weinberg (eds), *Deviance: The Interactionist Perspective*. New York: Macmillan.

ten Have, P. (1998) *Doing Conversation Analysis: A Practical Guide*. London: Sage.

ten Have, P. (2007) *Doing Conversation Analysis*, 2nd edn. London: Sage.

The Economist (2010) 'The disposable academic: why doing a PhD is often a waste of time'. 16 December.

Travers, M. (2006) 'New methods, old problems: a sceptical view of innovation in qualitative research'. Paper presented at Advances in Qualitative Research Practice, Mid-term Conference of ESA Qualitative Methods Research Network, 6–8 September, University of Cardiff.

Tucker-McLaughlin, M. and Campbell, K. (2012) 'A grounded theory analysis: Hillary Clinton represented as innovator and voiceless in TV news'. *Electronic News*, 6 (1), 3–19.

Venkatesh, S. (2008) *Gang Leader for a Day*. London: Allen Lane.

Wakeford, N. and Cohen, K. (2008) 'Fieldnotes in public: using blogs for research'. In N. Fielding, R. Lee and G. Blank (eds), *The SAGE Handbook of Online Research Methods*. London: Sage.

Walsh, D. (1998) 'Doing ethnography'. In C. Seale (ed.), *Researching Society and Culture* (pp. 225–38). London: Sage.

Ward, A. (2002) 'The writing process'. In S. Potter (ed.), *Doing Postgraduate Research* (pp. 71–116). London: Sage.

Watts, H.D. and White, P. (2000) 'Presentation skills'. In D. Burton (ed.), *Research Training for Social Scientists*. London: Sage.

Weinberg, M.S. (1994) 'The nudist management of respectability'. In P. Kollock and J. O'Brien (eds), *The Production of Reality: Essays and Readings in Social Psychology* (pp. 392–401). Thousand Oaks, CA: Sage.

Whittington, R. (2003) 'The work of strategizing and organizing: for a practice perspective'. *Strategic Organization*, 1 (1), 117–25.

Whyte, W.F. (1949) 'The social structure of the restaurant'. *American Journal of Sociology*, 54, 302–10.

Whyte, W.F. (1993) *Street Corner Society*, 4th rev. edn. Chicago: University of Chicago Press.

Wield, D. (2002) 'Planning and organizing a research project'. In S. Potter (ed.), *Doing Postgraduate Research* (pp. 35–70). London: Sage.

Wilkinson, S. (2011) 'Analysing focus group data'. In D. Silverman (ed.), *Qualitative Research: Theory, Method and Practice*, 3rd edn (pp. 168–84). London: Sage.

Wilkinson, S. (2016) 'Analysing focus group data'. In D. Silverman (ed.), *Qualitative Research: Theory, Method and Practice*, 3rd edn (pp.83–98). London: Sage.

Willis, P.E. (2000) *The Ethnographic Imagination*. Cambridge: Polity.

Wincup, E. (2017) *Criminological Research*, 2nd edn. London: Sage.

Wittgenstein, L. (1980) *Culture and Value*. Trans. P. Winch. Oxford: Blackwell.

Wolcott, H. (1990) *Writing Up Qualitative Research*. Newbury Park, CA: Sage.

Wolcott, H. (2009) *Writing Up Qualitative Research*, 3rd edn. London: Sage.

Ybema, S. (2009) *Organizational Ethnography: Studying the Complexities of Everyday Life*. Los Angeles: Sage.

Yin, R. (2009) *Case Study Research: Design and Methods*, 4th edn. Thousand Oaks, CA: Sage.

Author index

Subject Index